Kaplan Publishing are constantly finding new ways to make a difference to your studies and our exciting online resources really do offer something different to students looking for exam success.

This book comes with free MyKaplan online resources so that you can study anytime, anywhere

Having purchased this book, you have access to the following online study materials:

CONTENT	ACCA (including FFA,FAB,FMA)		FIA (excluding FFA,FAB,FMA)	
	Text	Kit	Text	Kit
iPaper version of the book	✓	✓	✓	✓
Interactive electronic version of the book	✓			
Progress tests with instant answers	✓			
Material updates	✓	✓	✓	✓
Latest official ACCA exam questions*		✓		
Extra question assistance using the signpost icon*		✓		
Timed questions with an online tutor debrief using the clock icon*		✓		
Interim assessment including questions and answers	✓		✓	
Technical articles	✓	✓	✓	✓

* Excludes F1, F2, F3, FFA, FAB, FMA

How to access your online resources

Kaplan Financial students will already have a MyKaplan account ar[illegible] available to you online. You do not need to register again, as this p[illegible] nrolled. If you are having problems accessing online materials, please ask your cours[illegible]

If you are already a registered MyKaplan user go to www.MyKaplan.co.uk and log in. Select the 'add a book' feature and enter the ISBN number of this book and the unique pass key at the bottom of this card. Then click 'finished' or 'add another book'. You may add as many books as you have purchased from this screen.

If you purchased through Kaplan Flexible Learning or via the Kaplan Publishing website you will automatically receive an e-mail invitation to MyKaplan. Please register your details using this email to gain access to your content. If you do not receive the e-mail or book content, please contact Kaplan Flexible Learning.

If you are a new MyKaplan user register at www.MyKaplan.co.uk and click on the link contained in the email we sent you to activate your account. Then select the 'add a book' feature, enter the ISBN number of this book and the unique pass key at the bottom of this card. Then click 'finished' or 'add another book'.

Your Code and Information

This code can only be used once for the registration of one book online. This registration and your online content will expire when the final sittings for the examinations covered by this book have taken place. Please allow one hour from the time you submit your book details for us to process your request.

Please scratch the film to access your MyKaplan code.

Please be aware that this code is case-sensitive and you will need to include the dashes within the passcode, but not when entering the ISBN. For further technical support, please visit www.MyKaplan.co.uk

ACCA

Paper P2 INT/UK

Corporate Reporting

Complete Text

British library cataloguing-in-publication data

A catalogue record for this book is available from the British Library.

Published by:
Kaplan Publishing UK
Unit 2 The Business Centre
Molly Millars Lane
Wokingham
Berkshire
RG41 2QZ

ISBN: 978-1-78415-037-2

Printed and bound in Great Britain

Acknowledgements

We are grateful to the Association of Chartered Certified Accountants and the Chartered Institute of Management Accountants for permission to reproduce past examination questions. The answers have been prepared by Kaplan Publishing.

Contents

		Page
Chapter 1	The Conceptual Framework	1
Chapter 2	The professional and ethical duty of the accountant	25
Chapter 3	Performance reporting	33
Chapter 4	Non-current assets, agriculture and inventories	71
Chapter 5	Foreign currency in individual financial statements	125
Chapter 6	Leases	141
Chapter 7	Events after the reporting period, provisions and contingencies	171
Chapter 8	Segment reporting	195
Chapter 9	Related parties	213
Chapter 10	Employee benefits	227
Chapter 11	Share-based payment	257
Chapter 12	Financial instruments	283
Chapter 13	Tax	345
Chapter 14	Group accounting – basic groups	371
Chapter 15	Complex groups	431
Chapter 16	Change in a group structure	467
Chapter 17	Group reorganisations	513
Chapter 18	Group accounting – foreign currency	521
Chapter 19	Group statement of cash flows	549
Chapter 20	Adoption of IFRS	601
Chapter 21	Specialised entities and specialised transactions	615

Chapter 22	Non-financial reporting	663
Chapter 23	Assessing financial performance and position	685
Chapter 24	Current issues	715
Chapter 25	Questions & Answers	723

Paper Introduction

How to Use the Materials

The nature of the P2 **Corporate Reporting** exam, is that of a 'pillar topic'. This means that students will need a good understanding of the basics of accounting as covered initially in F3 and then in F7.

The ACCA website www.accaglobal.com includes a useful FAQ section. Within this section the examiner recommends:

> *'It is important that students have done some pre-course work such as attempting as homework a past F7 exam as appropriate revision before starting work on P2. This message applies equally to students who have attempted and passed F7 and to those who have gained an exemption from F7'.*
>
> *P2 examiner – ACCA website*

These Kaplan Publishing learning materials have been carefully designed to make your learning experience as easy as possible and to give you the best chances of success in your examinations.

The product range contains a number of features to help you in the study process. They include:

(1) Detailed study guide and syllabus objectives

(2) Description of the examination

(3) Study skills and revision guidance

(4) Complete text or essential text

(5) Question practice

The sections on the study guide, the syllabus objectives, the examination and study skills should all be read before you commence your studies. They are designed to familiarise you with the nature and content of the examination and give you tips on how to best to approach your learning.

The **complete text or essential text** comprises the main learning materials and gives guidance as to the importance of topics and where other related resources can be found. Each chapter includes:

- The **learning objectives** contained in each chapter, which have been carefully mapped to the examining body's own syllabus learning objectives or outcomes. You should use these to check you have a clear understanding of all the topics on which you might be assessed in the examination.

- The **chapter diagram** provides a visual reference for the content in the chapter, giving an overview of the topics and how they link together.
- The **content** for each topic area commences with a brief explanation or definition to put the topic into context before covering the topic in detail. You should follow your studying of the content with a review of the illustration/s. These are worked examples which will help you to understand better how to apply the content for the topic.
- **Test your understanding** sections provide an opportunity to assess your understanding of the key topics by applying what you have learned to short questions. Answers can be found at the back of each chapter.
- **Summary diagrams** complete each chapter to show the important links between topics and the overall content of the paper. These diagrams should be used to check that you have covered and understood the core topics before moving on.
- **Question practice** is provided through this text.

Quality and accuracy are of the utmost importance to us so if you spot an error in any of our products, please send an email to mykaplanreporting@kaplan.com with full details, or follow the link to the feedback form in MyKaplan.

Our Quality Coordinator will work with our technical team to verify the error and take action to ensure it is corrected in future editions.

Icon Explanations

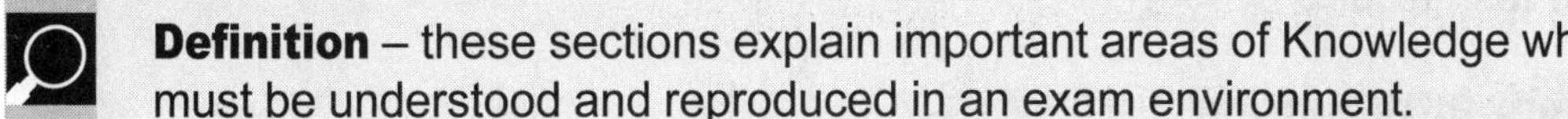

Definition – these sections explain important areas of Knowledge which must be understood and reproduced in an exam environment.

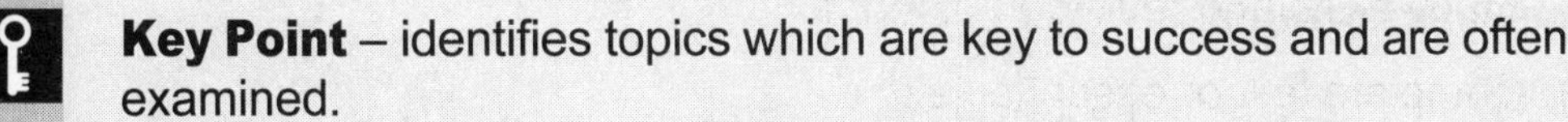

Key Point – identifies topics which are key to success and are often examined.

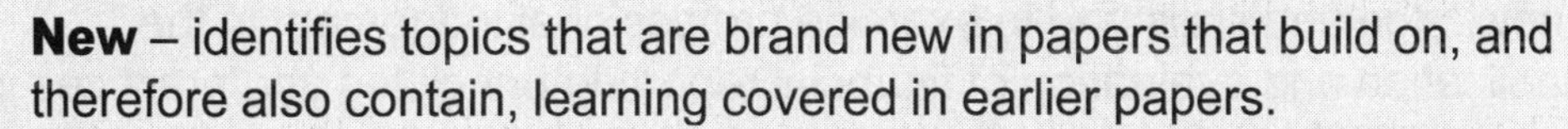

New – identifies topics that are brand new in papers that build on, and therefore also contain, learning covered in earlier papers.

Expandable Text – within the online version of the work book is a more detailed explanation of key terms, these sections will help to provide a deeper understanding of core areas. Reference to this text is vital when self studying.

Test Your Understanding – following key points and definitions are exercises which give the opportunity to assess the understanding of these core areas. Within the work book the answers to these sections are left blank, explanations to the questions can be found within the online version which can be hidden or shown on screen to enable repetition of activities.

Illustration – to help develop an understanding of topics and the test your understanding exercises the illustrative examples can be used.

Exclamation Mark – this symbol signifies a topic which can be more difficult to understand, when reviewing these areas care should be taken.

Tutorial note – included to explain some of the technical points in more detail.

Footsteps – helpful tutor tips.

On-line subscribers

Our on-line resources are designed to increase the flexibility of your learning materials and provide you with immediate feedback on how your studies are progressing.

If you are subscribed to our on-line resources you will find:

(1) On-line referenceware: reproduces your Complete or Essential Text on-line, giving you anytime, anywhere access.

(2) On-line testing: provides you with additional on-line objective testing so you can practice what you have learned further.

(3) On-line performance management: immediate access to your on-line testing results. Review your performance by key topics and chart your achievement through the course relative to your peer group.

Ask your local customer services staff if you are not already a subscriber and wish to join.

Paper introduction

Paper background

The aim of ACCA Paper P2 (INT), **Corporate reporting**, is to apply knowledge and skills and to exercise professional judgement in the application and evaluation of financial reporting principles and practices in a range of business contexts and situations.

Objectives of the syllabus

- Discuss the professional and ethical duties of the accountant
- Evaluate the financial reporting framework
- Advise on and report the financial performance of entities
- Prepare the financial statements of groups of entities in accordance with relevant accounting standards
- Explain reporting issues relating to specialised entities
- Discuss the implications of changes in accounting regulation on financial reporting
- Appraise the financial performance and position of entities
- Evaluate current developments.

Core areas of the syllabus

- The professional and ethical duty of the accountant
- The financial reporting framework
- Reporting the financial performance of entities
- Financial statements of groups of entities
- Specialised entities
- Implications of changes in accounting regulation on financial reporting
- The appraisal of financial performance and position of entities
- Current developments.

Approach to INT and UK syllabus elements

Both the International and UK P2 syllabus apply the principles of International Financial Reporting Standards (IFRS).

The international syllabus has been used as the basis of the text.

UK syllabus students are also required to outline and discuss the differences between the IFRS for small and medium entities and UK accounting standards. They must also have a knowledge of some of the requirements of the Companies Act. The examinable differences are covered in chapter 21 of this text.

Syllabus objectives

We have reproduced the ACCA's syllabus below, showing where the objectives are explored within this book. Within the chapters, we have broken down the extensive information found in the syllabus into easily digestible and relevant sections, called Content Objectives. These correspond to the objectives at the beginning of each chapter.

Syllabus learning objective/Chapter

A THE PROFESSIONAL AND ETHICAL DUTIES OF THE ACCOUNTANT

1 Professional behaviour and compliance with accounting standards

(a) Appraise and discuss the ethical and professional issues in advising on corporate reporting.[3] **Ch. 2**

(b) Assess the relevance and importance of ethical and professional issues in complying with accounting standards.[3] **Ch. 2**

2 Ethical requirements of corporate reporting and the consequences of unethical behaviour

(a) Appraise the potential ethical implications of professional and managerial decisions in the preparation of corporate reports.[3] **Ch. 2**

(b) Assess the consequences of not upholding ethical principles in the preparation of corporate reports.[3] **Ch. 2**

3 Social responsibility

(a) Discuss the increased demand for transparency in corporate reports, and the emergence of non-financial reporting standards.[3] **Ch. 22**

(b) Discuss the progress towards a framework for integrated reporting.[3] **Ch. 22**

B THE FINANCIAL REPORTING FRAMEWORK

1 The applications, strengths and weaknesses of an accounting framework

(a) Evaluate the valuation models adopted by standard setters.[3] **Ch. 1**

(b) Discuss the use of an accounting framework in underpinning the production of accounting standards.[3] **Ch. 1**

(c) Assess the success of such a framework in introducing rigorous and consistent accounting standards.[3] **Ch. 1**

2 Critical evaluation of principles and practices

(a) Identify the relationship between accounting theory and practice.[2] **Ch. 1**

(b) Critically evaluate accounting principles and practices used in corporate reporting.[3] **Ch. 1**

C REPORTING THE FINANCIAL PERFORMANCE OF ENTITIES

1 Performance reporting

(a) Prepare reports relating to corporate performance for external stakeholders.[3] **Ch. 3**

(b) Discuss the issues relating to the recognition of revenue.[3] **Ch. 3**

(c) Evaluate proposed changes to reporting financial performance.[3] **Ch. 3**

2 Non-current assets

(a) Apply and discuss the timing of the recognition of non-current assets and the determination of their carrying amounts including impairment and revaluations.[3] **Ch. 4**

(b) Apply and discuss the treatment of non-current assets held for sale.[3] **Ch. 4**

(c) Apply and discuss the accounting treatment of investment properties including classification, recognition and measurement issues.[3] **Ch. 4**

(d) Apply and discuss the accounting treatment of intangible assets including the criteria for recognition and measurement subsequent to acquisition and classification.[3] **Ch. 4**

3 Financial instruments

(a) Apply and discuss the recognition and derecognition of financial assets and financial liabilities.[2] **Ch. 12**

(b) Apply and discuss the classification of financial assets and financial liabilities and their measurement.[2] **Ch. 12**

(c) Apply and discuss the treatment of gains and losses arising on financial assets and financial liabilities.[2] **Ch. 12**

(d) Apply and discuss the treatment of impairment of financial assets.[2] **Ch. 12**

(e) Account for derivative financial instruments, and simple embedded derivatives.[2] **Ch. 12**

(f) Outline the principles of hedge accounting and account for fair value hedges and cash flow hedges including hedge effectiveness.[2] **Ch. 12**

4 Leases

(a) Apply and discuss the classification of leases and accounting for leases by lessors and lessees.[3] **Ch. 16**

(b) Account for and discuss sale and leaseback transactions.[3] **Ch. 16**

5 Segment reporting

(a) Determine the nature and extent of reportable segments.[3] **Ch. 8**

(b) Specify and discuss the nature of segment information to be disclosed. [3] **Ch. 8**

6 Employee benefits

(a) Apply and discuss the accounting treatment of short term and long term employee benefits.[3] **Ch. 10**

(b) Apply and discuss the accounting treatment of defined contribution and defined benefit plans.[3] **Ch. 10**

(c) Account for gains and losses on settlements and curtailments.[2] **Ch. 10**

(d) Account for the 'Asset Ceiling' test and the reporting of actuarial gains and losses.[2] **Ch. 10**

7 Income taxes

(a) Apply and discuss the recognition and measurement of deferred tax liabilities and deferred tax assets.[3] **Ch. 13**

(b) Determine the recognition of tax expense or income and its inclusion in the financial statements.[3] **Ch. 13**

8 Provisions, contingencies, events after the reporting date

(a) Apply and discuss the recognition, derecognition and measurement of provisions, contingent liabilities and contingent assets including environmental provisions.[3] **Ch. 7**

(b) calculate and discuss restructuring provisions.[3] **Ch. 7**

(c) Apply and discuss the accounting for events after the reporting date.[3] **Ch. 7**

(d) Determine and report going concern issues arising after the reporting date.[3] **Ch. 7**

9 Related parties

(a) Determine the parties considered to be related to an entity.[3] **Ch. 9**

(b) Identify the implications of related party relationships and the need for disclosure.[3] **Ch. 9**

10 Share-based payment

(a) Apply and discuss the recognition and measurement criteria for share-based payment transactions.[3] **Ch. 11**

(b) Account for modifications, cancellations and settlements of share-based payment transactions.[2] **Ch. 11**

11 Reporting requirements of small and medium-sized entities (SMEs)

(a) Discuss solutions to the problem of differential financial reporting.[3] **Ch. 21**

(b) Discuss the accounting treatments not allowable under the IFRS for SME's including the revaluation model for certain assets.[3] **Ch. 21**

(c) Discuss and apply the simplifications introduced by the IFRS for SMEs including accounting for goodwill and intangible assets, financial instruments, defined benefit schemes, exchange differences and associates and joint ventures.[3] **Ch. 21**

D FINANCIAL STATEMENTS OF GROUPS OF ENTITIES

1 Group accounting including statements of cash flow

(a) Apply the method of accounting for business combinations, including complex group structures.[3] **Ch. 14, 15 and 16**

(b) Apply the principles in determining the cost of a business combination. [3] **Ch. 14, 15 and 16**

(c) Apply the recognition and measurement criteria for identifiable acquired assets and liabilities and goodwill including step acquisitions. [3] **Ch. 14 and 15**

(d) Apply and discuss the criteria used to identify a subsidiary and an associate.[3] **Ch. 14**

(e) Determine and apply appropriate procedures to be used in preparing group financial statements.[3] **Ch. 14, 15 and 16**

(f) Identify and outline the circumstances in which a group is required to prepare consolidated financial statements; the circumstances when a group may claim an exemption from the preparation of consolidated financial statements, and why directors may not wish to consolidate a subsidiary and where this is permitted.[2] **Ch. 14**

(g) Apply the equity method of accounting for associates[3] **Ch. 14**

(h) Outline and apply the key definitions and accounting methods which relate to interests in joint arrangements.[3] **Ch. 14**

(i) Prepare and discuss group statements of cash flows.[3] **Ch. 19**

2 Continuing and discontinued interests

(a) Prepare group financial statements where activities have been discontinued, or have been acquired or disposed in the period.[3] **Ch. 16**

(b) Apply and discuss the treatment of a subsidiary which has been acquired exclusively with a view to subsequent disposal.[3] **Ch. 16**

3 Changes in group structures

(a) Discuss the reasons behind a group reorganisation.[3] **Ch. 17**

(b) Evaluate and assess the principal terms of a proposed group reorganisation.[3] **Ch. 17**

4 Foreign transactions and entities

(a) Outline and apply the translation of foreign currency amounts and transactions into the functional currency and the presentational currency.[3] **Ch. 18**

(b) Account for the consolidation of foreign operations and their disposal.[2] **Ch. 18**

E SPECIALISED ENTITIES AND SPECIALISED TRANSACTIONS

1 Financial reporting in specialised, not-for-profit and public sector entities

(a) Apply knowledge from the syllabus to straightforward transactions and events arising in specialised, not-for-profit, and public sector entities.[3] **Ch. 21**

2 Entity reconstructions

(a) Identify when an entity may no longer be viewed as a going concern or uncertainty exists surrounding the going concern status.[2] **Ch. 21**

(b) Identify and outline the circumstances in which a reconstruction would be an appropriate alternative to a company liquidation.[2] **Ch. 21**

(c) Outline the appropriate accounting treatment required relating to reconstructions.[2] **Ch. 21**

F IMPLICATIONS OF CHANGES IN ACCOUNTING REGULATION ON FINANCIAL REPORTING

1 The effect of changes in accounting standards on accounting systems

(a) Apply and discuss the accounting implications of the first time adoption of a body of new accounting standards.[3] **Ch. 20**

2 Proposed changes to accounting standards

(a) Identify the issues and deficiencies which have led to a proposed change to an accounting standard.[2] **Ch. 24**

G THE APPRAISAL OF FINANCIAL PERFORMANCE AND POSITION OF ENTITIES

1 The creation of suitable accounting policies

(a) Develop accounting policies for an entity which meets the entity's reporting requirements.[3] **Ch. 23**

(b) Identify accounting treatments adopted in financial statements and assess their suitability and acceptability.[3] **Ch. 23**

2 Analysis and interpretation of financial information and measurement of performance

(a) Select and calculate relevant indicators of financial and non-financial performance.[3] **Ch. 23**

(b) Identify and evaluate significant features and issues in financial statements.[3] **Ch. 23**

(c) Highlight inconsistencies in financial information through analysis and application of knowledge.[3] **Ch. 23**

(d) Make inferences from the analysis of information taking into account the limitation of the information, the analytical methods used and the business environment in which the entity operates.[3] **Ch. 23**

H CURRENT DEVELOPMENTS

1 Environmental and social reporting

(a) Appraise the impact of environmental, social, and ethical factors on performance measurement.[3] **Ch. 22**

(b) Evaluate current reporting requirements in the area, including the development of integrated reporting.[3] **Ch. 22**

(c) Discuss why entities might include disclosures relating to the environment and society.[3] **Ch. 22**

2 Convergence between national and international reporting standards

(a) Evaluate the implications of worldwide convergence with International Financial Reporting Standards.[3] **Ch. 20**

(b) Discuss the influence of national regulators on international financial reporting.[2] **Ch. 20**

3 Current reporting issues

(a) Discuss current issues in corporate reporting.[3] **Ch. 24**

The superscript numbers in square brackets indicate the intellectual depth at which the subject area could be assessed within the examination. Level 1 (knowledge and comprehension) broadly equates with the Knowledge module, Level 2 (application and analysis) with the Skills module and Level 3 (synthesis and evaluation) to the Professional level. However, lower level skills can continue to be assessed as you progress through each module and level.

The examination

Examination format

The syllabus is assessed by a three-hour paper-based examination. It examines professional competences within the corporate reporting environment.

Students will be examined on concepts, theories and principles and on their ability to question and comment on proposed accounting treatments.

Students should be capable of relating professional issues to relevant concepts and practical situations. The evaluation of alternative accounting practices and the identification and prioritisation of issues will be a key element of the paper. Professional and ethical judgement will need to be exercised, together with the integration of technical knowledge when addressing corporate reporting issues in a business context.

Global issues will be addressed via the current issues questions on the paper. Students will be required to adopt either a stakeholder or an external focus in answering questions and to demonstrate personal skills such as problem solving, dealing with information and decision making.

The paper also deals with specific professional knowledge appropriate to the preparation and presentation of consolidated and other financial statements from accounting data, to conform with accounting standards.

Section A will consist of one scenario based question worth 50 marks. It will deal with the preparation of consolidated financial statements including group statements of cash flows and with issues in financial reporting.

Students will be required to answer two out of three questions in Section B, which will normally comprise two questions which will be scenario or case-study based and one essay question which may have some computational element. Section B could deal with any aspects of the syllabus.

UK syllabus students will sit an exam that is identical in format to the International syllabus exam. The Examiner has indicated that the differences from the IFRS paper which may be examined in the UK paper will account for no more than 20% of that paper. The differences examined may be included within one or more questions in the examination paper.

	Number of marks
Section A	
Compulsory question	50
Section B	
Two from three 25-mark questions	50
	___
Total time allowed: 3 hours	100

Note that, in common with other ACCA Professional level papers, there will be a total of four professional marks available to candidates in each P2 examination paper. In the case of P2, the professional marks will be only available in section B, with two marks allocated to each of the three optional questions, with candidates required to attempt any two of those questions.

Study skills and revision guidance

This section aims to give guidance on how to study for your ACCA exams and to give ideas on how to improve your existing study techniques.

Preparing to study

Set your objectives

Before starting to study decide what you want to achieve – the type of pass you wish to obtain. This will decide the level of commitment and time you need to dedicate to your studies.

Devise a study plan

Determine which times of the week you will study.

Split these times into sessions of at least one hour for study of new material. Any shorter periods could be used for revision or practice.

Put the times you plan to study onto a study plan for the weeks from now until the exam and set yourself targets for each period of study – in your sessions make sure you cover the course, course assignments and revision.

If you are studying for more than one paper at a time, try to vary your subjects as this can help you to keep interested and see subjects as part of wider knowledge.

When working through your course, compare your progress with your plan and, if necessary, re-plan your work (perhaps including extra sessions) or, if you are ahead, do some extra revision/practice questions.

Effective studying

Active reading

You are not expected to learn the text by rote, rather, you must understand what you are reading and be able to use it to pass the exam and develop good practice. A good technique to use is SQ3Rs – Survey, Question, Read, Recall, Review:

(1) **Survey the chapter** – look at the headings and read the introduction, summary and objectives, so as to get an overview of what the chapter deals with.

(2) **Question** – whilst undertaking the survey, ask yourself the questions that you hope the chapter will answer for you.

(3) **Read** through the chapter thoroughly, answering the questions and making sure you can meet the objectives. Attempt the exercises and activities in the text, and work through all the examples.

(4) **Recall** – at the end of each section and at the end of the chapter, try to recall the main ideas of the section/chapter without referring to the text. This is best done after a short break of a couple of minutes after the reading stage.

(5) **Review** – check that your recall notes are correct.

You may also find it helpful to re-read the chapter to try to see the topic(s) it deals with as a whole.

Note-taking

Taking notes is a useful way of learning, but do not simply copy out the text. The notes must:

- be in your own words
- be concise
- cover the key points
- be well-organised
- be modified as you study further chapters in this text or in related ones.

Trying to summarise a chapter without referring to the text can be a useful way of determining which areas you know and which you don't.

Three ways of taking notes:

Summarise the key points of a chapter.

Make linear notes – a list of headings, divided up with subheadings listing the key points. If you use linear notes, you can use different colours to highlight key points and keep topic areas together. Use plenty of space to make your notes easy to use.

Try a diagrammatic form – the most common of which is a mind-map. To make a mind-map, put the main heading in the centre of the paper and put a circle around it. Then draw short lines radiating from this to the main sub-headings, which again have circles around them. Then continue the process from the sub-headings to sub-sub-headings, advantages, disadvantages, etc.

Highlighting and underlining – you may find it useful to underline or highlight key points in your study text, but do be selective. You may also wish to make notes in the margins.

Revision

The best approach to revision is to revise the course as you work through it. Also try to leave four to six weeks before the exam for final revision. Make sure you cover the whole syllabus and pay special attention to those areas where your knowledge is weak. Here are some recommendations:

Read through the text and your notes again and condense your notes into key phrases. It may help to put key revision points onto index cards to look at when you have a few minutes to spare.

Review any assignments you have completed and look at where you lost marks – put more work into those areas where you were weak.

Practise exam standard questions under timed conditions. If you are short of time, list the points that you would cover in your answer and then read the model answer, but do try to complete at least a few questions under exam conditions.

Also practise producing answer plans and comparing them to the model answer.

If you are stuck on a topic find somebody (a tutor) to explain it to you.

Read good newspapers and professional journals, especially ACCA's Student Accountant – this can give you an advantage in the exam.

Ensure you know the structure of the exam – how many questions and of what type you will be expected to answer. During your revision attempt all the different styles of questions you may be asked.

Further reading

You may find the following additional reading helpful:

'A student's guide to preparing financial statements' by Sally Baker

'A student's guide to group accounts' by Tom Clendon.

'A student's guide to International Financial Reporting Standards' by Clare Finch.

You can find further reading and technical articles within the student section of ACCA's website.

Technical update

This text has been updated to reflect Examinable Documents 2014 issued by ACCA. Documents and standards that are newly examinable from December 2014 include:

- IAS 41 Agriculture
- Consultation Draft of the International Integrated Reporting Framework
- FRS 100 – 102 (UK syllabus only)

There are also a number of discussion papers and exposure drafts that are newly examinable. These are outlined in Chapter 24.

chapter

1

The Conceptual Framework

Chapter learning objectives

Upon completion of this chapter you will be able to:

- evaluate models adopted by standards setters
- discuss the use of the 2010 Conceptual Framework for Financial Reporting (2010 Framework) in the production of accounting standards
- assess the success of the 2010 Framework in introducing rigorous and consistent accounting standards
- identify the relationship between accounting theory and practice
- critically evaluate accounting principles and practices used in corporate reporting
- explain the reasons for the introduction of IFRS 13 Fair value measurement together with application of the key principles to determine fair value measurement in specific situations.

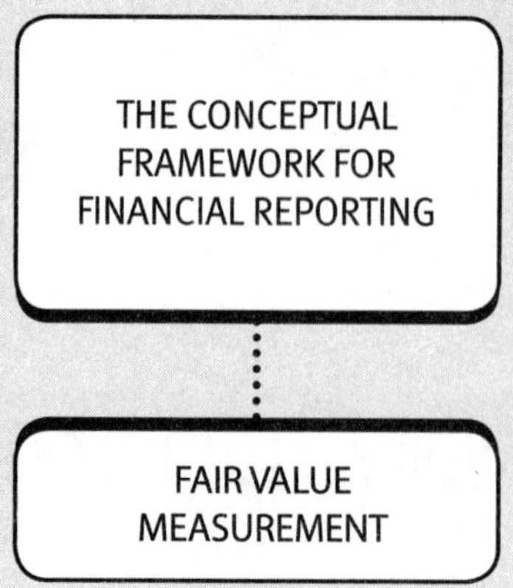

1 Conceptual Framework for Financial Reporting

Introduction: the need for a conceptual framework

A conceptual framework is a set of theoretical principles and concepts that underlie the preparation and presentation of financial statements.

If no conceptual framework existed, then it is more likely that accounting standards would be produced on a haphazard basis as particular issues and circumstances arose. These accounting standards might be inconsistent with one another, or perhaps even contradictory.

A strong conceptual framework therefore means that there is a set of principles in place from which all future accounting standards draw. It also acts as a reference point for the preparers of financial statements if there is no adequate accounting standard governing the types of transactions that an entity enters into this (this will be extremely rare).

This section of the text considers the contents of the Conceptual Framework for Financial Reporting ('the Framework') in more detail.

The purpose of the Framework

The Framework states that its purpose is to:

(a) assist in the development of future accounting standards and in the review of existing standards

(b) provide a basis for reducing the number of alternative accounting treatments permitted by international standards

(c) assist national standard setters in developing national standards

(d) assist preparers of financial statements in applying international standards and in dealing with issues not covered by international standards

(e) assist auditors in forming an opinion whether financial statements conform to international standards

(f) assist users of financial statements in interpreting the information contained in financial statements complying with international standards

(g) provide information about the IASB's approach to setting international standards.

The objective of financial reporting

The objective of financial reporting is to provide information about the reporting entity that is useful to existing and potential investors, lenders and other creditors in making decisions about providing resources to the entity.

Financial reports provide information about the financial position of a reporting entity, which is information about the entity's economic resources and the claims against the reporting entity. Financial reports also provide information about the effects of transactions and other events that change a reporting entity's economic resources and claims.

Underlying assumption

The Framework identifies one underlying assumption governing the preparation of financial statements:

- Going concern
  - The going concern basis assumes that the entity has neither the need nor the intention to liquidate or curtail materially the scale of its operations.

In previous versions of the Framework, accruals was also regarded as a fundamental assumption. Although it is still referred to within the Framework, it is no longer an underlying assumption.

Qualitative characteristics of useful financial information

The Framework identifies types of information that are useful to the users of financial statements.

It identifies two fundamental qualitative characteristics of useful financial information:

(1) **Relevance**

Information is relevant if it is capable of making a difference in decisions made by users of that information.

- Information will be regarded as being relevant if it has either predictive value or confirmatory value to a user

- Relevance is supported by materiality considerations
  - Information is regarded as material if its omission or misstatement could influence the decisions made by users of that information.

(2) **Faithful representation**

For financial information to be faithfully presented, it must be:

- complete
- neutral
- free from error.

Therefore, it must comprise information necessary for a proper understanding, it must be without bias or manipulation and clearly described.

In addition to the two fundamental qualitative characteristics, there are four enhancing qualitative characteristics of useful financial information. These should be maximised when possible:

(1) **Comparability**

Information is more useful if it can be compared with similar information about other entities, or even the same entity over different time periods.

- Consistency of methodology, approach or presentation helps to achieve comparability of financial information.
- Permitting different accounting treatments for similar items is likely to reduce comparability.

(2) **Verifiability**

Verifiability means that different, knowledgeable and independent observers could reach consensus, although not necessarily complete agreement, that a particular presentation of an item or items is a faithful representation.

- Verifiability of financial information provides assurance to users regarding its credibility and reliability.

(3) **Timeliness**

Information should be made available to users within a timescale which is likely to influence their decisions.

- Older information is generally less useful.

(4) **Understandability**

Understandability is enhanced if information is classified, characterised and presented clearly and concisely.

The cost constraint

It is important that the costs incurred in reporting financial information are justified by the benefits that the information brings to its users.

The elements of financial statements

The financial effects of a transaction can be grouped into one of five broad classes, known as the elements.

According to the Framework, the five elements of financial statements are as follows:

An **asset** is a resource controlled by the entity as a result of past events and from which future economic benefits are expected to flow to the entity.

A **liability** is a present obligation of the entity arising from past events, the settlement of which is expected to result in an outflow from the entity of resources embodying economic benefits.

Equity is the residual interest in an entity's assets after deducting all its liabilities.

Income is the increase in economic benefits during the accounting period.

Expenses are decreases in economic benefits during the accounting period.

Recognition of the elements of financial statements

An item should be recognised in the financial statements if:

- it meets one of the definitions of an element
- it is probable that any future economic benefit associated with the item will flow to or from the entity
- the item can be measured at a monetary amount (cost or value) with sufficient reliability.

The recognition of assets and liabilities falls into three stages:

- initial recognition (e.g. the purchase of a non-current asset)
- subsequent remeasurement (e.g. revaluation of the above asset)
- derecognition (e.g. sale of the asset).

Measurement of the elements of financial statements

Measurement is the process of determining the amount at which the elements should be recognised and carried at in the statement of financial position and the statement of profit or loss and other comprehensive income.

The Framework identifies four possible measurement bases:

Historical cost

Assets are recorded at the amount of cash or cash equivalents paid to acquire them.

Liabilities are recorded at the proceeds received in exchange for the obligation, or at the amounts expected to be paid to satisfy the liability.

Current cost

Assets are carried at their current purchase price.

Liabilities are carried at the undiscounted amount currently required to settle them.

Realisable value

Assets are carried at the amount that could currently be obtained by an orderly disposal. Liabilities are carried at their settlement values – the amount to be paid to satisfy them in the normal course of business.

Present value

Assets are carried at the present discounted value of the future net cash inflows that the item is expected to generate in the normal course of business. Liabilities are carried at the present discounted value of the expected cash outflows necessary to settle them.

Assessment of the Framework

- The Framework provides a conceptual underpinning for IFRS.
- One of the objectives of the Framework is to provide a basis for the formulation of IFRS.
- By providing definitions of assets, liabilities, etc. and guidance on recognition and measurement, the Framework forms a basis for dealing with any accounting issues that arise which are not covered by accounting standards.
- The Framework's approach builds corporate reporting around the definitions of assets and liabilities and the criteria for recognising and measuring them in the statement of financial position.
- This approach views accounting from the perspective of the statement of financial position ('a balance sheet perspective'), whereas most companies would not consider the measurement and recognition of assets and liabilities as the starting point for the determination of profit.
- In many jurisdictions, the financial statements form the basis of dividend payments, the starting point for the assessment of taxation, and often the basis for executive remuneration. A balance sheet fair value system, which the IASB favours, has major impacts on the above elements.

Current issues: The Framework

Discussion paper: A review of the conceptual framework for financial reporting

The IASB has identified a number of problems with the existing Framework:

- Important areas are not covered. For example, the existing Framework provides very little guidance on measurement.
- The guidance in some areas is unclear. For example, the existing definitions of assets and liabilities could be improved.
- Some aspects of the existing Framework are out of date and fail to reflect the current thinking of the IASB.

The discussion paper issued in July 2013 addresses these weaknesses and covers a number of other key areas:

The primary purpose of the framework

The primary purpose of the revised Framework is to assist the IASB by identifying concepts that the IASB will use consistently when developing and revising IFRSs.

Definitions of assets and liabilities

The discussion paper proposes the following definitions:

- An asset is a present economic resource controlled by the entity because of past events.
- A liability is a present obligation of the entity to transfer an economic resource because of past events.
- An 'economic resource' is a right, or other source of value, that is capable of producing economic benefits.

These differ from current definitions of assets and liabilities, which state that inflows or outflows of economic benefits should be probable.

Recognition and derecognition

The discussion paper says that all assets and liabilities should be recognised unless the IASB decides, when developing a standard, that recognition would not be relevant to the users or that faithful representation is impossible.

The existing Framework does not address derecognition. The IASB's view in the discussion paper is that an entity should derecognise an asset or a liability when it no longer meets the recognition criteria.

Defining equity and distinguishing equity from liabilities

The IASB have proposed that the existing definition of equity should remain.

In terms of distinguishing equity from liabilities, the IASB's preferred approach is that items should be classified as liabilities if there is an obligation to deliver economic resources.

Under IAS 32, some obligations to deliver equity instruments are currently classed as liabilities. However, per the discussion paper, all obligations to deliver equity instruments would be classified as equity.

Measurement

The IASB is aware that a single measurement basis for all assets and liabilities may not provide the most relevant information for users of financial statements. Therefore, when selecting which measurement to use for a particular item, the IASB should consider what information that measurement will produce in both the statement of financial position and the statement of profit or loss and OCI.

Presentation and disclosure

The existing Framework does not provide guidance on presentation and disclosure. The discussion paper proposes that greater guidance should be given.

Presentation in the statement of profit or loss and other comprehensive income

The current framework does not contain principles to determine the items to be recognised in profit or loss, and in OCI.

According to proposals, all items of income and expense should be recognised in profit or loss unless recognising an item in OCI enhances the relevance of profit or loss in that period. If an item is recognised in OCI, it must subsequently be reclassified to profit or loss when this results in relevant information.

The discussion paper says that recognising an item in OCI enhances relevance for:

- bridging items
- mismatched remeasurements.

Bridging items arise when measurement used in the statement of financial position differs from measurement in profit or loss. For instance, an asset may be held at fair value in the statement of financial position, but the profit or loss impact may be determined using amortised cost. The amount to be recognised in OCI would therefore be the difference (the 'bridge') between the two measures.

Mismatched remeasurements arise then there are linked assets or liabilities but only one item within the set is regularly remeasured to current value. It is proposed that the gain or loss on remeasurement of the single item should be recorded in OCI. This will be recycled to profit or loss later so that the effects of the two linked items are presented together.

The problem with this 'narrow' approach is that it contradicts certain accounting standards already in issue. For example, revaluation gains on property, plant and equipment are recorded in OCI, even though this not a bridging item or an accounting mis-match.

Therefore, a broad approach has also been proposed that would permit more items to be recognised in OCI.

Test your understanding 1 – Framework

In September 2010, the IASB issued the Conceptual Framework for Financial Reporting 2010 ('the Framework'). Nonetheless, proposals to restart work on the Framework quickly achieved a lot of support. This led to the release of a discussion paper in September 2013 that outlined further potential changes to the Framework. These discussions clearly highlight the importance of the Framework to the users and producers of International Financial Reporting Standards.

Required:

(a) **Explain the purpose of the Framework.**

(b) **How does the Framework define the elements relating to financial position, and why might these definitions be criticised?**

Test your understanding 2 – Applying the framework

Note: This question requires a knowledge of leases, deferred tax and financial instruments. You might prefer to study those accounting standards before completing this question.

During the year, Mineral, a listed company, signed a non-cancellable operating lease to use a photocopier for four years. The useful life of the machine is ten years and the lessor is responsible for its maintenance. Mineral pays the lessor annually in arrears.

Mineral owns a machine that is central to its production process. At the reporting date, the machine's carrying value exceeds it tax base. This difference is due to the revaluation of the asset to fair value in the financial statements. Due to its importance, it is extremely unlikely that the machine will be sold.

At the year-end, Mineral received $10m. In return, Mineral must issue ordinary shares in 12 month's time. The number of shares to be issued will be determined based on the quoted price of Mineral's shares at the issue date.

Required:

For each of the transactions above:

(i) **Briefly explain how it should be accounted for in accordance with International Financial Reporting Standards**

(ii) **Discuss why the accounting treatment could be argued to contradict the definition of the elements given by the Framework.**

2 Fair Value Measurement – IFRS 13

Introduction

The objective of IFRS 13 is to provide a single source of guidance for fair value measurement where it is required by a reporting standard, rather than it being spread throughout several reporting standards.

Scope

IFRS 13 does not apply to:

- share-based payment transactions within the scope of IFRS 2 Share-based Payment
- leasing transactions within the scope of IAS 17 Leases.
- measurements that are similar to fair value but which are not fair value, such as net realisable value (IAS 2 Inventories) or value in use (IAS 36 Impairment of Assets).

Fair value measurement and IFRS

The fair value of an asset or a liability may be required to be measured in a variety of circumstances as follows:

- Fair value upon **initial recognition** arises when a reporting standard requires fair value to be measured upon initial recognition.
  - For example, IFRS 3 Business Combinations (Revised) requires that the separable net assets of the acquired entity are measured at fair value to determine goodwill at acquisition.
- Fair value on a **recurring basis** arises when a reporting standard requires fair value to be measured on an ongoing basis.
  - Examples of this include IAS 40 Investment Property, or IFRS 9 Financial Instruments which require some financial assets and liabilities to be measured at fair value at each reporting date.
- Fair value on a **non-recurring basis** arises when a reporting standard requires fair value to be measured at fair value only in certain specified circumstances.
  - For example, IFRS 5 requires that assets classified as held for sale are measured at fair value less costs to sell.

As indicated by the above, a range of IFRSs require that assets and liabilities are measured at fair value at different times. Therefore, the introduction of IFRS 13 Fair Value Measurement has brought many benefits.

Reasons for the issue of IFRS 13

- To standardise the definition of fair value.
- To help users by providing additional disclosures relating to how fair value has been determined.
- To improve consistency of reported information
- To increase the extent of convergence between IFRS and US GAAP.

The definition of fair value

Fair value is defined by IFRS 13 as:

- the price that would be received to sell an asset or paid to transfer a liability in an orderly transaction between market participants at the measurement date

The basis of a fair value measurement

The following factors should be taken into consideration when measuring fair value:

- The asset or liability to be measured may be an individual asset (e.g. plot of land) or liability, or a group of assets and liabilities (e.g. a cash generating unit or business), depending upon exactly what is required to be measured.
- The measurement should reflect the price at which an **orderly transaction** between willing market participants would take place under current market conditions. It should not be a distress transaction.
- The value of the asset of liability should take into account the assumptions of **market participants**, who will generally want to maximise their own best interests
  - The valuation must therefore reflect the characteristics of the asset or liability (age, condition, location, and restrictions on use or sale) that are relevant to market participants.
- The entity must determine the **market** in which an orderly transaction would take place
  - This will normally be the **principal market**, which is the market in which the transaction would normally take place
  - In the absence of a principal market, the most **advantageous market** should be used

- Fair value is not adjusted for **transaction costs** because these are specific to the transaction and not a characteristic of the asset or liability
  - Transaction costs should, however, be taken into consideration if the entity needs to determine the most advantageous market for its assets or liabilities
  - Transaction costs do not include transport costs. Location is a characteristic of most assets and therefore fair value should be adjusted to reflect the costs of getting the asset to market.

Test your understanding 3 – Fair value

An asset is sold in two different active markets at different prices. An entity enters into transactions in both markets and can access the price in those markets for the asset at the measurement date as follows:

	Market 1	**Market 2**
	$	$
Price	26	25
Transaction costs	(3)	(1)
Transport costs	(2)	(2)
Net price received	21	22

Requirement:

What is the fair value of the asset if:

(a) **market 1 is the principal market for the asset?**

(b) **no principal market can be determined?**

3 Fair value hierarchy

In order to maximise verifiability, as well as to increase comparability, IFRS 13 states that an entity should maximise the use of observable inputs when determining fair value.

To aid with the application of the above, IFRS 13 establishes a hierarchy that categorises the inputs to valuation techniques used to measure fair value:

- **Level 1 inputs** comprise quoted prices ('observable') in active markets for identical assets and liabilities at the measurement date
  - This is regarded as providing the most reliable evidence of fair value and is likely to be used without adjustment.
- **Level 2 inputs** are observable inputs, other than those included within Level 1 above, which are observable directly or indirectly
  - This may include quoted prices for similar (not identical) asset or liabilities in active markets, or prices for identical or similar assets and liabilities in inactive markets. Typically, they are likely to require some degree of adjustment to arrive at a fair value measurement
  - An adjustment to a Level 2 input that is significant to the entire measurement might result in a fair value measurement categorised within Level 3 of the fair value hierarchy.
- **Level 3 inputs** are unobservable inputs for an asset or liability, based upon the best information available, including information that may be reasonably available relating to market participants
  - An entity shall develop unobservable inputs using the best information available in the circumstances, which might include the entity's own data.

IFRS 13 gives priority to level 1 inputs.

Inputs to determine fair value

Inputs into a valuation technique should be consistent with those which would be used by market participants, including control premiums or discounts for lack of control. Prices based upon bid-ask spreads should be the most representative of fair value from within that spread.

Prices may be provided by third parties, such as brokers, but the prices must be determined in accordance with the requirements of IFRS 13; e.g. they may be regarded as either observable or unobservable data.

Examples of inputs used to determine fair value include:

	Asset or liability	**Example**
Level 1	Equity shares in a listed entity	Unadjusted quoted prices in an active market
Level 2	Finished goods inventory at a retail outlet	Price paid by retail customers
	Licence acquired as part of a business combination which was recently negotiated with an unrelated party	The royalty rate contained within the contract
	Cash generating unit	Valuation multiple from observed transactions involving similar businesses
	Building held and used	Price per square metre for the building from observable market data, such as observed transactions for similar buildings in similar locations.
Level 3	Interest rate swap	Adjustment made to a mid-market non-binding price using data that cannot be directly observed or corroborated
	Decommissioning liability assumed upon a business combination	Use of own data to make estimates of expected future cash outflows to fulfil the obligation used to estimate the present value of that future obligation.
	Cash-generating unit	Profit or cash flow forecast using own data.

Valuation techniques

Valuation techniques should be used which are appropriate to the asset or liability at the measurement date and for which sufficient data is available, applying the fair value hierarchy to maximise the use of observable inputs as far as possible. IFRS 13 identifies three valuation approaches:

(1) Income approach – e.g. where estimated future cash flows may be converted into a single, current amount stated at present value.

(2) Market approach – e.g. where prices and other market-related data is used for similar or identical assets, liabilities or groups of assets and liabilities.

(3) Cost approach – e.g. to arrive at what may be regarded as current replacement cost to determine the cost that would be incurred to replace the service or operational capacity of an asset.

More than one valuation technique may be used in helping to determine fair value in a particular situation. Note that a change in valuation technique is regarded as a change of accounting estimate in accordance with IAS 8 which needs to be properly disclosed in the financial statements.

Specific application principles

Non-financial assets

The fair value of a non-financial asset is based upon highest and best use of that asset that would maximise its value, based upon uses which are physically possible, legally permissible and financially feasible. This is considered from the perspective of market participants, even if they may use the asset differently. Current use of a non-financial asset is presumed to be its highest and best use, unless there are factors that would suggest otherwise.

- Used in combination with other assets – fair value of an asset will be based upon what would be received if the asset was sold to another market participant, and that the complementary assets and liabilities they needed for highest and best use would be available to them.
- Used on a stand-alone basis – the price that would be received to sell the asset to a market participant who would use it on a stand-alone basis.

In either situation, it is assumed that the asset is sold individually, rather than as part of a collection of assets and liabilities.

Example — Land

An entity acquires land in a business combination. In accordance with IFRS 3 (revised), this must be stated at fair value at the date of acquisition to help determine the value of goodwill at that date. The land is currently developed for industrial use as a site for a factory. Alternatively, the site could be developed into a block of residential flats which, based upon evidence relating to adjoining plots of a similar size, appears to be a practical use of the site.

The current use of land is presumed to be its highest and best use unless market or other factors suggest a different use. In this situation, there is a possible alternative use which should be considered as follows:

The highest and best use of the land would be determined by taking the higher measurement from the two possible outcomes:

(a) the value of the land as currently developed for industrial use (i.e. the land would be used in combination with other assets, such as the factory, or with other assets and liabilities).

(b) the value of the land as a vacant site for residential use, taking into account the costs of demolishing the factory and other costs (including the uncertainty about whether the entity would be able to convert the asset to the alternative use, such as legal and planning issues) necessary to convert the land to a vacant site (i.e. the land is to be used by market participants on a stand-alone basis).

Example – Research and development project

An entity acquires a research and development (R&D) project in a business combination. The entity does not intend to complete the project as, if completed, the project would compete with one of its own projects (to provide the next generation of the entity's commercialised technology). Instead, the entity intends to hold (i.e. lock up) the project to prevent its competitors from obtaining access to the technology. In doing this the project is expected to provide defensive value, principally by improving the prospects for the entity's own competing technology and preventing access by competitors to the technology.

To measure the fair value of the project at initial recognition, the highest and best use of the project would be determined on the basis of its use by market participants. For example, the highest and best use of the R&D project could be:

(a) **to continue development** if market participants would continue to develop the project and that use would maximise the value of the group of assets or of assets and liabilities in which the project would be used (i.e. the asset would be used in combination with other assets or with other assets and liabilities). The fair value of the project would be measured on the basis of the price that would be received in a current transaction to sell the project, assuming that the R&D would be used with its complementary assets and the associated liabilities and that those assets and liabilities would be available to market participants.

(b) **to cease development for competitive reasons** if market participants would lock up the project and that use would maximise the value of the group of assets or of assets and liabilities in which the project would be used. The fair value of the project would be measured on the basis of the price that would be received in a current transaction to sell the project, assuming that the R&D would be used (i.e. locked up) with its complementary assets and the associated liabilities and that those assets and liabilities would be available to market participants.

(c) **to cease development if market participants would discontinue its development**. The fair value of the project would be measured on the basis of the price that would be received in a current transaction to sell the project on its own (which might be zero).

Liabilities and equity instruments

Ideally, fair value is measured using quoted prices for identical instruments – i.e. level one observable inputs. If this is not possible, it may be possible to use prices in an inactive market – level two observable inputs. If this is not possible, a valuation model should be used e.g. present value measurement.

Note that any fair value measurement of a liability should include non-performance or default risk. This may be different for different types of liability held by an entity; for example, default risk for a secured loan is less than default risk of an unsecured loan at any point in time. Also, be aware that this risk may change over time as an entity may or may not encounter financial and other commercial difficulties.

Fair value measurement of a liability or equity instrument assumes that it is transferred at the measurement date, and that both a liability and/or equity instrument would remain outstanding, rather than being settled or redeemed.

When a quoted price is not available for such an item, an entity shall measure fair value from the perspective of a market participant who holds the identical item as an asset at the measurement date. If there are no such observable prices, then an alternative valuation technique must be used.

Disclosures

Disclosures should provide information that enables users of financial statements to evaluate the inputs and methods used to determine how fair value measurements have been arrived at.

The level in the three-tier valuation hierarchy should be disclosed, together with supporting details of valuation methods and inputs used where appropriate. As would be expected, more detailed information is required where there is significant use of level-three inputs to arrive at a fair value measurement to enable users of financial statements to understand how such fair values have been arrived at.

Disclosure should also be made when there is a change of valuation technique to measure an asset or liability. This will include any change in the level of inputs used to determine fair value of particular assets and/or liabilities.

Chapter summary

The Framework

- Underpins accounting standards
- Fundamental qualitative characteristics of useful information are:
  - Relevance
  - Faithful representation
- Defines the elements of financial statements

↓

IFRS 13 Fair Value Measurement

- Provides single source of guidance where FV measurment is required
- Fair value hierachy - 3 levels

Test your understanding answers

Test your understanding 1 – Framework

(a) The Framework sets out the concepts that underlie the preparation and presentation of financial statements for external users.

The purpose of the Conceptual Framework is:

- to assist the IASB when developing or reviewing IFRSs
- to assist the Board in promoting the harmonisation of accounting standards
- to assist national standard-setting bodies in developing national standards
- to assist preparers of financial statements in applying IFRSs and in dealing with topics that have yet to form the subject of an IFRS
- to assist auditors in forming an opinion on whether financial statements comply with IFRSs
- to assist users of financial statements in interpreting the information contained in financial statements prepared in compliance with IFRSs
- to provide those who are interested in the work of the IASB with information about its approach to the formulation of IFRSs

Nothing in the Framework over-rides the requirements of a specific IFRS.

(b) An asset is a resource controlled by the entity as a result of past events and from which future economic benefits are expected to flow to the entity.

A liability is a present obligation of the entity arising from past events, the settlement of which is expected to result in an outflow from the entity of resources embodying economic benefits.

Equity is the residual interest in the assets of the entity after deducting all its liabilities.

The following criticisms could be made of these definitions:

- The definitions are inconsistently applied across the range of IFRSs
- The concept of 'control' is not clearly defined and can prove difficult to apply

- There is a lack of guidance about the meaning of an 'economic resource'
- The notion of 'expectation' is vague. Does it refer to the probability of an inflow/outflow or to a mathematical 'expected value'?
- The definitions do not offer enough guidance as to the difference between liabilities and equity. Further guidance here would benefit users, particularly when applying these concepts to financial instruments.

Test your understanding 2 – Applying the framework

Operating lease

In the financial statements of the lessee, the total payments made towards an operating lease are expensed to profit or loss on a straight line basis. The asset and the future lease payments are not recognised.

Operating lease commitments appear to meet the definition of a liability per the Framework. Signing the lease agreement would meet the definition of a 'past event'. Since the lease is non-cancellable, Mineral has an obligation to make payments to the lessor for several years.

The fact that no liability is recognised would therefore seem to contradict the Framework.

Deferred tax

The carrying value of the asset exceeds the tax base. A deferred tax liability will be recognised by multiplying the temporary difference by the tax rate. The tax charge will be recognised in other comprehensive income.

No obligation to pay tax has arisen as a result of the revaluation. Rather, deferred tax is an application of the accruals concept in that it recognises the tax effects of a transaction in the period when the transaction occurs. Moreover, Mineral has no plans to sell this asset so the payment of this tax is not probable.

The deferred tax liability does not appear to meet the Framework's definition of a liability

Financial instruments

IAS 32 states that a financial liability is any contract that may be settled in the entity's own equity instruments and is a non-derivative for which the entity is obliged to deliver a variable number of its own equity instruments

The contract requires that Mineral delivers as many of its own equity instruments as are equal in value to a certain amount. Per IAS 32, this contract should be classified as a financial liability.

An equity instrument is not a resource of an entity. This contract does not therefore represent an obligation to transfer a resource.

The financial liability does not satisfy the Framework's definition of a liability.

Test your understanding 3 – Fair value

(a) If Market 1 is the principal market for the asset (the market with the greatest volume and level of activity for the asset), the fair value of the asset would be measured using the price that would be received in that market, after taking into account transport costs. The fair value would therefore be $24 ($26 – $2). Transaction costs are ignored as they are not a characteristic of the asset.

(b) If neither market is the principal market for the asset, the fair value of the asset would be measured using the price in the most advantageous market. The most advantageous market is the market that maximises the amount that would be received to sell the asset, after taking into account transaction costs and transport costs (i.e. the net amount that would be received in the respective markets).

Because the maximum net amount that the entity would receive is $22 in Market 2 ($25 – $3), the fair value of the asset would be measured using prices in Market 2. This would result in a fair value measurement of $23 ($25 – $2). Although transaction costs are taken into account when determining which market is the most advantageous market, they are not factored into the fair value measurement itself.

chapter

2

The professional and ethical duty of the accountant

Chapter learning objectives

Upon completion of this chapter you will be able to:

- appraise the ethical and professional issues in advising on corporate reporting
- assess the relevance and importance of ethical and professional issues in complying with accounting standards
- appraise the potential ethical implications of professional and managerial decisions in the preparation of corporate reports
- assess the consequences of not upholding ethical principles in the preparation of corporate reports.

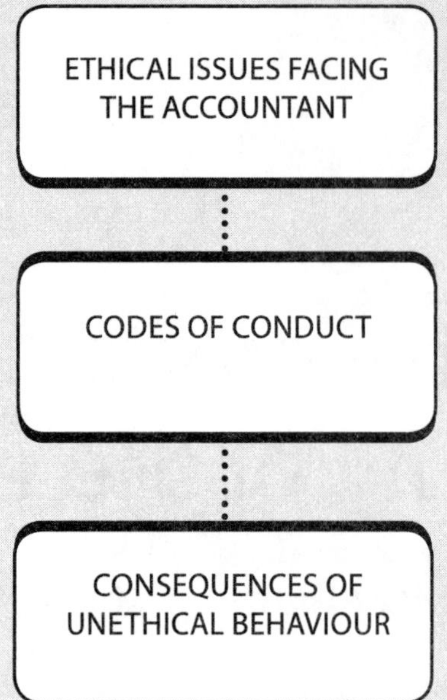

Accounting and ethics

A number of user groups rely on the financial statements to make economic decisions. It is important that these users are not misled.

However, the ethical beliefs of individual accountants may be too simplistic when dealing with real-life, complex ethical dilemmas. The study of ethics is therefore vital so that accountants can develop ethical reasoning skills that will help them to decide on the right course of action.

The ACCA requires its members to adhere to a code of professional ethics. This provides a set of moral guidelines for professional accountants. The fundamental principles of this code are:

(a) **Integrity** – to be straightforward and honest in all professional and business relationships.

(b) **Objectivity** – to not allow bias, conflict of interest or undue influence of others to override professional or business judgments.

(c) **Professional Competence and Due Care** – to maintain professional knowledge and skill at the level required to ensure that a client or employer receives competent professional services based on current developments in practice, legislation and techniques and act diligently and in accordance with applicable technical and professional standards.

(d) **Confidentiality** – to respect the confidentiality of information acquired as a result of professional and business relationships and, therefore, not disclose any such information to third parties without proper and specific authority, unless there is a legal or professional right or duty to disclose, nor use the information for the personal advantage of the professional accountant or third parties.

(e) **Professional behaviour** – to comply with relevant laws and regulations and avoid any action that discredits the profession.

Some of the elements of the ethical code are considered in more detail in the rest of this chapter.

Integrity

Acting with integrity involves being honest and straight-forward. Any attempt to conceal or hide transactions, either through omitting them or through inadequate or confusing disclosure, demonstrates a lack of integrity.

Later in this text, you will learn that forms of non-financial reporting are becoming increasingly important. Many entities prepare reports that detail their relationship with, and impact on, society and the environment. These issues could be combined in an integrated report. Such reports are voluntary. However, it could be argued that withholding information from users about a company's social and environmental impact lacks integrity. Moreover, failing to report issues about long-term sustainability may be just as misleading as incorrect information within the historical financial statements.

Objectivity

There are many times when an accountant might find that they have an incentive to represent the performance or position of a company in a particular way:

- **Profit related bonuses**: An accountant might be motivated to maximise profit in the current period in order to achieve their bonus. Alternatively, if current period targets have been met, an accountant might be motivated to shift profits into the next reporting period.
- **Financing**: An entity is more likely to be given a loan if it has valuable assets on which the loan can be secured. An incentive may therefore exist for the accountants to over-state assets on the statement of financial position.

- **Achieving a listing**: A company that is being listed on a stock exchange will want to maximise the amount that it receives from investors. Therefore, there may be an incentive for the accountants to over-state the assets and profits of a company before it lists.

Financial statements should faithfully represent the transactions that have occurred. The ethical code encourages accountants to not let bias or outside influence impact their judgements.

Areas of judgement in financial statements

One of the reasons why objectivity is such an important part of the ACCA ethical code is that accounting standards frequently involve the use of judgement. Bias would therefore have a direct impact on the financial statements produced. Some examples of the judgements required by IFRS are presented below:

- Many standards permit assets or liabilities to be held at fair value. IFRS 13 defines fair value as 'the price that would be received to sell an asset or paid to transfer a liability in an orderly transaction between market participants at the measurement date'. IFRS 13 stresses the importance of level 1 inputs – quoted prices for assets and liabilities in active markets – but, in the absence of these, permits more judgemental measures to be used.
- IAS 16 Property, Plant and Equipment states that entities should depreciate assets over their estimated useful life. By over-stating an asset's useful economic life, depreciation is charged more slowly to profit or loss.
- IAS 36 Impairment of Assets says that the recoverable amount of an asset is the higher of the fair value less costs to sell and the value in use. Both of these figures involve judgements about events that will happen in the future and are therefore open to manipulation.
- IFRS 2 Share-Based Payment requires entities to estimate the expense of an equity-settled share-based payment scheme based on the number of options expected to vest. By under-estimating the number of options expected to vest, profit in the short-term might be maximised.
- IAS 37 Provisions, Contingent Liabilities and Contingent Assets states that provisions should recorded at the best estimate of the expenditure to be incurred. Using lower than expected estimates will reduce the value of a provision and therefore maximise current year profits.

Unless an accountant understands and adheres to the code of ethics, then manipulation of these (and other) standards is likely. The financial statements would therefore not faithfully represent the performance and position of the entity and the users may be misled into making incorrect economic decisions.

Professional competence and due care

As you will be aware from your studies, new accounting standards are frequently issued and older standards are often updated or withdrawn. This means that accounting knowledge becomes out-of-date very quickly.

In order to comply with the code of ethics, accountants have a responsibility to ensure that they are aware of changes to accounting standards. This is often referred to as CPD (Continuing Professional Development).

CPD involves:

- Reading technical articles
- Attending seminars or presentations
- Attending training courses

Without up-to-date technical knowledge, it is unlikely that an accountant can produce financial statements that comply with IFRS. Material errors within financial statements will mislead the users.

Consequences of unethical behaviour

The journals and magazines of professional institutes regularly include details of professional disciplinary proceedings brought against individual members who were believed to have fallen short of the ethical standards expected of them.

The consequences of unethical behaviour in deliberately presenting incorrect financial information are severe. Many accountants have been fined or jailed for not fulfilling their professional duties.

The consequences for individuals include:

- Fines
- The loss of professional reputation

- Being prevented from acting as a director or officer of a public company in the future
- The possibility of being expelled by a professional accountancy body
- A prison sentence.

Ethics and the profit motive

It is commonly argued that the primary objective of a company is to maximise the wealth of its shareholders. Acting ethically might be seen to contradict this objective. For example, whilst it may be ethical to incur costs associated with looking after the environment, such costs reduce profits.

However, in modern society, companies are considered to be corporate citizens within society. Corporate social responsibility is increasingly important to investors and other stakeholders. It can attract 'green' investors, ethical consumers and employees and so in turn have a positive impact on financial results. Thus, it could be argued that the performance and sustainability of a company may not be maximised unless it behaves in an ethical manner.

Test your understanding 1 – Cookie

The directors of Cookie, a company, are very confident about the quality of the products that the company sells. Historically, the level of complaints received about product quality has been low. However, when calculating their warranty provision, they have over-estimated the number of items that will be returned as faulty. The directors believe that this is acceptable because it is important for financial statements to exhibit prudence.

Required:

Discuss the ethical issues raised by the treatment of the warranty provision.

Chapter summary

Ethical issues facing the accountant

- An accountant must be independent and must speak out if a client is following irregular accounting practices
- Accountants must follow the Codes of Ethics for the professional body of which they are a member
- Financial information must be prepared so that it meets accounting standards and shows a true and fair view/fair presentation of the financial position of the entity
- An employer may ask an accountant to act unethically by preparing the financial statements in a way that does not show the true picture

Codes of ethics

The principles in the ACCA Code of Ethics and Conduct are:

- Integrity
- Objectivity
- Professional competence and due care
- Confidentiality
- Professional behaviour

Consequences of unethical behaviour

The consequences of failing to act ethically are many and can be severe. They include:

- Prison sentence
- Fines or repayments of amounts taken fraudulently
- Loss of professional reputation
- Being prevented from acting in the same capacity in the future
- Investigation by professional accountancy body

Test your understanding answers

Test your understanding 1 – Cookie

Financial statements are important to a range of user groups, such as shareholders, banks, employees and suppliers. Prudence is important because over-stated assets or under-stated liabilities could mislead potential or current investors. However, excessive cautiousness means that the financial performance and position of an entity is not faithfully represented.

A faithful representation is often presumed to have been provided if accounting standards have been complied with. It would appear that the directors are not calculating the provision in line with the requirements of IAS 37, which requires provisions to be recognised at the 'best estimate' of the expenditure to be incurred. This may mean that profit is understated in the current period and then over-stated in subsequent periods.

Professional ethics is a vital part of the accountancy profession and ACCA members are bound by its Code of Ethics and Conduct. This sets out the importance of the fundamental principles of confidentiality, objectivity, professional behaviour, integrity, and professional competence and due care.

Integrity is defined as being honest and straight-forward. Over-estimating a provision in order to shift profits from one period to another demonstrates a lack of integrity.

If the provision is being over-stated in order to achieve bonus targets or profit expectations in the next financial period, then this demonstrates a lack of objectivity.

If the directors are unaware of the requirements of IAS 37, then they may not be sufficiently competent.

Financial statements should faithfully represent the transactions that have occurred. Compliance with the ethical code thus encourages accountants to ensure that they are technically capable and sufficiently independent to comply with the requirements of IFRS.

chapter

3

Performance reporting

Chapter learning objectives

Upon completion of this chapter you will be able to:

- prepare reports relating to corporate performance for external stakeholders
- discuss the issues relating to the recognition of revenue
- evaluate recent changes to reporting financial performance.

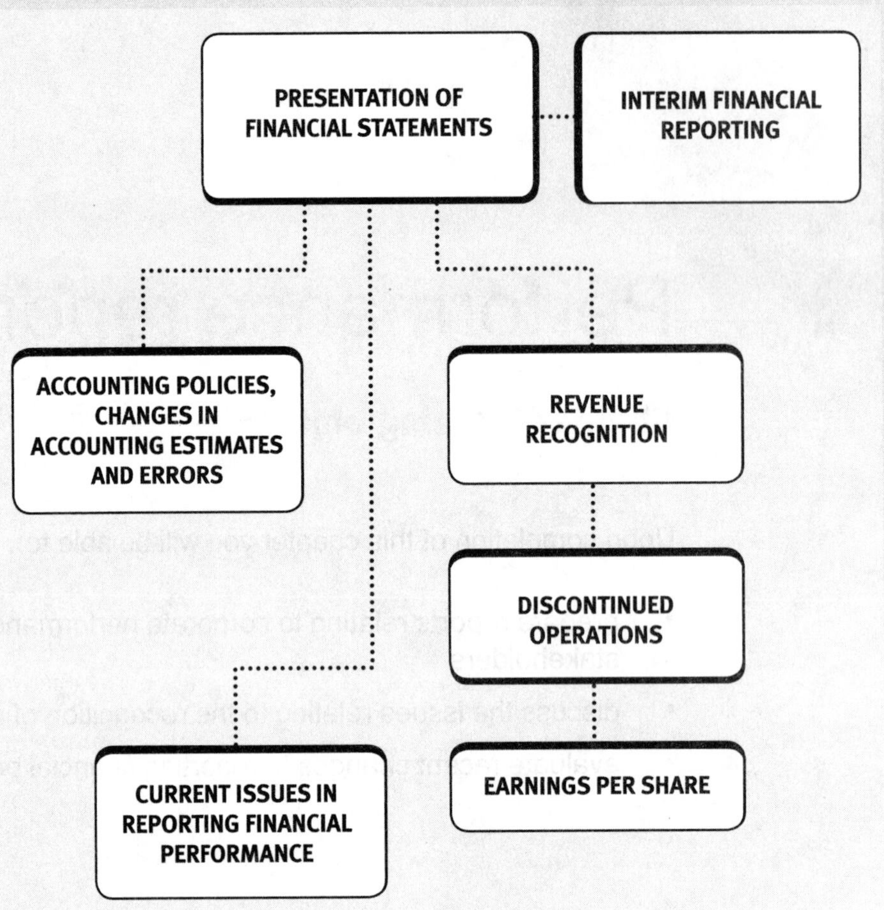

1 Presentation of financial statements (IAS 1 revised)

Components of financial statements

A complete set of financial statements has the following components:

- a statement of financial position at the end of the reporting period
- a statement of profit or loss and other comprehensive income (or statement of profit or loss with a separate statement of other comprehensive income)
- a statement of changes in equity for the period
- a statement of cash flows for the period (discussed in a later chapter)
- accounting policies note and other explanatory notes
- a statement of financial position at the beginning of the earliest comparative period when an entity applies an accounting policy retrospectively or corrects an error retrospectively

Other reports and statements in the annual report (such as a financial review, an environmental report or a social report) are outside the scope of IAS 1.

Statement of financial position

An entity shall classify an asset as current on the statement of financial position if:

- it expects to realise the asset, or intends to sell or consume it, in its normal operating cycle
- it holds the asset primarily for the purpose of trading
- it expects to realise the asset within twelve months after the reporting period.

All other assets are classified as non-current.

An entity shall classify a liability as current on the statement of financial position if:

- it expects to settle the liability in its normal operating cycle
- it holds the liability primarily for the purpose of trading
- the liability is due to be settled within twelve months after the reporting period
- it does not have an unconditional right to defer settlement of the liability for at least twelve months after the reporting period.

All other liabilities are classified as non-current.

Statement of profit or loss and other comprehensive income

Other comprehensive income (OCI) comprises income and expenses that are not recognised in profit or loss as required or permitted by other IFRSs.

Total comprehensive income is the realised profit or loss for the period plus all items of other comprehensive income for the period.

Items of OCI must be classified into two groups as follows:

- items that might be reclassified (or recycled) to profit or loss in subsequent accounting periods:
  - foreign exchange gains and losses arising on translation of a foreign operation (IAS 21)
  - effective parts of cash flow hedging arrangements (IAS 39)
- items that will not be reclassified (or recycled) to profit or loss in subsequent accounting periods:
  - changes in revaluation surplus (IAS 16 & IAS 38)
  - remeasurement components on defined benefit plans (IAS 19)
  - remeasurement of equity instruments designated to be classified as fair value through OCI (IFRS 9)

Entities can prepare one combined statement showing profit or loss for the year and OCI. Alternatively, an entity can prepare a statement of profit or loss and a separate statement of OCI. If the latter option is chosen, the statement of OCI should begin with profit or loss for the year so that there is no duplication or confusion as to which items are included within each statement.

Format one: statement of profit or loss and other comprehensive income

For illustration, one of the recommended formats is as follows:

XYZ Group – Statement of profit or loss and other comprehensive income for the year ended 31 December 20X3

	$000
Revenue	X
Cost of sales	(X)
Gross profit	X
Other operating income	X
Distribution costs	(X)
Administrative expenses	(X)
Other operating expenses	(X)
Profit from operations	X
Finance costs	(X)
Share of profit of associates	X

Profit before tax	X
Income tax expense	(X)
Profit or loss for the period	X
Other comprehensive income	
Items that will not be reclassified to profit or loss:	
Gains on property revaluation	X
Remeasurement or actuarial gains and losses on defined benefit pension plans	(X)
Financial assets designated to be accounted for through OCI	X
Income tax relating to items that will not be reclassified	(X)
Total – items that will not be reclassified to profit or loss net of tax:	**X**
Items that may be reclassified subsequently to profit or loss:	
Cash flow hedges	X
Exchange differences on translating foreign operations	X
Income tax relating to items that may be reclassified	(X)
Total – items that may be reclassified to profit or loss net of tax:	**X**
Total – other comprehensive income net of tax for the year	**(X)**
Total comprehensive income for the year	**X**
Profit attributable to:	
	$000
Owners of the parent	X
Non-controlling interest	X
	X
Total comprehensive income attributable to:	
Owners of the parent	X
Non-controlling interest	X
	X

Other comprehensive income and related tax

IAS 1 requires an entity to disclose income tax relating to each component of OCI. This may be achieved by either

- disclosing each component of OCI net of any related tax effect, or
- disclosing OCI before related tax effects with one amount shown for tax (as shown in the above examples).

The purpose of this is to provide users with tax information relating to these components, as they often have tax rates different from those applied to profit or loss.

Statement of changes in equity

IAS 1 requires all changes in equity arising from transactions with owners in their capacity as owners to be presented separately from non-owner changes in equity. This would include:

- Issues of shares
- Dividends.

Total comprehensive income is shown in aggregate only for the purposes of reconciling opening to closing equity.

XYZ Group – Statement of changes in equity for the year ended 31 December 20X3

	Equity capt'l	Ret'd earng's	Transl'n of for'gn operations	Financial assets thru' OCI	Cash flow hdg's	Reval'n surplus	Total
	$000	$000	$000	$000	$000	$000	$000
Balance at 1 Jan 20X3	X	X	(X)	X	X	–	X
Changes in accounting policy	–	X	–	–	–	–	X
Restated balance	X	X	X	X	X	X	X
Changes in equity for 20X3							
Dividends	–	(X)	–	–	–	–	(X)
Issue of equity capital	X	–	–	–	–	–	X
Total comprehensive income for year	–	X	X	X	X	X	X
Transfer to retained earnings	–	X	–	–	–	(X)	–
Balance at 31 December 20X3	X	X	X	X	X	X	X

In addition to these six columns, there should be columns headed:

(a) Non-controlling interest

(b) Total equity

A comparative statement for the prior period must also be published.

General features of financial statements

(a) **Going concern**

Once management have assessed that there are no material uncertainties as to the ability of an entity to continue for the foreseeable future, the financial statements should be prepared on the assumption that the entity will in fact continue. In other words, the financial statements will be prepared on a going concern basis.

(b) **Accruals basis of accounting**

The accruals basis of accounting means that transactions and events are recognised when they occur, not when cash is received or paid for them.

(c) **Consistency of presentation**

The presentation and classification of items in the financial statements should be retained from one period to the next unless:

- it is clear that a change will result in a more appropriate presentation
- a change is required by a standard (IAS or IFRS) or an interpretation (SIC or IFRIC).

(d) **Materiality and aggregation**

An item is material if its omission or misstatement could influence the economic decisions of users taken on the basis of the financial statements. Financial statements should therefore show material items separately, but immaterial items may be aggregated with amounts of a similar nature.

(e) **Offsetting**

Assets and liabilities, and income and expenses, should not be offset except when required or permitted by a standard or an interpretation.

(f) **Comparative information**

Comparative information for the previous period should be disclosed, unless a standard or an interpretation permits or requires otherwise.

(g) **Compliance with IFRS**

An entity whose financial statements comply with IFRS should make an explicit and unreserved statement of such compliance in the notes.

Accounting policies

The accounting policies note should describe:

- the measurement basis (or bases) used in preparing the financial statements (e.g. historical cost, fair value, etc)
- each significant accounting policy.

Sources of uncertainty

An entity should disclose information about the key sources of estimation uncertainty that may cause a material adjustment to assets and liabilities within the next year, e.g. key assumptions about the future.

Reclassification adjustments

Reclassification adjustments are amounts reclassified to profit or loss in the current period that were recognised in other comprehensive income in the current or previous periods. This is sometimes referred to as 'recycling'.

IAS 1 requires that reclassification adjustments should be disclosed, either on the face of the statement of profit or loss and other comprehensive income or in the notes.

This is necessary to inform users of amounts that are included as other comprehensive income in previous periods and in profit or loss in the current period, so that they can assess the effect of such reclassifications on profit or loss.

Dividends

Distributions to equity holders are disclosed in the statement of changes.

This requirement is in line with separate disclosure of owner and non-owner changes in equity discussed earlier.

2 Accounting policies, estimates and errors

IAS 8: Policies, estimates and errors

Accounting policies are the specific principles, bases, conventions, rules and practices applied by an entity in preparing and presenting financial statements.

Where a standard or interpretation exists in respect of a transaction, the accounting policy is determined by applying the standard or interpretation.

- Where there is no applicable standard or interpretation, management must use its judgement to develop and apply an accounting policy. The accounting policy selected must result in information that is relevant and reliable.
- Management should refer to the following:
  - standards and interpretations dealing with similar and related issues
  - the Framework.
- Provided they do not conflict with the sources above, management may also consider:
  - the most recent pronouncements of other standard-setting bodies that use a similar conceptual framework
  - other accounting literature and accepted industry practices.
- An entity must select and apply its accounting policies consistently for similar transactions.

Changes in accounting policies

An entity should only change its accounting policies if the change is required by a standard or interpretation, or it results in more reliable and relevant information.

- New accounting standards normally include transitional arrangements on how to deal with any resulting changes in accounting policy.
- If there are no transitional arrangements, the new policy should be applied retrospectively. The entity adjusts the opening balance of each affected component of equity, and the comparative figures are presented as if the new policy had always been applied.

- Where a change is applied retrospectively, IAS 1 revised requires an entity to include in its financial statements a statement of financial position at the beginning of the earliest comparative period. In practice this will result in 3 statements of financial position
  - at the reporting date
  - at the start of the current reporting period
  - at the start of the previous reporting period

Changes in accounting estimates

Making estimates is an essential part of the preparation of financial statements. For example, preparers may have to estimate allowances for receivables, inventory obsolescence or the useful lives of non-current assets.

- A change in an accounting estimate is not a change in accounting policy.
- The effect of a change in an accounting estimate must be recognised prospectively, by including it in the statement of profit or loss and other comprehensive income for the current period and any future periods that are also affected.

Prior period errors

Prior period errors are omissions from, and misstatements in, the entity's financial statements for one or more prior periods arising from a failure to use reliable information that was available when the financial statements were authorised for issue, and could reasonably be expected to have been taken into account.

- They include mistakes in applying accounting policies, oversights and the effects of fraud.
- Material prior period errors should be corrected retrospectively in the first set of financial statements authorised for issue after their discovery. Opening balances of equity, and the comparative figures, should be adjusted to correct the error.
- IAS 1 revised also requires that where a prior period error is corrected retrospectively, a statement of financial position is provided at the beginning of the earliest comparative period.

3 Revenue recognition (IAS 18)

Revenue

Revenue is the gross inflow of economic benefits during the period arising from the ordinary activities of the entity.

- Revenue can result from the sale of goods, the rendering of services and from the receipt of interest, royalties and dividends.
- 'Ordinary activities' means normal trading or operating activities.
- 'Revenue' presented in the statement of profit or loss should not include items such as proceeds from the sale of non-current assets, or sales tax.
- IAS 18 does not apply to rental and lease agreements (see IAS 17), associates (see IAS 28) or construction contracts (see IAS 11, which is outside of the P2 syllabus).

Measurement of revenue

Revenue should be measured at the fair value of the consideration received or receivable.

- For a cash sale, the revenue is the immediate proceeds of sale.
- For a credit sale, the revenue is the anticipated cash receivable.
- If the effect of the time value of money is material, the revenue should be discounted to present value.
- Revenue excludes sales taxes and similar items (these are not economic benefits for the reporting entity).

Revenue from the sale of goods

The following conditions must be satisfied before revenue from the sale of goods can be recognised:

- the seller transfers the significant risks and rewards of ownership to the buyer
- the seller does not retain management or control over the goods sold
- the amount of revenue can be measured reliably
- the transaction's economic benefits will probably flow to the seller
- the costs incurred or to be incurred can be measured reliably.

Revenue from services

If the following conditions are met, revenue from services is recognised according to the stage of completion:

- the revenue can be measured reliably
- the transaction's economic benefits will probably flow to the provider
- the stage of completion at the reporting date can be measured reliably
- the costs incurred and the costs to complete can be measured reliably.

If these conditions are not met, then revenue should be restricted to any recoverable costs incurred.

Interest, royalties and dividends

Revenue from these sources should be recognised when the receipt is probable and the revenues are measurable. Revenue should be recognised as follows:

- interest is recognised on a time proportion basis, taking into account the effective yield on the asset
- royalties are accrued in accordance with the relevant contract
- dividends are recognised when the shareholder's right to receive payment is established.

Illustration 1 – Car dealer revenue recognition

A car dealer sells a car on credit terms. When should the revenue be recognised?

Solution

This transaction gives rise to two different types of revenue – the trading profit and the finance income from the sale on credit. If the credit agreement is such that the user of the car becomes the legal owner either immediately or at some time in the future, then the risks and rewards are transferred to the user and the trading profit can be regarded as earned when the credit agreement is signed. However the finance income must be spread over the time period of the credit agreement.

Specific situations

Area	Guidance
Long-term contractual performance	Recognise in accordance with the performance of contractual obligations.
Separation or linking of contractual arrangements (e.g. the sale of goods with a maintenance contract)	Where the two components operate independently of each other, then recognise as separate transactions.
Bill and hold arrangements	Recognise revenue if the substance of the arrangement is that the goods represent an asset of the customer.
Sale with right of return	Exclude the sales value of estimated returns from revenue. Continue to monitor the accuracy of estimates with any changes reported within revenue.
Presentation of turnover as principal or agent	The issue is whether in a transaction on behalf of a third party a seller should record total turnover or merely the commission received from the third party (e.g. the on-line retailer of holidays through a website). IAS 18 states that the substance of the arrangement needs to be examined.

Specific situations: further details

IAS 18 includes an Appendix which gives guidance on specific situations:

(a) **Bill and hold arrangements**

This is a contract for the supply of goods, where the buyer accepts title to the goods but does not take physical delivery of them until a later date. Provided the goods are available for delivery, the buyer gives explicit instructions to delay delivery and there are no alterations to the terms on which the seller normally trades with the buyer, revenue should recognise when the buyer accepts title.

(b) **Payments for goods in advance (e.g. deposits)**

Revenue should be recognised when delivery of the goods to the buyer takes place. Until then, any payments in advance should be treated as liabilities.

(c) **Payments for goods by instalments**

Revenue is recognised when the significant risks and rewards of ownership have been transferred, which is usually when delivery is made. If the effect of the time value of money is material, the sale price should be discounted to its present value.

(d) **Sale or return**

Sometimes goods are delivered to a customer but the customer can return them within a certain time period. Revenue is normally recognised when the goods are delivered.

Revenue should then be reduced by an estimate of the returns. In most cases, a seller can estimate returns from past experience. For example, a retailer would know on average what percentage of goods were returned after the year end and could adjust revenue by the amount of expected returns.

(e) **Presentation of revenue as a principal or as agent**

The principal supplies goods or services on its own account, whilst the agent receives a fee or commission for arranging provision of goods or services by the principal. The principal is exposed to the risks and rewards of the transaction and therefore records revenue as the gross amount receivable. The agent only records the commission receivable on the transaction as revenue. An example would be a cosmetics agent who earns commission on the number of cosmetics sold. The agent owns no inventory, so is not exposed to obsolescence and therefore could only record commission as its revenue. The cosmetics company is exposed to inventory obsolescence and selling price changes, so would record the gross amount of the sale as revenue.

(f) **Separation and linking of contractual arrangements**

Sometimes businesses provide a number of different goods or services to customers as a package. For example, a customer might purchase software together with regular upgrades for one year. The problem here is whether the sale is one transaction or two separate transactions.

A 'package' such as this can only be treated as more than one separate transaction if each product or service is capable of being sold independently and if a reliable fair value can be assigned to each separate component.

Using the example above, if the support service is an optional extra and the software can be operated without it, the sale is two (or more) separate transactions. If the software cannot operate successfully without the upgrades, then the sale is one transaction and the amount of revenue recognised depends on the extent to which the seller has performed at the reporting date.

Test your understanding 1 – Revenue recognition

Skip is a company that sells printing equipment and provides printing services. It would like advice on how to recognise revenue from the following transactions in its financial statements for the year ended 31 December 20X1.

(1) During the year ended 31 December 20X1, Skip received $100,000 in deposits from customers who want to buy its latest product. These deposits are non-refundable, unless Skip is unable to fulfil the order. Skip expects to deliver the products on 1 February 20X2.

(2) On 31 December 20X1 Skip sold and delivered goods to its biggest customer. The goods normally sell for $50,000. The customer paid $25,000 upfront and will pay $25,000 on 31 December 20X2. This customer can borrow money at an annual interest rate of 10%.

(3) Skip signed a contract on 1 October 20X1 to print 12 issues of a new monthly magazine. It is expected that the magazine will grow rapidly in popularity over the next year. The contract value is $1m and this was received in advance. At 1 October 20X1 and 31 December 20X1, the total expected costs to fulfil the contract were estimated at $600,000. By 31 December 20X1, Skip had printed and delivered three issues of the magazine and had incurred total costs of $100,000.

(4) On 1 November 20X1, Skip sold some printing equipment to a customer and agreed to provide them with twelve months' of free technical support. Total consideration was $200,000 and this was received upfront. Skip would normally sell the technical support for $60,000.

Required:

Advise Skip on the accounting treatment of the above transactions in its financial statements for the year ended 31 December 20X1.

Revenue disclosure requirements

An entity should disclose:

- It's accounting policies for revenue including the methods adopted to determine the stage of completion of service transactions
- the amount of each significant category of revenue recognised during the period
- the amount of revenue arising from exchanges of goods or services.

Earnings management

Since IAS 18 was originally issued, businesses and transactions have become much more complex. Some entities have exploited the weaknesses in IAS 18 in order to artificially enhance revenue (a practice sometimes called 'aggressive earnings management'). For example, some software companies recognise sales when orders are made, well before it is reasonably certain that cash will be received.

The main issue is one of timing. At what point in a transaction should an entity recognise revenue?

Three questions can be helpful in dealing with an unusual transaction or situation:

- When is the 'critical event'? This is the point at which most or all of the uncertainty surrounding a transaction is removed.
- Has the seller actually performed? Transactions that give rise to revenue are legally contractual arrangements, regardless of whether a formal contract exists. Revenue can only be recognised when an entity has performed its obligations under the contract. For example, an entity cannot recognise revenue at the time that it receives payment in advance.
- Has the transaction increased the entity's net assets/equity? For example, when an entity makes a sale, its assets increase, because it has receivables (access to future economic benefits in the form of cash). Therefore it recognises a gain. This is one of the main principles in the Framework.

4 Discontinued operations

Discontinued operations (IFRS 5)

A discontinued operation is a component of an entity that either has been disposed of, or is classified as held for sale, and:

- represents a separate major line of business or geographical area of operations
- is part of a single co-ordinated plan to dispose of a separate major line of business or geographical area of operations
- is a subsidiary acquired exclusively with a view to resale.

If the component/operation has not already been sold, then it will only be a discontinued operation if it is held for sale.

An operation is held for sale if its carrying amount will not be recovered principally by continuing use. To be classified as held for sale (and therefore to be a discontinued operation) at the reporting date, it must meet the following criteria.

- The operation is available for immediate sale in its present condition.
- The sale is highly probable and is expected to be completed within one year.
- Management is committed to the sale.
- The operation is being actively marketed.
- The operation is being offered for sale at a reasonable price in relation to its current fair value.
- It is unlikely that the plan will change or be withdrawn.

Presentation

Users of the financial statements are more interested in future profits than past profits. They are able to make a better assessment of future profits if they are informed about operations that have been discontinued during the period.

IFRS 5 requires information about discontinued operations to be presented in the financial statements.

- A single amount should be presented on the face of the statement of profit or loss and other comprehensive income that is comprised of:
  - the total of the post-tax profit or loss of discontinued operations
  - the post-tax gain or loss on the measurement to fair value less costs to sell or on the disposal of the discontinued operation.
- An analysis of the single amount described above should be provided. This can be presented on the face of the statement of profit or loss and other comprehensive income or in the notes to the financial statements. The analysis must show:
  - the revenue, expenses and pre-tax profit or loss of discontinued operations
  - the related tax expense
  - the gain or loss recognised on the measurement to fair value less costs to sell or on the disposal of the discontinued operation
  - the related tax expense.
- The net cash flows attributable to the operating, investing and financing activities of discontinued operations must be shown, either on the face of the statement of cash flows or in the notes.
- If a decision to sell an operation is taken after the year-end but before the accounts are approved, this is treated as a non-adjusting event after the reporting date and disclosed in the notes. The operation does not qualify as a discontinued operation at the reporting date and separate presentation is not appropriate.
- In the comparative figures the operations are also shown as discontinued (even though they were not classified as such at the end of the previous year).

Example presentation

Statement of profit or loss (showing discontinued operations as a single amount, with analysis in the notes)

	20X2	20X1
	$m	$m
Revenue	100	90
Operating expenses	(60)	(65)
Profit from operations	40	25
Finance cost	(20)	(10)
Profit before tax	20	15
Income tax expense	(6)	(7)
Profit from continuing operations	14	8
Discontinued operations		
Loss from discontinued operations*	(25)	(1)
Profit/(loss) for the year	(11)	7

The entity did not recognise any components of other comprehensive income in the periods presented.

* The analysis of this loss would be given in a note to the accounts.

Illustration - Discontinued operations

The Portugal group of companies has a financial year-end of 30 June 20X4. The financial statements were authorised three months later. The group is disposing of many of its subsidiaries, each of which is a separate major line of business or geographical area.

- A subsidiary, England, was sold on 1 January 20X4.
- On 1 January 20X4, an announcement was made that there were advanced negotiations to sell subsidiary Switzerland and that, subject to regulatory approval, this was expected to be completed by 31 October 20X4.

- The board has also decided to sell a subsidiary called France. Agents have been appointed to find a suitable buyer but none have yet emerged. The agent's advice is that potential buyers are deterred by the expected price that Portugal hopes to achieve.
- On 10 July 20X4, an announcement was made that another subsidiary, Croatia, was for sale. It was sold on 10 September 20X4.

Required:

Explain whether each of these subsidiaries meets the definition of a 'discontinued operation' as defined by IFRS 5.

Solution

England has been sold during the year. It is a discontinued operation per IFRS 5.

Switzerland is a discontinued operation per IFRS 5. There is clear intention to sell, and the sale is highly probable within 12 months.

France is not a discontinued operation per IFRS 5. It does not seem that France is being offered for sale at a reasonable price in relation to its current fair value. The sale does not seem to be highly probable within 12 months.

Croatia is not a discontinued operation per IFRS 5. The conditions for classification as held for sale were not met until after the year end.

5 Earnings per share (IAS 33)

Earnings per share (IAS 33)

Scope and definitions

IAS 33 applies to entities whose equity shares are publicly traded. If private entities choose to disclose an earnings per share figure, it must have been calculated in accordance with IAS 33.

An **ordinary share** is an equity instrument that is subordinate to all other classes of equity instruments.

A potential ordinary share is a financial instrument or other contract that may entitle its holder to ordinary shares.

The basic calculation

The actual earnings per share (EPS) for the period is called the **basic EPS** and is calculated as:

$$\frac{\text{Profit or loss for the period attributable to equity shareholders}}{\text{Weighted average number of ordinary shares outstanding in the period}}$$

Profit for the period must be reduced (or a loss for the period must be increased) for any irredeemable preference dividends paid during the period.

If an entity prepares consolidated financial statements, then EPS will be based on the consolidated profit for the period attributable to the equity shareholders of the parent company (i.e. total consolidated profit less the profit attributable to the non-controlling interest).

The weighted average number of shares takes into account the timing of share issues during the year.

Illustration – Basic EPS

An entity issued 200,000 shares at full market price on 1 July 20X8.

Relevant information

	20X8	**20X7**
Profit attributable to the ordinary shareholders for the year ending 31 Dec	$550,000	$460,000
Number of ordinary shares in issue at 31 Dec	1,000,000	800,000

Required:

Calculate basic EPS for the years ended 31 December 20X7 and 20X8.

Solution

Calculation of earnings per share

20X7 = $460,000/800,000 = 57.5c

20X8 = $550,000/900,000 (W1) = 61.1c

(W1) **Weighted average number of shares in 20X8**

800,000 × 6/12 =	400,000
1,000,000 × 6/12 =	500,000
	900,000

Since the additional 200,000 shares were issued at full market price but have only contributed finance for half a year, a weighted average number of shares must be calculated. The earnings figure is not adjusted.

Bonus issues

If an entity makes a bonus issue of shares then share capital increases. However, no cash has been received and therefore there is no impact on earnings. This means that a bonus issue reduces EPS.

For the purpose of calculating basic EPS, the bonus issue shares are treated as if they have always been in issue. The easiest way to do this is multiply the number of shares outstanding before the bonus issue by the bonus fraction.

The bonus fraction is calculated as follows:

$$\frac{\text{Number of shares after bonus issue}}{\text{Number of shares before bonus issue}}$$

EPS for the comparative period must be restated. The easiest way to achieve this is to multiply the EPS figure from the prior year's financial statements by the inverse of the bonus fraction.

Illustration - Bonus issue

An entity made a bonus issue of one new share for every five existing shares held on 1 July 20X8.

Relevant information

	20X8	**20X7**
Profit attributable to the ordinary shareholders for the year ending 31 Dec	$550,000	$460,000
Number of ordinary shares in issue at 31 Dec	1,200,000	1,000,000

Required:

(a) **Calculate basic EPS for the year ended 31 December 20X8.**

(b) **Calculate the prior year comparative EPS figure as it would appear in the financial statements for the year ended 31 December 20X8.**

Solution

(a) EPS = $550,000/1,200,000 (W1) = 45.8c

(W1) **Weighted average number of shares**

1,000,000 × 6/12 × 6/5 (W2)	600,000
1,200,000 × 6/12	600,000
Weighted average number of shares	1,200,000

(W2) **Bonus fraction**

It was a one for five bonus issue.

A shareholder who had five shares before the bonus issue would have six shares after the bonus issue.

The bonus fraction is therefore 6/5.

(b) EPS in the financial statements for the year ended 31 December 20X7 would have been 46.0c ($460,000/1,000,000).

This is re-stated in the financial statements for the year ended 31 December 20X8 by multiplying it by the inverse of the bonus fraction.

The restated comparative is therefore 38.3c (46.0c × 5/6).

Rights issues

A rights issue of shares is normally made at less than the full market price. A rights issue therefore combines the characteristics of an issue at full market price with those of a bonus issue.

As already seen, the easiest way to deal with the bonus element is to calculate the bonus fraction and to apply this to all shares outstanding before the rights issue.

The bonus fraction for a rights issue is calculated as follows:

$$\frac{\text{Market price per share before rights issue}}{\text{Theoretical market price per share after the rights issue}}$$

EPS for the comparative period must be restated. The easiest way to achieve this is to multiply the EPS figure from the prior year's financial statements by the inverse of the bonus fraction.

Illustration – Rights issue

An entity issued one new share for every two existing shares at $1.50 per share on 1 July 20X8. The pre-issue market price was $3.00 per share.

Relevant information

	20X8	**20X7**
Profit attributable to the ordinary shareholders for the year ending 31 Dec	$550,000	$460,000
Number of ordinary shares in issue at 31 Dec	1,200,000	800,000

Required:

(a) **Calculate basic EPS for the year ended 31 December 20X8.**

(b) **Calculate the prior year comparative EPS figure as it would appear in the financial statements for the year ended 31 December 20X8.**

Solution

(a) EPS = $550,000/1,080,000 (W1) = 50.9c

(W1) **Weighted average number of shares**

800,000 × 6/12 × 3.00/2.50 (W2)	480,000
1,200,000 × 6/12	600,000
Weighted average number of shares	1,080,000

(W2) **Bonus fraction**

The bonus fraction is calculated as:

Share price before rights issue/Theoretical share price after rights issue.

The bonus fraction is $3.00/$2.50 (W3).

(W3) **Theoretical share price after rights issue**

	No. shares	Price per share	Market capitalisation
		$	$
Before rights issue	800,000	3.00	2,400,000
Rights issue	400,000	1.50	600,000
	1,200,000		3,000,000

The theoretical price per share after the rights issue is $2.50 ($3,000,000/1,200,000).

(b) EPS in the financial statements for the year ended 31 December 20X7 would have been 57.5c ($460,000/800,000).

This is restated in the financial statements for the year ended 31 December 20X8 by multiplying it by the inverse of the bonus fraction.

The restated comparative is therefore 47.9c (57.5c × 2.50/3.00).

Diluted earnings per share

Many companies issue convertible instruments, options and warrants that entitle their holders to purchase shares in the future at below the market price. When these shares are eventually issued, the interests of the original shareholders will be diluted. The dilution occurs because these shares will have been issued at below market price.

The Examiner has indicated that diluted earnings per share will not be examined in detail. However, students should have awareness of the topic as summarised below:

- Shares and other instruments that may dilute the interests of the existing shareholders are called potential ordinary shares.
- Examples of potential ordinary shares include:
  - debt and other instruments, including preference shares, that are convertible into ordinary shares
  - share warrants and options (instruments that give the holder the right to purchase ordinary shares)
  - employee plans that allow employees to receive ordinary shares as part of their remuneration and other share purchase plans
  - contingently issuable shares (i.e. shares issuable if certain conditions are met).
- Where there are dilutive potential ordinary shares in issue, the diluted EPS must be disclosed as well as the basic EPS. This provides relevant information to current and potential investors.
- Diluted EPS is calculated using current earnings but assuming that the worst possible dilution has already happened.
- The profit used in the basic EPS calculation is adjusted for any expenses that would no longer be paid if the convertible instrument were converted into shares, e.g. preference dividends, loan interest.
- The weighted average number of shares used in the basic EPS calculation is adjusted for the conversion of the potential ordinary shares. This is deemed to occur at the beginning of the period or the date of issue, if they were not in existence at the beginning of the period.

Presentation

An entity should present basic and diluted earnings per share on the face of the statement of profit or loss and other comprehensive income for each class of ordinary shares that has a different right to share in the net profit for the period.

- An entity should present basic and diluted earnings per share with equal prominence for all periods presented.
- If an entity has discontinued operations, it should also present basic and diluted EPS from continuing operations.
- An entity that reports a discontinued operation must disclose the basic and diluted EPS for the operation, either on the face of the statement of profit or loss or in the notes.
- IAS 33 also requires basic and diluted losses per share to be disclosed.
- In most cases, if basic EPS is a loss, then the diluted EPS will be the same as the basic EPS. This is because the loss per share will be diluted, and therefore reduced. Diluted EPS only relates to factors that decrease a profit or increase a loss.

Disclosure

An entity should disclose the following.

- The earnings used for basic and diluted EPS. These earnings should be reconciled to the net profit or loss for the period.
- The weighted average number of ordinary shares used for basic and diluted EPS. The two averages should be reconciled to each other.
- An entity may disclose an alternative EPS in addition to the IAS 33 requirements provided that:
  - the earnings figure is reconciled back to the statement of profit or loss and other comprehensive income
  - the same weighted average number of shares is used as for the IAS 33 calculations
  - basic and diluted EPS is disclosed
  - the alternative figure is shown in the notes, not on the face of the statement of profit or loss and other comprehensive income.

EPS as a performance measure

The EPS figure is used to compute the major stock market indicator of performance, the Price/Earnings ratio (P/E ratio). Rightly or wrongly, the stock market places great emphasis on the earnings per share figure and the P/E ratio. IAS 33 sets out a standard method of calculating EPS, which enhances the comparability of the figure.

However, EPS has limited usefulness as a performance measure.

- An entity's earnings are affected by its choice of accounting policies. Therefore, it may not always be appropriate to compare the EPS of different companies.
- EPS does not take account of inflation. Apparent growth in earnings may not be true growth.
- EPS does not provide predictive value. High earnings and growth in earnings may be achieved at the expense of investment, which would have generated increased earnings in the future.
- In theory, diluted EPS serves as a warning to equity shareholders that the return on their investment may fall in future periods. However, diluted EPS as currently required by IAS 33 is not intended to be forward-looking but is an additional past performance measure. Diluted EPS is based on current earnings, not forecast earnings. Therefore, diluted EPS is only of limited use as a prediction of future EPS.
- EPS is a measure of profitability. Profitability is only one aspect of performance. Concentration on earnings per share and 'the bottom line' arguably detracts from other important aspects of an entity's affairs, such as cash flow and stewardship of assets.

6 Interim reporting

Interim reporting (IAS 34)

Interim financial reports are prepared for a period shorter than a full financial year. Entities may be required to prepare interim financial reports under local law or listing regulations.

- IAS 34 does not require the preparation of interim reports, but sets out the principles that should be followed if they are prepared and specifies their minimum content.
- An interim financial report should include, as a minimum, the following components:
  - condensed statement of financial position as at the end of the current interim period, with a comparative statement of financial position as at the end of the previous financial year
  - condensed statement of profit or loss and other comprehensive income for the current interim period and cumulatively for the current financial year to date (if, for example the entity reports quarterly), with comparatives for the interim periods (current and year to date) of the preceding financial year
  - condensed statement showing changes in equity. This statement should show changes in equity cumulatively for the current year with comparatives for the corresponding period of the preceding financial year
  - condensed statement of cash flows cumulatively for the year to date, with a comparative statement to the same date in the previous year
  - selected explanatory notes
  - Improvements to IFRS issued May 2010 emphasises that there should be appropriate disclosures and reconciliation of events and transactions in interim statements with the most recent annual report. This could even be the first set of IFRS annual financial statements following adoption of IFRS for the first time.
- Condensed financial statements should include all of the headings and sub-totals used in the most recent annual financial statements.
- If an entity publishes a complete set of financial statements in its interim report, then they should comply with IAS 1 in full.
- Basic and diluted EPS should be presented on the face of interim statements of profit or loss and other comprehensive income for those entities within the scope of IAS 33.

7 Current issues

Current issues in performance reporting

Revenue from contracts with customers

Introduction

As part of a joint project between the IASB and US FASB, a revised ED dealing with revenue from contracts with customers was published in November 2011 (original ED published June 2010) with the objective to create a common revenue recognition standard for IFRS and US GAAP.

The reasons for developing a new reporting standard are as follows:

(a) to increase the extent of convergence between IFRS and US GAAP

(b) to improve comparability of revenue recognition practices between entities, across industries and capital markets

(c) to reduce complexity of revenue recognition principles and therefore simpler to prepare financial statements

(d) to enhance user benefits by improved disclosure requirements.

The current reporting standards dealing with revenue recognition (IAS 11 and IAS 18) are regarded as deficient as they do not provide a comprehensive framework for revenue recognition. Equally, simply amending either or both of these reporting standards will not achieve convergence between IFRS and US GAAP.

Revenue recognition proposals

The ED proposes a five-step approach to revenue recognition as follows:

(1) **Identify the contract(s) with the customer**. This would enable identification of enforceable rights and obligations within a contract. It may be possible to combine contracts and account for them as one set of enforceable rights and obligations.

(2) **Identify the separate enforceable obligations in a contract**. The various promises within a contract to transfer goods or services are referred to as performance obligations; where they are distinct, they should be accounted for separately. This will be the case if the goods or services are regularly sold separately. If a good or service is not sold separately, or is a part of in interrelated bundle, it is not regarded as distinct.

(3) **Determine the transaction price**. This is defined as the amount to which an entity expects to be entitled in exchange for transferring promised goods or services to a customer. The time value of money need not be taken into account if, at inception of the contract, the period between transfer of the promised goods or services and payment is expected to be within one year. Additionally, the transaction price will not include any allowance for risk of non-collection of the amount due.

(4) **Allocate the transaction price**. It is expected that revenue would be allocated to each separate performance obligation, based upon the relative selling prices of each distinct good or service. If there are no observable selling prices available, it would need to be estimated.

(5) **Recognise revenue when a performance obligation is satisfied**. Revenue should be recognised only when a performance obligation has been satisfied, with the amount required to satisfy the performance condition being the revenue recognised.
Where performance conditions are satisfied over time, as with the provision of services, there needs to be an appropriate measure of progress or provision to determine the extent to which a performance obligation has been satisfied and revenue recognised accordingly.

There would also be a limit on the cumulative amount of revenue that could be recognised to date to the amount to which an entity is reasonably assured it is entitled.

Other proposals

(1) Where performance obligations are to be satisfied over a period of time, and that time period exceeds one year, then any performance obligations regarded as onerous should result in recognition of a liability. In this context, onerous is defined as the lowest cost of settling a performance obligation exceeds the transaction price for that obligation.

(2) Where goods are transferred to a customer at a loss, this is an indication of impairment, and an impairment review should be performed. Where contracts are regarded as onerous, IAS 37 would continue to apply and provision for losses should be made.

(3) An asset may be recognised where costs have been incurred to obtain or fulfil a contract; such costs must:

- (a) relate to a specific contract,
- (b) generate or enhance resources that would be used in satisfying performance obligations relating to that contract, and
- (c) the costs are expected to be recovered.

(4) Enhanced qualitative and quantitative disclosures, particularly regarding significant judgements in applying the requirements of the standard, together with disclosures relating to recognition of assets

Summary

The revised ED provides the basis for a framework for revenue recognition that overcomes the current weaknesses of IAS 11 and IAS 18. This should result in similar transactions being accounted for on a consistent basis, irrespective of the entity applying the standard, the nature of the industry it operates in and whether IFRS or US GAAP is applied.

It is expected that the new IFRS governing revenue recognition will be issued during 2014.

8 Chapter summary

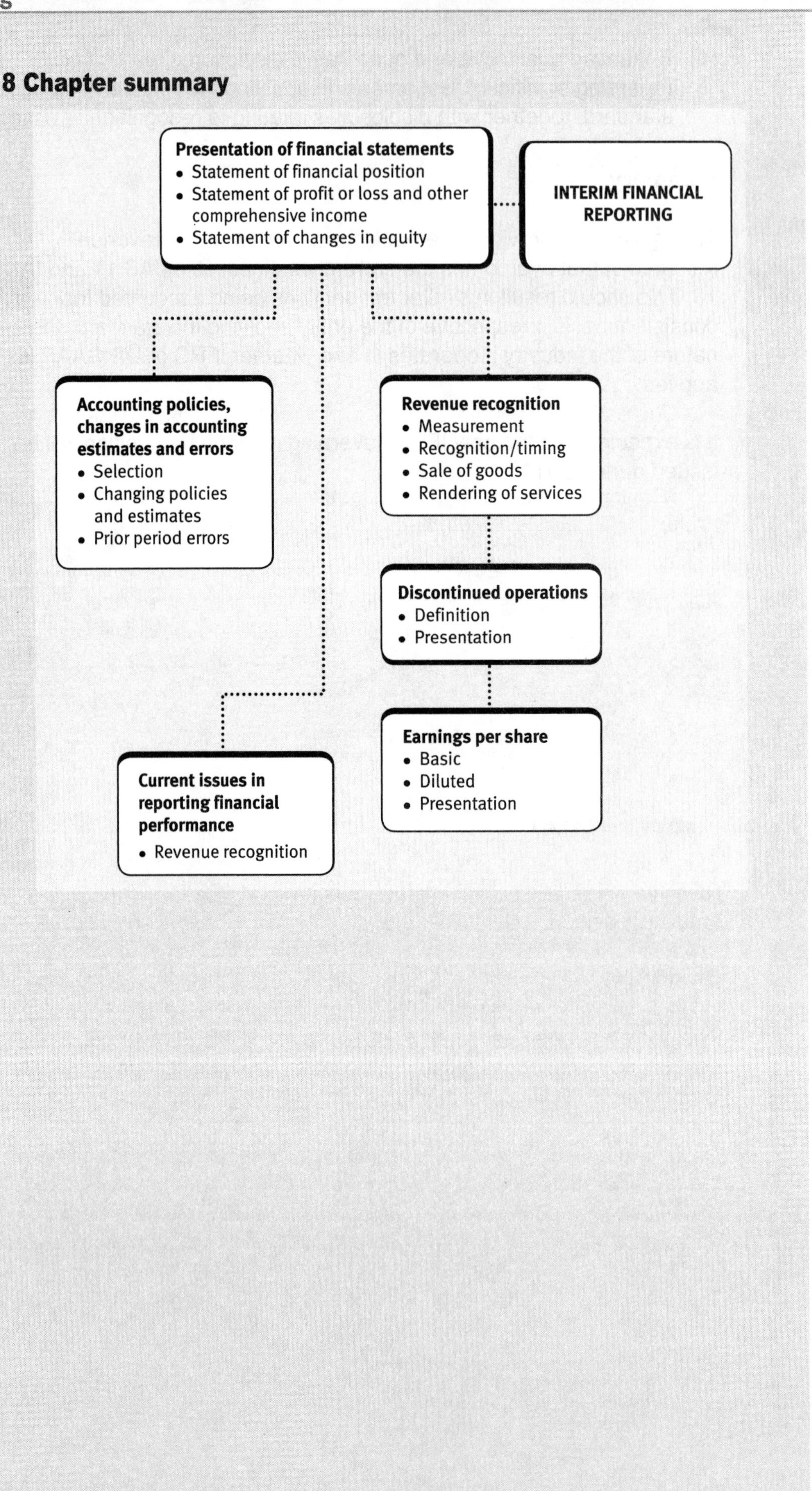

Test your understanding answers

Test your understanding 1 – Revenue recognition

Deposits

Revenue from the sale of a good should be recognised if:

- The entity has transferred the significant risks and rewards of ownership
- The entity does not retain continuing managerial involvement
- The amount of revenue can be measured reliably
- It is probable that economic benefits will flow to the entity
- The costs incurred or to be incurred can be measured reliably.

Although Skip has received payment there may be unanticipated events that will mean that the orders cannot be fulfilled and the deposits may need to be refunded. For instance, there might be quality issues with the product that prevent it from being shipped.

More importantly, Skip has not yet delivered the good to its customers. This means that the risks and rewards of ownership have not yet transferred.

Skip should not recognise any revenue from the deposits. The money received should be held as deferred income on the statement of financial position.

Credit sale

The good has been delivered to the customer and the revenues and costs can be measured reliably. Revenue should be recognised on 31 December 20X1.

According to IAS 18, revenue should be recognised at the fair value of the consideration received or receivable. This should be calculated by discounting expected receipts using the prevailing rate for a debt instrument issued by an entity with a similar credit rating to the customer.

The amount of revenue to be recognised on 31 December 20X1 is $47,727 (W1). Skip will need to recognise a receivable for $22,727 ($47,727 – $25,000).

(W1) **Present value of receipts**

Date	Cashflow	Discount rate	Present value
	$		$
31 December 20X1	25,000	1	25,000
31 December 20X2	25,000	1/1.1	22,727
			47,727

Printing services

Revenue should be recognised from the rendering of a service when:

- The amount of revenue can be measured reliably
- It is probable that economic benefits associated with the transaction will flow to the entity
- The stage of completion can be measured reliably
- The costs incurred and to complete the transaction can be measured reliably.

Total revenue is $1m, which has been received already. This means there are no doubts about its measurement or the likelihood of receipt. The entity can also measure the costs reliably. Stage of completion can be measured, based on either the number issues provided or the costs incurred. Therefore, Skip can recognise revenue from this transaction.

The amount of revenue to be recognised should be based on the stage of completion.

The contract is for 12 issues, and 3 issues have been printed. The contract could be said to be 25% complete (3 issues out of 12). On this basis, revenue of $250,000 ($1m × 25%) should be recognised.

However, this may be too simplistic, particularly as the magazine will increase in popularity over the 12 month contract period. This means that more work will be involved in printing the latter issues. It may therefore be more accurate to estimate the stage of completion on the basis of the proportion of total contract costs incurred.

Skip has incurred $100,000 out of total expected costs of $600,000. Using costs incurred as a basis to measure the stage of completion, the service is 1/6 complete ($100,000/$600,000) and revenue of $166,667 ($1m × 1/6) should be recognised.

This method of calculating the stage of completion may still over-estimate the proportion of the printing service performed. Most notably, it is likely that Skip will have incurred large up-front costs at the start of the contract.

The most accurate method of measuring the stage of completion is likely to be based on the total number of magazines printed to-date as a proportion of the total estimated number of magazines that will be printed. However, there is insufficient information presented to calculate the stage of completion under this method.

Sale of equipment and technical support

According to IAS 18, revenue from the sale of a good should be recognised when the risks and rewards of ownership transfer. Revenue from the provision of a service should be recognised according to the stage of completion. This transaction involves both the sale of a good (printing equipment) and the provision of a service (technical support) and therefore these components must be accounted for separately.

The service would normally retail for $60,000. This amount should be recognised according to the stage of completion. Based on the passage of time, 2/12 of the service has been provided by 31 December 20X1. This means that revenue of $10,000 ($60,000 × 2/12) should be recognised.

Revenue of $140,000 ($200,000 – $60,000) should be allocated to the sale of the equipment. This can be recognised in full on 1 November 20X1 because the risks and rewards of ownership transfer on this date.

Total revenue recognised from this transaction in the period is $150,000 ($10,000 + $140,000). A liability for deferred income of $50,000 ($200,000 – $150,000) should also be recognised on the statement of financial position.

chapter

4

Non-current assets, agriculture and inventories

Chapter learning objectives

Upon completion of this chapter you will be able to:

- apply and discuss the timing of the recognition of non-current assets and the determination of their carrying amounts including impairment and revaluations
- apply and discuss the treatment of non-current assets held for sale
- apply and discuss the accounting treatment of investment properties including classification, recognition and measurement issues
- apply and discuss the accounting treatment of intangible assets including the criteria for recognition and measurement subsequent to acquisition and classification
- apply and discuss the accounting treatment of inventories.

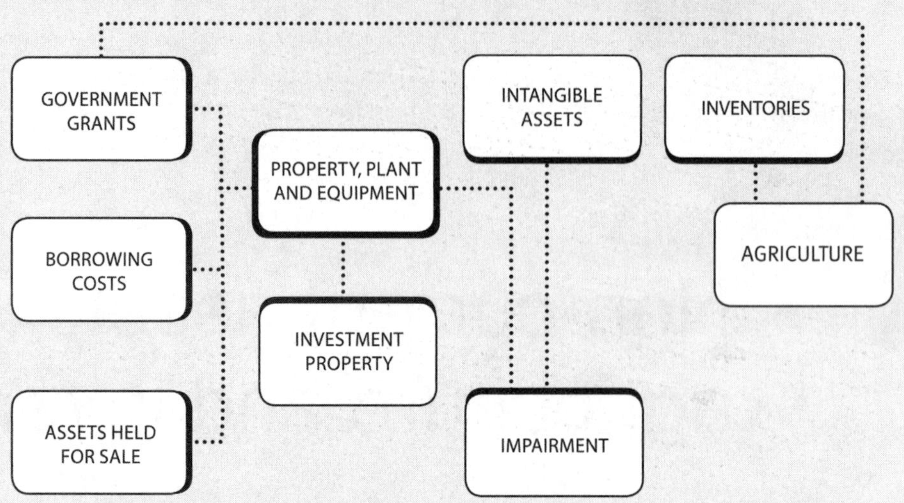

1 Property, plant and equipment

IAS 16 Property, plant and equipment: Initial recognition

Property, plant and equipment are tangible items that:

- are held for use in the production or supply of goods or services, for rental to others, or for administrative purposes
- are expected to be used during more than one period.

Tangible items have physical substance and can be touched.

An item of property, plant and equipment should be recognised as an asset when:

- it is probable that future economic benefits associated with the asset will flow to the entity
- the cost of the asset can be measured reliably.

Measurement on initial recognition

A tangible non-current asset should initially be measured at its cost. Its cost comprises:

- its purchase price
- any costs directly attributable to bringing the asset to the location and condition necessary for it to be capable of operating in the manner intended by management, i.e. it is ready for use (whether or not it is actually in use)

- the initial estimate of the costs of dismantling and removing the item and restoring the site on which it is located. This might apply where, for example, an entity has to recognise a provision for the cost of decommissioning an oil rig or a nuclear power station.

Directly attributable costs include commissioning costs (e.g. sea trials for a ship, testing a computer system before it goes live).

The following costs, specifically identified, should never be capitalised:

- administration and general overheads
- abnormal costs (repairs, wastage, idle time)
- costs incurred after the asset is physically ready for use (unless these costs increase the economic benefits the asset brings)
- costs incurred in the initial operating period (e.g. initial operating losses and any further costs incurred before a machine is used at its full capacity)
- costs of opening a new facility, introducing a new product (including advertising and promotional costs) and conducting business in a new location or with a new class of customer (including training costs)
- costs of relocating/reorganising an entity's operations.

Subsequent cost

Where additional costs are incurred after the asset becomes operational, the entity applies the normal recognition principle for assets: is it probable that future economic benefits will flow to the entity?

The costs of day-to-day servicing (repairs and maintenance) should not be capitalised. Rather than increasing economic benefits, they protect those expected at the time of the initial capitalisation. These costs should be recognised in profit or loss as they are incurred.

In contrast, the cost of replacing parts of items of property, plant and equipment is normally capitalised as it meets the recognition criteria. Examples:

- a furnace may require relining after a specified number of hours of use
- the interior walls of a building may need to be replaced.

Measurement after initial recognition

IAS 16 allows a choice between:

- the cost model
- the revaluation model.

Under the **cost model**, property, plant and equipment is valued at cost less accumulated depreciation.

Under the **revaluation model**, property, plant and equipment is carried at fair value less any subsequent accumulated depreciation.

- Revaluations must be made with 'sufficient regularity' to ensure that the carrying amount does not differ materially from the fair value at each reporting date.
- If an item is revalued, the entire class of assets to which the item belongs must be revalued.
- If a revaluation increases the value of an asset, the increase is presented as other comprehensive income (and disclosed as an item that will not be recycled to profit or loss in subsequent periods) and held within a 'revaluation surplus' within other components of equity.
- If a revaluation decreases the value of the asset, the decrease should be recognised immediately in profit or loss, unless there is a revaluation reserve representing a surplus on the same asset.

Depreciation

All assets with a finite useful life must be depreciated.

Depreciation is the systematic allocation of the depreciable amount of an asset over its useful life.

The depreciable amount of an asset is its cost less its residual value.

The residual value is the amount that the entity would currently obtain from disposal, net of selling costs, if the asset were already of the age and in the condition expected at the end of its useful life.

- IAS 16 does not prescribe a depreciation method, but the method used must reflect the pattern in which the asset's future economic benefits are expected to be consumed.

- Depreciation begins when the asset is available for use and continues until the asset is derecognised, even if it is idle.
- If an asset is measured at historical cost, the depreciation charge is based on historical cost.
- If an asset has been revalued, then the depreciation charge is based on the revalued amount.
- The residual value and the useful life of an asset should be reviewed at least at each financial year-end and revised if necessary. Depreciation methods should also be reviewed at least annually.
- Any adjustments are accounted for as a change in accounting estimate (under IAS 8 Accounting Policies, Changes in Accounting Estimates and Errors), rather than as a change in accounting policy. This means that they are reflected in the current and future statements of profit or loss and other comprehensive income.

Illustration: Change in depreciation estimates

An asset was purchased for $100,000 on 1 January 20X5 and straight line depreciation of $20,000 per annum was charged (five year life, no residual value). A general review of asset lives is undertaken and the remaining useful life of this asset as at 1 January 20X7 was deemed to be eight years.

Required:

What is the annual depreciation charge for 20X7 and subsequent years?

Solution

Carrying amount as at 1 January 20X7 (60% × $100,000)	$60,000
Remaining useful life as at 1 January 20X7	8 years
Annual depreciation charge ($60,000/8 years)	$7,500

Depreciation of separate components

Certain large assets are in fact a collection of smaller assets, each with a different cost and useful life. For example, an aeroplane consists of an airframe (which may last for 40 years or so) plus engines, radar equipment, seats, etc. all of which have a relatively short life. Instead of calculating depreciation on the aeroplane as a whole, depreciation is charged on each component (airframe, engines, etc.) instead.

For example, an entity buys a ship for $12m. The ship as a whole should last for 25 years. The engines, however, will need replacing after 7 years. The cost price of $12m included about $1.4m in respect of the engines.

The annual depreciation charge will be $624,000 made up as follows:

Engines: $1.4m over seven years = $200,000 pa, plus

The rest of the ship: $10.6m over 25 years = $424,000 pa.

Derecognition

Assets are derecognised on disposal, or when no future economic benefits are expected from their use or disposal.

- The gain or loss on derecognition of an asset is the difference between the net disposal proceeds, if any, and the carrying amount of the item.
- When a revalued asset is disposed of, any revaluation surplus may be transferred directly to retained earnings, or it may be left in equity under the heading revaluation surplus.

Disclosures

The following should be disclosed for each class of property, plant and equipment:

- the measurement bases used for determining the gross carrying amount
- the depreciation methods used
- the useful lives or the depreciation rates used
- the gross carrying amount and the accumulated depreciation (aggregated with accumulated impairment losses) at the beginning and end of the period
- a reconciliation of the carrying amount at the beginning and end of the period showing additions, disposals, increases or decreases resulting from revaluations and from impairment losses, depreciation, and other changes.

If items of property, plant and equipment are stated at revalued amounts, information about the revaluation should also be disclosed.

2 Impairment of assets (IAS 36)

Definition

Impairment is a reduction in the recoverable amount of an asset or cash-generating unit below its carrying amount.

An entity should carry out an impairment review at least annually if:

- an intangible asset is not being amortised because it has an indefinite useful life
- goodwill has arisen on a business combination.

Otherwise, an impairment review is required only where there is evidence that an impairment may have occurred.

Indications of impairment

Indications that an impairment might have happened can come from external or internal sources.

- **External sources of information**:
  - unexpected decreases in an asset's market value
  - significant adverse changes have taken place, or are about to take place, in the technological, market, economic or legal environment
  - increased interest rates have decreased an asset's recoverable amount
  - the entity's net assets are measured at more than its market capitalisation.
- **Internal sources of information**:
  - evidence of obsolescence or damage
  - there is, or is about to be, a material reduction in usage of an asset
  - evidence that the economic performance of an asset has been, or will be, worse than expected.

Calculating an impairment loss

An impairment occurs if the carrying amount of an asset is greater than its recoverable amount.

The **recoverable amount** is the higher of fair value less costs to sell and value in use.

Fair value is the price that would be received to sell an asset (or paid to transfer a liability) in an orderly transaction between market participants at the measurement date.

Costs to sell are incremental costs directly attributable to the disposal of an asset.

Value in use is the present value of future cash flows from using an asset, including its eventual disposal.

Carrying out an impairment test

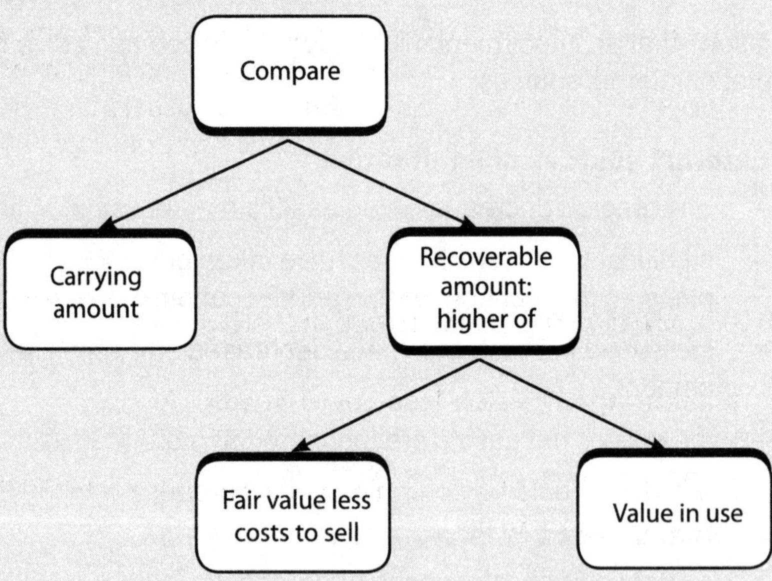

- If fair value less costs to sell is higher than the carrying amount, there is no impairment and no need to calculate value in use.

Illustration 1 – Impairment of item of plant

An item of plant is included in the financial statements at a carrying amount of $350,000. The present value of the future cash flows from continuing to operate the plant is $320,000. The plant could be sold for net proceeds of $275,000.

Required:

Is the item of plant impaired and, if so, by how much?

Solution

The recoverable amount is the greater of the fair value less costs to sell and the value in use. The fair value less costs to sell (net selling price) is $275,000 and the value in use is $320,000. The recoverable amount is therefore $320,000.

To determine whether the plant is impaired, the carrying amount is compared to the recoverable amount. The carrying amount of $350,000 is greater than the recoverable amount, so the asset must be written down to its recoverable amount. The impairment loss is $30,000 ($350,000 – $320,000).

Measurement of recoverable amount

(a) **Measuring fair value less costs to sell**

Fair value should be determined in accordance with IFRS 13 Fair Value Measurement.

Direct selling costs might include:

- legal costs
- stamp duty
- costs relating to the removal of a sitting tenant (in the case of a building).

Redundancy and reorganisation costs (e.g. following the sale of a business) are not direct selling costs.

(b) **Measuring value in use**

Value in use is calculated by estimating future cash inflows and outflows from the use of the asset and its ultimate disposal, and applying a suitable discount rate to these cash flows.

The discount rate should be a pre-tax rate that reflects current market assessments of:

- the time value of money, and
- the risks specific to the asset for which the future cash flow estimates have not been adjusted.

Test your understanding 1 – Impaired asset

Information about an asset is given below.

	$000
Carrying amount	500
Fair value less costs to sell	300
Future cash flows (per annum) for 2 years	200
Discount rate	10%

Required:

Determine the outcome of the impairment review.

Recognising impairment losses in the financial statements

An impairment loss is normally charged immediately in the statement of profit or loss and other comprehensive income.

- If the asset has previously been revalued upwards, the impairment is recognised as a component of other comprehensive income and is debited to the revaluation reserve until the surplus relating to that asset has been exhausted. The remainder of the impairment loss is recognised in profit or loss.
- The recoverable (impaired) amount of the asset is then depreciated/amortised over its remaining useful life.

Illustration 2 – Impairment of previously revalued asset

At 31 December 20X7, an item of property, plant and equipment has a carrying amount of $20,000. The asset had previously been revalued, and the remaining revaluation surplus relating to this asset is $10,000. An impairment review at 31 December 20X7 has determined that the asset is impaired by $12,000.

Required:

How should this loss be accounted for in the financial statements for the year ended 31 December 20X7?

Solution

A loss of $10,000 ($20,000 – $10,000) is recognised in other comprehensive income and debited to the revaluation surplus within other components of equity. The remaining loss of $2,000 is recognised as an expense in profit or loss for the period.

Cash-generating units

It is not usually possible to identify cash flows relating to particular assets. For example, a factory production line is made up of many individual machines, but the revenues are earned by the production line as a whole. This means that value in use must be calculated (and the impairment review performed) for groups of assets, rather than individual assets.

These groups of assets are called cash-generating units (CGUs).

Cash-generating units are segments of the business whose income streams are largely independent of each other.

- In practice they are likely to mirror the strategic business units used for monitoring the performance of the business.
- It could also include a subsidiary or associate within a corporate group structure.

Test your understanding 2 – Cash generating units

An entity has three stages of production:

- A – growing and felling trees
- B – creating parts of wooden furniture
- C – assembling the parts from B into finished goods.

The output of A is timber that is partly transferred to B and partly sold in an external market. If A did not exist, B could buy its timber from the market. The output of B has no external market and is transferred to C at an internal transfer price. C sells the finished product in an external market and the sales revenue achieved by C is not affected by the fact that the three stages of production are all performed by the entity.

Required:

Identify the cash-generating unit(s).

Allocating assets to cash-generating units

The carrying amount of a cash-generating unit includes the carrying amount of assets that can be attributed to the cash-generating unit and will generate the future cash inflows used in determining the cash-generating unit's value in use.

There are two problem areas:

- Corporate assets: assets that are used by several cash-generating units (e.g. a head office building or a research centre). They do not generate their own cash inflows, so do not themselves qualify as cash-generating units.
- Goodwill, which does not generate cash flows independently of other assets and often relates to a whole business.

Corporate assets and goodwill should be allocated to cash-generating units on a reasonable and consistent basis. A cash-generating unit to which goodwill has been allocated must be tested for impairment annually.

If no reasonable allocation of corporate assets or goodwill is possible, then a group of cash-generating units must be tested for impairment together in a two-stage process.

Illustration 3 – Impairment of CGU including goodwill

An entity acquires a business comprising three cash-generating units, D, E and F, but there is no reasonable way of allocating goodwill to them. After three years, the carrying amount and the recoverable amount of the net assets in the cash-generating units and the purchased goodwill are as follows:

	D	E	F	Goodwill	Total
	$000	$000	$000	$000	$000
Carrying amount	240	360	420	150	1,170
Recoverable amount	300	420	360		1,080

Step 1: Review the individual units for impairment.

F is impaired. A loss of $60,000 is recognised and its carrying amount is reduced to $360,000.

Step 2: Compare the carrying amount of the business as a whole, including the goodwill, with its recoverable amount.

The total carrying amount of the business is now $1,110,000 (1,170,000 – 60,000). A further impairment loss of $30,000 must then be recognised in respect of the goodwill (1,110,000 – 1,080,000).

Allocation of an impairment to the unit's assets

If an impairment loss arises in respect of a cash-generating unit, it is allocated among the assets in the unit in the following order:

- goodwill
- other assets pro rata to their carrying amount.

However, the carrying amount of an asset cannot be reduced below the highest of:

- its fair value less costs to sell (if determinable)
- its value in use (if determinable)
- zero.

Illustration 4 – Impairment allocation within CGU

Tinud has identified an impairment loss of $41m for one of its cash-generating units. The carrying amount of the unit's net assets was $150m, whereas the unit's recoverable amount was only $109m.

The draft values of the net assets of the unit are as follows:

	$m
Goodwill	13
Property	20
Machinery	49
Vehicles	35
Patents	14
Net monetary assets	19
	150

The net selling price of the unit's assets were insignificant except for the property, which had a market value of $35m. The net monetary assets will be realised in full.

Required:

How is the impairment loss allocated to the assets within the cash-generating unit?

Solution

Firstly, the impairment loss is allocated to the goodwill, reducing its carrying value to nil.

The impairment loss cannot be set against the property because its net selling price is greater than its carrying amount.

Likewise, the impairment loss cannot be set against the net monetary assets (receivables, cash, etc.) because they will be realised in full.

The balance of the impairment loss of $28m ($41m – $13m) is apportioned between the remaining assets on a pro rata basis. So, for example, the impairment allocated to the machinery is $14m ((49/(49 + 35 + 14)) × 28)

The table below shows how the impairment will be allocated.

	Draft values	Impairment loss	Revised value
	$m	$m	$m
Goodwill	13	(13)	–
Property	20	–	20
Machinery	49	(14)	35
Vehicles	35	(10)	25
Patents	14	(4)	10
Net monetary assets	19	–	19
	150	(41)	109

Test your understanding 3 – Factory explosion

There was an explosion in a factory. The carrying amounts of its assets were as follows:

	$000
Goodwill	100
Patents	200
Machines	300
Computers	500
Buildings	1,500
	2,600

The factory operates as a cash-generating unit. An impairment review reveals a net selling price of $1.2m for the factory and value in use of $1.95m. Half of the machines have been blown to pieces but the other half can be sold for at least their carrying amount. The patents have been superseded and are now considered worthless.

Required:

Discuss, with calculations, how any impairment loss will be accounted for.

Reversal of an impairment loss

The calculation of impairment losses is based on predictions of what may happen in the future. Sometimes, actual events turn out to be better than predicted. If this happens, the recoverable amount is re-calculated and the previous write-down is reversed.

- Impaired assets should be reviewed at each reporting date to see whether there are indications that the impairment has reversed.
- A reversal of an impairment loss is recognised immediately as income in profit or loss. If the original impairment was charged against the revaluation surplus, it is recognised as other comprehensive income and credited to the revaluation reserve.
- The reversal must not take the value of the asset above the amount it would have been if the original impairment had never been recorded. The depreciation that would have been charged in the meantime must be taken into account.
- The depreciation charge for future periods should be revised to reflect the changed carrying amount.

An impairment loss recognised for goodwill cannot be reversed in a subsequent period.

Impairment reversals

- External indicators of an impairment reversal are:

  (i) Increases in the asset's market value.

  (ii) Favourable changes in the technological, market, economic or legal environment.

  (iii) Decreases in interest rates.

- Internal indicators of an impairment reversal are:

  (i) Favourable changes in the use of the asset.

  (ii) Improvements in the asset's economic performance.

Reversing the impairment of a cash-generating unit: If the reversal relates to a cash-generating unit, the reversal is allocated to assets other than goodwill on a pro rata basis. The carrying amount of an asset must not be increased above the lower of:

- its recoverable amount (if determinable)
- the carrying amount that would have been determined (net of amortisation or depreciation) had no impairment loss been recognised for the asset in prior periods.

The amount that would otherwise have been allocated to the asset is allocated pro rata to the other assets of the unit, except for goodwill.

Reversals and goodwill: Impairment losses relating to goodwill can never be reversed. The reason for this is that once purchased goodwill has become impaired, any subsequent increase in its recoverable amount is likely to be an increase in internally generated goodwill, rather than a reversal of the impairment loss recognised for the original purchased goodwill. Internally generated goodwill cannot be recognised.

Test your understanding 4 – Boxer

Boxer purchased a non-current asset on 1 January 20X1 at a cost of $30,000. At that date, the asset had an estimated useful life of ten years. Boxer does not revalue this type of asset, but accounts for it on the basis of depreciated historical cost. At 31 December 20X2, the asset was subject to an impairment review and had a recoverable amount of $16,000.

At 31 December 20X5, the circumstances which caused the original impairment to be recognised have reversed and are no longer applicable, with the result that recoverable amount is now $40,000.

Required:

Explain, with supporting computations, the impact on the financial statements of the two impairment reviews.

Test your understanding 5 - CGUs and impairment reversals

On 31 December 20X2, an impairment review was conducted on a cash generating unit and the results were as follows:

Asset	Carrying value pre-impairment	Impairment	Carrying value post-impairment
	$000	$000	$000
Goodwill	100	(100)	Nil
Property, plant and equipment	300	(120)	180
	400	(220)	180

The property, plant and equipment was originally purchased for $400,000 on 1 January 20X1 and was attributed a useful economic life of 8 years.

At 31 December 20X3, the circumstances which caused the original impairment have reversed and are no longer applicable. The recoverable amount of the cash generating unit is now $420,000.

Required:

Explain, with supporting computations, the impact of the impairment reversal on the financial statements for the year ended 31 December 20X3.

IAS 36 disclosure requirements

The disclosure requirements of IAS 36 were amended in May 2013. The main disclosure requirements are:

- losses recognised during the period, and where charged in the statement of profit or loss and other comprehensive income
- reversals recognised during the period, and where credited in the statement profit or loss and other comprehensive income

- for each material loss or reversal:
  - the amount of loss or reversal and the events causing it
  - the nature of the asset (or cash-generating unit) and its reportable segment
  - the recoverable amount of the asset (or cash generating unit)
  - whether the recoverable amount is the fair value less costs to sell or value in use
  - the level of fair value hierarchy (per IFRS 13) used in determining fair value less costs to sell
  - the discount rate(s) used in estimating the value in use and, if applicable, fair value less costs to sell.

3 Government grants

IAS 20 Government grants: Definitions

Government grants are transfers of resources to an entity in return for past or future compliance with certain conditions. They exclude assistance that cannot be valued and normal trade with governments.

Government refers to government, government agencies and similar bodies whether local, national or international.

Government assistance is government action designed to provide an economic benefit to a specific entity. It does not include indirect help such as infrastructure development.

General principles

Grants should not be recognised until the conditions for receipt have been complied with and there is reasonable assurance that the grant will be received.

- Grants should be recognised in profit or loss so as to match them with the expenditure towards which they are intended to contribute.
- Income grants given to subsidise expenditure should be matched to the related costs.
- Income grants given to help achieve a non-financial goal (such as job creation) should be matched to the costs incurred to meet that goal.

Grants related to assets

Grants for purchases of non-current assets should be recognised over the expected useful lives of the related assets. There are two acceptable accounting policies for this:

- deduct the grant from the cost of the asset and depreciate the net cost
- treat the grant as deferred income and release to profit or loss over the life of the asset.

Repayments and other issues

A government grant that becomes repayable is accounted for as a revision of an accounting estimate.

(a) **Income-based grants**

Firstly, debit the repayment to any liability for deferred income. Any excess repayment must be charged to profits immediately.

(b) **Capital-based grants deducted from cost**

Increase the cost of the asset with the repayment. This will also increase the amount of depreciation that should have been charged in the past. This should be recognised and charged immediately.

(c) **Capital-based grants treated as deferred income**

Firstly, debit the repayment to any liability for deferred income. Any excess repayment must be charged against profits immediately.

Government assistance

As implied in the definition set out above, government assistance helps businesses through loan guarantees, loans at a low rate of interest, advice, procurement policies and similar methods. It is not possible to place reliable values on these forms of assistance, so they are not recognised.

Disclosure

The disclosure requirements of IAS 20 are:

- the accounting policy adopted for government grants, including the methods of presentation adopted in the financial statements
- the nature and extent of government grants recognised in the financial statements and other forms of government assistance received
- unfulfilled conditions and other contingencies attaching to government assistance that has been recognised.

Illustration – Government grants

On 1 June 20X1, Clock received written confirmation from a local government agency that it would receive a $1m grant towards the purchase price of a new office building. The grant becomes receivable on the date that Clock transfers the $10m purchase price to the vendor.

On 1 October 20X1 Clock paid $10m in cash for its new office building, which is estimated to have a useful life of 50 years. By 1 December 20X1, the building was ready for use. Clock received the government grant on 1 January 20X2.

Required:

Discuss the possible accounting treatments of the above in the financial statements of Clock for the year ended 31 December 20X1.

Solution

Government grants should be recognised when there is reasonable assurance that:

- The entity will comply with any conditions attached, and
- It is reasonably certain that the grant will be received.

The only condition attached to the grant is the purchase of the new building. Therefore, the grant should be accounted for on 1 October 20X1.

A receivable will be recognised for the $1m due from the local government. Clock could then choose to either:

(a) Reduce the cost of the building by $1m

In this case, the building will have a cost of $9m ($10m – $1m). This will be depreciated over its useful life of 50 years. The depreciation charge in profit or loss for the year ended 31 December 20X1 will be $15,000 (($9m/50 years) × 1/12) and the building will have a carrying value of $8,985,000 ($9m – $15,000) as at 31 December 20X1.

(b) Recognise deferred income of $1m.

In this case, the building is recognised at its cost of $10m. This will be depreciated over its useful life of 50 years. The depreciation charge in profit or loss for the year ended 31 December 20X1 will be $16,667 (($10m/50 years) × 1/12) and the building will have a carrying value of $9,983,333 ($10m – $16,667) as at 31 December 20X1.

The deferred income will be amortised to profit or loss over the building's useful economic life. Therefore, income of $1,667 (($1m/50) × 1/12) will be recorded in profit or loss for the year ended 31 December 20X1. The carrying value of the deferred income balance within liabilities on the statement of financial position will be $998,333 ($1m – $1,667) as at 31 December 20X1.

4 Borrowing costs

IAS 23 Borrowing costs

Borrowing costs are interest and other costs that an entity incurs in connection with the borrowing of funds.

Borrowing costs should be capitalised if they relate to the acquisition, construction or production of a **qualifying asset**. A qualifying asset is one that takes a substantial period of time to get ready for its intended use or sale.

Capitalisation period

Borrowing costs should only be capitalised while construction is in progress.

- Capitalisation of borrowing costs should commence when all of the following apply:
  - expenditure for the asset is being incurred
  - borrowing costs are being incurred
  - activities that are necessary to get the asset ready for use are in progress.
- Capitalisation of borrowing costs should cease when substantially all the activities that are necessary to get the asset ready for use are complete.
- Capitalisation of borrowing costs should be suspended during extended periods in which active development is interrupted.
- When construction of a qualifying asset is completed in parts and each part is capable of being used while construction continues on other parts, capitalisation of borrowing costs relating to a part should cease when substantially all the activities that are necessary to get that part ready for use are completed.

Borrowing costs eligible for capitalisation

Where a loan is taken out specifically to finance the construction of an asset, the amount to be capitalised is the interest payable on that loan, less any investment income on the temporary investment of the borrowings.

If construction of a qualifying asset is financed from an entity's general borrowings, the borrowing costs eligible to be capitalised are determined by applying a capitalisation rate to the expenditure incurred on the asset.

- The capitalisation rate is the weighted average of rates applicable to general borrowings outstanding in the period.
- General borrowings do not include loans for other specific purposes, such as constructing other qualifying assets.

IAS 23 is silent on how to arrive at the expenditure on the asset, but it would be reasonable to calculate it as the weighted average carrying amount of the asset during the period, including finance costs previously capitalised.

Disclosure requirements

The financial statements should disclose:

- the accounting policy adopted for borrowing costs
- the amount of borrowing costs capitalised during the period
- the capitalisation rate used.

Illustration – Borrowing costs

On 1 January 20X1, Hi-Rise obtained planning permission to build a new office building. Construction commenced on 1 March 20X1. To help fund the cost of this building, a loan for $5m was taken out from the bank on 1 April 20X1. The interest rate on the loan was 10% per annum.

Construction of the building ceased during the month of July due to an unexpected shortage of labour and materials.

By 31 December 20X1, the building was not complete. Costs incurred to date totalled $12m (excluding interest on the loan).

Requirement:

Discuss the accounting treatment of the above in the financial statements of Hi-Rise for the year ended 31 December 20X1.

Solution

An entity must capitalise borrowing costs that are directly attributable to the production of a qualifying asset. The new office building is a qualifying asset because it takes a substantial period of time to get ready for its intended use.

Hi-Rise should start capitalising borrowing costs when all of the following conditions have been met:

- It incurs expenditure on the asset – 1 March 20X1
- It incurs borrowing costs – 1 April 20X1
- It undertakes activities necessary to prepare the asset for intended use – 1 January 20X1.

Capitalisation of borrowing costs should therefore commence on 1 April 20X1. Capitalisation of borrowing costs ceases for the month of July because active development was suspended. In total, 8 months worth of borrowing costs should be capitalised in the year ended 31 December 20X1.

The total borrowing costs to be capitalised are $333,333 ($5m × 10% × 8/12). These will be added to the cost of the building, giving a carrying amount of $12,333,333 as at 31 December 20X1. The building is not ready for use, so no depreciation is charged.

5 Non-current assets held for sale (IFRS 5)

Classification as 'held for sale'

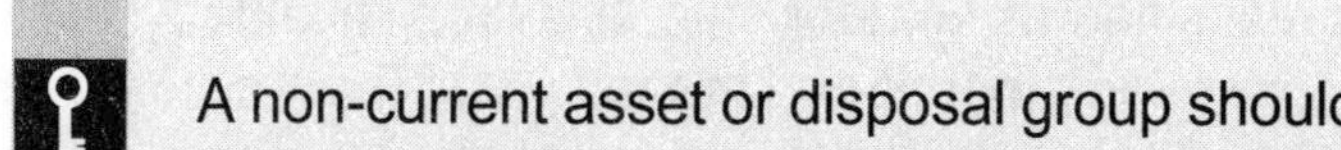

A non-current asset or disposal group should be classified as 'held for sale' if its carrying amount will be recovered principally through a sale transaction rather than through continuing use.

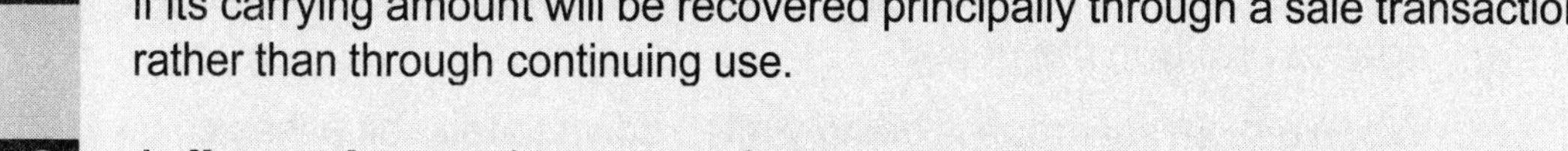

A **disposal group** is a group of assets (and possibly liabilities) that the entity intends to dispose of in a single transaction.

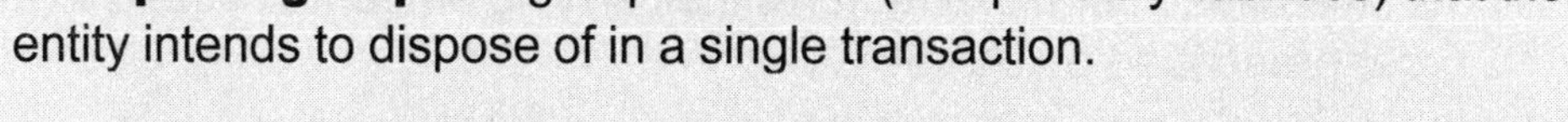

- IFRS 5 applies to disposal groups as well as to individual non-current assets that are held for sale.
- A disposal group may include goodwill acquired in a business combination if the group is a cash-generating unit to which goodwill has been allocated.
- Subsidiaries acquired exclusively with a view to resale are classified as disposal groups held for sale if they meet the conditions below.

IFRS 5 requires the following conditions to be met before an asset or disposal group can be classified as 'held for sale'.

- The item is available for immediate sale in its present condition
- The sale is highly probable
- Management is committed to a plan to sell the item
- An active programme to locate a buyer has been initiated
- The item is being actively marketed at a reasonable price in relation to its current fair value
- The sale is expected to be completed within one year from the date of classification
- It is unlikely that the plan will change significantly or be withdrawn.

Assets that are to be abandoned or wound down gradually cannot be classified as held for sale (although they may qualify as discontinued operations once they have been abandoned), because their carrying amounts will not be recovered principally through a sale transaction.

Measurement of assets and disposal groups held for sale

Items classified as held for sale should be measured at the lower of their carrying amount and fair value less costs to sell.

- Where fair value less costs to sell is lower than carrying amount, the item is written down and the write down is treated as an impairment loss.
- Where a non-current asset has been previously revalued and is now classified as being held for sale, it should be revalued to fair value immediately before it is classified as held for sale. It is then revalued again at the lower of the carrying amount and the fair value less costs to sell. The difference is the selling costs and these should be charged against profits in the period.
- When a disposal group is being written down to fair value less costs to sell, the impairment loss reduces the carrying amount of assets in the order prescribed by IAS 36
  - Impairments are firstly allocated to goodwill and then to other assets on a pro-rata basis.
- A gain can be recognised for any subsequent increase in fair value less costs to sell, but not in excess of the cumulative impairment loss that has already been recognised, either when the assets were written down to fair value less costs to sell or previously under IAS 36.
- An asset held for sale is not depreciated, even if it is still being used by the entity.

Test your understanding 6 – AB

On 1 January 20X1 AB acquires a building for $200,000 with an expected life of 50 years. On 31 December 20X4 AB puts the building up for immediate sale. On that date the building has a market value of $220,000 and expenses of $10,000 and tax of $5,000 will be payable on the sale.

Required:

Describe how the above transaction should be accounted for.

Test your understanding 7 – Nash

Nash purchased a building for its own use on 1 January 20X1 for $1m and attributed it a 50 year useful economic life. Nash uses the revaluation model to account for buildings.

On 31 December 20X2, this building was revalued to $1.2m.

On 31 December 20X3, the building met the criteria to be classified as held for sale. Its fair value was deemed to be $1.1m and the costs necessary to sell the building were estimated to be $50,000.

Nash does not make a reserves transfer in respect of excess depreciation.

Required:

Discuss the accounting treatment of the above.

Changes to a plan of sale

If a sale does not take place within one year, an asset (or disposal group) can still be classified as held for sale if:

- the delay has been caused by events or circumstances beyond the entity's control
- there is sufficient evidence that the entity is still committed to the sale.

If the criteria for 'held for sale' are no longer met, then the entity must cease to classify the assets or disposal group as held for sale. The assets or disposal group must be measured at the lower of:

- its carrying amount before it was classified as held for sale adjusted for any depreciation, amortisation or revaluations that would have been recognised had it not been classified as held for sale
- its recoverable amount at the date of the subsequent decision not to sell.

Any adjustment required is recognised in profit or loss as a gain or loss from continuing operations.

Presentation in the statement of financial position

IFRS 5 states that assets classified as held for sale should be presented separately from other assets in the statement of financial position. The liabilities of a disposal group classified as held for sale should be presented separately from other liabilities in the statement of financial position.

- Assets and liabilities held for sale should not be offset and presented as a single amount.
- The major classes of assets and liabilities classified as held for sale must be separately disclosed either on the face of the statement of financial position or in the notes.
- Where an asset or disposal group is classified as held for sale after the reporting date, but before the issue of the financial statements, details should be disclosed in the notes (this is a non-adjusting event after the reporting date).

Illustration 5 – Non-current assets held for sale (IFRS 5)

Statement of financial position (showing non-current assets held for sale)

	20X2	**20X1**
	$m	$m
ASSETS		
Non-current assets		
Property, plant and equipment	X	X
Goodwill	X	X
Financial assets	X	X
	X	X
Current assets		
Inventories	X	X
Trade receivables	X	X
Cash and cash equivalents	X	
Non-current assets classified as held for sale	X	X
	X	X
Total assets	X	X

Disclosures in notes to the accounts

In the period in which a non-current asset or disposal group has been either classified as held for sale, or sold, the notes to the accounts must include:

- a description of the non-current asset (or disposal group)
- a description of the facts and circumstances of the sale or expected sale
- any impairment losses or reversals recognised
- if applicable, the segment in which the non-current asset (or disposal group) is presented in accordance with IFRS 8 Operating Segments.

Test your understanding 8 – Hyssop

Hyssop is preparing its financial statements for the year ended 31 December 20X7.

(a) On 1 December 20X7, the entity became committed to a plan to sell a surplus office property and has already found a potential buyer. On 15 December 20X7 a survey was carried out and it was discovered that the building had dry rot and substantial remedial work would be necessary. The buyer is prepared to wait for the work to be carried out, but the property will not be sold until the problem has been rectified. This is not expected to occur until summer 20X8.

Required:

Can the property be classified as 'held for sale'?

(b) A subsidiary entity, B, is for sale at a price of $3 million. There has been some interest from prospective buyers but no sale as of yet. One buyer has made an offer of $2 million but the Directors of Hyssop rejected the offer. The Directors have just received advice from their accountants that the fair value of the business is $2.5 million. They have decided not to reduce the sale price of B at the moment.

Required:

Can the subsidiary be classified as 'held for sale'?

6 Investment property

IAS 40 Investment property: Definitions

Definition of investment property

Investment property is property (land or buildings) held (by the owner or by the lessee under a finance lease) to earn rentals or for capital appreciation or both.

Examples of investment property are:

- land held for long-term capital appreciation
- land held for undecided future use
- buildings leased out under an operating lease
- vacant buildings held to be leased out under an operating lease.

The following are **not** investment property:

- property held for use in the production or supply of goods or services or for administrative purposes (IAS 16 Property, Plant and Equipment applies)
- property held for sale in the ordinary course of business or in the process of construction of development for such sale (IAS 2 Inventories applies)
- property being constructed or developed on behalf of third parties (IAS 11 Construction Contracts applies)
- owner-occupied property (IAS 16 applies)
- property that is being constructed or developed for use as an investment property (IAS 16 currently applies until the property is ready for use, at which time IAS 40 starts to apply – see note below)
- property leased to another entity under a finance lease (IAS 17 Leases applies).

Measurement

On recognition, investment property shall be recognised at cost, measured along the lines of the principles in IAS 16.

After recognition an entity may choose either:

- the cost model
- the fair value model.

The policy chosen must be applied to all investment properties.

Change from one model to the other is permitted only if this results in a more appropriate presentation. IAS 40 notes that this is highly unlikely for a change from the fair value model to the cost model.

If the cost model is chosen, investment properties are held at cost less accumulated depreciation. No revaluations are permitted.

The fair value model

Under the fair value model, the entity remeasures its investment properties at fair value each year. There is no depreciation charge.

Fair value is defined in IFRS 13 as the amount that would be received to sell an asset (or paid to transfer a liability) in an orderly transaction between market participants at the measurement date.

- All gains and losses on revaluation are reported in as part of the profit for the period.
- The profit or loss on disposal of an investment property is the difference between the net disposal proceeds and the then carrying amount in the statement of financial position.

If, in exceptional circumstances, it is impossible to measure the fair value of an individual investment property reliably then the cost model should be adopted.

Operating leases

A property interest that is held by a lessee under an operating lease may be classified as an investment property, if, and only if, the property would meet the definition if it were not held under an operating lease.

- This classification is available on a property-by-property basis.
- The lessee accounts for the property as if it were a finance lease.
- Once the classification has been made for such property interest, the fair value model must be used for all investment properties held by the entity.

Transfers

Transfers to or from investment property can only be made if there is a change of use. There are several possible situations in which this might occur and the accounting treatment for each is set out below.

Transfer from investment property to owner-occupied property

Use the fair value at the date of the change for subsequent accounting under IAS 16.

Transfer from investment property to inventory

Use the fair value at the date of the change for subsequent accounting under IAS 2 Inventories.

Transfer from owner-occupied property to investment property to be carried at fair value

Normal accounting under IAS 16 (cost less depreciation) will have been applied up to the date of the change. On adopting fair value, there is normally an increase in value. This is recognised as other comprehensive income and credited to the revaluation surplus in equity in accordance with IAS 16. If the fair valuation causes a decrease in value, then it should be charged to profits.

Transfer from inventories to investment property to be carried at fair value

Any change in the carrying amount caused by the transfer should be recognised in profit or loss.

Illustration: Investment property

Lavender owns a property, which it rents out to some of its employees. The property was purchased for $40 million on 1 January 20X2 and had a useful life of 30 years at that date. On 1 January 20X7 it had a market value of $50 million and its remaining useful life remained unchanged. Management wish to measure properties at fair value where this is allowed by accounting standards.

Required:

How should the property be treated in the financial statements of Lavender for the year ended 31 December 20X7.

Solution

Property that is rented out to employees is deemed to be owner-occupied and therefore cannot be classified as investment property.

Management wish to measure the property at fair value, so Lavender adopts the fair value model in IAS 16 Property, Plant and Equipment, depreciating the asset over its useful life and recognising the revaluation gain in other comprehensive income.

Before the revaluation, the building had a carrying value of $25m ($30m × 25/30). The building would have been revalued to $50m on 1 January 20X7, with a gain of $25m ($50m – $25m) recognised in other comprehensive income.

The building would then be depreciated over its remaining useful life of 25 years (30 – 5), giving a depreciation charge of $2m ($50m/25) in the year ended 31 December 20X7. The carrying value of the asset as at 31 December 20X7 is $48m ($50m – $2m).

Illustration – ABC

ABC owns a building that it used as its head office. On 1 January 20X1, the building, which was measured under the cost model, had a carrying value of $500,000. On this date, when the fair value of the building was $600,000, ABC vacated the premises. However, the directors decided to keep the building in order to rent it out to tenants and to potentially benefit from increases in property prices. ABC measures investment properties at fair value. On 31 December 20X1, the property has a fair value of $625,000.

Required:

Discuss the accounting treatment of the building in the financial statements of ABC for the year ended 31 December 20X1.

Solution

When the building was owner-occupied, it was an item of property plant and equipment. From 1 January 20X1, the property was held to earn rental income and for capital appreciation so it should be reclassified as investment property.

Per IAS 40, if owner occupied property becomes investment property that will be carried at fair value, then a revaluation needs to occur under IAS 16 at the date of the change in use.

The building must be revalued from $500,000 to $600,000 under IAS 16. This means that the gain of $100,000 ($600,000 – $500,000) will be recorded in other comprehensive income and held in a revaluation reserve within equity.

Investment properties measured at fair value must be revalued each year end, with the gain or loss recorded in profit or loss. At year end, the building will therefore be revalued to $625,000 with a gain of $25,000 ($625,000 – $600,000) recorded in profit or loss.

Investment properties held at fair value are not depreciated.

7 Intangible assets

Definition and recognition criteria

An **intangible asset** is an identifiable non-monetary asset without physical substance.

An intangible asset should be recognised if all the following criteria are met.

- It is identifiable.
- It is controlled by the entity (the entity has the power to obtain economic benefits from it).
- It is expected to generate future economic benefits for the entity.
- It has a cost that can be measured reliably.

These recognition criteria apply whether an intangible asset is acquired externally or generated internally.

- An intangible asset is identifiable when it:
  - is separable (capable of being separated and sold, transferred, licensed, rented, or exchanged, either individually or as part of a package)
  - it arises from contractual or other legal rights, regardless of whether those rights are transferable or separable from the entity or from other rights and obligations.
- If an intangible asset does not meet the recognition criteria, then it should be charged to profits as it is incurred. Once the expenditure has been so charged, it cannot be capitalised at a later date.

Examples of intangible assets

Examples of possible intangible assets include:

- goodwill acquired in a business combination
- computer software
- patents
- copyrights
- motion picture films
- customer list
- mortgage servicing rights
- licences

- import quotas
- franchises
- customer and supplier relationships
- marketing rights.

Meeting the recognition criteria

(a) **Identifiability**

Intangible assets such as customer relationships cannot be separated from goodwill unless they:

- arise as a result of a legal right, if there are ongoing supply contracts, for example
- are separable, i.e. can be sold separately. This is unlikely unless there are legal contracts in existence, in which case they fall under the previous bullet point.

(b) **Control**

The knowledge that the staff have is an asset. It can be possible for the entity to control this knowledge. Patents, copyrights and restraint-of-trade agreements will give the entity legal rights to the future economic benefits and prevent other people from obtaining them. Therefore copyrights and patents can be capitalised.

(c) **Probable future economic benefits**

An intangible asset can generate future economic benefits in two ways. Owning a brand name can boost revenues, while owning the patent for a production process may help to reduce production costs. Either way, the entity's profits will be increased.

When an entity assesses the probability of future economic benefits, the assessment must be based on reasonable and supportable assumptions about conditions that will exist over the life of the asset.

(d) **Reliable measurement**

If the asset is acquired separately then this is straightforward. For example, the purchase price of a franchise should be capitalised, along with all the related legal and professional costs.

However, the cost of **internally generated intangible assets** cannot be distinguished from the cost of the entity's day-to-day operations. Therefore, internally generated intangible assets are not recognised on the statement of financial position unless they relate to research and development activity (see later in this chapter).

Measurement

When an intangible asset is initially recognised, it is measured at cost. After recognition, an entity must choose either the cost model or the revaluation model for each class of intangible asset.

- The cost model measures the asset at cost less accumulated amortisation and impairment.
- The revaluation model measures the asset at fair value less accumulated amortisation and impairment.

The revaluation model can only be adopted if fair value can be determined by reference to an **active market**. An active market is one where the products are homogenous, there are willing buyers and sellers to be found at all times, and prices are available to the public.

Active markets for intangible assets are rare. They may exist for assets such as:

- milk quotas
- European Union fishing quotas
- stock exchange seats.

Active markets are unlikely to exist for brands, newspaper mastheads, music and film publishing rights, patents or trademarks.

Revaluations should be made with sufficient regularity such that the carrying amount does not differ materially from actual fair value at the reporting date.

Revaluation gains and losses are accounted for in the same way as revaluation gains and losses of tangible assets under IAS 16.

Amortisation

An entity must assess whether the useful life of an intangible asset is finite or indefinite.

- An asset with a finite useful life must be amortised on a systematic basis over that life. Normally the straight-line method with a zero residual value should be used. Amortisation starts when the asset is available for use.
- An asset has an indefinite useful life when there is no foreseeable limit to the period over which the asset is expected to generate net cash inflows. It should not be amortised, but be subject to an annual impairment review.

Research and development expenditure

Research is original and planned investigation undertaken with the prospect of gaining new scientific or technical knowledge and understanding.

Development is the application of research findings or other knowledge to a plan or design for the production of new or substantially improved materials, devices, products, processes, systems or services before the start of commercial production or use.

- Research expenditure cannot be recognised as an intangible asset. (although tangible assets used in research should be recognised as plant and equipment).
- Development expenditure should be recognised as an intangible asset if an entity can demonstrate that:
  - the project is technically feasible
  - the entity intends to complete the intangible asset, and then use it or sell it
  - it is able to use or sell the intangible asset

- the intangible asset will generate future economic benefits. There must either be a market for the product or an internal use for it
- the entity has adequate technical, financial and other resources to complete the project
- it can reliably measure the attributable expenditure on the project.

Computer intangibles

Computer software

Some computer software is an integral part of the related hardware, for example the computer programme in a production-line robot or the operating system on a PC. The hardware will not work without the software, and so the software is capitalised as part of the hardware. This type of software is a tangible non-current asset subject to IAS 16.

Stand-alone computer software (for example an accounts package) is an intangible asset subject to IAS 38.

Test your understanding 9 – Innovate

Ten years ago, Innovate developed a new game called 'Our Sports'. This game sold over 10 million copies around the world and was extremely profitable. Due to its popularity, Innovate release a new game in the Our Sports series every year. The games continue to be best-sellers.

The directors have produced cash flow projections for the Our Sports series over the next five years. Based on these projections, they have prudently valued the Our Sports brand at $20 million and wish to recognise this in the statement of financial position as at 30 September 20X3.

On 30 September 20X3, Innovate also paid $1 million for the rights to the 'Pets & Me' videogame series after the original developer went into administration.

Required:

Discuss the accounting treatment of the above in the financial statements of Innovate for the year ended 30 September 20X3.

8 Agriculture

IAS 41 Agriculture applies to biological assets and to agricultural produce at the point of harvest.

Agricultural activity is the management of the biological transformation of biological assets for sale, into agricultural produce or into additional biological assets.

Biological transformation comprises the processes of growth, degeneration, production, and procreation that cause qualitative or quantitative changes in a biological asset.

A biological asset is a living plant or animal.

Agricultural produce is the harvested product of the entity's biological assets.

Harvest is the detachment of produce from a biological asset or the cessation of a biological asset's life processes.

Application of IAS 41

A farmer buys a dairy calf.	The calf is a biological asset.
The calf grows into a mature cow.	Growth is a type of biological transformation.
The farmer milks the cow.	The milk has been harvested. Milk is agricultural produce.

Biological assets

Recognition criteria

A biological asset should be recognised if:

- it is probable that future economic benefits will flow to the entity from the asset
- the cost or fair value of the asset can be reliably measured
- the entity controls the asset.

Initial recognition

Biological assets are initially measured at fair value less estimated costs to sell.

Gains and losses may arise in profit or loss when a biological asset is first recognised. For example:

- A loss can arise because estimated selling costs are deducted from fair value.
- A gain can arise when a new biological asset (such as a lamb or a calf) is born.

Subsequent measurement

At each reporting date, biological assets are revalued to fair value less costs to sell.

Gains and losses arising from changes in fair value are recognised in profit or loss for the period in which they arise.

Biological assets are presented separately on the face of the statement of financial position within non-current assets.

Physical changes and price changes

The fair value of a biological asset may change because of its age, or because prices in the market have changed.

IAS 41 recommends separate disclosure of physical and price changes because this information is likely to be of interest to users of the financial statements. However, this disclosure is not mandatory.

Inability to measure fair value

IAS 41 presumes that the fair value of biological assets should be capable of being measured reliably.

This presumption can be rebutted on the initial recognition of a biological asset if market prices are not readily available. If this is the case, the biological asset should be measured at cost less accumulated depreciation and accumulated impairment losses.

Once the asset's fair value can be measured reliably, it should be remeasured to fair value less costs to sell.

Test your understanding 10 – Cows

On 1 January 20X1, a farmer had a herd of 100 cows, all of which were 2 years old. At this date, the fair value less point of sale costs of the herd was $10,000. On 1 July 20X1, the farmer purchased 20 cows (each two and half years old) for $60 each.

As at 31 December 20X1, three year old cows sell at market for $90 each.

Market auctioneers have charged a sales levy of 2% for many years.

Required:

Discuss the accounting treatment of the above in the financial statements for the year ended 31 December 20X1.

Agricultural produce

At the date of harvest, agricultural produce should be recognised and measured at fair value less estimated costs to sell.

Gains and losses on initial recognition are included in profit or loss (operating profit) for the period.

After produce has been harvested, it becomes an item of inventory. Therefore, IAS 41 ceases to apply. The initial measurement value at the point of harvest is the deemed 'cost' for the purpose of IAS 2 Inventories, which is applied from then onwards.

Assets outside the scope of IAS 41

IAS 41 does not apply to intangible assets (such as production quotas) or to land related to agricultural activity.

- In accordance with IAS 38, intangible assets are measured at cost less amortisation or fair value less amortisation.
- Land is not a biological asset. It is treated as a tangible non-current asset and accounted for under IAS 16 Property, Plant and Equipment.
  - When valuing a forest, for example, the trees must be accounted for separately from the land that they grow on.

Test your understanding 11 – GoodWine

GoodWine is a company that grows and harvests grapes. The grapes are then sold to wine producers. GoodWine measures assets at fair value, when permitted by accounting standards.

GoodWine has one vineyard. On 1 July 20X1, the land has a fair value of $2m and the vines have a fair value of $500,000.

On 30 June 20X2, GoodWine harvests the grapes from its vines. The fair value of the grapes is $400,000, the fair value of the vines is $520,000 and the fair value of the land is $2.1m.

All selling costs are negligible and should be ignored.

Required:

Discuss the accounting treatment of the above in the financial statements of GoodWine for the year ended 30 June 20X2.

Agriculture and government grants

If a government grant relates to a biological asset measured at its cost less accumulated depreciation and accumulated impairment losses, it is accounted for under IAS 20 Accounting for Government Grants.

If a government grant relates to biological assets measured at fair value less costs to sell, then it is accounted for under IAS 41 Agriculture as follows:

- An **unconditional** government grant related to a biological asset measured at its fair value less costs to sell shall be recognised in profit or loss when it becomes receivable.
- A **conditional** government grant related to a biological asset measured at its fair value less costs to sell, shall be recognised in profit or loss when the conditions attaching to the government grant are met.
  - If a grant requires an entity to farm in a particular location for five years, and requires the entity to return all of the grant if it farms for a period shorter than five years, then the grant is not recognised in profit or loss until the five years have passed.
  - If the terms of the grant allow part of it to be retained according to the time that has elapsed, the entity recognises that part in profit or loss as time passes.

9 Inventories

IAS 2 Inventories

Inventories are measured at the lower of cost and net realisable value.

Cost includes all purchase costs, conversion costs and other costs incurred in bringing the inventories to their present condition and location.

- **Purchase costs** include the purchase price (less discounts and rebates), import duties, irrecoverable taxes, transport and handling costs and any other directly attributable costs.
- **Conversion costs** include all direct costs of conversion (materials, labour, expenses, etc), and a proportion of the fixed and variable production overheads. The allocation of production overheads must be based on the normal level of activity.
- Abnormal wastage, storage costs, administration costs and selling costs must be excluded from the valuation and charged as expenses in the period in which they are incurred.

Net realisable value is the expected selling price less the estimated costs of completion and sale.

- IAS 2 Inventories allows three methods of arriving at cost:
  - actual unit cost
  - first-in, first-out (FIFO)
  - weighted average cost (AVCO).
- Actual unit cost must be used where items of inventory are not ordinarily interchangeable.
- The same method of arriving at cost should be used for all inventories having similar nature and use to the entity. Different cost methods may be justified for inventories with different nature or use.
- Entities should disclose:
  - their accounting policy and cost formulae
  - total carrying amount of inventories by category
  - details of inventories carried at net realisable value.

Illustration – Valuation of inventories

An entity has the following items of inventory.

(a) Materials costing $12,000 bought for processing and assembly for a profitable special order. Since buying these items, the cost price has fallen to $10,000.

(b) Equipment constructed for a customer for an agreed price of $18,000. This has recently been completed at a cost of $16,800. It has now been discovered that, in order to meet certain regulations, conversion with an extra cost of $4,200 will be required. The customer has accepted partial responsibility and agreed to meet half the extra cost.

Required:

In accordance with IAS 2 Inventories, at what amount should the above items be valued?

Solution

(a) Inventory is valued at the lower of cost or net realisable value, not the lower of cost or replacement cost. Since the materials will be processed before sale there is no reason to believe that net realisable value will be below cost. Therefore the inventory should be valued at its cost of $12,000.

(b) The net realisable value is $15,900 (contract price $18,000 – constructor's share of modification cost $2,100). The net realisable value is below the cost price. Therefore the inventory should be held at $15,900.

10 Chapter summary

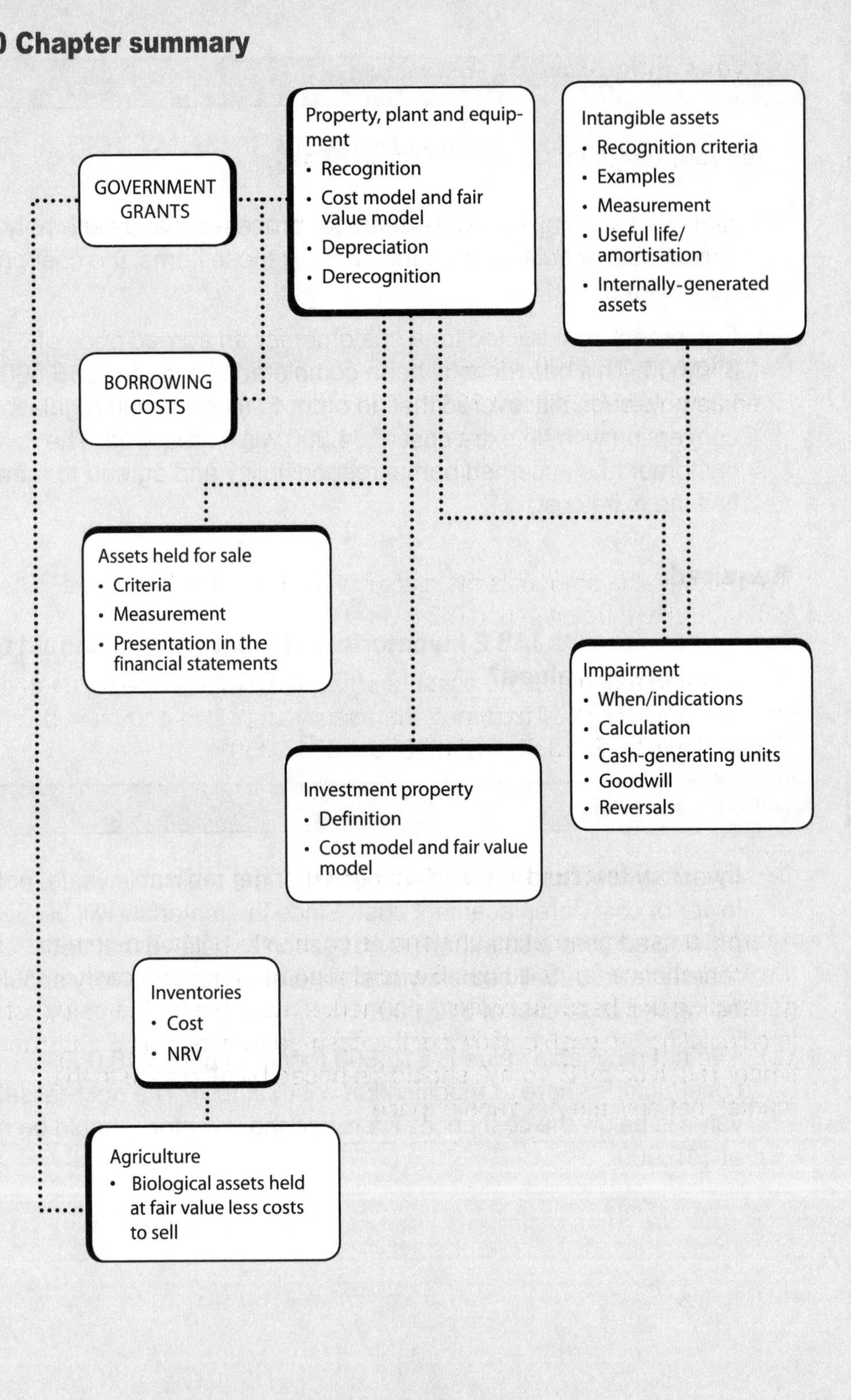

Test your understanding answers

Test your understanding 1 – Impaired asset

The value in use is calculated as the present value of the asset's future cash inflows and outflows.

	$000
Cash flow Year 1 (200 × 0.909)	182
Cash flow Year 2 (200 × 0.826)	165
	347

The recoverable amount is the higher of the fair value less costs to sell ($300,000) and value in use ($347,000).

The carrying amount of the asset of $500,000 exceeds the recoverable amount of $347,000. Therefore, the asset is impaired and must be written down by $153,000 ($500,000 – $347,000).

Test your understanding 2 – Cash generating units

A forms a cash-generating unit and its cash inflows should be based on the market price for its output. B and C together form one cash-generating unit because there is no market available for the output of B. In calculating the cash outflows of the cash-generating unit B + C, the timber received by B from A should be priced by reference to the market, not any internal transfer price.

Test your understanding 3 – Factory explosion

The patents have been superceded and have a recoverable amount of $nil. They therefore should be written down to $nil and an impairment loss of $200,000 must be charged to profit or loss.

Half of the machines have been blown to pieces. Therefore, half of the carrying value of the machines should be written off. An impairment loss of $150,000 will be charged to profit or loss.

The recoverable amount of the other assets cannot be determined so therefore they must be tested for impairment as part of their cash generating unit.

The carrying value of the CGU after the impairment of the patents and machines is $2,250,000 (see working below), whereas the recoverable amount is $1,950,000. A further impairment of $300,000 is therefore required.

This is firstly allocated to goodwill and then to other assets on a pro-rata basis. No further impairment should be alloacted to the machines as these have already been written down to their recoverable amount.

Allocation of impairment loss to CGU

	Draft	**Impairment**	**Revised**
	$000	$000	$000
Goodwill	100	(100)	Nil
Patents	nil	–	Nil
Machines	150	–	150
Computers	500	(50)	450
Buildings	1,500	(150)	1,350
	2,250	(300)	1,950

The total impairment charged to profit or loss is $650,000 ($200,000 + $150,000 + $300,000).

Test your understanding 4 – Boxer

Solution:

Year ended 31 December 20X2

	$
Asset carrying value ($30,000 × 8/10)	24,000
Recoverable amount	16,000
Impairment loss	8,000

The asset is written down to $16,000 and the loss of $8,000 is charged to profit or loss. The depreciation charge per annum in future periods will be $2,000 ($16,000 × 1/8).

Year ended 31 December 20X5

	$
Asset carrying value ($16,000 × 5/8)	10,000
Recoverable amount	40,000
Impairment loss	nil

There has been no impairment loss. In fact, there has been a complete reversal of the first impairment loss. The asset can be reinstated to its depreciated historical cost i.e. to the carrying value at 31 December 20X5 if there never had been an earlier impairment loss.

Year 5 depreciated historical cost (30,000 × 5/10) = $15,000

Carrying value: $10,000

Reversal of the loss: $5,000

The reversal of the loss is now recognised. The asset will be increased by $5,000 ($15,000 – $10,000) and a gain of $5,000 will be recognised in profit or loss.

It should be noted that the whole $8,000 original impairment cannot be reversed. The impairment can only be reversed to a maximum amount of depreciated historical cost, based upon the original cost and estimated useful life of the asset.

Test your understanding 5 - CGUs and impairment reversals

The goodwill impairment cannot be reversed.

The impairment of the PPE can be reversed. However, this is limited to the carrying value of the asset had no impairment loss been previously recognised.

The carrying value of PPE as at 31 December 20X3 is $150,000 ($180,000 × 5/6).

If the PPE had not been impaired, then its value at 31 December 20X3 would have been $250,000 ($400,000 × 5/8).

Therefore, the carrying amount of the PPE can be increased from $150,000 to $250,000. This will give rise to a gain of $100,000 in profit or loss.

Test your understanding 6 – AB

Until 31 December 20X4 the building is a normal non-current asset and its accounting treatment is prescribed by IAS 16. The annual depreciation charge was $4,000 ($200,000 / 50). The carrying amount at 31 December 20X4 is therefore $184,000 ($200,000 – (4 × $4,000)).

On 31 December 20X4 the building is reclassified as a non-current asset held for sale. It is measured at the lower of carrying amount ($184,000) and fair value less costs to sell ($220,000 – $10,000 = $210,000). Note that any applicable tax expense is excluded from the determination of costs to sell.

The building will therefore be measured at 31 December 20X4 at $184,000.

Test your understanding 7 – Nash

The building would have been recognised on 1 January 20X1 at its cost of $1m and depreciated over its 50 year life.

By 31 December 20X2, the carrying value of the building would have been $960,000 ($1m – (($1m/50) × 2 years)).

The building was revalued on 31 December 20X2 to $1.2m, giving a gain on revaluation of $240,000 ($1.2m – $960,000). This gain will have been recorded in other comprehensive income and held within a revaluation surplus (normally as a part of other components of equity).

The building would then have been depreciated over its remaining useful life of 48 years. Depreciation in the year ended 20X3 was therefore $25,000 ($1.2m/48). The building had a carrying value at 31 December 20X3 of $1,175,000 ($1.2m – $25,000).

At 31 December 20X3, the building is held for sale. Because it is held under the revaluation model, it must initially be revalued downwards to its fair value of $1,100,000. This loss of $75,000 ($1,175,000 – $1,100,000) is recorded in other comprehensive income because there are previous revaluation gains relating to this asset within equity.

The building will then be revalued to fair value less costs to sell. Therefore, the asset must be reduced in value by a further $50,000. This loss is charged to the statement of profit or loss.

Test your understanding 8 – Hyssop

(a) IFRS 5 states that in order to be classified as 'held for sale' the property should be available for immediate sale in its present condition. The property will not be sold until the work has been carried out, demonstrating that the facility is not available for immediate sale. Therefore the property cannot be classified as 'held for sale'.

(b) The subsidiary B does not meet the criteria for classification as 'held for sale'. Although actions to locate a buyer are in place, the subsidiary is not for sale at a price that is reasonable compared with its fair value. The fair value of the subsidiary is $2.5 million, but it is advertised for sale at $3 million. It cannot be classified as held for sale' until the sales price is reduced.

Test your understanding 9 – Innovate

According to IAS 38, an intangible asset can be recognised if:

- it is probable that expected future economic benefits attributable to the asset will flow to the entity
- the cost of the asset can be measured reliably.

Cash flow projections suggest that the Our Sports brand will lead to future economic benefits. However, the asset has been internally generated and therefore the cost of the asset cannot be measured reliably. This means that the Our Sports brand cannot be recognised in the financial statements.

The Pets & Me brand has been purchased for $1 million. Therefore, its cost can be measured reliably. An intangible asset should be recognised in respect of the Pets & Me brand at its cost of $1 million.

In subsequent periods, the Pets & Me brand will be amortised over its expected useful economic life.

Test your understanding 10 – Cows

Cows are biological assets and should be initially recognised at fair value less costs to sell.

The cows purchased in the year should be initially recognised at $1,176 ((20 × $60) × 98%). This will give rise to an immediate loss of $24 ((20 × $60) – $1,176) in the statement of profit or loss.

At year end, the whole herd should be revalued to fair value less costs to sell. Any gain or loss will be recorded in the statement of profit or loss.

The herd of cows will be held at $10,584 ((120 × $90) × 98%) on the statement of financial position.

This will give rise to a further loss of $592 (W1) in the statement of profit or loss.

(W1) **Loss on revaluation**

	$
Value at 1 January 20X1	10,000
New purchase	1,176
Loss (bal. fig)	(592)
Value at 31 December 20X1	10,584

Test your understanding 11 – GoodWine

Land is accounted for in accordance with IAS 16 Property, plant and equipment. If the revaluation model is chosen, then gains in the fair value of the land should be reported in other comprehensive income.

At 30 June 20X2, the land should be revalued to $2.1m and a gain of $100,000 ($2.1m – $2.0m) should be reported in other comprehensive income and held within a revaluation reserve in equity.

The vines are biological assets. They should be revalued at the year end to fair value less costs to sell with any gain or loss reported in profit or loss.

The vines should be revalued to $520,000 and held as a non-current asset on the statement of financial position. A gain of $20,000 ($520,000 – $500,000) should be reported in profit or loss.

The grapes are agricultural produce and should initially be recognised at fair value less costs to sell. Any gain or loss on initial recognition is reported in profit or loss.

The grapes should be initially recognised at $400,000 with a gain of $400,000 reported in profit or loss.

The grapes are now accounted for under IAS 2 Inventories. They will have a deemed cost of $400,000.

chapter

5

Foreign currency in individual financial statements

Chapter learning objectives

Upon completion of this chapter you will be able to:

- outline the principles for translating foreign currency amounts, including translations into the functional currency and presentation currency
- apply these principles

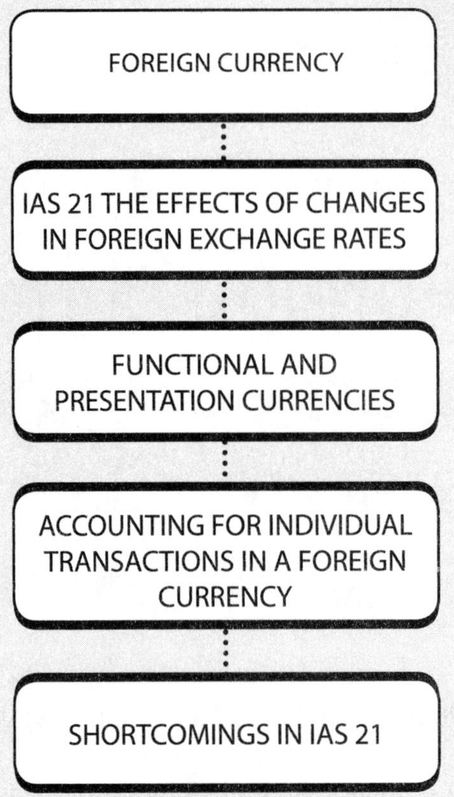

1 IAS 21 The effects of changes in foreign exchange rates

IAS 21 deals with:

- the definition of functional and presentation currencies
- accounting for individual transactions in a foreign currency
- translating the financial statements of a foreign operation.

Translating the financial statements of a foreign operation is covered in a later chapter.

Functional and presentation currencies

An entity maintains its day-to-day financial records in its functional currency.

The **functional currency** is the currency of the primary economic environment where the entity operates. In most cases this will be the local currency.

An entity should consider the following when determining its functional currency.

- The currency that mainly influences sales prices for goods and services.

- The currency of the country whose competitive forces and regulations mainly determine the sales price of goods and services.
- The currency that mainly influences labour, material and other costs of providing goods and services.

The **presentation currency** is the currency in which the entity presents its financial statements. This can be different from the functional currency.

Functional and presentation currencies

The **functional currency** is the currency an entity will use to record its day-to-day transactions. In addition to the points noted previously, IAS 21 also identifies that that an entity should consider the following factors in determining its functional currency:

- The currency in which funding from issuing debt and equity is generated.
- The currency in which receipts from operating activities are usually retained.

Let us consider an example to illustrate this point. Entity A operates in the UK. It sells goods throughout the UK and Europe with all transactions denominated in sterling. Cash is received from sales in sterling. It raises finance locally from UK banks with all loans denominated in sterling.

Looking at the factors listed above it is apparent that the functional currency for Entity A is sterling. It trades in this currency and raises finance in this currency.

Therefore Entity A would record its accounting transactions in sterling as its functional currency.

One complication in determining functional currency arises if an entity is a foreign operation. For example, if Entity A (from above) has a subsidiary Entity B located in Europe, Entity B will also have to determine its functional currency. The question arises as to whether this will be the same as the parent or will be the local currency where Entity B is located.

The factors that must be considered are:

- whether the activities of the foreign operation are carried out as an extension of the parent, rather than with a significant degree of autonomy
- whether transactions with the parent are a high or low proportion of the foreign operation's activities

- whether cash flows from the foreign operation directly affect the cash flows of the parent and are readily available for remittance to it
- whether cash flows from the activities of the foreign operation are sufficient to service existing debt obligations without funds being made available by the parent.

So, continuing with the example above, if Entity B operates as an independent operation, generating income and expenses in its local currency and raising finance in its local currency, then its functional currency would be its local currency and not that of Entity A. However, if Entity B was merely an extension of Entity A, only selling goods imported from Entity A and remitting all profits back to Entity A, then the functional currency should be the same as the parent. In this case Entity B would record its transactions in sterling and not its local currency.

Once a functional currency is determined it is not changed unless there is a change in the underlying circumstances that were relevant when determining the original functional currency.

IAS 21 states that whereas an entity is constrained by the factors listed above in determining its functional currency, it has a completely free choice as to the currency in which it presents its financial statements. If the **presentation currency** is different from the functional currency, then the financial statements must be translated into the presentation currency. For example, a group may have subsidiaries whose functional currencies are different to that of the parent. These must be translated into the presentation currency so that the consolidation procedure can take place. This process is covered in a later chapter.

2 Accounting for individual transactions designated in a foreign currency

Where an entity enters into a transaction denominated in a currency other than its functional currency, that transaction must be translated into the functional currency before it is recorded.

The exchange rate used to initially record transactions should be either:

- the spot exchange rate on the date the transaction occurred, or
- an average rate over a period of time, providing the exchange rate has not fluctuated significantly.

Cash settlement

When cash settlement occurs, such as when cash is received from an overseas credit customer, the settled amount should be translated into the functional currency using the spot exchange rate on the settlement date. If this amount differs from that used when the transaction occurred, there will be an exchange difference.

Exchange differences on settlement

IAS 21 requires that exchange gains or losses on settlement of individual transactions must be recognised in profit or loss in the period in which they arise.

IAS 21 is not definitive in stating where in profit or loss any such gains or losses are classified. It would seem reasonable to regard them as items of operating expense or income. However, other profit or loss headings may also be appropriate.

Illustration – Exchange differences on settlement

On 7 May 20X6 an entity with a functional currency of dollars ($) sold goods to a German entity for €48,000. On this date, the rate of exchange was $1 = € 3.2.

The sale is translated into the functional currency using the exchange rate in place on the transaction date.

	$
Dr Receivables (€48,000/3.2)	15,000
Cr Revenue	15,000

On 20 July 20X6 the customer paid the outstanding balance. On this date, the rate of exchange was $1 = €3.17.

The settlement is translated into the functional currency using the exchange rate in place on the settlement date.

	$
Dr Cash (€48,000/3.17)	15,142
Cr Receivables	15,000
Cr Profit or loss (exchange gain)	142

The $142 exchange gain forms part of the profit for the year.

Treatment of year-end balances

The treatment of any overseas items remaining in the statement of financial position at the year-end will depend on whether they are monetary or non-monetary:

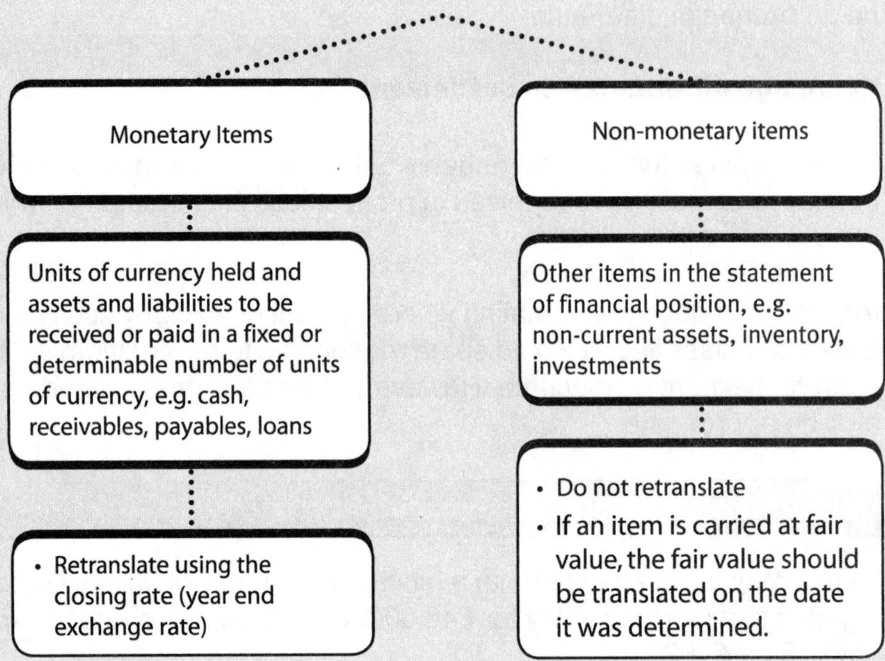

Exchange differences on retranslation of monetary items

As with exchange differences arising on settlement, IAS 21 requires that exchange differences arising on retranslation of monetary assets and liabilities must be recognised in profit or loss.

IAS 21 does not specify the heading(s) under which such exchange gains or losses should be classified. It would seem reasonable to regard them as items of operating income or operating expense as appropriate.

Illustration – Monetary items

On 7 May 20X6 an entity with a functional currency of dollars ($) sold goods to a German entity for €48,000. On this date, the rate of exchange was $1 = € 3.2.

The sale is translated into the functional currency using the exchange rate in place on the transaction date.

	$
Dr Receivables (€48,000/3.2)	15,000
Cr Revenue	15,000

By the reporting date of 31 July 20X6, the invoice had not been settled. On this date, the rate of exchange was $1 = €3.4.

Receivables are a monetary item so must be retranslated into the entity's functional currency at the year end using the closing exchange rate.

The receivable at year end should therefore be held at $14,118 (€48,000/3.4). The following entry is required:

	$
Dr Profit or loss (exchange loss)	882
Cr Receivables ($15,000 – $14,118)	882

Illustration – Non-monetary items

Olympic, which has a functional and presentation currency of the dollar ($), accounts for land using the cost model in IAS 16. On 1 July 20X5, Olympic purchased a plot of land in another country for 1.2 million dinars.

Relevant exchange rates:	Dinars to $1
1 July 20X5	4.0
30 June 20X6	3.0

The land is initially recognised at cost. This should be translated into the functional currency using the exchange rate on the purchase date. The land is therefore initially recorded at $300,000 (1.2m dinars /4.0).

Land is not a monetary item so is therefore not retranslated. In accordance with IAS 16, no depreciation is charged. This means that the land remains at $300,000.

Illustration – Non-monetary items at fair value

Pallot, which has a functional and presentation currency of the dollar ($), accounts for land using the revaluation model in IAS 16. On 1 July 20X5, Pallot purchased a plot of land in another country for 1.2 million dinars. At 30 June 20X6, the fair value of the plot of land was 1.5 million dinars.

Relevant exchange rates:	Dinars to $1
1 July 20X5	4.0
30 June 20X6	3.0

The land is initially recognised at cost. This should be translated into the functional currency using the exchange rate on the purchase date. The land is therefore initially recorded at $300,000 (1.2m dinars/4.0).

Land is not a monetary item so its cost is not retranslated. However, in accordance with the revaluation model in IAS 16, a fair value has been determined. This valuation is in dinars and so must be translated into the functional currency using the exchange rate in place when the fair value was determined. This means that the land will must be revalued to $500,000 (1.5m dinars/3.0).

The increase in the carrying value of the land of $200,000 ($500,000 – $300,000) will be reported as a revaluation gain in other comprehensive income for the year and a revaluation reserve will be included within other components of equity on the statement of financial position at the reporting date.

Test your understanding 1 – Butler, Waiter and Attendant

(a) An entity, Butler, has a reporting date of 31 December and a functional currency of dollars ($). On 27 November 20X6 Butler plc buys goods from a Swedish supplier for SwK 324,000.

On 19 December 20X6 Butler plc pays the Swedish supplier in full.

Exchange rates were as follows:

27 November 20X6 – SwK 11.15: $1
19 December 20X6 – SwK 10.93: $1

Required:

Describe how the above transaction should be accounted for in the financial statements of Butler for the year ended 31 December 20X6.

(b) An entity, Waiter, has a reporting date of 31 December and the dollar ($) as its functional currency. Waiter borrows in the foreign currency of the Kram (K). The loan of K120,000 was taken out on 1 January 20X7. A repayment of K40,000 was made on 1 March 20X7.

Exchange rates were as follows

1 January 20X7 – K1: $2
1 March 20X7 – K1: $3
31 December 20X7 – K1: $3.5

Required:

Describe how the above should be accounted for in the financial statements of Waiter for the year ended 31 December 20X7.

(c) An entity, Attendant, has a reporting date of 31 December and has the dollar ($) as its functional currency. Attendant purchased a plot of land overseas on 1 March 20X0. The entity paid for the land in the currency of the Rylands (R). The purchase cost of the land at 1 March 20X0 was R60,000. The value of the land at the reporting date was R80,000.

Exchange rates were as follows:

1 March 20X0 – R8 : $1
31 December 20X0 – R10 :$1

Required:

Describe how the above transaction should be accounted for in the financial statements of Attendant for the year ended 31 December 20X0 if the land is measured at:

- **cost**
- **fair value.**

Test your understanding 2 – Highlight

(a) Highlight is an entity whose functional currency is the dollar ($) and has an annual reporting date of 31 December.

On 1 July 20X3, Highlight purchased an item of plant and equipment on credit for Dn400,000. On 1 November 20X3, Highlight made a payment of Dn180,000 to the supplier. The balance of the invoice remains outstanding.

Highlight has a policy of applying historical cost accounting and depreciating plant and equipment at the rate of 20% per annum. The item of plant and equipment is not expected to have any residual value at the end of its useful life.

Relevant exchange rates to $1 are as follows:

	Dn
1 July 20X3	10.0
1 November 20X3	7.2
1 December 20X3	9.0
31 December 20X3	8.0

Required:

Prepare relevant extracts from Highlight's financial statements for the year ended 31 December 20X3 to illustrate the impact of the above transactions.

(b) During 20X3, Highlight entered into a number of transactions with Eraser, an overseas customer.

On 1 November 20X3, Highlight made credit sales to Eraser on 3 months credit for Dn360,000. On 1 December 20X3, Highlight made further credit sales to Eraser on 3 months credit for Dn540,000.

By 31 December 20X3, Highlight had received no payment from Eraser. As the receivables were still within their credit period, they were not regarded as being impaired.

Relevant exchange rates to $1 are as follows:

1 July 20X3	10.0
1 November 20X3	7.2
1 December 20X3	9.0
31 December 20X3	8.0

Required:

Prepare relevant extracts from Highlight's financial statements for the year ended 31 December 20X3 to illustrate the impact of the above transactions.

Shortcomings in IAS 21

There are a number of issues on which IAS 21 is either silent or fails to give adequate guidance.

(a) Under IAS 21 transactions should be recorded at the rate ruling at the date the transaction occurs (i.e. the date when the transaction qualifies for recognition in the accounts), but in some cases this date is difficult to establish. For example, it could be the order date, the date of invoice or the date on which the goods were received.

(b) IAS 21 states that average rates can be used if these do not fluctuate significantly, but what period should be used to calculate average rates? Should the average rate be adjusted to take account of material transactions?

(c) IAS 21 provides only limited guidance where there are two or more exchange rates for a particular currency or where an exchange rate is suspended. It has been suggested that companies should use whichever rate seems appropriate given the nature of the transaction and have regard to prudence if necessary.

(d) IAS 21 makes a distinction between the translation of monetary and non-monetary items, but in practice some items (such as progress payments paid against non-current assets or inventories, and debt securities held as investments) may have characteristics of both.

3 Chapter summary

FOREIGN CURRENCY

IAS 21 THE EFFECTS OF CHANGES IN FOREIGN EXCHANGE RATES

Functional currency:
The currency of the primary economic environment where the entity operates

Presentation currency:
The currency in which the entity presents its financial statements

Accounting for individual transactions in a foreign currency

- At transaction date
- On settlement
- At reporting date

Shortcomings in IAS21

Test your understanding answers

Test your understanding 1 – Butler, Waiter and Attendant

(a) The transaction on 27 November 20X6 must be translated using the exchange rate on the transaction date.

The transaction is recorded at $29,058 (SwK324,000/11.15).

Dr Purchases $29,058
Cr Payables $29,058

The cash settlement on 19 December 20X6 must be translated using the exchange rate on the settlement date.

The cash settlement is recorded at $29,643 (SwK324,000/10.93).

Dr Payables $29,058
Dr Profit or loss $585
Cr Cash $29,643

An exchange loss of $585 has arisen and this is recorded in the statement of profit or loss.

(b) On 1 January 20X7, money was borrowed in Krams. This must be translated into the functional currency using the exchange rate on the transaction date.

The transaction is recorded at $240,000 (K120,000 × 2).

Dr Cash $240,000
Cr Loans $240,000

The cash settlement on 1 March 20X7 must be translated into the functional currency using the exchange rate on the settlement date.

The cash settlement is recorded at $120,000 (K40,000 × 3).

Dr Loans $120,000
Cr Cash $120,000

Loans are a monetary liability. At the reporting date, the remaining loan of K80,000 (K120,000 – K40,000) must be translated at the year end exchange rate. This gives a closing liability of $280,000 (K80,000 × 3.5).

The exchange loss on retranslation is calculated as follows:

	K	Rate	$
1 January 20X7	120,000	2.0	240,000
1 March 20X7	(40,000)	3.0	(120,000)
Exchange loss (bal. fig)			160,000
31 December 20X7	80,000	3.5	280,000

The double entry to record this loss:

Dr Profit or loss $160,000
Cr Loans $160,000

(c) The asset is initially recognised at cost. This should be translated into the functional currency using the exchange rate on the purchase date. The land is therefore initially recorded at $7,500 ($60,000/8).

Land is not a monetary item so is therefore not retranslated. If held under the cost model, it will remain at $7,500

If the land is held at fair value, then the valuation must be translated into dollars using the exchange rate in place when determined. Therefore, the land will be revalued to $8,000 (R80,000/10).

The carrying value of the land must be increased by $500 ($8,000 – $7,500).

If the land is held under IAS 40 Investment Property, then the gain will be recorded in profit or loss.

If the land is held under IAS 16 Property, Plant and Equipment, then the gain will be recorded in other comprehensive income.

Test your understanding 2 – Highlight

(a) Both the purchase of plant and equipment and the associated payable are recorded using the rate ruling at the date of the transaction (Dn10 = $1), giving a value of $40,000. The part-payment made on 1 November is recorded using the rate applicable on that date, with the remaining dinar liability being restated in dollars at the closing rate at the reporting date. The exchange difference, in this case a loss of $12,500 (see calculation below), is taken to profit or loss as an operating expense.

		Dn	Rate	$
1/7/X3	Payable recorded	400,000	10.0	40,000
1/11/X3	Part-payment made	(180,000)	7.2	(25,000)
	Exchange loss (bal. fig.)			12,500
31/12/X3	Payable outstanding	220,000	8.0	27,500

Plant and equipment, as a non-monetary item, is accounted for at historic cost and is therefore not retranslated. The depreciation charge is $4,000 ($40,000 × 1/5 × 6/12).

Extracts of the financial statements for the year ended 31 December 20X3 are as follows:

Statement of profit or loss:	$
Cost of sales (depreciation)	(4,000)
Operating expenses (exchange loss)	(12,500)

Statement of financial position:	
Property, plant and equipment ($40,000 – $4,000)	36,000
Current liabilities	27,500

(b) Each of the sales invoices denominated in Dn must be translated into $ using the spot rate on the date of each transaction. Each transaction will result in recognition of revenue and a trade receivable at the following amounts:

1 November 20X3: Dn360,000/7.2 = $50,000
1 December 20X3: Dn540,000/9.0 = $60,000

Both amounts remain outstanding at the reporting date and must be restated into dollars using the closing rate of Dn8 = $1. The exchange difference, in this case a gain of $2,500 (see calculation below), is taken to profit or loss as an item of other operating income.

		Dn	Rate	$
1/11/X3	Receivable recorded	360,000	7.2	50,000
1/12/X3	Receivable recorded	540,000	9.0	60,000
	Exchange gain (bal. fig.)			2,500
31/12/X3	Receivable outstanding	900,000	8.0	112,500

Extracts of the financial statements for the year ended 31 December 20X3 are as follows:

Statement of profit or loss:	$
Revenue ($50,000 + $60,000)	110,000
Other operating income (exchange gain)	2,500
Statement of financial position:	
Receivables	112,500

chapter

6

Leases

Chapter learning objectives

Upon completion of this chapter you will be able to:

- apply and discuss the classification of leases and accounting by lessors and lessees
- account for and discuss the accounting for sale and leaseback transactions.

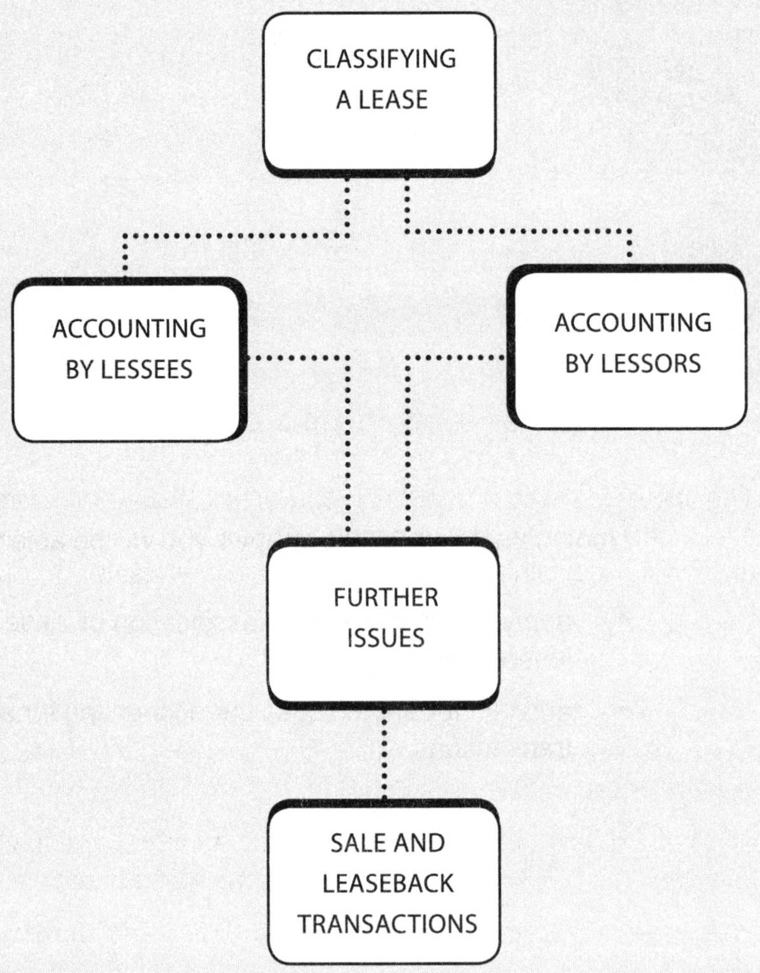

1 Classifying a lease

Definitions

A **lease** is an agreement whereby the lessor conveys to the lessee in return for a payment or series of payments the right to use an asset for an agreed period of time.

A **finance lease** is a lease that transfers substantially all the risks and rewards incidental to ownership of an asset.

An **operating lease** is a lease other than a finance lease.

A lease is classified as an operating lease or a finance lease at inception. Whether a lease is a finance lease or an operating lease depends on the substance of the agreement.

- A finance lease is essentially a way of financing the use of an asset by spreading the payment over the life of the asset instead of paying the full amount all at once
- An operating lease is similar to a rental agreement. The entity normally rents the asset for only part of its useful life.

How to classify a lease

IAS 17 Leases explains that a lease is probably a finance lease if one or more of the following apply:

- Ownership is transferred to the lessee at the end of the lease
- The lessee has the option to purchase the asset for less than its expected fair value at the date the option becomes exercisable and it is reasonably certain that the option will be exercised
- The lease term (including any secondary periods) is for the major part of the asset's economic life
- At the inception of the lease, the present value of the minimum lease payments amounts to at least substantially all of the fair value of the leased asset
- The leased assets are of a specialised nature so that only the lessee can use them without major modifications being made
- The lessee will compensate the lessor if the lease is cancelled
- Gains or losses from fluctuations in the fair value of the residual fall to the lessee (for example, by means of a rebate of lease payments)
- The lessee has the ability to continue the lease for a secondary period at a rent that is substantially lower than market rent.

How to classify a lease

In most cases, it should be fairly easy to tell whether or not any of the above situations apply. The exception is the fourth item, comparing the present value of the minimum lease payments with the fair value of the leased asset. The present value of the minimum lease payments normally has to be calculated, using an appropriate discount rate.

Test your understanding 1–- Lease classification

DanBob is considering whether or not to lease a building.

The building, if purchased outright, would have a useful economic life of 50 years. The lease term, which would commence on 1 January 20X0, is for 30 years.

DanBob would pay 40% of the asset's value upfront. At the end of each of the 30 years, there is also an annual rental payment due. This is equivalent to 6% of the asset's value as at 1 January 20X0 or, if higher, the year end.

Legal title at the end of the lease remains with the lessor, but DanBob can continue to lease the asset indefinitely at a rental that is substantially below its market value. If Danbob cancels the lease, it must make a payment to the lessor to recover their remaining investment.

Required:

Per IAS 17 Leases, should the lease be classified as an operating lease or a finance lease?

Leases of land and buildings

Land and buildings are often leased together, but IAS 17 requires the land and buildings elements to be classified separately.

- The land element is normally classified as an operating lease unless title passes to the lessee at the end of the lease term.
- The buildings element may be classified as either a finance or an operating lease depending upon the nature of the lease contract.
- The minimum lease payments are allocated between the land and buildings elements in proportion to their relative fair values.

Note, however, that IAS 17 has been amended to require that leases of land and buildings are evaluated based upon the commercial substance of the whole transaction. This may result, for example, in a long-term lease of land and buildings (e.g. for 900 years) being accounted for as a finance lease as substantially all of the risks and rewards associated with the lease have been transferred.

2 Accounting by lessees

Finance leases

IAS 17 requires the lessee to report the substance of the transaction.

- At the beginning of the lease term, the lessee recognises the leased asset and a liability for future lease payments in the statement of financial position.
- The asset and the liability are measured at the lower of:
  - the fair value of the asset
  - the present value of the minimum lease payments (discounted at the interest rate implicit in the lease, if practicable, or else at the entity's incremental borrowing rate).
- A finance cost is charged on the lease liability, increasing its value.
- The lease payments reduce the lease liability.
- The leased asset is depreciated over the shorter of:
  - its useful life
  - the lease term (including secondary period).

Test your understanding 2 – Finance leases

A machine delivered at the beginning of year 1 has a fair value of $1,700,000 and a useful life of six years. The lease contract requires an annual payment of $400,000 for six years. Significant risks and rewards have been transferred to the lessee.

Required:

Prepare extracts from the statement of profit and loss and the statement of financial position for year one assuming that the instalments are paid in:

(a) **arrears (implicit rate of interest 10.84%)**

(b) **advance (implicit rate of interest 16.32%)**

Operating leases

The substance of the transaction is that the lessee uses an asset, but does not own or control it.

- The lessee does not recognise the leased asset in its statement of financial position.
- Rentals are charged as an expense on a straight line basis over the term of the lease unless another systematic and rational basis is more appropriate.
- Any difference between the amount charged to profit or loss and the cash payments should be recognised as a prepayment or an accrual.

Test your understanding 3 – Operating leases

A company hires a machine under an operating lease for three years. Payments are due annually in arrears, as follows:

	$
Year 1	5,000
Year 2	10,000
Year 3	6,000

Required:

Prepare extracts from the statement of profit and loss and the statement of financial position for each of the three years

Leases: off-balance sheet finance

If an entity leases a lot of its assets, accounting for them as finance leases can have a significant impact on the financial statements.

- Return on capital employed decreases, because of the additional assets.
- Earnings (and earnings per share) may be lower in early years of a lease due to high finance costs.
- Gearing increases, because of the additional liabilities (obligations to pay future rentals).

An entity may already have a high level of long-term debt, or need to raise additional finance, or may be in danger of breaching loan covenants (agreements). Loan covenants often include a clause stating that the gearing ratio or the ratio of assets to liabilities must not exceed a certain figure. Therefore, management may have an incentive to try to keep lease assets and liabilities of the statement of financial position ('off balance sheet').

The classification of leases is subjective, meaning that there is scope for manipulation. Moreover, it is possible to structure a lease agreement so that the lease appears to be an operating lease when it is actually a finance lease. This is a form of 'creative accounting'. IAS 17 requires that the classification of a lease should always reflect the **substance** of the agreement.

3 Accounting by lessors

Finance leases

The lessee, not the lessor, has control of the asset.

- The lessor must derecognise the leased asset.
- The lessor recognises a lease receivable. The carrying value of the receivable is the lessor's net investment in the lease.
- The net investment in the lease is the total of:
  - the present value of the minimum lease payments receivable
  - the present value of any unguaranteed residual value accruing to the lessor (e.g. the residual value of the leased asset when it is repossessed at the end of the lease).
- Assuming that there is no unguaranteed residual value, the lessor's net investment in the lease is the same as the lessee's lease liability.
- Finance income is recognised on the receivable, increasing its value.
- Cash receipts reduce the value of the receivable.

Illustration 1 – Lessors and finance leases

Vache leases machinery to Toro. The lease is for four years at an annual cost of $2,000 payable annually in arrears. The normal cash price (and fair value) of the asset is $5,900. The present value of the minimum lease payments is $5,710. The implicit rate of interest is 15%.

Required:

How should Vache account for their net investment in the lease?

Solution

Vache recognises the net investment in the lease as a receivable. This is the present value of the minimum lease payments of $5,710.

The receivable is increased by finance income. The receivable is reduced by the cash receipts.

Year	Opening balance	Finance income (15%)	Cash received	Closing balance
	$	$	$	$
1	5,710	856	(2,000)	4,566
2	4,566	685	(2,000)	3,251
3	3,251	488	(2,000)	1,739
4	1,739	261	(2,000)	–

Extract from the statement of financial position at the end of Year 1

	$
Non-current assets:	
Net investment in finance leases (see note)	3,251
Current assets:	
Net investment in finance leases	1,315

Note: the current asset is the next instalment less next year's interest ($2,000 – $685). The non-current asset is the remainder ($4,566 – $1,315).

Operating leases

If a lessor has an operating lease, it continues to recognise the leased asset.

- Assets held under operating leases are recognised in the statement of financial position as non-current assets. They should be presented according to the nature of the asset and depreciated in the normal way.
- Rental income from operating leases is recognised in profit or loss on a straight-line basis over the term of the lease, unless another systematic and rational basis is more appropriate.
- Any difference between the income recognised and the cash received should be recognised as a receivable or as deferred income.

Illustration 2 – Lessors and operating leases

Oroc hires out industrial plant on long-term operating leases. On 1 January 20X1, it entered into a seven-year lease on a mobile crane. The terms of the lease are $175,000 payable on 1 January 20X1, followed by six rentals of $70,000 payable on 1 January 20X2 – 20X7. The crane will be returned to Oroc on 31 December 20X7. The crane originally cost $880,000 and has a 25-year useful life with no residual value.

Required:

Discuss the accounting treatment of the above in the year ended 31 December 20X1.

Solution

Oroc holds the crane in its statement of financial position and depreciates it over its useful life. The annual depreciation charge is $35,200 ($880,000/25 years).

Rental income must be recognised in profit or loss on a straight line basis. Total lease receipts are $595,000 ($175,000 + ($70,000 × 6 years)). Annual rental income is therefore $85,000 ($595,000/7 years). The statement of financial position includes a liability for deferred income of $90,000 ($175,000 – $85,000).

Summary

Finance lease

- Substance = lessee has the asset
- Substance = financing agreement
- Lessee recognises asset in SFP
- Lessee recognises liability for future rentals
- Lessor recognises net investment in lease (a receivable)
- Interest accrues on outstanding amount and is paid by lessee/received by lessor
- Lease receivable/liability is reduced by lease rentals over the term of the lease

Operating lease

- Substance = lessor has the asset
- Substance = rental agreement
- Lessor recognises asset in SFP
- Lessor recognises lease rentals as income
- Lessee recognises lease rentals as an expense

Further issues in accounting for leases

Initial direct costs

Initial direct costs are costs that are directly attributable to negotiating and arranging a lease, for example, commissions, legal fees and premiums. Both lessees and lessors may incur these costs. The treatment is summarised below.

	Costs incurred by lessee	Costs incurred by lessor
Finance lease	Add to amount recognised as an asset; depreciate over asset's useful life	Include in initial measurement of receivable; reduce income receivable over lease term
Operating lease	Treat as part of lease rentals; expense over lease term on straight line basis	Add to carrying amount of leased asset; expense over lease term on same basis as lease income

- Exclude general overheads (these are not directly attributable to arranging the lease).

Operating leases: incentives

An operating lease agreement may include incentives for the lessee to sign the lease. Typical incentives include an up-front cash payment to the lessee (a reverse premium), rent-free periods, or contributions by the lessor to the lessee's relocation costs.

- Any incentives given by the lessor should be recognised over the life of the lease on a straight line basis. This applies to the financial statements of both the lessee and the lessor.

Depreciation of leased assets

Leased assets should be depreciated on the same basis as similar assets that the entity owns. This applies in the accounts of both the lessee (under a finance lease) and the lessor (under an operating lease).

Manufacturer or dealer lessors

Finance leases can be arranged with a third party, such as a bank, or they can be provided by the manufacturer or dealer of the goods. A manufacturer or dealer may offer customers the option to lease an asset as a way of encouraging sales.

A finance lease results in two transactions:

- a sale on normal terms (see below) giving rise to sales income and a profit or loss
- the provision of finance, giving rise to finance income.

The sales proceeds are measured at the lower of:

- fair value (i.e. the normal sales price)
- the present value of the minimum lease payments discounted at a commercial rate of interest (regardless of the rate of interest quoted to the customer). The requirement to use a commercial rate of interest prevents companies inflating the value of their sales and their profits by claiming to offer low rates of finance.

The cost of sales is the cost (or carrying amount) of the asset sold, less the present value of any unguaranteed residual value. All initial direct costs are charged when the sale is made.

Determining whether an arrangement contains a lease

Sometimes transactions or arrangements do not take the legal form of a lease but convey rights to use assets in return for a payment or series of payments. Examples of such arrangements include:

- outsourcing arrangements
- telecommunication contracts that provide rights to capacity
- take-or-pay contracts, in which purchasers must make specified payments whether or not they take delivery of the contracted products or services.

4 Sale and leaseback transactions

Introduction

Under a sale and leaseback transaction an entity sells one of its own assets and immediately leases the asset back.

- This is a common way of raising finance whilst retaining the use of the related assets. The buyer and lessor is normally a bank.
- There are two key questions to ask when assessing the substance of these transactions:
  - is the new lease a finance lease or an operating lease
  - if the new lease is an operating lease, was the original sale at fair value or not?
- The leaseback is classified in accordance with the usual criteria set out in IAS 17.

Sale and leaseback under a finance lease

In accordance with IAS 17, a sale and finance leaseback arrangement is, in essence, a financing arrangement. The substance of the arrangement is that the asset has been used as security for a loan. The accounting treatment required by IAS 17 is as follows:

- The lessee defers any gain on the disposal of the asset, and amortises this to profit or loss over the lease term
- The lessee recognises both a finance lease asset and a finance lease obligation.
- The finance lease asset is depreciated over the lease term
- A finance cost is charged based on the outstanding lease liability
- The finance lease repayments reduce the outstanding lease liability.

Test your understanding 4 – Sale and finance leaseback

Lash owns a machine with a carrying value of $750,000. On 1 January 20X4, this was sold to a bank for its fair value of $1m and then leased back for five years.

The remaining useful life of the machine is 5 years. Lease payments of $277,409 are to be made annually in arrears. The implicit rate of interest is 12%.

Required:

Prepare extracts from Lash's statement of profit or loss and statement of financial position for the year ended 31 December 20X4.

Value of sales proceeds

The accounting treatment of a sale and finance leaseback is not affected if the sales proceeds are above or below the carrying value of the asset. The asset is only being used as security for the loan, and so it is up to the lender as to whether they are prepared to lend more or less than the value of the security.

However, if the sales proceeds are significantly lower than the asset's carrying amount, this suggests that the entity needs to carry out an impairment review. Alternatively, if sales proceeds are significantly higher than carrying amount, the entity may consider revaluing the asset. These adjustments are dealt with in the normal way and they do not affect the substance of the sale and leaseback transaction itself.

Sale and leaseback under an operating lease

A sale and operating leaseback transfers the risks and rewards incident to ownership to the buyer/lessor. The accounting treatment is as follows:

- Operating lease rentals are recognised as an expense in profit or loss.
- The asset is removed from the seller's statement of financial position.
- Any gain on disposal is recognised in accordance with the guidance provided in IAS 17. This is summarised in the following diagram.

Summary

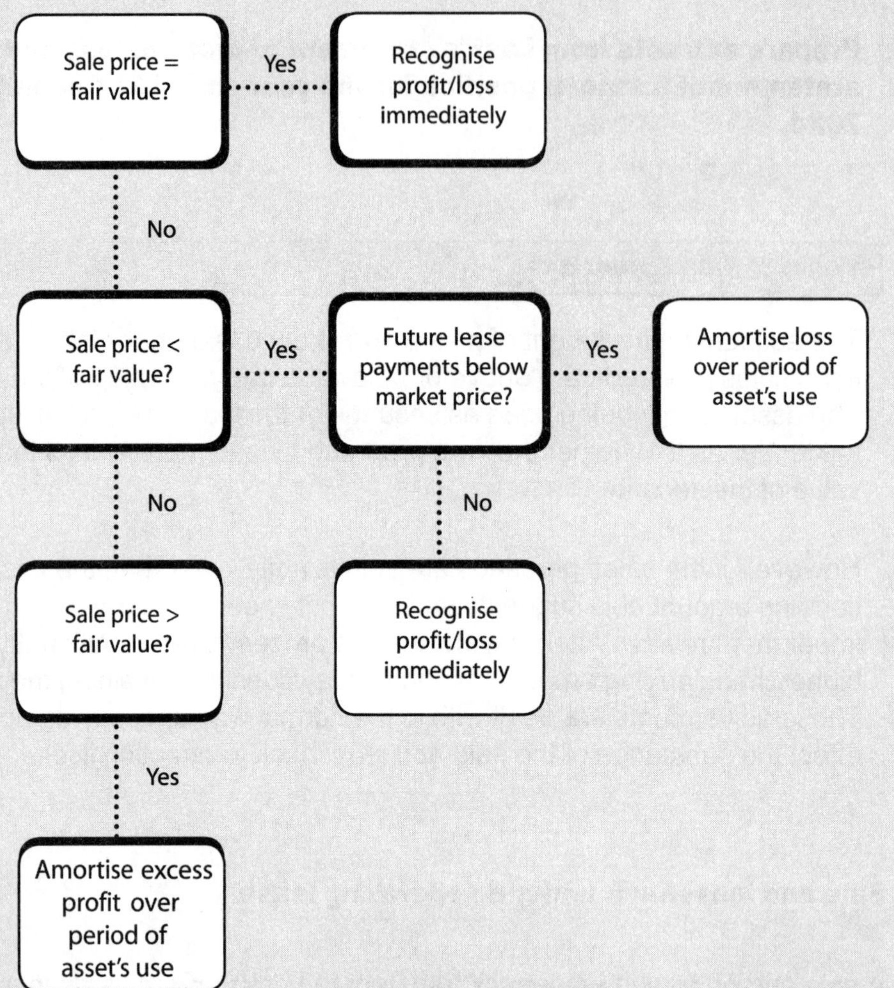

Excess profit is the difference between the sale price and the fair value of the asset.

Sale and operating leaseback illustration

On 1 January 20X4, Crash sold its freehold office premises and leased them back on a 20-year operating lease. The details of the scheme are as follows:

Proceeds of sale	$8,000,000
Fair value of the asset at the time of sale	$15,000,000
Carrying amount at the time of sale	$12,000,000
Annual operating lease rentals (on a 20 year lease)	$650,000

Required:

Prepare all relevant extracts from Crash's statement of profit or loss and statement of financial position for the year ending 31 December 20X4, assuming that the future lease rentals are:

(a) **at market rate**

(b) **below market rate.**

Solution

(a) **Future rentals at market rate**

If the rentals are at market rate (or above), then the loss must be recognised immediately.

Statement of profit or loss for the year ended 31 December 20X4

		$
Loss on disposal	($8m – $12m)	4,000,000
Operating lease rentals	Amount paid	650,000

(b) **Future rentals at below market rate**

If the rentals are below market rate, the loss is deferred and amortised over the life of the lease.

Statement of profit or loss for the year ended 31 December 20X4

	$	$
Loss on disposal		Nil
Operating lease rentals		
Amount paid	650,000	
Plus: amortisation of deferred loss $4m / 20 years	200,000	
Amount charged P/L		850,000

Statement of financial position as at 31 December 20X4

Assets	$
Deferred loss on disposal	
Brought forward	–
Arising during the year	4,000,000
Amortised	(200,000)
Carried down	3,800,000

$3,600,000 of this loss would be disclosed as a non-current asset.

Sale price less than fair value

If a loss on disposal arises because the proceeds are less than the fair value of the asset, then the loss can only be deferred if the future operating lease rentals are also at below the market rate. This is because deferring a loss gives rise to an asset in the statement of financial position, and assets can only be recognised if there are future economic benefits. The economic benefits that will justify deferring this loss are reduced rentals.

If a loss is deferred.

- The loss should be amortised over the period the asset is expected to be used.
- It would be wise to conduct regular impairment reviews on such assets, because changes in market rentals and/or interest rates could easily impair the benefit of the reduced rent. For instance, if the lease rentals were $650,000 per year and the market rate for a property fell to $600,000 per year, then there would no longer be any benefit to be had from an agreed rent of $650,000. If there are no future benefits, then there is no asset to recognise.

If the sale proceeds are less than the fair value, and the fair value is less than the carrying value of the asset, then only the difference between the proceeds and the fair value can be deferred. The difference between the fair value and the carrying value must be recognised as a loss immediately.

For example, if a building with a carrying value of $9m and a fair value of $7m was sold for $4m, then a loss of $2m would be recognised on disposal, and the $3m difference between the proceeds and the fair value would be deferred.

Sale and operating leaseback illustration

Ash sells its freehold office premises and leases them back on a 20-year operating lease. The sale took place on 1 January 20X4, and the company has a 31 December year-end.

The details of the scheme are as follows:

Proceeds of sale	$10,000,000
Fair value of the asset at the time of sale	$9,000,000
Carrying amount at the time of sale	$3,500,000
Lease payments (annual rental)	$480,000
Market rate for similar premises (annual rental)	$410,000

(a) **Calculate the profit on disposal that Ash should claim in 20X4.**

(b) **Calculate the annual rental that Ash will charge in its statement of profit or loss.**

(c) **Prepare all relevant extracts from Ash's statement of profit or loss and statement of financial position for the year ending 31 December 20X4.**

Solution

(a) Ash can only claim a profit on disposal based upon the fair value of the asset. This will give a profit on disposal of $5,500,000 ($9,000,000 fair value less $3,500,000 CV).

(b) The $1m difference between the proceeds and the fair value is credited to deferred income and released over the life of the lease on a straight line basis. The annual release will be $50,000 ($1m / 20 years). This reduces the rent charged to $430,000 ($480,000 – $50,000).

(c) **Statement of profit or loss for the year ended 31 December 20X4**

	$
Profit on disposal at fair value	5,500,000
Operating lease rentals ($480,000 – $50,000)	(430,000)

Statement of financial position as at 31 December 20X4

	$
Deferred income ($1,000,000 – $50,000)	950,000

$900,000 of this liability is non-current and $50,000 is current.

Test your understanding 5 – Sale and leaseback

Details of several sale and operating leaseback transactions are shown below. In all situations, the sale occured on 1 January 20X1, the lease term is 20 years and annual lease rentals are $400,000.

The rentals for lease 2 are below market rate.

	Sale value	Fair value	Carrying amount
	$000	$000	$000
(1)	10,000	10,000	8,000
(2)	10,000	15,000	12,000
(3)	15,000	10,000	8,000

Required:

Explain how the seller should account for each sale and leaseback transaction in the year ended 31 December 20X1.

Current issue

Criticisms of IAS 17

If a lease is classified as a finance lease, then a liability is recognised at the lower of the asset's fair value and the present value of the minimum lease payments. If a lease is classified as an operating lease, then no liability is recognised.

The problem that arises is that the same leasing arrangement may be accounted differently by two entities depending upon their perception and interpretation of the relevant risks and rewards criteria.

IAS 17 has also been criticised for its inconsistencies with the Framework. Per the Framework a liability is:

- an obligation
- from a past event
- that will lead to an outflow of economic resources

Operating leases are often non-cancellable. As a result of signing an agreement in the past, an entity is obliged to make payments to the lessor for several years. Therefore, operating lease commitments do meet the definition of a liability. However, no liability is recognised in the lessee's financial statements.

As a result, the quality of financial information provided to the users suffers. Shareholders and lenders have to analyse the detail of disclosure notes to get a true sense of the commitments of the reporting entity.

Long-term finance leases can also be packaged as operating leases to secure the benefits of 'off balance sheet finance'.

New Proposals – ED/2013/6

Lessee accounting

Under the proposals outlined in the leases exposure draft, issued in May 2013, there will be no distinction between an operating lease and a finance lease. An asset and liability will be recognised in the books of the lessee for all leases that exceed 12 months. It is believed that this will present a more faithful representation of the financial position of the lessee to the users.

Assets and liabilities will be accounted for on a discounted basis, at the present value of the lease payments. This is therefore comparable with the measurement of other financial liabilities.

The Exposure Draft recognises that accounting for all leases in the same way would ignore the wide variety of lease contracts that exist. Therefore, leases will be split into:

- Type A leases (mainly equipment)
- Type B leases (mainly property).

For an equipment lease, the lessee is paying to use and consume the asset. For a building, which will have a much greater useful economic life than equipment, the lessee is merely paying to use the asset. Therefore, the proposed accounting treatment of 'type A' leases leads to a greater expense in the earlier years of the lease, since the consumption of the asset will be greater in those years. Under a type B lease, the total lease expense will be recognised in profit or loss on a straight line basis over the lease term.

Lessor accounting

Lessor accounting for finance leases and for buildings under an operating lease will essentially remain unchanged.

There will be significant changes for entities who lease out machines and vehicles under leases that would be categorised as 'operating leases' under IAS 17. It is proposed that these entities will:

- Derecognise the underlying asset
- Recognise a lease receivable and a retained interest in the underlying asset, and
- Recognise interest income on both the lease receivable and the residual asset over the lease term.

Numerical Example – Lessee accounting

A company leases an asset for 3 years for $10,000 per year, paid annually in arrears. The company can borrow at a rate of 5%. Under IAS 17, the lease would have been classified as an operating lease.

Let's compare the accounting treatment of the lease under IAS 17 with the new proposed approach.

IAS 17 – Operating lease

The asset, and associated liability, is not recognised. Instead, the lease rentals are expensed on a straight line basis over the lease term. Therefore, an expense of $10,000 will be recorded in the statement of profit or loss for each year of the lease.

New Proposals – Type A

If the asset was an item of machinery, then the company will consume its economic benefits over the lease term. The lease would therefore be classified as a type A lease.

An asset and liability will be recognised at the present value of the lease payments. The discount rate should be the rate charged by the lessor to the lessee. If this is unknown, then the rate at which the lessee can borrow should be used. This means that an asset and liability should be recognised at $27,232 (W1)

The benefits provided by the asset will be higher in the earlier years, and therefore the expense should be higher in the initial years.

This is achieved by charging interest on the liability using the actuarial method. The finance cost in the statement of profit or loss will be $1,362 and the liability on the statement of financial position will be $18,594 (W2).

The asset will be depreciated over the lease term. The depreciation charged to the statement of profit or loss will be $9,077 ($27,232/3 years) and the asset will be held on the statement of financial position at $18,155 ($27,232 – $9,077).

New Proposals – Type B

If the leased asset was property, it would have been classified as a type B lease. The asset and liability would have been initially recognised at the same value as above ($27,232).

Property is not consumed as rapidly as machinery meaning that the consumption of the asset by the lessee would be relatively insignificant. Therefore, the total expense of the lease should be recognised on a straight line basis over the lease term.

The total expense to be recognised over the 3 years is $30,000, of which $10,000 will be recognised in profit or loss in each year.

In the first year of the lease, this will be made of $1,362 of 'interest' (as with the type A lease). The balance of $8,638 ($10,000 – $1,362) will be a depreciation expense. The asset will therefore be held at $18,594 ($27,232 – $8,638).

The interest cost is not shown as a finance cost in the statement of profit or loss. Instead, the full $10,000 will be presented within operating expenses.

(W1) **Present value of lease payments**

Time	Cash flow	Discount factor (5%)	Present value
	$		$
Year 1	10,000	0.952	9,524
Year 2	10,000	0.907	9,070
Year 2	10,000	0.864	8,638
			27,232

(W2) **Lease liability**

Bfd	Interest (5%)	Cash	Cfd
$	$	$	$
27,232	1,362	(10,000)	18,594

Technical article

The P2 Examiner wrote an article discussing the accounting treatment of leases 'Lease – operating or finance?' dated September 2012 for the Student Accountant magazine. You can access this article from the ACCA website (www.accaglobal.com).

5 Chapter summary

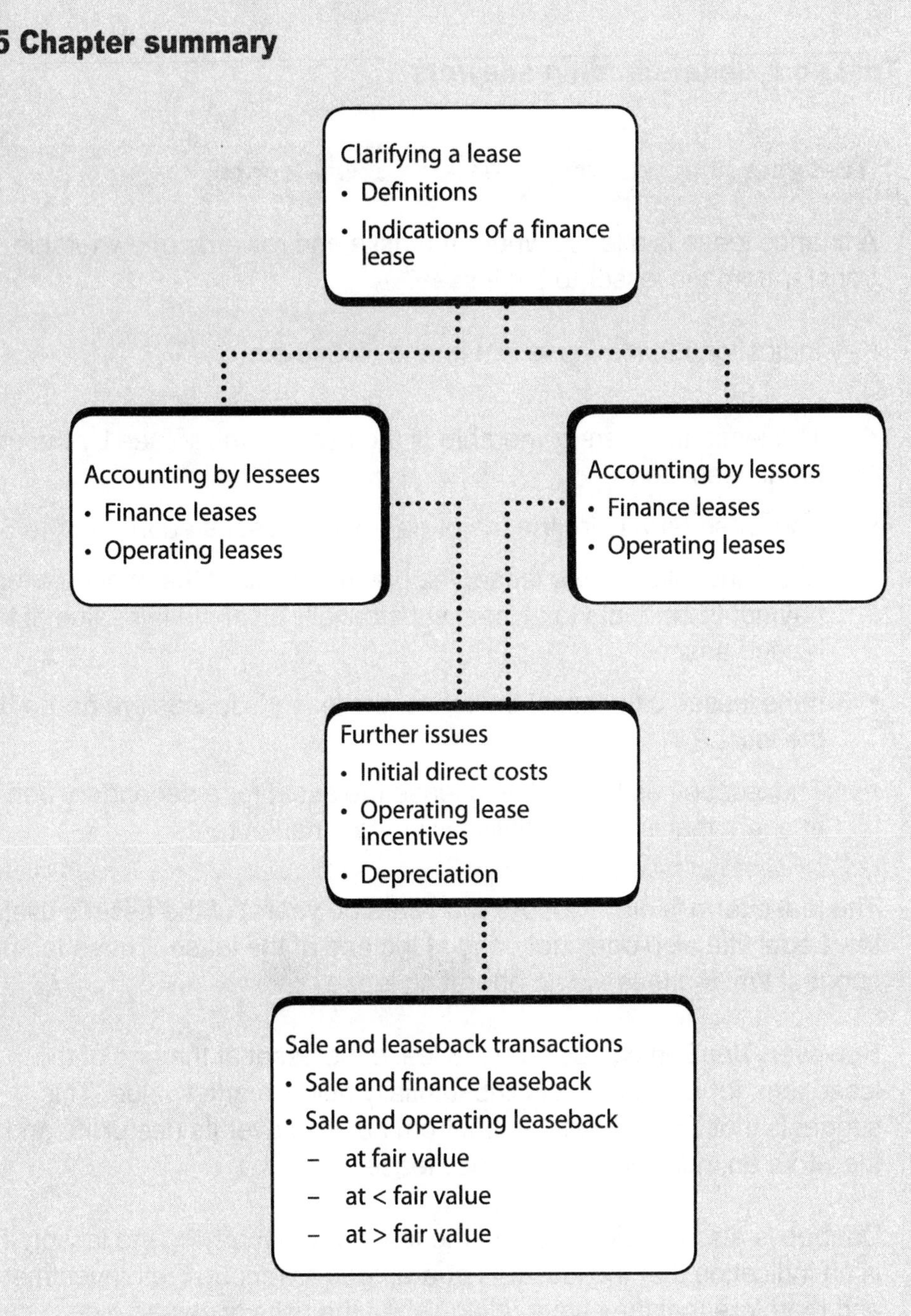

Test your understanding answers

Test your understanding 1–- Lease classification

A finance lease is a lease where the risks and rewards of ownership transfer from the lessor to the lessee.

Key indications that a lease is a finance lease are:

- The lease transfers ownership of the asset to the lessee by the end of the lease term
- The lease term is for the major part of the asset's economic life
- At the inception of the lease, the present value of the minimum lease payments amounts to at least substantially all of the fair value of the leased asset
- If the lessee can cancel the lease, the lessor's losses are borne by the lessee
- The lessee has the ability to lease the asset for a secondary period at a rent that is substantially lower than market rent.

The lease term is only for 60% (30 years/50 years) of the asset's useful life. Legal title also does not pass at the end of the lease. These factors suggest that the lease is an operating lease.

However, DanBob can continue to lease the asset at the end of the lease term for a value that is substantially below market value. This suggests that Danbob will benefit from building over its useful life and is therefore an indication of a finance lease.

Danbob is also unable to cancel the lease without paying the lessor. This is an indication that the lessor is guaranteed to recoup their investment and therefore that they have relinquished the risks of ownership.

It also seems likely that the present value of the minimum lease payments will be substantially all of the asset's fair value. Contingent rentals should be excluded from minimum lease payments – the impact of the potential rental increase should be ignored as this is contingent upon a future event. The minimum lease payments (ignoring discounting) equate to 40% of the fair value, payable upfront, and then another 180% (30 years × 6%) of the fair value over the lease term. Therefore this again suggests that the lease is a finance lease.

The fact that there is a contingent rental can be suggestive of an operating or a finance lease. This must be examined more closely to see whether it suggests a transfer of the risks and rewards of ownership. In this particular case, an increase in the value of the building will mean that the lessor receives greater payments from the lessee. However, a decrease in the value of the building will mean that the rent is fixed at 6% of the fair value at inception. This appears to be guaranteeing the lessor their required return on the investment, suggesting that the risks of ownership have been transferred to the lessee.

All things considered, it would appear that the lease is a finance lease.

Test your understanding 2 – Finance leases

Extracts from statement of profit or loss for year 1

	(a) Arrears	(b) Advance
	$000	$000
Depreciation ($1,700,000/6 years)	283	283
Finance cost	184	212

Extracts from statement of financial position at the end of Year 1

	(a) Arrears	(b) Advance
	$000	$000
Non-current asset		
Property, plant and equipment ($1,700,000 – $283,000)	1,417	1,417
Non-current liabilities		
Finance lease obligations (W1/W2)	1,245	1,112
Current liabilities		
Finance lease obligations (W1/W2)	239	400

(W1) **Arrears**

Year	Opening	Interest (10.84%)	Payments	Closing
	$000	$000	$000	$000
1	1,700	184	(400)	1,484
2	1,484	161	(400)	1,245

The finance cost for year 1 is $184,000.

The total liability at the end of year 1 is $1,484,000.

Of this liability, $1,245,000 is non-current and $239,000 ($1,484,000 – $1,245,000) is current.

(W2) **Advance**

Year	Opening	Payment	Total	Interest (16.32%)	Closing
	$000	$000	$000	$000	$000
1	1,700	(400)	1,300	212	1,512
2	1,512	(400)	1,112	182	1.294

The finance cost for year 1 is $212,000

The total liability at the end of year 1 is $1,512,000.

Of this liability, $1,112,000 is non-current and $400,000 ($1,512,000 – $1,112,000) is current.

Test your understanding 3 – Operating leases

The total lease payments are $21,000 ($5,000 + $10,000 + $6,000).

The annual lease expense in profit or loss is therefore $7,000 ($21,000/3 years).

Extracts from statement of profit or loss

	Year 1	Year 2	Year 3
	$	$	$
Operating lease expense	7,000	7,000	7,000

By the end of year one, a total of $7,000 has been charged to the statement of profit and loss but only $5,000 has been paid. As such, an accrual of $2,000 is required at the end of year 1.

By the end of year 2, a total of $14,000 has been charged to the statement of profit and loss and $15,000 ($5,000 + $10,000) has been paid. Therefore a prepayment of $1,000 will be required at the end of year 2.

By the end of year 3, a total of $21,000 has been charged to the statement of profit and loss and $21,000 ($5,000 + $10,000 + $6,000) has been paid. This means that no accrual or prepayment is required.

Extracts from statement of financial position

	Year 1	Year 2	Year 3
	$	$	$
Prepayments	–	1,000	–
Accruals	2,000	–	–

Test your understanding 4 – Sale and finance leaseback

Sale of the asset

	$
Proceeds	1,000,000
Carrying value	(750,000)
	250,000

This gain on disposal is credited to deferred income and then amortised to the statement of profit or loss over the lease term.

Income of $50,000 ($250,000/5 years) will be recorded in the current year. The balance on the deferred income account at the year end is therefore $200,000 ($250,000 – $50,000) of which $50,000 is a current liability and $150,000 is a non-current liability.

Recording and depreciating the asset

The asset and finance lease obligation are recognised at the fair value of $1m.

The asset is depreciated over the shorter of the lease term and the useful economic life. Depreciation of $200,000 ($1m/5 years) will be charged to the statement of profit or loss and the asset will have a carrying value at the year end of $800,000 ($1m – $200k).

Accounting for the lease liability

Interest is charged on the lease liability using the implicit rate. The cash payments reduce the liability.

Year	Bfd	Interest at 12%	Cash	Cfd
	$	$	$	$
20X4	1,000,000	120,000	(277,409)	842,591
20X5	842,591	101,111	(277,409)	666,293

In the current year, there will be a finance cost charged to the statement of profit or loss of $120,000. The lease liability at the year end is $842,591. Of this, $666,293 is a non-current liability and $176,298 ($842,591 – $666,293) is current.

Statement of financial position:

	20X4
Non-current assets	$
Property, plant and equipment	800,000
Non-current liabilities:	
Finance lease liabilities	666,293
Deferred income	150,000
Current liabilities	
Finance lease liabilities	176,298
Deferred income	50,000

Statement of profit or loss

	20X4
	$
Amortisation of deferred income	(50,000)
Depreciation charge	200,000
Finance cost	120,000

Test your understanding 5 – Sale and leaseback

(i) **Sale at fair value**

The asset is derecognised and the gain on disposal of $2m ($10m – $8m) can be recognised in profit or loss immediately.

Operating lease rentals paid of $400,000 are charged to the statement of profit or loss.

(ii) **Sale at below fair value**

The asset is derecognised.

The future rentals are below market value. The loss on disposal of $2m ($10m – $12m) must be deferred and released to the statement of profit or loss over the period of the asset's use. Therefore, $100,000 ($2m/20 years) will be charged to profit or loss in the current year. The deferred loss remaining on the statement of financial position is $1,900,000 ($2,000,000 – $100,000).

Operating lease rentals paid of $400,000 are charged to the statement of profit or loss.

(iii) **Sale at above fair value**

The asset is derecognised.

The excess profit, the difference between the sales price and the fair value, is $5m ($15m – $10m). This is held on the statement of financial position as deferred income and released to profit or loss over the period in which the asset is used. Therefore, $250,000 ($5m/20 years) will be credited to the statement of profit or loss in the current year. The deferred income remaining on the statement of financial position is $4,750,000 ($5,000,000 – $250,000).

The remainder of the profit, the difference between fair value and the carrying value, of $2m ($10m – $8m) is recognised in profit or loss immediately.

Operating lease rentals paid of $400,000 are charged to the statement of profit or loss.

chapter

7

Events after the reporting period, provisions and contingencies

Chapter learning objectives

Upon completion of this chapter you will be able to:

- apply and discuss accounting for events after the reporting date
- determine and report going concern issues arising after the reporting date
- apply and discuss the recognition, derecognition and measurement of provisions, contingent liabilities and contingent assets including environmental provisions
- calculate and discuss restructuring provisions.

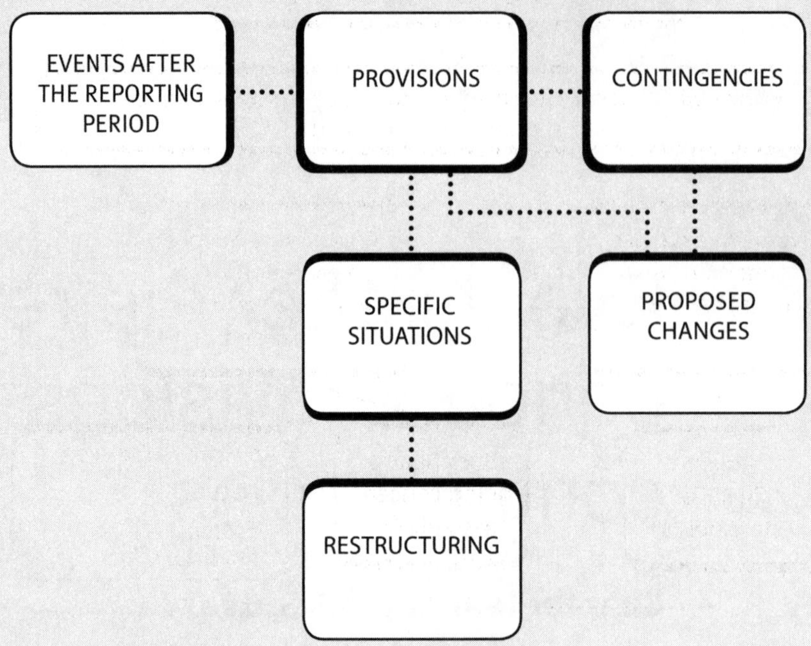

1 Events after the reporting period

Definition

Events after the reporting period are those events, both favourable and unfavourable, that occur between the reporting date and the date on which the financial statements are authorised for issue.

There are two types of event after the reporting period:

- adjusting events
- non-adjusting events.

Financial statements are prepared on the basis of conditions existing at the reporting date.

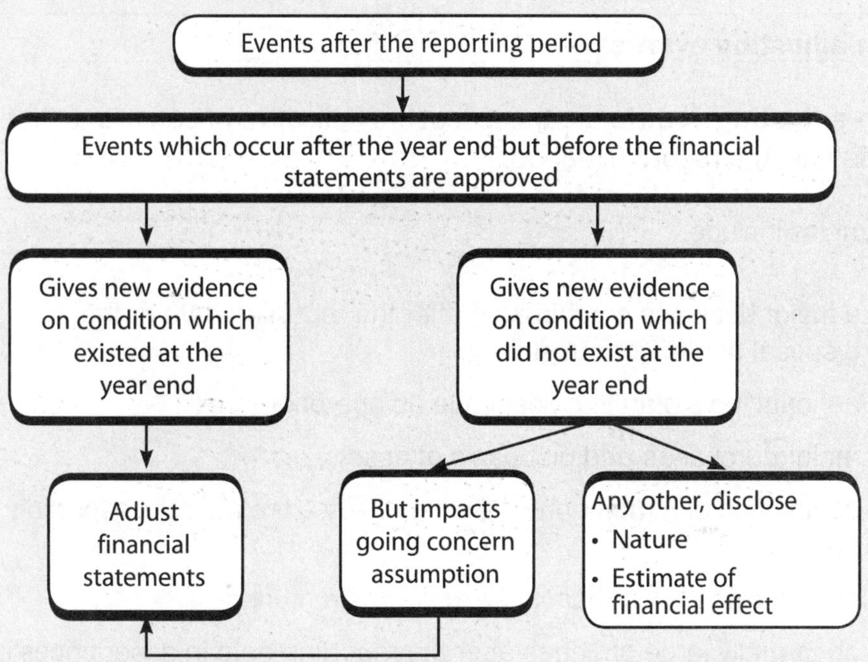

Adjusting and non-adjusting events

Adjusting events

Adjusting events provide evidence of conditions that existed at the reporting date.

Examples include:

- the sale of inventory after the reporting date which gives evidence about its net realisable value at the reporting date
- the bankruptcy of a customer after the reporting date that confirms that an allowance is required against an outstanding balance at the reporting date
- the discovery of fraud or errors that show that the financial statements are incorrect
- the settlement after the reporting period of a court case that confirms that the entity had a present obligation at the reporting date.

Adjusting events result in changes to the figures recognised in the financial statements.

Non-adjusting events

Non-adjusting events are those that are indicative of conditions that arose after the reporting period.

Examples include:

- a major business combination after the reporting date or the disposal of a major subsidiary
- announcing a plan to discontinue an operation
- major purchases and disposals of assets
- destruction of a major production plant by a fire after the reporting date
- announcing or commencing a major restructuring
- abnormally large changes after the reporting date in asset prices or foreign exchange rates.

Non-adjusting events do not affect any items in the statement of financial position or the statement of profit or loss and other comprehensive income. However, material non-adjusting events must be disclosed, otherwise the financial statements could be misleading.

- The following should be disclosed for material non-adjusting events:
  - the nature of the event
  - an estimate of the financial effect, or a statement that such an estimate cannot be made.
- Equity dividends declared or proposed after the year-end are not a liability at the year-end (because no obligation to pay a dividend exists at that time). They should be disclosed in a note to the financial statements. This is a non-adjusting event.

Date of authorisation for issue

The date when the financial statements were authorised for issue, and who gave that authorisation, should be disclosed in the financial statements.

- If the entity's owners or others have the power to amend the financial statements after issue, this must also be disclosed.
- It is important that the authorisation date is disclosed as the financial statements do not reflect events occurring after this date.

Problems with events after the reporting period

(a) **'Window dressing'**

Window dressing is the practice of entering into certain transactions before the year-end and reversing those transactions after the year-end. The objective of window dressing is to artificially improve the view given by the financial statements. Management may have a particular incentive to enter into window dressing transactions, where there is a need to boost year-end profitability and liquidity (for example, where loan agreements specify that the current ratio should not fall below a certain level, or where directors' remuneration depends upon meeting certain targets).

Typical examples include.

- Obtaining a loan before the year-end and presenting it as a non-current liability on the understanding that it will be repaid soon after the year-end. This will improve the current ratio at the year-end.
- Selling goods before the year-end on the understanding that they will be returned (and a credit note raised) after the year-end. This will boost the profits for the year.

IAS 10 does not refer to window dressing. However, if IAS 10 is applied correctly, users of the financial statements should be made aware of any unusual transactions that reverse after the year-end. In addition, IAS 1 and the Framework require that entities report the substance of their transactions, rather than the strict legal form.

(b) **Adjusting or non-adjusting?**

Sometimes it can be difficult to determine whether an event took place before the reporting date or whether or not it provides evidence of conditions existing at the reporting date.

For example, suppose that a non-current asset is valued shortly after the year-end and this valuation reveals a significant fall in value. It is probably reasonable to assume that the fall in value occurred over a period of several months beforehand. The loss would then be an adjusting event. However, there may be evidence that the fall in value occurred after the year-end (perhaps as a result of a particular event). It is important to look at all the circumstances surrounding an event after the reporting period.

Test your understanding 1 – Adjusting events

The following material events have occurred after the reporting period and prior to the date of approval of the financial statements by the directors.

(i) The insolvency of a major credit customer

(ii) The uninsured loss of inventory in a fire

(iii) The proposal of a final equity dividend

(iv) A change in foreign exchange rates.

Required:

State whether the above are adjusting or non-adjusting events.

Going concern issues arising after the reporting date

There is an exception to the rule that the financial statements reflect conditions at the reporting date. If, after the reporting date, management decides to liquidate the entity or cease trading (or decides that it has no realistic alternative to these actions), the financial statements cannot be prepared on a going concern basis.

- In accordance with IAS 1, management must disclose any material uncertainties relating to events or conditions that cast significant doubt upon an entity's ability to continue trading. This applies if the events have arisen since the reporting period.
- If the going concern assumption is no longer appropriate, the effect is so pervasive that there must be a fundamental change in the basis of accounting.
- If the financial statements are not prepared on a going concern basis, that fact must be disclosed.

Going concern considerations

IAS 1 states that management should assess whether the going concern assumption is appropriate. Management should take into account all available information about events within at least twelve months of the end of the reporting period.

Where there is uncertainty, management should consider all available information about the future, including current and expected profitability, debt repayment finance and potential sources of alternative finance. If there is greater doubt or uncertainty, then more work will be required to evaluate whether or not the entity can be regarded as a going concern. Here, 'the future' means at least twelve months from the reporting date.

2 Provisions

Introduction

Liabilities are obligations arising from a past event that will lead to an outflow of economic resources.

Most liabilities can be measured accurately. For example, if you take out a bank loan then you know exactly how much you have to repay, and when the repayments are due. Provisions, however, involve more uncertainty.

A provision is a liability of uncertain timing or amount.

Recognition

IAS 37 Provisions, Contingent Liabilities and Contingent Assets requires that a provision should be recognised when and only when:

- an entity has a present obligation (legal or constructive) as a result of a past event
- it is probable that an outflow of resources embodying economic benefits will be required to settle the obligation
- a reliable estimate can be made of the amount of the obligation.

An obligation is something that cannot be avoided:

- **A constructive obligation** arises from an entity's established pattern of past practice, published policies or a sufficiently specific current statement, that indicate to other parties that it will accept certain responsibilities and, as a result, the entity has created a valid expectation on the part of those other parties that it will discharge those responsibilities.
- **A legal obligation** arises from a contract or from laws and legislation.

An outflow of economic benefits is regarded as probable if it is more likely than not to occur. Only in extremely rare cases is it impossible to make a reliable estimate of the amount of the obligation.

Measurement

The amount recognised as a provision should be the best estimate of the expenditure required to settle the obligation that existed at the reporting date.

The best estimate of a provision will be:

- the most likely amount payable for a single obligation (such as a court case)
- an expected value for a large population of items (such as a warranty provision).

An entity should use its own judgement in deriving the best estimate, supplemented by past experience and the advice of experts (such as lawyers).

Future events that may affect the amount required to settle an obligation shall be reflected in the amount of a provision where there is sufficient objective evidence that they will occur.

- This might include, for example, future changes in technology that are reasonably expected to occur and which will reduce the costs which the provision is associated with.

If the effect of the time value of money is material, then the provision should be discounted. The discount rate should be pre-tax and risk-specific.

Test your understanding 2 – Warranty

Clean sells domestic appliances such as washing machines.

On 31 December 20X1, Clean decides to start selling washing machines with a warranty. Under the terms of the warranty, Clean will repair washing machines at no charge to the customer if they break within the warranty period. The entity estimates, based on past-correspondence with customers, that 20% of the washing machines sold will require repair within the warranty period at an average cost to Clean of $50 per machine.

Clean sold 200 washing machines on 31 December 20X1.

The time value of money should be ignored.

Required:

Calculate the warranty provision required.

Subsequent measurement

If a provision has been discounted to present value, then the discount must be unwound and presented in finance costs in the statement of profit or loss:

Dr Finance costs (P/L)
Cr Provisions (SFP)

Provisions should be reviewed at each reporting date and adjusted to reflect the current best estimate.

Derecognition

Provisions should be used only for expenditure that relates to the matter for which the provision was originally recognised.

At the reporting date, a provision should be reversed if it is no longer probable that an outflow of economic benefits will be required to settle the obligation.

Provisions and 'creative accounting'

Before IAS 37 was issued, provisions were recognised on the basis of prudence. Little guidance was given as to when a provision should be recognised and how it should be measured. This gave rise to inconsistencies, and also allowed profits to be manipulated.

In particular, provisions could be created when profits were high and released when profits were low, in order to smooth reported results. This was common where an entity made an acquisition. The acquirer would create excessive provisions for the cost of integrating a new subsidiary's operations into the group. When the provisions were released, the profits reported by the group as a whole would be artificially inflated.

As well as disguising poor performance in a particular year, profit smoothing can also create an impression that profits are less volatile (and therefore less risky), than they really are. This tends to boost share prices.

IAS 37 prevents entities from recognising excessive provisions by focusing on the statement of financial position and applying the definitions and recognition criteria in the Framework for the preparation and presentation of financial statements. A provision cannot be recognised unless it represents a genuine liability.

3 Contingent liabilities

A contingent liability is

- a possible obligation that arises from past events and whose existence will be confirmed only by the outcome of one or more uncertain future events not wholly within the control of the entity
- a present obligation that arises from past events, but does not meet the criteria for recognition as a provision. This is either because an outflow of economic benefits is not probable or (more rarely) because it is not possible to make a reliable estimate of the obligation.

A contingent liability should not be recognised.

- Instead, it should be disclosed, unless the possibility of a future outflow of economic benefits is remote.
- Contingent liabilities should be reviewed regularly. If an outflow of economic benefits becomes probable, then they must be reclassified as provisions.

4 Contingent assets

A contingent asset is a possible asset that arises from past events and whose existence will be confirmed only by the outcome of one or more uncertain future events, not wholly within the control of the entity.

A contingent asset should not be recognised.

- A contingent asset should be disclosed if the future inflow of economic benefits is probable.
- If the future inflow of benefits is virtually certain, then it ceases to be a contingent asset and should be recognised as a normal asset.

Summary

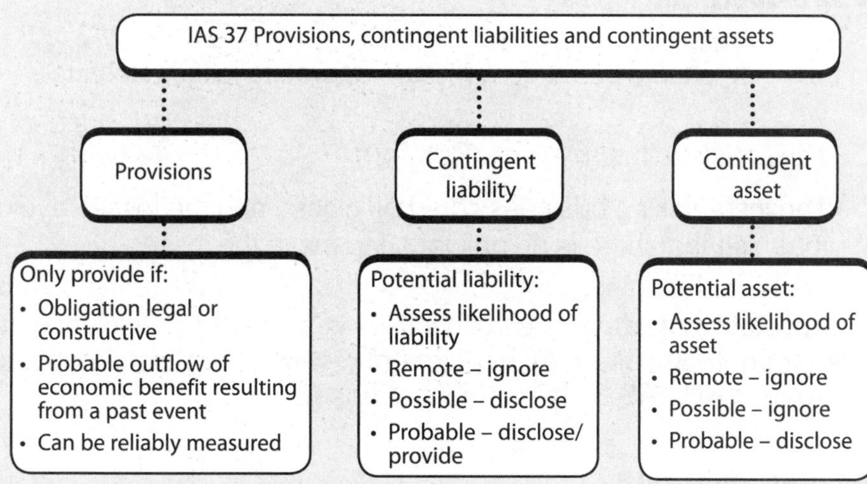

Problems in applying IAS 37

(a) **Definition of contingent liability**

The definition of a contingent liability gives particular problems, because 'possible' is not defined. However, IAS 37 says that 'probable' means 'more likely than not'. Because probable means 'more than 50% likely' it is reasonable to assume that 'possible' means 'less than 50% likely'.

Therefore, a contingent liability is often taken to be a liability whose existence is less than 50% likely or where the probability of an outflow of economic benefits is less than 50%.

(b) **'Virtually certain' and 'remote'**

Contingent assets should be recognised if they are virtually certain and contingent liabilities should not be disclosed if they are remote. There is no definition of 'virtually certain' or 'remote'.

However, it is usually assumed that 'virtually certain' means more than 95% probable and 'remote' means less than 5% probable.

5 Provisions and contingencies: specific situations

Future operating losses

No provision should be made for future operating losses because:

- They relate to future events
- The loss-making business could be closed and the losses avoided, meaning that there is no obligation to make the losses.

An expectation of future operating losses is, however, an indication that assets may be impaired. An impairment review should be conducted in accordance with IAS 36 Impairment of Assets.

Onerous contracts

An **onerous contract** is a contract in which the unavoidable costs of meeting the contract exceed the economic benefits expected to be received under it.

- A common example of an onerous contract is a lease on a surplus factory. The leaseholder signed a lease agreement in the past that has legally obliged them to carry on paying the rent on the factory. However, no benefits will be obtained from using the factory.
- If an entity has an onerous contract, a provision should be recognised for the present obligation under the contract.
- The provision is measured at the least net cost: the lower of the cost of fulfilling the contract or of terminating it and suffering any penalty payments.
- Some assets may have been bought specifically for use in fulfilling the onerous contract. These should be reviewed for impairment before any separate provision is made for the contract itself.

Test your understanding 3 – Danboy

Danboy is a company that owns several shops and which has a year end of 31 December 20X1.

One of the shops is loss-making. At 31 December 20X1, Danboy forecasts that this shop will make a loss of $50,000 in the year ended 31 December 20X2.

On 31 December 20X1, Danboy closed down a different shop. At that date, there were still three years left to run on the shop's lease. Lease rentals are $100,000 per annum. The landlord will allow Danboy to cancel the lease if it pays a one-off fee of $200,000.

Required:

Discuss the accounting treatment of the above in the financial statements for the year ended 31 December 20X1.

Future repairs to assets

Some assets need to be repaired or to have parts replaced every few years. For example, an airline may be required by law to overhaul all its aircraft every three years.

- Provisions cannot normally be recognised for the cost of future repairs or replacement parts
- Even if the future expenditure is required by law, the entity could sell the asset and avoid the expense
- Instead, the expenditure should be capitalised when incurred and depreciated over its useful life.

Test your understanding 4 – Repairs

An entity has a reporting date of 31 December 20X7 and intends to repair an item of plant next year. The cost has been reliably estimated at the reporting date at $10,000. The repair is made in the following accounting period at a cost $12,000.

Required:

What provision (if any) should be recognised in the statement of financial position in the year ended 20X7?

Test your understanding 5 – Smoke filters

Under new legislation, an entity is required to fit smoke filters to its factories by 31 December 20X7. At the reporting date of 30 June 20X7, the entity has not fitted the smoke filters.

Required:

Should a provision be made at the reporting date for the estimated cost of fitting the filter?

Environmental provisions

Environmental provisions are often referred to as clean-up costs because they usually relate to the cost of decontaminating and restoring an industrial site after production has ceased.

A provision is recognised if a past event has created an obligation to repair environmental damage:

- A provision can only be set up to rectify environmental damage that has already happened. There is no obligation to restore future environmental damage because the entity could cease its operations.
- Merely causing damage or intending to clean-up a site does not create an obligation.
  - An entity may have a constructive obligation to repair environmental damage if it publicises policies that include environmental awareness or explicitly undertakes to clean up the damage caused by its operations

The full cost of an environmental provision should be recognised as soon as the obligation arises.

- The effect of the time value of money is usually material. Therefore, an environmental provision is normally discounted to its present value.
- If the expenditure results in future economic benefits then an equivalent asset can be recognised. This is depreciated over its useful life, which is the same as the 'life' of the provision.

Test your understanding 6 – Environmental provisions

(a) An entity has a policy of only carrying out work to rectify damage caused to the environment when it is required to do so by local law. For several years the entity has been operating an overseas oil rig which causes environmental damage. The country in which the oil rig is located has not had legislation in place that required this damage to be rectified.

A new government has recently been elected in the country. At the reporting date, it is virtually certain that legislation will be enacted that will require damage rectification. This legislation will have retrospective effect.

(b) Under a licence granted by a local government, an entity has constructed a rock-crushing plant to process material mined from the surrounding area. Mining activities have already started. Under the terms of the licence, the entity must remove the rock-crushing plant when mining activities have been completed and must landscape the mined area, so as to create a national park.

Required:

For each of the situations, explain whether a provision should be recognised.

Test your understanding 7 – Scrubber

On 1 January 20X6, Scrubber spent $5m on erecting infrastructure and machinery near to an area of natural beauty. These assets will be used over the next three years. Scrubber is well-known for its environmentally friendly behaviour and is therefore expected to restore the site after its use.

The estimated cost of removing these assets and cleaning up the area on 1 January 20X9 is $3m.

The pre-tax, risk-specific discount rate is 10%.

Required:

Explain how the above should be treated in the financial statements of Scrubber.

6 Restructuring provisions

Definition

A **restructuring** is a programme that is planned and controlled by management and has a material effect on:

- the scope of a business undertaken by the reporting entity in terms of the products or services it provides
- the manner in which a business undertaken by the reporting entity is conducted.

A restructuring could include:

- sale or termination of a line of business
- the closure of business locations in a country or region or the relocation of business activities from one country or region to another
- changes in management structure, for example, eliminating a layer of management
- fundamental reorganisations that have a material effect on the nature and focus of the entity's operations.

When can a provision be recognised?

A restructuring provision can only be recognised where an entity has a **constructive obligation** to carry out the restructuring.

A board decision alone does not create a constructive obligation. A constructive obligation exists only if:

- there is a detailed formal plan for restructuring, that identifies the businesses, locations and employees affected as well as an estimate of the cost and timings involved
- the employees affected have a valid expectation that the restructuring will be carried out, either because the plan has been formally announced or because the plan has started to be implemented.

The constructive obligation must exist at the reporting date. An obligation arising after the reporting date requires disclosure as a non-adjusting event under IAS 10 Events after the Reporting Period.

Measuring a restructuring provision

A restructuring provision should only include the direct costs of restructuring. These must be both:

- necessarily entailed by the restructuring
- not associated with the ongoing activities of the entity.

The following costs must **not** be included in a restructuring provision:

- retraining or relocating staff
- marketing
- investment in new systems and distribution networks
- future operating losses (unless these arise from an onerous contract)
- profits on disposal of assets

The amount recognised should be the best estimate of the expenditure required and it should take into account expected future events. This means that expenses should be measured at their actual cost, where this is known, even if this was only discovered after the reporting date (this is an adjusting event after the reporting period per IAS 10).

Test your understanding 8 – Restructuring provisions

On 15 January 20X5, the Board of Directors of Shane voted to proceed with two reorganisation schemes involving the closure of two factories. Shane's reporting date is 31 March, and the financial statements will be authorised for issue on 30 June.

Scheme 1

The closure costs will amount to $125,000. The factory is rented on a short-term lease, and there will be no gains or losses arising on this property. The closure will be announced in June, and will commence in August.

Scheme 2

The costs will amount to $45,000 (after crediting $105,000 profit on disposal of certain machines). The closure will take place in July, but redundancy negotiations began with the staff in March.

Required:

For each of the two schemes discuss whether a provision should be recognised and, if so, at what amount.

Test your understanding 9 – Delta

On 30 June 20X2, the directors of Delta decided to close down a division. This decision was announced to the employees affected on 15 July 20X2 and the actual closure occurred on 31 August 20X2, prior to the 20X2 financial statements being authorised for issue on 15 September.

Expenses and other items connected with the closure were as follows:

	$m
Redundancy costs (estimated)	22
Staff retraining (actual)	10
Operating loss for the 2 months to 31 August 20X2	
(estimated at 30 June)	12
Profit on sale of property	5

The actual redundancy costs were $20 million and the actual operating loss for the two months to 31 August 20X2, was $15 million.

Required:

What is the amount of the restructuring provision to be recognised in the financial statements of Delta plc for the year ended 31 July 20X2?

Current issues

The IAS 37 project

In June 2005, the IASB published an ED of the proposed amendments to IAS 37. In January 2010 it published a second ED, setting out proposed new measurement guidance. However, it was decided later in the same year that this was not an urgent project and work was deferred.

In 2012, the Board decided to make IAS 37 a research project. The project will focus on identifying aspects of IAS 37 that cause difficulties in application. These will be used as test cases for developing the Conceptual Framework.

7 Chapter summary

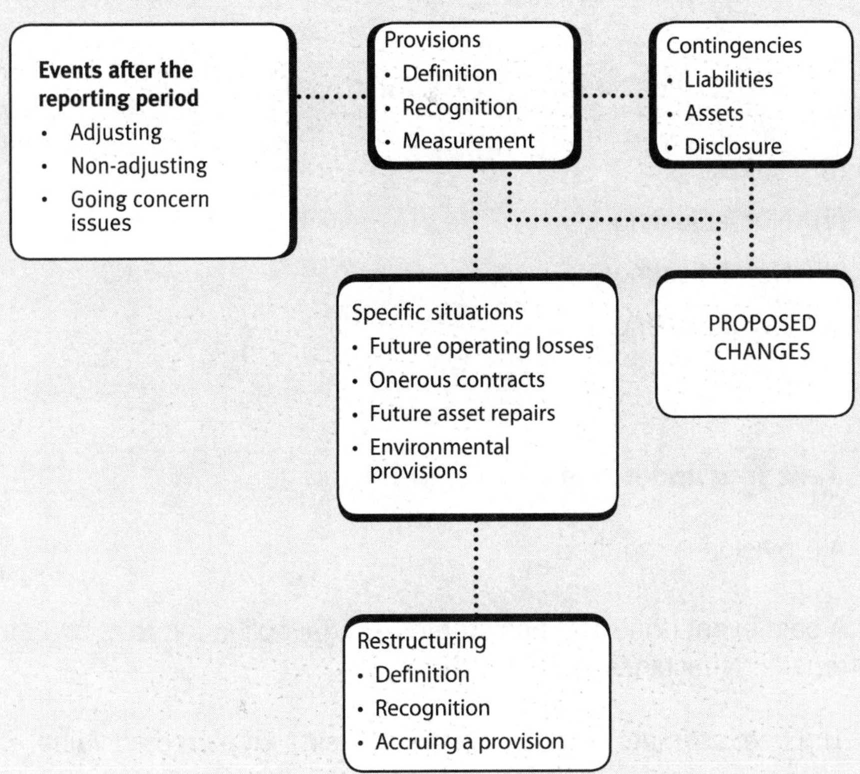

Test your understanding answers

Test your understanding 1 – Adjusting events

(i) Adjusting.

(ii) Non-adjusting.

(iii) Non-adjusting.

(iv) Non-adjusting.

Test your understanding 2 – Warranty

A provision is required.

A past event (the sale) has created a legal obligation to spend money on repairing machines in the future.

The best estimate can be determined using an expected value:

200 machines × 20% × $50 = $2,000.

Test your understanding 3 – Danboy

IAS 37 states that no provision should be made for future operating losses. Therefore, no provision should be made for the $50,000 forecast losses.

The second shop is held under an onerous lease. Provisions can be made for onerous contracts because there is an obligation arising from a past event. A provision should be recognised for the lower of the cost of fulfilling the lease and the cost of terminating the lease.

Fulfilling the lease will cost Danboy $300,000 ($100,000 × 3 years), but it will only cost $200,000 to terminate the lease. This means that a provision should be made for $200,000.

Test your understanding 4 – Repairs

The standard states that no provision should be made for future repairs despite it being probable and capable of being reliably measured. This is because there has been no relevant past event and there is no obligation at the year end.

Repairs expenditure is expensed to profit or loss as it is incurred.

Test your understanding 5 – Smoke filters

No provision should be made for this future expenditure despite it being probable and capable of being reliably measured. There has been no obligating past event (the fitting of the filters).

Test your understanding 6 – Environmental provisions

For each situation, ask two questions.

(a) Is there a present obligation as the result of a past event?

(b) Is an outflow of economic benefits probable as a result?

A provision should be recognised if the answer to both questions is yes. In the absence of information to the contrary, it is assumed that any future costs can be estimated reliably.

(a) Present obligation? Yes. Because the new legislation with retrospective effect is virtually certain to be enacted, the damage caused by the oil rig is the past event that gives rise to a present obligation.

Outflow of economic benefits probable? Yes.

Conclusion – Recognise a provision.

(b) Present obligation? Yes. There is a legal obligation under the licence to remove the rock-crushing plant and to make good damage caused by the mining activities to date (but not any that may be caused by these activities in the future, because mining activities could be stopped and no such damage caused).

Outflow of economic benefits probable? Yes.

Conclusion – Recognise a provision for the best estimate of the eventual costs of rectifying the damage caused up to the reporting date.

Test your understanding 7 – Scrubber

Scrubber has a constructive obligation to restore the area to its original condition as a result of a past event (erecting the infrastructure). Therefore, it should recognise a provision at 1 January 20X6. The best estimate of the expenditure is $3m, but this must be discounted to its present value of $2,253,000 ($3m × 0.751).

Scrubber could not carry out its operations without incurring the clean-up costs. This means that incurring the costs gives it access to future economic benefits. The estimated clean-up costs are therefore included in the cost of the property, plant and equipment (PPE):

Dr PPE	$2,253,000
Cr Provisions	$2,253,000

Each year, the discount unwinds and the provision increases. The unwinding of the discount is charged to the statement of profit or loss as a finance cost.

Movement on provision	20X6	20X7	20X8	20X9
	$000	$000	$000	$000
Opening balance	2,253	2,478	2,727	3,000
Finance cost at 10%	225	249	273	–
Utilisation	–	–	–	(3,000)
Closing balance	2,478	2,727	3,000	–

Initial cost of PPE	$000
Cash paid 1 January 20X6	5,000
PV of clean-up costs	2,253
Total	7,253

The effect on the financial statements is shown below:

Statements of profit or loss	**20X6**	**20X7**	**20X8**	**20X9**
	$000	$000	$000	$000
Operating costs				
Depreciation ($7,253/3 years)	2,418	2,418	2,417	–
Finance costs				
Unwinding of discount	225	249	273	–

Statement of financial position	$000	$000	$000	$000
PPE				
Cost	7,253	7,253	7,253	–
Depreciation	(2,418)	(4,836)	(7,253)	–
Carrying value	4,835	2,417	–	–
Liabilities				
Clean-up provision	2,478	2,727	3,000	–

Test your understanding 8 – Restructuring provisions

Scheme 1

The obligating event is the announcement of the plan, which occurs in June. This is after the year-end, so there can be no provision. However, the announcement in June should be disclosed as a non-adjusting event after the reporting date.

Scheme 2

Although the closure will not begin until July, the employees will have had a valid expectation that it would happen when the redundancy negotiations began in March. Therefore, a provision should be recognised. The provision will be for $150,000 because the expected profit on disposal cannot be netted off against the expected costs.

Test your understanding 9 – Delta

The only item which can be included in the provision is the redundancy costs, measured at their actual amount of $20 million.

IAS 37 prohibits the recognition of future operating losses, staff retraining and profits on disposals of assets.

chapter

8

Segment reporting

Chapter learning objectives

Upon completion of this chapter you will be able to:

- determine the nature and extent of reportable segments
- specify and discuss the nature of segment information to be disclosed.

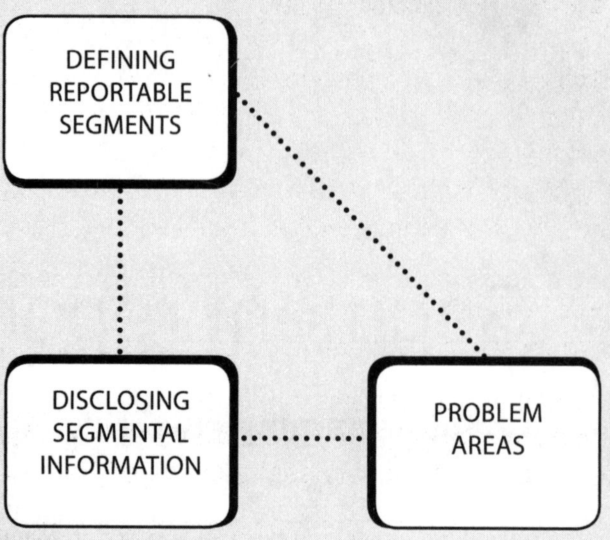

1 Defining reportable segments

Introduction

Segmental reports are designed to reveal significant information that might otherwise be hidden by the process of presenting a single statement of profit or loss and other comprehensive income and statement of financial position for an entity.

IFRS 8 Operating Segments requires certain entities to disclose information about each of its operating segments that will enable users of the financial statements to evaluate the nature and financial effects of the business activities in which it engages and the economic environments in which it operates.

IFRS 8 applies to entities which:

- trade debt or equity instruments in a public market
- file, or are in the process of filing, financial statements with a securities commission or other regulatory organisation for the purpose of issuing any class of instruments in a public market.

IFRS 8 defines an **operating segment** as a component of an entity:

- that engages in business activities from which it may earn revenues and incur expenses
- whose operating results are regularly reviewed by the entity's chief operating decision maker to make decisions about resources to be allocated to the segment and assess its performance
- for which discrete financial information is available.

How to define reportable segments

Under IFRS 8, an operating segment is a component whose results are regularly reviewed by the entity's chief operating decision maker. This means that the segments reported in the financial statements are the same as those that are disclosed and reviewed in internal management reports. In other words, it is management that identifies the operating segments.

- A part of an entity that only sells goods to other parts of the entity is a reportable segment if management treats it as one
- Management may use more than one set of segment information. For example, they might analyse information by classes of business (different products or services) and by geographical areas.
- If management uses more than one set of segment information, it should identify a **single** set of components on which to base the segmental disclosures. The basis of reporting information should be the one that best enables users to understand the business and the environment in which it operates.

Not every part of an entity is necessarily an operating segment or part of an operating segment:

- Corporate headquarters and other similar departments do not earn revenue and are therefore not operating segments
- An entity's pension plan is not an operating segment.

Two or more operating segments can be reported as a single operating segment provided that they have similar economic characteristics, and are similar in the following respects:

- the nature of the products and services
- the nature of the production processes
- the type of class of customer for their products and services
- the methods used to distribute their products or provide their services.

Test your understanding 1 – E-Games

E-Games is a UK based company that sells computer games and hardware. Sales are made through the E-Games website as well as through high street stores. The products sold online and in the stores are the same. E-Games sells new releases for $40 in its stores, but for $30 online.

Internal reports used by the chief operating decision maker show the results of the online business separately from the stores. However, they will be aggregated together for disclosure in the financial statements.

Required:

Should the online business and the high street stores be aggregated into a single segment in the operating segments disclosure?

Quantitative thresholds

An entity must separately report information about an operating segment that meets any of the following quantitative thresholds:

- its reported revenue, including both sales to external customers and inter-segment sales, is ten per cent or more of the combined revenue of all operating segments
- its reported profit or loss is ten per cent or more of the greater, in absolute amount, of:
  - the combined reported profit of all operating segments that did not report a loss and
  - the combined reported loss of all operating segments that reported a loss.
- its assets are ten per cent or more of the combined assets of all operating segments.

At least 75% of the entity's external revenue must be included in reportable segments. Other segments should be identified as reportable segments until 75% of external revenue is reported.

Information about other business activities and operating segments that are not reportable are combined into an 'all other segments' category.

There is no precise limit to the number of segments that can be disclosed, but if there are more than ten, the resulting information may become too detailed.

Although IFRS 8 defines a reportable segment in terms of size, size is not the only criterion to be taken into account. There is some scope for subjectivity.

Test your understanding 2 – Identifying reportable segments

The management of a company have identified operating segments based on geographical location. Information for these segments is provided below:

Segment	Total revenue $000	External revenue $000	Internal revenue $000	Profit/ (loss) $000	Assets $000
Europe	260	140	120	98	3,400
Middle East	78	33	45	(26)	345
Asia	150	150	–	47	995
North America	330	195	135	121	3,800
Central America	85	40	45	(15)	580
South America	97	54	43	12	880
	1,000	612	388	237	10,000

Requried:

According to IFRS 8, which segments must be reported?

Approaches to identify reportable segments

There are two main approaches to identifying reportable segments:

- the 'risks and returns' approach
- the 'managerial' approach.

The 'risks and returns' approach identifies segments on the basis of different risks and returns arising from different lines of business and geographical areas. Broadly speaking, this was the approach adopted by IAS 14 Segment Reporting which has been replaced by IFRS 8.

The 'managerial' approach identifies segments corresponding to the internal organisation structure of the entity. This is the approach adopted by IFRS 8.

The 'risks and returns' approach

The 'risks and returns' approach is believed to have the following advantages:

- it produces information that is more comparable between companies and consistent over time than the 'managerial' approach
- it assists in the assessment of profitability and the risks and returns of the component parts of the entity
- it reflects the approach taken in the financial statements for external reporting.

The main disadvantage of the approach is that defining segments can be difficult in practice and also subjective. This affects comparability.

The 'managerial' approach

The 'managerial' approach bases both the segments reported and the information reported about them on the information used internally for decision making. This means that management defines the reportable segments.

Arguments for the 'managerial approach' include the following.

- Segments based on an entity's internal structure are less subjective than those identified by the 'risks and returns' approach
- It highlights the risks and opportunities that management believes are important
- It provides information with predictive value because it enables users of the financial statements to see the entity through the eyes of management
- The cost of providing the information is low (because it should already have been provided for management's use)
- It will produce segment information that is consistent with the way in which management discuss their business in other parts of the annual report (e.g. in the Chairman's Statement and the Operating and Financial Review)

Arguments against the 'managerial approach' include the following.

- Segments based on internal reporting structures are unlikely to be comparable between entities and may not be comparable from year to year for an individual entity. (For example, organisation structures, or the way in which they are perceived, may change as a result of new managers being appointed)
- The information is likely to be commercially sensitive (because entities are organised strategically)
- In theory, segmental information could be given other than by products or services or geographically. This might be more difficult to analyse
- Using the managerial approach could lead to segments with different risks and returns being combined

However, it should be remembered that for many entities, the risks and returns approach and the managerial approach will probably identify exactly the same reportable segments.

2 Disclosing reportable segments

General information

IFRS 8 requires disclosure of the following.

- Factors used to identify the entity's reportable segments, including the basis of organisation (for example, whether segments are based on products and services, geographical areas or a combination of these).
- The types of products and services from which each reportable segment derives its revenues.

Information about profit or loss and other segment items

For each reportable segment an entity should report:

- a measure of profit or loss
- a measure of total assets
- a measure of total liabilities (if such an amount is regularly used in decision making).

IFRS 8 requires segmental reports to be based on the information reported to and used by management, even where this is prepared on a different basis from the rest of the financial statements.Therefore, an entity must provide explanations of the measurement of segment profit or loss, segment assets and segment liabilities.

The following amounts must also be disclosed if regularly provided to the chief operating decision maker:

- revenues from external customers
- revenues from inter-segment transactions
- interest revenue
- interest expense
- depreciation and amortisation
- material items of income and expense (exceptional items)
- interests in the profit or loss of associates and joint ventures accounted for by the equity method
- income tax expense
- material non-cash items other than depreciation or amortisation.

An entity must provide reconciliations between amounts disclosed in the segment report and amounts reported in the financial statements for the following:

- revenue
- profit or loss (before tax and discontinued operations unless these items are allocated to segments)
- assets
- liabilities
- other material items of segment information disclosed.

Entity wide disclosures

IFRS 8 also requires the following disclosures about the entity as a whole, even if it only has one reportable segment.

- The revenues from external customers for each product and service or each group of similar products and services.
- Revenues from external customers split between the entity's country of domicile and all foreign countries in total.

- Non-current assets split between those located in the entity's country of domicile and all foreign countries in total.
- Revenue from a single external customer which amounts to ten per cent or more of an entity's revenue. The identity of the customer does not need to be disclosed.

Preparing segmental reports

The illustration provides a useful format to follow when preparing a segmental report.

Illustration

	Segment A	Segment B	Segment C	Segment D	All other	Totals
	$000	$000	$000	$000	$000	$000
Revenues from external customers	5,000	9,500	12,000	5,000	1,000	32,500
Revenues from inter-segment transactions	–	3,000	1,500	–	–	4,500
Interest revenue	800	1,000	1,500	1,000	–	4,300
Interest expense	600	700	1,100	–	–	2,400
Depreciation and amortisation	100	50	1,500	900	–	2,550
Exceptional costs	–	–	–	200	–	200
Segment profit	70	900	2,300	500	100	3,870
Impairment of assets	200	–		–	–	200
Segment assets	5,000	3,000	12,000	57,000	2,000	79,000
Additions to non-current assets	700	500	800	600	–	2,600
Segment liabilities	3,000	1,800	8,000	30,000	–	42,800

Notes

(1) The 'all other' column shows amounts relating to segments that fall below the quantitative thresholds.

(2) Impairment of assets is disclosed as a material non-cash item.

(3) Comparatives should be provided. These should be restated if an entity changes the structure of its internal organisation so that its reportable segments change, unless the information is not available and the cost of preparing it would be excessive.

3 Problem areas in segmental reporting

Segmental reports provide useful information, but they also have limitations.

- IFRS 8 states that segments should reflect the way in which the entity is managed. This means that segments are defined by the directors. Arguably, this provides too much flexibility. It also means that segmental information is only useful for comparing the performance of the same entity over time, not for comparing the performance of different entities.
- Common costs may be allocated to different segments on whatever basis the directors believe is reasonable. This can lead to arbitrary allocation of these costs.
- A segment's operating results can be distorted by trading with other segments on non-commercial terms.

To counter the above, IFRS 8 requires disclosure about the way in which common costs are allocated and the basis of accounting for inter-segment transactions.

Further problem areas

Determining reportable segments

IFRS 8 only requires one segmental report. If management uses more than one set of segment information, it should identify a single set of components on which to base the segmental disclosures. In practice, this may be both difficult to do, and subjective. For example, some entities adopt a 'matrix' form of organisation in which some managers are responsible for different products worldwide, while others are responsible for particular geographical areas.

Disclosure of segment information

Some information (for example, segment liabilities) is only required if it is regularly provided to the chief operating decision maker. In theory, it would be possible to avoid disclosing 'bad news' or other sensitive information on the grounds that the information was not used in decision making.

Measurement of segment results and segment assets

IFRS 8 does not define segment results and segment assets. Although the standard requires disclosure of certain figures if these are included in the totals, the amounts will not necessarily be measured on the same basis as the amounts in the main financial statements. This may be a particular issue in countries such as the UK, where the consolidated financial statements are prepared using IFRSs but internal financial information may still follow local GAAP. Totals must be reconciled to the main financial statements, but users may still find it difficult to understand the disclosures.

Changes to the way in which an entity is organised

One of the disadvantages of the IFRS 8 approach is that if a company changes the way in which it is organised, its reportable segments may also change. IFRS 8 requires an entity to restate its comparative information for earlier periods unless the information is not available and the cost of developing it would be excessive. If an entity does not restate its comparative figures, segment information for the current period must be disclosed both on the old basis and on the new basis. The disclosures should help users to understand the effect of the change, but some users may find it difficult to analyse the information, particularly where an entity undergoes frequent restructurings.

Test your understanding 3 – Segments

An entity has prepared the following segmental report:

Operating segments

	Fruit grow'g		Canning		Other		Group	
	20X2	**20X1**	**20X2**	**20X1**	**20X2**	**20X1**	**20X2**	**20X1**
	$000	$000	$000	$000	$000	$000	$000	$000
Total revenue	13,635	15,188	20,520	16,200	5,400	4,050	39,555	35,438
Less inter-segment revenue.	3,485	1,688	2,970	3,105			6,455	4,793
External. revenue	10,150	13,500	17,550	13,095	5,400	4,050	33,100	30,645
Segment. profit	3,565	3,375	4,725	3,600	412	540	8,702	7,515
Seg. assets	33,750	32,400	40,500	33,750	18,765	17,563	93,015	83,713
Unallocated (common) assets							13,500	11,003
Total assets							106,515	94,716

Required:

Identify areas where the above segmental report does not disclose useful information.

4 Chapter summary

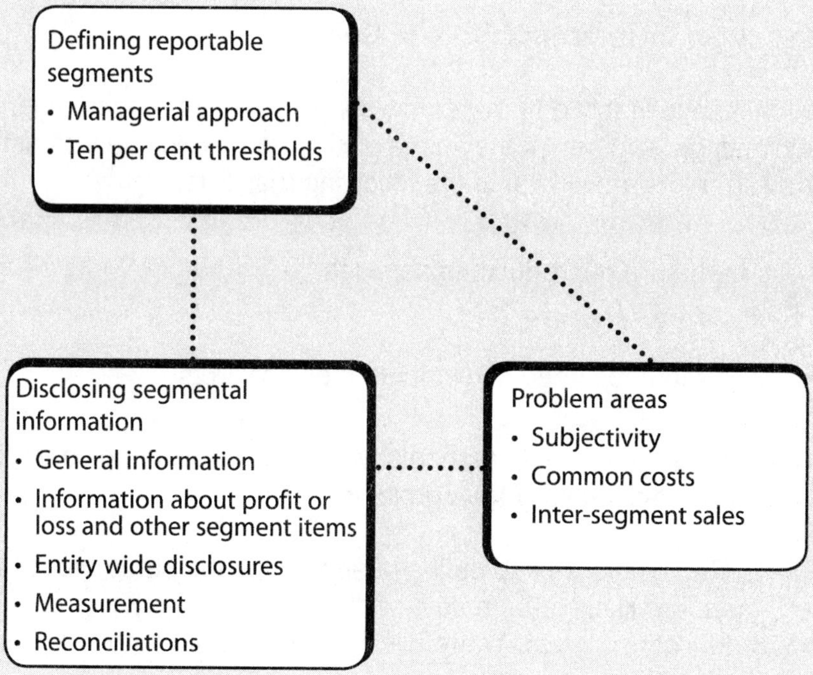

Defining reportable segments
- Managerial approach
- Ten per cent thresholds

Disclosing segmental information
- General information
- Information about profit or loss and other segment items
- Entity wide disclosures
- Measurement
- Reconciliations

Problem areas
- Subjectivity
- Common costs
- Inter-segment sales

Test your understanding answers

Test your understanding 1 – E–Games

IFRS 8 says that two or more operating segments may be aggregated into a single segment if they have similar economic characteristics and the segments are similar in the following respects:

- The nature of products or services
- The type of customer
- The methods used to distribute their products

The standard says that segments with similar economic characteristics would have similar long-term gross margins.

The E-Games stores and online business sell the same types of product, and there are likely to be no major differences in the types of customer (individual consumers). Therefore, in these respects, the segments are similar.

However, customers will collect their goods from the stores, but E-Games will deliver the products sold online. This means that distribution methods are different.

Moreover, there are different sales prices between the stores and the online business, giving rise to significant differences in gross margin. This suggests dissimilarity in terms of economic characteristics.

This means that it might be more appropriate to disclose these two segments separately.

Note:

There is no 'right' or 'wrong' answer here. There are numerous retailers who do not disclose their online operations as a separate segment. However, the IASB has noted in the post-implementation review of IFRS 8 that many companies are over-aggregating segments. For exam purposes, it is important to state the relevant recognition criteria and then to apply these to the information given in the question.

Test your understanding 2 – Identifying reportable segments

The 10% tests

Segment	10% total revenue (W1)	10% results test (W2)	10% assets (W3)	Report?
Europe	Y	Y	Y	Y
Middle East	N	N	N	N
Asia	Y	Y	N	Y
North America	Y	Y	Y	Y
Central America	N	N	N	N
South America	N	N	N	N

Based on the 10% tests, Europe, Asia and North America are reportable. However, we must check whether they comprise at least 75% of the company's external revenue.

The 75% test

	External revenue $000
Europe	140
Asia	150
North America	195
Total	485

The external revenue of reportable segments is 79% ($485,000/ $612,000) of total external revenue. The 75% test is met and no other segments need to be reported.

Conclusion

The reportable segments are Europe, Asia and North America.

(W1) **10% of total sales**

10% × $1m = $100,000.

All segments whose total sales exceed $100,000 are reportable.

(W2) **10% of results**

10% of profit making segments:

10% × ($98,000 + $47,000 + $121,000 + $12,000) = $27,800

10% of loss making segments:

10% × ($26,000 + $15,000) = $4,100

Therefore, all segments which make a profit or a loss of greater than $27,800 are reportable.

(W3) **10% of total assets**

10% × $10m = $1m.

All segments whose assets exceed $1m are reportable.

Test your understanding 3 – Segments

Your answer may have included some of the following:

(i) **Definition of segments:** It would be helpful to know whether there are any other classes of business included within the three operating segments supplied by the company which are material. This is particularly important when one looks at the Canning segment and notices that it comprises 50% of the total sales to customers outside the group.

(ii) **Inter-segment sales:** The inter-segment sales for fruit growing are a relatively high percentage (at around 25% ($3,485/13,635)) of its total revenue. In assessing the risk and economic trends it might well be that those of the receiving segment are more useful in predicting future prospects than those of the segment from which the sale originated.

(iii) **Analysis of assets:** Users often need to calculate a return on capital employed for each segment. Therefore, it is important to ensure that the segment profit and assets are appropriately defined, so that segment profit can be usefully related to the assets figure to produce a meaningful ratio. This means that both the operating profit and assets figure need to be precisely defined. If, for example, the assets are the gross assets, then the operating profits should be before deduction of interest. This means that the preparer of the segmental report needs to be aware of the reader's information needs.

(iv) **Unallocated items:** The information provided includes unallocated assets that represent around 12% of the total assets. It is not clear what these assets represent.

(v) **Treatment of interest:** It would be useful to know if there has been any interest charge incurred and to ascertain whether it is material and whether it can be reasonably identified as relating to any particular segment. As mentioned in (iii) above, it is not clear how segment profit is defined or how it has been derived.

chapter

9

Related parties

Chapter learning objectives

Upon completion of this chapter you will be able to:

- determine the parties considered to be related to an entity
- identify the implications of related party relationships and the need for disclosure.

1 The need for disclosure of related parties

A **related party transaction** is the transfer of resources, services or obligations between related parties, regardless of whether a price is charged.

- Transactions between related parties are a normal feature of business.
- However, a related party relationship can affect the performance and financial position of an entity as shown by its financial statements.
- Users of the financial statements therefore need to know about these transactions.

Illustration – the need for related party disclosures

Company A owns 75% of the equity shares of B. A sells goods to B at prices significantly above market rate. As a result, the profit of A is more than it would have been had it sold all of its goods to a third party.

Company A is therefore not comparable with that of similar companies. Its performance has been distorted because it trades with an entity over which it has control. This has enabled it to charge prices that are not equivalent to those in arm's length transactions.

Companies A and B are related parties. Users of the financial statements, such as investors and banks, need to be made aware of the transactions that have occurred between these two companies to enable them to make a proper assessment of the financial statements.

Examples of related party transactions

Related party transactions could include:

- purchases or sales of goods
- purchases or sales of non-current assets
- giving or receiving of services e.g. accounting or management services
- leasing arrangements
- transfers of research and development
- financing arrangements (including loans)
- provision of guarantees or collateral
- settlement of liabilities on behalf of the entity.

A related party relationship can affect the financial position and operating results of an entity in a number of ways, particularly in a group situation.

- An entity may enter into transactions which may not have occurred if the relationship did not exist
  - For example, a subsidiary may sell most of its production to its parent, where it might have found an alternative customer if the parent company had not purchased the goods.
- An entity may enter into transactions on different terms from those with an unrelated party
  - For example, a subsidiary may lease equipment to another group company on terms imposed by the parent, possibly at a low rent or for no rent.
- Transactions with third parties may be affected by the existence of the relationship
  - For example, a parent could instruct a subsidiary to sell goods to a particular customer or to close down a particular operation.

Directors may not want to disclose related party transactions. Sometimes this is because they believe that disclosure will give users of the financial statements the impression of poor stewardship or wrong-doing. Other times it may be that disclosure of related party transactions would cast doubt about the true financial performance and position of a company.

2 Definition of a related party

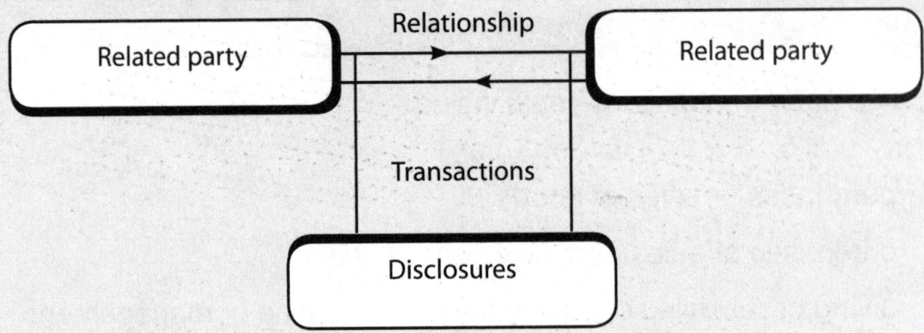

A related party is a person or entity that is related to the entity that is preparing its financial statements.

IAS 24 gives the following rules which should be used to determine the existence of related party relationships:

(a) **A person or a close member of that person's family is related to a reporting entity** if that person:

- (i) has control or joint control of the reporting entity
- (ii) has significant influence over the reporting entity
- (iii) is a member of the key management personnel of the reporting entity or of a parent of the reporting entity.

(b) **An entity is related to a reporting entity** if any of the following conditions apply:

- (i) The entity and the reporting entity are members of the same group (which means that each parent, subsidiary and fellow subsidiary is related to the others)
- (ii) One entity is an associate or joint venture of the other entity (or an associate or joint venture of a member of a group of which the other entity is a member)
- (iii) Both entities are joint ventures of the same third party
- (iv) One entity is a joint venture of a third entity and the other entity is an associate of the third entity
- (v) The entity is a post-employment benefit plan for the benefit of employees of either the reporting entity or an entity related to the reporting entity. If the reporting entity is itself such a plan, the sponsoring employers are also related to the reporting entity

(vi) The entity is controlled or jointly controlled by a person identified in (a)

(vii) A person identified in (a)(i) has significant influence over the entity or is a member of the key management personnel of the entity (or of a parent of the entity)

(viii) The entity, or any member of a group of which it is a part, provides key management personnel services to the reporting entity or to the parent of the reporting entity.

Group accounting is covered in a later chapter. You may therefore find the following definitions useful:

- A **subsidiary** is an entity over which an investor has control.
- A **joint venture** is an entity over which an investor has joint control.
- An **associate** is an entity over which an investor has significant influence.

In the definition of a related party, an associate includes subsidiaries of the associate and a joint venture includes subsidiaries of the joint venture. Therefore, an associate's subsidiary and the investor that has significant influence over the associate are related to each other.

The standard notes that the following should not be considered related parties:

- two entities simply because they have a director or other member of key management personnel in common or because a member of key management personnel of one entity has significant influence over the other entity
- two joint venturers simply because they share joint control of a joint venture
- a customer or supplier with whom an entity transacts a significant volume of business, simply by virtue of the resulting economic dependence.

IAS 24 stresses the importance of substance over form when deciding if two parties are related.

Related parties summary

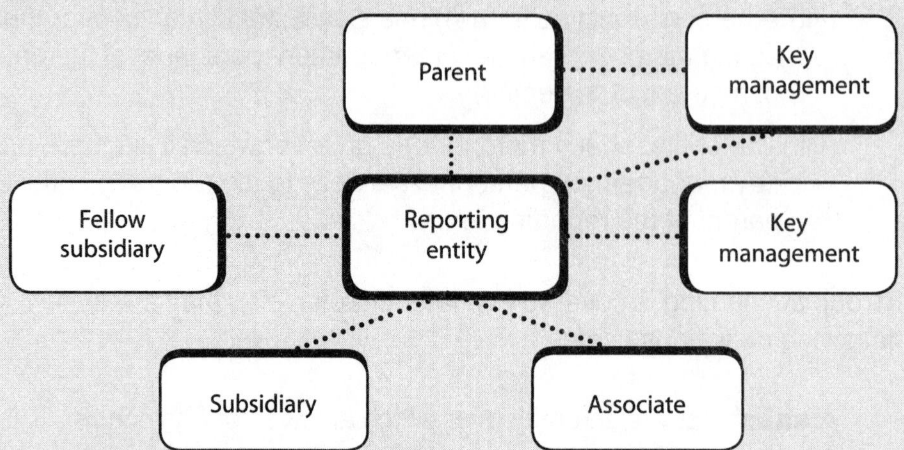

Further detail on definitions

Close members of the family of a person are those family members who may be expected to influence, or be influenced by, that person in their dealings with the entity and include:

- that person's children and spouse or domestic partner
- children of that person's spouse or domestic partner
- dependants of that person or that person's spouse or domestic partner

Control is defined in IFRS 10. An investor **controls an investee** when:

- the investor has power over the investee, and
- the investor is exposed, or has rights, to variable returns from its involvement with the investee, and
- the investor has the ability to affect those returns through its power over the investee.

In simple terms, control is normally assumed when one entity owns more than half of the equity shares of another entity.

Significant influence is defined in IAS 28 Investments in Associates and Joint Ventures as the power to participate in, but not control, the financial and operating policy decisions of an entity. Significant influence is normally assumed when an entity owns between 20% and 50% of the equity shares of another entity.

Joint control is defined in IFRS 11 Joint Arrangements as the contractually agreed sharing of control of an arrangement, which exists only when decisions about the relevant activities require the unanimous consent of the parties sharing control.

Key management personnel are those persons having authority and responsibility for planning, directing and controlling the activities of the entity, directly or indirectly, including any director (whether executive or otherwise) of that entity.

Test your understanding 1 – Group structures

Consider the following structure:

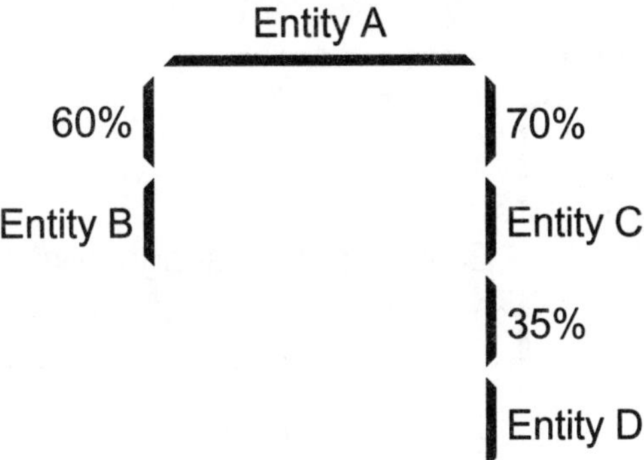

Required:

Identify the related party relationships within the above structure.

Test your understanding 2 – Individual shareholdings

Consider each of the following situations:

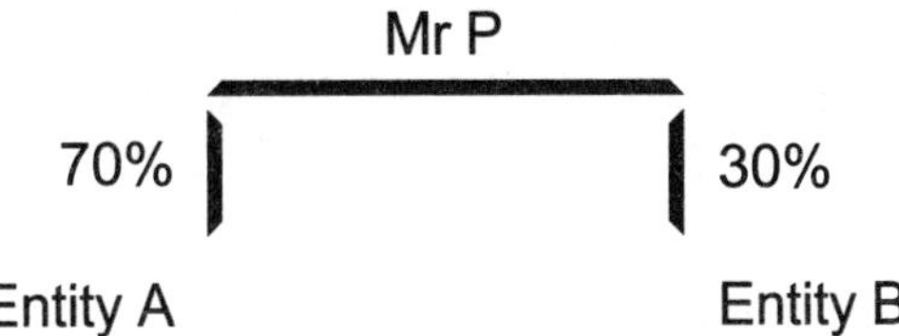

Mr P controls entity A and is able to exert significant influence over entity B.

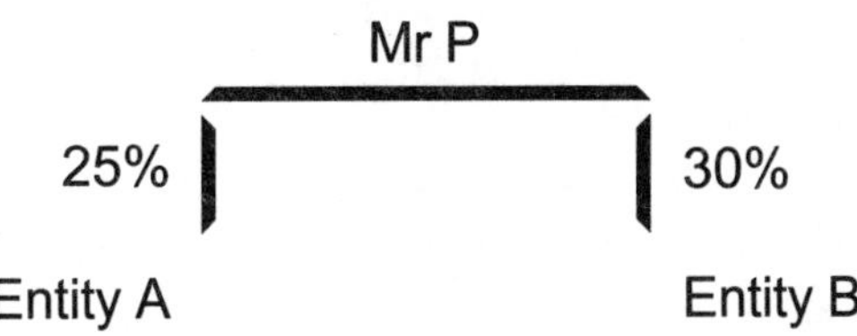

Mr P is able to exert significant influence over entity A and entity B.

Required:

For each situation explain whether or not entity A and entity B are related parties.

Test your understanding 3 – Key management personnel

Consider the following situation:

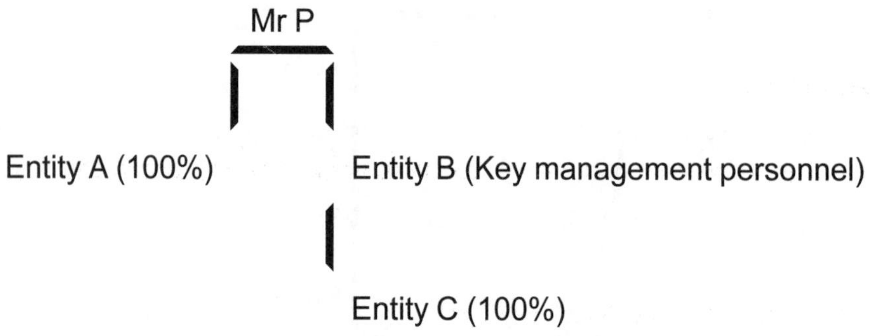

Mr P owns all of the issued share capital of entity A. He also is a member of the key management personnel of entity B which, in turn, owns all of the issued share capital of entity C.

Required:

Discuss the related party relationships arising from the above structure.

Test your understanding 4 – Family members

Consider the following situation:

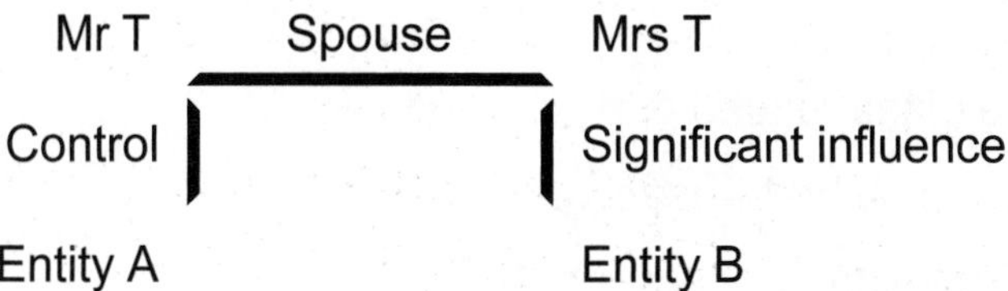

Mr T controls entity A. His spouse, Mrs T, exercises significant influence over entity B.

Required:

Discuss the related party relationships arising from the above.

3 Disclosure of related parties

Disclosure of related parties

Parent and subsidiary relationships

IAS 24 requires that relationships between parents and subsidiaries should always be disclosed. The name of the parent and, if different, the ultimate controlling party should be given. This applies regardless of whether or not any transactions have taken place between the parties during the period.

The disclosure requirements of IFRS 12 Disclosure of Interests in Other Entities (covered later in this text) also apply

Key management personnel

Compensation granted to key management personnel should be disclosed in total and for each of the following categories:

- short-term employee benefits
- post-employment benefits
- other long-term benefits
- termination benefits
- share-based payment.

Disclosure of transactions and balances

If there have been transactions between related parties, and if there are balances outstanding between the parties, the following should be disclosed:

- the nature of the related party relationship
- a description of the transactions
- the amounts of the transactions
- the amounts and details of any outstanding balances
- allowances for receivables in respect of the outstanding balances
- the irrecoverable debt expense in respect of outstanding balances.

Disclosure should be made whether or not a price was charged.

An entity may only disclose that related party transactions were made on terms equivalent to those that prevail in arm's length transactions if such terms can be substantiated.

Test your understanding 5 – Picture and Frame

Joanne Smith has owned 60% of the equity shares of Picture and 70% of the equity shares of Frame for many years. On 1 January 20X4, Picture entered into a lease agreement with Frame. Under the terms of the lease, Picture would lease one of its unused warehouses, with a remaining useful life of 20 years, to Frame for five years. Consideration payable by Frame would be $10,000 a year in arrears. Market rentals for similar sized warehouses tend to be around $100,000 per year.

Required:

Discuss how the above transaction should be treated in Picture's financial statements for the year ended 30 June 20X4.

4 Chapter summary

The need for disclosure of related parties

- Users need to be aware of related party relationships because transactions may not have happened at normal market rates.

Disclosure of related parties

- Parent/subsidiary relationships
- Disclosure of transactions and balances
- Key management compensation

Test your understanding answers

Test your understanding 1 – Group structures

Entity A:

Entities that are within the same group are related to one another. Entities B and C are therefore related parties of A.

D is an associate of C. C is a member of A's group. This means that D is a related party of A.

Entity B:

Entities that are within the same group are related to one another. Entities A and C are therefore related parties of B.

D is an associate of C. C is a member of the same group as B. This means that D is a related party of B

Entity C:

Entities that are within the same group are related to one another. Entities A and B are therefore related parties of C.

Entities are related if one is an associate of another. C and D are therefore related parties.

Entity D:

Entities are related if one is an associate of another. D and C are therefore related parties.

Entities are related if one is an associate of a member of a group of which the other entity is also a member. D is an associate of C. Companies A and B are in the same group as C. This means that D is also a related party of A and B.

Test your understanding 2 – Individual shareholdings

Situation A:

Mr P is a related party of both entity A and entity B as he is able to exercise either control or significant influence over each entity.

Mr P controls entity A and has significant influence over entity B. Therefore, A and B are related parties.

Situation B:

Mr P is a related party of both entity A and entity B as he is able to exercise significant influence over each entity.

Mr P does not control either entity A or entity B. Therefore, A and B are not related parties.

Test your understanding 3 – Key management personnel

Mr P has control over entity A, meaning that Mr P is a related party of A.

Mr P is a member of key management personnel of B, so is a related party of B.

A and B are related parties, because Mr P controls A and is a member of key management personnel of B.

Entity B controls entity C so B and C are related parties.

Mr P is a member of key management personnel of the parent of C, so Mr P and C are related parties.

This means that entities A and C are also related parties (Mr P controls A and is a member of key management personnel of the parent company of C).

Test your understanding 4 – Family members

Mr T and Mrs T are close family.

Mr T controls entity A. Mr T and Mrs T are related parties of entity A.

Mrs T has significant influence over entity B. Mrs T and Mr T are related parties of entity B.

Mr and Mrs T control entity A and have significant influence over entity B. A and B are related parties.

Test your understanding 5 – Picture and Frame

According to IAS 17, a finance lease is a lease where the risks and rewards of ownership transfer. This lease between Picture and Frame is only for a fraction of the asset's remaining useful life and the lease payments are insignificant. The lease is therefore an operating lease. Picture should recognise lease income on a straight line basis over the lease term. Therefore, $5,000 ($10,000 × 6/12) should be recognised in the current year's statement of profit or loss, as well as corresponding accrued income on the SFP.

A related party transaction is defined by IAS 24 as a transfer of resources, services or obligations between a reporting entity and a related party. An entity is related to the reporting entity if they are under joint control. An entity must disclose if it has entered into any transactions with a related party.

Picture and Frame are under joint control of Joanne Smith, so this means that they are related parties. Disclosure is required of all transactions between Picture and Frame during the financial period. Picture must disclose details of the leasing transaction and the income of $5,000 from Frame during the year.

Disclosures that related party transactions were made on terms equivalent to an arm's length transaction can only be made if they can be substantiated. The lease rentals are only 10% of normal market rate meaning that this disclosure cannot be made.

chapter

10

Employee benefits

Chapter learning objectives

Upon completion of this chapter you will be able to:

- apply and discuss the accounting treatment of short term and long term employee benefits
- apply and discuss the accounting treatment of defined contribution and defined benefit plans
- account for gains and losses on settlements and curtailments
- account for the 'asset ceiling' test and the reporting of remeasurement gains and losses.

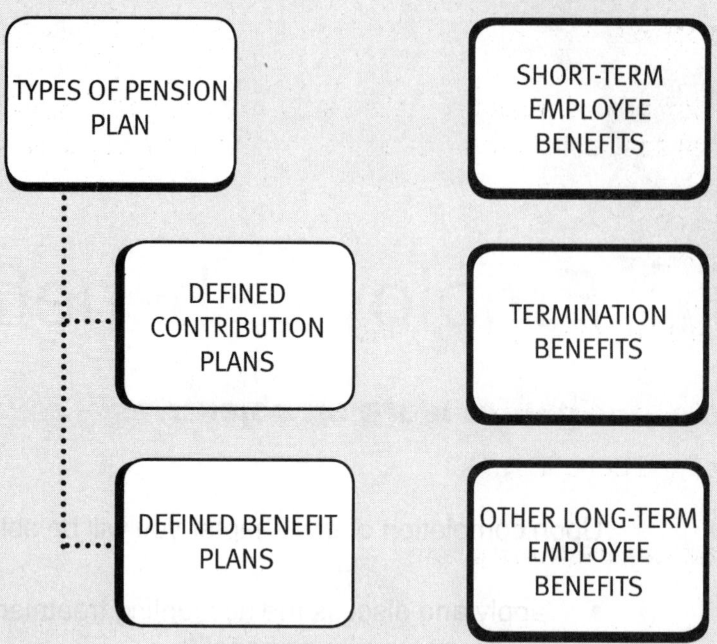

1 Introduction

Types of employee benefit

IAS 19 identifies four types of employee benefit as follows:

- **Post-employment benefits**. This normally relates to retirement benefits, which will typically take the form of either a defined contribution plan or a defined benefit plan (sometimes referred to as a defined benefit scheme).
- **Short-term employee benefits**. This includes wages and salaries, bonuses and other benefits.
- **Termination benefits**. Termination benefits arise when benefits become payable upon employment being terminated, either by the employer or by the employee accepting terms to have employment terminated.
- **Other long-term employee benefits**. This comprises other items not within the above classifications and will include long-service leave or awards, long-term disability benefits and other long-service benefits.

Each will be considered within this chapter, with particular emphasis upon post-employment defined benefit plans.

2 Post-employment benefit plans

Introduction

A pension plan (sometimes called a post-employment benefit plan or scheme) consists of a pool of assets, together with a liability for pensions owed. Pension plan assets normally consist of investments, cash and (sometimes) properties. The return earned on the assets is used to pay pensions.

There are two main types of pension plan:

- defined contribution plans
- defined benefit plans.

Defined contribution plans

The pension payable on retirement depends on the contributions paid into the plan by the employee and the employer:

- The employer's contribution is usually a fixed percentage of the employee's salary. The employer has no further obligation after this amount is paid.
- Therefore, the annual cost to the employer is reasonably predictable.
- Defined contribution plans present few accounting problems, other than ensuring that an accrual is made, where required, for contributions due, but not yet paid, at the reporting date.

In this situation, the employee bears the uncertainty regarding the value of the pension that will be paid upon retirement.

Defined benefit plans

The pension payable on retirement normally depends on either the final salary or the average salary of the employee during their career.

- The employer undertakes to finance a pension income of a certain amount,
  - e.g. 2/3 × final salary × (years of service/40 years)
- The employer has an ongoing obligation to make sufficient contributions to the plan to fund the pensions that have been promised.

- An actuary calculates the amount that must be paid into the plan each year in order to provide the promised pension. The calculation is based on various estimates and assumptions, such as the following:
  - **Life expectancy.** If employees are expected to live for a long time post-retirement, then there will need to be lots of assets in the pension plan to fund their pension.
  - **Investment returns.** If investment returns are low, the company will need to pay more cash into the pension plan to cover retirement benefits.
  - **Wage inflation**. If wage inflation is high, then employees will have larger salaries on retirement. This means they will be due higher pension payments.
- The actuary will re-assess their assumptions over time. Therefore, defined benefit pension plans are less predictable than defined contribution plans.

The actual contribution paid by the employer into a defined benefit plan during an accounting period does not usually represent the true cost to the employer of providing pensions in that period. The financial statements must reflect the true cost of providing pensions, rather than accounting only for the cash contributions made into the pension plan.

Multi-employer plans

Often a small entity does not have the resources to run a pension plan in-house, so it pays pension contributions over to an insurance company which runs a multi-employer plan. Such a plan can be either of a defined contribution nature or a defined benefit nature. Alternatively, a group may operate a plan for the employees of all subsidiaries within the group.

3 Accounting for post-employment benefit plans

Defined contribution plans

The expense of providing pensions in the period is normally the same as the amount of contributions paid.

- The entity should charge the agreed pension contribution to profit or loss as an employment expense in each period.
- An asset or liability for pensions only arises if the cash paid does not equal the value of contributions due for the period.
- IAS 19 requires disclosure of the amount recognised as an expense in the period.

Test your understanding 1 – Defined contribution scheme

An entity makes contributions to the pension fund of employees at a rate of 5% of gross salaries. For convenience, the entity pays $10,000 per month into the pension scheme with any balance being paid in the first month of the following accounting year. The wages and salaries for 20X6 are $2.7m.

Required:

Calculate the pension expense for 20X6, and the accrual/ prepayment at the end of the year.

Defined benefit plans: the basic principles

The actuary values the liability for future pension payments and the plan assets by applying carefully developed estimates and assumptions:

- If the liability exceeds the assets, there is a plan deficit (the usual situation) and a liability is reported in the statement of financial position.
- If the plan assets exceed the liability, there is a surplus and an asset is reported in the statement of financial position.
- In simple terms, the movement in the net liability (or asset) from one reporting date to the next is reflected in the statement of profit or loss and other comprehensive income for the year.

Measuring the plan assets and liabilities

In practice, the actuary measures the plan assets and liabilities by applying carefully developed estimates and assumptions relevant to the defined benefit pension plan.

- The plan liability is measured at the present value of the defined benefit obligation, using the Projected Unit Credit Method. This is an actuarial valuation method.
- Discounting is necessary because the liability will be settled many years in the future and, therefore, the effect of the time value of money is material. The discount rate used should be determined by market yields on high quality corporate bonds at the start of the reporting period, and applied to the net liability or asset at the start of the reporting period.
- Plan assets are measured at fair value. IFRS 13 Fair Value measurement provides a framework for determining how fair value should be established.

- IAS 19 does not prescribe a maximum time interval between valuations. However, valuations should be carried out with sufficient regularity to ensure that the amounts recognised in the financial statements do not differ materially from actual fair values at the reporting date.
- Where there are unpaid contributions at the reporting date, these are not included in the plan assets. Unpaid contributions are treated as a liability owed by the entity/employer to the plan.

Defined benefit plan movement

The following proforma shows the movement on the defined benefit deficit (surplus) over a reporting period:

	$000
Net deficit/(asset) brought forward (Obligation bfd – assets bfd)	X/(X)
Net interest component	X/(X)
Service cost component	X
Contributions into plan	(X)
Benefits paid	–
	X/(X)
Remeasurement component (bal. fig)	X/(X)
Net deficit/(asset) carried forward (Obligation cfd – assets cfd)	X/(X)

- **The net interest component**, which is charged (or credited) to profit or loss, is the change in the net pension liability (or asset) due to the passage in time. It is computed by applying the discount rate at the start of the year to the net defined benefit liability (or asset).
- **The service cost component** is charged to profit or loss. It is comprised of three elements:
  - The current service cost, which is the increase in the present value of the obligation arising from employee service in the current period.
  - The past service cost, which is the change in the present value of the obligation for employee service resulting from plan amendments or curtailments.
  - Any gain or loss on settlement.
- **Contributions into the plan** are the cash payments paid into the plan during the reporting period. This has no impact on the statement of profit or loss and other comprehensive income.

- **Benefits paid** are the amounts paid out of the plan assets to retired employees during the period. These payments reduce both the plan obligation and the plan assets. Therefore, this no overall impact on the net pension deficit (or asset).

After accounting for the above, the net pension deficit will differ from the amount calculated by the actuary. This is for a number of reasons, that include the following:

- The actuary's calculation of the value of the plan obligation and assets is based on assumptions, such as life expectancy and final salaries, and these will have changed year-on-year.
- The actual return on plan assets is different from the amount taken to profit or loss as part of the net interest component.

An adjustment, known as the **remeasurement component**, must therefore be posted. This is charged or credited to other comprehensive income for the year and identified as an item that will not be reclassified to profit or loss in future periods.

Explanation of terms

A **past service cost** is the change in the present value of the defined benefit obligation for employee service in prior periods, resulting from a plan amendment or a curtailment. In this context, a plan amendment is defined as the introduction of, or withdrawal of, or changes to a post-employment benefit plan.

- Past service costs could arise when there has been an improvement in the benefits to be provided under the plan. This will apply whether or not the benefits have vested (i.e. whether or not employees are immediately entitled to those enhanced benefits), or whether they are obliged to provide additional work and service to become eligible for those enhanced benefits.
- Past service costs are part of the service cost component for the year and are recognised at the earlier of the following dates:
  - when the plan amendment or curtailment occurs
  - when the entity recognises related restructuring costs or termination benefits.

A curtailment is a significant reduction in the number of employees covered by a pension plan. This may be a consequence of an individual event such as plant closure or discontinuance of an operation, which will typically result in employees being made redundant.

A settlement occurs when an entity enters into a transaction to eliminate the obligation for part or all of the benefits under a plan. For example, an employee may leave the entity for a new job elsewhere, and a payment is made from that pension plan to the pension plan operated by the new employer.

- The gain or loss on settlement comprises the difference between the fair value of the plan assets paid out and the reduction in the present value of the defined benefit obligation and is included as part of the service cost component.
- The gain or loss on settlement is recognised when the settlement occurs. This is the date when the entity eliminates the obligation for all or part of the benefits provided under the defined benefit plan.

Separate disclosure of the plan assets and obligation

For the purposes of the P2 exam it will be quicker to account for the net pension obligation, as outlined in the section above.

However, in a set of published financial statements that are prepared in accordance with IFRS, an entity should disclose separate reconciliations for the defined benefit obligation and the plan assets, showing the movement between the opening and closing balances.

These would appear as follows:

	Obligation $000	Assets $000
Brought forward	X	X
Interest on obligation	X	
Interest on plan assets		X
Service cost component	X	
Contributions into plan		X
Benefits paid	(X)	(X)
	X	X
Remeasurement component (bal. fig)	X/(X)	X/(X)
Carried forward	X	X

Summary of the amounts recognised in the financial statements

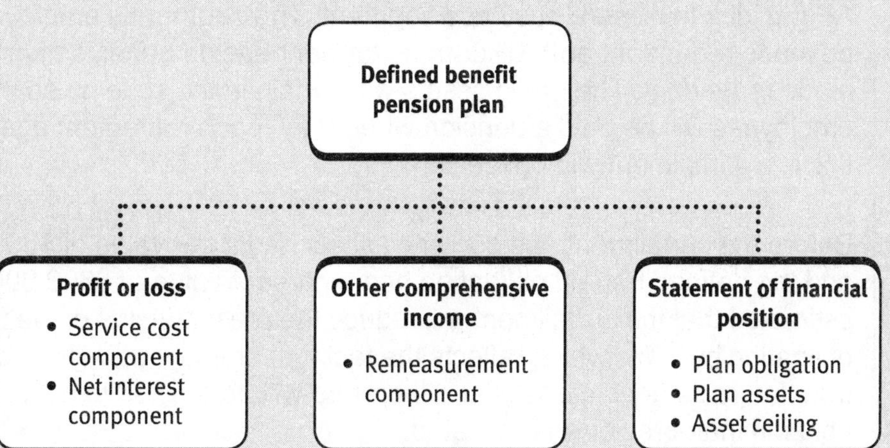

Illustration 1 – Accounting for past service costs

An entity operates a pension plan that provides a pension of 2% of final salary for each year of service. On 1 January 20X5, the entity improves the pension to 2.5% of final salary for each year of service, including service before this date. Employees must have worked for the entity for at least five years in order to obtain this increased benefit. At the date of the improvement, the present value of the additional benefits for service from 1 January 20X1 to 1 January 20X5, is as follows:

	$000
Employees with more than five years' service at 1.1.X5	150
Employees with less than five years' service at 1.1.X5 (average length of service: two years)	120
	270

Required:

Explain how the additional benefits are accounted for in the financial statements of the entity.

Solution

The entity recognises all $270,000 immediately as an increase in the defined benefit obligation following the amendment to the plan on 1 January 20X5. This will form part of the service cost component. Whether or not the benefits have vested by the reporting date is not relevant to their recognition as an expense in the financial statements.

Illustration 2 – Settlements and curtailments

AB decides to close a business segment. The segment's employees will be made redundant and will earn no further pension benefits after being made redundant. Their plan assets will remain in the scheme so that the employees will be paid a pension when they reach retirement age (i.e. this is a curtailment without settlement).

Before the curtailment, the scheme assets had a fair value of $500,000, and the defined benefit obligation had a present value of $600,000. It is estimated that the curtailment will reduce the present value of the future obligation by 10%, which reflects the fact that employees will not benefit from future salary increases and therefore will be entitled to a smaller pension than previously estimated.

Required:

What is net gain or loss on curtailment and how will this be treated in the financial statements?

Solution

The obligation is to be reduced by 10% × $600,000 = $60,000, with no change in the fair value of the assets as they remain in the plan. The reduction in the obligation represents a gain on curtailment which should be included as part of the service cost component and taken to profit or loss for the year. The net position of the plan following curtailment will be:

	Before	**On curtailment**	**After**
	$000	$000	$000
Present value of obligation	600	(60)	540
Fair value of plan assets	(500)	–	(500)
Net obligation in SOFP	100	(60)	40

The gain on curtailment is $60,000 and this will be included as part of the service cost component in profit or loss for the year.

Illustration 3 – Defined benefit plan – Celine

The following information is provided in relation to a defined benefit plan operated by Celine. At 1 January 20X4, the present value of the obligation was $140 million and the fair value of the plan assets amounted to $80 million.

	20X4	20X5
Discount rate at start of year	4%	3%
Current and past service cost ($m)	30	32
Benefits paid ($m)	20	22
Contributions into plan ($m)	25	30
Present value of obligation at 31 December ($m)	200	230
Fair value of plan assets at 31 December ($m)	120	140

Required:

Determine the amounts to be taken to profit or loss and other comprehensive income for both financial years, together with the net plan obligation or asset at 31 December 20X4 and 20X5.

Solution

The remeasurement component on the net obligation

This is calculated by analysing the change in the net pension deficit for the period.

- The net interest component reflects the growth in the plan assets and obligation due to the passage of time.
- The service cost component increases the plan obligation and thus the net deficit.
- The benefits paid during the year reduce both the plan obligation and plan assets and thus have no impact on the net deficit.
- The contributions into the scheme increase the plan assets and thus reduce the net plan deficit.

Reconciliation of the net obligation for 20X4 and 20X5

	20X4	20X5
	$m	$m
Obligation bal b/fwd 1 January	140.0	200.0
Asset bal b/fwd at 1 January	(80.0)	(120.0)
Net obligation b/fwd at 1 January	60.0	80.0
Service cost component	30.0	32.0
Net interest component		
4% × $60m	2.4	
3% × $80m		2.4
Contributions into plan	(25.0)	(30.0)
Benefits paid	–	–
Net remeasurement component on obligation (W1)	12.6	5.6
Net obligation c/fwd at 31 December	80.0	90.0

The statement of financial position

	20X4	20X5
	$m	$m
PV of plan obligation	200.0	230.0
FV of plan assets	(120.0)	(140.0)
Closing net liability	80.0	90.0

The statement of profit or loss and other comprehensive income

Both the service cost component and the net interest component are charged to profit or loss for the year. The remeasurement component, which comprises actuarial gains and losses, together with returns on plan assets to the extent that they are not included within the net interest component, is taken to other comprehensive income.

	20X4	20X5
Profit or loss	$m	$m
Service cost component	30.0	32.0
Net interest component	2.4	2.4
	32.4	34.4
Other comprehensive income		
Remeasurement component	12.6	5.6
Total comprehensive income charge for year	45.0	40.0

Test your understanding 2 – Fraser

The following information relates to a defined benefit plan operated by Fraser. At 1 January 20X1, the present value of the obligation was $1,000,000 and the fair value of the plan assets amounted to $900,000.

	20X1	20X2	20X3
Discount rate at start of year	10%	9%	8%
Current and past service cost ($000)	125	130	138
Benefits paid ($000)	150	155	165
Contributions paid into plan ($000)	90	95	105
PV of obligation at 31 December ($000)	1,350	1,340	1,450
FV of plan assets at 31 December ($000)	1,200	1,150	1,300

Required:

Show how the defined benefit plan would be shown in the financial statements for each of the years ended 31 December 20X1, 20X2 and 20X3 respectively.

Test your understanding 3 – TC

TC has a defined benefit pension plan and prepares financial statements to 31 March each year. The following information is relevant for the year ended 31 March 20X3:

- The net pension obligation at 31 March 20X3 was $55 million. At 31 March 20X2, the net obligation was $48 million, comprising the present value of the plan obligation stated at $100 million, together with plan assets stated at fair value of $52 million.
- The discount rate relevant to the net obligation was 6.25% and the actual return on plan assets for the year was $4 million.
- The current service cost was $12 million.
- At 31 March 20X3, TC granted additional benefits to those currently receiving benefits that are due to vest over the next four years and which have a present value of $4 million at that date. They were not allowed for in the original actuarial assumptions.
- During the year, TC made pension contributions of $8 million into the scheme and the scheme paid pension benefits in the year amounting to $3 million.

Required:

Explain the accounting treatment of the TC pension scheme for the year to 31 March 20X3, together with supporting calculations.

Test your understanding 4 - Mickleover

On 1 July 20X3 Mickleover started a defined benefit pension scheme for its employees and immediately contributed $4m cash into the scheme. The actuary has stated that the net obligation was $0.4m as at 30 June 20X4. The interest rate for good quality corporate bonds was 10% at 1 July 20X3 but 12% by 30 June 20X4. The actual return on the plan assets was 11%. The increased cost from the employee's service in the year was $4.2m which can be assumed to accrue at the year end.

On 30 June 20X4 Mickleover paid $0.3m in settlement of a defined benefit obligation with a present value of $0.2m. This related to staff that were to be made redundant although, as at 30 June 20X4, they still had an average remaining employment term of one month. The redundancies were not foreseen at the start of the year.

Required:

Discuss the correct accounting treatment of the above transaction in the financial statements of Mickleover for the year ended 30 June 20X4.

Criticisms of IAS 19

Retirement benefit accounting continues to be a controversial area. Commentators have perceived the following problems with the IAS 19 approach.

- Fair values of plan assets may be volatile, or even difficult to measure reliably depending upon the nature of the plan assets; consequently there may be significant fluctuations in the statement of financial position.
- IAS 19 requires plan assets to be valued at fair value (normally market value). Fair values of plan assets are not relevant to the economic reality of most pension schemes. Under the requirements of IAS 19, assets are valued at short-term amounts, but most pension scheme assets and liabilities are held for the long term. The actuarial basis of valuing plan assets would better reflect the long-term costs of funding a pension scheme. However, such a move would be a departure from IFRS 13 Fair Value Measurement which seeks to standardise the application of fair value measurement when it is required by a particular reporting standard.
- The treatment of pension costs in the statement of profit or loss and other comprehensive income is complex and may not be easily understood by users of the financial statements. It has been argued that all the components of the pension cost are so interrelated that it does not make sense to present them separately.
- Where there is a net pension plan surplus (rather than net obligation) at a reporting date, then IAS 19 treats it as if it 'belongs' to the employer. However, in practice, the situation is that the surplus perhaps 'belongs' to the members of the plan and must be applied for their benefit. IAS 19 may therefore not reflect the legal and economic reality of this situation.

Multi-employer plans

Multi-employer plans are defined contribution plans or defined benefit plans that:

- pool the assets contributed by various entities that are not under common control, an
- use those assets to provide benefits to employees of more than one entity, on the basis that contribution and benefit levels are determined without regard to the identity of the entity that employs the employees.

Defined contribution multi-employer plans do not pose a problem because the employer's cost is limited to the contributions payable.

Defined benefit multi-employer plans expose participating employers to the actuarial risks associated with the current and former employees of other entities. There are also potential problems because an employer may be unable to identify its share of the underlying assets and liabilities.

IAS 19 states that where a multi-employer plan is a defined benefit plan, the entity accounts for its proportionate share of the obligations, benefits and costs associated with the plan in the same way as usual. However, where sufficient information is not available to do this, the entity accounts for the plan as if it were a defined contribution plan and discloses:

- the fact that the plan is a defined benefit plan
- the reason why sufficient information is not available to account for the plan as a defined benefit plan.

In this situation, the revised standard requires additional disclosures to be made regarding the defined benefit plan, some of which may be quite onerous for preparers of financial statements.

4 The asset ceiling

Sometimes the deduction of plan assets from the pension obligation results in a negative amount: i.e. an asset. IAS 19 states that pension plan assets (surpluses) are measured at the lower of:

- the amount calculated as normal per earlier examples and illustrations
- the total of the present value of any economic benefits available in the form of refunds from the plan or reductions in future contributions to the plan.

Applying the 'asset ceiling' means that a surplus can only be recognised to the extent that it will be recoverable in the form of refunds or reduced contributions in future.

Illustration 4 – The asset ceiling

The following information relates to a defined benefit plan:	$000
Fair value of plan assets	950
Present value of pension liability	800
Present value of future refunds and reductions in future contributions	70

Required:

What is the value of the asset that recognised in the financial statements?

Solution

The amount that can be recognised is the lower of:

	$000
Present value of plan obligation	800
Fair value of plan assets	(950)
	(150)

	$000
PV of future refunds and/or reductions in future contributions	(70)

Therefore the asset that can be recognised is restricted to $70,000.

Test your understanding 5 – Arc

The following information relates to the defined benefit plan operated by Arc for the year ended 30 June 20X4:

	$m
FV of plan assets b/fwd at 30 June 20X3	2,600
PV of obligation b/fwd at 30 June 20X3	2,000
Current service cost for the year	100
Benefits paid in the year	80
Contributions into plan	90
FV of plan assets at 30 June 20X4	3,100
PV of plan obligation at 30 June 20X4	2,400

Discount rate for the defined benefit obligation – 10%

Arc has identified that the asset ceiling at 30 June 20X3 and 30 June 20X4, based upon the present value of future refunds from the plan and/or reductions in future contributions amounts to $200m at 30 June 20X3 and 30 June 20X4.

Required:

(a) **Explain, with supporting calculations, the accounting treatment of the pension scheme for the year ended 30 June 20X4.**

(b) **Explain the purpose of the asset ceiling, together with its impact upon accounting for the defined benefit plan operated by Arc.**

Disclosure requirements

IAS 19 has extensive disclosure requirements. An entity should disclose the following information about defined benefit plans:

- explanation of the regulatory framework within which the plan operates, together with explanation of the nature of benefits provided by the plan
- explanation of the nature of the risks the entity is exposed to as a consequence of operating the plan, together with explanation of any plan amendments, settlements or curtailments in the year

- the entity's accounting policy for recognising actuarial gains and losses, together with disclosure of the significant actuarial assumptions used to determine the net defined benefit obligation or assets. Although there is no longer a choice of accounting policy for actuarial gains and losses, it may still be helpful to users to explain how they have been accounted for within the financial statements.
- a general description of the type of plan operated
- a reconciliation of the assets and liabilities recognised in the statement of financial position
- a reconciliation showing the movements during the period in the net liability (or asset) recognised in the statement of financial position
- the charge to total comprehensive income for the year, separated into the appropriate components
- analysis of the remeasurement component to identify returns on plan assets, together with actuarial gains and losses arising on the net plan obligation
- sensitivity analysis and narrative description of how the defined benefit plan may affect the nature, timing and uncertainty of the entity's future cash flows.

Other employee benefits

IAS 19 covers a number of other issues in addition to post-employment benefits as follows:

Short-term employee benefits – This includes a number of issues including:

- **Wages and salaries and bonuses and other benefits**. The general principle is that wages and salaries costs are expenses as they are incurred on a normal accruals basis, unless capitalisation is permitted in accordance with another reporting standard, such as IAS 16 or IAS 38. Bonuses and other short-term payments are recognised using normal criteria of establishing an obligation based upon past events which can be reliably measured.

- **Compensated absences**. This covers issues such as holiday pay, sick leave, maternity leave, jury service, study leave and military service. The key issue is whether the absences are regarded as being accumulating or non-accumulating:
  - accumulating benefits are earned over time and are capable of being carried forward. In this situation, the expense for future compensated absences is recognised over the period services are provided by the employee. This will typically result in the recognition of a liability at the reporting date for the expected cost of the accumulated benefit earned but not yet claimed by an employee. An example of this would be a holiday pay accrual at the reporting date where unused holiday entitlement can be carried forward and claimed in a future period.
  - for non-accumulating benefits, an expense should only be recognised when the absence occurs. This may arise, for example, where an employee continues to receive their normal remuneration whilst being absent due to illness or other permitted reason. A charge to profit or loss would be made only when the authorised absence occurs; if there is no such absence, there will be no charge to profit or loss.
- **Benefits in kind**. Recognition of cost should be based on the same principles as benefits payable in cash; it should be measured based upon the cost to the employer of providing the benefit and recognised as it is earned.

Termination benefits

Termination benefits may be defined as benefits payable as a result of employment being terminated, either by the employer, or by the employee accepting voluntary redundancy. Such payments are normally in the form of a lump sum; entitlement to such payments is not accrued over time, and only become available in a relatively short period prior to any such payment being agreed and paid to the employee.

The obligation to pay such benefits is recognised either when the employer can no longer withdraw the offer of such benefits (i.e. they are committed to paying them), or when it recognises related restructuring costs (normally in accordance with IAS 37). Payments which are due to be paid more than twelve months after the reporting date should be discounted to their present value.

Other long-term employee benefits

This comprises other items not within the above classifications and will include long-service leave, long-term disability benefits and other long-service benefits. These employee benefits are accounted for in a similar manner to accounting for post-employment benefits, typically using the projected unit credit method, as benefits are payable more than twelve months after the period in which services are provided by an employee.

5 Chapter summary

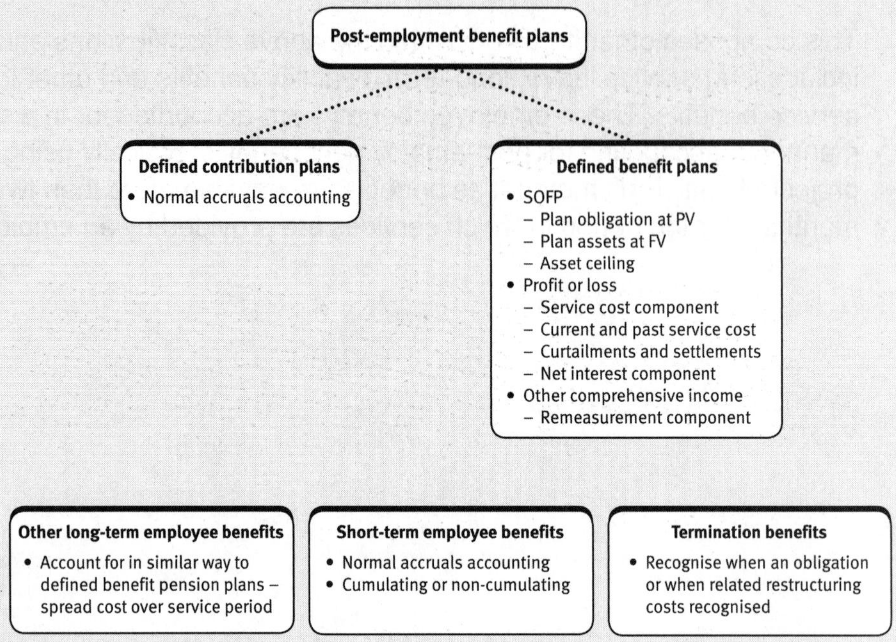

Post-employment benefit plans

Defined contribution plans
- Normal accruals accounting

Defined benefit plans
- SOFP
  - Plan obligation at PV
  - Plan assets at FV
  - Asset ceiling
- Profit or loss
  - Service cost component
  - Current and past service cost
  - Curtailments and settlements
  - Net interest component
- Other comprehensive income
  - Remeasurement component

Other long-term employee benefits
- Account for in similar way to defined benefit pension plans – spread cost over service period

Short-term employee benefits
- Normal accruals accounting
- Cumulating or non-cumulating

Termination benefits
- Recognise when an obligation or when related restructuring costs recognised

Test your understanding answers

Test your understanding 1 – Defined contribution scheme

This appears to be a defined contribution scheme.

The charge to profit or loss should be:

$2.7m × 5% = $135,000

The statement of financial position will therefore show an accrual of $15,000, being the difference between the $135,000 expense and the $120,000 ($10,000 × 12 months) cash paid in the year.

Test your understanding 2 – Fraser

The remeasurement component on the net obligation

	20X1	20X2	20X3
	$000	$000	$000
Net obligation at start of the year	100	150	190
Net interest component (10% X1/9% X2/8% X3)	10	14	15
Service cost component	125	130	138
Contributions into plan	(90)	(95)	(105)
Remeasurement (gain) loss – bal.fig	5	(9)	(88)
Net obligation at end of the year	150	190	150

Statement of financial position

	20X1	20X2	20X3
	$000	$000	$000
Net pension (asset) liability	150	190	150

Profit or loss and other comprehensive income for the year

	20X1	20X2	20X3
	$000	$000	$000
Profit or loss			
Service cost component	125	130	138
Net interest component	10	14	15
Charge to profit or loss	135	144	153
Other comprehensive income:			
Remeasurement component	5	(9)	(88)
Total charge to comprehensive income	140	135	65

Test your understanding 3 – TC

		$m
Net obligation brought forward		48
Net interest component (6.25% × 48)		3
Service cost component:		
Current service cost	12	
Past service cost	4	
		16
Contributions into the plan		(8)
Benefits paid		–
Remeasurement component (bal fig)		(4)
Net obligation carried forward		55

Explanation:

- The discount rate is applied to the net obligation brought forward. The net interest component is $3m and this is charged to profit or loss.
- The current year service cost, together with the past service cost forms the service cost component. Past service cost is charged in full, usually when the scheme is amended, rather than when the additional benefits vest. The total service cost component is $16m and this is charged to profit or loss.
- To the extent that there has been a return on assets in excess of the amount identified by application of the discount rate to the fair value of plan assets, this is part of the remeasurement component (i.e. $4m – $3.25m ($52m × 6.25%) = $0.75m).
- Contributions paid into the plan during the year of $8m reduce the net obligation.
- Benefits paid of $3 million will reduce both the scheme assets and the scheme obligation, so have no impact on the net obligation.
- The statement of financial position as at 31 March 20X3 will show a net deficit (a liability) of $55m.

Test your understanding 4 - Mickleover

The accounting treatment of a defined benefit plan is as follows:

- the amount recognised in the statement of financial position is the present value of the defined benefit obligation less the fair value of the plan assets as at the reporting date.
- The opening net position should be unwound using a discount rate that applies to good quality corporate bonds. This should be charged/credited to profit or loss.
- The increased cost from the employees' service during the past year is known as a current service cost. This should be expensed against profits as part of the service cost component and credited to the pension scheme obligation.
- Curtailments should be recognised at the earlier of when the curtailment occurs or when the related termination benefits are recognised.
- The remeasurement component should be included in other comprehensive income and identified as an item which will not be reclassified to profit and loss in future periods.

In relation to Mickleover:

- The net liability on the statement of financial position as at 30 June 20X4 is $0.4m.
- Although this is the first year of the scheme cash of $4m was introduced at the start of the year and so this should be unwound at 10%.
- The net interest component credited to profit and loss will therefore be $0.4m (10% × $4m). The service cost arises at the year end and so is not unwound.
- Although the employees have not yet been made redundant, the costs related to the redundancy will have been recognised during the current reporting period. Therefore, a loss on curtailment of $0.1m ($0.3m – $0.2m) should also be recognised in the current year. As the curtailment was not foreseen and would not have been included within the actuarial assumptions, the $0.1m should be charged against profits within the service cost component.
- The remeasurement loss, which includes the difference between the actual returns on plan assets and the amount taken to profit or loss as part of the net interest component, is $0.5m (W1).

(W1) **Remeasurement component**

		$m
Net obligation brought forward		0
Contributions		(4)
Net interest component (10% × $4m)		(0.4)
Service cost component:		
Current service cost	4.2	
Loss on curtailment	0.1	
		4.3
Benefits paid		–
Remeasurement component (bal fig)		**0.5**
Net obligation carried forward		0.4

Test your understanding 5 – Arc

(a)

	Net plan asset before ceiling adj	Ceiling adj*	Net plan asset after ceiling adj	Note
	$m	$m	$m	
Balance b/fwd	(600)	400	(200)	1
Net interest component (10%)	(60)	40	(20)	2
Service cost component	100	–	100	3
Benefits paid	–	–	–	4
Contributions in	(90)	–	(90)	5
Sub-total:	(650)	440	(210)	
Remeasurement component:	(50)	60	10	6
Balance c/fwd	(700)	500	(200)	

* note that this is effectively a balancing figure.

Explanation:

(1) The asset ceiling adjustment at the previous reporting date of 30 June 20X3 measures the net defined benefit asset at the amount recoverable by refunds and/or reduced future contributions, stated at $200m. In effect, the value of the asset was reduced for reporting purposes at 30 June 20X3.

(2) Interest charged on the obligation or earned on the plan assets is based upon the discount rate for the obligation, stated at 10%. This will then require adjustment to agree with the net return on the net plan asset at the beginning of the year. Net interest earned is taken to profit or loss for the year.

(3) The current year service cost increases the plan obligation, which therefore reduces the net plan asset. The current year service cost is taken to profit or loss for the year.

(4) Benefits paid in the year reduce both the plan obligation and the plan assets by the same amount.

(5) Contributions into the plan increase the fair value of plan assets, and also the net plan asset during the year.

(6) The remeasurement component, including actuarial gains and losses for the year, is identified to arrive at the present value of the plan obligation and the fair value of the plan assets at 30 June 20X4. As there is a net asset of $700m ($3,100m – $2,400m) for the defined benefit pension plan, the asset ceiling test is applied to restrict the reported asset to the expected future benefits in the form of refunds and/or reduced future contributions. This is stated in the question to be $200m. To the extent that an adjustment is required to the net asset at the reporting date, this is part of the net remeasurement component.

Statement of financial position

	$000
Net pension asset	200

Profit or loss and other comprehensive income for the year

	$000
Profit or loss	
Service cost component	100
Net interest component	(20)
Charge to profit or loss	80
Other comprehensive income:	
Remeasurement component	(10)
Total charge to comprehensive income	70

(b) The asset ceiling test is designed to ensure that any net pension asset is not overstated on the statement of financial position. If it can be reliably measured based upon the present value of future economic benefits to be received, either in the form of reduced future contributions or refunds of contributions already paid, this will comply with the definition of an asset from the Conceptual Framework for Financial Reporting.

If the asset ceiling test was not applied there would be a net asset for the defined benefit plan amounting to $700m ($3,100 – $2,400) at 30 June 20X4. However, this amount would not be fully represented by the right to receive future economic benefits in the form of refunds of amounts already paid or reductions in future contributions into the plan. Consequently, the asset would be overstated.

chapter

11

Share-based payment

Chapter learning objectives

Upon completion of this chapter you will be able to:

- apply and discuss the recognition and measurement criteria for share-based payment transactions
- account for modifications, cancellations and settlements of share-based payment transactions.

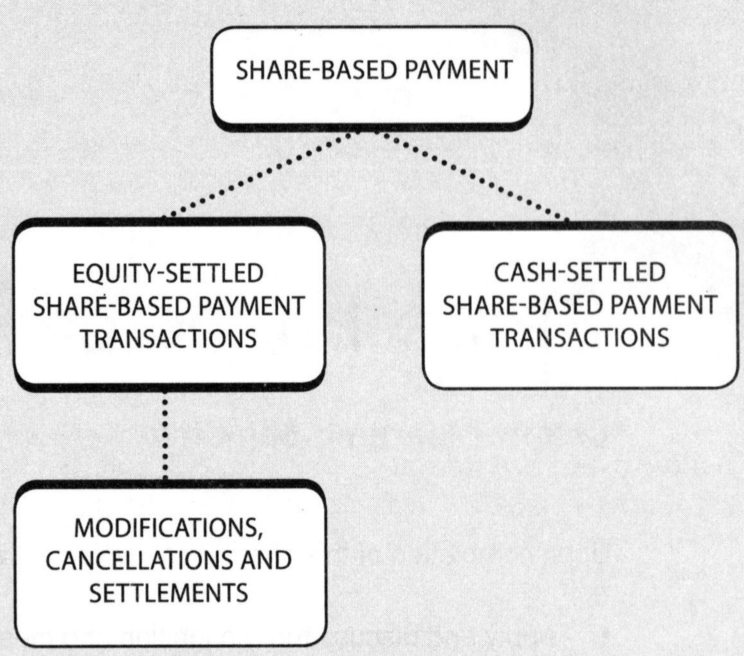

1 Share-based payment

Introduction

Share-based payment has become increasingly common. Share-based payment occurs when an entity buys goods or services from other parties (such as employees or suppliers) and:

- settles the amounts payable by issuing shares or share options, or
- incurs liabilities for cash payments based on its share price.

The problem

If a company pays for goods or services in cash, an expense is recognised in profit or loss. If a company 'pays' for goods or services in share options, there is no cash outflow and therefore, under traditional accounting, no expense would be recognised.

If a company issues shares to employees, a transaction has occurred. The employees have provided a valuable service to the entity, in exchange for the shares/options. It is inconsistent not to recognise this transaction in the financial statements.

IFRS 2 Share-based Payment was issued to deal with this accounting anomaly. IFRS 2 requires that all share-based payment transactions must be recognised in the financial statements when the transaction takes place.

Arguments against recognising share-based payments

There are a number of arguments against recognising share-based payments. IFRS 2 rejects them all.

No cost therefore no charge

A charge for shares or options should not be recognised because the entity does not have to sacrifice cash or other assets. There is no cost to the entity.

This argument ignores the fact that a transaction has occurred. The employees have provided valuable services to the entity in return for valuable shares or options. If this argument were accepted, the financial statements would fail to reflect the economic transactions that had occurred.

Earnings per share would be hit twice

The charge to profit for the employee services consumed reduces the entity's earnings. At the same time there is an increase in the number of shares issued.

However, the double impact on earnings per share simply reflects the two economic events that have occurred: the entity has issued shares, thus increasing the denominator of the EPS calculation, and it has also consumed the resources it received for those shares, thus reducing the numerator. Issuing shares to employees, instead of paying them in cash, requires a greater increase in the entity's earnings in order to maintain its earnings per share. Recognising the transaction ensures that its economic consequences are reported.

Adverse economic consequences

Recognition of employee share-based payment might discourage entities from introducing or continuing employee share plans.

However, accounting for share-based payments avoids the economic distortion created when entities consume resources without having to account for such transactions.

Types of transaction

IFRS 2 applies to all share-based payment transactions. There are two main types.

- **Equity-settled share-based payments:** the entity acquires goods or services in exchange for equity instruments of the entity (e.g. shares or share options)
- **Cash-settled share-based payments:** the entity acquires goods or services in exchange for amounts of cash measured by reference to the entity's share price.

The most common type of share-based payment transaction is where share options are granted to employees or directors as part of their remuneration.

2 Equity-settled share-based payment transactions

Accounting treatment

When an entity receives goods or services as a result of an equity-settled share-based payment transaction, it posts the following double entry:

Dr Expense/asset
Cr Equity (usually reported in 'other components of equity')

Measurement

The basic principle is that all transactions are measured at fair value.

How fair value is determined:

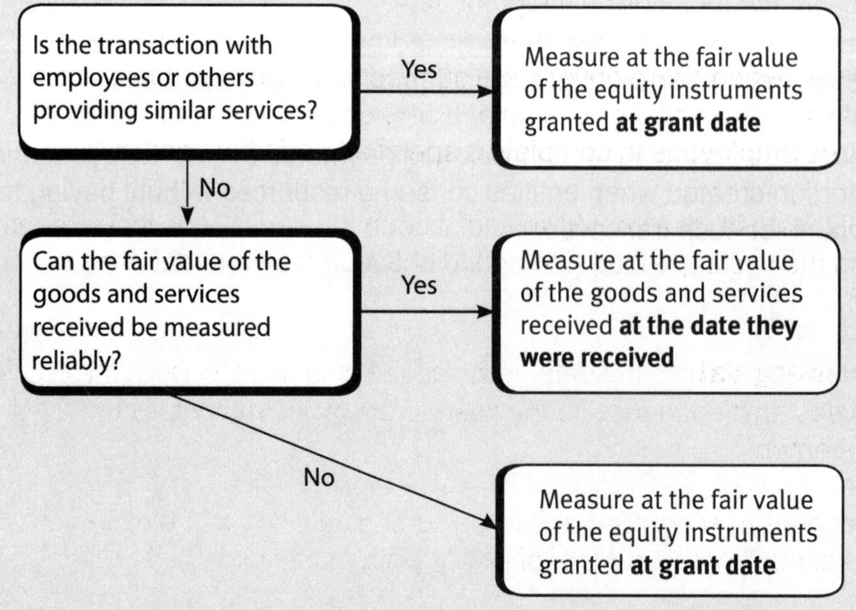

The **grant date** is the date at which the entity and another party agree to the arrangement.

Determining fair value

Where a share-based payment transaction is with parties other than employees, it is assumed that the fair value of the goods and services received can be measured reliably, at their cash price for example.

Where shares or share options are granted to employees as part of their remuneration, it is not usually possible to arrive at a reliable value for the services received in return. For this reason, the entity measures the transaction by reference to the fair value of the equity instruments granted.

The fair value of equity instruments is market value, if this is available. Where no market price is available (for example, if the instruments are unquoted), a valuation technique or model is used.

The fair value of share options is harder to determine. In rare cases there may be publicly quoted traded options with similar terms, whose market value can be used as the fair value of the options we are considering. Otherwise, the fair value of options must be estimated using a recognised option-pricing model. IFRS 2 does not require any specific model to be used. The most commonly used is the Black-Scholes model.

Allocating the expense to reporting periods

Some equity instruments vest immediately. In other words, the holder is unconditionally entitled to the instruments. In this case, the transaction should be accounted for in full on the grant date.

However, when share options are granted to employees, there are normally conditions attached. For example, a service condition may exist that requires employees to complete a specified period of service.

IFRS 2 states that an entity should account for services as they are rendered during the vesting period (the period between the grant date and the vesting date).

The **vesting date** is the date on which the counterparty (e.g., the employee) becomes entitled to receive the cash or equity instruments under the arrangement.

The expense recognised at each reporting date should be based on the best estimate of the number of equity instruments expected to vest.

On the vesting date, the entity shall revise the estimate to equal the number of equity instruments that ultimately vest.

Illustration 1 – When to recognise the transaction

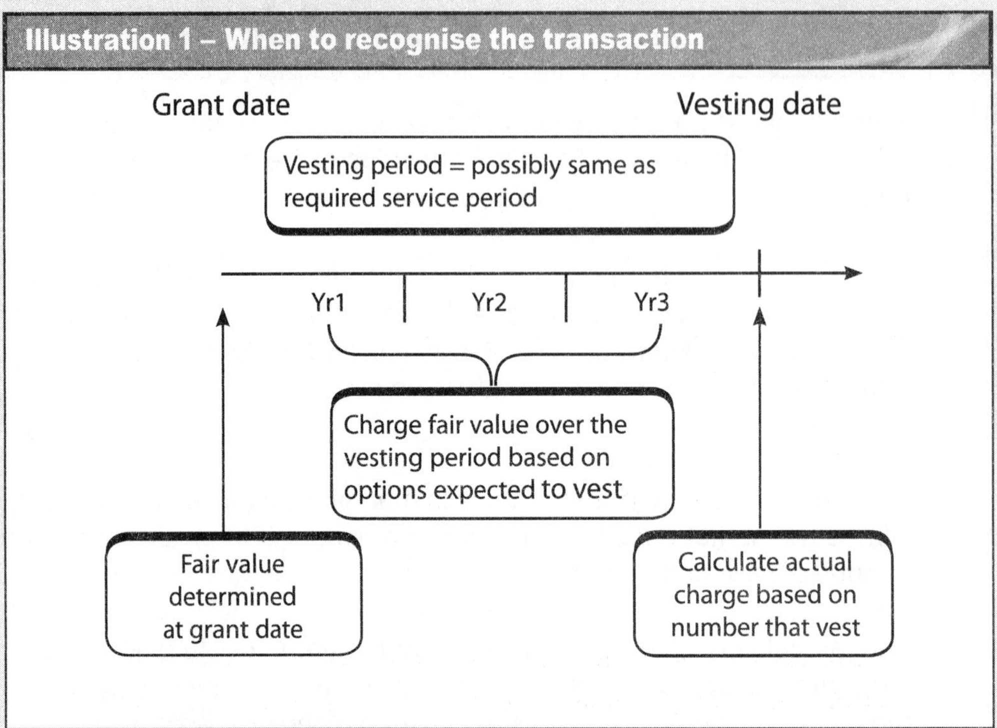

Test your understanding 1 – Equity-settled share-based

An entity has a reporting date of 31 December.

On 1 January 20X1 it grants 100 share options to each of its 500 employees. Each grant is conditional upon the employee working for the entity until 31 December 20X3. At the grant date the fair value of each share option is $15.

During 20X1, 20 employees leave and the entity estimates that a total of 20% of the 500 employees will leave during the three-year period.

During 20X2, a further 20 employees leave and the entity now estimates that only 15% of the original 500 employees will leave during the three-year period.

During 20X3, a further 10 employees leave.

Required:

Calculate the remuneration expense that will be recognised in each of the three years of the share-based payment scheme.

Performance conditions

In addition to service conditions, some share based payment schemes have **performance conditions** that must be satisfied before they vest, such as:

- achieving a specified increase in the entity's profit
- the completion of a research project
- achieving a specified increase in the entity's share price.

Performance conditions can be classified as either market conditions or non-market conditions.

- A **market condition** is defined by IFRS 2 as 'one that is related to the market price of the entity's equity instruments.' An example of a market condition is that the entity must attain a minimum share price by the vesting date for scheme members to be eligible to participate in the share-based payment scheme.
- **Non-market performance conditions** are not related to the market price of the entity's equity instruments. Examples of non-market performance conditions include EPS or profit targets.

Conditions attaching to share-based payment transactions: a summary

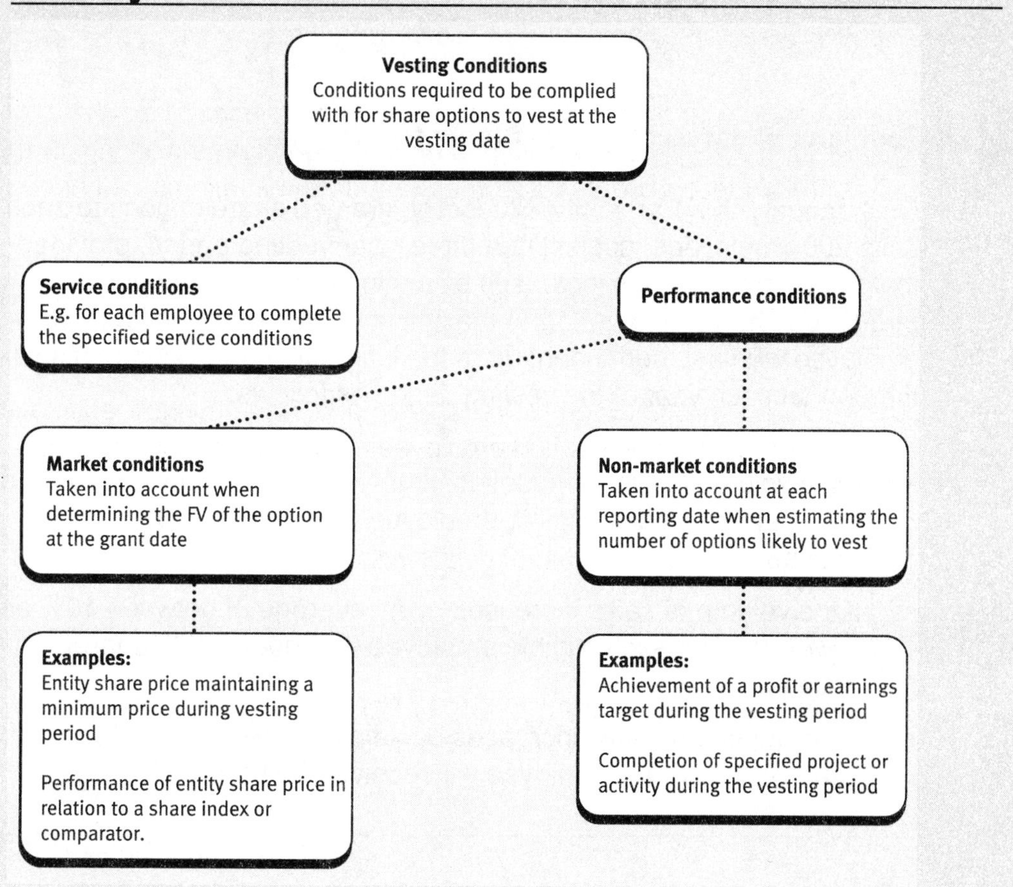

The impact of performance conditions

- **Market based conditions** have already been factored into the fair value of the equity instrument at the grant date. Therefore, an expense is recognised irrespective of whether market conditions are satisfied
- **Non-market based conditions** must be taken into account in determining whether an expense should be recognised in a reporting period.

Test your understanding 2 – Market based conditions

On 1 January 20X1, one hundred employees were given 50 share options each. These will vest if the employees still work for the entity on 31 December 20X2 and if the share price on that date is more than $5.

On 1 January 20X1, the fair value of the options was $1. The share price on 31 December 20X1 was $3 and it was considered unlikely that the share price would rise to $5 by 31 December 20X2. Ten employees left during the year ended 31 December 20X1 and a further ten are expected to leave in the following year.

Required:

How should the above transaction be accounted for in the year ended 31 December 20X1?

Test your understanding 3 – Blueberry

On 1 January 20X4 an entity, Blueberry, granted share options to each of its 200 employees, subject to a three-year vesting period, provided that the volume of sales increases by a minimum of 5% per annum throughout the vesting period. A maximum of 300 share options per employee will vest, dependent upon the increase in the volume of sales throughout each year of the vesting period as follows:

- If the volume of sales increases by an average of between 5% and 10% per year, each eligible employee will receive 100 share options.
- If the volume of sales increases by an average of between 10% and 15% per year, each eligible employee will receive 200 share options.
- If the volume of sales increases by an average of over 15% per year, each eligible employee will receive 300 share options.

At the grant date, Blueberry estimated that the fair value of each option was $10 and that the increase in the volume of sales each year would be between 10% and 15%. It was also estimated that a total of 22% of employees would leave prior to the end of the vesting period. At each reporting date within the vesting period, the situation was as follows:

Reporting date	Employees leaving in year	Further leavers expected prior to vesting date	Annual increase in sales volume	Expected sales volume increase over remaining vesting period	Average annual increase in sales volume to date
31 Dec X4	8	18	14%	14%	14%
31 Dec X5	6	4	18%	16%	16%
31 Dec X6	2		16%		16%

Required:

Calculate the impact of the above share-based payment scheme on Blueberry's financial statements in each reporting period.

Accounting after the vesting date

IFRS 2 states that no further adjustments to **total equity** should be made after the vesting date. This applies even if some of the equity instruments do not vest (for example, because a market based condition was not met).

Entities may, however, transfer any balance from 'other components of equity' to retained earnings.

Test your understanding 4 – Beginner

Beginner offered directors an option scheme conditional on a three-year period of service. The number of options granted to each of the ten directors at the inception of the scheme was 1 million. The options were exercisable shortly after the end of the third year. Upon exercise of the share options, those directors eligible would be required to pay $2 for each share of $1 nominal value.

The fair value of the options and the estimates of the number of options expected to vest were:

Year	Rights expected to vest	Fair value of the option $
Start of Year One	8m	0.30
End of Year One	7m	0.33
End of Year Two	8m	0.37
End of Year Three	9m	0.74

Required:

(a) **Show how the option scheme will affect the financial statements for each of the three years of the vesting period.**

(b) **Show the accounting treatment at the vesting date for each of the following situations:**

(i) **The fair value of a share was $5 and all eligible directors exercised their share options immediately.**

(ii) **The fair value of a share was $1.50 and all eligible directors allowed their share options to lapse.**

Modifications to the terms on which equity instruments are granted

An entity may alter the terms and conditions of share option schemes during the vesting period. For example:

- it might increase or reduce the exercise price of the options (the price that the holder of the options has to pay for shares when the options are exercised). This makes the scheme less favourable or more favourable to employees.
- it might change the vesting conditions, to make it more likely or less likely that the options will vest.

If a modification to an equity-settled share-based payment scheme occurs, the entity must continue to recognise the grant date fair value of the equity instruments in profit or loss, unless the instruments do not vest because of a failure to meet a non-market based vesting condition.

If the modification increases the fair value of the equity instruments, then an extra expense must be recognised:

- The difference between the fair value of the new arrangement and the fair value of the original arrangement (the incremental fair value) at the date of the modification must be recognised as a charge to profit or loss. The extra expense is spread over the period from the date of the change to the vesting date.

Test your understanding 5 – Modifications

An entity grants 100 share options to each of its 500 employees, provided that they remain in service over the next three years. The fair value of each option is $20.

During year one, 50 employees leave. The entity estimates that a further 60 employees will leave during years two and three.

At the end of year one the entity reprices its share options because the share price has fallen. The other vesting conditions remain unchanged. At the date of repricing, the fair value of each of the original share options granted (before taking the repricing into account) was $10. The fair value of each repriced share option is $15.

During year two, a further 30 employees leave. The entity estimates that a further 30 employees will leave during year three.

During year three, a further 30 employees leave.

Required:

Calculate the amounts to be recognised in the financial statements for each of the three years of the scheme.

Further illustration on modifications

An entity grants 100 share options to each of the 15 employees in its sales team, on condition that they remain in service over the next three years. There is also a performance condition: the team must sell more than 40,000 units of a particular product over the three-year period. At the grant date the fair value of each option is $20.

During Year 2, the entity increases the sales target to 70,000 units. By the end of Year 3, only 60,000 units have been sold and the share options do not vest.

All 15 employees remain with the entity for the full three years.

Required:

Calculate the amounts to be recognised in the financial statements for each of the three years of the scheme.

Solution

IFRS 2 states that when a share option scheme is modified, the entity must recognise, as a minimum, the services received measured at the fair value at the grant date. The employees have not met the modified sales target, but **did** meet the original target set on grant date.

This means that the entity must recognise the expense that it would have incurred had the original scheme continued in force.

The total amount recognised in equity is $30,000 (15 × 100 × 20). The entity recognises an expense of $10,000 for each of the three years.

Cancellations and settlements

An entity may cancel or settle a share option scheme before the vesting date.

- If the cancellation or settlement occurs during the vesting period, the entity immediately recognises the amount that would otherwise have been recognised for services received over the vesting period (an acceleration of vesting).
- Any payment made to employees up to the fair value of the equity instruments granted at cancellation or settlement date is accounted for as a deduction from equity.
- Any payment made to employees in excess of the fair value of the equity instruments granted at the cancellation or settlement date is accounted for as an expense in profit or loss.

Test your understanding 6 – Cancellations and settlements

An entity introduced an equity-settled share-based payment scheme on 1 January 20X0 for its 5 directors. Under the terms of the scheme, the entity will grant 1,000 options to each director if they remain in employment for the next three years. All five directors are expected to stay for the full three years. The fair value of each option at the grant date was $8.

On 30 June 20X1, the entity decided to base its share-based payment schemes on profit targets instead. It therefore cancelled the existing scheme. On 30 June 20X1, it paid compensation of $10 per option to each of the 5 directors. The fair value of the options at 30 June 20X1 was $9.

Required:

Explain, with calculations, how the cancellation and settlement of the share-based payment scheme should be accounted for in the year ended 31 December 20X1.

3 Cash-settled share-based payment transactions

Examples of cash-settled share-based payment transactions include:

- share appreciation rights (SARs), where employees become entitled to a future cash payment based on the increase in the entity's share price from a specified level over a specified period of time
- the right to shares that are redeemable, thus entitling the holder to a future payment of cash.

Accounting treatment

The double entry for a cash-settled share-based payment transaction is:

Dr Profit or loss
Cr Liabilities

Measurement

The entity remeasures the fair value of the liability arising under a cash-settled scheme at each reporting date.

- This is different from accounting for equity-settled share-based payments, where the fair value is fixed at the grant date.

Allocating the expense to reporting periods

Where services are received in exchange for cash-settled share-based payments, these are recognised over the period that the employees render the services (the vesting period).

- This is the same principle as for equity-settled transactions.

Illustration 2 – Cash-settled share-based payment transactions

An entity has a reporting date of 31 December.

On 1 January 20X1 the entity grants 100 share appreciation rights (SARs) to each of its 300 employees, on the condition that they continue to work for the entity until 31 December 20X3.

During 20X1, 20 employees leave. The entity estimates that a further 40 will leave during 20X2 and 20X3.

During 20X2, 10 employees leave. The entity estimates that a further 20 will leave during 20X3.

During 20X3, 10 employees leave.

The fair value of a SAR at each reporting date is shown below:

	$
20X1	10.00
20X2	12.00
20X3	15.00

Required:

Calculate the expense for each of the three years of the scheme, and the liability to be recognised in the statement of financial position as at 31 December for each of the three years.

Solution

Year	**Liability at year-end**	**Expense for year**
	$000	$000
20X1 ((300 – 20 – 40) × 100 × $10 × 1/3)	80	80
20X2 ((300 – 20 – 10 – 20) × 100 × $12 × 2/3)	200	120
20X3 ((300 – 20 – 10 – 10) × 100 × $15)	390	190

Note that the fair value of the liability is remeasured at each reporting date. This is then spread over the vesting period.

The value of share appreciation rights (SARs)

SARs may be exercisable over a period of time. The fair value of each SAR comprises the intinsic value (the cash amount payable based upon the share price at that date) together with its time value (based upon the fact that the share price will vary over time).

When SARs are exercised, they are accounted for at their intrinsic value at the exercise date. The fair value of a SAR could exceed its intrinsic value at this date. This is because SAR holders who do not exercise their rights at that time have the ability to benefit from future share price rises.

At the end of the exercise period, the intrinsic value of a SAR will equal its fair value. The liability will be cleared and any remaining balance taken to profit or loss.

Test your understanding 7 – Growler

On 1 January 20X4 Growler granted 200 share appreciation rights (SARs) to each of its 500 employees, on condition that they continue to work for the entity for four years. At 1 January 20X4, the entity expects that 25 of those employees will leave each year.

During 20X4, 20 employees leave Growler. The entity expects that this number will leave in each future year of the scheme.

During 20X5, 24 employees leave, and the entity expects that a total of 44 employees will leave over the remaining two-year period of the scheme.

During 20X6, eighteen employees leave, with a further 20 expected to leave in the final year. During 20X7, only 10 employees leave.

The SARs vest on 31 December 20X7 and can be exercised during 20X8 and 20X9. On 31 December 20X8, 257 of the eligible employees exercised their SARs in full and the remaining eligible employees exercised their SARs in full on 31 December 20X9.

The fair value and intrinsic value of each SAR was as follows:

Reporting date	FV per SAR	Intrinsic value per SAR
31 December 20X4	$5	
31 December 20X5	$7	
31 December 20X6	$8	
31 December 20X7	$9	
31 December 20X8	$11	$10
31 December 20X9	$12	$12

Required:

(a) **Calculate the amount to be recognised as a remuneration expense in the statement of profit or loss and other comprehensive income, together with the liability to be recognised in the statement of financial position for each of the four years to the vesting date.**

(b) **Calculate the amount to be recognised as a remuneration expense and reported as a liability in the financial statements for each of the two years ended 31 December 20X8 and 20X9.**

Hybrid transactions

If a share-based payment transaction gives the entity a choice over whether to settle in cash or by issuing equity instruments then:

- The scheme should be accounted for as a cash-settled share-based payment transaction if the entity has an obligation to settle in cash.
- If no obligation exists to settle in cash, then the entity accounts for the transaction as an equity-settled share-based payment scheme.

Some entities enter into share-based payment transactions that give the counterparty the choice of settling in cash or in equity instruments. In this case, the entity has granted a compound financial instrument that must be split accounted (part is recorded as debt and part is recorded as equity).

Group share-based payment transactions

A subsidiary might receive goods or services from employees or suppliers but the parent (or another entity in the group) might issue equity or cash settled share-based payments as consideration.

Under IFRS 2, the entity that receives goods or services in a share-based payment arrangement must account for those goods or services irrespective of which entity in the group settles the transaction, or whether the transaction is settled in shares or cash.

Disclosures

Entities should disclose information that enables users of the financial statements to understand the nature and extent of share-based payment arrangements that existed during the period. The main disclosures are as follows:

- a description of each type of share-based payment arrangement that existed at any time during the period
- the number and weighted average exercise prices of share options:
  - (i) outstanding at the beginning of the period
  - (ii) granted during the period
  - (iii) forfeited during the period
  - (iv) exercised during the period
  - (v) expired during the period
  - (vi) outstanding at the end of the period
  - (vii) exercisable at the end of the period.
- for share options exercised during the period, the weighted average share price at the date of exercise
- for share options outstanding at the end of the period, the range of exercise prices and weighted average remaining contractual life.

IFRS 2 also requires disclosure of information that enables users of the financial statements to understand how the fair value of the goods or services received, or the fair value of the equity instruments granted, during the period was determined.

Entities should also disclose information that enables users of the financial statements to understand the effect of share-based payment transactions on the entity's profit or loss for the period and on its financial position, that is:

- the total expense recognised for the period arising from share-based payment transactions
- for liabilities arising from share-based payment transactions:
  - – the total carrying amount at the end of the period
  - – the total intrinsic value at the end of the period of liabilities for which the counterparty's right to cash or other assets had vested by the end of the period.

4 Chapter summary

Share-based payment
- What it is
- Types of transaction
- Basic principles

Equity-settled share-based payment transactions
- Measurement
- Allocating the expense to reporting periods

Cash-settled share-based payment transactions
- Measurement
- Accounting treatment

Modifications, cancellations and settlements
- Accounting treatment of modifications
- Accounting treatment of cancellations and settlements

Test your understanding answers

Test your understanding 1 – Equity-settled share-based

The total expense recognised is based on the fair value of the share options granted at the grant date (1 January 20X1). The entity recognises the remuneration expense as the employees' services are received during the three-year vesting period.

Year ended 31 December 20X1

At 31 December 20X1, the entity must estimate the number of options expected to vest by predicting how many employees will remain in employment until the vesting date. It believes that 80% of the employees will stay for the full three years and therefore calculates an expense based on this assumption:

(500 employees × 80%) × 100 options × \$15 FV × 1/3 = \$200,000

Therefore, an expense is recognised for \$200,000 together with a corresponding increase in equity.

Year ended 31 December 20X2

The estimate of the number of employees staying for the full three years is revised at each year end. At 31 December 20X2, it is estimated that 85% of the 500 employees will stay for the full three years. The calculation of the share based payment expense is therefore as follows:

	$
(500 employees × 85%) × 100 options × \$15 FV × 2/3	425,000
Less previously recognised expense	(200,000)
Expense in year ended 31 December 20X2	225,000

Equity will be increased by \$225,000 to \$425,000 (\$200,000 + \$225,000).

Year ended 31 December 20X3

A total of 50 (20 + 20+ 10) employees left during the vesting period. The expense recognised in the final year of the scheme is as follows:

	$
(500 – 50 employees) × 100 options × $15 FV × 3/3	675,000
Less previously recognised expense	(425,000)
Expense in year ended 31 December 20X3	250,000

The financial statements will include the following amounts:

Statement of profit or loss	20X1	20X2	20X3
	$	$	$
Staff costs	200,000	225,000	250,000

Statement of financial position	20X1	20X2	20X3
	$	$	$
Other components of equity	200,000	425,000	675,000

Test your understanding 2 – Market based conditions

The expense recognised is based on the fair value of the options at the grant date. This should be spread over the vesting period.

There are two types of conditions attached to the share based payment scheme:

- A service condition (employees must complete a minimum service period)
- A market based performance condition (the share price must be $5 at 31 December 20X2).

Although it looks unlikely that the share price target will be hit, this condition has already been factored into the fair value of the options at the grant date. Therefore, this condition can be ignored when determining the charge to the statement of profit or loss.

The expense to be recognised should therefore be based on how many employees are expected to satisfy the service condition only. The calculation is as follows:

(100 employees – 10 – 10) × 50 options × $1 FV × 1/2 = $2,000.

The entry to recognise this is:

Dr Profit or loss	$2,000
Cr Equity	$2,000

Test your understanding 3 – Blueberry

Rep. date	**Calculation of equity**	**Equity**	**Expense**	**Note**
		$000	$000	
31/12/X4	(174 × 200 × $10) × 1/3	116	116	1
31/12/X5	(182 × 300 × $10) × 2/3	364	248	2
31/12/X6	(184 × 300 × $10) × 3/3	552	188	3

Notes:

(1) At 31/12/X4 a total of 26 employees (8 + 18) are expected to leave by the vesting date meaning that 174 are expected to remain. Blueberry estimates that average annual growth in sales volume will be 14%. Consequently, it is estimated that eligible employees would each receive 200 share options at the vesting date

(2) At 31/12/X5, a total of 18 employees (8 + 6 + 4) are expected to leave by the vesting date meaning that 182 are expected to remain. Blueberry estimates that the average growth in sales volume will be 16%. Consequently, it is estimated that eligible employees will each receive 300 share options at the vesting date.

(3) A t 31/12/X6, it is known that total of 16 employees (8 + 6 + 2) have left at some point during the vesting period, leaving 184 eligible employees. As average annual growth in sales volume over the vesting period was 16%, eligible employees are entitled to 300 share options each.

Test your understanding 4 – Beginner

Year		**Equity**	**Expense**
		$000	$000
Year 1	(7m × $0.3 × 1/3)	700	700
Year 2	(8m × $0.3 × 2/3)	1,600	900
Year 3	(9m × $0.3)	2,700	1,100

Note: Equity-settled share-based payments are measured using the fair value of the instrument at the grant date (the start of year one).

(i) All eligible directors exercised their options:

The entity will post the following entry:

Dr Cash (9m × $2)	$18.0m
Dr Equity reserve	$2.7m
Cr Share capital (9m × $1)	$9.0m
Cr Share premium (bal. fig.)	$11.7m

(ii) No options are exercised

The amount recognised in equity ($2.7m) remains. The entity can choose to transfer this to retained earnings.

Test your understanding 5 – Modifications

The repricing means that the total fair value of the arrangement has increased and this will benefit the employees. This in turn means that the entity must account for an increased remuneration expense. The increased cost is based upon the difference in the fair value of the option, immediately before and after the repricing. Under the original arrangement, the fair value of the option at the date of repricing was $10, which increased to $15 following the repricing of the options, for each share estimated to vest. The additional cost is recognised over the remainder of the vesting period (years two and three).

The amounts recognised in the financial statements for each of the three years are as follows:

	Equity	**Expense**
	$	$
Year one original		
(500 – 50 – 60) × 100 × $20 × 1/3	260,000	260,000
Year two original		
(500 – 50 – 30 – 30) × 100 × $20 × 2/3	520,000	260,000
Incremental		
(500 – 50 – 30 – 30) × 100 × $5 × 1/2	97,500	97,500
	617,500	357,500
Year three original		
(500 – 50 – 30 – 30) × 100 × $20	780,000	260,000
Incremental		
(500 – 50 – 30 – 30) × 100 × $5	195,000	97,500
	975,000	357,500

Test your understanding 6 – Cancellations and settlements

The share option scheme has been cancelled. This means that all the expense not yet charged through profit or loss must now be recognised in the year ended 31 December 20X1:

	$
Total expense (5 directors × 1,000 options × $8)	40,000
Less expense recognised in year ended 31 December 20X0 (5 directors × 1,000 options × $8 × 1/3)	(13,333)
Expense to be recognised	26,667

To recognise the remaining expense, the following entry must be posted:

Dr Profit or loss	$26,667
Cr Equity	$26,667

Any payment made in compensation for the cancellation that is up to the fair value of the options is recognised as a deduction to equity. Any payment in excess of the fair value is recognised as an expense.

The compensation paid to the director for each option exceeded the fair value by $1 ($10 – $9). Therefore, an expense of $1 per option should be recognised in profit or loss.

The following accounting entry is required:

Dr Equity (5 directors × 1,000 options × $9)	$45,000
Dr Profit or loss (5 directors × 1,000 options × $1)	$5,000
Cr Cash (5 directors × 1,000 options × $10)	$50,000

Test your understanding 7 – Growler

(a) The liability is remeasured at each reporting date, based upon the current information available relating to known and expected leavers, together with the fair value of the SAR at each date. The remuneration expense recognised is the movement in the liability from one reporting date to the next as summarised below:

Rep. date	Workings	Liability (SFP)	Expense (P/L)
		$	$
31/12/X4	(500 – 20 – 20 – 20 – 20) × 200 × $5 × 1/4	105,000	105,000
31/12/X5	(500 – 20 – 24 – 44) × 200 × $7 × 2/4	288,400	183,400
31/12/X6	(500 – 20 – 24 – 18 – 20) × 200 × $8 × 3/4	501,600	213,200
31/12/X7	(500 – 20 – 24 – 18 – 10) × 200 × $9 × 4/4	770,400	268,800

(b) The number of employees eligible for a cash payment is 428 (500 – 20 – 24 – 18 – 10). Of these, 257 exercise their SARs at 31/12/X8 and the remaining 171 exercise their SARs at 31/12/X9.

The liability is measured at each reporting date, based upon the current information available at that date, together with the fair value of each SAR at that date. Any SARs exercised are reflected at their intrinsic value at the date of exercise.

Year ended 31/12/X8

	$
Liability b/fwd	770,400
Cash payment (257 × 200 × $10)	(514,000)
Profit or loss (bal. fig)	119,800
Liability c/fwd (171 × 200 × $11)	376,200

Year ended 31/12/X9

	$
Liability b/fwd	376,200
Cash payment (171 × 200 × $12)	(410,400)
Profit or loss (bal. fig)	34,200
Liability c/fwd	nil

chapter

12

Financial instruments

Chapter learning objectives

Upon completion of this chapter you will be able to:

- apply and discuss the recognition and derecognition of financial assets or financial liabilities
- apply and discuss the classification of financial assets or financial liabilities and their measurement
- apply and discuss the treatment of gains and losses arising on financial assets and financial liabilities
- apply and discuss the treatment of impairment of financial assets
- account for derivative financial instruments, and simple embedded derivatives
- outline the principle of hedge accounting, and account for fair value hedges and cash flow hedges including hedge effectiveness.

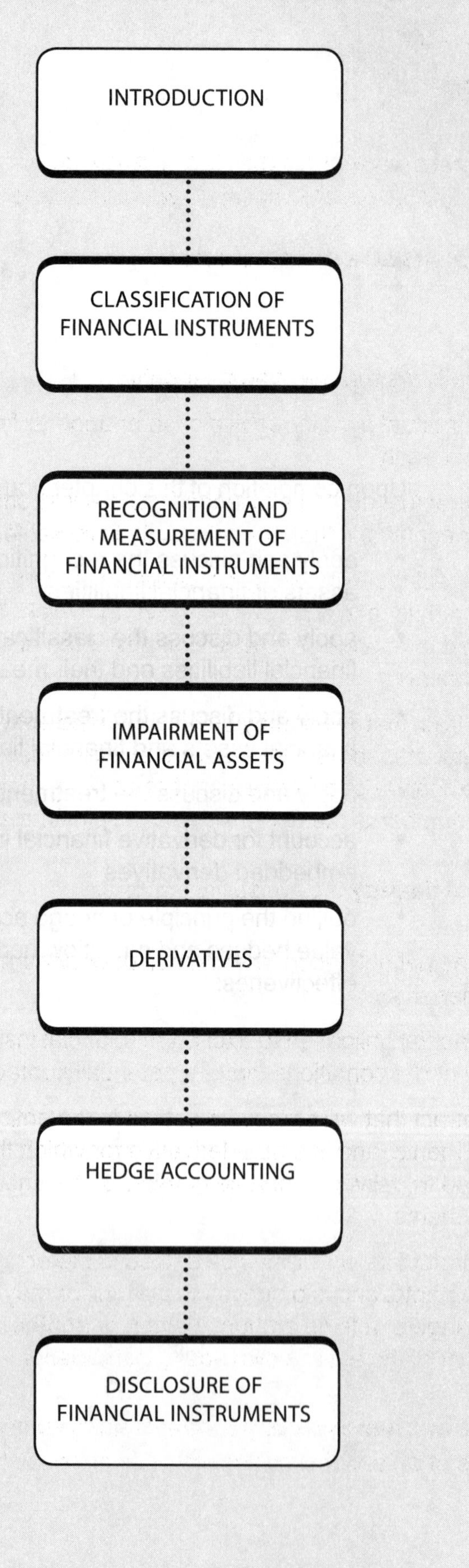
INTRODUCTION
CLASSIFICATION OF FINANCIAL INSTRUMENTS
RECOGNITION AND MEASUREMENT OF FINANCIAL INSTRUMENTS
IMPAIRMENT OF FINANCIAL ASSETS
DERIVATIVES
HEDGE ACCOUNTING
DISCLOSURE OF FINANCIAL INSTRUMENTS

1 Introduction

Definitions

A **financial instrument** is any contract that gives rise to a financial asset of one entity and a financial liability or equity instrument of another entity.

A **financial asset** is any asset that is:

- cash
- an equity instrument of another entity
- a contractual right to receive cash or another financial asset from another entity
- a contractual right to exchange financial instruments with another entity under conditions that are potentially favourable
- a contract that will or may be settled in the entity's own equity instruments, and is a non-derivative for which the entity is or may be obliged to receive a variable number of the entity's own equity instruments
- a contract that will or may be settled in the entity's own equity instruments, and is a derivative that will or may be settled other than by the exchange of a fixed amount of cash or another financial asset for a fixed number of the entity's own equity instruments.

A **financial liability** is any liability that is a:

- contractual obligation to deliver cash or another financial asset to another entity
- contractual obligation to exchange financial instruments with another entity under conditions that are potentially unfavourable
- a contract that will or may be settled in the entity's own equity instruments, and is a non-derivative for which the entity is or may be obliged to deliver a variable number of the entity's own equity instruments
- a contract that will or may be settled in the entity's own equity instruments, and is a derivative that will or may be settled other than by exchange of a fixed amount of cash or another financial asset for a fixed number of the entity's own equity instruments.

An **equity instrument** is any contract that evidences a residual interest in the assets of an entity after deducting all of its liabilities.

Reporting standards

There are four reporting standards that deal with financial instruments:

- IAS 32 Financial Instruments: Presentation
- IAS 39 Financial Instruments: Recognition and Measurement
- IFRS 7 Financial Instruments: Disclosures
- IFRS 9 Financial Instruments

IAS 32 deals with the classification of financial instruments and their presentation in financial statements.

Most of IAS 39 has been replaced by IFRS 9, but parts of IAS 39 dealing with impairments, derivatives and hedge accounting continue to apply.

IFRS 7 deals with the disclosure of financial instruments in financial statements.

IFRS 9 is concerned with the initial and subsequent measurement of financial instruments.

First time adoption of IFRS 9

IFRS 9 is effective for accounting periods commencing on or after 2015, although earlier adoption is permitted. Where early adoption is taken up, to the extent that IFRS 9 has not yet been fully updated, the provisions of the earlier standards continue to apply. IAS 39 will eventually be withdrawn following further additions to IFRS 9 dealing with impairment, derivatives and hedge accounting.

Entities applying IFRS 9 for the first time therefore have a choice as to when to apply the standard as follows:

- For accounting periods commencing before 1 January 2015:
  - IAS 39 can continue to be applied in full, or
  - IFRS 9 (2009) dealing only with financial assets can be applied, together with the remaining provisions of IAS 39 not yet replaced, or
  - IFRS 9 (2010) dealing with both financial assets and financial liabilities can be applied, together with the remaining provisions of IAS 39 not yet replaced.
- For accounting periods commencing on or after 1 January 2015, IFRS 9 must be applied in full, together with any remaining provisions of IAS 39 not yet replaced.

It is therefore possible that the provisions of IFRS 9 relating to financial assets may be applied in one accounting period, with application relating to financial liabilities applied in a subsequent accounting period.

2 Classification of financial liabilities and equity

IAS 32 provides rules on classifying financial instruments.

The issuer of a financial instrument must classify it as a financial liability, financial asset or equity instrument on initial recognition according to its substance. Financial assets are considered later in this chapter.

Financial liabilities

The instrument will be classified as a financial liability if the issuer has:

(a) A contractual obligation:

- to deliver cash (or another financial asset) to the holder
- to exchange financial instruments on potentially unfavourable terms.

(b) A contract that will or may be settled in the entity's own equity instruments and is:

- a non-derivative for which the entity is or may be obliged to deliver a variable number of the entity's own equity instruments, or
- a derivative that will or may be settled other than by the exchange of a fixed amount of cash or another financial asset for a fixed number of the entity's own equity instruments.

A redeemable preference share will be classified as a liability, because the issuer has the contractual obligation to deliver cash to the holders on the redemption date.

Equity instruments

A financial instrument is only an equity instrument if both of the following conditions are met:

(a) The instrument includes no contractual obligation to deliver cash or another financial asset to another entity, or to exchange financial assets or liabilities with another entity under conditions that are potentially unfavourable to the issuer.

(b) If the instrument will or may be settled in the issuer's own equity instruments, it is either:

   (i) a non-derivative that includes no contractual obligation for the issuer to deliver a variable number of its own equity instruments

   (ii) a derivative that will be settled only by the issuer exchanging a fixed amount of cash or another financial asset for a fixed number of its own equity shares.

Test your understanding 1 – Liabilities or equity?

Coasters wishes to purchase a new ride for their 'Animation Galaxy' theme park. In order to fund this, they have had to obtain extra funding. On 30 September 20X3, Coasters issued the following dividend-free preference shares:

- 1,000,000 preference shares for $3 each. Coasters will redeem the preference shares in three year's time by issuing ordinary shares worth $3 million. The exact number of ordinary shares issuable will be based on their fair value on 30 September 20X6.
- 2,000,000 preference shares for $2.80 each. The preference shares will be redeemed in two year's time by issuing 3,000,000 ordinary shares.

Required:

Discuss whether these financial instruments should be classified as financial liabilities or equity in the financial statements of Coasters for the year ended 30 September 20X3.

Classification of rights issues

Rights issues denominated in a currency other than the functional currency of the issuer were previously accounted for as derivative liabilities. However, provided certain conditions are met, such rights issues are now classified as equity regardless of the currency in which the exercise price is denominated.

Interest, dividends, losses and gains

The accounting treatment of interest, dividends, losses and gains relating to a financial instrument follows the treatment of the instrument itself.

- Dividends paid in respect of preference shares classified as a liability will be charged as a finance expense through profit or loss

- Dividends paid on shares classified as equity will be reported in the statement of changes in equity.

Offsetting a financial asset and a financial liability

IAS 32 states that a financial asset and a financial liability may only be offset in very limited circumstances. The net amount may only be reported when the entity:

- has a legally enforceable right to set off the amounts
- intends either to settle on a net basis, or to realise the asset and settle the liability simultaneously.

3 Recognition and measurement of financial liabilities

Initial recognition of financial liabilities

At initial recognition, financial liabilities are measured at fair value.

- If the financial liability will be held at fair value through profit or loss, transaction costs should be expensed to the statement of profit or loss
- If the financial liability will not be held at fair value through profit or loss, transaction costs should be deducted from its carrying value.

Subsequent measurement of financial liabilities

The subsequent treatment of a financial liability is that they can be measured at either:

- fair value through profit or loss
- amortised cost.

Financial liabilities incurred for trading, as well as derivatives, are measured at fair value through profit or loss. These liabilities are remeasured to fair value at each reporting date with gains or losses recorded in the statement of profit or loss.

Most other financial liabilities, such as borrowings, are subsequently measured at amortised cost using the effective interest method. This is considered in more detail below.

It is possible to opt to measure a liability ('FV option') at fair value when it would normally be measured at amortised cost. This would be applicable, for example, to eliminate or reduce an accounting mismatch. When this applies, the fair value of the liability is established by discounting the outstanding cashflows to their present value using the current market rate of interest at each reporting date.

Amortised cost

Assume that a company takes out a $10m bank loan for 5 years. Interest of 10% is payable annually in arrears:

- The interest payable each year is $1m ($10m × 10%)
- The total cost of the loan is $5m ($1m × 5 years).

Now assume that a company issues a bond. This has a nominal value of $10m and interest of 10% is payable annually in arrears. However, the company issues the bond for only $9m and has agreed to repay $12m to the bond holders in five years time.

- Interest of $1m ($10m × 10%) will be paid per year
- Total interest payments over the life of the bond are $5m ($1m × 5 years).
- On top of this interest, the entity must pay back $3m more ($12m – $9m) than it received.

The total cost of the loan is actually $8m ($5m + $3m) and, in accordance with the accruals concept, this should be spread over the 5 year period. This is achieved by charging interest on the liability using the **effective rate of interest**. The effective rate is the internal rate of return of the investment.

Calculating amortised cost

The initial carrying amount of an 'other' financial liability is the net proceeds of issue.

A finance cost is charged on the liability using the effective rate of interest. This will increase the carrying value of the liability:

Dr Finance cost (P/L)
Cr Liability

The liability is reduced by any cash payments made during the year:

Dr Liability
Cr Cash

Amortised cost table

In the exam, assuming interest is paid in arrears, you might find the following working useful:

Opening liability	**Finance cost** (op.liability × effective %)	**Cash payments** (nom. value × coupon %)	**Closing Liability**
X	X	(X)	X

The finance cost is charged to the statement of profit or loss.

The cash payment will be part of 'interest paid' in the statement of cash flows.

The closing liability will appear on the statement of financial position.

Illustration 1 – Loan issues at a discount

On 1 January 20X1 James issued a loan note with a $50,000 nominal value. It was issued at a discount of 16% of nominal value. The costs of issue were $2,000. Interest of 5% of the nominal value is payable annually in arrears. The bond must be redeemed on 1 January 20X6 (after 5 years) at a premium of $4,611.

The effective rate of interest is 12% p.a.

Required:

How will this be reported in the financial statements of James over the period to redemption?

Solution

The liability will be initially recognised at the net proceeds received:

	$
Face value	50,000
Less: 16% discount	(8,000)
Less: Issue costs	(2,000)
Initial recognition of liability	40,000

The liability is then measured at amortised cost:

Year	Opening balance	Finance cost (Liability × 12%)	Cash payments ($50,000 × 5%)	Closing balance
	$	$	$	$
1	40,000	4,800	(2,500)	42,300
2	42,300	5,076	(2,500)	44,876
3	44,876	5,385	(2,500)	47,761
4	47,761	5,731	(2,500)	50,992
5	50,992	6,119	(2,500)	54,611
		27,111	(12,500)	
		To: Profit or loss	To: Statement of cash flows	To: SOFP

According to the above working, the total cost of the loan over the five year period is $27,111.

This is made up as follows:

	$	$
Repayments:		
Capital	50,000	
Premium	4,611	
		54,611
Interest ($50,000 × 5% × 5 years)		12,500
		67,111
Cash received		(40,000)
Total finance cost		27,111

The finance charge taken to profit or loss in each year is greater than the actual interest paid. This means that the value of the liability increases over the life of the instrument until it equals the redemption value at the end of its term.

In Years 1 to 4 the balance shown as a liability is less than the amount that will be payable on redemption. Therefore the full amount payable must be disclosed in the notes to the accounts.

Test your understanding 2 – Hoy

Hoy raised finance on 1 January 20X1 by the issue of a two-year 2% bond with a nominal value of $10,000. It was issued at a discount of 5% and is redeemable at a premium of $1,075. Issue costs can be ignored. The bond has an effective rate of interest of 10%.

Wiggins raised finance by issuing $20,000 6% four-year loan notes on 1 January 20X4. The loan notes were issued at a discount of 10%, and will be redeemed after four years at a premium of $1,015. The effective rate of interest is 12%. The issue costs were $1,000.

Cavendish raised finance by issuing zero coupon bonds at par on 1 January 20X5 with a nominal value of $10,000. The bonds will be redeemed after two years at a premium of $1,449. Issue costs can be ignored. The effective rate of interest is 7%.

The reporting date for each entity is 31 December.

Required:

Illustrate and explain how these financial instruments should be accounted for by each company.

Presentation of compound instruments

The issuer of a financial instrument must classify it as a financial liability or equity instrument on initial recognition according to its substance.

A **compound instrument** is a financial instrument that has characteristics of both equity and liabilities. An example would be debt that can be redeemed either in cash or in equity shares.

- IAS 32 requires compound financial instruments be split into two components:
  - a financial liability (the liability to repay the debt holder in cash)
  - an equity instrument (the option to convert into shares).
- These two elements must be shown separately in the financial statements.

The initial recognition of compound instruments

On initial recognition, a compound instrument must be split into a liability component and an equity component:

- The liability component is calculated as the present value of the repayments, discounted at a market rate of interest for a similar instrument without conversion rights
- The equity component is calculated as the difference between the cash proceeds from the issue of the instrument and the value of the liability component.

Further examples of compound instruments

Irredeemable preference shares would normally be regarded as equity as there is no obligation to repay or redeem them. However, if there is a requirement (i.e an obligation) to pay an annual dividend, then the irredeemable preference share would be regarded as a compound instrument which must be split between liability and equity elements. The annual compulsory dividend would be regarded as part of the liability element.

Illustration 2 – Compound instruments

On 1 January 20X1 Daniels issued a $50m three-year convertible bond at par.

- There were no issue costs.
- The coupon rate is 10%, payable annually in arrears on 31 December.
- The bond is redeemable at par on 1 January 20X4.
- Bondholders may opt for conversion in the form of shares. The terms of conversion are two 25-cent equity shares for every $1 owed to each bondholder on 1 January 20X4.
- Bonds issued by similar entities without any conversion rights currently bear interest at 15%.
- Assume that all bondholders opt for conversion in shares.

Required:

How will this be accounted for by Daniels?

Solution

On initial recognition, the proceeds received must be split between liabilities and equity.

- The liability component is calculated as the present value of the cash repayments at the market rate of interest for an instrument similar in all respects, except that it does not have conversion rights.
- The equity component is the difference between the proceeds of the issue and the liability component.

(1) **Splitting the proceeds**

The cash payments on the bond should be discounted to their present value using the interest rate for a bond without the conversion rights, i.e. 15%.

Date		**Cash flow**	**Discount factor (15%)**	**Present value**
		$000		$000
31-Dec-X1	Interest	5,000	1/1.15	4,347.8
31-Dec-X2	Interest	5,000	$1/1.15^2$	3,780.7
31-Dec-X3	Interest	5,000	$1/1.15^3$	3,287.6
1-Jan-X4	Principal	50,000	$1/1.15^3$	32,875.8
Liability component		A		44,291.9
Net proceeds of issue		B		50,000.0
Equity component		B – A		5,708.1

(2) **Measuring the liability at amortised cost**

The liability component is measured at amortised cost. The working below shows the finance costs recorded in the statement of profit or loss for each year as well as the carrying value of the liability in the statement of financial position at each reporting date.

	Opening bal.	**Finance cost (15%)**	**Payments**	**Closing bal.**
	$000	$000	$000	$000
20X1	44,291.9	6,643.8	(5,000)	45,935.7
20X2	45,935.7	6,890.4	(5,000)	47,826.1
20X3	47,826.1	7,173.9	(5,000)	50,000.0

(3) **The conversion of the bond**

The carrying amounts at 1 January 20X4 are:

	$000
Equity	5,708.1
Liability – bond	50,000.0
	55,708.1

The conversion terms are two 25-cent equity shares for every $1. Therefore 100m shares ($50m × 2), will be issued which have a nominal value of $25m. The remaining $30,708,100 should be classified as the share premium, also within equity. There is no remaining liability, because conversion has extinguished it.

The double entry is as follows:

	$000
Dr Other components of equity	5,708.1
Dr Liability	50,000.0
Cr Share capital	25,000.0
Cr Share premium	30,708.1

Test your understanding 3 – Craig

Craig issues a $100,000 4% three-year convertible loan on 1 January 20X6. The market rate of interest for a similar loan without conversion rights is 8%. The conversion terms are one equity share ($1 nominal value) for every $2 of debt. Conversion or redemption at par takes place on 31 December 20X8.

Required:

How should this be accounted for:

(a) **if all holders elect for the conversion?**

(b) **no holders elect for the conversion?**

'Fair value option' for financial liabilities

Accounting treatment

IFRS 9 permits entities to designate liabilities which would normally be measured at amortised cost as fair value through profit or loss (Fair value Option (FVO)). This designation, if made, must be made upon initial recognition and is irrevocable. Where an entity opts for this treatment, any change in fair value of the liability must be separated into two elements as follows:

- Changes in fair value due to own credit risk, which are taken to other comprehensive income, and
- Other changes in fair value, which are taken to profit or loss.

Own credit risk

Own credit risk can be considered to be similar to the risk of default on a liability – it is the risk that an entity will be unable to discharge a particular liability. It will not necessarily be the same for all liabilities incurred by an entity. For example, if an entity issues both secured and unsecured debt, the risk of default on the secured debt is likely to be low and relatively stable, particularly if the loan agreement includes performance and other criteria which protect the position of the lender. However, the risk of default attaching to the unsecured debt will certainly be higher and will almost certainly vary over time, due to trading performance and other factors, until the liability is settled.

One possible approach to identifying a fair value change due to own credit risk is to separate the interest rate charged on the financial liability into a benchmark rate (such as LIBOR) and an instrument-specific rate. Any change in the fair value of the liability which is not wholly due to the change in the benchmark rate must therefore be due to a change in own credit risk. The movement in fair value can then be split into the two separate elements.

'Fair value option' illustration

On 1 January 20X8 an entity issues a 7 year bond at par value of $300,000 and annual fixed coupon rate of 9%, which is also the market rate, when LIBOR is 6%. Therefore the instrument-specific element of IRR = (9% – 6%) is 3%.

At 31 December 20X8, LIBOR has moved to 5.5%, thus making the benchmark interest rate (5.5% + 3%) 8.5% (i.e. LIBOR plus the instrument-specific element of IRR). If the fair value of the liability is consistent with a market interest rate of, say, 8.3%, then any change in the fair value of the liability from the benchmark rate to fair value must be due to something other than the change in the benchmark rate – i.e. it must be due to the change in the liability's credit risk.

Required:

Calculate the amounts to be included within the financial statements for the year ended 31 December 20X8.

Solution

IFRS 9 requires that the change in the fair value of the liability as a result of own credit risk is taken to other comprehensive income. This can be quantified by calculating the present value (PV) of the liability using the benchmark rate and comparing it with the PV of the liability using the market rate as follows:

PV at benchmark rate 8.5%	**Cash flow**	**Factor**	**PV**
Year	$		$
1 – 6	27,000	4.5533	122,939
6	300,000	0.6129	183,870
			306,809

PV at market rate 8.3%	**Cash flow**	**Factor**	**PV**
Year	$		$
1 – 6	27,000	4.5811	123,690
6	300,000	0.6197	185,910
			309,600

Therefore, the change in the fair value of the liability which is not due to the change in the benchmark rate must be due to the change in the liability's credit risk.

	$
PV of liability at market rate of 8.3% (on SOFP at reporting date)	309,600
PV of liability at benchmark rate of 8.5%	306,809
Other comprehensive income	2,791

The only exception to this accounting treatment arises where the outcome would create or enlarge an accounting mismatch in profit or loss. If this is the case, then an entity will present all changes in fair value on that liability in profit or loss.

4 Recognition and measurement of financial assets

Initial recognition of financial assets

IFRS 9 deals with recognition and measurement of financial assets. An entity should recognise a financial asset on its statement of financial position when, and only when, the entity becomes party to the contractual provisions of the instrument.

Examples of this principle are as follows:

- A trading commitment to buy or sell goods is not recognised until one party has fulfilled its part of the contract. For example, a sales order will not be recognised as revenue and a receivable until the goods have been delivered.
- Forward contracts are accounted for as derivative financial assets and are recognised on the commitment date, not on the date when the item under contract is transferred from seller to buyer. (A forward contract is a commitment to buy or sell a financial instrument or a commodity at a later date.)
- Option contracts are accounted for as derivative financial assets and are recognised on the date the contract is entered into, not on the date when the item subject to the option is acquired if the option is exercised at a later date,

Initial measurement of financial assets

At initial recognition, all financial assets are measured at fair value. This should include transaction costs unless the financial asset will be measured at fair value through profit or loss.

Subsequent measurement of financial assets

The subsequent measurement of a financial asset depends on whether it is a debt instrument or an equity instrument.

Debt instruments

Debt instruments would normally be measured at fair value through profit or loss (FVTPL). However, an entity can choose to measure debt instruments at amortised cost if the following two tests are passed:

(1) **The business model test** establishes whether the entity holds the financial asset to collect the contractual cash flows or whether the objective is to sell the financial asset prior to maturity to realise changes in fair value.

   – If an entity plans to hold the asset, there will be no or few sales of such financial assets from a portfolio prior to their maturity date. If this is the case, the test is passed.

   – If disposals are more common, this may be a response to changes in the fair value of the assets. In this situation, the test is failed and the financial asset cannot be measured at amortised cost.

(2) **The contractual cash flow characteristics test** determines whether the contractual terms of the financial asset give rise to cash flows on specified dates that are solely payments of principal and interest based upon the principal amount outstanding. If this is not the case, the test is failed and the financial asset cannot be measured at amortised cost.

   – For example, the interest on convertible bonds is lower than market rate, because the holder of the bond gets the benefit of choosing to take redemption in the form of cash or shares. The contractual cash flows are therefore not solely payments of principal and interest on the principal amount outstanding. This means that an investment in convertible bonds would fail the test and be accounted for as fair value through profit or loss.

If both of the tests are passed, then a financial asset can be measured at amortised cost.

If an entity changes its business model for managing financial assets, it must reclassify its debt instruments as fair value through profit or loss. This is applied prospectively.

Even if the two tests are passed, it is still possible to designate a debt instrument as fair value through profit or loss if doing so eliminates or significantly reduces a measurement or recognition inconsistency (i.e. accounting mismatch) that would otherwise arise from measuring assets or liabilities or from recognising the gains or losses on them on different bases.

Test your understanding 4 – Paloma

Paloma purchased a new financial asset on 31 December 20X3. The asset is a bond that will mature in three years. Paloma buys debt investments with the intention of holding them to maturity although has, on occasion, sold some investments if cash flow deteriorated beyond acceptable levels. The bond pays a market rate of interest. The Finance Director is unsure as to whether this financial asset can be measured at amortised cost.

Required:

Advise the Finance Director on the accounting treatment of the bond.

Equity instruments

Equity instruments (such as an investment in the ordinary shares of another entity) are measured at either:

- fair value either through profit or loss, or
- fair value through other comprehensive income.

The normal expectation is that equity instruments will have the designation of fair value through profit or loss, with the price paid to acquire the financial asset (excluding transaction costs) initially regarded as fair value.

It is possible to designate an equity instrument as fair value through other comprehensive income, provided that the following conditions are complied with:

- the equity instrument must not be held for trading, and
- there must have been an irrevocable choice for this designation upon initial recognition of the asset.

Changes in the fair value of a financial asset held at fair value through other comprehensive income will be recognised in other comprehensive income. Dividends must be taken to profit or loss, unless they represent a recovery of part of the investment.

Overview of recognition and measurement of financial assets

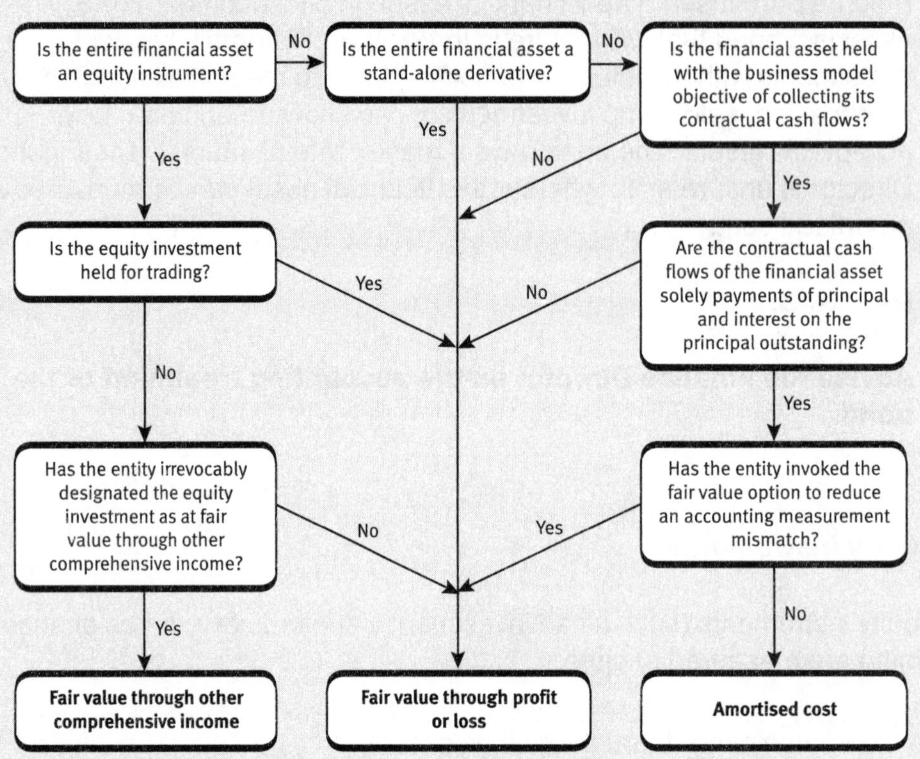

Test your understanding 5 – Ashes' financial assets

Ashes holds the following financial assets:

(1) Trade receivables

(2) Investments in ordinary shares that are held for short-term speculation

(3) Investments in ordinary shares that, from the purchase date, are intended to be held for the long term

Required:

How should Ashes classify and account for its financial assets?

5 Derecognition of financial instruments

A **financial asset** should be derecognised if one of the following has occurred:

- the contractual rights to the cash flows of the financial asset have expired.
  - For example, an option held by the entity may have lapsed and become worthless.
- the financial asset has been sold and the transfer qualifies for derecognition because substantially all the risks and rewards of ownership have been transferred from the seller to the buyer.

The analysis of where the risks and rewards of ownership lie after a transaction is critical. If an entity has retained substantially all of the risks and rewards of a financial asset then it should not be derecognised, even if it has been legally 'sold' to another entity.

A **financial liability** should be derecognised when, and only when, the obligation specified in the contract is discharged, cancelled or has expired.

On derecognition, the difference between the carrying amount of the asset or liability and the amount received or paid for it should be recognised in profit or loss for the period.

For financial assets held at fair value through other comprehensive income, the cumulative gains and losses recognised in other comprehensive income are **not** recycled to profit or loss on disposal.

Test your understanding 6 – Ming

Ming has two receivables that it has factored to a bank in return for immediate cash proceeds. Both receivables are due from long standing customers who are expected to pay in full and on time. Ming had agreed a three-month credit period with both customers.

The first receivable is for $200,000. In return for assigning the receivable, Ming has received $180,000 from the factor. Under the terms of the factoring arrangement, Ming will not have to repay this money, even if the customer does not settle the debt (the factoring arrangement is said to be 'without recourse').

The second receivable is for $100,000. In return for assigning the receivable, Ming has received $70,000 from the factor. The terms of this factoring arrangement state that Ming will receive a further $5,000 if the customer settles the account on time.

If the customer does not settle the account in accordance with the agreed terms then the receivable will be reassigned back to Ming who will then be obliged to refund the factor with the original $70,000 (this factoring arrangement is said to be 'with recourse').

Required:

Discuss the accounting treatment of the two factoring arrangements.

Test your understanding 7 – Case

Case holds equity investments at fair value through profit or loss. Due to short-term cash flow shortages, Case sold some equity investments for $5 million when the carrying value was $4m. The terms of the disposal state that Case has the right to repurchase the shares at any point over the next two years at their fair value on the repurchase date. Case has not derecognised the investment because its directors believe that a repurchase is highly likely.

Required:

Advise the directors of Case as to the acceptability of the above accounting treatment.

Test your understanding 8 – Jones

Jones bought an investment for $40 million plus associated transaction costs of $1 million. The asset was designated upon initial recognition as fair value through other comprehensive income. At the reporting date the fair value of the financial asset had risen to $60 million. Shortly after the reporting date the financial asset was sold for $70 million.

Required:

(a) **How should the investment be accounted for?**

(b) **How would the answer have been different if the investment had been classified as at fair value through profit and loss?**

6 Impairment of financial assets

The impairment of financial assets is governed by IAS 39. This standard specifies the following:

- Financial assets that are measured at fair value through profit or loss are not subject to an impairment review. Remeasurement of fair value at each reporting date will automatically take account of any impairment.
- Financial assets measured at fair value through other comprehensive income are not subject to an impairment review. Any changes in fair value, including those which may relate to impairment, are recognised in other comprehensive income.
- Financial assets measured at amortised cost must be assessed at each reporting date as to whether there is objective evidence of impairment. For instance, an event may have occurred that has had a negative impact on the expected future cash flows of the asset.
  - The event causing the negative impact must have already happened. An event causing an impairment in the future must not be anticipated.

Test your understanding 9 – Straw

On 30 April 20X4, Straw loaned $1 million to a key supplier. The loan was at a market rate of interest. Straw has made loans to other suppliers in the past and has, on average, written off 20% of the amounts that it was owed. Based on these past experiences, Straw believes that it should immediately write this new loan asset down to $800,000.

Required:

Discuss the correct accounting treatment of the above transaction in the financial statements of Straw for the year ended 30 April 20X4.

Impairment review of financial assets measured at amortised cost

Examples of objective evidence of impairment at the reporting date include:

- significant financial difficulty of the borrower
- the failure of the borrower to make interest payments on the due date.

If there is objective evidence of an impairment at the reporting date then an impairment review must be performed.

An impairment loss on a financial asset measured at amortised cost is calculated as follows:

	$
Carrying value of the asset per the financial statements	X
Less:	
PV of the estimated future cash flows discounted at the original effective interest rate	(X)
Impairment loss	X

Any impairment loss is recognised as an expense in profit or loss.

- If the recoverable amount exceeds the carrying value, the asset is not impaired.

Illustration 3 – Impairment of financial assets

On 1 February 20X6, Eve makes a four-year loan of $10,000 to Fern. The coupon rate on the loan is 6%, the same as the effective rate of interest. Interest is received at the end of each year.

On 1 February 20X9, Fern tells Eve that it is in financial difficulties. At this time the current market interest rate is 8%.

Eve estimates that it will receive no more interest from Fern. It also estimates that only $6,000 of the capital will be repaid on the redemption date.

Required:

How should this be accounted for?

Solution

Because the coupon and the effective interest rate are the same, the carrying amount of the principal will remain constant at $10,000.

The recoverable amount of the asset can be calculated as the present value of the future cash flows. The discount rate should be the original effective rate (6%).

The recoverable amount of the financial asset is therefore $5,660 ($6,000 × 1/1.06).

The asset must be written down from \$10,000 to \$5,660 and an impairment loss of \$4,340 (\$10,000 – \$5,660) is charged as an expense to the statement of profit or loss.

The asset will continue to be accounted for using amortised cost, based on the revised carrying amount of the loan. In the last year of the loan, the interest income of \$340 (5,660 × 6%) will be recognised in profit or loss.

Reversals of impairment losses

The reversal of an impairment loss is only permitted as a result of an event occurring after the impairment loss has been recognised.

- An example would be the credit rating of a customer being revised upwards by a credit rating agency.

Reversal of impairment losses in respect of financial assets measured at amortised cost are recognised in profit or loss.

7 Derivatives

Definitions

A derivative is a financial instrument with the following characteristics:

(a) Its value changes in response to the change in a specified interest rate, security price, commodity price, foreign exchange rate, index of prices or rates, a credit rating or credit index or similar variable (called the 'underlying')

(b) It requires little or no initial net investment relative to other types of contract that have a similar response to changes in market conditions

(c) It is settled at a future date.

The problems of derivatives

- Derivatives were originally designed to hedge against fluctuations in agricultural commodity prices on the Chicago Stock Exchange. A speculator would pay a small amount (say $100) now for the contractual obligation to buy a thousand units of wheat in three months' time for $10,000. If in three months time one thousand units of wheat costs $11,000, then the speculator would make a profit of $900 (11,000 – 100 – 10,000). This would be a 900% return on the original investment over 3 months, which is one of the attractions of derivatives to speculators. But if the price had dropped to $9,000, then the trader would have made a loss of $1,100 (100 + 1,000) despite the initial investment only having been $100.
- This shows that losses on derivatives can be far greater than their historical cost. Therefore, shareholders need to be given additional information about derivatives in order to assess the entity's exposure to loss.
- It is important that derivatives are recognised and disclosed in the financial statements as they have very little initial outlay but can expose the entity to significant gains and losses.

Typical derivatives

Derivatives include the following types of contracts:

Forward contracts

- The holder of a forward contract is obliged to buy or sell a defined amount of a specific underlying asset, at a specified price at a specified future date.
- For example, a forward contract for foreign currency might require £100,000 to be exchanged for $150,000 in three months time. Both parties to the contract have both a financial asset and a financial liability. For example, one party has the right to receive $150,000 and the obligation to pay £100,000.
- Forward currency contracts may be used to minimise the risk on amounts receivable or payable in foreign currencies.

Forward rate agreements

- Forward rate agreements can be used to fix the interest charge on a floating rate loan.

- For example, an entity has a $1m floating rate loan, and the current rate of interest is 7%. The rates are reset to the market rate every six months, and the entity cannot afford to pay more than 9% interest. The entity enters into a six-month forward rate agreement (with, say, a bank) at 9% on $1m. If the market rates go up to 10%, then the bank will pay them $5,000 (1% of $1m for 6 months) which in effect reduces their finance cost to 9%. If the rates only go up to 8% then the entity pays the bank $5,000. The forward rate agreement effectively fixes the interest rate payable at 9% for the period.

Futures contracts

- Futures contracts oblige the holder to buy or sell a standard quantity of a specific underlying item at a specified future date.
- Futures contracts are very similar to forward contracts. The difference is that futures contracts have standard terms and are traded on a financial exchange, whereas forward contracts are tailor-made and are not traded on a financial exchange. Also, whilst forward contracts will always be settled, a futures contract will rarely be held to maturity.

Swaps

- Two parties agree to exchange periodic payments at specified intervals over a specified time period.
- For example, in an interest rate swap, the parties may agree to exchange fixed and floating rate interest payments calculated by reference to a notional principal amount.
- This enables companies to keep a balance between their fixed and floating rate interest payments without having to change the underlying loans.

Options

- These give the holder the right, but not the obligation, to buy or sell a specific underlying asset on or before a specified future date.

Measurement of derivatives

- On initial recognition, derivatives should be measured at fair value. Transaction costs are expensed to the statement of profit or loss.
- At the reporting date, derivatives are remeasured to fair value. Movements in fair value are recognised in profit or loss.

Accounting for derivatives

Entity A has a reporting date of 30 September. It enters into an option on 1 June 20X5, to purchase 10,000 shares in another entity on 1 November 20X5 for $10 per share. The purchase price of each option is $1. This is recorded as follows:

Debit	Option (10,000 × $1)	$10,000
Credit	Cash	$10,000

By 30 September the fair value of each option has increased to $1.30. This increase is recorded as follows:

Debit	Option (10,000 × ($1.30 – 1))	$3,000
Credit	Profit or loss	$3,000

On 1 November, the fair value per option increases to $1.50. The share price on the same date is $11.50. A exercises the option on 1 November and the shares are classified at fair value through profit or loss. Financial assets are recognised at their fair value so the shares are initially measured at $115,000 (10,000 × $11.50):

Debit	Investment in shares (at fair value)	$115,000
Credit	Cash (10,000 × $10)	$100,000
Credit	Option ($10,000 + $3,000)	$13,000
Credit	Profit or loss (gain on option)	$2,000

Test your understanding 10 – Hoggard

Hoggard buys 100 options on 1 January 20X6 for $5 per option. Each option gives Hoggard the right to buy a share in Rowling on 31 December 20X6 for $10 per share.

Required:

How should this be accounted for, given the following outcomes?

(a) **The options are sold on 1 July 20X6 for $15 each.**

(b) **On 31 December 20X6, Rowling's share price is $8 and Hoggard lets the option lapse unexercised.**

(c) **The option is exercised on 31 December when Rowling's share price is $25. The shares are classified as held for trading.**

Further points on derivatives

The need for a financial reporting standard

Many derivatives have no cost and may not appear in a traditional historical cost statement of financial position, even if they represent substantial assets or liabilities of the entity. However, their values change rapidly, exposing holders to the risk of large profits or losses.

Consequently, there is great debate regarding the accounting for derivatives, together with ensuring that there are adequate disclosures for users to fully understand and appreciate their impact upon the reported financial performance and position of an entity.

Measurement of derivatives

As already noted, derivatives should initially be measured at fair value in the statement of financial position (usually cost). Subsequent measurement will involve the derivative being remeasured to fair value with gains and losses recorded through profit or loss.

The arguments for using fair value for these items rather than historical cost are as follows.

(a) Sometimes these items have no historical cost, and so they are ignored by conventional accounting.

(b) Remeasuring to fair value reports gains and losses as they arise, not just when they are realised in cash. This gives a better and more objective indication of an entity's performance.

(c) Comparability is enhanced. All derivatives will be carried at their fair value at the reporting date, rather than at out-of-date historical costs. Different entities will also be using the same up-to-date fair values.

(d) Fair values have more predictive value.

(e) Derivatives are traded on active markets and are therefore easy to value.

However, some people still disagree with using fair values. Some of the arguments against fair values are as follows.

(a) Reporting changes in fair value will result in volatile profits.

(b) Some of the changes in fair value might never be realised. Therefore, the profit or loss will include losses that never arise and profits that are never realised.

(c) It may not always be possible to value all derivatives reliably.

Embedded derivatives

An embedded derivative is a component of a hybrid contract that also includes a non-derivative host, with the effect that some of the cash flows of the combined instrument vary in a way similar to a stand-alone derivative.

With regards to the accounting treatment of an embedded derivative, if the host contract is within the scope of IFRS 9 then the entire contract must be classified and measured in accordance with that standard.

If the host contract is not within the scope of IFRS 9 (i.e. it is not a financial asset or liability), then the embedded derivative can be separated out and measured at fair value through profit or loss if:

(i) the economic risks and characteristics of the embedded derivative are not closely related to those of the host contract

(ii) a separate instrument with the same terms as the embedded derivative would meet the definition of a derivative, and

(iii) the entire instrument is not measured at fair value with changes in fair value recognised in profit or loss.

Because of the complexity involved in splitting out and measuring an embedded derivative, IFRS 9 permits a hybrid contract where the host element is outside the scope of IFRS 9 to be measured at fair value through profit or loss in its entirety.

Therefore, for the vast majority of embedded derivatives, the whole contract will simply be measured at fair value through profit or loss.

Embedded derivatives: an example

An entity has an investment in a convertible bond, which can be converted into a fixed number of equity shares at a specified future date. The bond is a non-derivative host contract and the option to convert to shares is therefore a derivative element.

The host contract, the bond, is a financial liability and so is within the scope of IFRS 9. This means that the rules of IFRS 9 must be applied to the entire contract.

The bond would fail the contractual cash flow characteristics test and therefore the entire contract should be measured at fair value through profit or loss.

8 Hedge accounting

The need for hedge accounting

An entity has inventories of gold that cost $8m and whose value has increased to $10m. The entity is worried that the fair value of this inventory will fall, so it enters into a futures contract on 1 October 20X1 to sell the inventory for $10m in 6 months time.

By the reporting date, the fair value of the inventory had fallen by $1m to $9m. There was a $1m increase in the fair value of the derivative.

In accordance with IFRS 9, the $1m gain on the derivative will be recognised through profit or loss:

Dr Derivative	$1m
Cr Profit or loss	$1m

In accordance with IAS 2, the $1m decline in the inventory's fair value will not be recognised (inventories are measured at the lower of cost ($8m) and NRV ($9m, assuming no selling costs).

The derivative has created volatility in profit or loss. However, if the entity had chosen to apply hedge accounting, this volatility would have been eliminated. This section of the text will outline the criteria for, and accounting treatment of, hedge accounting in more detail.

Definitions

Hedge accounting is a method of managing risk by designating one or more hedging instruments so that their change in fair value is offset, in whole or in part, by the change in fair value or cash flows of a hedged item.

A **hedged item** is an asset or liability that exposes the entity to risks of changes in fair value or future cash flows (and is designated as being hedged). There are 3 types of hedged item:

- A recognised asset or liability
- An unrecognised firm commitment – a binding agreement for the exchange of a specified quantity of resources at a specified price on a specified future date or dates
- A highly probable forecast transaction – an uncommitted but anticipated future transaction.

A **hedging instrument** is a designated derivative whose fair value or cash flows are expected to offset changes in fair value or future cash flows of the hedged item.

Hedge accounting under IAS 39

As at 31 August 2013, IFRS 9 did not contain requirements relating to hedge accounting. Accordingly, the requirements specified in IAS 39 continue to apply in the P2 exam.

IAS 39 identifies three types of hedge. Two of these are within the P2 syllabus:

(1) **Fair value hedge**: a hedge of the exposure to changes in fair value of a recognised asset or liability or an unrecognised firm commitment that is attributable to a particular risk and could affect profit or loss.

(2) **Cash flow hedge**: a hedge of the exposure to variability in cash flows that is attributable to a particular risk associated with a recognised asset or liability or a highly probable forecast transaction and that could affect profit or loss.

Criteria for hedge accounting

Under IAS 39, hedge accounting rules can only be applied if the hedging relationship meets the following criteria:

(1) At the inception of the hedge there must be formal documentation identifying the hedged item and the hedging instrument

(2) The hedge is expected to be highly effective

(3) The effectiveness of the hedge can be measured reliably (i.e. the fair value/cash flows of the item and the instrument can be measured reliably)

(4) The hedge has been assessed on an on-going basis and is determined to have been effective

(5) If the hedged item is a foreast transaction, then the transaction must be highly probable.

Hedge effectiveness

In order to hedge account, the hedge must be highly effective. IAS 39 describes effectiveness as the degree to which the changes in fair value or cash flows of the hedged item are offset by changes in the fair value or cash flows of the hedging instrument.

A hedge is viewed as being highly effective if actual results are within a range of 80% to 125%.

Illustration 4 – Hedge effectiveness

Joseph uses hedging transactions to minimise the risk of exposure to foreign exchange fluctuations. He buys goods from overseas and takes out forward contracts to fix the price of his inputs.

The gain on his forward contract for November was $570. The loss on a foreign currency payable was $600.

The effectiveness of the hedge is determined by dividing $570 by $600 or $600 by $570.

This gives an effectiveness percentage of 95% and 105% respectively. The hedge meets the criteria of 80–125% and is therefore highly effective.

Accounting treatment of a fair value hedge

- The hedging instrument will be remeasured to fair value, with all gains and losses reported in profit or loss for the year.
- The carrying value of the hedged item will be adjusted for the change in fair value since the inception of the hedge. The gain or loss will be reported in profit or loss for the year.

As a result of the above, the gain (or loss) on the hedging instrument and the loss (or gain) on the hedged item will largely net off in profit or loss. Therefore, the volatility in profit or loss that is created by entering into derivative contracts is minimised.

Simple fair value hedge

An entity has inventories of gold that cost $8m but whose value has increased to $10m. The entity is worried that the fair value of this inventory will fall, so it enters into a futures contract on 1 October 20X1 to sell the inventory for $10m in 6 months time. This was designated as a fair value hedge.

By the reporting date of 31 December 20X1, the fair value of the inventory had fallen from $10m to $9m. There was a $1m increase in the fair value of the derivative.

In order to hedge account, the hedge must have been highly effective throughout the reporting period. This hedge is 100% ($1m/$1m) effective and, as such, hedge accounting is permitted.

Under a fair value hedge, the movement in the fair value of the item and instrument since the inception of the hedge are accounted for through profit or loss.

The $1m gain on the future and the $1m loss on the inventory will be accounted for as follows:

Dr Derivative	$1m
Cr Profit or loss	$1m
Dr Profit or loss	$1m
Cr Inventory	$1m

By applying hedge accounting, the profit impact of remeasuring the derivative to fair value has been offset by the movement in the fair value of the inventory. Volatility has, in this example, been eliminated.

Note that the inventory will now be held at $7m (cost of $8m – $1m fair value decline). This is neither cost nor NRV. The normal accounting treatment of inventory has been changed by applying hedge accounting rules.

Test your understanding 11 – Fair value hedge

On 1 January 20X8 an entity purchased equity instruments for their fair value of $900,000. They were designated upon initial recognition to be classified as fair value through other comprehensive income.

At 30 September 20X8, the equity instrument was still worth $900,000 but the entity became worried about the risk of a decline in value. It therefore entered into a futures contract to sell the shares for $900,000 in six months time. It identified the futures contract as a hedging instrument as part of a fair value hedging arrangement. The fair value hedge was correctly documented and designated upon initial recognition and was expected to be a highly effective hedging arrangement.

By the reporting date of 31 December 20X8, the fair value of the equity instrument had fallen to $800,000, and the fair value of the futures contract had risen by $90,000.

Required:

Illustrate and explain the accounting treatment for the fair value hedge arrangement based upon the available information.

Test your understanding 12 – Firm commitments

Chive has a firm commitment to buy an item of machinery for CU2m on 31 March 20X2. The Directors are worried about the risk of exchange rate fluctuations.

On 1 October 20X1, when the exchange rate is CU2:$1, Chive enters into a futures contract to buy CU2m for $1m on 31 March 20X2.

At 31 December 20X1, CU2m would cost $1,100,000. The fair value of the futures contract has risen to $95,000.

Required:

Explain the accounting treatment of the above in the financial statements for the year ended 31 December 20X1 if:

(a) **Hedge accounting was not used.**

(b) **On 1 October 20X1, the futures contract was designated as a fair value hedge of the movements in the fair value of the firm commitment to purchase the machine.**

Accounting treatment of a cash flow hedge

- The hedging instrument will be remeasured to fair value at the reporting date. The gain (or loss) on the portion of the instrument that is deemed to be an effective hedge will be recorded in other comprehensive income and held in a separate component of equity.
- Any movement in the fair value of the hedging instrument that is in excess of the movement in the fair value of the hedged item will be reported immediately in profit or loss.

Test your understanding 13 – Cash flow hedge

A company enters into a derivative contract in order to protect its future cash inflows relating to a recognised financial asset. At inception, when the fair value of the hedging instrument was nil, the relationship was documented as a cash flow hedge.

By the reporting date, the loss in respect of the future cash flows amounted to $9,100 in fair value terms

Required:

Explain the accounting treatment of the cash flow hedge if the fair value of the hedging instrument at the reporting date is:

(a) **$7,000**

(b) **$8,500**

(c) **$10,000.**

- If the hedged item eventually results in the recognition of a financial asset or a financial liability, the gains or losses that were recognised in equity shall be reclassified to profit or loss as a reclassification adjustment in the same period during which the hedged forecast cash flows affect profit or loss.
- If the hedged item eventually results in the recognition of a non-financial asset or liability, the gain or loss held in equity must be recycled in one of the two following ways:
  - the gain/loss is adjusted against the carrying amount of the non-financial asset/liability, or
  - the gain/loss is transferred to profit and loss in line with the consumption of the non-financial asset/liability.

Test your understanding 14 – Bling

On 31 October 20X1, Bling had inventories of gold which cost $6.4m to buy and which could be sold for $7.7m. The management of Bling are concerned about the risk of fluctuations in future cash inflows from the sale of this gold.

To mitigate this risk, Bling entered into a futures contract on 31 October 20X1 to sell the gold for $7.7m. The contracts mature on 31 March 20X2. The hedging relationship was designated and documented at inception as a cash flow hedge.

On 31 December 20X1, the fair value of the gold was $8.6m. The fair value of the futures contract had fallen by $0.9m.

There is no change in fair value of the gold and the futures contract between 31 December 20X1 and 31 March 20X2. On 31 March 20X2, the inventory is sold for its fair value and the futures contract is settled net with the bank.

Required:

(a) **Discuss the accounting treatment of the hedge in the year ended 31 December 20X1.**

(b) **Outline the accounting treatment of the inventory sale and the futures contract settlement on 31 March 20X2.**

Test your understanding 15 – Grayton

In January, Grayton, whose functional currency is the dollar ($), decided that it was highly probable that it would buy an item of plant in one year's time for KR 200,000. As a result of being risk averse, it wished to hedge the risk that the cost of buying KRs would rise and so entered into a forward rate agreement to buy KR 200,000 in one year's time for the fixed sum of $100,000. The fair value of this contract at inception was zero and it was designated as a hedging instrument.

At Grayton's reporting date on of 31 July, the KR had depreciated and the value of KR 200,000 was $90,000. The fair value of the derivative had declined by $10,000. These values remained unchanged until the plant was purchased.

Required:

How should this be accounted for?

9 Discontinuing hedge accounting

An entity must cease hedge accounting if any of the following occur:

- The hedging instrument expires or is exercised, sold or terminated
- The hedge no longer meets the hedging criteria
- The designation as a hedge is revoked
- A 'highly probable' future transaction is no longer expected to occur.

The discontinuance should be accounted for prospectively (entries posted to date are not reversed).

Upon discontinuing a cash flow hedge, the treatment of the accumulated gains or losses on the hedging instrument within reserves depends on the reason for the discontinuation:

- If the forecast transaction is no longer expected to occur, gains and losses recognised in other comprehensive income must be taken to profit or loss immediately
- If the transaction is still expected to occur, the gains and losses will be retained in equity until the former hedged item affects profit or loss.

10 Disclosure of financial instruments

IFRS 7 provides the disclosure requirements for financial instruments. A summary of the requirements is detailed below.

The two main categories of disclosures required are:

(1) Information about the significance of financial instruments.

(2) Information about the nature and extent of risks arising from financial instruments.

The disclosures made should be made by each class of financial instrument.

Significance of financial instruments

- An entity must disclose the **significance** of financial instruments for their financial position and performance. The disclosures must be made for each class of financial instruments.
- An entity must disclose items of income, expense, gains, and losses, with separate disclosure of gains and losses from each class of financial instrument.

Nature and extent of risks arising from financial instruments

Qualitative disclosures

The qualitative disclosures describe:

- risk exposures for each type of financial instrument
- management's objectives, policies, and processes for managing those risks
- changes from the prior period.

Quantitative disclosures

The quantitative disclosures provide information about the extent to which the entity is exposed to risk, based on information provided internally to the entity's key management personnel. These disclosures include:

- summary quantitative data about exposure to each risk at the reporting date
- disclosures about credit risk, liquidity risk, and market risk as further described below
- concentrations of risk.

IFRS 7 Disclosures

Introduction

IFRS 7 was issued in August 2005 and replaced the disclosure elements of IAS 32. The presentation elements of IAS 32 remain the same. It adds to the disclosures that were required by IAS 32 and includes both quantitative and qualitative disclosures. IFRS 7 was also amended in October 2010 to require enhanced disclosures dealing with aspects of derecognition and off-balance sheet activities.

Additionally, some of the disclosure requirements have been amended following the introduction of IFRS 9. In principle, there should be sufficient information to enable users of financial statements to fully understand:

- how financial assets and liabilities have been designated
- the date, reason and effect of any reclassification of financial assets

The two main categories of disclosures required are:

(1) Accounting policies applied in respect of accounting for financial instruments

(2) Information about the significance of financial instruments upon the financial performance and position of the entity.

(3) Information about the nature and extent of risks arising from financial instruments.

(4) Detailed disclosures relating to the nature and extent of accounting for fair value and cash flow hedging arrangements.

Types of risk

There are four types of financial risk:

(1) **Market risk** – This refers to the possibility that the value of an asset (or burden of a liability) might go up or down. Market risk includes three types of risk: currency risk, interest rate risk and price risk.

(a) **Currency risk** is the risk that the value of a financial instrument will fluctuate because of changes in foreign exchange rates.

(b) Fair value **interest rate risk** is the risk that the value of a financial instrument will fluctuate due to changes in market interest rates. This is a common problem with fixed interest rate bonds. The price of these bonds goes up and down as interest rates go down and up.

(c) Price risk refers to other factors affecting price changes. These can be specific to the enterprise (bad financial results will cause a share price to fall), relate to the sector as a whole (all Tech-Stocks boomed in the late nineties, and crashed in the new century) or relate to the type of security (bonds do well when shares are doing badly, and vice versa).

Market risk embodies not only the potential for a loss to be made but also a gain to be made.

(2) **Credit risk** – The risk that one party to a financial instrument fails to discharge its obligations, causing a financial loss to the other party. For example, a bank is exposed to credit risk on its loans, because a borrower might default on its loan.

(3) **Liquidity risk** – This is also referred to as funding risk. This is the risk that an enterprise will be unable to meet its commitments on its financial instruments. For example, a business may be unable to repay its loans when they fall due.

(4) **Cash flow interest rate risk** – This is the risk that future cash flows associated with a monetary financial instrument will fluctuate in amount due to changes in market interest rates. For example, the cash paid (or received) on floating rate loans will fluctuate in line with market interest rates.

Offsetting financial assets and financial liabilities

Following a joint project between the IASB and US FASB, IFRS 7 was amended in December 2011.

The initial objectives, as reflected in the ED issued in January 2011, were to agree a common offsetting model, agree presentation in the statement of financial position and to agree supporting disclosures.

The use of different offsetting models, together with amounts presented in the statement of financial position made it difficult for users of financial statements to compare the financial performance and position of entities. This was compounded by less than full disclosure of amounts which had been offset together with their associated accounting treatment. In addition, the application of offsetting can significantly reduce the values of assets and liabilities reported in the statement of financial position.

Although a common offsetting model could not be agreed between IASB and US FASB, and is therefore excluded from the approved amendments, there was agreement on common disclosures required in the financial statements which should enable users of those financial statements to better compare the financial position and performance of entities.

In principle, the following must be disclosed:

- gross amounts before offsetting,
- gross amounts set-off,
- net amounts presented in the statement of financial position,
- other amounts not set off, and
- net amounts

As the amounts set-off will depend upon the offsetting model, disclosure is required of the basis of offsetting, together with accounting treatment adopted.

The amendments are effective for accounting periods commencing on or after 1 January 2013, with retrospective application required.

Current issues – expected credit losses

ED/2013/3 Expected credit losses

Under IAS 39, a financial asset should only be impaired if there is objective evidence at the end of the reporting period about whether a financial asset or group of financial assets is impaired. This is known as the **incurred loss model**. Following the 'credit crunch', it became apparent that many banks had not written down assets, despite having little expectation of receiving any benefits. This resulted in profit and assets being overstated.

As a result of this, it has been proposed that financial asset impairments should be accounted for under an **expected loss model**. This model has been detailed in an exposure draft issued in 2013.

Expected credit losses: a three stage approach

The exposure draft published in March 2013 proposed that entities determine and account for expected credit losses from the date an asset is acquired rather than wait for an actual default. Expected credit losses are defined as the expected shortfall in contractual cash flows.

The Exposure Draft suggests a three stage approach to accounting for the impairment of financial assets using an expected loss model.

- Stage 1: When a financial asset is first recognised, an entity would create an allowance equal to 12-months' expected credit losses. Interest income is still recognised based on the gross carrying value of the asset.
- Stage 2: If the credit quality of a financial asset deteriorates after initial recognition, then an allowance should be made for the present value of expected lifetime credit losses. A discount rate should be used that is between the risk-free rate and the effective interest rate. Interest income is still recognised based on the gross carrying value of the asset.
- Stage 3: When credit losses actually occur (i.e. if an actual default happens), then the entity still recognises an allowance for lifetime credit losses. However, the interest income recognised in profit or loss should now be based on the net carrying value of the financial asset (gross carrying value under the amortised cost basis less the allowance.

Simplifications

To reduce the cost and time involved in applying these new rules, the exposure draft suggests that entities can choose to always recognise lifetime expected credit losses for trade receivables and lease receivables.

Benefits and drawbacks

Switching to the expected loss model is in accordance with prudence, since it is less likely that assets will be over-stated.

It will also provider timelier information to the users of the financial statements, who will be warned about expected losses earlier.

However, the expected loss model will require more judgement than the incurred loss model. This reduces verifiability and also increases the potential to manipulate profits.

There are differences in the IASB's and the FASB's proposals that might lead to material differences in accounting treatments and thus reduce comparability between companies.

The costs of implementing the new model may be very high, particularly for banks.

Current issues – expected credit loss example

On 1 January 2013, Company A loaned Company B $1,000,000. The coupon rate of interest was 10%, which was equal to the effective rate of interest. Interest repayments were due on 31 December each year. The loan was due for repayment on 31 December 2015.

On 1 January 2013, Company A believed that there was a 0.5% chance that Company B would default on payments due in the first 12 months.

During the year ended 31 December 2013, there were no defaults. However, at 31 December 2013, Company A believes that there has been a significant deterioration in the industry in which Company B operates. Company A estimates that there is a 20% chance that Company B will default on the remaining payments. Due to the risk level, this financial asset is now below 'investment grade'.

Required:

According to the 2013 Exposure Draft, how would Company A account for the above in the year ended 31 December 2013?

Solution

The financial asset will initially be recognised at the proceeds advanced of $1,000,000.

When a financial asset is first recognised, Company A must create an allowance equal to 12-months' expected credit losses. In this example, at 1 January 2013, 12 month expected credit losses are $500 (0.5% × ($1,000,000 × 10%))

The financial asset is still held at $1,000,000 but an allowance would be recorded for $500 and an impairment of $500 would be charged to the statement of profit or loss.

The financial asset is measured at amortised cost and therefore investment income of $100,000 ($1,000,000 × 10%) would have been recognised in the statement of profit or loss for the year ended 31 December 2013. The asset would have a gross carrying value of $1,000,000.

At 31 December 2013, there has been a decline in the creditworthiness of the borrowing company. Company A must now allow for lifetime expected credit losses.

An allowance should be calculated at the present value of the expected credit losses over the remaining life of the asset.

The discount rate used should be between the risk-free rate and the effective rate of the asset. In the absence of further information, the effective rate of 10% should be used.

Company A will therefore need to increase the allowance for impairment from $500 to $200,000 (W1). A further impairment loss of $199,500 ($200,000 – $500) will be recognised in the statement of profit or loss. The allowance will be netted off the value of the asset to reduce its carrying value to $800,000 ($1,000,000 – $200,000) in the statement of financial position.

(W1) **Present value of expected credit losses**

Date	Potential credit loss	Probability of default	Expected credit loss	Discount factor	PV of expected credit loss
	$		$		$
31 December 2014	100,000	20%	20,000	0.909	18,182
31 December 2015	1,100,000	20%	220,000	0.826	181,818
					200,000

Current issues – hedge accounting

IFRS 9 - Draft chapter 6 - Hedge accounting

Hedging activities have become increasingly sophisticated since the issue of IAS 39. Therefore, the IASB have recognised that an overhaul of hedge accounting requirements is essential.

Since 2008, the IASB has released a number of discussion papers and exposure drafts on potential changes to the hedge accounting requirements. A draft of the forthcoming hedge accounting requirements, to be included in IFRS 9, was posted on the IASB's website in September 2012. This draft is an examinable document for P2.

Hedging components of non-financial items

Under IAS 39, a component of a non-financial item cannot be designated as a hedged item. One common example of this is the oil price component of jet fuel. Although an airline may enter into derivative contracts in order to manage the risk of oil price fluctuations, it is not permitted to hedge account for this. This creates volatility in profit or loss that is not consistent with the economic situation. In fact, it actually makes the financial statements of companies which have entered into risk management strategies appear more volative (and therefore more risky) than those who have taken no measures to manage their risks.

Under the new hedge accounting requirements, an entity will be able to designate components of a non-financial item as a hedged item.

Hedge effectiveness

Under IAS 39, hedge accounting is permitted if a hedge is highly effective. IAS 39 deems a hedge to be highly effective if the gain (or loss) on the hedging instrument is within 80 to 125% of the loss (or gain) on the hedged item. This has been criticised as an arbitary measure of effectiveness. Furthermore, these metrics are only used for accounting purposes and therefore increase the cost and burden of hedge accounting.

The draft hedge accounting chapter requires an entity to determine whether a hedge is effective by using information and data that will already be produced internally for risk management purposes. The draft states that a hedge is effective if:

- there is an economic relationship between the hedged item and the hedging instrument
- the effect of credit risk does not dominate the value changes that result from that economic relationship
- the hedge ratio of the hedging relationship should reflect the actual quantity of hedging instrument used to hedge the actual quantity of hedge item.

Entities will still be required to assess effectiveness at the inception of the hedging relationship, and on an ongoing basis.

Technical articles

Tony Sweetman of Kaplan Publishing wrote an article discussing financial instruments for the August 2011 edition of Student Accountant magazine.

Tom Clendon of Kaplan Financial wrote a two-part article discussing the accounting treatment of financial assets and liabilities 'What is a financial instrument?' dated July 2012 for the Student Accountant magazine.

An article about the proposed new accounting treatment of financial asset impairments was published in Student Accountant magazine in 2013.

You can access all these articles from the ACCA website (www.accaglobal.com).

11 Chapter summary

Classification of liabilities and equity:
- Liabilities include a contractual obligation to pay cash or exchange financial instruments
- Equity – no such obligation

Financial liabilities measured at either:
- Fair value through profit or loss, or
- Amortised cost

Note there is option to measure liabilities at FV to reduce accounting mismatch.

Derivatives (assets and liabilities):
- Include options, swaps, forward contracts and future contracts
- Categorised as fair value through profit or loss, unless used as a hedge
  - Fair value hedge
  - Cash flow hedge
- Embedded derivatives are included within another non-derivative contract – need to split from host contract

Financial assets:
- Initial recognition at fair value
- Subsequent measurement depends upon categorisation:
  - Fair value through profit or loss is the default categorisation
  - Fair value through other comprehensive income - elect upon recognition for equity instruments only
  - Amortised cost – elect upon initial recognition provided two tests passed:
- Business model test
- Cash flow characteristics test

Impairment of financial assets:
- Need to review annually for evidence of impairment
- If measured at FV, then impairment taken to profit or loss or other comprehensive income to follow categorisation
- If measured at amortised cost, then impairment taken to profit or loss.

Disclosure requirements:
- Significance of financial instruments
- Nature and extents of risks
- Qualitative and quantitative issues

Test your understanding answers

Test your understanding 1 – Liabilities or equity?

IAS 32 states that a financial liability is any contract that may be settled in the entity's own equity instruments and is a non-derivative for which the entity is obliged to deliver a variable number of its own equity instruments.

Therefore, a contract that requires the entity to deliver as many of the entity's own equity instruments as are equal in value to a certain amount should be treated as debt.

Coasters must redeem the first set of preference shares by issuing ordinary shares equal to the value of $3 million. The $3 million received from the preference share issue should be classified as a liability on the statement of financial position.

An equity instrument is any contract that evidences a residual interest in the net assets of an entity after deducting all of its liabilities.

A contract that will be settled by the entity receiving (or delivering) a fixed number of its own equity instruments in exchange for a fixed amount of cash or another financial asset is an equity instrument.

Coasters will redeem the second preference share issue with a fixed number of ordinary shares. Therefore, the $5.6 million from the second preference share issue should be classified as equity in the statement of financial position.

Test your understanding 2 – Hoy

Hoy has a financial liability to be measured at amortised cost.

The financial liability is initially recorded at the fair value of the consideration received (the net proceeds of issue). This amount is then increased each year by interest at the effective rate and reduced by the actual repayments.

Hoy has no issue costs, so the net proceeds of issue were $9,500 ($10,000 less 5%). The annual cash payment is $200 (the 2% coupon rate multiplied by the $10,000 nominal value of the debt).

	Bal b/fwd	Finance costs (10%)	Cash paid	Bal c/fwd
Rep date	$	$	$	$
31 Dec X1	9,500	950	(200)	10,250
31 Dec X2	10,250	1,025	(200)	
			(11,075)	
		1,975		

Wiggins has a liability that will be classified and accounted for at amortised cost and thus initially measured at the fair value of consideration received less the transaction costs:

	$
Cash received ($20,000 × 90%)	18,000
Less the transaction costs	(1,000)
Initial recognition	17,000

The effective rate is used to determine the finance cost for the year - this is charged to profit or loss. The coupon rate is applied to the nominal value of the loan notes to determine the cash paid to the holder of the loan notes:

	Bal b/fwd	Finance costs (12%)	Cash paid	Bal c/fwd
Rep date	$	$	$	$
31 Dec X4	17,000	2,040	(1,200)	17,840
31 Dec X5	17,840	2,141	(1,200)	18,781
31 Dec X6	18,781	2,254	(1,200)	19,835
31 Dec X7	19,835	2,380	(1,200)	
			(21,015)	
		8,815		

Cavendish has a financial liability to be measured at amortised cost.

It is initially recorded at the fair value of the consideration received. There is no discount on issue, nor is there any issue costs to deduct from the initial measurement.

The opening balance is increased each year by interest at the effective rate. The liability is reduced by the cash repayments - there are no interest repayments in this example because it is a zero rate bond.

	Bal b/fwd	Finance costs (7%)	Cash paid	Bal c/fwd
Rep date	$	$	$	$
31 Dec X5	10,000	700	Nil	10,700
31 Dec X6	10,700	749	(11,449)	

Test your understanding 3 – Craig

Up to 31 December 20X8, the accounting entries are the same under both scenarios.

(1) **Splitting the proceeds**

The cash payments on the bond should be discounted to their present value using the interest rate for a bond without the conversion rights, i.e. 8%.

Date		**Cash flow**	**Discount factor (8%)**	**Present value**
		$		$
31/12/X6	Interest	4,000	1/1.08	3,704
31/12/X7	Interest	4,000	$1/1.08^2$	3,429
31/12/X8	Interest and principal	104,000	$1/1.08^3$	82,559
Liability component			A	89,692
Net proceeds of issue were			B	100,000
Equity component			B – A	10,308

(2) **The annual finance costs and year end carrying amounts**

	Opening balance	Finance cost (8%)	Cash paid	Closing balance
	$	$	$	$
X6	89,692	7,175	(4,000)	92,867
X7	92,867	7,429	(4,000)	96,296
X8	96,296	7,704	(4,000)	100,000

(3) (a) **Conversion**

The carrying amounts at 31 December 20X8 are:

	$
Equity	10,308
Liability – bond	100,000
	110,308

If the conversion rights are exercised, then 50,000 ($100,000 ÷ 2) equity shares of $1 are issued and $60,308 is classified as share premium.

(b) **Redemption**

The carrying amounts at 31 December 20X8 are the same as under 3a. On redemption, the $100,000 liability is extinguished by cash payments. The equity component remains within equity, probably as a non-distributable reserve.

Test your understanding 4 – Paloma

A debt instrument can be held at amortised cost if two tests are passed: the business model test and the contractual cash flow characteristics test.

The business model test is passed if the entity intends to hold the financial asset to collect contractual cash flows, rather than selling it to realise fair value changes. The contractual cash flow characteristics test is passed if the contractual terms of the asset give rise to cash flows that are solely payments of principal and interest based upon the principal amount outstanding.

If these tests are failed, a debt instrument would normally be held at fair value through profit or loss.

Paloma's objective is to hold the financial assets and collect the contractual cash flows. Making some sales when cash flow deteriorates does not contradict that objective.

The bond pays a market level of interest, and therefore the interest payments received provide adequate compensation for the time value of money or the credit risk associated with the principal amount outstanding.

The business model test and the contractual cash flow characteristics test are both passed and so the asset can be measured at amortised cost.

Test your understanding 5 – Ashes' financial assets

(1) Trade receivables will be recognised until the cash that is due has been collected. As such they meet both the business model and cash flow characteristics tests specified by IFRS 9 and so they are classified and accounted for at amortised cost.

(2) Investments held for short-term speculative purposes must be classified and accounted for as fair value through profit or loss. Such assets are initially recognised at fair value (excluding transaction costs). They are remeasured to fair value at the reporting date with the gains and losses on remeasurement recognised in profit or loss.

(3) Investments that, from the outset, are going to be held indefinitely may be irrevocably designated upon initial recognition as fair value through other comprehensive income. Such assets are initially recognised at fair value (including transaction costs). They are remeasured to fair value at the reporting date and gains and losses on remeasurement are recognised in other comprehensive income. If no such election on purchase is made then the investment must be classified and accounted for as fair value through profit or loss (see (2) above).

Test your understanding 6 – Ming

The principle at stake with derecognition or otherwise of receivables is whether, under the factoring arrangement, the risks and rewards of ownership pass from Ming to the factor. The principal risk with regard to receivables is the risk of bad debt.

In the first arrangement the $180,000 has been received as a one-off, non refundable sum. This is factoring without recourse for bad debts. The risk of bad debt has clearly passed from Ming to the factoring bank. Accordingly Ming should derecognise the receivable and there will be an expense of $20,000 recognised.

In the second arrangement the $70,000 is simply a payment on account. More may be received by Ming implying that Ming retains an element of reward. The monies received are refundable in the event of default and as such represent an obligation. This means that the risk of slow payment and bad debt remains with Ming who is liable to repay the monies so far received. Despite the passage of legal title the receivable should remain recognised in the accounts of Ming. In substance Ming has borrowed $70,000 and this loan should be recognised immediately. This will increase the gearing of Ming.

Test your understanding 7 – Case

An entity has transferred a financial asset if it has transferred the contractual rights to receive the cash flows of the asset.

If an entity has transferred an asset, it must evaluate the extent to which it has retained the significant risks and rewards of ownership. If the entity transfers substantially all the risks and rewards of ownership of the financial asset, the entity must derecognise the financial asset.

Gains and losses on the disposal of a financial asset are recognised in the statement of profit or loss.

Case is under no obligation to buy back the shares and is therefore protected from future share price declines. Moreoever, If Case does repurchase the shares, this will be at fair value rather than a pre-fixed price and therefore Case does not retain the risks and rewards related to price fluctuations.

The risks and rewards of ownership have been transferred and, as such, Case should derecognise the financial asset. A profit of $1m ($5m – $4m) should be recognised in profit or loss.

Test your understanding 8 – Jones

(a) On purchase the investment is recorded at the consideration paid. The asset is classified as fair value through other comprehensive income and, as such, transaction costs are included in the initial value:

Dr	Asset	41m
Cr	Cash	41m

At the reporting date the asset is remeasured to fair value and the gain of $19m ($60m – $41m) is recognised in other comprehensive income and taken to equity:

Dr	Asset	19m
Cr	Other components of equity	19m

On disposal, the asset is derecognised. The profit or loss on disposal, recorded in the statement of profit or loss, is determined by comparing disposal proceeds with the carrying value of the asset:

Dr	Cash	70m
Cr	Asset	60m
Cr	Profit or loss	10m

Note that the any gains or losses previously taken to equity are **not** recycled upon derecognition, although they may be reclassified within equity.

(b) If Jones had designated the investment as fair value through profit and loss, the transaction costs would have been recognised as an expense in profit or loss. The entry posted on the purchase date would have been:

Dr	Asset	40m
Cr	Cash	40m
Dr	Profit or loss	1m
Cr	Cash	1m

At the reporting date, the asset is remeasured to fair value and the gain of $20m ($60m – $40m) is recognised in the statement of profit or loss:

Dr	Asset	20m
Cr	Profit or loss	20m

On disposal the asset is derecognised and the profit on disposal is recorded in the statement of profit or loss:

Dr	Cash	70m
Cr	Asset	60m
Cr	Profit or loss	10m

Note that the reported profit on derecognition of $10 million is the same whether the asset was designated as fair value through profit or loss or fair value through other comprehensive income.

Test your understanding 9 – Straw

Under IAS 39, an entity should assess at the end of each reporting period if there is objective evidence that a financial asset has been impaired.

Objective evidence may include the following:

- Significant financial difficulties of the issuer
- A breach of contract
- Granting concessions to the borrower

According to IAS 39, losses expected as a result of future events, no matter how likely, must not be recognised.

No objective evidence exists that this particular supplier is experiencing financial difficulties, and no actual default of payments has occurred. No impairment loss should be accounted for. The asset should be recognised at its fair value of $1 million.

Test your understanding 10 – Hoggard

In all scenarios the cost of the derivative on 1 January 20X6 is $500 ($5 × 100) and an asset is recognised in the statement of financial position.

Dr	Asset – option	$500
Cr	Cash	$500

Outcome A

If the option is sold for $1,500 (100 × $15) before the exercise date, it is derecognised at a profit of $1,000.

Dr	Cash	$1,500
Cr	Asset – option	$500
Cr	Profit or loss	$1,000

Outcome B

If the option lapses unexercised, then it is derecognised and there is a loss to be taken to profit or loss:

Dr	Profit or loss	$500
Cr	Asset – option	$500

Outcome C

If the option is exercised then the option is derecognised, the entity records the cash paid upon exercise, and the investment in shares is recognised at fair value. An immediate profit is recognised:

Dr	Asset – investment (100 × $25)	$2,500
Cr	Cash (100 × $10)	$1,000
Cr	Asset – option	$500
Cr	Profit or loss	$1,000

Test your understanding 11 – Fair value hedge

Hedge accounting is permitted if, at the reporting date, the hedge has been highly effective.

The fair value of the hedging instrument has risen by $90,000. The fair value of the hedged item has fallen by $100,000. Hedge effectiveness is 90% ($90,000/$100,000). This falls within the range 80% – 125%, so the hedge is regarded as highly effective.

The increase in the fair value of the derivative of $90,000 will be accounted for through profit or loss.The fall in fair value of the equity interest of $100,000 since the inception of the hedge is also taken to profit or loss.

Dr Derivative	$90,000
Cr Profit or loss	$90,000
Dr Profit or loss	$100,000
Cr Equity investment	$100,000

There is a small net expense of $10,000 in profit or loss. Volatility has been reduced but not entirely eliminated. This is because the hedge was not 100% effective.

Test your understanding 12 – Firm commitments

(a) The futures contract is a derivative and is measured at fair value with all movements being accounted for through profit or loss.

The fair value of the futures contract at 1 October 20X1 was nil. By the year end, it had risen to $95,000. Therefore, at 31 December 20X1, Chive will recognise an asset at $95,000 and a gain of $95,000 will be recorded in profit or loss.

(b) If the relationship had been designated as a fair value hedge and it was found to be highly effective, the movement in the fair value of the hedging instrument (the future) and the fair value of the hedged item (the firm commitment) since inception of the hedge are accounted for through profit or loss.

The derivative has increased in fair value from $nil at 1 October 20X1 to $95,000 at 31 December 20X1. Purchasing CU2 million at 31 December 20X1 would cost Chive $100,000 more than it would have done at 1 October 20X1. Therefore the fair value of the firm commitment has fallen by $100,000.

Hedge effectiveness is 95% ($95,000/$100,000). This falls between 80% and 125%. The hedge is therefore highly effective and hedge accounting is permitted.

At year end, the derivative will be held at its fair value of $95,000, and the gain of $95,000 will be recorded in profit or loss.

The $100,000 fall in the fair value of the commitment will also be accounted for, with an expense recognised in profit or loss.

In summary, the double entries are as follows:

Dr Derivative	$95,000
Cr Profit or loss	$95,000
Dr Profit or loss	$100,000
Cr Firm commitment	$100,000

The gain on the derivative and the loss on the firm commitment largely net off. There is a residual $5,000 ($100,000 – $95,000) net expense in profit or loss due to hedge ineffectiveness. Nonetheless, financial statement volatility is far less than if hedge accounting had not been used.

Test your understanding 13 – Cash flow hedge

(a) The effectiveness of the hedge is 76.9% ($7,000/$9,100). This does not fall within the 80% – 125% range and so the hedge is not highly effective. Hedge accounting is not permitted and normal accounting rules must be applied.

The derivative will be remeasured from its initial fair value of nil to its year end fair value of $7,000. The gain of $7,000 will be reported in profit or loss.

Dr Derivative	$7,000
Cr Profit or loss	$7,000

(b) The effectiveness of the hedge is 93.4% ($8,500/$9,100). It is a highly effective hedge and, as such, hedge accounting is permitted.

The movement on the hedging instrument is less than the movement on the hedged item. Therefore, the instrument is remeasured to fair value and the gain is recognised in other comprehensive income.

Dr Derivative	$8,500
Cr OCI	$8,500

(c) The effectiveness of the hedge is 109.9% ($10,000/$9,100). It is a highly effective hedge and, as such, hedge accounting is permitted.

The movement on the hedging instrument is more than the movement on the hedged item. The excess movement of $900 ($10,000 – $9,100) is recognised in the statement of profit or loss.

Dr Derivative	$10,000
Cr Profit or loss	$900
Cr OCI	$9,100

Test your understanding 14 – Bling

(a) Hedge accounting is permitted if, at the reporting date, the hedge has been highly effective.

Between 1 October 20X1 and 31 December 20X1, the fair value of the futures contract had fallen by $0.9m. Over the same time period, the hedged item (the estimated cash receipts from the sale of the inventory) had increased by $0.9m ($8.6m – $7.7m).

Hedge effectiveness is 100% ($0.9m/$0.9m). The hedge is highly effective and hedge accounting is therefore permitted.

Under an effective cash flow hedge, the movement in the fair value of the hedging instrument is accounted for through other comprehensive income. Therefore, the following entry is required:

Dr Other comprehensive income $0.9m
Cr Derivative $0.9m

The loss recorded in other comprehensive income will be held in a cash flow hedging reserve within equity.

(b) The following entries are required:

Dr Cash	$8.6m
Cr Revenue	$8.6m
Dr Cost of sales	$6.4m
Cr Inventory	$6.4m

To record the sale of the inventory at fair value

Dr Derivative	$0.9m
Cr Cash	$0.9m

To record the settlement of the futures contract.

Dr Profit or loss	$0.9m
Cr Hedging reserve	$0.9m

To recycle the losses held in equity through profit or loss in the same period as the hedged item affects profit or loss.

Test your understanding 15 – Grayton

The forward rate agreement has no fair value at its inception so is initially recorded at $nil.

This is a cash flow hedge. The derivative has fallen in value by $10,000 but the cash flows have increased in value by $10,000 (it is now $10,000 cheaper to buy the asset). The hedge is 100% effective, which falls within the range 80% – 125%. Hedge accounting is therefore permitted.

Because it has been designated a cash flow hedge, the movement in the value of the hedging instrument is recognised in other comprehensive income:

Dr	Other comprehensive income	$10,000
Cr	Derivative	$10,000

(Had this not been designated a hedging instrument, the loss would have been recognised immediately in profit or loss.)

The forward contract will be settled and closed when the asset is purchased.

Property, plant and equipment is a non-financial item. The loss on the hedging instrument held within equity can be recycled by either:

- adjusting it against the carrying value of the plant
- transferring it to profit or loss as the plant is consumed (depreciated).

Assuming that the first option is chosen, the following entries would be posted:

Dr	Liability – derivative	$10,000
Dr	Plant	$90,000
Cr	Cash	$100,000

Being the settlement of the derivative and the purchase of the plant.

Dr	Plant	$10,000
Cr	Other components of equity	$10,000

Being the recycling of the losses held within equity against the carrying value of the plant. Notice that the plant will be held at $100,000 ($90,000 + $10,000) and the cash spent in total was $100,000. This was the position that the derivative guaranteed.

chapter

13

Tax

Chapter learning objectives

Upon completion of this chapter you will be able to:

- apply and discuss the recognition and measurement of deferred tax liabilities and deferred tax assets
- determine the recognition of tax expense or income and its inclusion in the financial statements.

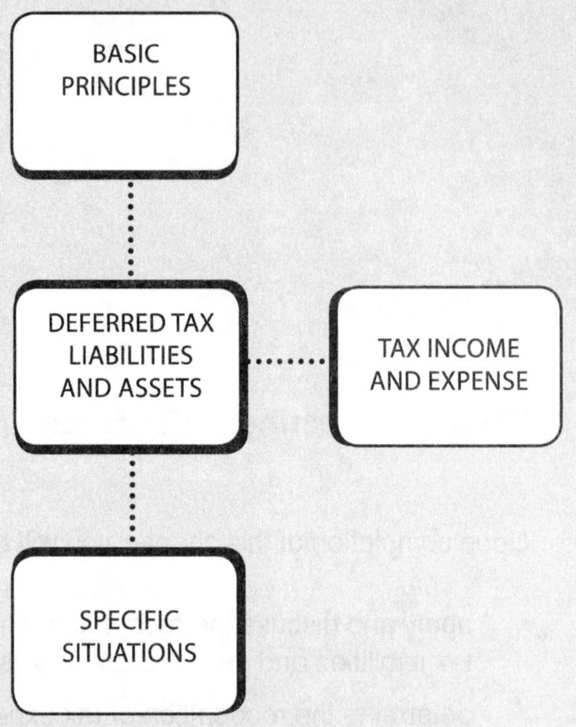

1 Basic principles of tax

Taxation

Taxation is a major expense for business entities. There are two elements to tax that an entity may have to deal with:

- **Current tax** – the amount payable to the tax authorities in relation to the trading activities of the current period.
- **Deferred tax** – an accounting measure used to match the tax effects of transactions with their accounting treatment. It is not a tax that is levied by the government that needs to be paid, but simply an application of the accruals concept.

In summary, the tax expense for an entity is calculated as follows:

Tax expense = current tax +/– movement in deferred tax

2 Current tax

Accounting for current tax

Current tax is the amount expected to be paid to the tax authorities by applying the tax laws and tax rates in place at the reporting date.

Current tax is recognised in the financial statements by posting the following entry:

Dr Tax expense (P/L)
Cr Tax payable (SFP)

Current tax expense and income

IAS 12 contains the following requirements relating to current tax.

- Unpaid tax for current and prior periods should be recognised as a liability. Overpaid current tax is recognised as an asset.
- Current tax should be accounted for in profit or loss unless the tax relates to an item that has been accounted for in equity.
- If the item was disclosed as an item of other comprehensive income and accounted for in equity, then the tax should be disclosed as relating to other comprehensive income and allocated to equity.
- Tax is measured at the amount expected to be paid. Tax rates used should be those that have been enacted or substantively enacted by the reporting date.

3 Basic principles of deferred tax

The need to provide for deferred tax

There are generally differences between accounting standards (such as IFRS) and the tax rules of a particular jurisdiction. This means that accounting profits are normally different from taxable profits.

Some differences between accounting and tax treatments are permanent:

- Fines, political donations and entertainment costs would be expensed to the statement of profit or loss but are normally disallowed by the tax authorities. Therefore, these costs are eliminated ('added back') in the company's tax computation.

Some differences between accounting and tax treatments are temporary:

- Capital assets might be written down at different rates for tax purposes than they are in the financial statements.

Temporary differences may mean that profits are reported in the financial statements before they are taxable. Conversely, it might mean that tax is payable even though profits have not yet been reported in the financial statements.

According to the accruals concept, the tax effect of a transaction should be reported in the same accounting period as the transaction itself. Therefore, an adjustment to the tax charge may be required. This gives rise to deferred tax.

Deferred tax only arises on temporary differences. It is not accounted for on permanent differences.

A **temporary difference** is the difference between the carrying amount of an asset or liability and its tax base.

The **tax base** is the amount attributed to an asset or liability for tax purposes.

Illustration 1 – Basic principles of deferred tax

Prudent prepares financial statements to 31 December each year. On 1 January 20X0, the entity purchased a non-current asset for $1.6 million that had an anticipated useful life of four years. This asset qualified for immediate tax relief of 100% of the cost of the asset.

For the year ending 31 December 20X0, the draft accounts showed a profit before tax of $2 million. The directors anticipate that this level of profit will be maintained for the foreseeable future.

Prudent pays tax at a rate of 30%. Apart from the differences caused by the purchase of the non-current asset in 20X0, there are no other differences between accounting profit and taxable profit or the tax base and carrying amount of net assets.

Required:

Compute the pre, and post-tax profits for Prudent for each of the four years ending 31 December 20X0–20X3 inclusive and for the period as a whole assuming:

(a) **that no deferred tax is recognised**

(b) **that deferred tax is recognised.**

Solution

(a) **No deferred tax**

First of all, it is necessary to compute the taxable profits of Prudent for each period and the current tax payable:

	Year ended 31 December				**Total**
	20X0	**20X1**	**20X2**	**20X3**	
	$000	$000	$000	$000	$000
Accounting profit	2,000	2,000	2,000	2,000	8,000
Add back Depreciation	400	400	400	400	1,600
Deduct Capital allowances	(1,600)	–	–	–	(1,600)
Taxable profits	800	2,400	2,400	2,400	8,000
Current tax at 30%	240	720	720	720	2,400

The differences between the accounting profit and the taxable profit that occur from one year to another, cancel out over the four years as a whole.

The statements of profit or loss for each period and for the four years as a whole, are given below:

	Year ended 31 December				**Total**
	20X0	**20X1**	**20X2**	**20X3**	
	$000	$000	$000	$000	$000
Profit before tax	2,000	2,000	2,000	2,000	8,000
Current tax	(240)	(720)	(720)	(720)	(2,400)
Profit after tax	1,760	1,280	1,280	1,280	5,600

Ignoring deferred tax produces a performance profile that suggests a declining performance between 20X0 and 20X1.

In fact the decline in profits is caused by the timing of the current tax charge on them.

In 20X0, some of the accounting profit escapes tax, but the tax is only postponed until 20X1, 20X2 and 20X3, when the taxable profit is more than the accounting profit.

(b) **Deferred tax is recognised**

The deferred tax figures that are required in the statement of financial position are given below:

	Year ended 31 December			
	20X0	**20X1**	**20X2**	**20X3**
	$000	$000	$000	$000
Carrying amount	1,200	800	400	Nil
Tax base	Nil	Nil	Nil	Nil
Temporary difference at year end	1,200	800	400	Nil
Closing deferred tax liability (30%)	360	240	120	Nil
Opening deferred tax liability	Nil	(360)	(240)	(120)
So charge/(credit) to income	360	(120)	(120)	(120)

The statements of profit or loss for the four year period including deferred tax are shown below:

	Year ended 31 December				Total
	20X0	**20X1**	**20X2**	**20X3**	
	$000	$000	$000	$000	$000
Profit before tax	2,000	2,000	2,000	2,000	8,000
Current tax	(240)	(720)	(720)	(720)	(2,400)
Deferred tax	(360)	120	120	120	Nil
Profit after tax	1,400	1,400	1,400	1,400	5,600

A more meaningful performance profile is presented.

Examples of temporary differences

Examples of temporary differences include (but are not restricted to):

- Tax deductions for the cost of non-current assets that have a different pattern to the write-off of the asset in the financial statements, i.e. accelerated capital allowances.
- Pension liabilities that are accrued in the financial statements, but are allowed for tax only when the contributions are made to the pension fund at a later date.
- Intra-group profits in inventory that are unrealised for consolidation purposes yet taxable in the computation of the group entity that made the unrealised profit.
- A loss is reported in the financial statements and the related tax relief is only available by carry forward against future taxable profits.
- Assets are revalued upwards in the financial statements, but no adjustment is made for tax purposes.
- Development costs are capitalised and amortised to profit or loss in future periods, but were deducted for tax purposes as incurred.
- The cost of granting share options to employees is recognised in profit or loss, but no tax deduction is obtained until the options are exercised.

Calculating temporary differences

Deferred tax is calculated by comparing the carrying value of an asset or liability to its tax base. The tax base is the amount attributed to the asset or liability for tax purposes.

- If the carrying amount exceeds the tax base, deferred tax must be provided for, and the temporary difference is said to be a **taxable** temporary difference (a liability).
- If the tax base exceeds the carrying amount, the temporary difference is a **deductible** temporary difference (an asset).

Test your understanding 1 – Dive (temporary differences)

An entity, Dive, provides the following information regarding its assets and liabilities as at 31 December 20X1.

	Carrying value	Tax base	Temporary difference
Assets			
A machine cost $100,000. Depreciation of $18,000 has been charged to date. Capital allowances of $30,000 have been claimed.			
Interest receivable in the statement of financial position is $1,000. The interest will be taxed when received.			
Trade receivables have a carrying amount of $10,000.The revenue has already been included in taxable profit.			
Inventory has been written down by $500 to $4,500 in the financial statements. The reduction is ignored for tax purposes until the inventory is sold.			
Liabilities			
Current liabilities include accrued expenses of $1,000. This is deductible for tax on a cash paid basis.			
Accrued expenses have a carrying amount of $5,000. The related expense has been deducted for tax purposes.			

Required:

Complete the table with carrying value, tax base and temporary difference for each of the assets and liabilities.

4 Deferred tax liabilities and assets

Recognition

IAS 12 Income Taxes states that deferred tax should be provided for on all taxable temporary differences, unless the deferred tax liability arises from:

- goodwill, for which amortisation is not tax deductible
- the initial recognition of an asset or liability in a transaction, which is not a business combination, and at the time of the transaction affects neither accounting profit nor taxable profit. An example is expenditure on a finite life intangible asset, which attracts no tax allowances. Accounting profit is only affected after the transaction (by subsequent amortisation), while taxable profit is never affected.

Deferred tax assets should be recognised on all deductible temporary differences unless the exceptions above also apply, provided that taxable profit will be available against which the deductible temporary difference can be utilised.

- It is appropriate to offset deferred tax assets and liabilities when presenting them in the statement of financial position as long as:
  - the entity has a legally enforceable right to set off **current** tax assets and **current** tax liabilities
  - the deferred tax assets and liabilities relate to tax levied by the same tax authority on either the same taxable entity or different taxable entities which settle **current** tax balances on a net basis.

Measurement

The tax rate in force (or expected to be in force) when the asset is realised or the liability is settled, should be applied to the temporary difference to calculate the deferred tax balance.

- This rate must be based on tax rates and legislation that has been enacted or substantively enacted by the reporting date.
- Deferred tax assets and liabilities should not be discounted to present value.

The entry to profit or loss and other comprehensive income in respect of deferred tax is the difference between the net liability at the beginning of the year and the net liability at the end of the year.

- If the item giving rise to the deferred tax is dealt with in profit or loss, the related deferred tax should also be presented in profit or loss.

- If the item giving rise to the deferred tax is dealt with in other comprehensive income, the related deferred tax should also be recorded in other comprehensive income and held within equity.

Test your understanding 2 – Dive (deferred tax calculation)

Required:

Using the information in 'test your understanding 1', calculate Dive's deferred tax balance as at 31 December 20X1. The applicable tax rate is 30%.

Test your understanding 3 – Brick

Brick is a company with a reporting date of 30 April 20X4. The company obtains tax relief for research and development expenditure on a cash paid basis. The recognition of a material development asset during the year, in accordance with IAS 38, created a significant taxable temporary difference as at 30 April 20X4.

The tax rate for companies as at the reporting period was 22%. On 6 June 20X4, the government passed legislation to lower the company tax rate to 20% from 1 January 20X5.

Required:

Explain which tax rate should have been used to calculate the deferred tax liability for inclusion in the financial statements for the year ended 30 April 20X4.

5 Specific situations

Revaluations

Deferred tax should be recognised on the revaluation of property, plant and equipment even if:

- there is no intention to sell the asset
- any tax due on the gain made on any sale of the asset can be deferred by being 'rolled over' against the cost of a replacement asset.

Revaluation gains are recorded in other comprehensive income and so any deferred tax arising on the revaluation must also be recorded in other comprehensive income.

Test your understanding 4 – Dodge

An entity, Dodge, owns property, plant and equipment that cost $100,000 when purchased. Depreciation of $40,000 has been charged up to the reporting date of 31 March 20X1. The entity has claimed total tax allowances on the asset of $50,000. On 31 March 20X1, the asset is revalued to $90,000. The tax rate is 30%.

Required:

Explain the deferred tax implications of this situation.

Investment properties

It is presumed that the carrying value of investment properties measured at fair value will be recovered from a sale transaction, unless there is evidence to the contrary.

- This latter situation may arise, for example, when the relevant asset is included within a business model whose objective is to consume most of the economic benefits over time, rather than recovery of economic value through disposal.

The deferred tax calculation must take into consideration how the asset is measured together with how the entity expects to recover its value.

IAS 40 illustration

Melbourne has an investment property, which is measured using the fair value model in accordance with IAS 40, comprising the following elements:

	Cost	**Fair value**
	$000	$000
Land	800	1,200
Building	1,200	1,800
	2,000	3,000

Further information is as follows:

- Accumulated tax allowances claimed on the building to date are $600,000.
- Unrealised changes in the carrying value of investment property do not affect taxable profit.

- If an investment property is sold for more than cost, the reversal of accumulated depreciation will be included in taxable profit and taxed at the standard rate.
- The standard rate of tax is 30%, but for asset disposals in excess of cost, the tax rate is 20%, unless the asset has been held for less than two years, when the tax rate is 25%.

Required:

Calculate the deferred tax provision required if:

(a) **Melbourne expects to hold the investment property for more than two years.**

(b) **Melbourne expects to sell the investment property within two years.**

IAS 40 solution

A summary of cost, fair value, and accumulated allowances claimed to date, together with tax base and temporary difference is as follows:

	(a)	(b)	(c)	(a) - (c) = (d)	(b) - (d) = (e)
	Cost	**Fair value**	**Tax allowances claimed**	**Tax base**	**Temp. diff**
	$000	$000	$000	$000	$000
Land	800	1,200	–	800	400
Building	1,200	1,800	(600)	600	1,200
	2,000	3,000	(600)	1,400	1,600

Note that the tax rate to apply in each situation will be the tax rate expected to apply when the investment property is sold.

(a) **If Melbourne expects to hold the investment property for more than two years:**

The reversal of the accumulated depreciation charged on the building element will be charged at the standard rate of 30%, whilst the proceeds in excess of cost will be charged at 20% as follows:

		$000
Accumulated depreciation	(600 × 30%)	180
Proceeds in excess of cost	(1,000 × 20%)	200
Deferred tax liability		380

(b) **If Melbourne expects to sell the investment property within two years:**

The reversal of the accumulated depreciation charged on the building element will be charged at the standard rate of 30%, whilst the proceeds in excess of cost will be charged at 25% as follows:

		$000
Accumulated depreciation	(600 × 30%)	180
Proceeds in excess of cost	(1,000 × 25%)	250
Deferred tax liability		430

Share option schemes

Accounting for share option schemes involves recognising an annual remuneration expense in profit or loss throughout the vesting period. Tax relief is not normally granted until the share options are exercised. The amount of tax relief granted is based on the intrinsic value of the options (the difference between the market price of the shares and the exercise price of the option).

This delayed tax relief means that equity-settled share-based payment schemes give rise to a deferred tax asset.

The following pro-forma can be used to calculate the deferred tax asset arising on an equity-settled share-based payment scheme:

	$	$
Carrying value of share-based payment	Nil	
Less:		
Tax base of the share-based payment*	(X)	
× Tax rate %	X	
Deferred tax asset		X

* The tax base is the expected future tax relief (based on the intrinsic value of the options) that has accrued by the reporting date.

Where the amount of the estimated future tax deduction exceeds the accumulated remuneration expense, this indicates that the tax deduction relates partly to the remuneration expense and partly to equity. Therefore, the deferred tax must be recognised partly in profit or loss and partly in equity.

Test your understanding 5 – Splash

An entity, Splash, established a share option scheme for its four directors. This scheme commenced on 1 July 20X8. Each director will be entitled to 25,000 share options on condition that they remain with Splash for four years, from the date the scheme was introduced.

Information regarding the share options is provided below:

Fair value of option at grant date	$10
Fair value of option at 30 June 20X9	$12
Exercise price of option	$5

The market value (i.e. fair value) of the shares at 30 June 20X9 was $17 per share.

A tax deduction is only given for the share options when they are exercised. The allowable deduction will be based on the intrinsic value of the options. Assume a tax rate of 30%.

Required:

Calculate and explain the amounts to be included in the financial statements of Splash for the year ended 30 June 20X9, including explanation and calculation of any deferred tax implications.

Unused tax losses

Where an entity has unused tax losses, IAS 12 allows a deferred tax asset to be recognised only to the extent that it is probable that future taxable profits will be available against which the unused tax losses can be utilised.

IAS 12 advises that the deferred tax asset should only be recognised after considering:

- whether an entity has sufficient taxable temporary differences against which the unused tax losses can be offset.
- whether it is probable the entity will have taxable profits before the unused tax losses expire.
- whether the tax losses result from identifiable causes which are unlikely to recur (otherwise, the existence of unused tax losses is strong evidence that future taxable profits may not be available).
- whether tax planning opportunities are available to the entity that will create taxable profit in the period that the tax losses can be utilised.

Test you understanding 6 – Red

As at 31 December 20X1, Red has tax adjusted losses of $4m which arose from a one-off restructuring exercise. Under tax law, these losses may be carried forward to relieve taxable profits in the future. Red has produced forecasts that predict total future taxable profits over the next three years of $2.5m. However, the accountant of Red is not able to reliably forecast profits beyond that date.

The tax rate for profits earned during the year ended 31 December 20X1 is 30%. However, the government passed legislation during the reporting period that lowered the tax rate to 28% from 1 January 20X2.

Required:

Explain the deferred tax implications of the above.

Business combinations

A business combination can have several deferred tax consequences.

- The identifiable assets and liabilities of the acquired subsidiary are consolidated at fair value but the tax base derives from the values in the subsidiary's individual financial statements. A temporary difference is created, giving rise to deferred tax in the consolidated financial statements.
- The deferred tax recognised on this difference is treated as part of the net assets acquired and, as a result, impacts upon the amount of goodwill recognised on the acquisition of the subsidiary.
- The goodwill itself does not give rise to deferred tax because IAS 12 specifically excludes it.
- The acquirer may be able to utilise the benefit of its own unused tax losses against the future taxable profit of the acquiree. In such cases, the acquirer recognises a deferred tax asset, but does not take it into account in determining the goodwill arising on the acquisition.

Test your understanding 7 – Tom

On 30 June 20X1 Tom acquired 100% of the shares of Jones for $300,000. At this date, the carrying value of the net assets of Jones were $250,000. Included in this net asset figure is inventory which cost $50,000 but which had a replacement cost of $55,000. The applicable tax rate is 30%.

Required:

Explain the deferred tax implications of the above in the consolidated financial statements of the Tom group.

Provisions for unrealised profit

When one company within a group sells inventory to another group company, unrealised profits remaining within the group at the reporting date must be eliminated. The following adjustment is required in the consolidated financial statements:

Dr Cost of sales (P/L)
Cr Inventory (SFP)

This adjustment reduces the carrying value of inventory in the consolidated financial statements but the tax base of the inventory is its cost in the individual financial statements of the purchasing company.

- A deductible temporary difference is created, giving rise to a deferred tax asset in the consolidated financial statements.

Note: you may find it easier to think of this adjustment in terms of profits. The unrealised profit on the intra-group transaction is removed from the consolidated financial statements and therefore the tax charge on this profit must also be removed.

Test your understanding 8 – Mug

Mug has owned 80% of the ordinary shares of Glass for many years. During the current year, Mug sold inventory to Glass for $250,000 making a gross profit margin of 40%. One quarter of this inventory remains unsold by Glass at the reporting date.

The tax rate is 20%.

Required:

Discuss the deferred tax implications of the above transaction.

Unremitted earnings

A temporary difference arises when the carrying amount of investments in subsidiaries, branches, associates or joint ventures is different from the tax base.

- The carrying amount in consolidated financial statements is the investor's share of the net assets of the investee, plus purchased goodwill, but the tax base is usually the cost of the investment. Unremitted earnings (i.e. undistributed profits) in the accounts of subsidiaries, branches, associates or joint ventures, will lead to a temporary difference.
- Deferred tax should be recognised on these temporary differences except when:
  - the parent, investor or venturer is able to control the timing of the reversal of the temporary difference and
  - it is probable that the temporary difference will not reverse (i.e the profit will not be distributed) in the foreseeable future.
- An investor can control the dividend policy of a subsidiary, but not always that of other types of investment. This means that deferred tax does not arise on investments in subsidiaries, but may arise on investments in associates and joint ventures.

Trade investments may give rise to deferred tax if they are revalued.

Arguments for recognising deferred tax

If a deferred tax liability is ignored, profits are inflated and the obligation to pay an increased amount of tax in the future is also ignored. The arguments for recognising deferred tax are summarised below.

- The accruals concept requires tax to be matched to profits as they are earned.
- The deferred tax will eventually become an actual tax liability.
- Ignoring deferred tax overstates profits, which may result in:
  - over-optimistic dividend payments based on inflated profits
  - distortion of earnings per share and of the price/earnings ratio, both important indicators of an entity's performance
  - shareholders being misled.

Arguments for not recognising deferred tax

Some people believe that the 'temporary difference' approach is conceptually wrong. The framework for the preparation and presentation of financial statements defines a liability as an obligation to transfer economic benefits, as the result of a past event. In practice, a liability for deferred tax is often recognised before the entity actually has an obligation to pay the tax.

For example, suppose that an entity revalues a non-current asset and recognises a gain. It will not be liable for tax on the gain until the asset is sold. However, IAS 12 requires that deferred tax is recognised immediately on the revaluation gain, even if the entity has no intention of selling the asset (and realising the gain) for several years.

As a result, the IAS 12 approach could lead to the build-up of liabilities that may only crystallise in the distant future, if ever.

An alternative approach

An alternative approach to recognising deferred tax focuses on timing differences rather than temporary differences.

Timing differences arise because some gains and losses are recognised in the financial statements in different accounting periods from those in which they are assessed to tax. This results in differences between an entity's reported profit in the financial statements and its taxable profit. Timing differences originate in one period and may reverse in one or more subsequent periods.

The timing differences approach focuses on profit and loss for the period and on the actual tax expense. It is normally simpler to apply than the temporary differences approach, as it is usually easy to identify timing differences from tax computations.

Current issues

Accounting for deferred tax is an area that the IASB and FASB have identified as in need of convergence. In the October 2009 joint meeting, both boards indicated that they would consider undertaking a fundamental review of accounting for income taxes in the future.

In the meantime, the IASB has made some small amendments to IAS 12. For example, in December 2010, the IASB issued an amendment to IAS 12 dealing with accounting for deferred tax on investment property measured at fair value. This amendment is included within the content of this chapter.

6 Chapter summary

Basic principles
- Temporary differences
- Examples
- Calculations

Deferred tax liabilities and assets
- Recognition
- Measurement

Tax income andexpense
- Current tax
- Deferred tax

Specific situations
- Revaluations
- Business combinations
- Unremitted earnings
- Losses

Test your understanding answers

Test your understanding 1 – Dive (temporary differences)

	Carrying value	Tax base	Temp. difference
	$	$	$
Non-current asset	82,000	70,000	12,000
Interest receivable	1,000	Nil	1,000
Receivables	10,000	10,000	Nil
Inventory	4,500	5,000	(500)
Accrual (cash basis for tax)	(1,000)	Nil	(1,000)
Accrual (already had tax relief)	(5,000)	(5,000)	Nil

Test your understanding 2 – Dive (deferred tax calculation)

The net temporary difference as at the reporting date is as follows:

	$
Non-current assets	12,000
Interest receivable	1,000
Receivables	–
Inventory	(500)
Accrual (cash basis for tax)	(1,000)
Accrual (already had tax relief)	–
	11,500

There will be a deferred tax liability because the carrying value of the net assets and liabilities exceeds their net tax base. The deferred tax liability is calculated by applying the relevant tax rate to the temporary difference.

The deferred tax liability is therefore $3,450 ($11,500 × 30%).

Assuming that there is no opening deferred tax liability, the following accounting entry is required:

Dr Tax expense (P/L)	$3,450
Cr Deferred tax liability (SFP)	$3,450

Test your understanding 3 – Brick

Deferred tax liabilities and assets should be measured using the tax rates expected to apply when the asset is realised. This tax rate must have been enacted or substantively enacted by the end of the reporting period.

The government enacted the 20% tax rate after the period end. Therefore, it should not be used when calculating the deferred tax liability for the year ended 30 April 20X4. The current 22% rate should be used instead.

Per IAS 10, changes in tax rates after the end of the reporting period are a non-adjusting event. However, if the change in the tax rate is deemed to be material then Brick should disclose this rate change and an estimate of the financial impact.

Test your understanding 4 – Dodge

The carrying value of the asset is $90,000 and the tax base is $50,000 ($100,000 – $50,000). The carrying value exceeds the tax base by $40,000 ($90,000 – $50,000).

This temporary difference will give rise to a deferred tax liability of $12,000 ($40,000 × 30%).

Prior to the revaluation, the carrying value of the asset was $60,000. The asset was then revalued to $90,000. Therefore, $30,000 ($90,000 – $60,000) of the temporary difference relates to the revaluation. Revaluation gains are recorded in other comprehensive income and so the deferred tax charge relating to this gain should also be recorded in other comprehensive income. This means that the tax charged to other comprehensive income is $9,000 ($30,000 × 30%).

The following accounting entry is required:

Dr Other comprehensive income	$9,000
Dr Profit or loss (bal. fig.)	$3,000
Cr Deferred tax liability	$12,000

Test your understanding 5 – Splash

The expense recognised for an equity-settled share-based payment scheme is calculated based on the fair value of the options at the grant date. This expense is spread over the vesting period. At each reporting date, the entity should reassess the number of options expected to vest.

The expense for the scheme in the year ended 30 June 20X9 is $250,000 (4 × 25,000 × $10 × 1/4).

For tax purposes, tax relief is allowed based on the intrinsic value of the options at the date they are exercised.

At the reporting date, the shares have a market value of $17 but the options allow the holders to purchase these shares for $5. The options therefore have an intrinsic value of $12 ($17 – $5).

The deferred tax asset is calculated as follows:

	$	$
Carrying value of share-based payment	Nil	
Tax base of the share-based payment (4 × 25,000 × ($17 – $5) × 1/4)	(300,000)	
× Tax rate 30%	(300,000)	
Deferred tax asset		90,000

Where the amount of the estimated future tax deduction exceeds the accumulated remuneration expense, this indicates that the tax deduction relates partly to the remuneration expense and partly to equity.

In this case, the estimated future tax deduction is $300,000 whereas the accumulated remuneration expense is $250,000. Therefore, $50,000 of the temporary difference is deemed to relate to an equity item, and the deferred tax relating to this should be credited to equity.

The following entry is required:

Dr Deferred tax asset	$90,000
Cr Equity ($50,000 × 30%)	$15,000
Cr Profit or loss ($250,000 × 30%)	$75,000

If the deferred tax asset is to be recognised, it must be capable of reliable measurement and also be regarded as recoverable.

Test you understanding 6 – Red

The tax adjusted losses have no carrying value in the financial statements. However, they will reduce taxable profits in the future and therefore they have a tax base.

A deferred tax asset can be recognised based on this temporary difference if it is deemed probable that future taxable profits will be available against which the unused losses can be utilised.

The tax losses have arisen from an exceptional event, suggesting that the entity will return to profitability. Forecasts produced by the accountant confirm this.

Red is only able to reliably forecast future profits of $2.5m. This limits the deferred tax asset that can be recognised.

Deferred tax should be calculated using the tax rate that is expected to be in force when the temporary difference reverses based on the rates enacted by the reporting date. This means that the 28% rate should be used.

The deferred tax asset that can be recognised is therefore $700,000 ($2.5m × 28%). There will be a corresponding credit to the tax expense in the statement of profit or loss.

Test your understanding 7 – Tom

According to IFRS 3, the net assets of the subsidiary at the acquisition date must be consolidated at fair value. The carrying value of the inventory in the group financial statements will be $55,000. The tax base of the inventory is based on its carrying value of $50,000 in the individual financial statements. Therefore, there is a temporary difference of $5,000 that arises on consolidation.

A deferred tax liability must be recognised in the consolidated financial statements for $1,500 ($5,000 × 30%). This is treated as a reduction in the subsidiary's net assets at the acquisition date, which will increase the goodwill arising on acquisition.

	$	$
Consideration		300,000
Net assets:		
Carrying value	250,000	
Fair value uplift	5,000	
Deferred tax liability	(1,500)	
		(253,500)
Goodwill at acquisition		46,500

Test your understanding 8 – Mug

There has been an intra-group sale and some of the inventory remains within the group at the reporting date. The profits held within this unsold inventory must therefore be removed from the consolidated statements.

The profit on the sale was \$100,000 (\$250,000 × 40%). Of this, \$25,000 (\$100,000 × 25%) remains within the inventory of the group.

The adjustment required to eliminate the unrealised profits is:

Dr Cost of sales	\$25,000
Cr Inventory	\$25,000

The carrying value of inventory in the consolidated financial statements is now \$25,000 lower than its tax base, creating a deductible temporary difference of \$25,000. This gives rise to a deferred tax asset of \$5,000 (\$25,000 × 20%) in the consolidated statement of financial position as well as a corresponding reduction to the tax expense in the consolidated statement of profit or loss.

The adjustment required to account for the deferred tax is:

Dr Deferred tax asset	\$5,000
Cr Tax expense	\$5,000

chapter

14

Group accounting – basic groups

Chapter learning objectives

Upon completion of this chapter you will be able to:

- apply the method of accounting for business combinations
- apply the principles in determining the cost of a business combination
- apply the recognition and measurement criteria for identifiable acquired assets and liabilities and goodwill
- apply and discuss the criteria used to identify a subsidiary and an associate
- determine and apply appropriate procedures to be used in preparing group financial statements
- Identify and outline:
  - the circumstances in which a group is required to prepare consolidated financial statements
  - the circumstances when a group may claim an exemption from the preparation of consolidated financial statements
  - why directors may not wish to consolidate a subsidiary and where this is permitted
- apply the equity method of accounting for associates
- outline and apply the key definitions and accounting methods which relate to interests in joint arrangements
- discuss current issues in group accounting.

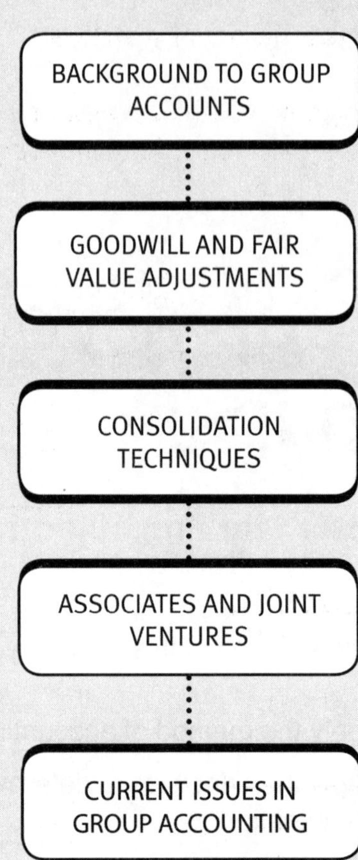
BACKGROUND TO GROUP ACCOUNTS
GOODWILL AND FAIR VALUE ADJUSTMENTS
CONSOLIDATION TECHNIQUES
ASSOCIATES AND JOINT VENTURES
CURRENT ISSUES IN GROUP ACCOUNTING

1 Overview of interests in other entities

The following diagram presents an overview of the varying types of interests in other entities, together with identification of applicable reporting standards.

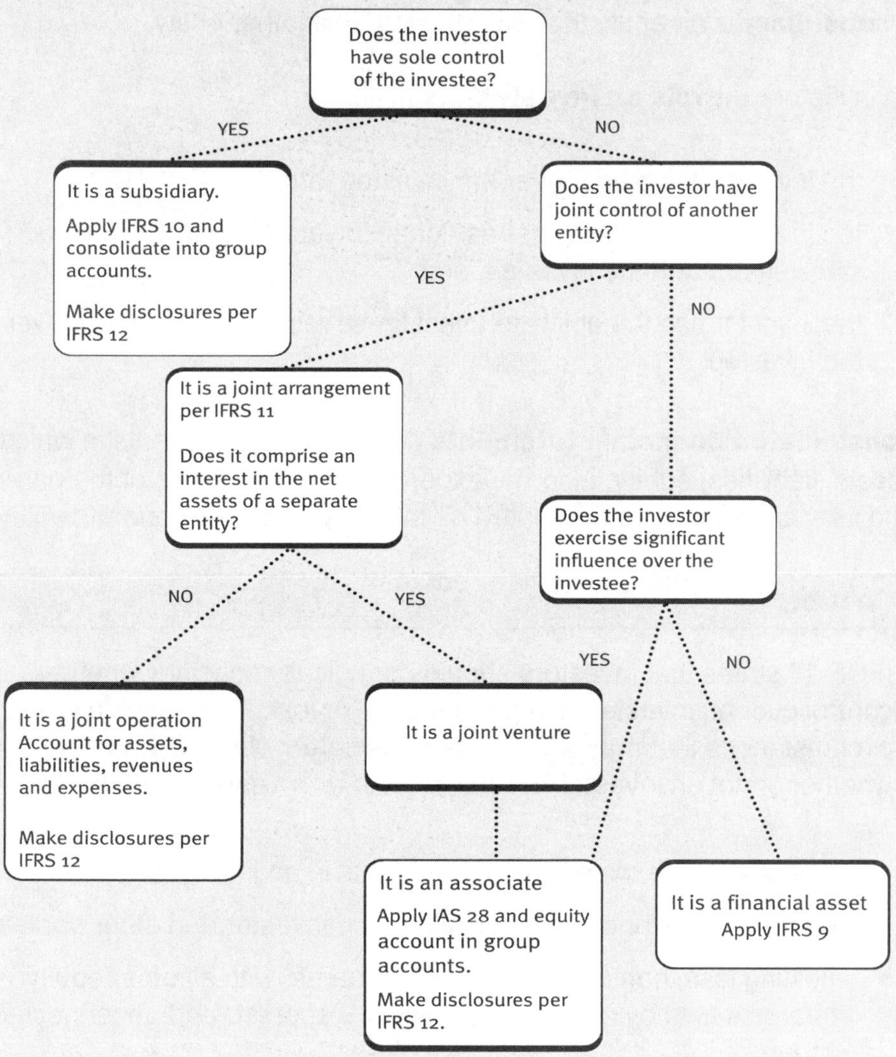

The standards referred to in the diagram above cover a range of group accounting issues:

- IFRS 10 Consolidated Financial Statements
- IFRS 11 Joint Arrangements
- IFRS 12 Disclosure of Interests in Other Entities
- IAS 28 Investments in Associates and Joint Ventures

These standards, as well as IFRS 3 Business Combinations, are covered in this chapter. IFRS 9 Financial Instruments was dealt with earlier in the publication.

2 Definitions

An entity that is a parent is required to prepare consolidated financial statements.

A **parent** is an entity that controls one or more entities.

A **subsidiary** is an entity that is controlled by another entity.

An investor **controls an investee** when:

- the investor has power over the investee, and
- the investor is exposed, or has rights, to variable returns from its involvement with the investee, and
- the investor has the ability to affect those returns through its power over the investee.

Consolidated financial statements are financial statements in which the assets, liabilities, equity, income, expenses and cash flows of the parent and its subsidiaries are presented as those of a single economic entity.

Control

IFRS 10 states that investors should periodically consider whether control over an investee has been gained or lost. It identifies a range of circumstances that may need to be considered when determining whether or not an investor has power over an investee, such as:

- exercise of the majority of voting rights in an investee
- contractual arrangements between the investor and other parties
- holding less than 50% of the voting shares, with all other equity interests held by a numerically large, dispersed and unconnected group
- holding potential voting rights (such as convertible loans) that are currently capable of being exercised
- the nature of the investor's relationship with other parties that may enable that investor to exercise control over an investee
- the exercise of control over a portion of another entity could lead to consolidation of only part of a separate entity over which control is exercised (this is referred to in IFRS 10 as a 'silo').

Application of IFRS 10 control definition

Example 1:

An investor acquires 48 per cent of the voting rights of an investee. The remaining voting rights are held by thousands of shareholders, none individually holding more than 1 per cent of the voting rights. None of the shareholders has any arrangements to consult any of the others or make collective decisions. When assessing the proportion of voting rights to acquire, on the basis of the relative size of the other shareholdings, the investor determined that a 48 per cent interest would be sufficient to give it control.

In this case, on the basis of the absolute size of its holding and the relative size of the other shareholdings, the investor concludes that it has a sufficiently dominant voting interest to meet the power criterion without the need to consider any other evidence of power.

Example 2:

Investor A holds 40 per cent of the voting rights of an investee and twelve other investors each hold 5 per cent of the voting rights of the investee. A shareholder agreement grants investor A the right to appoint, remove and set the remuneration of management responsible for directing the relevant activities. To change the agreement, a two-thirds majority vote of the shareholders is required.

In this case, investor A decides that the absolute size of its holding and the relative size of the other shareholdings alone are not conclusive in determining whether it has control. However, investor A determines that the combination of its voting rights and ability to appoint or remove management is sufficient to conclude that it has control over the investee.

Test your understanding 1 – Control

Parsley has a 40% holding in the ordinary shares of Oregano. Another investor has a 10% shareholding in Oregano whilst the remaining voting rights are held by thousands of shareholders, none of whom individually hold more than 1 per cent of the voting rights. Parsley also holds debt instruments that, as at 30 April 20X4, are convertible into ordinary shares of Oregano at a price of $4 per share. At 30 April 20X4, the shares of Oregano trade at $3.80 per share. If the debt was converted into ordinary shares, Parsley would hold 60% of the voting rights in Oregano. Parsley and Oregano undertake similar activities and would benefit from synergies.

Required:

Discuss how Parsley's investment in the ordinary shares of Oregano should be treated in the consolidated financial statements for the year ended 30 April 20X4.

Exemptions from consolidation

Intermediate parent companies

An intermediate parent entity is an entity which has a subsidiary but is also itself a subsidiary of another entity. For example:

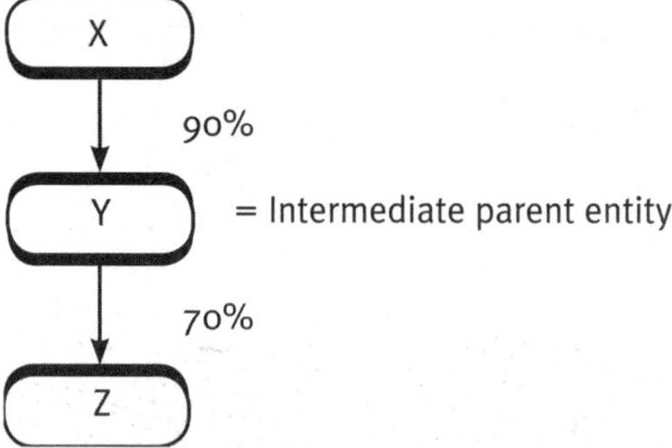

IFRS 10 permits a parent entity not to present group financial statements provided all of the following conditions apply:

- it is a wholly-owned, or partially-owned subsidiary where owners of the non-controlling interest do not object to the non-preparation
- its debt or equity instruments are not currently traded in a domestic or foreign market
- it is not in the process of having any of its debt or equity instruments traded on a domestic or foreign market

- the ultimate parent entity produces consolidated financial statements that comply with IFRS and which are available to the public.

If this is the case, IAS 27 Separate Financial Statements requires that the following disclosures are made:

- the fact that consolidated financial statements have not been presented
- a list of significant investments (subsidiaries, joint ventures and associates) including percentage shareholdings, principal place of business and country of incorporation
- the bases on which those investments listed above have been accounted for in its separate financial statements.

Investment entities

An investment entity is defined by IFRS 10 as an entity that:

(a) obtains funds from one or more investors for the purpose of providing those investor(s) with investment management services, and

(b) commits to its investor(s) that its business purpose is to invest funds solely for returns from capital appreciation, investment income, or both, and

(c) measures and evaluates the performance of substantially all of its investments on a fair value basis.

Amendments to IFRS 10, IFRS 12 and IAS 27 that were issued in October 2012 state that investment entities do not consolidate an investment over which they have control. Instead, the investment is measured at fair value through profit or loss.

Particular situations

IFRS 10 and IAS 27 do not specify any other circumstances when subsidiaries must be excluded from consolidation. However, the following circumstances merit consideration:

(a) **Acquired for resale**

A subsidiary acquired exclusively with a view to disposal within 12 months will probably meet the conditions in IFRS 5 Non-current assets held for sale and discontinued activities for classification as held for sale. If it does, it is accounted for under IFRS 5, with all of its assets presented as a single line item below current assets and all of its liabilities presented as a single line item below current liabilities. The subsidiary is therefore still consolidated, but in a different way.

(b) **Materiality**

Accounting standards do not normally apply to immaterial items, meaning that an immaterial subsidiary need not be consolidated. However, this would need to be kept under review from year to year, and the parent would need to consider each subsidiary to be excluded on this basis, both individually and collectively. Ideally, a parent should consolidate all subsidiaries which it controls in all accounting periods, rather than report changes in the corporate structure from one period to the next.

Invalid reasons to exclude a subsidiary from consolidation

In addition to the valid reasons to exclude a subsidiary from consolidation considered earlier, directors of the parent entity may seek to exclude a subsidiary from group accounts for several invalid reasons, including:

- **Long-term restrictions on the ability to transfer funds to the parent**. This exclusion from consolidation is not permitted as it may still be possible to control a subsidiary in such circumstances.
- The **subsidiary undertakes different activities** and/or operates in different locations, thus being distinctive from other members of the group. This is not a valid reason for exclusion from consolidation. Indeed it could be argued that inclusion within the group accounts of such a subsidiary will enhance the relevance and reliability of the information contained within the group accounts.
- The **subsidiary has made losses or has significant liabilities** which the directors would prefer to exclude from the group accounts to improve the overall reported financial performance and position of the group. This could be motivated, for example, by determination of directors' remuneration based upon group financial performance. This is not a valid reason for exclusion from consolidation.

- The directors may seek to **disguise the true ownership of the subsidiary**, perhaps to avoid disclosure of particular activities or events, or to avoid disclosure of ownership of assets. This could be motivated, for example, by seeking to avoid disclosure of potential conflicts of interest which may be perceived adversely by users of financial statements.
- The directors may seek to exclude a subsidiary from consolidation in order for the group to **disguise its true size and extent**. This could be motivated, for example, by trying to avoid legal and regulatory compliance requirements applicable to the group or individual subsidiaries. This is not a valid reason for exclusion from consolidation.

3 The acquisition method

Per IFRS 3 Business Combinations, all business combinations should be accounted for using the acquisition method.

The acquisition method has four requirements:

- Identifying the acquirer
- Determining the acquisition date
- Recognising and measuring the identifiable assets acquired, the liabilities assumed and any non-controlling interest in the acquiree
- Recognising and measuring goodwill or a gain from a bargain purchase.

Identifying the acquirer

The acquirer is the entity that has assumed control over another entity.

In a business combination, it is normally clear which entity has assumed control. If it is not clear as to which entity is the acquirer, IFRS 3 provides some guidance:

- The acquirer is normally the entity that has transferred cash or other assets within the business combination
- If the business combination has not involved the transfer of cash or other assets, the acquirer is usually the entity that issues its equity interests.

Other factors to consider are as follows:

- The acquirer is usually the entity whose (former) management dominates the management of the combined entity
- The acquirer is usually the entity whose owners retain or receive the largest portion of the voting rights in the combined entity
- The acquirer is normally the entity whose size is greater than the other entities.

Test your understanding 2 – Identifying the acquirer

Abacus and Calculator are two public limited companies. The fair values of the net assets of these two companies are $100 million and $60 million respectively.

On 31 October 20X1, Abacus incorporates a new company, Phone, in order to effect the combination of Abacus and Calculator. Phone issues its shares to the shareholders of Abacus and Calculator in return for their equity interests.

After this, Phone is 60% owned by the former shareholders of Abacus and 40% owned by the former shareholders of Calculator. On the board of Phone are 4 of the former directors of Abacus and 2 of the former directors of Calculator.

Required:

With regards to the above business combination, identify the acquirer.

The acquisition date

The acquisition date is the date on which the acquirer obtains control over the acquiree.

Identifiable assets, liabilities and the non-controlling interest

The acquirer shall measure the identifiable assets acquired and the liabilities assumed at their fair values at the acquisition date.

At the acquisition date, the acquirer shall measure the non-controlling interests in the acquiree at either:

(a) fair value or

(b) the non-controlling interest's share of the fair value of the identifiable net assets acquired.

Goodwill

Goodwill should be recognised on a business combination. This is calculated as the difference between:

(1) The aggregate of the fair value of the consideration transferred and the non-controlling interest in the acquiree at the acquisition date, and

(2) The fair value of the acquiree's identifiable net assets and liabilities.

4 The fair value of net assets

IFRS 3 requires that the identifiable net assets of the subsidiary are measured at their fair values at the date of acquisition.

Goodwill in the subsidiary's individual financial statements is not an identifiable asset because it cannot be separately disposed of.

Fair value of the identifiable net assets of the acquiree

Identifiable assets

An asset is identifiable if:

- It is capable of disposal separately from the business owning it, or
- It arises from contractual or other legal rights, regardless of whether those rights can be sold separately.

The identifiable assets and liabilities of the subsidiary should be recognised at fair value where:

- they meet the definitions of assets and liabilities in the Conceptual Framework for Financial Reporting, and
- they are exchanged as part of the business combination rather than a separate transaction.

Items that are not identifiable or do not meet the definitions of assets or liabilities are subsumed into the calculation of purchased goodwill.

Fair value – exceptions

There are certain exceptions to the requirement to measure the subsidiary's net assets at fair value when accounting for business combinations:

- The assets and liabilities falling within the scope of IAS 12 Income Taxes, IAS 19 Employee Benefits, IFRS 2 Share-based Payment and IFRS 5 Non-current Assets Held for Sale and Discontinued Operations are required to be valued according to those standards
- Leases are required to be classified on the basis of factors at the inception date rather than factors at the acquisition date of the subsidiary.

Contingent liabilities

Contingent liabilities that are present obligations arising from past events and that can be measured reliably are recognised at fair value at the acquisition date. This is true even where an economic outflow is not probable. The fair value will incorporate the probability of an economic outflow.

Provisions

A provision for future operating losses cannot be created as this is a post-acquisition item. Similarly, restructuring costs are only recognised to the extent that a liability actually exists at the date of acquisition.

Test your understanding 3 – Fair value of identifiable net assets

P purchased 60% of the shares of S on 1 January 20X1. At the acquisition date, S had share capital of $10,000 and retained earnings of $190,000.

The property, plant and equipment of S includes land with a carrying value of $10,000 but a fair value of $50,000.

Included within the intangible assets of S is goodwill of $20,000 which arose on the purchase of the trade and assets of a sole-trader business. S has an internally generated brand that is not recognised (in accordance with IAS 38). The directors of P believe that this brand has a fair value of $150,000.

In accordance with IAS 37, the financial statements of S disclose the fact that a customer has initiated legal proceedings against them. If the customer wins, which lawyers have advised is unlikely, estimated damages would be $1m. The fair value of this contingent liability has been assessed as $100,000 at the acquisition date.

The directors of P wish to close one of the divisions of S. They estimate that this will cost $200,000 in redundancy payments.

Required:

What is the fair value of S's identifiable net assets at the acquisition date?

5 Non-controlling interest

IFRS 3 revised provides a choice in valuing the non-controlling interest at acquisition:

EITHER:	OR:
Method 1 - The proportionate share of net assets method NCI % × Fair value of the net assets of the subsidiary at the acquisition date	**Method 2 - The fair value method** Fair value of NCI at date of acquisition. This is usually given in the question.

Non-controlling interest

Choice of method

The standard indicates that the method used to measure the NCI should be decided on a transaction by transaction basis. This means that, within the same group, the NCI in some subsidiaries may have been measured at fair value at acquisition, whilst the NCI in other subsidiaries may have been measured at acquisition using the proportionate basis.

Subsequent measurement of the NCI

In subsequent years the NCI is increased by the proportion of post-acquisition retained earnings and any other reserves (e.g. revaluation reserve) due to the NCI. This is true regardless of which method is used to value the NCI at acquisition.

6 Purchase consideration

The purchase consideration transferred to acquire control of a subsidiary must be measured at fair value at the acquisition date.

- Contingent consideration should be included at fair value, even if payment is not deemed probable. The fair value will incorporate the probability of payment occurring.
- Acquisition costs are excluded from the calculation of purchase consideration.
  - Legal and professional fees are expensed to profit or loss as incurred
  - Debt or equity issue costs are accounted for in accordance with IFRS 9 Financial Instruments.

Contingent consideration

IFRS 3 says that contingent consideration is:

'Usually, an obligation of the acquirer to transfer additional assets or equity interests to the former owners of an acquiree as part of the exchange for control of the acquiree if specified future events occur or conditions are met. However, contingent consideration also may give the acquirer the right to the return of previously transferred consideration if specified conditions are met.'

In an examination question the acquisition date fair value of any contingent consideration (or details of how to calculate it) would be given.

The payment of contingent consideration may be in the form of equity or a liability (issuing a debt instrument or cash) and should be recorded as such under the rules of IAS 32 Financial Instruments: Presentation (or other applicable standard).

Changes in the fair value of any contingent consideration after the acquisition date are also dealt with in IFRS 3.

- Changes due to additional information obtained after the acquisition date that affects the facts or circumstances as they existed at the acquisition date are accounted for retrospectively. This means that the liability (and goodwill) are remeasured. This further information must have been obtained within twelve months of the acquisition date.

- Changes due to events after the acquisition date (for example, meeting an earnings target which triggers a higher payment than was provided for at acquisition) are treated as follows:
  - Contingent consideration classified as equity shall not be remeasured. Its subsequent settlement shall be accounted for within equity (e.g. Cr share capital/share premium Dr retained earnings).
  - Contingent consideration classified as an asset or a liability shall be remeasured with the movement recognised in profit or loss.

Note: Although contingent consideration is usually a liability, it may be an asset if the acquirer has the right to a return of some of the consideration transferred if certain conditions are met.

Test your understanding 4 – Purchase consideration

Following on from TYU 3, the purchase consideration transferred by P in exchange for the shares in S was as follows:

- Cash paid of $300,000
- Cash to be paid in one year's time of $200,000
- 10,000 shares in P. These had a nominal value of $1 and a fair value at 1 January 20X1 of $3 each
- $250,000 to be paid in one year's time if S makes a profit before tax of more than $2m. There is a 50% chance of this happening. The fair value of this contingent consideration can be measured as the present value of the expected value

Legal fees associated with the acquisition were $10,000.

Where required, a discount rate of 10% should be used.

Required:

Per IFRS 3, what is the fair value of the consideration transferred to acquire control of S?

7 Goodwill

The calculation of goodwill will depend on the method chosen to value the non-controlling interest at the acquisition date.

If the NCI is valued at acquisition as their proportionate share of the acquisition net assets, then only the acquirer's goodwill will be calculated.

- Where an exam question requires the use of this method, it will state that 'it is group policy to value the non-controlling interest at its proportionate share of the fair value of the subsidiary's identifiable net assets'.

If the NCI is valued at acquisition at fair value, then goodwill attributable to both the acquirer and the NCI will be calculated. This is known as the 'full goodwill method'.

- Where an exam question requires the use of this method, it will state that 'it is group policy to value the non-controlling interest using the full goodwill method' or that 'the non-controlling interest is measured at fair value'.

Test your understanding 5 – Goodwill

Following on from 'Test your understandings' 3 and 4, the fair value of the non-controlling interest at the acquisition date is $160,000.

Required:

Calculate the goodwill arising on the acquisition of S if the non-controlling interest at the acquisition date is valued at:

(a) **fair value**

(b) **its proportion of the fair value of the subsidiary's identifiable net assets.**

Measurement period

During the measurement period, the acquirer in a business combination must retrospectively adjust the provisional amounts recognised at the acquisition date to reflect new information obtained about facts and circumstances that existed as of the acquisition date.

- Goodwill arising on acquisition must therefore be recalculated.

The measurement period ends no later than twelve months after the acquisition date.

Measurement period illustration

P bought 100% of the shares of S on 31 December 20X1 for $60,000. On the acquisition date, it was estimated that the fair value of S's net assets were $40,000.

For the year ended 31 December 20X1, P would consolidate S's net assets of $40,000 and would also show goodwill of $20,000 ($60,000 – $40,000).

However, P receives further information on 30 June 20X2 which indicates that the fair value of S's net assets at the acquisition date was actually $50,000. This information was determined within the measurement period and so is retrospectively adjusted for.

Therefore, the financial statements for the year ended 31 December 20X1 will be adjusted. P will now consolidate S's net assets of $50,000 and will show goodwill of $10,000 ($60,000 – $50,000).

Bargain purchases

If the share of net assets acquired exceeds the consideration given, then a gain on bargain purchase ('negative goodwill') arises on acquisition. The accounting treatment for this is as follows:

- IFRS 3 says that negative goodwill is rare and therefore it may mean that an error has been made in determining the fair values of the consideration and the net assets acquired. The figures must be reviewed for errors.
- If no errors have been made, the negative goodwill is credited immediately to profit or loss.

8 Impairment of goodwill

IAS 36 requires that goodwill is tested for impairment annually.

Goodwill does not generate independent cash inflows. Therefore, it is tested for impairment as part of a cash generating unit.

- A cash generating unit is the smallest identifiable group of assets that generates cash inflows that are largely independent of the cash inflows from other assets or groups of assets.

For exam purposes, a subsidiary is normally designated as a cash generating unit.

Accounting for an impairment

An **impairment loss** is the amount by which the carrying amount of an asset or a cash generating unit exceeds its recoverable amount.

Recoverable amount is the higher of fair value less costs to sell and value in use.

Impairment losses on a subsidiary will firstly be allocated against goodwill and then against other assets on a pro-rata basis.

Accounting for an impairment with a non-controlling interest

Full method of valuing NCI

- Goodwill calculated under the fair value method represents full goodwill. It can therefore be added together with the other net assets of the subsidiary and compared to the recoverable amount of the subsidiary's net assets on a like for like basis.
- Any impairment of goodwill is allocated between the group and the NCI based upon their respective shareholdings.

Illustration 1 – Impairment of full goodwill

A owns 80% of B. At 31 October 20X6 the carrying amount of B's net assets is $60 million, excluding goodwill of $8 million that arose on the original acquisition. The non-controlling interest is valued using the fair value method.

Calculate the impairment loss if the recoverable amount of the net assets of B is:

(a) $64 million

(b) $50 million

Solution

Solution (a)

	$m
Goodwill	8
Net assets	60
Carrying value	68
Recoverable amount	64
Impairment	4

The impairment loss will be allocated against goodwill, reducing it from $8m to $4m.

The $4m impairment expense will be charged to profit or loss. Of this, $3.2m ($4m × 80%) is attributable to the group and $0.8m ($4m × 80%) is attributable to the NCI.

Solution (b)

	$m
Goodwill	8
Net assets	60
Carrying value	68
Recoverable amount	50
Impairment	18

The impairment loss is firstly allocated to goodwill, thus writing it down to $nil. The remaining $10m ($18m – $8m) is set against other assets on a pro-rata basis, unless there is further information available regarding the recoverable amount of other individual assets.

The total impairment of $18m is charged to profit or loss. Of this, $14.4m ($18m × 80%) is attributable to the group and $3.6m ($18m × 20%) is attributable to the NCI.

Proportionate method of valuing NCI

If the NCI is valued at acquisition at its share of the subsidiary's net assets then only the goodwill attributable to the group is calculated. This means that the NCI share of goodwill is not reflected in the group accounts. As such, any comparison between the carrying value of the subsidiary (including goodwill) and the recoverable amount of its net assets will not be on a like for like basis.

- In order to address this problem, goodwill must be grossed up to include goodwill attributable to the NCI prior to conducting the impairment review
- This grossed up goodwill is known as 'total notional goodwill'.
- Once any impairment loss is determined, it should be allocated firstly to the total notional goodwill and then to the subsidiary's assets on a pro rata basis.
- As only the parent's share of the goodwill is recognised in the group accounts, only the parent's share of the goodwill impairment loss should be recognised.

Illustration 2 – NCI on proportionate basis

A owns 80% of B. At 31 October 20X6 the carrying amount of B's net assets is $60 million, excluding goodwill of $8 million that arose on the original acquisition. The non-controlling interest is valued using the proportion of net assets method.

Calculate the impairment loss if the recoverable amount of B's net assets is:

(a) $64 million

(b) $50 million

Solution

Solution (a)

	$m	$m
Goodwill	8	
Unrecognised NCI (20/80 × $8m)	2	
Total notional goodwill		10
Net assets		60
Carrying value		70
Recoverable amount		64
Impairment		6

The impairment loss is allocated against the total notional goodwill.

Only the group's share of goodwill has been recognised in the financial statements and therefore only the group's share (80%) of the impairment is recognised. The impairment charged to profit or loss is therefore $4.8m and goodwill will be reduced to $3.2m ($8m – $4.8m).

Solution (b)

	$m	$m
Goodwill	8	
Unrecognised NCI (20/80 × $8m)	2	
Total notional goodwill		10
Net assets		60
Carrying value		70
Recoverable amount		50
Impairment		20

The impairment loss is firstly allocated to the notional goodwill, reducing it from $10m to nil. However, as only $8m of the goodwill was recognised in the financial statements, only $8m of the impairment is recognised. This will be charged to profit or loss and is all attributable to the owners of the group.

The remaining impairment of $10 million ($20m – $10m) is allocated to other net assets and charged to profit or loss. Of this $10m, $8m is attributable to the owners of the group and $2m is attributable to the NCI.

Therefore, the total impairment charged to profit or loss is $18m.

Test your understanding 6 – Happy

On 1 January 20X5, Lucky group purchased 80% of Happy for $500,000. The fair value of the identifiable net assets of Happy at the date of acquisition amounted to $560,000. It is Lucky Group policy to value the non-controlling interest at its proportionate share of the fair value of the subsidiary's identifiable net assets.

The carrying amount of Happy's net assets at 31 December is $520,000 (excluding goodwill). Happy is a cash-generating unit.

At 31 December 20X5 the recoverable amount of Happy's net assets is $510,000.

Required:

Calculate the impairment loss and explain how this would be dealt with in the financial statements of the Lucky group.

9 Associates

Associates

Accounting for associates was dealt with as part of your ACCA Paper F7 (or equivalent) studies and is defined and explained in the following commentary.

Definitions

- An **associate** is an entity over which the investor has **significant influence** and which is neither a subsidiary nor a joint venture of the investor.
- **Significant influence** is the power to participate in, but not control, the financial and operating policy decisions of an entity.
  - Significant influence is usually evidenced by representation on the board of directors, which allows the investing entity to participate in policy decisions.

- A holding between 20% and 50% of the voting power is presumed to give significant influence, unless it can be clearly demonstrated that this is not the case.
- Conversely, it is presumed that a holding of less than 20% does not give significant influence, unless such influence can be clearly demonstrated.

Accounting for associates

Associates are not consolidated because the parent does not have control. Instead they are accounted for using the **equity method**.

Statement of financial position

IAS 28 requires that the carrying value of the associate is determined as follows:

	$000
Cost	X
Add: P% of increase in reserves	X
Less: impairment losses	(X)
Less: P% of unrealised profits if P is the seller	(X)
Less: P% of excess depreciation on fair value adjustments	(X)
Investment in associate	X

The investment in the associate is shown in the non-current assets section of the consolidated statement of financial position.

Statement of profit or loss

For an associate, a single line item is presented in the statement of profit or loss below operating profit. This is made up as follows:

	$
P% of associate's profit after tax	X
Less: Current year impairment loss	(X)
Less: P% of unrealised profits if associate is the seller	(X)
Less: P% of excess depreciation on fair value adjustments	(X)
Share of profit of associate	X

Within consolidated other comprehensive income, the group should present its share of the associate's other comprehensive income (if applicable).

General points and disclosures

- The equity method is not used when:
  - the investment is classified as held for sale in accordance with IFRS 5 Non-current assets held for sale and discontinued operations
  - the investor is itself a subsidiary, its owners do not object to the equity method not being applied and its debt and equity securities are not publicly traded. In this case, the investor's parent must present consolidated financial statements that do use the equity method.
- Transactions and balances between the associate and the parent company are not eliminated because the associate is not a part of the group.
- Dividends received from the associate must be removed from the consolidated statement of profit or loss.
- The group share of any unrealised profit arising on transactions between the group and the associate must be eliminated.
  - If the associate is the seller:
    - Dr Share of the associate's profit (P/L)/Retained earnings (SFP)
    - Cr Inventories (SFP)
  - If the associate is the purchaser:
    - Dr Cost of sales (P/L)/Retained earnings (SFP)
    - Cr Investment in the associate (SFP)
- The financial statements used to equity account for the associate should be drawn up to the investor's reporting date. If this is not possible, then the difference in reporting dates should be less than three months.
- The associate's accounting policies should be harmonised with those of its investor.
- The investor should disclose its share of the associate's contingencies.
- A list and description of significant associates should be disclosed. This will note the ownership interests and voting interests for each associate.

Test your understanding 7 – Paint

Paint has several investments in subsidiary companies. On 1 July 20X1, it acquires 30% of the ordinary shares of Animate for $2m. This holding gives Paint significant influence over Animate.

At the acquisition date, the fair value of Animate's net assets approximate to their carrying values with the exception of a building. This building, with a remaining useful life of 10 years, had a carrying value of $1m but a fair value of $1.8m.

Between 1 July 20X1 and 31 December 20X1, Animate sold goods to Paint for $1 million making a profit of $100,000. All of these goods remain in the inventory of Paint. This sale was made on credit and the invoice has not yet been settled.

Animate made a profit after tax of $800,000 for the year ended 31 December 20X1. At 31 December 20X1, the directors of Paint believe that the investment in the associate needs impairing by $50,000.

Required:

Prepare extracts from the consolidated statement of financial position and the consolidated statement of profit or loss showing the treatment of the associate for the year ended 31 December 20X1.

10 Consolidation techniques

Consolidated statement of financial position

Producing a consolidated statement of financial position involves five standard workings. These will help you to understand the structure of the group and to calculate goodwill, the non-controlling interest and group reserves.

The first step in any examination question should be to determine the group structure.

(W1) **Group structure**

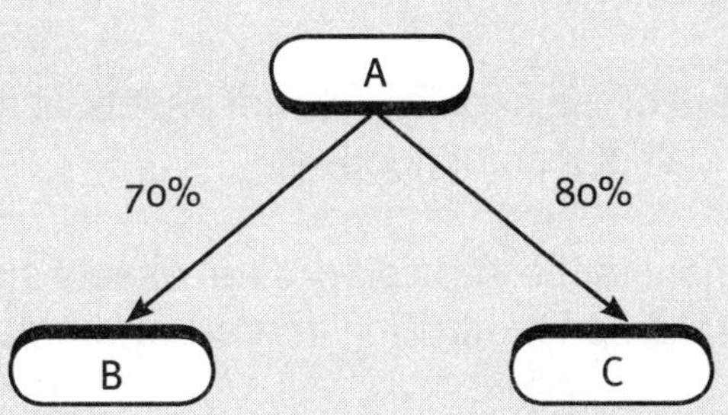

This working is useful to decide whether the question involves subsidiaries, associates, joint ventures, or simple trade investments. You may also want to include the dates of acquisitions and disposals.

Once the group structure has been determined, set up a proforma statement of financial position.

- Eliminate the carrying value of the parent's investments in its subsidiaries. These will be replaced by goodwill.
- The assets and liabilities of the parent and its subsidiaries should be added together in full.
- Only include the parent company's share capital and share premium.
- The following standard workings will help you to determine goodwill, NCI and group reserves.

(W2) **Net assets of each subsidiary**

This working sets out the fair value of the subsidiary's identifiable net assets at acquisition date and at the reporting date.

	At acquisition	**At reporting date**
	$000	$000
Equity capital	X	X
Share premium	X	X
Other components of equity	X	X
Retained earnings	X	X
Goodwill in the accounts of the sub.	(X)	(X)
Fair value adjustments (FVA)	X	X
Post acq'n dep'n/amort. on FVA		(X)
PURP if the sub is the seller		(X)
	X	X
	(to W3)	

Remember to update the face of the statement of financial position for adjustments made to the net assets at the reporting date (such as fair value uplifts and PURPs).

The fair value of the subsidiary's net assets at the acquisition date are used in the calculation of goodwill.

The movement in the subsidiary's net assets since acquisition is used to calculate the non-controlling interest and group reserves.

(W3) **Goodwill**

According to IFRS 3, goodwill can either be calculated on a full basis or a proportionate ("net") basis. One template can be used to calculate goodwill under both methods.

	$000
Fair value of purchase consideration	X
NCI at acquisition**	X
	X
Less: fair value of identifiable net assets at acquisition (per net assets working)	(X)
Goodwill at acquisition	X
Less: impairment to date	(X)
Goodwill to consolidated SFP	X

**if full goodwill method adopted, NCI value = FV of NCI at date of acquisition. This will normally be given in a question.

**if proportionate basis adopted, NCI value = NCI % of the fair value of the net assets at acquisition (per net assets working).

(W4) **Non-controlling interest**

	$000
NCI value at acquisition (W3)	X
NCI % of post-acquisition movement in net assets (W2)	X
Less: NCI % of goodwill impairment (fair value method only)	(X)
NCI to consolidated SFP	X

(W5) **Group reserves**

Retained earnings

	$000
Parent's retained earnings (100%)	X
For each subsidiary: group share of post-acquisition retained earnings (W2)	X
Add: gain on bargain purchase (W3)	X
Less: goodwill impairment** (W3)	(X)
Less: PURP if the parent was the seller	(X)
Retained earnings to consolidated SFP	X

** If the NCI was valued at fair value at the acquisition date, then only the parent's share of the goodwill impairment is deducted from retained earnings.

Other components of equity

	$000
Parent's other components of equity (100%)	X
For each subsidiary: group share of post-acquisition other components of equity (W2)	X
Other components of equity to consolidated SFP	X

Illustration 3 – Consolidated statement of financial position

On 1 April 20X7 Pauline acquired the following non-current investments:

- 6 million equity shares in Sonia by an exchange of two shares in Pauline for every four shares in Sonia plus $1.25 per acquired Sonia share in cash. The market price of each Pauline share at the date of acquisition was $6 and the market price of each Sonia share at the date of acquisition was $3.25.
- 30% of the equity shares of Arthur at a cost of $7.50 per share in cash.

Only the cash consideration of the above investments has been recorded by Pauline. In addition $1,000,000 of professional costs relating to the acquisition of Sonia is included in the cost of the investment.

The summarised draft statements of financial position of the three companies at 31 March 20X8 are presented below:

	Pauline	Sonia	Arthur
	$000	$000	$000
Assets			
Non-current assets			
Property, plant and equipment	36,800	20,800	36,000
Investments in Sonia and Arthur	26,500	–	–
Financial assets	13,000	–	–
	76,300	20,800	36,000
Current assets			
Inventories	13,800	12,400	7,200
Trade receivables	6,400	3,000	4,800
Total assets	96,500	36,200	48,000
Equity and liabilities			
Equity shares of $1 each	20,000	8,000	8,000
Retained earnings			
– at 31 March 20X7	32,000	12,000	22,000
– for year ended 31 March 20X8	18,500	5,800	10,000
	70,500	25,800	40,000
Non-current liabilities			
7% Loan notes	10,000	2,000	2,000
Current liabilities			
Trade payables	16,000	8,400	6,000
	96,500	36,200	48,000

The following information is relevant to the preparation of the consolidated statement of financial position:

(i) At the date of acquisition Sonia had an internally generated brand name. The directors of Pauline estimate that this brand name has a fair value of $2 million, an indefinite life and has not suffered any impairment.

(ii) On 1 April 20X7, Pauline sold an item of plant to Sonia at its agreed fair value of $5 million. Its carrying amount prior to the sale was $4 million. The estimated remaining life of the plant at the date of sale was five years.

(iii) During the year ended 31 March 20X8 Sonia sold goods to Pauline for $5.4 million. Sonia had marked up these goods by 50% on cost. Pauline had a third of the goods still in its inventory at 31 March 20X8. There were no intra-group payables or receivables at 31 March 20X8.

(iv) Pauline has a policy of valuing non-controlling interests at fair value at the date of acquisition. For this purpose the share price of Sonia at this date should be used. Impairment tests on 31 March 20X8 concluded that neither consolidated goodwill or the value of the investment in Arthur were impaired.

(v) The financial assets in Pauline's statement of financial position are classified as fair value through profit or loss. In the draft financial statements, they are held at their fair value on 1 April 20X7. They have a fair value of $18 million at 31 March 20X8.

(vi) No dividends were paid during the year by any of the companies.

Required:

Prepare the consolidated statement of financial position for the Pauline group as at 31 March 20X8.

Solution

Consolidated statement of financial position as at 31 March 20X8

	$000
Assets	
Non-current assets	
Property, plant and equipment ($36,800 + $20,800 – $800 (W8))	56,800
Goodwill (W3)	10,000
Intangible assets (W2)	2,000
Investment in associate (W6)	21,000
Financial assets (W9)	18,000
	107,800
Current assets	
Inventories ($13,800 + $12,400 – $600 (W7))	25,600
Trade receivables ($6,400 + $3,000)	9,400
Total assets	142,800
Equity and liabilities	
Equity attributable to equity holders of the parent	
Equity shares of $1 each ($20,000 + $3,000 (W3))	23,000
Share premium (W3)	15,000
Retained earnings (W5)	60,600
	98,600
Non-controlling interest (W4)	7,800
Total equity	106,400
Non-current liabilities	
7% Loan notes ($10,000 + $2,000)	12,000
Current liabilities	
Trade payables ($16,000 + $8,400)	24,400
Total equity and liabilities	142,800

Workings

(W1) **Group structure**

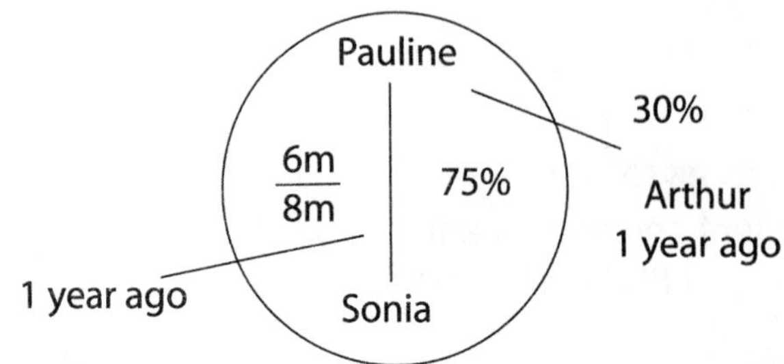

(W2) **Net assets – Sonia**

	At acquisition date	**At reporting date**
	$000	$000
Equity capital	8,000	8,000
Retained earnings	12,000	17,800
Fair value adj:		
Brand	2,000	2,000
PURP (W7)		(600)
	22,000	27,200

(W3) **Goodwill**

	Sonia
Fair value of consideration	$000
Share exchange (6m × 2/4 × $6)	18,000
Cash paid (6m × $1.25)	7,500
	25,500
FV of NCI at acquisition (2m × $3.25)	6,500
	32,000
Less FV of net assets at acquisition (W2)	(22,000)
	10,000

The 3 million shares issued by Pauline in the share exchange at a value of $6 each would be recorded as $1 per share in equity capital and $5 per share in share premium. This gives an increase in equity capital of $3 million and a share premium of $15 million.

(W4) **NCI**

	$000
Fair value of NCI at acquisition (W3)	6,500
NCI share of post-acquisition net asset movement (25% × ($27,200 – $22,000)) (W2)	1,300
	7,800

(W5) **Group retained earnings**

	$000
100% of Pauline's retained earnings ($32,000 + $18,500)	50,500
Professional costs written off	(1,000)
Gain on financial assets (W9)	5,000
P% of Sonia's post-acquisition retained earnings** (75% × (($17,800 – $600) – $12,000) (W2))	3,900
P% of Arthur's post-acquisition retained earnings (30% × $10,000)	3,000
PPE PURP (W8)	(800)
	60,600

** It is worth noting that, if the subsidiary has no 'other components of equity', then you could simply take P's share of the subsidiary's post-acquisition net assets movement:

75% × ($27,200 – $22,000 (W2)) = $3,900.

(W6) **Investment in associate**

	$000
Cost (8,000 × 30% × $7.50)	18,000
P's share post-acquisition reserves ($10,000 × 30%)	3,000
	21,000

(W7) **PURP in inventory**

Intra-group sales are $5.4 million on which Sonia made a profit of $1,800,000 ($5,400,000 × 50/150).

The unrealised profit still in inventory is therefore $600,000 ($1,800,000 × 1/3).

Sonia is the seller so the profit must be removed from Sonia's retained earnings in W2.

The adjusting entry is:

Dr Retained earnings (W2)	$600,000
Cr Inventories	$600,000

(W8) **PURP in PPE**

The carrying value of the PPE is $4m ($5m – ($5m/5 years)).

If no group transfer had happened, then the carrying value would have been $3.2m ($4m – ($4m/5 years).

PPE must therefore be reduced by $800,000 ($4m – $3.2m). Pauline is the seller so the profit impact must be adjusted against Pauline's retained earnings in W5. The adjusting entry is:

Dr Retained earnings (W5)	$800,000
Cr PPE	$800,000

(W9) **Financial assets**

The financial assets must be remeasured to fair value and the gain recorded through profit or loss.

The gain on revaluation to fair value is $5m ($18m – $13m). This will be recorded in profit or loss and will increase group retained earnings in W5.

Consolidated statement of profit or loss and other comprehensive income

Step 1: Group structure

This working is useful to decide whether the question involves subsidiaries, associates, joint ventures, or simple trade investments. You may also want to include the dates of acquisitions and disposals.

Step 2: Pro-forma

Once the group structure has been determined, set up a proforma statement of profit or loss and other comprehensive income.

Remember to leave space at the bottom to show the profit and total comprehensive income (TCI) attributable to the owners of the parent company and the profit and TCI attributable to the non-controlling interest.

Step 3: Complete the pro-forma

Add together the parent and subsidiary's incomes and expenses and items of other comprehensive income on a line-by-line basis.

- If the subsidiary has been acquired mid-year, make sure that you pro-rate the results of the subsidiary so that only post-acquisition incomes, expenses and other comprehensive income are consolidated.
- Ensure that you eliminate intra-group incomes and expenses, unrealised profits on intra-group transactions, as well as any dividends received from the subsidiary.

Step 4: Calculate the profit/TCI attributable to the non-controlling interest

Remember, profit for the year and TCI for the year must be split between the group and the non-controlling interest. The following proforma will help you to calculate the profit and TCI attributable to the non-controlling interest.

	Profit	TCI
	$	$
Profit/TCI of the subsidiary for the year (pro-rated for mid-year acquisition)	X	X
PURP (if S is the seller)	(X)	(X)
Excess depreciation/amortisation	(X)	(X)
Goodwill impairment (under FV model only)	(X)	(X)
× NCI %	X	X
Profit/TCI attributable to the NCI	X	X

Illustration 4 – Consolidated statement of profit or loss

H has owned 80% of the ordinary shares of S and 30% of the ordinary shares of A for many years. The information below is required to prepare the consolidated statement of profit or loss for the year ended 30 June 20X8.

Statements of profit or loss for the year ended 30 June 20X8

	H	S	A
	$	$	$
Revenue	500,000	200,000	100,000
Cost of sales	(100,000)	(80,000)	(40,000)
Gross profit	400,000	120,000	60,000
Distribution costs	(160,000)	(20,000)	(10,000)
Administrative expenses	(140,000)	(40,000)	(10,000)
Profit from operations	100,000	60,000	40,000
Tax	(23,000)	(21,000)	(14,000)
Profit after tax	77,000	39,000	26,000

Note: There were no items of other comprehensive income in the year.

At the date of acquisition, the fair value of S's plant and machinery, which at that time had a remaining useful life of ten years, exceeded the book value by $10,000.

During the year S sold goods to H for $10,000 at a margin of 50%. By the year-end H had sold 80% of these goods.

The group accounting policy is to measure non-controlling interests using the proportion of net assets method. The current year goodwill impairment loss was $1,200, and this should be charged to administrative expenses.

By 30 June 20X8 the investment in A had been impaired by $450, of which the current year loss was $150.

On 1 January 20X8, H signed a contract to provide a customer with support services for the following twelve months. H received the full fee of $30,000 in advance and recognised this as revenue.

Required:

Prepare the consolidated statement of profit or loss for the year ended 30 June 20X8.

Solution

Group statement of profit or loss for the year ended 30 June 20X8

	$
Revenue ($500,000 + $200,000 – $10,000 (W3) – $15,000 (W4))	675,000
Cost of sales ($100,000 + $80,000 + $1,000 (W2) – $10,000 (W3) + $1,000 (W3))	(172,000)
Gross profit	503,000
Distribution costs ($160,000 + $20,000)	(180,000)
Administrative expenses ($140,000 + $40,000 + $1,200 GW imp)	(181,200)

Profit from operations	141,800
Share of profit of associate ((30% × $26,000) – $150 impairment)	7,650
Profit before tax	149,450
Tax ($23,000 + $21,000)	(44,000)
Profit for the period	105,450
Attributable to:	
Equity holders of the parent (bal. fig)	98,050
Non-controlling interest (W5)	7,400
Profit for the period	105,450

Note: There were no items of other comprehensive income in the year.

Workings

(W1) **Group structure**

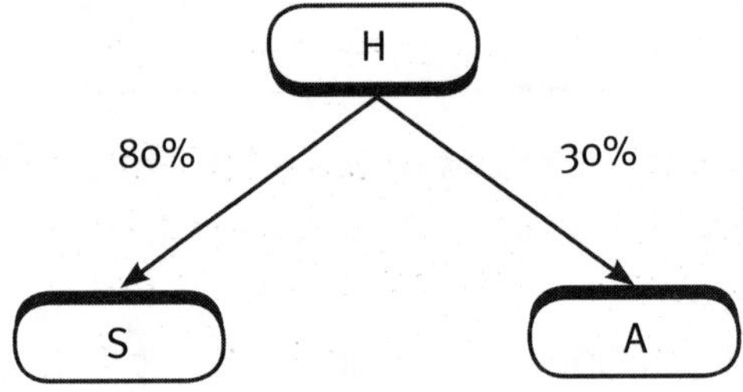

(W2) **Excess depreciation**

$10,000/10 years = $1,000.

The adjusting entry is:

Dr Cost of sales	$1,000
Cr PPE	$1,000

(W3) **Inter company trading**

The $10,000 trading between S and H must be eliminated:

Dr Revenue	$10,000
Cr Cost of sales	$10,000

The profit on the sale was $5,000 (50% × $10,000). Of this, $1,000 ($5,000 × 20%) remains within the inventories of the group. The PURP adjustment is therefore:

Dr Cost of sales	$1,000
Cr Inventories	$1,000

(W4) **Revenue**

Based on the passage of time, the contract is 50% (6/12) complete so only 50% of the revenue should be recognised by the reporting date. Therefore $15,000 ($30,000 × 50%) should be removed from revenue and held as deferred income on the SFP.

Dr Revenue	$15,000
Cr Deferred income	$15,000

(W5) **Profit attributable to NCI**

	$	
S's profit for the year	39,000	
PURP (W3)	(1,000)	
Excess depreciation (W2)	(1,000)	
	37,000	
× 20%		
Profit attributable to NCI		7,400

Note: If the parent had sold goods to the subsidiary then the PURP adjustment would not be included when calculating the profit attributable to the NCI.

Goodwill has been calculated using the share of net assets method. Therefore, none of the impairment loss is attributable to the NCI.

Test your understanding 8 – Borough High Street

Summarised financial statements for three entities for the year ended 30 June 20X8 are as follows:

Statements of financial position

	Borough	High	Street
Assets	$	$	$
Property, plant and equipment	100,000	80,000	60,000
Investments	121,000	–	–
Inventories	22,000	30,000	15,000
Receivables	70,000	10,000	2,000
Cash and cash equivalents	47,000	25,000	3,000
	360,000	145,000	80,000
Equity and liabilities			
Equity capital ($1 shares)	100,000	75,000	35,000
Retained earnings	200,000	50,000	40,000
Other components of equity	10,000	5,000	–
Liabilities	50,000	15,000	5,000
	360,000	145,000	80,000

Statements of profit or loss

	Borough	High	Street
	$	$	$
Revenue	500,000	200,000	100,000
Cost of sales	(300,000)	(140,000)	(60,000)
Gross profit	200,000	60,000	40,000
Administrative expenses	(50,000)	(10,000)	(10,000)
Profit from operations	150,000	50,000	30,000
Investment income	10,000	–	–
Finance costs	–	(10.000)	–
Profit before tax	160,000	40,000	30,000
Tax	(60,000)	(20,000)	(15,000)
Profit for the year	100,000	20,000	15,000

Note: There are no items of other comprehensive income.

On 1 July 20X7, Borough purchased 45,000 shares in High for $100,000. At that date, High had retained earnings of $30,000 and no other components of equity. High's net assets had a fair value of $120,000 and the fair value of the non-controlling interest was $55,000.

The excess of the fair value of High's net assets over their carrying values at the acquisition date relates to property, plant and equipment. This had a remaining estimated useful life of five years at the acquisition date. It is group policy to value the non-controlling interest using the full goodwill method. Goodwill has been subject to an impairment review and it was determined that, at the reporting date, the recoverable amount of the net assets of High was $170,000.

On 1 July 20X7, Borough purchased 10,500 equity shares in Street for $21,000. At that date, Street had retained earnings of $25,000 and no other components of equity.

During the year Borough sold goods to High for $10,000 at a margin of 50%. By the reporting date, High had only sold 80% of these goods.

During the year Borough gave High short-term loans, most of which were repaid shortly before the year-end. The final balance of $5,000 was repaid on 10 July 20X8. The finance cost in High's statement of profit or loss and the investment income in Borough's statement of profit or loss represents interest on this loan.

On 5 July 20X8, Borough received notification that an employee was claiming damages against them as a result of a work-place accident that took place on 30 April 20X8. Lawyers have advised that there is a 60% chance that Borough will lose the case and will be required to pay damages of $30,000.

Required:

Prepare the consolidated statement of profit or loss for the year ended 30 June 20X8 and the consolidated statement of financial position as at 30 June 20X8.

11 IFRS 11 – Joint arrangements

IFRS 11 Joint Arrangements adopts the definition of control as included in IFRS 10 (see earlier within this chapter) as a basis for determining whether there is joint control.

Joint arrangements are defined as arrangements where two or more parties have joint control. This will only apply if the relevant activities require unanimous consent of those who collectively control the arrangement.

Joint arrangements may take the form of either:

- joint operations
- joint ventures.

The key distinction between the two forms is based upon the parties' rights and obligations under the joint arrangement.

IFRS 11 Joint arrangements

Joint operations are defined as joint arrangements whereby the parties that have joint control have rights to the assets and obligations for the liabilities. Normally, there will not be a separate entity established to conduct joint operations.

Example of a joint operation

A and B decide to enter into a joint operation to produce a new product. A undertakes one manufacturing process and B undertakes the other. A and B have agreed that decisions regarding the joint operation will be made unanimously and that each will bear their own expenses and take an agreed share of the sales revenue from the product.

Joint ventures are defined as joint arrangements whereby the parties have joint control of the arrangement and have rights to the net assets of the arrangement. This will normally be established in the form of a separate entity to conduct the joint venture activities.

Example of a joint venture

A and B decide to set up a separate entity, C, to enter into a joint venture. A will own 55% of the equity capital of C, with B owning the remaining 45%. A and B have agreed that decision-making regarding the joint venture will be unanimous. Neither party will have direct right to the assets, or direct obligation for the liabilities of the joint venture; instead, they will have an interest in the net assets of entity C set up for the joint venture.

Joint control is defined as contractually agreed sharing of control of an arrangement which exists only when the decisions about the relevant activities require the unanimous consent of the parties sharing control. The key aspects of joint control are described as follows:

- Contractually agreed – contractual arrangements are usually, but not always, written, and provide the terms of the arrangement.
- Control and relevant activities – IFRS 10 describes how to assess whether a party has control, and how to identify the relevant activities.
- Unanimous consent – exists when the parties to an arrangement have collective control over the arrangement and no single party has control.

Accounting for joint arrangements

Joint operations

The individual financial statements of each joint operator will recognise all of:

- the assets that it controls and the liabilities that it incurs
- the expenses that it incurs
- share of the revenue that it earns from the sale of goods or services by the joint venture.

This may also include amounts due to and from the other joint operators.

As the income, expenses, assets and liabilities of the joint venture are included in the individual financial statements they will automatically flow through to the consolidated financial statements.

Joint ventures

The individual financial statements of each joint venture party will recognise:

- the cost of the investment in the joint venture entity (e.g. the share capital subscribed for), and
- any returns received in the form of dividends from the joint venture entity.

In the consolidated financial statements, the interest in the joint venture entity will be accounted for under the equity method as required by IAS 28. The treatment of a joint venture in the consolidated financial statements is therefore identical to the treatment of an associate.

Illustration 5 – Joint operation – Blast

Blast has a 30% share in a joint operation. The assets, liabilities, revenues and costs of the joint operation are apportioned on the basis of shareholdings. The following information relates to the joint arrangement activity for the year ended 30 November 20X2:

- The manufacturing facility cost $30m to construct and was completed on 1 December 20X1 and is to be dismantled at the end of its estimated useful life of 10 years. The present value of this dismantling cost to the joint arrangement at 1 December 20X1, using a discount rate of 8%, was $3m.
- During the year ended 30 November 20X2, the joint operation entered into the following transactions:
  - goods with a production cost of $36m were sold for $50m
  - other operating costs incurred amounted to $1m
  - administration expenses incurred amounted to $2m.

Blast has only accounted for its share of the cost of the manufacturing facility, amounting to $9m. The revenue and costs are receivable and payable by the two other joint operation partners who will settle amounts outstanding with Blast after each reporting date.

Required:

Show how Blast will account for the joint operation within its financial statements for the year ended 30 November 20X2.

Solution – Blast

Profit or loss impact:	$m
Revenue ($50m × 30%)	15.000
Cost of sales ($36m × 30%)	(10.800)
Operating costs ($1m × 30%)	(0.300)
Depreciation (($30m + 3m) × 1/10 × 30%)	(0.990)
Administration expenses ($2m × 30%)	(0.600)
Finance cost ($3m × 8% × 30%)	(0.072)
Share of net profit re joint operation (include in retained earnings within SOFP)	2.238

Statement of financial position impact:	$m
Property, plant and equipment (amount paid = share of cost)	9.000
Dismantling cost ($3m × 30%)	0.900
Depreciation ($33m × 1/10 × 30%)	(0.990)
	8.910
Trade receivables (i.e. share of revenue due)	15.000
Non-current liabilities:	
Dismantling provision (($3m × 30%) + $0.072)	0.972
Current liabilities:	
Trade payables ($10.8m + $0.3m + $0.6m) (i.e. share of expenses to pay)	11.700

The amounts calculated above should be classified under the appropriate headings within the statement of profit or loss for the year or statement of financial position as appropriate.

Note also that where there are amounts owed to and from a joint operating partner, it may be acceptable to show just a net amount due to or from each partner.

IFRS 12 Disclosure of Interests in Other Entities

IFRS 12 is the single source of disclosure requirements for business combinations. Disclosure requirements include:

- disclosure of significant assumptions and judgements made in determining whether an investor has control, joint control or significant influence over an investee
- disclosure of the nature, extent and financial effects of its interests in joint arrangements and associates
- additional disclosures relating to subsidiaries with non-controlling interests, joint arrangements and associates that are individually material
- significant restrictions on the ability of the parent to access and use the assets or to settle the liabilities of its subsidiaries
- extended disclosures relating to "structured entities", previously referred to as special-purpose entities, to enable a full understanding of the nature of the arrangement and associated risks, such as the terms on which an investor may be required to provide financial support to such an entity.

IAS 27 Separate Financial Statements

IAS 27 applies when an entity has interests in subsidiaries, joint ventures or associates and either elects to, or is required to, prepare separate non-consolidated financial statements.

Disclosures required when separate, non-consolidated, financial statements have been prepared by the parent entity include:

- the fact that exemption from consolidation has been used (usually as an intermediate holding company), together with the name, place of business and country of incorporation of the ultimate holding company who have prepared group financial statements in compliance with IFRS, and an address from which those financial statements can be obtained
- in other cases than being an intermediate holding company, the fact that they are separate financial statements, together with the reason why separate financial statements have been prepared
- a list of names, interests in equity capital and principal place of business for each significant subsidiary, associate and joint venture, including details of how they have been accounted for in the separate financial statements

If the financial statements are not consolidated, they must therefore present interests in other entities at cost or in accordance with IFRS 9 Financial Instruments.

Current issues

The following exposure drafts, relating to group accounting issues, are examinable in P2.

ED/2012/3 Equity method: share of other net asset changes

The IASB have noted that IAS 28 does not state whether the investor should account for its share of other net asset changes of an associate or joint venture that are not recognised in profit or loss or other comprehensive income of the investee, or that are not distributions received ('other net asset changes'). Examples would include the issue of share capital, and some share based payment transactions.

The IASB wish to clarify that an investor initially recognises its investment in an associate or a joint venture at cost. Thereafter, the carrying amount is increased or decreased to recognise changes in the investor's share of the investee's net assets. The investor's share of the investee's net asset changes, other than profit or loss or other comprehensive income and distributions received, is recognised in the investor's equity.

When an investor discontinues equity accounting, they shall reclassify to profit or loss the cumulative amount of equity that had previously been recognised.

ED/2012/6 Sale or contribution of assets between an investor and its associate or joint venture

Some users of IFRS noted an inconsistency in the treatment of the gain or loss that arises on the disposal of certain investments. IAS 27 requires a full gain or loss recognition on the loss of control of a subsidiary, whereas SIC-13 requires a partial gain or loss recognition in transactions between an investor and its associate or joint venture.

The IASB proposes to amend IAS 28 so that the current requirements for the partial gain or loss recognition for transactions between an investor and its associate or joint venture only apply to the gain or loss resulting from the sale or contribution of assets that do not constitute a 'business' (as defined in IFRS 3 Business Combinations). Gains or losses that arise from the disposal of assets that constitute a 'business' would be recognised in full.

ED/2012/7 Acquisition of an interest in a joint operation

The IASB notes that there is a lack of guidance on accounting for the acquisition of an interest in a joint operation in which the activity of the joint operation constitutes a business. This has led to significant diversity in practice.

As a result, the IASB proposes to amend IFRS 11 and IFRS 1 First-time Adoption of International Financial Reporting Standards so that a joint operator accounting for the acquisition of an interest in a joint operation in which the activity of the joint operation constitutes a business applies the relevant principles for business combinations accounting in IFRS 3.

This will make it mandatory to recognise the identifiable assets and liabilities of the joint operation at fair value and to recognise the difference between the consideration transferred and the fair value of the identifiable net assets acquired as goodwill. It also clarifies that all acquisition related costs should be recognised as an expense (except for the costs of issuing debt or equity that are recognised in accordance with IAS 32 and IFRS 9).

12 Chapter summary

Background to group accounts

- Consolidated accounts show the results of the group
- Intercompany transactions and balances must be eliminated
- All companies in the group should use the same accounting policies and have the same reporting date

Goodwill and fair value adjustments

- Goodwill is calculated as the excess of consideration + the NCI over the fair value of the net assets of the subsidiary
- The NCI is valued as:
  - NCI at acquisition + NCI% × post acquisition movement in net assets
- All assets, liabilities and contingent liabilities at the acquisition date (including those not recognised in the subsidiary's financial statements) must be recognised at fair value

Consolidation techniques

- A methodical approach is the best way to complete a group accounting question
- The following workings should be used:
  - group structure
  - net assets
  - goodwill
  - non-controlling interest
  - group retained earnings

Associates and joint arrangements

- Associates are accounted for using the equity method
- Joint arrangements are accounted for according to the type of arrangement
- Joint ventures that are separate entities are be accounted for using the equity method

Current issues in group accounting

Test your understanding answers

Test your understanding 1 – Control

An investor controls an investee if the investor has:

- power over the investee
- exposure, or rights, to variable returns from its involvement with the investee
- the ability to use its power over the investee to affect the amount of the investor's returns.

When assessing control, an investor considers its potential voting rights. Potential voting rights are rights to obtain voting rights of an investee, such as those arising from convertible instruments or options.

Potential voting rights are considered if the rights are substantive. This would mean that the rights need to be currently exercisable. Other factors that should be considered in determining whether potential voting rights are substantive include:

- whether the exercise price creates a financial barrier that would prevent (or deter) the holder from exercising its rights
- whether the party or parties that hold the rights would benefit from the exercise of those rights.

Parsley has voting rights that are currently exercisable and these should be factored into an assessment of whether control exists. The fact that the exercise price on the convertible instrument is out of the money (i.e. the exercise price is higher than the current market price) could potentially deter Parsley from taking up these voting rights. However, these options are not deeply out of the money. This may also be compensated by the fact that synergies would arise on the acquisition. This would suggest that it is likely that Parsley will exercise the options. The potential voting rights should therefore be considered substantive.

Based on the above, Parsley has control over Oregano. Oregano should be treated as a subsidiary and consolidated.

Test your understanding 2 – Identifying the acquirer

If the business combination has not involved the transfer of cash or other assets, the acquirer is usually the entity that issues its equity interests. This might point towards Phone being the acquirer, since Phone has issued shares in exchange for the shares of Abacus and Calculator.

However, other circumstances must be considered:

- The acquirer is usually the entity whose (former) management dominates the management of the combined entity.
- The acquirer is usually the entities whose owners retain or receive the largest portion of the voting rights in the combined entity.
- The acquirer is normally the entity whose size is greater than the other entities.

All three of these circumstances would point towards Abacus being the acquirer. This would appear to reflect the substance of the transaction since Phone has been incorporated by Abacus as a way of enabling a business combination with Calculator.

Test your understanding 3 – Fair value of identifiable net assets

	$
Share capital	10,000
Retained earnings	190,000
Fair value uplift ($50,000 – $10,000)	40,000
Goodwill	(20,000)
Brand	150,000
Contingent liability	(100,000)
Fair value of identifiable net assets at acquisition	270,000

Goodwill in the subsidiary's own financial statements is not an identifiable asset because it cannot be disposed of separately from the rest of the business.

No adjustment is made to the fair value of the net assets for the estimated redundancy provision. This is because no obligation exists at the acquisition date.

Test your understanding 4 – Purchase consideration

	$
Cash paid	300,000
Deferred cash ($200,000 × (1/1.1))	181,818
Shares (10,000 × $3)	30,000
Contingent consideration ($250,000 × 50% × (1/1.1))	113,636
Fair value of consideration	625,454

The legal fees are expensed to the statement of profit or loss.

Test your understanding 5 – Goodwill

	Fair value method $	Net assets method $
Consideration (TYU 4)	625,454	625,454
Add: NCI at acquisition (part b = 40% × $270,000)	160,000	108,000
	785,454	733,454
FV of identifiable net assets at acquisition (TYU 3)	(270,000)	(270,000)
	515,454	463,454

The fair value method calculates both the group's goodwill and the goodwill attributable to the non-controlling interest. Therefore, goodwill is higher under this method.

The proportion of net assets method only calculates the goodwill attributable to the group. Goodwill is lower under this method.

Test your understanding 6 – Happy

Goodwill arising on acquisition:

	$000
Fair value of consideration paid	500
NCI share of net assets at acquisition (20% × $560,000)	112
	612
Less: fair value of net assets at acquisition	(560)
Goodwill	52

Impairment review:

	$000	$000
Goodwill	52	
Unrecognised NCI (20/80 × $52,000)	13	
Total notional goodwill		65
Net assets		520
Carrying value		585
Recoverable amount		(510)
Impairment		75

The impairment loss is firstly allocated to the notional goodwill, reducing it from $65,000 to nil. However, as only $52,000 of the goodwill was recognised in the financial statements, only $52,000 of the impairment is recognised. This will be charged to profit or loss and is all attributable to the owners of the group.

The remaining impairment of $10,000 ($75,000 – $65,000) is allocated to other net assets and charged to profit or loss. Of this $10,000, $8,000 is attributable to the owners of the group and $2,000 is attributable to the NCI.

Therefore, the total impairment charged to profit or loss is $62,000 ($52,000 + $10,000).

Test your understanding 7 – Paint

Consolidated statement of financial position	$
Investment in associate (W1)	2,058,000

Consolidated statement of profit or loss	
Share of profit of associate (W2)	28,000

Note: No adjustment is required for receivables and payables held between Paint and Animate.

(W1) **Investment in associate**

	$
Cost	2,000,000
Share of post-acquisition profit (30% × $800,000 × 6/12)	120,000
Share of excess depreciation (30% × (($1.8m – $1m)/10 years) × 6/12)	(12,000)
Impairment	(50,000)
Investment in associate	2,058,000

The inventory is held within the group so the parent's share of the PURP is credited against inventory rather than the investment in the associate.

(W2) **Share of associate's profit**

	$
P's share of A's profit after tax (30% × $800,000 × 6/12)	120,000
Impairment	(50,000)
P's share of excess depreciation (30% × (($1.8m – $1m)/10 years) × 6/12)	(12,000)
P's share of PURP (30% × $100,000)	(30,000)
Share of profit of associate	28,000

Test your understanding 8 – Borough High Street

Borough Group statement of profit or loss for the year ended 30 June 20X8

	$
Revenue ($500,000 + $200,000 – $10,000 inter.co)	690,000
Cost of Sales ($300,000 + $140,000 – $10,000 inter.co + $1,000 (W7) + $3,000 (W2))	(434,000)
Gross profit	256,000
Administrative expenses ($50,000 + $10,000 + $7,000 (W6) + $30,000 (W10))	(97,000)
Profit from operations	159,000
Investment income	–
Finance costs	–
Income from associate (W9)	4,500
Profit before tax	163,500
Tax ($60,000 + $20,000)	(80,000)
Profit for the year	83,500
Attributable to owners of parent (bal. fig)	79,500
Attributable to NCI (W11)	4,000
	83,500

Borough Group statement of financial position as at 30 June 20X8

	$
Non Current Assets	
Goodwill (W3)	28,000
Property, plant and equipment ($100,000 + $80,000 + $15,000 (W2) – $3,000 (W2))	192,000
Investment in Associate (W8)	25,500
Current Assets	
Inventories ($22,000 + $30,000 – $1,000 (W7))	51,000
Receivables ($70,000 + $10,000 – $5,000 inter.co)	75,000
Cash and cash equivalents ($47,000 + $25,000)	72,000
	443,500
Equity capital	100,000
Retained earnings (W5)	179,500
Other components of equity (W5)	13,000
Non-controlling interest (W4)	61,000
Total equity	353,500
Liabilities ($50,000 + $15,000 – $5,000 inter.co + $30,000 (W10))	90,000
	443,500

(W1) **Group structure**

Borough is the parent

High is a 60% subsidiary (45/75)

Street is a 30% associate (10.5/35)

Both acquisitions took place a year ago

(W2) **Net assets of High**

	Acq	Rep date
	$	$
Equity capital	75,000	75,000
Other components of equity	–	5,000
Retained earnings	30,000	50,000
Fair value adjustment (FVA)	15,000*	15,000
Depreciation on FVA ($15,000/5)	–	(3,000)
*bal fig	120,000	142,000

(W3) **Goodwill**

	$
Consideration	100,000
FV of NCI at acquisition	55,000
	155,000
FV of net assets at acquisition (W2)	(120,000)
Goodwill at acquisition	35,000
Impairment (W6)	(7,000)
Goodwill at the reporting date	28,000

(W4) **Non-controlling interest**

	$
Fair value of NCI at acquisition (given)	55,000
NCI % of post-acquisition net assets (40% × ($142,000 – $120,000) (W2))	8,800
NCI share of goodwill impairment (40% × $7,000 (W6))	(2,800)
	61,000

(W5) **Group reserves**

Group retained earnings

	$
Parent	200,000
Provision (W10)	(30,000)
Share of post-acquisition retained earnings:	
High: 60% × (($50,000 – $3,000) – $30,000) (W2)	10,200
Street: 30% × ($40,000 – $25,000)	4,500
Group share of goodwill impairment (60% × $7,000 (W6))	(4,200)
PURP (W7)	(1,000)
	179,500

Other components of equity

	$
Parent	10,000
Share of post-acquisition other components of equity:	
High: 60% × ($5,000 – $nil) (W2)	3,000
	13,000

(W6) **Impairment**

	$
Net assets of High at reporting date (W2)	142,000
Goodwill (W3)	35,000
	177,000
Recoverable amount	(170,000)
Impairment	7,000

The impairment is allocated against goodwill (W3).

(W7) **Provision for unrealised profit**

The profit on the intra-group sale was $5,000 (50% × $10,000).

The unrealised profit still in inventory is $1,000 (20% × $5,000).

The parent was the seller, so retained earnings is adjusted in (W5)

Dr Cost of sales/retained earnings	$1,000
Cr Inventories	$1,000

(W8) **Investment in the associate**

	$
Cost	21,000
Share of increase in retained earnings (30% × ($40,000 – $25,000))	4,500
	25,500

(W9) **Income from the associate**

	$
Group share of the associate's profit after tax (30% × $15,000)	4,500

(W10) **Provision**

The obligating event, the accident, happened during the reporting period.

This means that there is an obligation from a past event, and a probable outflow of resources that can be measured reliably. A provision is therefore required for the best estimate of the amount payable, which is $30,000.

Dr Administrative expenses/retained earnings	$30,000
Cr Provisions	$30,000

(W11) **Profit attributable to NCI**

	$	
High's profit for the year	20,000	
Excess depreciation (W2)	(3,000)	
Goodwill impairment	(7,000)	
	10,000	
× 40%		
Profit attributable to NCI		4,000

Note: If High had sold goods to Borough then the PURP adjustment would have been included when calculating the profit attributable to the NCI.

Goodwill has been calculated using the fair value method. Therefore, the NCI must be allocated their share of the impairment loss.

chapter

15

Complex groups

Chapter learning objectives

Upon completion of this chapter you will be able to:

- apply the method of accounting for business combinations, including complex group structures
- determine and apply appropriate procedures to be used in preparing group financial statements.

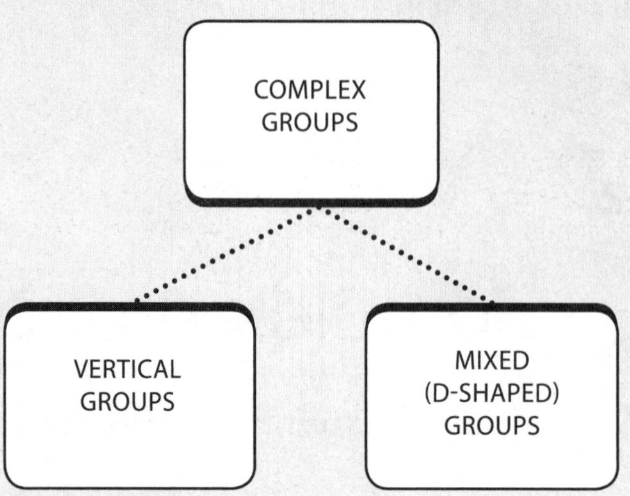

1 Complex group structures

Complex group structures exist where a subsidiary of a parent entity owns a shareholding in another entity which makes that other entity also a subsidiary of the parent entity.

Complex structures can be classified under two headings:

- Vertical groups
- Mixed groups.

2 Vertical groups

Definition

A **vertical group** arises where a subsidiary of the parent entity holds shares in a further entity such that control is achieved. The parent entity therefore controls both the subsidiary entity and, in turn, its subsidiary (often referred to as a sub-subsidiary entity).

Look at the following two situations:

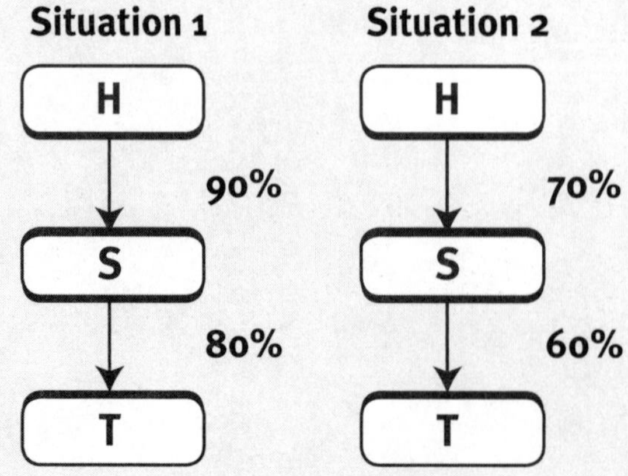

In both situations, H controls S, and S controls T. H is therefore able to exert control over T by virtue of its ability to control S. All three companies form a vertical group.

Both companies that are controlled by the parent are consolidated.

The basic techniques of consolidation are the same as seen previously, with some changes to the goodwill, NCI and group reserves calculations.

Approach to a question

When establishing the group structure, follow these steps:

- Control - which entities does the parent control directly or indirectly?
- Percentages - what are the effective ownership percentages for consolidation?
- Dates - when did the parent achieve control over the subsidiary and the sub-subsidiary?

Illustration 1 – Vertical group structure

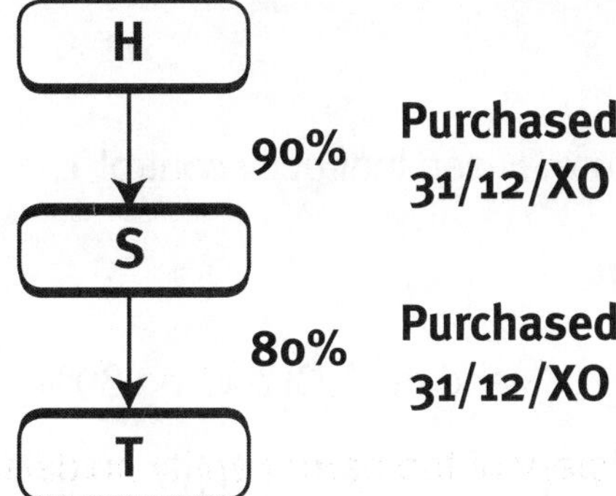

Control

H controls S and S controls T. Therefore, H can indirectly control T.

Effective consolidation percentage

S will be consolidated with H owning 90% and the NCI owning 10%.

T will be consolidated with H owning 72% (90% × 80%) and the NCI owning 28% (100% – 72%).

These effective ownership percentages will be used in standard workings (W4) and (W5).

Dates

S will be consolidated from 31 December 20X0.

When H acquires control of S, it also acquires indirect control over T. Therefore H will consolidate T from 31 December 20X0.

e.g

Illustration 2 – Vertical group structure

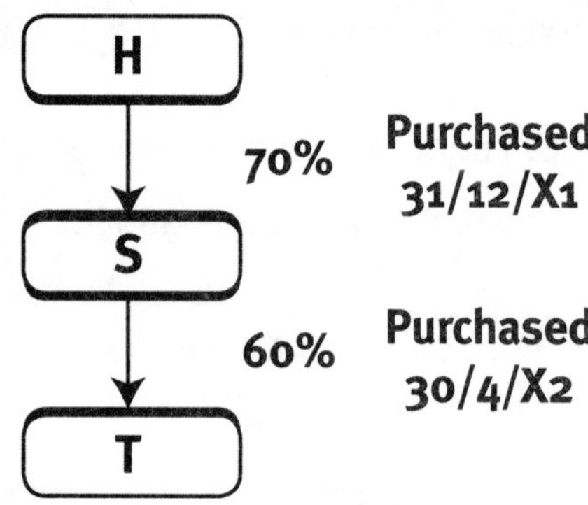

Control

H controls S and S controls T. Therefore, H can indirectly control T.

Effective consolidation percentage

S will be consolidated with H owning 70% and the NCI owning 30%.

T will be consolidated with H owning 42% (70% × 60%) and the NCI owning 58% (100% – 42%).

The effective ownership percentages will be used in standard workings (W4) and (W5).

Do not be put off by the fact that the effective group interest in T is less than 50%, and that the effective non-controlling interest in T is more than 50%.

Dates

S will be consolidated from 31 December 20X1.

However, S did not gain control of T until 30 April 20X2 meaning that H does not indirectly control T until this date. Therefore, T is consolidated into the H group from 30 April 20X2.

Indirect holding adjustment

Accounting for a sub-subsidiary requires an **indirect holding adjustment**.

- Goodwill in the sub-subsidiary is calculated from the perspective of the ultimate parent company. Therefore, the cost of the investment in the sub-subsidiary should be the parent's share of the amount paid by its subsidiary.
  - The NCI's share of the cost of the investment in the sub-subsidiary must be eliminated from the goodwill calculation.
- The value of the non-controlling interest in the subsidiary includes the NCI's share of the cost of the investment in the sub-subsidiary.
  - The NCI's share of the cost of the investment in the sub-subsidiary must be eliminated from the NCI calculation.

Illustration 3 – Indirect holding adjustment

On 31 December 20X1, A purchased 90% of the equity shares in B for $150,000 and B purchased 80% of the equity shares in C for $100,000.

At this date, the fair value of the net assets of B and C were $144,000 and $90,000 respectively. The fair value of the non-controlling interest in B and C was $17,000 and $15,000 respectively.

Required:

Calculate goodwill and the non-controlling interest for inclusion in the consolidated statement of financial position as at 31 December 20X1.

Solution

Goodwill

	B	C
	$	$
Consideration	150,000	100,000
Indirect holding adjustment (10% × $100,000)		(10,000)
Add: FV of non-controlling interest at acquisition	17,000	15,000
	167,000	105,000
Less: Net assets at acquisition	(144,000)	(90,000)
Goodwill at acquisition	23,000	15,000

Non-controlling interest

	$
B: NCI at acquisition (W3)	17,000
B: Indirect holding adjustment (W3)	(10,000)
C: NCI at acquisition (W3)	15,000
Non-controlling interest	22,000

Note: In subsequent years, the NCI will be adjusted for its share of the post-acquisition net asset movement of each subsidiary.

The NCI % in B is 10% (100% – 90%).

The NCI % in C is 28% (100% – (90% × 80%))

Illustration 4 – Vertical group 1

The draft statements of financial position of David, Colin and John, as at 31 December 20X4, are as follows:

	D	C	J
	$000	$000	$000
Sundry assets	280	180	130
Shares in subsidiary	120	80	
	400	260	130
Equity capital ($1 shares)	200	100	50
Retained earnings	100	60	30
Liabilities	100	100	50
	400	260	130

The following information is also available:

- David acquired 75,000 $1 shares in Colin on 1 January 20X4 when the retained earnings of Colin amounted to $40,000. At that date, the fair value of the non-controlling interest in Colin was valued at $38,000.
- Colin acquired 40,000 $1 shares in John on 30 June 20X4 when the retained earnings of John amounted to $25,000. The retained earnings of John had been $20,000 on the date of David's acquisition of Colin. On 30 June 20X4, the fair value of the non-controlling interest in John (both direct and indirect), based upon effective shareholdings, was $31,000.
- Goodwill has suffered no impairment. It is group policy to use the full goodwill method.

Required:

Produce the consolidated statement of financial position of the David group as at 31 December 20X4.

Solution

Statement of financial position for the David group at 31 December 20X4

	$000
Goodwill ($18 + $16) (W3)	34
Sundry assets ($280 + $180 + $130)	590
	624
Equity and liabilities:	
Equity capital	200
Retained earnings (W5)	118
	318
Non-controlling interest (W4)	56
Total equity	374
Liabilities ($100 + $100 + $50)	250
	624

(W1) **Group structure**

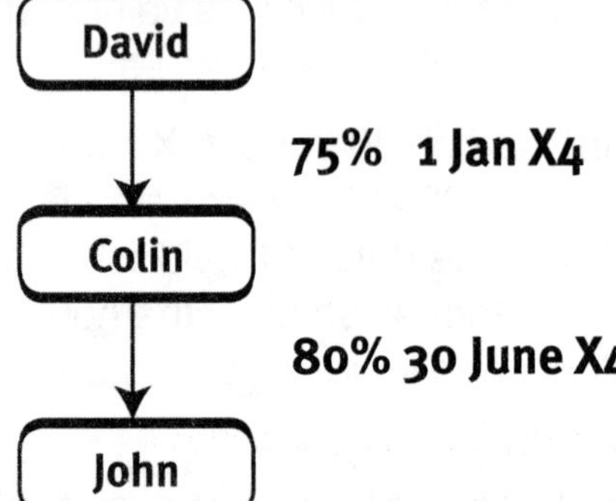

Control

David controls Colin and Colin controls John. Therefore, David can indirectly control John.

Effective consolidation percentage

Colin will be consolidated with David owning 75% and the NCI owning 25%.

John will be consolidated with David owning 60% (75% × 80%) and the NCI owning 40% (100% – 60%).

The effective ownership percentages will be used in standard workings (W4) and (W5).

Dates

Colin will be consolidated from 1 Jan 20X4.

However, Colin did not gain control of John until 30 June X4. Therefore, David does not indirectly control John until this date. As such, John is consolidated from 30 June 20X4.

(W2) **Net assets**

The acquisition date will be the date on which David (the parent company) gained control over each entity:

- Colin: 1 January 20X4
- John: 30 June 20X4

This means that the information given regarding John's retained earnings at 1 January 20X4 is irrelevant in this context.

Net assets of subsidiaries

	Colin		**John**	
	At acq'n	**At rep date**	**At acq'n**	**At rep date**
	$000	$000	$000	$000
Equity capital	100	100	50	50
Retained earnings	40	60	25	30
	140	160	75	80

(W3) **Goodwill**

A separate goodwill calculation is required for each subsidiary.

For the sub-subsidiary, goodwill is calculated from the perspective of the ultimate parent entity (David) rather than the immediate parent (Colin). Therefore, the effective cost of John is only David's share of the amount that Colin paid for John, i.e. $80,000 × 75% = $60,000.

	Colin	**John**
	$000	$000
Cost of investment in subsidiary	120	80
Indirect holding adjustment (25% × $80,000)	–	(20)
Fair value of NCI	38	31
	158	91
FV of net assets (W2)	(140)	(75)
	18	16

(W4) **Non-controlling interest**

	$000
Colin: NCI at acquisition (W3)	38
Colin: NCI share of post-acq'n net assets (25% × $20,000 (W2))	5
Less: Indirect holding adjustment (25% × 80,000)	(20)
John: NCI at acquisition (W3)	31
John NCI share of post acq'n net assets (40% × $5,000 (W2))	2
	56

(W5) **Group retained earnings**

	$000
David	100
Colin: 75% × $20,000 (W2)	15
John: 60% × $5,000 (W2)	3
	118

Note that only the group's effective share (60%) is taken of John's post-acquisition retained earnings.

Illustration 5 – Vertical group 2

The draft statements of financial position of Daniel, Craig and James as at 31 December 20X4 are as follows:

	D	C	J
	$000	$000	$000
Sundry assets	180	80	80
Shares in subsidiary	120	80	
	300	160	80
Equity capital	200	100	50
Retained earnings	100	60	30
	300	160	80

- Craig acquired 40,000 $1 shares in James on 1 January 20X4 when the retained earnings of James amounted to $25,000.
- Daniel acquired 75,000 $1 shares in Craig on 30 June 20X4 when the retained earnings of Craig amounted to $40,000 and those of James amounted to $30,000.

It is group policy to value the non-controlling interest using the proportion of net assets method.

Required:

Produce the consolidated statement of financial position of the Daniel group at 31 December 20X4.

Solution

Consolidated statement of financial position of the Daniel group at 31 December 20X4

Assets:	$000
Goodwill ($15 + $12) (W3)	27
Sundry assets ($180 + $80 + $80)	340
	367
Equity and liabilities:	
Equity capital	200
Retained earnings (W5)	115
Non-controlling interest (W4)	52
	367

(W1) **Group structure**

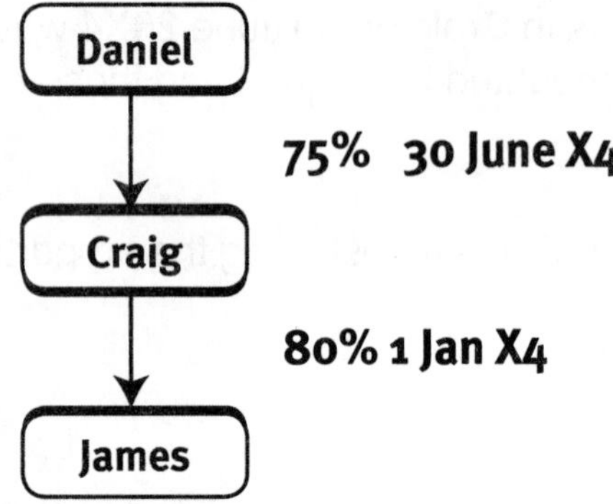

Control

Daniel controls Craig and Craig controls James. Therefore, Daniel can indirectly control James.

Effective consolidation percentage

Craig will be consolidated with Daniel owning 75% and the NCI owning 25%.

James will be consolidated with Daniel owning 60% (75% × 80%) and the NCI owning 40% (100% – 60%).

The effective ownership percentages will be used in standard workings (W4) and (W5). They will also be used in (W3) to calculate goodwill, as the group policy is to use the proportion of net assets method.

Dates

Craig will be consolidated from 30 June 20X4.

When Daniel acquires control of Craig, it also acquires indirect control over James. Therefore Daniel will consolidate James from 30 June 20X4.

(W2) **Net assets**

	Craig		James	
	Acq'n date	Rep date	Acq'n date	Rep date
	$000	$000	$000	$000
Share capital	100	100	50	50
Retained earnings	40	60	30	30
	140	160	80	80

(W3) **Goodwill**

	Craig	James
	$000	$000
Cost of investment	120	80
Indirect holding adjustment (25% × $80,000)	–	(20)
NCI at acquisition: Craig: 25% × $140,000 (W2) James: 40% × $80,000 (W2)	35	32
	155	92
FV of NA at acquisition (W2)	(140)	(80)
Goodwill	15	12

(W4) **Non-controlling interest**

	$000
Craig: NCI at acquisition (W3)	35
Craig: NCI % post-acq'n net assets (25% × ($160,000 – $140,000)) (W2)	5
Less: indirect holding adjustment (W3)	(20)
James: NCI at acquisition (W3)	32
James: NCI % post-acq'n net assets (40% × ($80,000 – $80,000)) (W2)	–
	52

(W5) **Group retained earnings**

	$000
Daniel	100
Craig: 75% × ($60,000 – $40,000) (W2)	15
James: 60% × ($30,000 – $30,000) (W2)	–
	115

Test your understanding 1 – H, S & T

The following are the statements of financial position at 31 December 20X7 for H group companies:

	H	**S**	**T**
	$	$	$
45,000 shares in S	65,000	–	–
30,000 shares in T	–	55,000	–
Sundry assets	280,000	133,000	100,000
	345,000	188,000	100,000
Equity share capital ($1 shares)	100,000	60,000	50,000
Retained earnings	45,000	28,000	25,000
Liabilities	200,000	100,000	25,000
	345,000	188,000	100,000

All the shareholdings were acquired on 1 January 20X1 when the retained earnings of S were $10,000 and those of T were $8,000. At that date, the fair value of the non-controlling interest in S was $20,000. The fair value of the total non-controlling interest (direct and indirect) in T was $50,000. It is group policy to value the non-controlling interest using the full goodwill method. Goodwill was fully written off in an earlier period.

Required:

Prepare the consolidated statement of financial position for the H group at 31 December 20X7.

Test your understanding 2 – Grape, Vine and Wine

The statements of financial position of three entities at 30 June 20X6 were as follows:

	Grape	Vine	Wine
	$000	$000	$000
Investment	110	60	–
Sundry assets	350	200	120
	460	260	120
Equity share capital	100	50	10
Retained earnings	210	110	70
Liabilities	150	100	40
	460	260	120

Grape purchased 40,000 of the 50,000 $1 shares in Vine on 1 July 20X5, when the retained earnings of that entity were $80,000. At that time, Vine held 7,500 of the 10,000 $1 shares in Wine. These had been purchased on 1 January 20X5 when Wine's retained earnings were $65,000. On 1 July 20X5, Wine's retained earnings were $67,000.

At 1 July 20X5, the fair value of the non-controlling interest in Vine was $27,000, and that of Wine (both direct and indirect) was $31,500. It is group policy to value the non-controlling interest using the full goodwill method.

The equity share capital of Grape includes $20,000 received from the issue of 20,000 class B shares on 30 June 20X6. These shares entitle the holders to fixed annual dividends. The holders of these B shares can also demand the repayment of their capital from 30 June 20X9.

Included in the liabilities of Grape are $100,000 proceeds from the issue of a loan on 1 July 20X5. There are no annual interest payments and Grape therefore believes that no further accounting entries are required until the repayment date. The loan is repayable on 30 June 20X8 at a premium of 100%. The effective rate of interest on the loan is 26.0%.

Required:

Prepare the consolidated statement of financial position for the Grape group at 30 June 20X6.

3 Mixed (D-shaped) groups

Definition

In a mixed group situation the parent entity has a direct controlling interest in at least one subsidiary. In addition, the parent entity and the subsidiary together hold a controlling interest in a further entity.

For example:

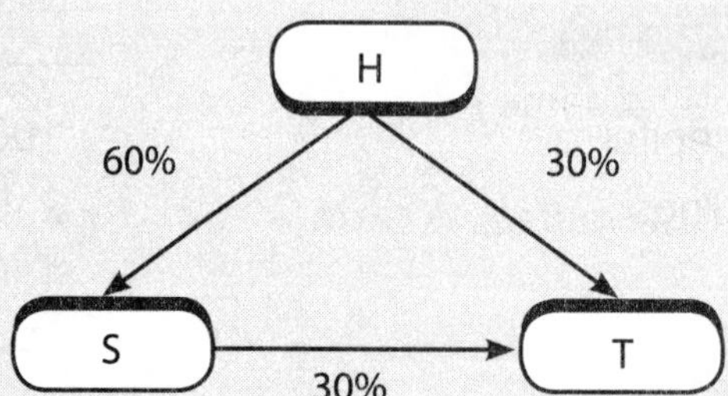

- H has 60% of the shares of S. S is therefore a subsidiary of H.
- H has a 30% direct holding in T. H also controls S, who has a 30% holding in T. H therefore controls T through its direct and indirect holdings. This means that T is part of H's group and must be consolidated.

Accounting for a mixed group is similar to accounting for a vertical group.

Approach to a question

Follow the same steps as with a vertical group when establishing group structure:

- Control
- Percentages of ownership
- Dates of acquisition

Illustration 6 – Mixed group structure

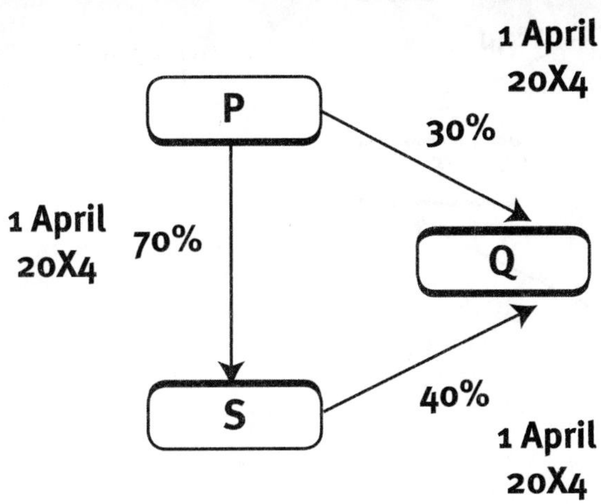

P acquired a 70% interest in S on 1 April 20X4, and acquired a 30% interest in Q on the same date.

S acquired a 40% interest in Q on 1 April 20X4.

Control

P controls S. This makes S a subsidiary of P.

P is able to direct 30% + 40% = 70% of the voting rights of Q. Q is a sub-subsidiary of P.

Effective consolidation percentage

S will be consolidated with P owning 70% and the NCI owning 30%.

P's effective interest in Q is calculated as follows:

Direct	30%
Indirect (70% × 40%)	28%
P's effective interest in Q	58%

The NCI interest in Q is therefore 42% (100% – 58%).

Dates

The date of acquisition for S and Q is 1 April 20X4.

Illustration 7 – Mixed group structure

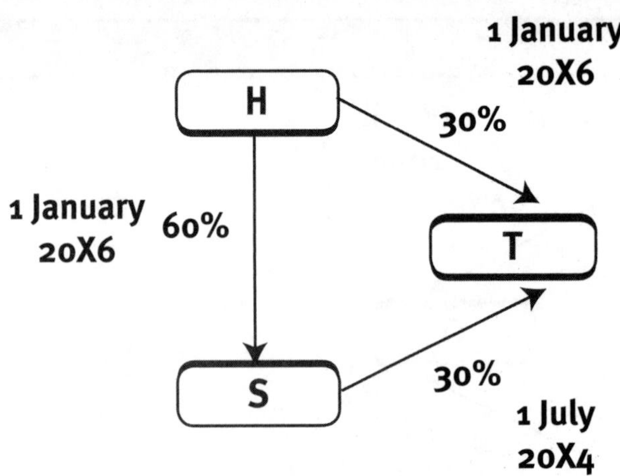

H acquired a 60% interest in S on 1 January 20X6, and acquired a 30% interest in T on the same date.

S acquired a 30% interest in T on 1 July 20X4.

Control

H controls S. This makes S a subsidiary of H.

H is able to direct 30% + 30% = 60% of the voting rights of T. T is a sub-subsidiary of H.

Effective consolidation percentage

S will be consolidated with H owning 60% and the NCI owning 40%.

H's effective interest in T is calculated as follows:

Direct	30%
Indirect (60% × 30%)	18%
H's effective interest in T	48%

The NCI interest in T is therefore 52% (100% – 48%).

Dates

The date of acquisition for S and T is 1 January 20X6.

Further detail on mixed groups

Note that the definition of a mixed group does not include the situation where the parent and an associate together hold a controlling interest in a further entity.

E.g.

H owns 35% of S, S owns 40% of W and H owns 40% of W.

This is **not** a mixed group situation. Neither S nor W is a member of the H group, although S and W may both be 'associates' of H.

H's interest in W might be calculated as before as (35% × 40%) + 40% = 54%. Although H has an arithmetic interest in W that is more than 50%, it does not have parent entity control of W, as it does not control S's 40% stake in W.

Consolidation

All consolidation workings are the same as those used in vertical group situations, with the exception of goodwill.

The goodwill calculation for the sub-subsidiary differs slightly from a vertical group. The cost of the sub-subsidiary must include the following:

- the cost of the parent's holding (the direct holding)
- the cost of the subsidiary's holding (the indirect holding)
- the indirect holding adjustment.

Illustration 8 – H, S, C

The statements of financial position of H, S and C as at 31 December 20X5 were as follows:

	H	S	C
	$	$	$
45,000 shares in S	72,000	–	–
16,000 shares in C	25,000	–	–
12,000 shares in C	–	20,000	–
Sundry assets	125,000	120,000	78,000
	222,000	140,000	78,000
Equity share capital ($1 shares)	120,000	60,000	40,000
Retained earnings	95,000	75,000	35,000
Liabilities	7,000	5,000	3,000
	222,000	140,000	78,000

All shares were acquired on 31 December 20X2 when the retained earnings of S amounted to $30,000 and those of C amounted to $10,000.

It is group accounting policy to value the non-controlling interest on a proportionate basis.

Required:

Prepare the statement of financial position for the H group as at 31 December 20X5.

Solution

Group statement of financial position for H group as at 31 December 20X5

	$
Goodwill ($4,500 + $8.750) (W3)	13,250
Sundry assets ($125,000 + $120,000 + $78,000)	323,000
	336,250

Equity and liabilities:	$
Equity share capital	120,000
Retained earnings (W5)	144,375
Non-controlling interest (W4)	56,875
Total equity	321,250
Liabilities ($7,000 + $5,000 + $3,000)	15,000
	336,250

(W1) **Group structure**

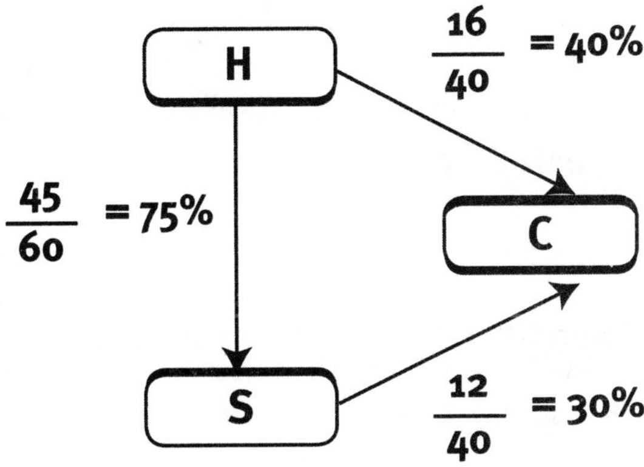

H's interest in S in 75%. The NCI interest in S is 25%.

H's effective interest in C:	
Direct	40.0%
Indirect (75% × 30%)	22.5%
	62.5%

The NCI interest in C is 37.5% (100% – 62.5%).

(W2) **Net assets**

S's net assets	At acq'n	At rep date
	$	$
Equity capital	60,000	60,000
Retained earnings	30,000	75,000
	90,000	135,000

C's net assets		
	$	$
Equity capital	40,000	40,000
Retained earnings	10,000	35,000
	50,000	75,000

(W3) **Goodwill**

Goodwill arising on acquisition of S	
	$
Cost of H's investment	72,000
NCI at acquisition (25% × $90,000 (W2))	22,500
	94,500
Less: FV of net assets at acquisition (W2)	(90,000)
Goodwill	4,500

Goodwill arising on acquisition of C	
	$
Cost of H's investment	25,000
Cost of S's investment	20,000
Indirect holding adjustment (25% × $20,000)	(5,000)
NCI at acquisition (37.5% × $50,000 (W2))	18,750
	58,750
Less: FV of net assets at acquisition (W2)	(50,000)
Goodwill	8,750

(W4) **Non-controlling interest**

	$
S – NCI at acquisition (W3)	22,500
S – NCI % of post acquisition net assets (25% × $45,000 (W2))	11,250
Indirect holding adjustment (W3)	(5,000)
C – NCI at acquisition (W3)	18,750
C – NCI % of post acquisition net assets (37.5% × $25,000 (W2))	9,375
	56,875

(W5) **Retained earnings**

	$
100% of H's retained earnings	95,000
Group share of S's post acquisition retained earnings (75% × $45,000 (W2))	33,750
Group share of C's post acquisition retained earnings (62.5% × $25,000 (W2))	15,625
	144,375

Test your understanding 3 – T, S & R

The following are the summarised statements of financial position of T, S and R as at 31 December 20X4.

	T	**S**	**R**
	$	$	$
Non-current assets	140,000	61,000	170,000
Investments	200,000	65,000	–
Current assets	30,000	28,000	15,000
	370,000	154,000	185,000
Equity shares of $1 each	200,000	80,000	100,000
Retained earnings	150,000	60,000	80,000
Other components of equity	10,000	8,000	–
Liabilities	10,000	6,000	5,000
	370,000	154,000	185,000

On 1 January 20X3 S acquired 35,000 ordinary shares in R at a cost of $65,000 when the retained earnings of R amounted to $40,000.

On 1 January 20X4 T acquired 64,000 shares in S at a cost of $120,000 and 40,000 shares in R at a cost of $80,000. On this date, the retained earnings of S and R amounted to $50,000 and $60,000 respectively. S also had other components of equity of $3,000. The fair value of the NCI in S on 1 January 20X4 was $27,000. The fair value of the NCI (direct and indirect) in R was $56,000. The non-controlling interest is measured using the full goodwill method. At the reporting date, goodwill has not been impaired.

On 1 January 20X4, T obtained use of a machine under a two year lease. The machine has a useful economic life of ten years. No payment was due during 20X4 so no accounting entries have been posted. A payment of $10,000 must be made on 31 December 20X5.

On 1 January 20X4, T granted 100 share appreciation rights (SARs) to 60 managers. These entitle the holders to a cash bonus based on the share price of T. The SARs vest if the managers are still employed by T at 31 December 20X7. Five managers left during 20X4 and it is expected that another 15 will leave prior to 31 December 20X7. The fair value of each SAR was $10 on 1 January 20X4 and $14 on 31 December 20X4.

Required:

Prepare the consolidated statement of financial position of the T group as at 31 December 20X4.

4 Chapter summary

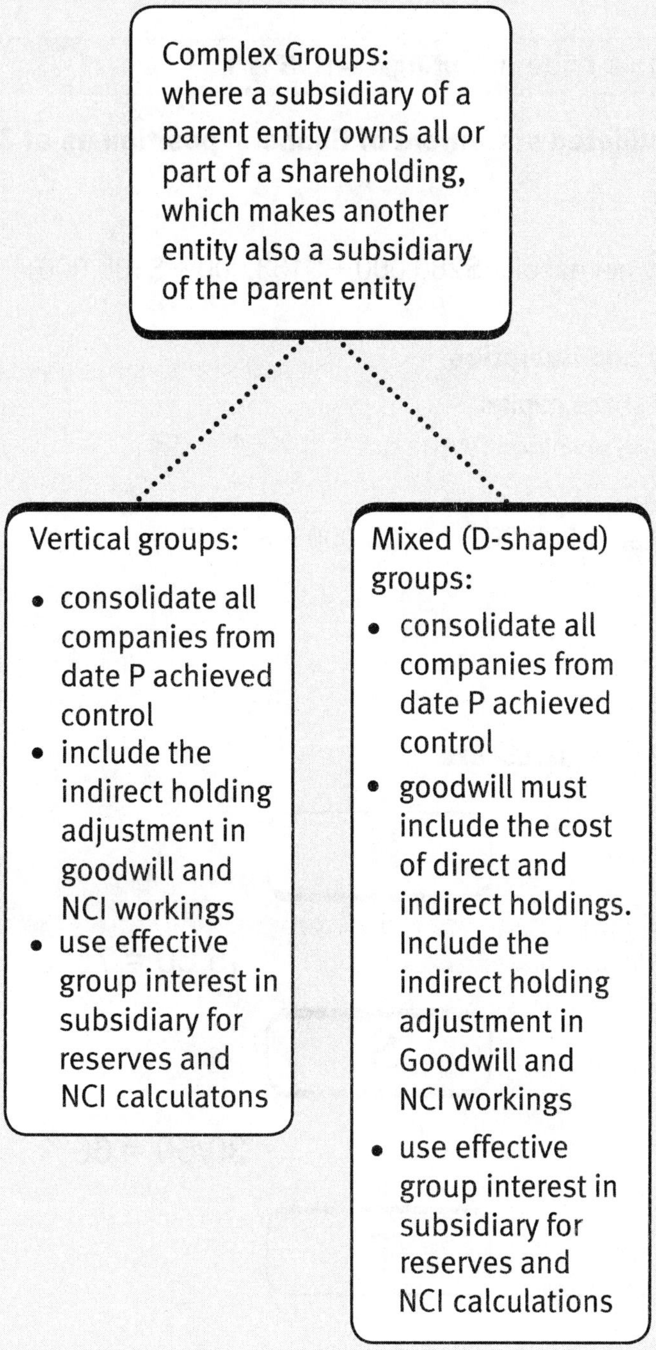

Complex Groups: where a subsidiary of a parent entity owns all or part of a shareholding, which makes another entity also a subsidiary of the parent entity

Vertical groups:

- consolidate all companies from date P achieved control
- include the indirect holding adjustment in goodwill and NCI workings
- use effective group interest in subsidiary for reserves and NCI calculatons

Mixed (D-shaped) groups:

- consolidate all companies from date P achieved control
- goodwill must include the cost of direct and indirect holdings. Include the indirect holding adjustment in Goodwill and NCI workings
- use effective group interest in subsidiary for reserves and NCI calculations

Test your understanding answers

Test your understanding 1 – H, S & T

Consolidated statement of financial position as at 31 December 20X7

	$
Sundry net assets ($280,000 + $133,000 + $100,000)	513,000
Equity and liabilities	
Equity share capital	100,000
Retained earnings (W5)	39,938
NCI (W4)	48,062
Liabilities ($200,000 + $100,000 + $25,000)	325,000
	513,000

(W1) **Group structure**

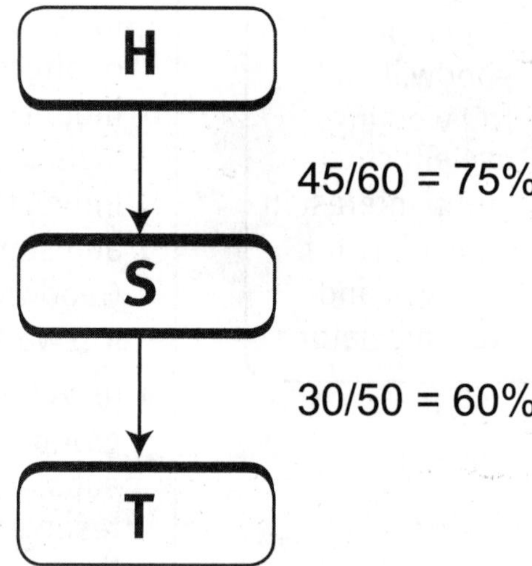

		%
S:	Group share	75
	NCI	25
T:	Group share (75% × 60%)	45
	NCI (100% – 45%)	55

(W2) **Net assets**

	S		T	
	acq'n	rep date	acq'n	rep date
	$	$	$	$
Equity capital	60,000	60,000	50,000	50,000
Retained earnings	10,000	28,000	8,000	25,000
	70,000	88,000	58,000	75,000

(W3) **Goodwill**

	S	T
	$	$
Consideration paid	65,000	55,000
FV of NCI	20,000	50,000
Indirect Holding Adjustment (25% × $55,000)	–	(13,750)
	85,000	91,250
FV of NA at acquisition	(70,000)	(58,000)
Goodwill at acquisition	15,000	33,250
Less: Impairment	(15,000)	(33,250)
Goodwill at reporting date	Nil	Nil

(W4) **Non-controlling interest**

	$
S – FV at date of acquisition	20,000
S – NCI % of post-acq'n net assets (25% × $18,000 (W2))	4,500
Indirect Holding Adjustment (W3)	(13,750)
T – FV at date of acquisition	50,000
T – NCI % of post-acq'n net assets (55% × $17,000 (W2))	9,350
NCI % of S's goodwill impairment (25% × $15,000 (W3))	(3,750)
NCI % of T's goodwill impairment (55% × $33,250 (W3))	(18,288)
	48,062

(W5) **Consolidated retained earnings**

	$
Retained earnings of H	45,000
Group % of post-acquisition retained earnings:	
S – (75% × $18,000 (W2))	13,500
T – (45% × $17,000 (W2))	7,650
H's % of S's goodwill impairment (75% × $15,000)	(11,250)
H's % of T's goodwill impairment (45% × $33,250)	(14,963)
	39,938

Test your understanding 2 – Grape, Vine and Wine

Consolidated statement of financial position as at 30 June 20X6

	$
Goodwill ($7,000 + $2,500 (W3))	9,500
Sundry assets ($350,000 + $200,000 + $120,000)	670,000
	679,500

Equity and liabilities	$
Equity share capital ($100,000 – $20,000 (W6))	80,000
Retained earnings (W5)	209,800
Non-controlling interest (W4)	53,700
Liabilities ($150,000 + $100,000 + $40,000 + $20,000 (W6) + $26,000 (W7))	336,000
	679,500

(W1) **Group structure**

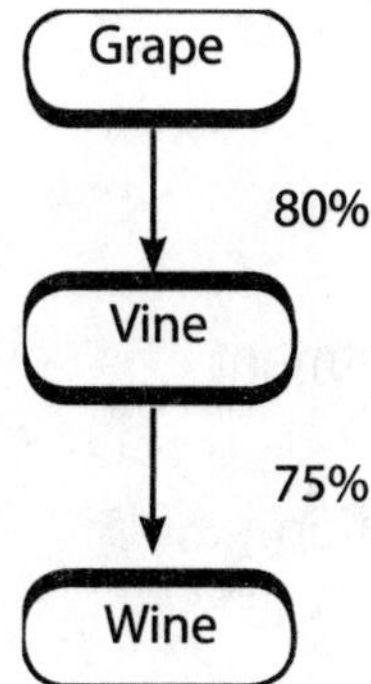

Effective consolidation percentage

Vine will be consolidated with Grape owning 80% and the NCI owning 20%.

Wine will be consolidated with Grape owning 60% (80% × 75%) and the NCI owning 40% (100% – 60%).

The effective ownership percentages will be used in standard workings (W4) and (W5).

Dates

Grape gained control over Vine and Wine on 1 July 20X5.

(W2) **Net assets**

	Vine		Wine	
	acq'n	rep. date	acq'n	rep. date
	$	$	$	$
Equity capital	50,000	50,000	10,000	10,000
Retained earnings	80,000	110,000	67,000	70,000
	130,000	160,000	77,000	80,000

The acquisition date for both entities is the date they joined the Grape group, i.e. 1 July 20X5.

(W3) **Goodwill**

	Vine	Wine
	$	$
Consideration paid	110,000	60,000
Indirect holding adjustment (20% × $60,000)		(12,000)
FV of NCI at acquisition	27,000	31,500
	137,000	79,500
FV of net assets at acquisition (W2)	(130,000)	(77,000)
Goodwill	7,000	2,500

(W4) **Non-controlling interest**

	$
V – NCI at acquisition (W3)	27,000
V – NCI share of post acq'n net assets (20% × $30,000 (W2))	6,000
Indirect holding adjustment (W3)	(12,000)
W – NCI at acquisition (W3)	31,500
W – NCI share of post acq'n net assets (40% × $3,000 (W2))	1,200
	53,700

(W5) **Consolidated retained earnings**

	$
Retained earnings of Grape	210,000
Interest on liability (W7)	(26,000)
Group share of post-acquisition retained earnings	
V (80% × $30,000 (W2))	24,000
W (60% × $3,000 (W2))	1,800
	209,800

(W6) **Shares**

A financial liability exists if there is an obligation to deliver cash.

The class B shares are a financial liability and must be reclassified:

Dr Equity share capital	$20,000
Cr Liabilities	$20,000

(W7) **Loan**

The loan will be measured at amortised cost. A finance cost must be charged using the effective rate. The finance cost for the year is $26,000 ($100,000 × 26%).

Dr Finance costs/retained earnings (W5)	$26,000
Cr Liabilities	$26,000

Test your understanding 3 – T, S & R

T consolidated statement of financial position as at 31 December 20X4

	$
Goodwill ($14,000 + $28,000 (W3))	42,000
Non-current assets ($140,000 + $61,000 + $170,000)	371,000
Current assets ($30,000 + $28,000 + $15,000)	73,000
	486,000

	$
Equity share capital	200,000
Retained earnings (W5)	152,600
Other components of equity (W5)	14,000
	366,600
Non-controlling interest (W4)	79,400
Liabilities ($10,000 + $6,000 + $5,000 + $5,000 (W6) + $14,000 (W7))	40,000
	486,000

(W1) **Group structure**

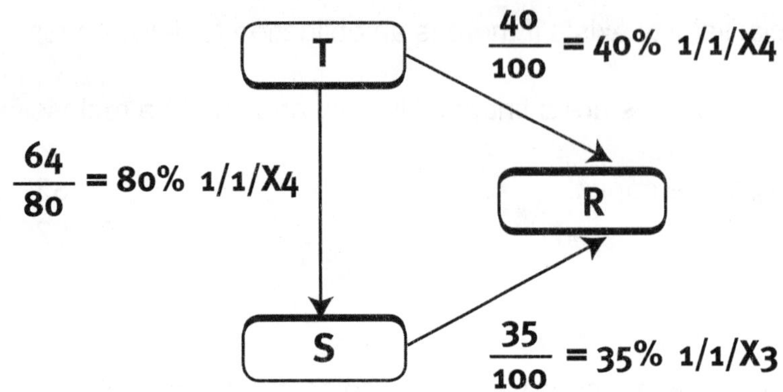

T has an 80% holding in S. The NCI holding is 20%.

T's effective holding in R is calculated as follows:

Direct	40%
Indirect (80% × 35%)	28%
	68%

The NCI holding in R is 32% (100% – 68%).

T's acquisition date for both entities is 1 January 20X4.

(W2) **Net assets**

S's Net assets	At acq'n	At rep date
	$	$
Equity share capital	80,000	80,000
Retained earnings	50,000	60,000
Other components of equity	3,000	8,000
	133,000	148,000

R's Net assets		
	$	$
Equity share capital	100,000	100,000
Retained earnings	60,000	80,000
	160,000	180,000

(W3) **Goodwill**

Goodwill arising on the acquisition of S

	$
Consideration paid	120,000
FV of NCI	27,000
	147,000
FV of net assets at acquisition (W2)	(133,000)
Goodwill	14,000

Goodwill arising on the acquisition of R

	$
Cost of T's investment	80,000
Cost of S's investment	65,000
Indirect holding adjustment (20% × 65,000)	(13,000)
Fair value of NCI at acquisition	56,000
	188,000
FV of net assets at acquisition (W2)	(160,000)
Goodwill	28,000

(W4) **Non-controlling interest**

	$
S – FV of NCI at acquisition	27,000
NCI share of S's post acquisition net assets (20% × ($148,000 – $133,000) (W2))	3,000
Indirect holding adjustment (W3)	(13,000)
R – FV of NCI at acquisition	56,000
NCI share of R's post acquisition net assets (32% × ($180,000 – $160,000) (W2))	6,400
	79,400

(W5) **Group retained earnings**

	$
100% of T's retained earnings	150,000
Operating lease (W6)	(5,000)
Share-based payment (W7)	(14,000)
Group share of S's post acquisition retained earnings (80% × ($60,000 – $50,000) (W2))	8,000
Group share of R's post acquisition retained earnings (68% × ($80,000 – $60,000) (W2))	13,600
	152,600

Other components of equity

	$
100% of T's other components of equity	10,000
Group share of S's post acquisition other components (80% × ($8,000 – $3,000) (W2))	4,000
Group share of R's post acquisition other components (68% × nil (W2))	–
	14,000

(W6) **Operating lease**

The lease term is much shorter than the useful life of the asset so it appears to be an operating lease. The total lease payments should be expensed to the statement of profit or loss on a straight line basis.

The annual operating lease expense is $5,000 ($10,000/2 years).

The adjusting entry is:

Dr Profit or loss/Retained earnings (W5)	$5,000
Cr Liabilities (accruals)	$5,000

(W7) **Share-based payments**

This is a cash-settled share-based payment scheme.

The expense should be spread across the vesting period. The expense to be recognised is based on the fair value of the scheme at the period end and the number of SARs that are expected to vest.

(60 employees – 5 – 15) × 100 × $14 × 1/4 = $14,000

The adjusting entry is:

Dr Profit or loss/Retained earnings (W5)	$14,000
Cr Liabilities	$14,000

chapter

16

Change in a group structure

Chapter learning objectives

Upon completion of this chapter you will be able to:

- prepare group financial statements where activities have been discontinued, or have been acquired or disposed of in the period
- apply and discuss the treatment of a subsidiary which has been acquired exclusively with a view to subsequent disposal.

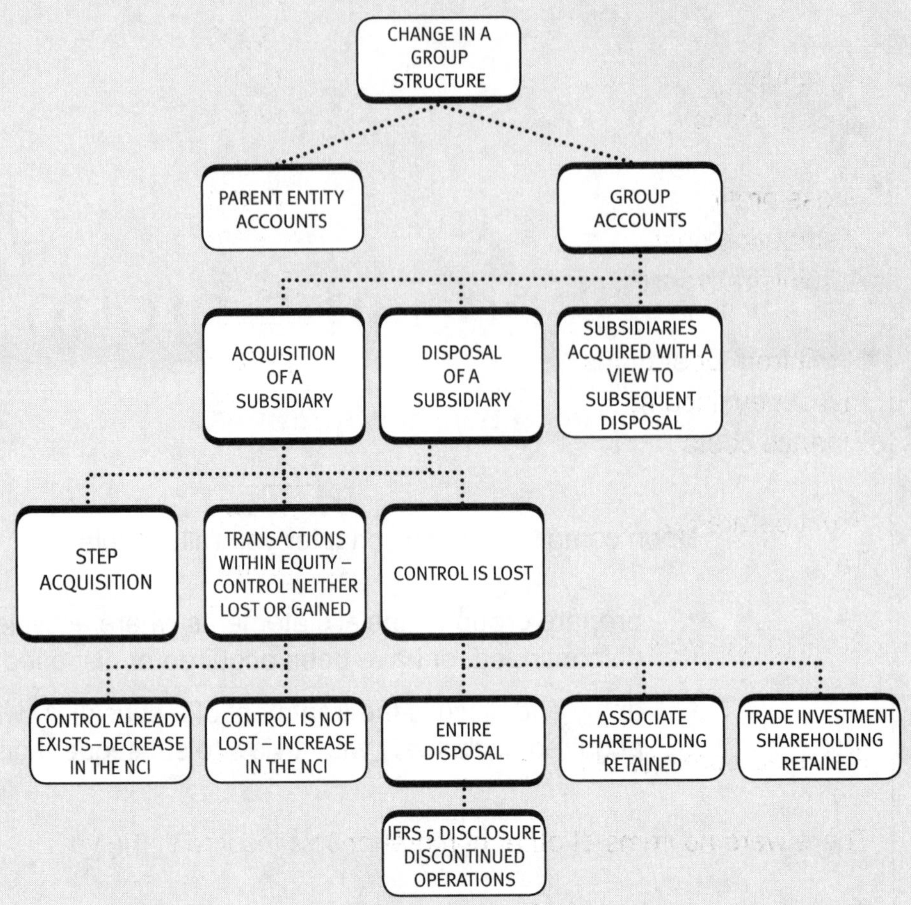

1 Acquisition of a subsidiary

A parent entity consolidates a subsidiary from the date that it achieves control. If this happens partway through the reporting period then it will be necessary to pro-rate the results of the subsidiary so that only the post-acquisition incomes and expenses are consolidated into the group statement of profit or loss.

Illustration 1 – Tudor – mid-year acquisition of a subsidiary

On 1 July 20X4 Tudor purchased 1,600,000 of the 2,000,000 $1 equity shares of Windsor for $10,280,000. On the same date it also acquired 1,000,000 of Windsor's $1 10% loan notes. At the date of acquisition the retained earnings of Windsor were $6,150,000.

The statements of profit or loss for each entity for the year ended 31 March 20X5 were as follows.

	Tudor	Windsor
	$000	$000
Revenue	60,000	24,000
Cost of sales	(42,000)	(20,000)
Gross profit	18,000	4,000
Distribution costs	(2,500)	(50)
Administrative expenses	(3,500)	(150)
Profit from operations	12,000	3,800
Investment income	75	–
Finance costs	–	(200)
Profit before tax	12,075	3,600
Tax	(3,000)	(600)
Profit for the year	9,075	3,000
Retained earnings bfd	16,525	5,400

There were no items of other comprehensive income in the year.

The following information is relevant:

(1) The fair values of Windsor's net assets at the date of acquisition were equal to their carrying values with the exception of plant and equipment, which had a carrying value of $2,000,000 but a fair value of $5,200,000. The remaining useful life of this plant and equipment was four years at the date of acquisition. Depreciation is charged to cost of sales and is time apportioned on a monthly basis.

(2) During the post-acquisition period Tudor sold goods to Windsor for $12 million. The goods had originally cost $9 million. During the remaining months of the year Windsor sold $10 million (at cost to Windsor) of these goods to third parties for $13 million.

(3) Incomes and expenses accrued evenly throughout the year.

(4) Tudor has a policy of valuing non-controlling interests using the full goodwill method. The fair value of non-controlling interest at the date of acquisition was $2,520,000.

(5) The recoverable amount of the net assets of Windsor at the reporting date was $14,150,000. Any goodwill impairment should be charged to administrative expenses.

Required:

Prepare a consolidated statement of profit or loss for Tudor group for the year ended 31 March 20X5.

Solution

Tudor group statement of profit or loss for the year ended 31 March 20X5

	$000
Revenue ($60,000 + (9/12 × $24,000) – $12,000)	66,000
Cost of sales ($42,000 + (9/12 × $20,000) – $12,000 + $600 (W6) + $500 (W5))	(46,100)
Gross profit	19.900
Distribution costs ($2,500 + (9/12 × $50))	(2,538)
Administrative expenses ($3,500 + (9/12 × $150) + $300 (W3))	(3,912)
Profit from operations	13,450
Investment income ($75 – $75)	–
Finance costs ((9/12 × $200) – $75)	(75)
Profit before tax	13,375
Tax ($3,000 + (9/12 × $600))	(3,450)
Profit after tax for the year	9,925
Profit attributable to:	
Owners of the parent (bal. fig)	9,655
Non-controlling interest (W7)	270
	9,925

There were no items of other comprehensive income in the year.

(W1) **Group structure – Tudor owns 80% of Windsor**

- the acquisition took place three months into the year
- nine months is post-acquisition

(W2) **Goodwill impairment**

	$000
Net assets of the subsidiary (W3)	13,000
Goodwill (W4)	1,450
	14,450
Recoverable amount	(14,150)
Impairment	300

The impairment will be allocated against goodwill and charged to the statement of profit or loss.

Goodwill has been calculated using the fair value method so the impairment needs to be factored in when calculating the profit attributable to the NCI (W7).

(W3) **Net assets**

	Acq'n date	**Rep. date**
	$000	$000
Equity capital	2,000	2,000
Retained earnings (Rep date = $5,400 bfd + $3,000)	6,150	8,400
Fair value adjustment – PPE ($5.2m – $2.0m)	3,200	3,200
Depreciation on FVA (W6)	–	(600)
	11,350	13,000

(W4) **Goodwill**

	$000
Consideration	10,280
FV of NCI at acquisition	2,520
	12,800
FV of net assets at acquisition (W3)	(11,350)
Goodwill pre-impairment review (W2)	1,450

(W5) **PURP**

$2 million ($12m – $10m) of the $12 million intra-group sale remains in inventory.

The profit that remains in inventory is $500,000 (($12m – $9m) × 2/12).

(W6) **Excess depreciation**

Per W3, there has been a fair value uplift in respect of PPE of $3,200,000.

This uplift will be depreciated over the four year remaining life.

The depreciation charge in respect of this uplift in the current year statement of profit or loss is $600,000 (($3,200,000/4 years) × 9/12).

(W7) **Profit attributable to the NCI**

	$000	$000
Profit of Windsor (9/12 × $3,000)	2,250	
Excess depreciation (W6)	(600)	
Goodwill impairment (W2)	(300)	
	1,350	
× 20%		
Profit attributable to the NCI		270

2 Step acquisitions

Step acquisitions

A step acquisition occurs when the parent company acquires control over the subsidiary in stages. This is achieved by buying blocks of shares at different times. Acquisition accounting is only applied at the date when control is achieved.

- Any pre-existing equity interest in an entity is accounted for according to:
  - IFRS 9 in the case of simple investments
  - IAS 28 in the case of associates and joint ventures
  - IFRS 11 in the case of joint arrangements other than joint ventures
- At the date when the equity interest is increased and control is achieved:
  (1) re-measure the previously held equity interest to fair value

  (2) recognise any resulting gain or loss in profit or loss for the year

  (3) calculate goodwill and non-controlling interest on either a partial or full basis. For the purposes of the goodwill calculation, the consideration will be the fair value of the previously held equity interest plus the cost of the most recent purchase of shares at the acquisition date. You may wish to use the following proforma:

	$
Fair value of previously held interest	X
Fair value of consideration for additional interest	X
NCI at acquisition	X
	X
Less: FV of net assets at acquisition	(X)
Goodwill at acquisition	X

- If there has been re-measurement of any previously held equity interest that was recognised in other comprehensive income, any changes in value recognised in earlier years are now reclassified to retained earnings.
- Purchasing further shares in a subsidiary after control has been acquired (for example taking the group interest from 60% to 75%) is regarded as a transaction between equity holders. Goodwill is not recalculated. This situation is dealt with separately within this chapter.

Illustration 2 – Ayre and Byrne

Ayre holds a 10% investment in Byrne at $24,000 in accordance with IFRS 9. On 1 June 20X7, it acquires a further 50% of Byrne's equity shares at a cost of $160,000. The non-controlling interest is calculated using the fair value method.

On 1 June 20X7, fair values were as follows:

- Byrne's net assets – $200,000
- The non-controlling interest – $100,000
- The original 10% investment – $26,000

Required:

Calculate the goodwill arising when control is obtained over Byrne?

Solution

(W1) **Group Structure**

Ayre
|
| 60% (10% + 50%)
|
Byrne

This is a step acquisition. The previous investment in shares must be revalued to fair value. The gain on revaluation is recorded in the statement of profit or loss.

Dr	Investment ($26,000 – $24,000)	2,000
Cr	Profit or loss	2,000

(W2) **Net assets**

	At date of acquisition 1 June 20X7
	$
Net assets	200,000

(W3) **Goodwill**

	$
FV of previously held interest	26,000
FV of consideration for additional interest	160,000
NCI at acquisition date	100,000
	286,000
FV of net assets at acquisition (W2)	(200,000)
Goodwill	86,000

Test your understanding 1 – Major and Tom

The statements of financial position of two entities, Major and Tom, as at 31 December 20X6 are as follows:

	Major	**Tom**
	$000	$000
Investment	160	
Sundry assets	350	250
	510	250
Equity share capital	200	100
Retained earnings	250	122
Liabilities	60	28
	510	250

Major acquired 40% of Tom on 31 December 20X1 for $90,000. At this time, the retained earnings of Tom stood at $76,000. A further 20% of shares in Tom was acquired by Major three years later for $70,000. On this date, the fair value of the existing holding in Tom was $105,000. Tom's retained earnings were $100,000 on the second acquisition date. The NCI should be valued using the proportion of net assets method.

Required:

Prepare the consolidated statement of financial position for the Major group as at 31 December 20X6.

3 Further share purchase after control is obtained

When a parent company increases its shareholding in a subsidiary, this is not treated as an acquisition in the group financial statements. Instead, it is accounted for as a decrease in the non-controlling interest.

For example if the parent holds 80% of the shares in a subsidiary and buys 5% more then the relationship remains one of a parent and subsidiary. However, the NCI holding has decreased from 20% to 15%.

The accounting treatment is as follows:

- There is a decrease in the NCI.
- The difference between the consideration paid for the extra shares and the decrease in the NCI is accounted for within equity (normally, in 'other components of equity').
- No profit or loss arises on the purchase of the additional shares.
- Goodwill is not recalculated.

The following proforma will help to calculate the adjustments required to NCI and other components of equity:

	$	
Cash paid	X	Cr
Decrease in NCI	(X)	Dr
Decrease/(increase) to other components of equity	X/(X)	Dr/Cr (bal. entry)

The decrease in NCI will represent the proportionate reduction in the carrying value of the NCI at the date of the group's additional purchase of shares

- For example, if the NCI shareholding reduces from 30% to 20%, then the carrying value of the NCI must be reduced by one-third.

Test your understanding 2 – Gordon and Mandy

Gordon has owned 80% of Mandy for many years.

Gordon is considering acquiring more shares in Mandy. The NCI of Mandy currently has a carrying value of $20,000, with the net assets and goodwill having a value of $125,000 and $25,000 respectively.

Gordon is considering the following two scenarios:

(i) Gordon could buy 20% of the Mandy shares leaving no NCI for $25,000, or

(ii) Gordon could buy 5% of the Mandy shares for $4,000 leaving a 15% NCI.

Required:

Calculate the adjustments required to NCI and other components of equity.

4 Disposal scenarios

During the year, one entity may sell some or all of its shares in another entity.

Possible situations include:

(1) the disposal of all the shares held in the subsidiary

(2) the disposal of part of the shareholding, leaving a residual holding after the sale, which is regarded as an associate

(3) the disposal of part of the shareholding, leaving a residual holding after the sale, which is regarded as a trade investment

(4) the disposal of part of the shareholding, leaving a controlling interest after the sale.

5 Investing entity's financial statements

Profit or loss on disposal in the individual financial statements

In all of the above scenarios, the profit on disposal in the investing entity's individual financial statements is calculated as follows:

	$
Sales proceeds	X
Carrying amount (usually cost) of shares sold	(X)
Profit/(loss) on disposal	X/(X)

The profit or loss may need to be reported as an exceptional item. If so, it must be disclosed separately on the face of the parent's statement of profit or loss for the year.

There may be tax to pay on this gain, depending on the tax laws in place in the parent's jurisdiction. This would result in an increase to the parent company's tax expense in the statement of profit or loss.

6 Consolidated financial statements

In the consolidated financial statements, the accounting treatment of the sale of shares in a subsidiary will depend on whether or not the transaction causes control over the subsidiary to be lost.

Accounting for a disposal where control is lost

- Where control is lost (i.e. the subsidiary is completely disposed of or becomes an associate or investment), the group:
  - Recognises:
    - the consideration received
    - any investment retained in the former subsidiary at fair value on the date of disposal
  - Derecognises:
    - the assets and liabilities of the subsidiary at the date of disposal
    - goodwill in the subsidiary at the date of disposal
    - the non-controlling interest at the date of disposal.
  - The difference between these amounts is a profit or loss on disposal that is recorded in the consolidated statement of profit or loss.

Where control of a subsidiary has been lost, the following template should be used for the calculation of the profit or loss on disposal:

	$	$
Disposal proceeds		X
Fair value of retained interest		X
		X
Less interest in subsidiary disposed of:		
Net assets of subsidiary at disposal date	X	
Goodwill at disposal date	X	
Less: Carrying value of NCI at disposal date	(X)	
		(X)
Profit/(loss) to the group		X/(X)

There are two ways of presenting the results of the disposed subsidiary:

(i) **Time-apportionment line-by-line**

In the consolidated statement of profit or loss, the income and expenses of the subsidiary are consolidated up to the date of disposal. The traditional way is to time apportion each line of the disposed subsidiary's results.

The profit or loss on disposal of the subsidiary would be presented as an exceptional item.

(ii) **Discontinued operation**

If the subsidiary qualifies as a discontinued operation in accordance with IFRS 5 then its results are aggregated into a single line on the face of the statement of profit or loss. This is presented immediately after profit for the period from continuing operations.

This single figure comprises:

- the profit or loss of the subsidiary up to the disposal date
- the profit or loss on the disposal of the subsidiary.

7 Group accounts – entire disposal

Entire disposal

Illustration 3 – Rock – entire disposal

Rock has held a 70% investment in Dog for two years. Goodwill has been calculated using the full goodwill method. There have been no goodwill impairments to date.

Rock disposes of all of its shares in Dog. The following information has been provided:

	$
Cost of investment	2,000
Dog – Fair value of net assets at acquisition	1,900
Dog – Fair value of the non-controlling interest at acquisition	800
Sales proceeds	3,000
Dog – Net assets at disposal	2,400

Required:

Calculate the profit or loss on disposal in:

(a) **Rock's individual financial statements**

(b) **the consolidated financial statements.**

Solution

(a) **Rock's individual financial statements**

	$
Sales proceeds	3,000
Cost of shares sold	(2,000)
Profit on disposal	1,000

(b) **Consolidated financial statements**

	$	$
Sales proceeds		3,000
Interest in subsidiary disposed of:		
Net assets at disposal	2,400	
Goodwill at disposal (W1)	900	
Less: carrying value of NCI at disposal (W2)	(950)	
		(2,350)
Profit on disposal		650

(W1) **Goodwill**

	$
Consideration	2,000
FV of NCI at acquisition	800
	2,800
FV of net assets at acquisition	(1,900)
Goodwill	900

(W2) **NCI at disposal date**

	$
NCI at acquisition	800
NCI % of post acquisition net assets (30% × ($2,400 – $1,900))	150
	950

Test your understanding 3 – Snooker

Snooker purchased 80% of the shares in Billiards for $100,000 when the net assets of Billiards had a fair value of $50,000. Goodwill at acquisition was $60,000 and has not suffered any impairment to date. This was calculated using the share of net assets method. Snooker has just disposed of its entire shareholding in Billiards for $300,000, when the net assets were stated at $110,000.

Required:

(a) **Calculate the profit or loss arising to the parent entity on disposal of the shares in Billiards.**

(b) **Calculate the profit or loss arising to the group on disposal of the shares in Billiards.**

Test your understanding 4 – Padstow

Padstow purchased 80% of the shares in St Merryn four years ago for $100,000. On 30 June it sold all of these shares for $250,000. The net assets of St Merryn at the acquisition date were $69,000 and at the disposal date were $88,000. Fifty per cent of the goodwill arising on acquisition had been written off in an earlier year. The fair value of the non-controlling interest in St Merryn at the date of acquisition was $15,000. It is group policy to account for goodwill using the full goodwill method.

Tax is charged at 30%.

Required:

(a) **Calculate the profit or loss arising to the parent entity on the disposal of the shares.**

(b) **Calculate the profit or loss arising to the group on the disposal of the shares.**

8 Group accounts – Subsidiary to associate

A part disposal of shares could result in a subsidiary becoming an associate. For example, a 90% holding might be reduced to a 40% holding.

After the disposal the incomes, expenses, assets and liabilities of the ex-subsidiary can no longer be consolidated on a line by line basis. Instead the investment must be accounted for in the consolidated financial statements under the equity method.

Consolidated statement of profit or loss and other comprehensive income

- Consolidate the results line by line up to the date of disposal
- Calculate the group profit or loss on the disposal of the subsidiary
- Equity account for the results after the date of disposal by including a single line representing the group's share of the associate's profits

Consolidated statement of financial position

- Equity account for the associate at the year end, by including a single line representing the fair value of the investment retained plus the group's share of profits and other comprehensive income earned since the date that the investment became an associate.

Illustration 4 – Thomas and Percy

Thomas disposed of a 25% holding in Percy on 30 June 20X6 for $125,000. A 70% holding in Percy had been acquired five years prior to this. Thomas uses the full goodwill method. Goodwill was impaired and written off in full prior to the year of disposal.

Details of Percy are as follows:

	$
Net assets at disposal date	340,000
Fair value of a 45% holding at 30 June 20X6	245,000

The carrying value of the NCI is $80,000 at the disposal date.

Required:

What is the profit or loss on disposal for inclusion in the consolidated statement of profit or loss for the year ended 31 December 20X6?

Solution

The group's holding in Percy has reduced from 70% to 45%. Control over Percy has been lost and a profit or loss on disposal must be calculated.

The profit on disposal to be included in the consolidated statement of profit or loss is calculated as follows:

	$	$
Proceeds		125,000
FV of retained interest		245,000
		370,000
Net assets recognised at disposal	340,000	
Goodwill at disposal	–	
Less: NCI at disposal date	(80,000)	
		(260,000)
Profit on disposal		110,000

From 30 June 20X6, the investment in Percy will be accounted for using the equity method in the consolidated financial statements.

Test your understanding 5 – Hague

Hague has held a 60% investment in Maude for several years, using the full goodwill method to value the non-controlling interest. Half of the goodwill has been impaired prior to the date of disposal of shares by Hague. Details are as follows:

	$000
Cost of investment	6,000
Maude – Fair value of net assets at acquisition	2,000
Maude – Fair value of a 40% investment at acquisition date	1,000
Maude – Net assets at disposal	3,000
Maude – Fair value of a 25% investment at disposal date	3,500

Required:

(a) **Assuming a full disposal of the holding and proceeds of $10 million, calculate the profit or loss arising:**

(i) **in Hague's individual financial statements**

(ii) **in the consolidated financial statements.**

Tax is 25%.

(b) **Assuming a disposal of a 35% holding and proceeds of $5 million:**

(i) **calculate the profit or loss arising in the consolidated financial statements**

(ii) **explain how the residual shareholding will be accounted for.**

Ignore tax.

Test your understanding 6 – Kathmandu

The statements of profit or loss and extracts from the statements of changes in equity for the year ended 31 December 20X9 are as follows:

Statements of profit or loss for the year ended 31 December 20X9:

	Kathmandu Group	**Nepal**
	$	$
Revenue	553,000	450,000
Operating costs	(450,000)	(400,000)
Operating profits	103,000	50,000
Investment income	8,000	–
Profit before tax	111,000	50,000
Tax	(40,000)	(14,000)
Profit for the period	71,000	36,000

Extracts from SOCIE for year ended 31 December 20X9

	Kathmandu group	Nepal
	$	$
Retained earnings b/f	100,000	80,000
Profit for the period	71,000	36,000
Dividend paid	(25,000)	(10,000)
Retained earnings c/f	146,000	106,000

There were no items of other comprehensive income during the year.

Additional information

- The accounts of the Kathmandu group do not include the results of Nepal.
- On 1 January 20X5 Kathmandu acquired 70% of the shares of Nepal for $100,000 when the fair value of Nepal's net assets was $110,000. Nepal has equity capital of $50,000. At that date, the fair value of the non-controlling interest was $40,000. It is group policy to measure the NCI at fair value at the date of acquisition.
- Nepal paid its 20X9 dividend in cash on 31 March 20X9.
- Goodwill has not been impaired.

Required:

(a) (i) Prepare the group statement of profit or loss for the year ended 31 December 20X9 for the Kathmandu group on the basis that Kathmandu plc sold its holding in Nepal on 1 July 20X9 for $200,000. This disposal is not yet recognised in any way in Kathmandu group's statement of profit or loss. Assume that Nepal does not represent a discontinued operation per IFRS 5.

(ii) Calculate the group's retained earnings as at 31 December 20X9.

(iii) Explain and illustrate how the results of Nepal are presented in the group statement of profit or loss in the event that Nepal represented a discontinued activity per IFRS 5.

Ignore tax on the disposal.

(b) (i) Prepare the group statement of profit or loss for the year ended 31 December 20X9 for the Kathmandu group on the basis that Kathmandu sold half of its holding in Nepal on 1 July 20X9 for $100,000 This disposal is not yet recognised in any way in Kathmandu group's statement of profit or loss. The residual holding of 35% has a fair value of $100,000 and leaves the Kathmandu group with significant influence over Nepal.

(ii) Calculate the group's retained earnings as at 31 December 20X9.

Ignore tax on the disposal.

9 Group accounts – Disposal with trade investment retained

In this situation, a disposal of shares means that control over a subsidiary is lost and the group is instead left with a simple trade investment. For example, a 90% shareholding is reduced to a 10% shareholding.

Consolidated statement of profit or loss

- Consolidate the results line by line up to the date of disposal
- Calculate the group profit or loss on the disposal of the subsidiary
- Include dividend income after the date of disposal, as well as any gains or losses recorded in accordance with IFRS 9 Financial Instruments.

Consolidated statement of financial position

- Recognise the residual holding retained as an investment. This will initially be at fair value at the disposal date but will be subsequently remeasured under the rules of IFRS 9 Financial Instruments.

10 Disposal where control is not lost (increase in NCI)

From the perspective of the group accounts, a sale of shares which results in the parent retaining control over the subsidiary is simply a transaction between shareholders. The parent's shareholding in the subsidiary decreases and the NCI's shareholding increases.

If the parent company holds 80% of the shares of a subsidiary but then sells a 5% holding, a relationship of control still exists. As such, the subsidiary will still be consolidated in the group financial statements. However, the NCI has risen from 20% to 25%.

Where there is such an increase in the non-controlling interest:

- No profit or loss on disposal is calculated
- No adjustment is made to the carrying value of goodwill
- The difference between the proceeds received and change in the non-controlling interest is accounted for in other components of equity as follows:

	$	
Cash proceeds received	X	Dr
Increase in NCI	(X)	Cr
Increase/(Decrease) to other components of equity	X/ (X)	Cr/Dr (bal. entry)

The increase in the NCI will be the share of the net assets (always) and goodwill (fair value method only) of the subsidiary at the date of disposal which the parent has effectively sold to the NCI.

- For example, if the NCI shareholding increases from 20% to 30%, then the carrying value of the NCI must be increased by 10% of the subsidiary's net assets and, if using the fair value method, goodwill.

Illustration 5 – No loss of control – Juno

Until 30 September 20X7, Juno held 90% of Hera. On that date it sold a 10% interest in the equity capital for $15,000. At the date of the share disposal, the carrying value of net assets and goodwill of Juno were $100,000 and $20,000 respectively. At acquisition, the NCI was valued at fair value.

Required:

How should the sale of shares be accounted for in the Juno Group's financial statements?

Solution

	$
Cash proceeds	15,000 Dr
Increase in NCI: 10% × ($100,000 + $20,000)	(12,000) Cr
Increase in other components of equity (bal. fig)	3,000 Cr

There is no gain or loss to the group as there has been no loss of control. Note that, depending upon the terms of the share disposal, there could be either an increase or decrease in equity.

Disposal with no loss of control

In this situation, the subsidiary remains a subsidiary, albeit the shareholding is reduced, e.g. 90% holding is reduced to a 60% holding.

Consolidated statement of profit or loss and other comprehensive income

- Consolidate the subsidiary's results for the whole year.
- Calculate the non-controlling interest relating to the periods before and after the disposal separately and then add together:
- e.g. (X/12 × profit × 10%) + (Y/12 × profit × 40%)

Consolidated statement of financial position

- Consolidate the assets and liabilities of the parent and subsidiary as normal
- Be careful in your calculation of NCI (W4) and retained earnings (W5)
  - The NCI would be allocated 10% of the subsidiary's net asset movement between acquisition and the date of the share disposal. They would then be allocated 40% of the net asset movement from the date of the share disposal
  - In group retained earnings, the group would be allocated 90% of the subsidiary's retained earnings movement between acquisition and the date of the share disposal. From the date of the share disposal, the group would be allocated 60% of the subsidiary's retained earnings movement.
- Take the difference between the proceeds and the change in the NCI to other components of equity as discussed above.

Test your understanding 7 – David and Goliath

David has owned 90% of Goliath for many years and is considering selling part of its holding, whilst retaining control of Goliath.

At the date of considering disposal of part of the shareholding in Goliath, the NCI has a carrying value of $7,200 and the net assets and goodwill have a carrying value of $70,000 and $20,000 respectively. The NCI was valued at fair value at the acquisition date.

(i) David could sell 5% of the Goliath shares for $5,000 leaving it holding 85% and increasing the NCI to 15%, or

(ii) David could sell 25% of the Goliath shares for $20,000 leaving it holding 65% and increasing the NCI to 35%.

Required:

Calculate the difference arising that will be taken to equity for each situation.

Test your understanding 8 – Pepsi

Statements of financial position for three entities at the reporting date are as follows:

	Pepsi	Sprite	Tango
	$000	$000	$000
Assets	1,000	800	500
Investment in Sprite	326	–	–
Investment in Tango	165	–	–
Total assets	1,491	800	500
Equity			
Ordinary share capital ($1)	500	200	100
Retained earnings	391	100	200
	891	300	300
Liabilities	600	500	200
Total equity and liabilities	1,491	800	500

Pepsi acquired 80% of Sprite when Sprite's retained earnings were $25,000, paying cash consideration of $300,000. It is group policy to measure NCI at fair value at the date of acquisition. The fair value of the NCI holding in Sprite at acquisition was $65,000.

At the reporting date, Pepsi purchased an additional 8% of Sprite's equity shares for cash consideration of $26,000. This amount has been debited to Pepsi's investment in Sprite.

Pepsi acquired 75% of Tango when Tango's retained earnings were $60,000, paying cash consideration of $200,000. The fair value of the NCI holding in Tango at the date of acquisition was $50,000.

At the reporting date, Pepsi sold 10% of the equity shares of Tango for $35,000. The cash proceeds have been credited to Pepsi's investment in Tango.

Required:

Prepare the consolidated statement of financial position of the Pepsi group.

11 Subsidiaries acquired exclusively with a view to subsequent disposal

A subsidiary acquired exclusively with a view to resale is not exempt from consolidation. However, if it meets the 'held for sale' criteria in IFRS 5:

- it is presented in the financial statements as a disposal group classified as held for sale. This is achieved by amalgamating all its assets into one line item and all its liabilities into another
- it is measured, both on acquisition and at subsequent reporting dates, at fair value less costs to sell. (IFRS 5 sets down a special rule for such subsidiaries, requiring the deduction of costs to sell. Normally, it requires acquired assets and liabilities to be measured at fair value).

The 'held for sale' criteria include the requirements that:

- the subsidiary is available for immediate sale
- the sale is highly probable
- it is likely to be disposed of within one year of the date of its acquisition.

A newly acquired subsidiary which meets these held for sale criteria automatically meets the criteria for being presented as a discontinued operation.

Illustration: IFRS 5

David acquires Rose on 1 March 20X7. Rose is a holding entity with two wholly-owned subsidiaries, Mickey and Jackie. Jackie is acquired exclusively with a view to resale and meets the criteria for classification as held for sale. David's year-end is 30 September.

On 1 March 20X7 the following information is relevant:

- the identifiable liabilities of Jackie have a fair value of $40m
- the acquired assets of Jackie have a fair value of $180m
- the expected costs of selling Jackie are $5m.

On 30 September 20X7, the assets of Jackie have a fair value of $170m.

The liabilities have a fair value of $35m and the selling costs remain at $5m.

Discuss how Jackie will be treated in the David Group financial statements on acquisition and at 30 September 20X7.

Solution

On acquisition the assets and liabilities of Jackie are measured at fair value less costs to sell in accordance with IFRS 5:

	$m
Assets	180
Less selling costs	(5)
	175
Liabilities	(40)
Fair value less costs to sell	135

At the reporting date, the assets and liabilities of Jackie are remeasured to update the fair value less costs to sell.

	$m
Assets	170
Less selling costs	(5)
	165
Liabilities	(35)
Fair value less costs to sell	130

The fair value less costs to sell has decreased from $135m on 1 March to $130m on 30 September. This $5m reduction in fair value must be presented in the consolidated statement of profit or loss as part of the single line item entitled 'discontinued operations'. Also included in this line is the post-tax profit or loss earned/incurred by Jackie in the March – September 20X7 period.

The assets and liabilities of Jackie must be disclosed separately on the face of the statement of financial position. Jackie's assets will appear below the subtotal for the David group's current assets:

	$m
Non-current assets classified as held for sale	165

Jackie's liabilities will appear below the subtotal for the David group's current liabilities:

	$m
Liabilities directly associated with non-current assets classified as held for sale	35

No other disclosure is required.

12 Chapter summary

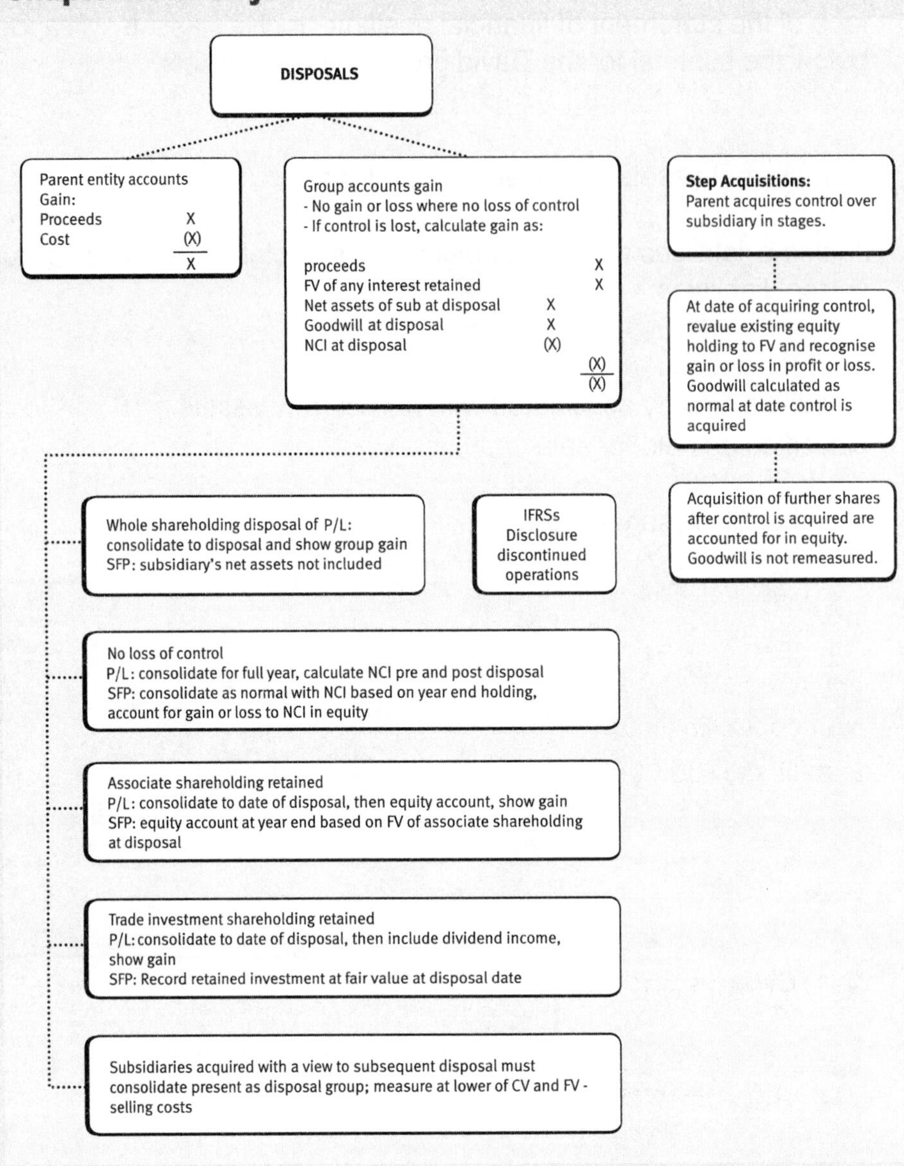

Test your understanding answers

Test your understanding 1 – Major and Tom

Consolidated statement of financial position for Major as at 31 December 20X6

	$
Goodwill (W3)	55,000
Sundry assets ($350,000 + $250,000)	600,000
	655,000

Equity and liabilities	$
Equity share capital	200,000
Retained earnings (W5)	278,200
Non-controlling interest (W4)	88,800
Liabilities ($60,000 + $28,000)	88,000
	655,000

(W1) **Group structure**

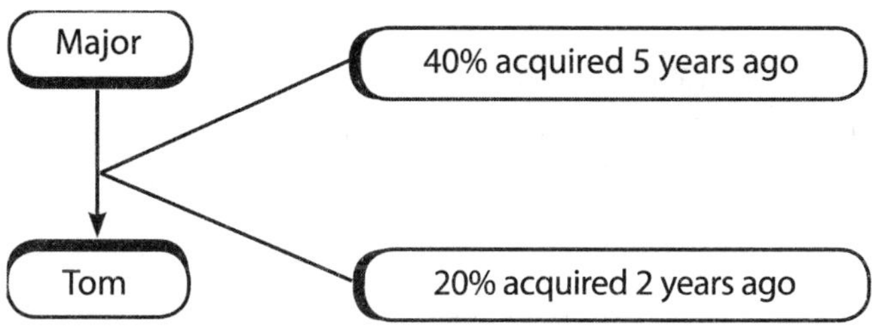

Tom becomes a subsidiary of Major from December 20X4.

The previously held investment must be revalued to fair value with the gain or loss recorded in the statement of profit or loss.

Dr Investment ($105,000 – $90,000)	15,000
Cr Profit or loss	15,000

(W2) **Net assets**

	At Acquisition 20X4	At Reporting date
	$	$
Share capital	100,000	100,000
Retained earnings	100,000	122,000
	200,000	222,000

(W3) **Goodwill**

	$
Fair value of previously held interest	105,000
Fair value of consideration for additional interest	70,000
	175,000
NCI at acquisition (40% × $200,000)	80,000
Less: FV of net assets at acquisition (W2)	(200,000)
	55,000

(W4) **Non-controlling interest**

	$
NCI at acquisition date	80,000
NCI % of post-acquisition net assets (40% × $22,000 (W2))	8,800
	88,800

(W5) **Group Retained earnings**

	$
Major	250,000
Gain on revaluation of investment (W1)	15,000
Tom (60% × $22,000 (W2))	13,200
	278,200

Test your understanding 2 – Gordon and Mandy

(i) **Purchase of 20% of Mandy shares**

	$	
Cash paid	25,000	Cr
Decrease in NCI ((20%/20%) × 20,000)	(20,000)	Dr
Decrease in other components of equity	5.000	Dr

(ii) **Purchase of 5% of Mandy shares**

	$	
Cash paid	4,000	Cr
Decrease in NCI ((5%/20%) × 20,000)	(5,000)	Dr
Increase in other components of equity	(1,000)	Cr

Test your understanding 3 – Snooker

(a) **Profit to Snooker**

	$000
Sales proceeds	300
Cost of shares sold	(100)
Profit on disposal	200

(b) **Consolidated financial statements**

		$000
Proceeds		300
FV of retained interest		nil
		300
Net assets of subsidiary at disposal date	110	
Unimpaired goodwill at disposal date	60	
Less: NCI carrying value at disposal date (W1)	(22)	
		(148)
Profit on disposal		152

(W1) **NCI at disposal date**

	$000
NCI at acquisition ($50,000 × 20%)	10
NCI % of increase in net assets to disposal date (20% × ($110,000 – $50,000))	12
	22

Test your understanding 4 – Padstow

(a) **Profit to Padstow**

	$000
Sales proceeds	250
Cost of shares sold	(100)
Profit on disposal	150

The tax due on the profit on disposal is: ($150,000 × 30%)	45

The profit on disposal will be disclosed as an exceptional item in the statement of profit or loss.

The tax on the gain will be charged to the statement of profit or loss as part of the year's current tax charge.

(b) **Consolidated accounts**

	$000	$000
Sales proceeds		250
Net assets at disposal date	88.0	
Goodwill at disposal date (W1)	23.0	
Less: NCI at disposal date (W2)	(14.2)	
		(96.8)
Profit on disposal		153.2

The tax of $45,000 that arose on the disposal in the parent's financial statements will be consolidated into the group financial statement

(W1) **Goodwill**

	$000
Consideration	100.0
NCI at acquisition	15.0
	115.0
FV of net assets at acquisition	(69.0)
Goodwill at acquisition	46.0
Impairment ($46 × 50%)	(23.0)
Goodwill at disposal date	23.0

(W2) **NCI at disposal date**

	$000
NCI at acquisition	15.0
NCI % of post-acq'n net assets movement (20% × ($88.0 – $69.0))	3.8
NCI % of impairment (20% × $23.0 (W1))	(4.6)
	14.2

Test your understanding 5 – Hague

(a) **Full disposal**

(i) **Profit in Hague's individual financial statements**

	$000
Sale proceeds	10,000
Cost of shares	(6,000)
Profit on disposal	4,000
Tax charge on disposal: (25% × $4,000)	(1,000)

(ii) **Profit in consolidated financial statements**

	$000	$000
Sale proceeds		10,000
FV of retained interest		nil
CV of subsidiary at disposal:		
Net Assets at disposal:	3,000	
Goodwill at disposal (W1)	2,500	
Less: NCI at disposal date (W2)	(400)	
		(5,100)
Profit on disposal		4,900

(W1) **Goodwill**

	$000
Consideration	6,000
NCI at acquisition	1,000
	7,000
FV of NA at acquisition (given)	(2,000)
Goodwill at acquisition	5,000
Impaired (50%)	(2,500)
Goodwill at disposal	2,500

(W2) **NCI at disposal date**

	$000
NCI at acquisition	1,000
NCI share of post-acquisition net assets (40% × ($3,000 – $2,000))	400
Less: NCI share of goodwill impairment (40% × $2,500) (W1)	(1,000)
	400

(b) **Disposal of a 35% shareholding**

(i) **Profit in consolidated financial statements**

	$000	$000
Disposal proceeds		5,000
FV of retained interest		3,500
		8,500
CV of subsidiary at disposal date:		
Net assets at disposal	3,000	
Goodwill at disposal (W1)	2,500	
	5,500	
Less: NCI at disposal date (W2)	(400)	
		(5,100)
Profit on disposal		3,400

(ii) After the date of disposal, the residual holding will be accounted for using the equity method in the consolidated financial statements:

- The statement of profit or loss will show the group's share of the current year profit earned by the associate from the date significant influence was obtained.
- The statement of financial position will show the carrying value of the investment in the associate. This will be the fair value of the retained shareholding at the disposal date plus the group's share of the increase in reserves from this date.

Test your understanding 6 – Kathmandu

(a) (i) **Consolidated statement of profit or loss – full disposal**

	$
Revenue ($553,000 + (6/12 × $450,000))	778,000
Operating costs ($450,000 + (6/12 × $400,000))	(650,000)
Operating profit	128,000
Investment income ($8,000 – ($10,000 × 70%))	1,000
Profit on disposal (W4)	80,400
Profit before tax	209,400
Tax ($40,000 + (6/12 × $14,000))	(47,000)
Profit for the period	162,400
Attributable to:	
Equity holders of Kathmandu (bal. fig)	157,000
Non-controlling interest (W5)	5,400
	162,400

There were no items of other comprehensive income during the year.

(ii) **Group retained earnings at 31 December 20X9 – full disposal**

	$
Brought forward	
Kathmandu	100,000
Group % of Nepal's post acquisition retained earnings b/f (70% × ($130,000 (W1) – $110,000) (per Q))	14,000
	114,000
Profit for year attributable to equity holders	157,000
Less dividend paid	(25,000)
Retained earnings carried forward	246,000

(iii) Group statement of profit or loss – discontinued operations presentation

	$
Revenue	553,000
Operating costs	(450,000)
Operating profit	103,000
Investment income ($8,000 – (70% × $10,000))	1,000
Profit before tax	104,000
Tax	(40,000)
Profit for the period from continuing operations	64,000
Profit from discontinued operations (($36,000 × 6/12)+ $80,400 (W4))	98,400
	162,400
Attributable to:	
Equity holders of Kathmandu (bal. fig)	157,000
Non-controlling interest (W5)	5,400
	162,400

There were no items of other comprehensive income during the year.

Notice that the post-tax results of the subsidiary up to the date of disposal are presented as a one-line entry in the group statement of profit or loss. There is no line-by-line consolidation of results when this method of presentation is adopted.

(b) (i) **Consolidated statement of profit or loss – part disposal with residual interest**

	$
Revenue ($553,000 + (6/12 × $450,000)	778,000
Operating costs ($450,000 + (6/12 × $400,000))	(650,000)
Operating profit	128,000
Investment income ($8,000 – (70% × $10,000)	1,000
Income from associate (35% × $36,000 × 6/12)	6,300
Profit on disposal (W4)	80,400
Profit before tax	215,700
Tax ($40,000 + (6/12 × $14,000))	(47,000)
Profit for the period	168,700

There were no items of other comprehensive income during the year.

Attributable to:	
Equity holders of Kathmandu (bal. fig)	163,300
Non-controlling interest (W5)	5,400
	168,700

(ii) **Group retained earnings at 31 December 20X9 – part disposal**

	$
Brought forward	
Kathmandu	100,000
Group % of Nepal's post acquisition retained earnings b/f	
(70% × (130,000 (W1) – 110,000) (per Q))	14,000
	114,000
Profit for the period attributable to equity holders	163,300
Less dividend paid	(25,000)
	252,300

Alternatively:

	$
Kathmandu c/fwd	146,000
Parent gain on disposal of shares	
($100,000 – (50% × $100,000))	50,000
Gain on remeasurement of residual holding	
($100,000 – $50,000)	50,000
Share of associate profit (6/12 × 35% × $36,000)	6,300
	252,300

Workings

(W1) **Net assets – Nepal**	**Net assets at disposal**	**Net assets b/f**
	$	$
Share capital	50,000	50,000
Retained earnings		
B/f	80,000	80,000
6/12 × 36,000	18,000	
Less Dividend	(10,000)	–
	138,000	130,000

(W2) **Goodwill**

	$
Consideration	100,000
FV of NCI at date of acquisition	40,000
	140,000
FV of net assets at date of acquisition	(110,000)
Goodwill	30,000

(W3) **NCI at disposal date**

FV of NCI at date of acquisition	40,000
NCI share of post-acquisition net assets (30% × ($138,000 – $110,000)	8,400
	48,400

(W4) **Profit on full disposal (a)(i)**

	$	$
Proceeds		200,000
Interest in subsidiary disposed of:		
Net assets at disposal (W1)	138,000	
Goodwill at disposal (W2)	30,000	
	168,000	
NCI at date of disposal (W3)	(48,400)	
		(119,600)
Profit on disposal		80,400

(W5) **Profit attributable to NCI**

	$	$
Profit of Nepal (6/12 × $36,000)	18,000	
× 30%	18,000	
Profit attributable to NCI		5,400

(W6) **Profit on part disposal (b)(i)**

	$	$
Proceeds		100,000
FV of retained interest (per question)		100,000
		200,000
Net assets at disposal (W1)	138,000	
Unimpaired goodwill at disposal date (W2)	30,000	
	168,000	
NCI at date of disposal (W3)	(48,400)	
		(119,600)
Profit on disposal		80,400

Test your understanding 7 – David and Goliath

(i) **Sale of 5% of Goliath shares**

	$	
Cash proceeds	5,000	Dr
Increase in NCI (5% × ($70,000 + $20,000)	(4,500)	Cr
Increase in other components of equity	500	Cr

(ii) **Sale of 25% of Goliath shares**

	$	
Cash proceeds	20,000	Dr
Increase in NCI (25% × ($70,000 + $20,000)	(22,500)	Cr
Decrease in other components of equity	(2,500)	Dr

Note that in both situations, Goliath remains a subsidiary of David after the sale of shares. There is no gain or loss to the group – the difference arising is taken to equity. Goliath would continue to be consolidated within the David Group like any other subsidiary. There is no change to the carrying value of goodwill. The only impact will be the calculation of NCI share of retained earnings for the year – this would need to be time-apportioned based upon the NCI percentage pre- and post-disposal during the year.

Test your understanding 8 – Pepsi

Consolidated statement of financial position

	$000
Assets ($1,000 + $800 + $500)	2,300
Goodwill ($140 + $90) (W3)	230
Total assets	2,530
Equity	
Ordinary share capital ($1)	500
Retained earnings (W5)	556
Other components of equity ($6 – $4) (W6, W7)	2
	1,058
Non-controlling interests ($48 + $124) (W4)	172
	1,230
Liabilities ($600 + $500 + $200)	1,300
Total equity and liabilities	2,530

Workings

(W1) **Group structure**

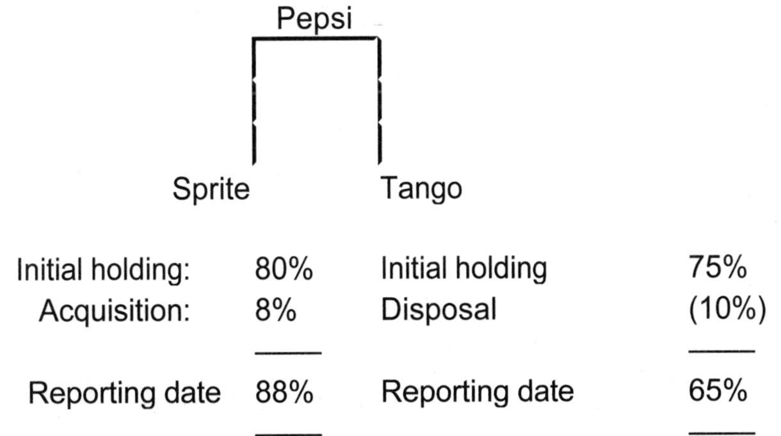

(W2) **Net Assets of subsidiaries**

Sprite	Acquisition date	Reporting date
	$000	$000
Share capital	200	200
Retained earnings	25	100
	225	300

Tango	Acquisition date	Reporting date
	$000	$000
Share capital	100	100
Retained earnings	60	200
	160	300

(W3) **Goodwill**

Sprite	$000
Consideration	300
FV of NCI at acquisition	65
Fair value of net assets at acquisition (W2)	(225)
	140

Tango	$000
Consideration	200
FV of NCI at acquisition	50
Fair value of net assets at acquisition (W2)	(160)
	90

(W4) **Non-controlling interest**

Sprite	$000
NCI at acquisition (W3)	65
NCI% × post acquisition net assets (20% × $75 (W2))	15
NCI before control to control adjustment	80
Decrease in NCI (W6)	(32)
	48

Tango	$000
NCI at acquisition (W3)	50
NCI% × post acquisition net assets (25% × $140 (W2))	35
NCI before control to control adjustment	85
Increase in NCI (W7)	39
	124

(W5) **Retained earnings**

	$000
Pepsi's retained earnings	391
Pepsi's % of Sprite's post acquisition retained earnings (80% × $75 (W2))	60
Pepsi's % of Tango's post acquisition retained earnings (75% × $140 (W2))	105
	556

(W6) **Control to control adjustment – Sprite**

	$000	
Cash paid	26	Cr
Decrease in NCI (8/20 × $80 (W4))	(32)	Dr
Increase to other components of equity	(6)	Cr

(W7) **Control to control adjustment – Tango**

	$000	
Cash received	35	Dr
Increase in NCI (10% × ($300 (W2) + $90 (W3))	(39)	Cr
Decrease to other components of equity	(4)	Dr

chapter

17

Group reorganisations

Chapter learning objectives

Upon completion of this chapter you will be able to:

- discuss the reasons behind a group reorganisation
- evaluate and assess the principal terms of a proposed group reorganisation.

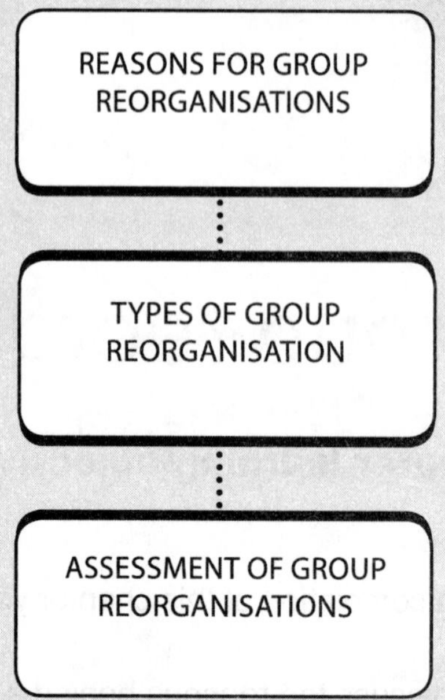

Definition of a group reorganisation

A group reorganisation (or restructuring) is any of the following:

(a) the transfer of shares in a subsidiary from one group entity to another

(b) the addition of a new parent entity to a group

(c) the transfer of shares in one or more subsidiaries of a group to a new entity that is not a group entity but whose shareholders are the same as those of the group's parent

(d) the combination into a group of two or more companies that before the combination had the same shareholders

(e) the acquisition of the shares of another entity that itself then issues sufficient shares so that the acquired entity has control of the combined entity.

Reasons for a reorganisation

There are a number of reasons why a group may wish to reorganise. These include the following.

- A group may wish to list on a public stock exchange. This is usually facilitated by creating a new holding company and keeping the business of the group in subsidiary entities.
- The ownership of subsidiaries may be transferred from one group company to another. This is often the case if the group wishes to sell a subsidiary, but retain its trade.
- The group may decide to transfer the assets and trades of a number of subsidiaries into one entity. This is called divisionalisation and is undertaken in order to simplify the group structure and save costs. The details of divisionalisation are not examinable at P2.
- There may be corporate tax advantages to reorganising a group structure, particularly if one or more subsidiaries within the group is loss-making.
- The group may split into two or more parts; each part is still owned by the same shareholders but is not related to the other parts. This is a demerger and is often done to enhance shareholder value. By splitting the group, the value of each part is realised whereas previously the stock market may have undervalued the group as a whole. The details of demergers are not examinable at P2.
- An unlisted entity may purchase a listed entity with the aim of achieving a stock exchange listing itself. This is called a reverse acquisition.

Types of group reorganisation

There are a number of ways of effecting a group reorganisation. The type of reorganisation will depend on what the group is trying to achieve.

New holding company

A group might set up a new holding entity for an existing group in order to improve co-ordination within the group or as a vehicle for flotation.

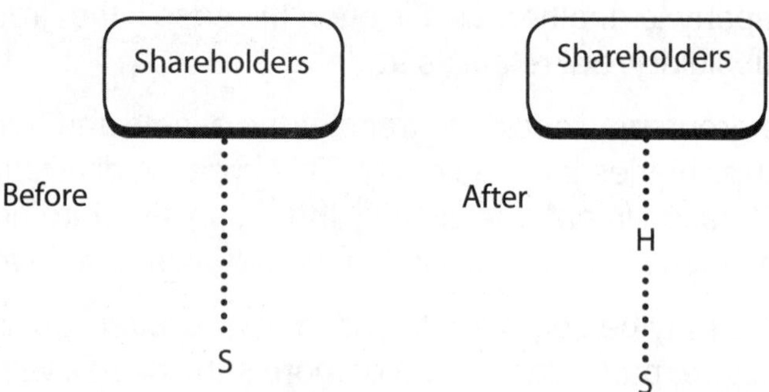

- H becomes the new holding entity of S.
- Usually, H issues shares to the shareholders of S in exchange for shares of S, but occasionally the shareholders of S may subscribe for shares in H and H may pay cash for S.

IFRS 3 excludes from its scope any business combination involving entities or businesses under 'common control', which is where the same parties control all of the combining entities/businesses both before and after the business combination.

As there is no mandatory guidance in accounting for these items, the acquisition method should certainly be used in examination questions.

Change of ownership of an entity within a group

This occurs when the internal structure of the group changes, for example, a parent may transfer the ownership of a subsidiary to another of its subsidiaries.

The key thing to remember is that the reorganisation of the entities within the group should not affect the group accounts, as shareholdings are transferred from one company to another and no assets will leave the group.

The individual accounts of the group companies will need to be adjusted for the effect of the transfer.

The following are types of reorganisation:

(a) **Subsidiary moved up**

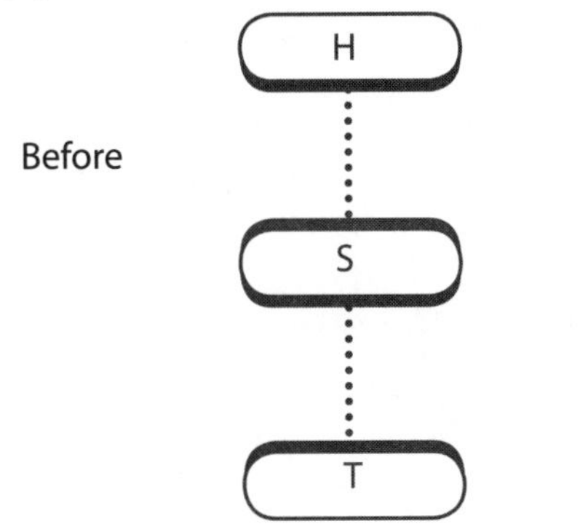

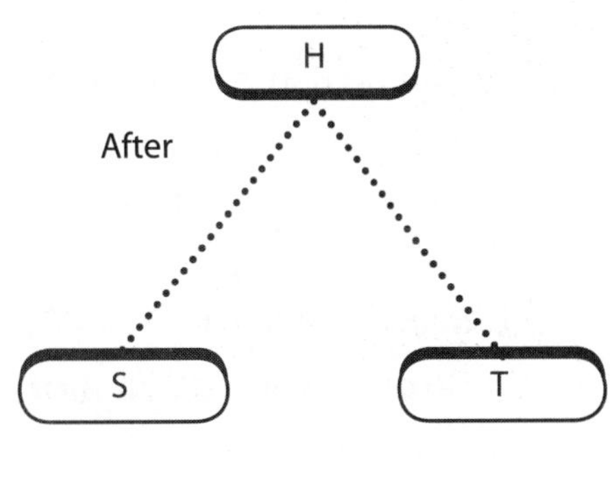

This can be achieved in one of two ways.

(a) S transfers its investment in T to H as a dividend in specie. If this is done then S must have sufficient distributable profits to pay the dividend.

(b) H purchases the investment in T from S for cash. In practice the purchase price often equals the fair value of the net assets acquired, so that no gain or loss arises on the transaction.

Usually, it will be the carrying value of T that is used as the basis for the transfer of the investment, but there are no legal rules confirming this.

A share-for-share exchange cannot be used as in many jurisdictions it is illegal for a subsidiary to hold shares in the parent company.

(b) **Subsidiary moved down**

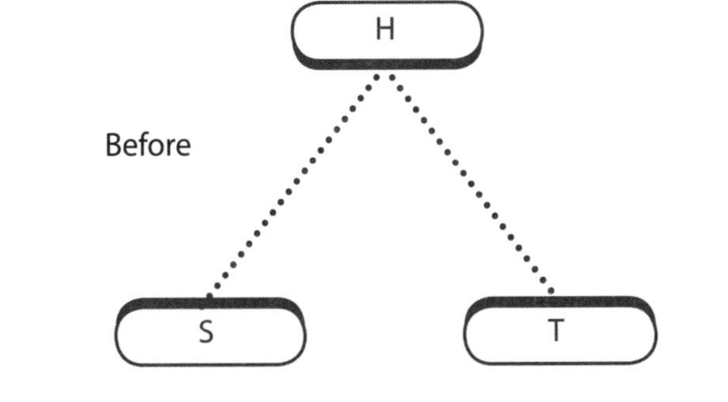

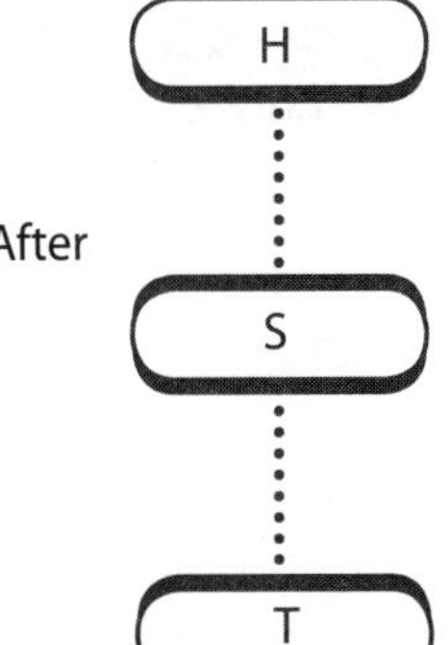

This reorganisation may be carried out where there are tax advantages in establishing a 'sub-group', or where two or more subsidiaries are linked geographically.

This can be carried out either by:

(a) a share-for-share exchange (S issues shares to H in return for the shares in T)

(b) a cash transaction (S pays cash to H).

(c) **Subsidiary moved along**

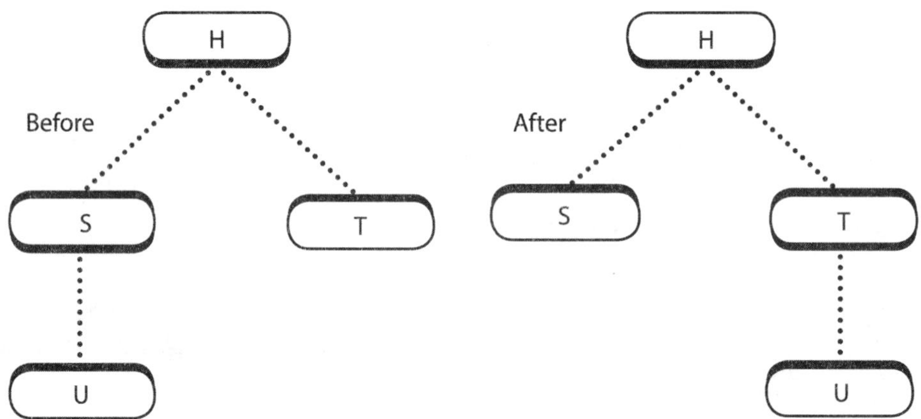

This is carried out by T paying cash (or other assets) to S. The consideration would not normally be in the form of shares because a typical reason for such a reconstruction would be to allow S to be managed as a separate part of the group or even disposed of completely. This could not be achieved effectively were S to have a shareholding in T.

If the purpose of the reorganisation is to allow S to leave the group, the purchase price paid by T should not be less than the fair value of the investment in U, otherwise S may be deemed to be receiving financial assistance for the purchase of its own shares, which is illegal in many jurisdictions.

Reverse acquisitions

Definition

A **reverse acquisition** occurs when an entity obtains ownership of the shares of another entity, which in turn issues sufficient shares so that the acquired entity has control of the combined entity.

Reverse acquisitions are a method of allowing unlisted companies to obtain a stock exchange quotation by taking over a smaller listed company.

For example, a private company arranges to be acquired by a listed company. This is effected by the public entity issuing shares to the private company so that the private company's shareholders end up controlling the listed entity. Legally, the public entity is the parent, but the substance of the transaction is that the private entity has acquired the listed entity.

Assessment of group reorganisations

Previous examination questions testing group reorganisations have provided a scenario with a group considering a number of reorganisation options. The questions have then asked for an evaluation and recommendation of a particular proposal.

In order to do this, you will need to consider the following:

- the impact of the proposal on the individual accounts of the group entities
- the impact of the proposal on the group accounts
- the purpose of the reorganisation
- whether there is any impairment of any of the group's assets
- whether any impairment loss should be recognised in relation to the investment in subsidiaries in the parent company accounts.

1 Chapter summary

Reasons for group reorganisations

- Transfer of shares in a subsidiary from one group entity to another
- Addition of a new parent entity to a group
- Transfer of shares in one or more subsidiaries of a group to a new entity that is not a group entity, but whose shareholders are the same as those of the group's parent
- Combination into a group of two or more companies that before the combination had the same shareholders

Types of group reorganisations

- New holding company
- Change of ownership of an entity within the group
- Reverse acquisition

Assessment of group reorganisations

- Look for the effect on the group and individual financial statements
- Look for any impairment of assets in the group
- Look for any impairment of investments in the parent company

chapter

18

Group accounting – foreign currency

Chapter learning objectives

Upon completion of this chapter you will be able to:

- account for the consolidation of foreign operations and their disposal.

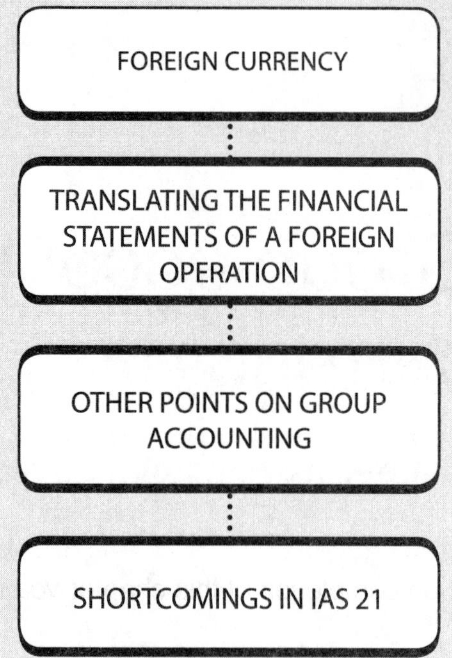

1 Key definitions

Foreign currency transactions in the individual financial statements of a company were covered in Chapter 5.

Below is a reminder of some key definitions:

The **functional currency** is the currency of the primary economic environment where the entity operates. In most cases this will be the local currency.

The **presentation currency** is the currency in which the entity presents its financial statements. This can be different from the functional currency.

2 Consolidation of a foreign operation

The functional currency used by a subsidiary to prepare its own individual accounting records and financial statements may differ from the presentation currency used for the group financial statements. Therefore, prior to adding together the assets, liabilities, incomes and expenses of the parent and subsidiary, the financial statements of an overseas subsidiary must be translated.

Translating the subsidiary's financial statements

The rules for translating an overseas subsidiary into the presentation currency of the group are as follows:

- **Incomes, expenses and other comprehensive income** are translated at the rate in place at the date of each transaction. The average rate for the year may be used as an approximation.
- **Assets and liabilities** are translated at the closing rate.

Illustration 1 – Dragon

This example runs through the chapter and is used to illustrate the basic steps involved in consolidating an overseas subsidiary.

Dragon bought 90% of the ordinary shares of Tattoo for DN180m on 31 December 20X0. The retained earnings of Tattoo at this date were DN65m. The fair value of the non-controlling interest at the acquisition date was DN14m.

The financial statements of Dragon and Tattoo for the year ended 31 December 20X1 are presented below:

Statements of profit or loss for year ended 31 December 20X1

	Dragon $m	Tattoo DNm
Revenue	1,200	600
Costs	(1,000)	(450)
Profit	200	150

Statements of financial position as at 31 December 20X1

	Dragon $m	Tattoo DNm
Property, plant and equipment	290	270
Investments	60	–
Current assets	150	130
	500	400

Share capital	10	5
Retained earnings	290	215
Liabilities	200	180
	–––	–––
	500	400
	–––	–––

There has been no intra-group trading. Goodwill arising on the acquisition of Tattoo is not impaired. The presentation currency of the consolidated financial statements is the dollar ($).

Exchange rates are as follows:

	DN to $
31 December 20X0	3.0
31 December 20X1	2.0
Average for year to 31 December 20X1	2.6

Required:

For inclusion in the consolidated statement of profit or loss and other comprehensive income for the year ended 31 December 20X1, calculate:

- **Revenue**
- **Costs**

For inclusion in the consolidated statement of financial position as at 31 December 20X1, calculate:

- **Property, plant and equipment**
- **Investments**
- **Current assets**
- **Share capital**
- **Liabilities**

Solution

	$m
Revenue ($1,200 + (DN600/2.6))	1,430.8
Costs ($1,000 + (DN450/2.6))	(1,173.1)
PPE ($290 + (DN270/2))	425.0
Investments (eliminated on consolidation)	–
Current assets ($150 + (DN130/2))	215.0
Share capital (Dragon only)	10.0
Liabilities ($200 + (DN180/2))	290.0

Remember, the incomes and expenses of an overseas subsidiary are translated at the average rate. The assets and liabilities are translated at the closing rate.

Translating goodwill

Goodwill should be calculated in the functional currency of the subsidiary.

According to IAS 21, goodwill should be treated like other assets of the subsidiary and therefore translated at the reporting date using the closing rate.

As with all consolidated statement of financial position questions, it may be helpful to produce a table showing the subsidiary's net assets (at fair value) at both the year end and acquisition date ('Working 2'). This should be completed in the functional currency of the subsidiary.

Illustration 2 – Goodwill

Required:

Using the information in illustration 1, calculate goodwill for inclusion in the consolidated statement of financial position for the Dragon group as at 31 December 20X1.

Solution

Goodwill calculation

	DNm
Consideration	180
NCI at acquisition	14
Net assets at acquisition (W)	(70)
	124
Goodwill impairments	–
	124

Goodwill is translated at the closing rate to give a value of $62m (DN124/2).

(W1) **Net assets of Tattoo**

	Acquisition date	Reporting date	Post-acquisition
	DNm	DNm	DNm
Share capital	5	5	
Retained earnings	65	215	
	70	220	150

Exchange Differences

The process of translating an overseas subsidiary gives rise to exchange gains and losses. These gains and losses arise for the following reasons:

- **Goodwill**: Goodwill is retranslated each year-end at the closing rate. It will therefore increase or decrease in value simply because of exchange rate movements.
- **Opening net assets**: At the end of the prior year, the net assets of the subsidiary were translated at the prior year closing rate. This year, those same net assets are translated at this year's closing rate. Therefore, opening net assets will have increased or decreased simply because of exchange rate movements.

- **Profit**: The incomes and expenses (and, therefore, the profit) of the overseas subsidiary are translated at the average rate. However, making a profit increases the subsidiary's assets which are translated at the closing rate. This disparity creates an exchange gain or loss.

Current year exchange gains or losses on the translation of an overseas subsidiary and its goodwill are recorded in other comprehensive income.

Goodwill translation

The proforma for calculating the current year gain or loss on the retranslation of goodwill is as follows:

	DN	Exchange Rate	$
Opening goodwill	X	Opening rate	X
Impairment loss in year	(X)	Average rate	(X)
Exchange gain/(loss)	–	**Bal fig.**	X/(X)
Closing goodwill	X	Closing rate	X

If the subsidiary was purchased part-way through the current year, then substitute 'opening goodwill' for 'goodwill at acquisition'. This would then be translated at the rate of exchange on the acquisition date.

It is important to pay attention to the method of goodwill calculation:

- If the full goodwill method has been used, gain and losses will need to be apportioned between the group and the non-controlling interest.
- If the proportionate goodwill method has been used, then all of the exchange gain or loss on goodwill is attributable to the group.

Illustration 3 – Translating goodwill

Required:

Using the information in illustration 1, calculate the exchange gain or loss arising on the translation of the goodwill that will be credited/charged through other comprehensive income in the year ended 31 December 20X1.

Who is this gain or loss attributable to?

Solution

	DNm	Exchange Rate	$m
Opening goodwill	124.0	3.0	41.3
Impairment loss in year	–	2.6	–
Exchange gain	–	**Bal fig.**	20.7
Closing goodwill	124.0	2.0	62.0

The total translation gain of $20.7m will be credited to other comprehensive income.

This is then allocated to the group and NCI based on their respective shareholdings:

Group: $20.7m × 90% = $18.6m
NCI: $20.7m × 10% = $2.1m

Opening net assets and profit

The exchange gains or losses arising on the translation of opening net assets and profit for the year are generally calculated together.

The proforma for calculating the current year exchange gain or loss on the translation of the opening net assets and profit is as follows:

	DN	Exchange Rate	$
Opening net assets	X	Opening rate	X
Profit/(loss) for the year	X/(X)	Average rate	X/(X)
Exchange gain/(loss)	–	**Bal fig.**	X/(X)
Closing net assets	X	Closing rate	X

If the subsidiary was purchased part-way through the current year, then substitute 'opening net assets' and 'opening rate' for 'acquisition net assets' and 'acquisition rate'.

The gain or loss on translation of the opening net assets and profit is apportioned between the group and non-controlling interest based on their respective shareholdings.

Illustration 4 – Opening net assets and profit

Required:

Using the information in illustration 1, calculate the exchange gain or loss arising on the translation of the opening net assets and profit of Tattoo that will be credited/charged through other comprehensive income in the year ended 31 December 20X1.

Who are these gains or losses attributable to?

Solution

	DN	Exchange Rate	$
Opening net assets*	70	3.0	23.3
Profit/(loss) for the year*	150	2.6	57.7
Exchange gain/(loss)	–	**Bal fig.**	29.0
Closing net assets*	220	2.0	110.0

*These figures are taken from the net assets working, which can be found in the solution to illustration 2.

The total translation gain of $29.0m will be credited to other comprehensive income.

This is then allocated to the group and NCI based on their respective shareholdings:

Group: 29.0 × 90% = $26.1m
NCI: 29.0 × 10% = $2.9m

Exchange differences on the statement of financial position

Exchange gains and losses arising from the translation of goodwill and the subsidiary's opening net assets and profit which are attributable to the group are normally held in a translation reserve, a separate component within equity.

Illustration 5 – Reserves

Required:

Using the information in illustration 1, calculate the non-controlling interest, retained earnings and the translation reserve for inclusion in the consolidated statement of financial position as at 31 December 20X1.

Solution

Non-controlling interest

	$m
NCI at acquisition (DN14/3 opening rate)	4.7
NCI % of Tattoo's post-acquisition profits (10% × (DN150/2.6 average rate))	5.7
NCI % of goodwill translation (illustration 3)	2.1
NCI % of net assets and profit translation (illustration 4)	2.9
	15.4

Retained earnings

	$m
100% of Dragon	290.0
90% of Tattoo's post-acquisition profits (90% × (DN150/2.6))	51.9
	341.9

Translation reserve

	$m
Group share of goodwill forex (illustration 3)	18.6
Group share of net assets and profit forex (illustration 4)	26.1
	44.7

Illustration 6 – Completing the financial statements

Required:

Using the information in illustration 1, complete the consolidated statement of financial position and the statement of profit or loss and other comprehensive income for the Tattoo group for the year ended 31 December 20X1.

Solution

Statement of profit or loss and other comprehensive income for year ended 31 December 20X1

	$m
Revenue (illustration 1)	1,430.8
Costs (illustration 1)	(1,173.1)
Profit for the year	257.7
Other comprehensive income – items that may be classified to profit or loss in future periods	
Exchange differences on translation of foreign subsidiary ($20.7 (illustration 3) + $29.0 (illustration 4))	49.7
Total comprehensive income for the year	307.4
Profit attributable to:	
Owners of Dragon (bal. fig.)	251.9
Non-controlling interest (10% × (DN150/2.6 avg. rate))	5.8
Profit for the year	257.7
Other comprehensive income attributable to:	
Owners of Dragon (bal. fig.)	296.6
Non-controlling interest ($5.8 (profit) + $2.1 (illustration 3) + $2.9 (illustration 4))	10.8
Total comprehensive income for the year	307.4

Statement of financial position as at 31 December 20X1

	$m
Property, plant and equipment (illustration 1)	425.0
Goodwill (illustration 2)	62.0
Current assets (illustration 1)	215.0
	702.0
Share capital (illustration 1)	10.0
Retained earnings (illustration 5)	341.9
Translation reserve (illustration 5)	44.7
	396.6
Non-controlling interest (illustration 5)	15.4
	412.0
Liabilities (illustration 1)	290.0
	702.0

Test your understanding 1 – Parent & Overseas

Parent is an entity that owns 80% of the equity shares of Overseas, a foreign entity that has the Shilling as its functional currency. The subsidiary was acquired at the start of the current accounting period on 1 January 20X7 when its retained earnings were 6,000 Shillings.

At that date the fair value of the net assets of the subsidiary was 20,000 Shillings. This included a fair value adjustment in respect of land of 4,000 Shillings that the subsidiary has not incorporated into its accounting records and still owns.

Goodwill, which is unimpaired at the reporting date, is to be accounted for using the full goodwill method. At the date of acquisition, the non-controlling interest in Overseas had a fair value of 5,000 Shillings.

Statements of financial position:

	Parent	Overseas
	$	Shillings
Investment (20,999 shillings)	3,818	
Assets	9,500	40,000
	13,318	40,000
Equity and liabilities		
Equity capital	5,000	10,000
Retained earnings	6,000	8,200
Liabilities	2,318	21,800
	13,318	40,000

Statement of profit or loss for the year:

	Parent	Overseas
	$	Shillings
Revenue	8,000	5,200
Costs	(2,500)	(2,600)
Profit before tax	5,500	2,600
Tax	(2,000)	(400)
Profit for the year	3,500	2,200

Neither entity recognised any other comprehensive income in their individual financial statements during the reporting period.

Relevant exchange rates (Shillings to $1) are:

Date	**Shillings: $1**
1 January 20X7	5.5
31 December 20X7	5.0
Average for year to 31 December 20X7	5.2

Required:

Prepare the consolidated statement of financial position at 31 December 20X7, together with a consolidated statement of profit or loss and other comprehensive income for the year ended 31 December 20X7

Test your understanding 2 – Saint and Albans

On the 1 July 20X1 Saint acquired 60% of Albans, whose functional currency is Ds. The presentation currency of the Saint group is the dollar ($). The financial statements of both entities are as follows.

Statements of financial position as at 30 June 20X2

	Saint	**Albans**
Assets	$	D
Investment in Albans	5,000	–
Loan to Albans	1,400	–
Property, plant and equipment	10,000	15,400
Inventories	5,000	4,000
Receivables	4,000	500
Cash and cash equivalents	1,600	560
	27,000	20,460
Equity and liabilities	$	D
Equity capital ($1 / D1)	10,000	1,000
Share premium	3,000	500
Retained earnings	4,000	12,500
Non-current liabilities	5,000	5,460
Current liabilities	5,000	1,000
	27,000	20,460

Statements of profit or loss for the year ended 30 June 20X2

	Saint	**Albans**
	$	D
Revenue	50,000	60,000
Cost of sales	(20,000)	(30,000)
Gross profit	30,000	30,000
Distribution and Administration expenses	(20,000)	(12,000)
Profit before tax	10,000	18,000
Tax	(8,000)	(6,000)
Profit for the year	2,000	12,000

Note: There were no items of other comprehensive income within the individual financial statements of either entity.

The following information is applicable.

(i) Saint purchased the shares in Albans for D10,000 on the first day of the accounting period. At the date of acquisition the retained earnings of Albans were D500 and there was an upward fair value adjustment of D1,000. The fair value adjustment is attributable to plant with a remaining five-year life as at the date of acquisition. This plant remains held by Albans and has not been revalued.

(ii) Just before the year-end Saint acquired some goods from a third party at a cost of $800, which it sold to Albans for cash at a mark up of 50%. At the reporting date all these goods remain in the inventories of Albans.

(iii) On 1 June X2 Saint lent Albans $1,400. The liability is recorded at the historic rate within the non-current liabilities of Albans.

(iv) No dividends have been paid.

(v) Goodwill is to be accounted using the full goodwill method. An impairment review was performed and goodwill had reduced in value by 10% at 30 June 20X2. Impairment is to be charged to cost of sales. The fair value of the non-controlling interest at the date of acquisition was D5,000.

(vi) On 1 July 20X1, Saint received a government grant for $4,000. This grant was provided as a contribution towards the costs of training employees over the next two years. Saint has reduced its administrative expenses by the full $4,000.

(vii) On 30 June 20X2, Saint sold $2,000 of receivables to a factor for $1,500. Saint must reimburse the factor with any amounts not collected by 31 December 20X2. Saint has credited the proceeds received against receivables.

(viii) Exchange rates are as follows:

	D: $1
1 July 20X1	2.00
Average rate	3.00
1 June 20X2	3.90
30 June 20X2	4.00

Required:

Prepare the group statement of financial position as at 30 June 20X2 and the group statement of profit or loss and other comprehensive income for the year ended 30 June 20X2.

3 Other points on group accounting

Disposal of a foreign entity

On the disposal of a foreign subsidiary, the cumulative exchange differences recognised as other comprehensive income and accumulated in a separate component of equity become realised.

IAS 21 requires that these exchanges differences are recycled (i.e. reclassified) on the disposal of the subsidiary as part of the profit/loss on disposal.

Test your understanding 3 – LUMS Group

The LUMS group has sold its entire 100% holding in an overseas subsidiary for proceeds of $50,000. The net assets at the date of disposal were $20,000 and the carrying value of goodwill at that date was $10,000. The cumulative balance on the group foreign currency reserve is a gain of $5,000.

Required:

Calculate the gain arising on the disposal of the foreign subsidiary in the consolidated statement of profit or loss.

Equity accounting

The principles used to translate an overseas subsidiary's financial statements also apply to the financial statements of an overseas associate.

Once the results are translated, the carrying amount of the associate (cost (at the closing rate) plus the share of post-acquisition retained earnings) can be calculated together with the group's share of the profits for the period and included in the group financial statements.

Shortcomings in IAS 21

Retranslating the opening reserves at the closing rate gives a difference that goes direct to reserves under the closing rate method. The reasoning behind this is that these exchange differences do not result from the operations of the group. To include them in profit or loss would be to distort the results of the group's trading operations. However, some commentators consider that all such gains and losses are part of a group's profit and should be recorded in profit or loss.

4 Chapter summary

FOREIGN CURRENCY

IAS 21 THE EFFECTS OF CHANGES IN FOREIGN EXCHANGE RATES

Translating the financial statements of a foreign operation

Assets and liabilities translate at closing rate

Incomes and expenses translate at average rate

Calculation of exchange difference

Consolidation of a foreign operation

- Calculation of goodwill
- Calculation of non-controlling interests
- Calculation of group reserves

Other points on group accounting

- Disposal of foreign entity
- Equity accounting

Shortcomings in IAS 21

Test your understanding answers

Test your understanding 1 – Parent & Overseas

Group statement of financial position

Note: The assets and liabilities of Overseas have been translated at the closing rate.

	$
Goodwill (W3)	1,200
Assets ($9,500 + ((Sh40,000 + Sh4,000 FVA)/5.0))	18,300
	19,500
Equity and liabilities	$
Equity capital	5,000
Retained earnings (W5)	6,338
Translation reserve (W6)	392
	11,730
Non-controlling interest (W4)	1,092
Total equity	12,822
Liabilities ($2,318 + (Sh21,800/5.0))	6,678
	19,500

Group statement of profit or loss and other comprehensive income for the year

Note: The income and expenses for Overseas have been translated at the average rate.

	$
Revenue ($8,000 + (Sh5,200/5.2))	9,000
Costs ($2,500 + (Sh2,600/5.2))	(3,000)
Profit before tax	6,000
Tax ($2,000 + (Sh400/5.2))	(2,077)
Profit for the year	3,923

Other comprehensive income	
Items that may be reclassified to profit or loss in future periods	
Exchange differences on translation of foreign subsidiary ($109 (W3) + $381 (W6))	490
Total comprehensive income for the year	4,413
Profit for the year attributable to:	
Owners of Parent (bal. fig.)	3,838
Non-controlling interest (20% × (Sh2,200/5.2))	85
	3,923
Total comprehensive income attributable to:	
Owners of Parent (bal. fig.)	4,230
Non-controlling interest $85 (profit) + $22(W3) + $76(W7)	183
	4,413

Workings

(W1) **Group structure**

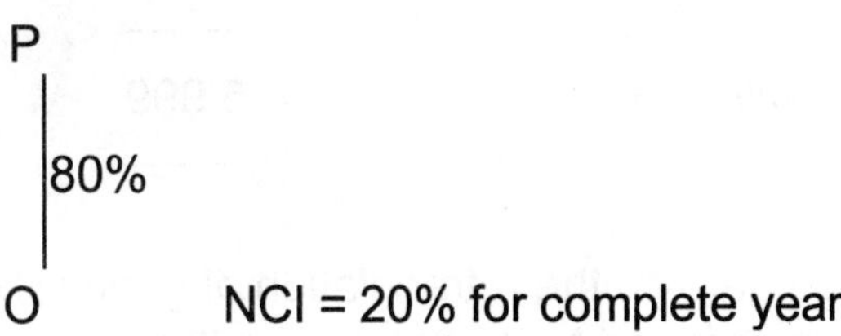

(W2) **Net assets of subsidiary in functional currency**

	Acq'n date Shillings	Rep date Shillings	Shillings
Share capital	10,000	10,000	
Retained earnings	6,000	8,200	
Fair value adjustment – land	4,000	4,000	
	20,000	22,200	2,200

(W3) **Goodwill calculation and forex**

Calculation of goodwill

Full goodwill:	Shillings
Cost of investment $3,818 @ 5.5	20,999
FV of NCI at acquisition	5,000
	25,999
FV of NA at acquisition (W2)	(20,000)
Full goodwill at acquisition	5,999
Translate at closing rate @ 5.0	$1,200

Goodwill forex

	Shillings	Exchange rate	$
Goodwill at acquisition	5,999	5.5	1,091
Impairment	–		–
Exchange gain		**bal. fig**	**109**
Closing goodwill	5,999	5.0	1,200

The exchange gain on the retranslation of goodwill is allocated between the group and NCI based upon their respective shareholdings:

Group: 80% × $109 = $87 (W7)
NCI: 20% × $109 = $22 (W4)

(W4) **Non-controlling interest**

	$
NCI fair value at acquisition (Sh5,000/5.5 op. rate)	909
NCI share of post-acquisition profit (20% × (Sh2,200 (W2)/5.2 avg rate))	85
NCI share of exchange gain on retranslation of goodwill (W3)	22
NCI share of exchange gain on retranslation of net assets (W7)	76
	1,092

(W5) **Retained earnings**

	$
Parent	6,000
Group share of post-acquisition profit (80% × (2,200(W2)/5.2 avg. rate))	338
	6,338

(W6) **Translation reserve**

	$
Group share of goodwill forex (W3)	87
Group share of net assets and profit forex (W7)	305
	392

(W7) **Forex on net assets and profit**

	Shillings	Rate	$
Net assets at acquisition (W2)	20,000	5.5	3,636
Retained profit for the year (W2)	2,200	5.2	423
Exchange gain	**bal fig**		**381**
Closing net assets	22,200	5.0	4,440

Note that the total exchange gain on retranslation of the opening net assets and profit must be allocated between the group and NCI based upon their respective shareholdings as follows:

Group: 80% × $381 = $305 (W6)
NCI: 20% × $381 = $76 (W4)

Test your understanding 2 – Saint and Albans

Saint Group

Note: The assets and liabilities of Albans have been translated at the closing rate.

Group statement of financial position at 30 June 20X2

	$
Goodwill (W3)	2,700
Loan to Albans ($1,400 – $1,400 interco)	Nil
Property, plant and equipment ($10,000 + D14,500/4 + D1,000 (W2)/4 – D200 (W2)/4)	14,050
Inventories ($5,000 + D4,000/4 – $400 (W8))	5,600
Receivables ($4,000 + D500/4 + $1,500 (W10))	5,625
Cash and cash equivalents ($1,600 + D560/4)	1,740
	29,715

	$
Equity capital	10,000
Share premium	3,000
Retained earnings (W5)	3,692
Translation reserve (W7)	(2,773)
	13,919
Non-controlling interest (W4)	2,046
Total equity	15,965
Non-current liabilities ($5,000 + D5,460/4 + D140/4 – $1,400 interco)	5,000
Current liabilities ($5,000 + D1,000/4 + $2,000 (W9) + $1,500 (W10))	8,750
	29,715

Note: The income and expenses of Albans have been translated at the average rate for the year.

Group statement of profit or loss and other comprehensive income for the year ended 30 June 20X2

	$
Revenue ($50,000 + D60,000/3 – $1,200 interco)	68,800
Cost of sales ($20,000 + D30,000/3 + D200/3 (W2) + $400 (W3) + $400 (W8) – $1,200 interco)	(29,667)
Gross profit	39,133
Admin expenses ($20,000 + D12,000/3 + D140/3 (W2) + $2,000 (W9))	(26,047)
Profit before tax	13,086
Tax ($8,000 + D6,000/3)	(10,000)
Profit for the year:	3,086
Other comprehensive income – items that may be reclassified to profit or loss in future periods:	
Exchange loss on translation of foreign subsidiary (($2,900) (W3) + ($1,722) (W6))	(4,622)
Total comprehensive income for the year	(1,536)
Profit for the year:	
Attributable to Group (bal fig.)	1,691
Attributable to NCI ((40% × (D11,660 (W2)/3 avg. rate)) – $160 GW impairment (W3))	1,395
	3,086
Total comprehensive income for the year:	$
Attributable to Group (bal fig.)	(1,082)
Attributable to NCI ($1,395 profit – $1,160 (W3) – $689 (W6))	(454)
	(1,536)

Workings

(W1) **Group structure**

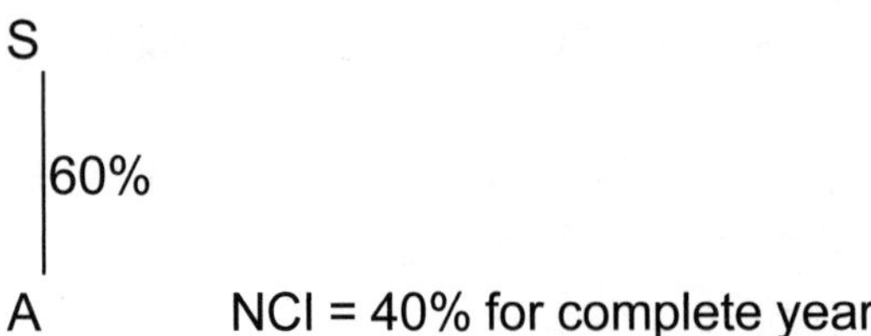

(W2) **Net assets of subsidiary in functional currency**

	At acquisition	Rep date	Post-acq'n
	D	D	D
Equity capital	1,000	1,000	
Share premium	500	500	
Retained earnings	500	12,500	
Fair value adjustment – plant	1,000	1,000	
FVA – dep'n on plant (1/5)		(200)	
Exchange loss on loan*		(140)	
Post acquisition movement	3,000	14,660	11,660

***Exchange loss on loan received by Albans**

The loan was initially recorded at D5,460 ($1,400 × 3.9)

The loan needs to be retranslated using the closing rate to D5,600 ($1,400 × 4.0)

There is therefore an exchange loss of D140 (D5,600 – D5,460).

Dr Profit or loss/retained earnings (W2) D140
Cr Non-current liabilities D140

(W3) **Goodwill**

Goodwill calculation

	D
Cost to parent ($5,000 × 2.0)	10,000
FV of NCI at acquisition	5,000
	15,000
FV of NA at acquisition (W2)	(3,000)
Full goodwill at acquisition	12,000
Impairment – 10%	(1,200)
Unimpaired goodwill at reporting date	10,800

Exchange gain (loss) on retranslation of goodwill

	D	Rate	$
Goodwill at acquisition	12,000	2.0	6,000
Impairment	(1,200)	3.0	(400)
Exchange gain (loss)		**Bal fig**	**(2,900)**
Goodwill at reporting date	10,800	4.0	2,700

The impairment loss on the goodwill is allocated between the group and NCI based on their respective shareholdings:

Group: 60% × $400 = $240 (W5)
NCI: 40% × $400 = $160 (W4)

The exchange loss on retranslation of goodwill is allocated between the group and NCI based on their respective shareholdings:

Group: 60% × $2900 = $1,740 (W7)
NCI: 40% × $2900 = $1,160 (W4)

(W4) **Non-controlling interest**

	$
FV at acquisition per question (D5,000/2)	2,500
NCI % of post-acquisition profit 40% × (D11,660/3 avg rate) (W2)	1,555
NCI % of goodwill impairment (W3)	(160)
NCI % of retranslation loss on goodwill (W3)	(1,160)
NCI % of retranslation loss on net assets (W6)	(689)
	2,046

(W5) **Group retained earnings**

	$
Parent retained earnings	4,000
Government grant (W9)	(2,000)
Group share of goodwill impairment (W3)	(240)
Group share of post-acq'n profit 60% × (D11,660/ 3 avg. rate) (W2)	2,332
PURP (W8)	(400)
	3,692

(W6) **Exchange differences on retranslation of net assets**

	D	Rate	$
Acquisition net assets	3,000	2.0	1,500
Profit for year	11,660	3.0	3,887
Exchange gain/(loss)		**bal fig**	**(1,722)**
Closing net assets	14,660	4.0	(3,665)

The exchange loss is allocated between the group and NCI based upon respective shareholdings:

Group: 60% × $1,722 = $1,033 (W7)
NCI: 40% × $1,722 = $689 (W4)

(W7) **Translation reserve**

	$
Group share of forex on net assets and profit (W6)	(1,033)
Group share of forex on goodwill (W3)	(1,740)
	(2,773)

(W8) **PURP**

The profit on the intra-group sale is $400 ((50/100) × $800).

All of these items remain in group inventory. Therefore the adjustment required is:

Dr Cost of sales/retained earnings $400
Cr Inventories $400

(W9) **Government grant**

This is a revenue grant. It should be recognised in profit or loss on a systematic basis. The grant is intended to cover training costs over a two year period and so it should be recognised in profit or loss over two years.

Saint should increase its expenses by $2,000 (1/2 × $4,000) and record the balance as deferred income on the SFP.

Dr Administrative expenses/retained earnings $2,000
Cr Current liabilities $2,000

(W10) **Receivables factoring**

The risks and rewards of ownership have not transferred from Saint to the factor so the receivable should not be derecognised. The proceeds received should instead be shown as a liability.

The correcting entry is:

Dr Receivables $1,500
Cr Liabilities $1,500

Test your understanding 3 – LUMS Group

		$
Proceeds		50,000
Net assets recorded prior to disposal:		
Net assets	20,000	
Goodwill	10,000	
		(30,000)
Realisation of the group exchange difference, reclassified to profit as part of the gain		5,000
		25,000

chapter

19

Group statement of cash flows

Chapter learning objectives

Upon completion of this chapter you will be able to:

- prepare and discuss group statements of cash flows.

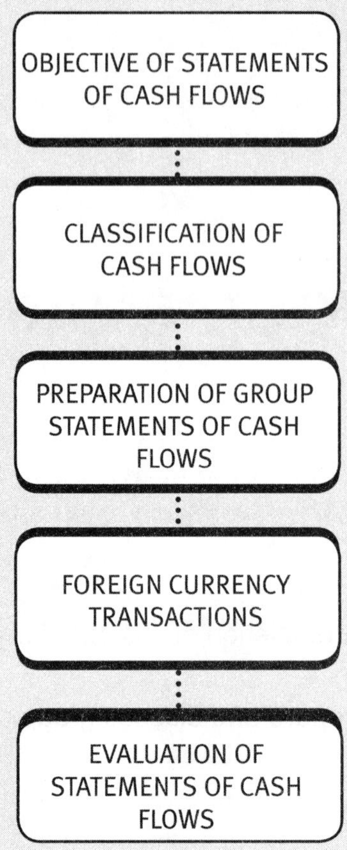

1 Objective of statements of cash flows

- IAS 7 Statement of Cash Flows provides guidance on the preparation of a statement of cash flow.
- The objective of a statement of cash flows is to provide information on an entity's changes in cash and cash equivalents during the period.
- The statement of financial position and statement of profit or loss are prepared on an accruals basis and do not show how the business has generated and used cash in the reporting period.
- The statement of profit or loss may show profits even though the company is suffering severe cash flow problems.
- Statements of cash flows enable users of the financial statements to assess the liquidity, solvency and financial adaptability of a business.

Definitions:

- **Cash** consists of cash in hand and deposits repayable upon demand, less overdrafts. This includes cash held in a foreign currency.
- **Cash equivalents** are short-term, highly liquid investments that are readily convertible to known amounts of cash and are subject to an insignificant risk of changes in value.
- **Cash flows** are inflows and outflows of cash and cash equivalents.

2 Classification of cash flows

IAS 7 does not prescribe a specific format for the statement of cash flows, although it requires that cash flows are classified under three headings:

- **cash flows from operating activities**, defined as the entity's principal revenue earning activities and other activities that do not fall under the next two headings
- **cash flows from investing activities**, defined as the acquisition and disposal of long-term assets and other investments (excluding cash equivalents)
- **cash flows from financing activities**, defined as activities that change the size and composition of the entity's equity and borrowings.

Proforma statement of cash flow per IAS 7

	$	$
Cash flows from operating activities		
Profit before tax	X	
Add: finance costs	X	
Less: investment income	(X)	
Less: income from associate	(X)	
Adjust for non-cash items dealt with in arriving at operating profit:		
Add: depreciation	X	
Less: gain on disposal of subsidiary	(X)	
Add: loss on disposal of subsidiary	X	
Add: loss on impairment charged to PorL	X	
Add: loss on disposal of non-current assets	X	
Add: increase in provisions	X	
	X/(X)	
Changes in working capital:		
Increase in inventory	(X)	
Increase in receivables	(X)	
Decrease in payables	(X)	
Cash generated/used from operations	X/(X)	
Interest paid	(X)	
Taxation paid	(X)	
Net cash Inflow/(outflow) from operating activities		X/(X)

Cash flows from investing activities		
Payments to purchase NCA	(X)	
Receipts from NCA disposals	X	
Net cash paid to acquire subsidiary	(X)	
Net cash proceeds from subsidiary disposal	X	
Dividend received from associate	X	
Interest received	X	
Net cash inflow/(outflow) from investing activities		X/(X)
Cash flows from financing activities		
Proceeds from share issue	X	
Proceeds from loan or debenture issue	X	
Cash repayment of loans or debentures	(X)	
Finance lease repayments	(X)	
Equity dividend paid by parent	(X)	
Dividend paid to NCI	(X)	
Net cash inflow/(outflow) from financing activities		X/(X)
Increase/(decrease) in cash and equivalents		X/(X)
Cash and equivalents brought forward		X/(X)
Cash and equivalents carried forward		X/(X)

Classification of cash flows

Cash flows from operating activities

There are two methods of calculating cash generated from operations.

- The **direct method** shows operating cash receipts and payments. This includes cash receipts from customers, cash payments to suppliers and cash payments to and on behalf of employees. The Examiner has indicated that the direct method is unlikely to be examined in detail, although you may be required to explain key similarities and differences between the two methods.
- The **indirect method** starts with profit before tax and adjusts it for non-cash charges and credits, to reconcile it to the net cash flow from operating activities.

IAS 7 permits either method, although encourages the use of the direct method. The methods differ only in respect of derivation of the item 'net cash inflow from operating activities'. Subsequent inflows and outflows for investing and financing activities are the same. A comparison between the direct and indirect method to arrive at cash generated from operations is shown below.

Direct method:	$m	**Indirect method:**	$m
Cash receipts from customers	15,424	Profit before tax	6,022
Cash payments to suppliers	(5,824)	Depreciation charges	899
Cash payments to and on behalf of employees	(2,200)	Increase in inventories	(194)
Other cash payments	(511)	Increase in receivables	(72)
		Increase in payables	234
Cash generated from operations	6,889	Cash generated from operations	6,889

The principal advantage of the direct method is that it discloses operating cash receipts and payments. Knowledge of the specific sources of cash receipts and the purposes for which cash payments have been made in past periods may be useful in assessing and predicting future cash flows.

Under the **indirect method,** typically begin with profit before tax and then make adjustments for a number of items, the most frequently occurring of which are:

- depreciation or amortisation charges in the year
- impairment charged to profit or loss in the year
- profit or loss on disposal of non current assets
- change in inventories
- change in receivables
- change in payables.

Cash flows from investing activities

Cash flows to appear under this heading include:

- cash paid for property, plant and equipment and other non-current assets
- cash received on the sale of property, plant and equipment and other non-current assets

- cash paid for investments in or loans to other entities (excluding movements on loans from financial institutions, which are shown under financing)
- cash received for the sale of investments or the repayment of loans to other entities (again excluding loans from financial institutions).

Cash flows from financing activities

Financing cash flows mainly comprise receipts or repayments of principal from or to external providers of finance.

Financing cash inflows include:

- receipts from issuing shares or other equity instruments
- receipts from issuing debentures, loans, notes and bonds and from other long-term and short-term borrowings (other than overdrafts, which are normally included in cash and cash equivalents).

Financing cash outflows include:

- repayments of amounts borrowed (other than overdrafts)
- the capital element of finance lease rental payments
- payments to reacquire or redeem the entity's shares.

Interest and dividends

There are different opinions as to how interest and dividends should be classified in the statement of cash flows. Some regard them as part of operating activities, because they are as much part of the day to day activities as receipts from customers, payments to suppliers and payments to staff. Others regard them as part of financing activities, the heading under which the instruments giving rise to the payments and receipts are classified. Still others believe they are part of investing activities, because this is what the long-term finance raised in this way is used for.

IAS 7 allows interest and dividends, whether received or paid, to be classified under any of the three headings, provided the classification is consistent from period to period.

The practice adopted in this text is to classify:

- interest received as a cash flow from investing activities
- interest paid as a cash flow from operating activities
- dividends received as a cash flow from investing activities
- dividends paid as a cash flow from financing activities.

3 Cash and cash equivalents

The statement of cash flows reconciles cash and cash equivalents at the start of the reporting period to the end of the reporting period.

- Cash equivalents are short-term, highly liquid investments that are readily convertible to known amounts of cash and are subject to an insignificant risk of changes in value.
- 'Cash equivalents' are held in order to meet short-term cash commitments. They are not held for investment purposes.
- IAS 7 does not define 'readily convertible' but notes that an investment would qualify as a cash equivalent if it had a short maturity of 'three months or less from the date of acquisition'.
- Equity investments are generally excluded from being included in cash equivalents because there is a significant risk of a change in value. IAS 7 makes an exception for preference shares with a short period to maturity and a specified redemption date.

Test your understanding 1 – Cash and cash equivalents

The accountant for Minted, a company, is preparing a statement of cash flows. She would like advice about whether the following items can be included within 'cash and cash equivalents'.

- An overdraft of $100,000.
- A balance of $500,000 held in a high-interest account. Minted must give 28 days notice in order to access this money, which is held with the intention of meeting working capital shortages.
- An investment in the ordinary shares of Moolah. The shares are listed and therefore could be sold immediately. The shares have a fair value of $1m.

Required:

Advise the accountant of Minted whether the above items qualify as 'cash and cash equivalents'.

Unusual items and non-cash transactions

Unusual cash flows

Where cash flows are unusual because of their size or incidence, sufficient disclosure should be given to explain their cause and nature.

For a cash flow to be unusual on the grounds of its size alone, it must be unusual in relation to cash flows of a similar nature.

Discontinued activities

Cash flows relating to discontinued activities are required by IFRS 5 to be shown separately, either on the face of the statement of cash flows or in a disclosure note.

Major non-cash transactions

Material transactions not resulting in movements of cash should be disclosed in the notes to the statement of cash flows if disclosure is necessary for an understanding of the underlying transactions.

Consideration for transactions may be in a form other than cash. The purpose of a statement of cash flows is to report cash flows, and non-cash transactions should therefore not be reported in a statement of cash flows. However, to obtain a full picture of the alterations in financial position caused by the transactions for the period, separate disclosure of material non-cash transactions is also necessary.

4 Preparation of a consolidated statement of cash flows

A consolidated statement of cash flows shows the cash flows between a group and third parties. It is prepared using the consolidated statement of financial position and the consolidated statement of profit or loss. This means that intra-group transactions have already been eliminated.

When producing a consolidated statement of cash flows, there are three extra elements that need to be considered:

- cash paid to non-controlling interests
- associates
- acquisitions and disposals of subsidiaries.

Cash paid to non-controlling interests

- When a subsidiary that is not wholly owned pays a dividend, some of that dividend is paid outside of the group to the non-controlling interest.
- Dividends paid to non-controlling interests should be disclosed separately in the statement of cash flows.
- To calculate the dividend paid, reconcile the non-controlling interest in the statement of financial position from the opening to the closing balance. You can use a T-account or a schedule to do this.

Illustration 1 – Cash paid to NCI

The following information has been extracted from the consolidated financial statements of WG, which has a year end of the 31 December:

	20X7	**20X6**
	$000	$000
Statement of financial position:		
Equity:		
Non-controlling interest	780	690
Statement of profit or loss:		
Profit for the period attributable to the non-controlling interest	120	230

Required:

What is the dividend paid to non-controlling interest in the year ended 31 December 20X7?

Solution

	$000
NCI b/fwd	690
Add: NCI re sub acquired in year	XX
Add: NCI share of profit for the year	120
Less: NCI derecognised due to subsidiary disposal	(XX)
Cash dividend paid in year (bal. fig)	(30)
NCI c/fwd	780

Watch out if a subsidiary has been acquired or disposed of during the year. This will affect the NCI and will need to be factored into the schedule as indicated.

Alternatively, a T account can be used:

Non-controlling interests

	$000		$000
NCI derecognised re sub disposal	XX	NCI Balance b/fwd	690
Dividends paid (bal fig)	30	NCI recognised re acq'n of sub	XX
NCI Balance c/fwd	780	Share of profits in year	120
	810		810

Associates

An associate is a company over which an investor has significant influence. Associates are not part of the group and therefore cash flows between the group and the associate must be reported in the statement of cash flows.

Cash flows relating to associates that need to be separately reported within the statement of cash flows are as follows:

- dividends received from an associate
- loans made to associates
- cash payments to acquire associates
- cash receipts from the sale of associates.

These cash flows should be presented as cash flows from investing activities.

Remember, associates are accounted for using the equity method. In the consolidated statement of profit or loss, the group records its share of the associate's profit for the year. This is a non-cash income and so must be deducted in the indirect reconciliation between profit before tax and cash generated from operations.

Illustration 2 – Associates

The following information has been extracted from the consolidated financial statements of H:

Extract from consolidated statement of profit or loss for year ended 31 December 20X1

	$000
Profit from operations	734
Share of profit of associate	48
Profit before tax	782
Tax	(304)
Profit for the year	478

Extracts from consolidated statement of financial position as at 31 December 20X1 (with comparatives)

	20X1	**20X0**
	$000	$000
Non-current assets		
CV of interest in associate	466	456
Loan to associate	380	300
Current assets		
Receivables	260	190
Included within group receivables is the following amount:		
Current account with associate	40	70

Required:

Calculate the relevant figures to be included in the group statement of cash flows for the year ended 31 December 20X1.

Solution

Extracts from statement of cash flows

	$000
Cash flows from operating activities	
Profit before tax	782
Share of profit of associate	(48)
Investing activities	
Dividend received from associate (W1)	38
Loan to associate (380 – 300)	(80)

(W1) **Dividend received from associate**

When dealing with the dividend from the associate, the process is the same as we have already seen with the non-controlling interest.

Set up a schedule or T account and include all the balances that relate to the associate. The balancing figure will be the cash dividend received from the associate.

	$000
Balance b/fwd	456
Share of profit of associate	48
Cash dividend received **(bal fig)**	(38)
Balance c/fwd	466

Note that the current account with the associate remains within receivables and the loan made to the associate is dealt with separately.

Instead of a schedule, a T-account could be used:

Associate

	$000		$000
Balance b/fwd	456	Dividend received (bal fig)	38
Share of profit of associate	48	Balance c/fwd	466
	504		504

Acquisitions and disposals of subsidiaries

Acquisitions

- In the statement of cash flows we must record the actual cash flow for the purchase of the subsidiary net of any cash held by the subsidiary that is now controlled by the group
- The assets and liabilities of the acquired subsidiary must be included in any workings to calculate the cash movement for an item during the year.

Illustration – Acquisition of a subsidiary

Sparkling buys 70% of the equity shares of Still for $500,000 in cash. At the acquisition date, Still had cash and cash equivalents of $25,000.

Although Sparkling paid $500,000 for the shares, it also gained control of Still's cash of $25,000. In the consolidated statement of cash flows, this would be presented as follows:

Cash flows from investing activities	$000
Acquisition of subsidiary, net of cash acquired ($500,000 – $25,000)	(475)

Disposals

- The statement of cash flows will show the cash received from the sale of the subsidiary, net of any cash held by the subsidiary that the group has lost control over
- The assets and liabilities of the disposed subsidiary must be included in any workings to calculate the cash movement for an item during the year.

Illustration – Disposal of a subsidiary

Sparkling owned 80% of the equity shares of Fizzy. During the period, these shares were sold for $800,000 in cash. At the disposal date, Fizzy had cash and cash equivalents of $70,000.

Although Sparkling received $800,000 for the shares, it lost control of Fizzy's cash of $70,000. In the consolidated statement of cash flows, this would be presented as follows:

Cash flows from investing activities	$000
Disposal of subsidiary, net of cash disposed of ($800,000 – $70,000)	730

Disclosure

- A note to the statement of cash flows should show a summary of the effects of acquisitions and disposals of subsidiaries, indicating how much of the consideration comprised cash and cash equivalents, and the assets and liabilities acquired or disposed of.

Illustration 3 – Acquisitions and disposals

Extracts from a group statement of financial position are presented below:

	20X8	**20X7**
	$000	$000
Inventories	74,666	53,019
Trade receivables	58,246	62,043
Trade payables	93,678	86,247

During 20X8, Subsidiary A was acquired and all shares in Subsidiary B were disposed of.

Details of the working capital balances of these two subsidiaries are provided below:

	Working capital of Subsidiary A at acquisition	Working capital of Subsidiary B at disposal
	$000	$000
Inventories	4,500	6,800
Trade receivables	7,900	6,700
Trade payables	8,250	5,740

Required:

Calculate the movement in inventories, trade receivables and trade payables for inclusion in the group statement of cash flows.

Solution

The net assets of Subsidiary A are being consolidated at the end of the year, but they were not consolidated at the start of the year. Conversely, the net assets of Subsidiary B are not consolidated at the end of the year, but they were consolidated at the start of the year. The working capital balances brought forward and carried forward are therefore not directly comparable.

Comparability can be achieved by calculating the movement between the closing and opening figures and then:

- Deducing the subsidiary's balances at the acquisition date for a subsidiary acquired during the year
- Adding the subsidiary's balances at the disposal date for a subsidiary disposed of during the year.

	Inventories	Trade receivables	Trade payables
	$000	$000	$000
Bal c/fwd	74,666	58,246	93,678
Bal b/fwd	(53,019)	(62,043)	(86,247)
	21,647	(3,797)	7,431
Less:sub acquired in year	(4,500)	(7,900)	(8,250)
Add:sub disposed in year	6,800	6,700	5,740
Movement in the year	inc 23,947	dec (4,997)	inc 4,921
Impact on cash flow	Outflow	Inflow	Inflow

Test your understanding 2 – Extracts

Calculate the required cash flows in each of the following scenarios:

(1)	20X0	20X1
	$	$
Property, plant and equipment (PPE)	100	250

During the year depreciation charged was $20, a revaluation surplus of $60 was recorded, PPE with a carrying value of $15 was disposed of and PPE acquired subject to finance leases had a carrying value of $30.

Required:

How much cash was spent on property, plant and equipment in the period?

(2)	20X0	20X1
	$	$
Deferred tax liability	50	100
Income tax liability	100	120

The income tax charge in the statement of profit or loss was $180.

Required:

How much tax was paid in the period?

(3)	20X0	20X1
	$	$
Non-controlling interest	440	840

The group statement of profit or loss and other comprehensive income reported total comprehensive income attributable to the non-controlling interest of $500.

Required:

How much was the cash dividend paid to the non-controlling interest?

(4)	20X0	20X1
	$	$
Non-controlling interest	500	850

The group statement of profit or loss and other comprehensive income reported total comprehensive income attributable to the non-controlling interest of $600.

Required:

How much was the cash dividend paid to the non-controlling interest?

(5)	20X0	20X1
	$	$
Investment in associate	200	500

The group statement of profit or loss reported 'share of profit of associates' of $750.

Required:

How much was the cash dividend received by the group?

(6)	20X0	20X1
	$	$
Investment in associate	600	3200

The group statement of profit or loss reported 'share of profit of associates' of $4,000.

In addition, the associate revalued its non-current assets during the period. The group share of this gain is $500.

Required:

How much was the cash dividend received by the group?

(7)	20X0	20X1
	$	$
Property, plant and equipment (PPE)	150	500

During the year depreciation charged was $50, and the group acquired a subsidiary with PPE of $200.

Required:

How much cash was spent on property, plant and equipment in the period?

(8)	20X0	20X1
	$	$
Loan	2,500	1,000

The loan is denominated in an overseas currency, and a loss of $200 has been recorded on the retranslation.

Required:

How much of the loan was repaid in cash?

Test your understanding 3 – AH Group

Extracts from the consolidated financial statements of the AH Group for the year ended 30 June 20X5 are given below:

Consolidated statement of profit or loss for the year ended 30 June 20X5

	$000
Revenue	85,000
Cost of sales	(60,750)
Gross profit	24,250
Operating expenses	(5,650)
Profit from operations	18,600
Finance cost	(1,400)
Profit before disposal of property	17,200
Disposal of property (note 2)	1,250
Profit before tax	18,450
Tax	(6,250)

Profit for the period		12,200
Attributable to:		
Non-controlling interest		405
Owners of the parent		11,795
		12,200

Note: There were no items of other comprehensive income

Statement of financial position, with comparatives, at 30 June 20X5

		20X5		**20X4**
	$000	$000	$000	$000
Non-current assets				
Property, plant and equipment	50,600		44,050	
Goodwill (note 3)	5,910		4,160	
		56,510		48,210
Current assets				
Inventories	33,500		28,750	
Trade receivables	27,130		26,300	
Cash and cash equivalents	1,870		3,900	
		62,500		58,950
		119,010		107,160
Equity and liabilities	$000	$000	$000	$000
Equity shares	20,000		18,000	
Share premium	12,000		10,000	
Retained earnings	24,135		18,340	
		56,135		46,340
Non-controlling interest		3,875		1,920
Total equity		60,010		48,260
Non-current liabilities				
Interest-bearing borrowings		18,200		19,200

Current liabilities				
Trade payables	33,340		32,810	
Interest payables	1,360		1,440	
Tax	6,100		5,450	
		40,800		39,700
		119,010		107,160

Notes:

(1) Several years ago, AH acquired 80% of the issued equity shares of its subsidiary, BI. On 1 January 20X5, AH acquired 75% of the issued equity shares of CJ in exchange for a fresh issue of 2 million of its own $1 equity shares (issued at a premium of $1 each) and $2 million in cash. The net assets of CJ at the date of acquisition were assessed as having the following fair values:

	$000
Property, plant and equipment	4,200
Inventories	1,650
Trade receivables	1,300
Cash and cash equivalents	50
Trade payables	(1,950)
Tax	(250)
	5,000

(2) During the year, AH disposed of property, plant and equipment for proceeds of $2,250,000. The carrying value of the asset at the date of disposal was $1,000,000. There were no other disposals of property, plant and equipment. Depreciation of $7,950,000 was charged to the consolidated statement of profit or loss in the year.

(3) Goodwill on acquisition relates to the acquisition of two subsidiaries. Entity BI was acquired many years ago, and goodwill relating to this acquisition was calculated on a proportion of net assets basis. Goodwill relating to the acquisition of entity CJ during the year was calculated on the full goodwill basis. On 1 January 20X5 when CJ was acquired, the fair value of the non-controlling interest was $1,750,000. Any impairment of goodwill during the year was accounted for within operating expenses.

Required:

Prepare the consolidated statement of cash flows of the AH Group for the year ended 30 June 20X5 using the indirect method.

Test your understanding 4 – Pearl

Below are the consolidated financial statements of the Pearl Group for the year ended 30 September 20X2:

Consolidated statements of financial position

	20X2	**20X1**
	$000	$000
Non-current assets		
Goodwill	1,930	1,850
Property, plant and equipment	2,545	1,625
Investment in associate	620	540
	5,095	4,015
Current assets		
Inventories	470	435
Trade receivables	390	330
Cash and cash equivalents	210	140
	6,165	4,920
Equity and liabilities		
Share capital ($1 shares)	1,500	1,500
Retained earnings	1,755	1,085
Other reserves	750	525
	4,005	3,110
Non-controlling interest	310	320
	4,315	3,430
Non-current liabilities:		
Loans	500	300
Deferred tax	150	105

Current liabilities:		
Trade payables	800	725
Tax payable	400	360
	6,165	4,920

Consolidated statement of profit or loss and other comprehensive income for the year ended 30 September 20X2

	$000
Revenue	2,090
Operating expenses	(1,155)
Profit from operations	935
Gain on disposal of subsidiary	100
Finance cost	(35)
Share of profit of associate	115
Profit before tax	1,115
Tax:	(225)
Profit for the period	890
Other comprehensive income	200
Other comprehensive income from associate	50
Total comprehensive income	1,140
Profit for the year attributable to:	
Owners of the parent	795
Non-controlling interests	95
	890
Total comprehensive income for the year attributable to:	
Owners of the parent	1,020
Non-controlling interests	120
	1,140

Consolidated statement of changes in equity

	Attributable to owners of the parent	Attributable to the NCI
	$000	$000
Equity brought forward	3,110	320
Total comprehensive income	1,020	120
Acquisition of subsidiary	–	340
Disposal of subsidiary	–	(420)
Dividends	(125)	(50)
Equity carried forward	4,005	310

(1) Depreciation totalling $385,000 was charged during the year. Plant with a carrying value of $250,000 was sold for $275,000. The gain on disposal was recognised in operating costs. Certain properties were revalued during the year resulting in a revaluation gain of $200,000 being recognised.

(2) During the year, Pearl acquired 80% of the equity share capital of Gem paying cash consideration of $1.5 million. The NCI holding was measured at its fair value of $340,000 at the date of acquisition. The fair value of Gem's net assets at acquisition was made up as follows:

	$000
Property, plant and equipment	1,280
Inventories	150
Trade receivables	240
Cash and cash equivalents	80
Trade payables	(220)
Tax payable	(40)
	1,490

(3) During the year, Pearl disposed of its 60% equity shareholding in Stone for cash proceeds of $850,000. The subsidiary has been acquired several years ago for cash consideration of $600,000. The NCI holding was measured at its fair value of $320,000 at acquisition and the fair value of Stone's net assets were $730,000. Goodwill had not suffered any impairment. At the date of disposal, the net assets of Stone had carrying values in the consolidated statement of financial position as follows:

	$000
Property, plant and equipment	725
Inventories	165
Trade receivables	120
Cash and cash equivalents	50
Trade payables	(80)
	980

Required:

Prepare the consolidated statement of cash flows for the Pearl group for the year ended 30 September 20X2.

Exchange gains and losses

- The values of assets and liabilities denominated in an overseas currency will increase or decrease partly due to movements in exchange rates.
- The values of the assets and liabilities of an overseas subsidiary when translated into the group's presentation currency will increase or decrease partly due to movements in exchange rates.
- These movements must be factored into your workings in order to determine the actual cash payments and receipts during the year.
- If cash balances are partly denominated in a foreign currency, the effect of exchange rate movements on cash is reported in the statement of cash flows in order to reconcile the cash balances at the beginning and end of the period. This amount is presented separately from cash flows from operating, investing and financing activities.

Illustration 4 – Cash flows and foreign exchange

A group had the following working capital as at 31 December 20X1 and 20X0:

	20X1	20X0
	$	$
Inventories	100	200
Trade receivables	300	200
Trade payables	500	200

During the period ended 31 December 20X1, the group acquired a subsidiary with the following working capital.

Inventories	50
Trade receivables	200
Trade payables	40

During this period the group disposed of a subsidiary with the following working capital.

Inventories	25
Trade receivables	45
Trade payables	20

During this period the group experienced the following exchange rate differences.

Inventories	11	Gain
Trade receivables	21	Gain
Trade payables	31	Loss

Required:

Calculate the movements in inventories, trade receivables and trade payables as they would appear in the indirect reconciliation between profit before tax and cash generated from operations for the period ended 31 December 20X1.

Solution

	Inventories	Trade receivables	Trade payables
	$000	**$000**	**$000**
Bal c/fwd	100	300	500
Bal b/fwd	(200)	(200)	(200)
	(100)	100	300
Less:sub acquired in year	(50)	(200)	(40)
Add:sub disposed in year	25	45	20
Adjustment for forex	(11)	(21)	(31)
Movement in the year	dec (136)	dec (76)	inc 249
Impact on cash flow	Inflow	Inflow	Inflow

Be careful with foreign exchange gains and losses:

- Assets are increased by a foreign exchange gain
- Liabilities are increased by a foreign exchange loss.

Illustration 5 – Changes in group with foreign exchange

The following are extracts from a group's financial statements

	Closing balance	Opening balance
	$000	$000
Consolidated statement of financial position extracts		
Property, plant and equipment	500	400
Loans	300	600
Tax	200	300
Consolidated statement of profit or loss extracts		
Depreciation	50	
Loss on disposal of property, plant and equipment (sold for $30,000)	10	
Tax charge	200	

During the accounting period, one subsidiary was sold, and another acquired. Extracts from the statements of financial position are as follows:

	Sold	Acquired
	$000	$000
Property, plant and equipment	60	70
Loans	110	80
Tax	45	65

During the accounting period, the following net exchange gain arose in respect of the net assets of an overseas subsidiary:

	$000
Property, plant and equipment	40
Loans	(5)
Tax	(5)
Net exchange gain	30

Required:

Calculate the cash flows for property, plant and equipment, loans and tax for inclusion in the consolidated statement of cash flows.

Solution

Property, plant and equipment

	$000
Opening balance	400
Depreciation	(50)
CV of disposed asset (30 + 10)	(40)
Disposal of subsidiary	(60)
Acquisition of subsidiary	70
Exchange gain	40
Cash acquisitions (bal figure)	140
Closing balance	500

Loans

Opening balance	600
Disposal of subsidiary	(110)
Acquisition of subsidiary	80
Exchange loss	5
Cash repaid (bal. fig)	(275)
Closing balance	300

Tax

Opening balance	300
Charge for the year	200
Disposal of subsidiary	(45)
Acquisition of subsidiary	65
Exchange loss	5
Cash paid (bal. fig)	(325)
Closing balance	200

Illustration - Overseas subsidiary

B Group recognised a gain of $160,000 on the translation of the financial statements of a 75% owned foreign subsidiary for the year ended 31 December 20X7. This gain is found to be made up as follows

	$
Gain on opening net assets:	
Non-current assets	90,000
Inventories	30,000
Receivables	50,000
Payables	(40,000)
Cash	30,000
	160,000

The overseas subsidiary made no profit or loss in the year. No goodwill arose on acquisition.

B Group recognised a loss of $70,000 on retranslating the parent entity's foreign currency loan. This loss has been recorded in the statement of profit or loss.

Consolidated statements of financial position as at 31 December

	20X7	**20X6**
	$000	$000
Non-current assets	2,100	1,700
Inventories	650	480
Receivables	990	800
Cash	500	160
	4,240	3,140
Share capital	1,000	1,000
Group reserves	1,600	770
	2,600	1,770
Non-controlling interest	520	370
Equity	3,120	2,140
Long-term loan	250	180
Payables	870	820
	4,240	3,140

There were no non-current asset disposals during the year.

Consolidated statement of profit or loss for the year ended 31 December 20X7

	$000
Profit before tax (after depreciation of $220,000)	2,100
Tax	(650)
Group profit for the year	1,450
Profit attributable to:	
Owners of the parent	1,190
Non-controlling interest	260
Net profit for the period	1,450

Note: The dividend paid by the parent company of the B group during the year was $480,000.

Prepare a statement of cash flows for the year ended 31 December 20X7.

Solution

Statement of cash flows for the year ended 31 December 20X7

Cash flows from operating activities

		$000
Profit before tax		2,100
Forex loss on loan		70
Depreciation charges		220
Increase in inventory (650 – 480 – 30)		(140)
Increase in receivables (990 – 800 – 50)		(140)
Increase in payables (870 – 820 – 40)		10
Cash generated from operations		2,120
Income taxes paid		(650)
Net cash from operating activities		1,470
Cash flows from investing activities		
Purchase of non-current assets (W1)	(530)	
		(530)
Cash flows from financing activities		
Dividends paid to non-controlling interests (W2)	(150)	
Dividends paid	(480)	
		(630)
Exchange gain on cash		30
Increase in cash and cash equivalents		340
Cash and cash equivalents at 1 Jan 20X7		160
Cash cash equivalents at 31 Dec 20X7		500

Note: There have been no proceeds from loans during the year. The loan balance has increased by $70,000 ($250,000 – $180,000) as a result of the foreign exchange loss.

(W1) **Non-current assets**

	$000
Bal b/fwd	1,700
Exchange gain	90
Depreciation	(220)
Additions (bal. fig.)	530
Bal c/fwd	2,100

(W2) **Non-controlling interest**

	$000
Bal b/fwd	370
Total comprehensive income*	300
Dividend paid (bal. fig.)	(150)
Bal c/fwd	520

* This is the NCI share of the subsidiary's profit after tax ($260,000) as well as the NCI share of the foreign exchange gain (25% × $160,000)

Test your understanding 5 – Boardres

Set out below is a summary of the accounts of Boardres, a public limited company, for the year ended 31 December 20X7.

Consolidated statement of profit or loss and other comprehensive income for the year ended 31 December 20X7

	$000
Revenue	44,754
Cost of sales and other expenses	(39,613)
Profit from operations	5,141
Income from associates	30
Finance cost	(305)

Profit before tax	4,866
Tax:	(2,038)
Profit for the period	2,828
Other comprehensive income: Items that may be reclassified to profit or loss in future periods	
Total exchange difference on retranslation of foreign operations (note 5)	302
Total comprehensive income	3,130
Profit for the year attributable to:	
Owners of the parent	2,805
Non-controlling interests	23
	2,828
Total comprehensive income for the year attributable to:	
Owners of the parent (2,805 + 302)	3,107
Non-controlling interests	23
	3,130

Summary of changes in equity attributable to the owners of the parent for the year

	$000
Equity b/f	14,164
Profit for year	2,805
Dividends paid	(445)
Exchange differences	302
Equity c/f	16,826

Consolidated statements of financial position at 31 December

	Note	20X7 $000	20X6 $000
Non-current assets			
Goodwill		500	–
Property, plant and equipment	(1)	11,157	8,985
Investment in associate		300	280
		11,957	9,265
Current assets			
Inventories		9,749	7,624
Receivables		5,354	4,420
Short-term investments	(2)	1,543	741
Cash		1,013	394
		29,616	22,444
Equity share capital		1,997	1,997
Share premium		5,808	5,808
Retained earnings		9,021	6,359
		16,826	14,164
Non-controlling interest		170	17
Total equity		16,996	14,181
Non-current liabilities			
Loans		2,102	1,682
Provisions	(4)	1,290	935
Current liabilities	(3)	9,228	5,646
		29,616	22,444

Notes to the accounts

(1) **Property, plant and equipment**

Property, plant and equipment movements include the following:

	$000
Carrying value of disposals	305
Proceeds from disposals	854
Depreciation charge for the year	907

(2) **Short-term investments**

The short-term investments are readily convertible into cash and there is an insignificant risk that their value will change.

(3) **Current liabilities**

	20X7	**20X6**
	$000	$000
Bank overdrafts	1,228	91
Trade payables	4,278	2,989
Tax	3,722	2,566
	9,228	5,646

(4) **Provisions**

	Legal provision	**Deferred taxation**	**Total**
	$000	$000	$000
At 31 December 20X6	246	689	935
Exchange rate adjustment	29	–	29
Increase in provision	460	–	460
Decrease in provision	–	(134)	(134)
At 31 December 20X7	735	555	1,290

(5) **Liberated**

During the year, the company acquired 82% of the issued equity capital of Liberated for a cash consideration of $1,268,000. The fair values of the assets of Liberated were as follows:

	$000
Property, plant and equipment	208
Inventories	612
Trade receivables	500
Cash in hand	232
Trade payables	(407)
Debenture loans	(312)
	833

(6) **Exchange gains**

The net exchange gain on translating the financial statements of a wholly-owned subsidiary has been taken to equity and comprises differences on the retranslation of the following:

	$000
Property, plant and equipment	138
Legal provision	(29)
Inventories	116
Trade receivables	286
Trade payables	(209)
Net exchange gain	302

(7) **Non-controlling interest**

The non-controlling interest is valued using the proportion of net assets method.

Required:

Prepare a statement of cash flows for the year ended 31 December 20X7.

5 Evaluation of statements of cash flows

Usefulness of the statement of cash flows

A statement of cash flows can provide information that is not available from the statement of financial position or statement of profit or loss and other comprehensive income.

(a) It may assist users of financial statements in making judgements on the amount, timing and degree of certainty of future cash flows.

(b) It gives an indication of the relationship between profitability and cash generating ability, and thus of the quality of the profit earned.

(c) Analysts and other users of financial information often, formally or informally, develop models to assess and compare the present value of the future cash flow of entities. Historical cash flow information could be useful to check the accuracy of past assessments.

(d) A statement of cash flow in conjunction with a statement of financial position provides information on liquidity, solvency and adaptability. The statement of financial position is often used to obtain information on liquidity, but the information is incomplete for this purpose as the statement of financial position is drawn up at a particular point in time.

(e) Cash flows cannot easily be manipulated and are not affected by judgement or by accounting policies.

Limitations of the statement of cash flows

Statements of cash flows should normally be used in conjunction with statements of profit and loss and other comprehensive income and statements of financial position when making an assessment of future cash flows.

(a) Statements of cash flows are based on historical information and therefore do not provide complete information for assessing future cash flows.

(b) There is some scope to 'window dress' cash flows. For example, a business may delay paying suppliers until after the period-end, or it may sell assets before the period-end and then immediately repurchase them at the start of the next period.

(c) Cash flow is necessary for survival in the short term, but in order to survive in the long term a business must be profitable. It is often necessary to sacrifice cash flow in the short term in order to generate profits in the long term (e.g. by investment in non-current assets). A substantial cash balance is not a sign of good management if the cash could be invested elsewhere to generate profit.

Neither cash flow nor profit provides a complete picture of an entity's performance when looked at in isolation.

6 Chapter summary

Objective of statements of cash flows

- To provide information on changes in cash and cash equivalents
- To enable users to assess the liquidity, solvency and financial adaptability of a business

Classifications of cash flows

- IAS 7 only requires 3 headings:
  - Operating activities
  - Investing activities
  - Financing activities

Preparation of group statements of cash flows

- Three additional elements:
  - Cash paid to non-controlling interest
  - Associates
  - Acquisition and disposal of subsidiaries/ associates

Foreign currency transactions

- Exchange gains must be taken out of the statement of financial position movements as they are not cash

Evaluation of statements of cash flows

- Proivdes information not available in the statement of financial position and the statement of profit or loss
- Shows relationship between profitability and cash generating ability

Test your understanding answers

Test your understanding 1 – Cash and cash equivalents

To qualify as a cash equivalent, an item must be readily convertible to cash and have an insignificant risk of a change in value. Furthermore, it should be held for the purpose of meeting short-term cash commitments.

Bank overdrafts are an integral part of most company's cash management. They are therefore generally treated as a component of cash.

The balance of $500,000 in a high interest account is readily available (only 28 days notice is required to access it). This money is also held to meet short-term needs. Assuming that there is not a significant penalty for accessing this money, it should be included within cash equivalents.

The shares are not a cash equivalent. Shares are investments rather than a way of meeting short-term cash requirements. Moreover, there is a significant risk that the value of the shares will change. Any cash spent on shares in the period should be shown within cash flows from investing activities.

Test your understanding 2 – Extracts

(1) **Property, plant and equipment**

	$
Bal b/fwd	100
Revaluation	60
Finance leases	30
Depreciation	(20)
Disposals	(15)
Additions (bal. fig.)	95
Bal c/fwd	250

(2) **Tax**

	$
Bal b/fwd (50 + 100)	150
Profit or loss charge	180
Tax paid (bal. fig.)	(110)
Bal c/fwd (100 + 120)	220

(3) **Non-controlling interest**

	$
Bal b/fwd	440
Total comprehensive income	500
Dividend paid (bal. fig.)	(100)
Bal c/fwd	840

(4) **Non-controlling interest**

	$
Bal b/fwd	500
Total comprehensive income	600
Dividend paid (bal. fig.)	(250)
Bal c/fwd	850

(5) **Associate**

	$
Bal b/fwd	200
Profit or loss	750
Dividend received (bal. fig.)	(450)
Bal c/fwd	500

(6) **Associate**

	$
Bal b/fwd	600
Profit or loss	4,000
Revaluation	500
Dividend received (bal. fig.)	(1,900)
Bal c/fwd	3,200

(7) **Property, plant and equipment**

	$
Bal b/fwd	150
New subsidiary	200
Depreciation	(50)
Additions (bal. fig.)	200
Bal c/fwd	500

(8) **Loan**

	$
Bal b/fwd	2,500
Exchange loss	200
Cash paid (bal. fig.)	(1,700)
Bal c/fwd	1,000

Test your understanding 3 – AH Group

Consolidated statement of cash flows for the year ended 30 June 20X5

	$000	$000
Cash flows from operating activities		
Profit before tax	18,450	
Less: profit on disposal of property (2,250 – 1,000)	(1,250)	
Add: finance cost	1,400	
Adjustment for non-cash items dealt with in arriving at operating profit:		
Depreciation	7,950	
Decrease in trade receivables (27,130 – 26,300 – 1,300)	470	
Increase in inventories (33,500 – 28,750 – 1,650)	(3,100)	
Decrease in trade payables (33,340 – 32,810 – 1,950)	(1,420)	
Goodwill impaired (W5)	1,000	
Cash generated from operations	23,500	
Interest paid (W1)	(1,480)	
Income taxes paid (W2)	(5,850)	
Net cash from operating activities		16,170
Cash flows from investing activities		
Acquisition of subsidiary net of cash acquired (2,000 – 50)	(1,950)	
Purchase of property, plant, and equipment (W3)	(11,300)	
Proceeds from sale of property	2,250	
Net cash used in investing activities		(11,000)

Cash flows from financing activities

Repayment of long-term borrowings (18,200 – 19,200)	(1,000)	
Dividend paid by parent (W7)	(6,000)	
Dividends paid to NCI (W6)	(200)	
Net cash used in financing activities		(7,200)
Net decrease in cash and cash equivalents		(2,030)
Cash and cash equivalents at 1 July 20X4		3,900
Cash and cash equivalents at 30 June 20X5		1,870

(W1) **Interest paid**

	$000
Bal b/fwd	1,440
Profit or loss	1,400
Interest paid (bal. fig.)	(1,480)
Bal c/fwd	1,360

(W2) **Income taxes paid**

	$000
Bal b/fwd	5,450
Profit or loss	6,250
New subsidiary	250
Tax paid (bal. fig.)	(5,850)
Bal c/fwd	6,100

(W3) **Property, plant and equipment**

	$000
Bal b/fwd	44,050
New subsidiary	4,200
Depreciation	(7,950)
Disposals	(1,000)
Additions (bal. fig.)	11,300
Bal c/fwd	50,600

(W4) **Goodwill arising on acquisition of subsidiary**

	$000
Fair value of shares issued (2m × $2)	4,000
Cash consideration	2,000
	6,000
Fair value of NCI at acquisition	1,750
	7,750
Fair value of net assets at acquisition	(5,000)
Goodwill at acquisition	2,750

(W5) **Goodwill**

	$000
Bal b/fwd	4,160
Goodwill on sub acquired (W4)	2,750
Impairment in year (bal. fig.)	(1,000)
Bal c/fwd	5,910

(W6) **Non-controlling interest**

	$000
Bal b/fwd	1,920
NCI arising on subsidiary acquired	1,750
Profit or loss	405
Dividend paid (bal. fig.)	(200)
Bal c/fwd	3,875

(W7) **Retained earnings**

	$000
Bal b/fwd	18,340
Profit or loss	11,795
Dividend paid (bal. fig.)	(6,000)
Bal c/fwd	24,135

Test your understanding 4 – Pearl

Consolidated statement of cash flows

	$000	$000
Cash flows from operating activities		
Profit before tax	1,115	
Finance cost	35	
Profit on sale of subsidiary	(100)	
Income from associates	(115)	
Depreciation	385	
Impairment (W1)	80	
Gain on disposal of PPE ($275 – $250)	(25)	
Increase in inventories ($470 – $435 – $150 + $165)	(50)	
Decrease in receivables ($390 – $330 – $240 + $120)	60	
Decrease in payables ($800 – $725 – $220 + $80)	(65)	
	1,320	
Interest paid	(35)	
Tax paid (W4)	(180)	
		1,105
Cash flows from investing activities		
Proceeds from sale of PPE	275	
Purchases of PPE (W5)	(800)	
Dividends received from associate (W6)	85	
Acquisition of subsidiary ($1,500 – $80)	(1,420)	
Disposal of subsidiary ($850 – $50)	800	
		(1,060)

Cash flows from financing activities

Proceeds from loans ($500 – $300)	200	
Dividends paid to shareholders of the parent (per CSOCIE)	(125)	
Dividends paid to NCI (per CSOCIE)	(50)	
		25
Increase in cash and cash equivalents		70
Opening cash and cash equivalents		140
Closing cash and cash equivalents		210

Workings

(W1) **Goodwill**

	$000
Balance b/f	1,850
Acquisition of subsidiary (W2)	350
Disposal of subsidiary (W3)	(190)
Impairment (bal fig)	(80)
Balance c/f	1,930

(W2) **Goodwill on acquisition of subsidiary**

	$000
Cost of investment	1,500
Fair value of NCI at acquisition	340
Fair value of net assets at acquisition	(1,490)
	350

(W3) **Goodwill at disposal date**

	$000
Cost of investment	600
Fair value of NCI at acquisition	320
Fair value of net assets at acquisition	(730)
	190

(W4) **Tax**

	$000
Balance b/f ($360 + $105)	465
Acquisition of subsidiary	40
Disposal of subsidiary	–
Profit or loss	225
Cash paid	(180)
Balance c/f ($400 + $150)	550

(W5) **PPE**

	$000
Balance b/f	1,625
Depreciation	(385)
Revaluation gain	200
Disposal of plant	(250)
Acquisition of subsidiary	1,280
Disposal of subsidiary	(725)
Cash paid (bal. fig)	800
Balance c/f	2,545

(W6) **Dividend from associate**

	$000
Balance b/f	540
Share of profit of associate	115
OCI from associate	50
Dividend received (bal. fig)	(85)
Balance c/f	620

Test your understanding 5 – Boardres

Statement of cash flows for the year ended 31 December 20X7

	$000	$000
Cash flows from operating activities		
Profit before tax	4,866	
Finance cost	305	
Income from associates	(30)	
Depreciation	907	
Goodwill (W7)	85	
Profit on disposal of PPE (W1)	(549)	
Increase in legal provision	460	
	6,044	
Change in working capital		
Increase in inventory		
(9,749 – 7,624 – 612 acq – 116 ex diff)	(1,397)	
Increase in receivables		
(5,354 – 4,420 – 500 acq – 286 ex diff)	(148)	
Increase in payables		
(4,278 – 2,989 – 407 acq – 209 ex diff)	673	
	5,172	
Interest paid	(305)	
Tax paid (W2)	(1,016)	
Cash flows from investing activities		
Purchase of non-current assets (W3)	(3,038)	
Proceeds on disposal	854	
Cash consideration paid on acquisition of subsidiary, net of cash acquired (1,268 – 232)	(1,036)	
Dividend received from associate (W4)	10	
		(3,210)

Cash flows from financing activities

Dividends paid	(445)	
Dividends paid to NCI (W6)	(20)	
Proceeds from debt issue (W5)	108	
		(357)
Change in cash and cash equivalents		284
Opening cash and cash equivalents (394 + 741 – 91)		1,044
Closing cash and cash equivalents (1,013 + 1,543 – 1,228)		1,328

Workings

(W1) **Profit on disposal of property, plant and equipment**

	$000
Sales proceeds	854
CV	(305)
Profit on disposal	549

(W2) **Tax paid**

	$000
Bal b/fwd (2,566 + 689)	3,255
Profit or loss	2,038
Tax paid (bal. fig.)	(1,016)
Bal c/fwd (3,722 + 555)	4,277

(W3) **Property, plant and equipment**

	$000
Bal b/fwd	8,985
Exchange gain	138
Acquisition of subsidiary	208
Depreciation	(907)
Disposal	(305)
Additions (bal. fig.)	3,038
Bal c/fwd	11,157

(W4) **Dividends from associates**

	$000
Bal b/fwd	280
Profit or loss	30
Dividend received (bal. fig.)	(10)
Bal c/fwd	300

(W5) **Debentures**

	$000
Bal b/fwd	1,682
Acquisition of subsidiary	312
Cash received (bal. fig.)	108
Bal c/fwd	2,102

(W6) **Non-controlling interest**

	$000
Bal b/fwd	17
Total comprehensive income	23
Acquisition of subsidiary (18% × 833)	150
Dividend paid (bal. fig.)	(20)
Bal c/fwd	170

(W7) **Goodwill**

	$000
Cost of investment	1,268
NCI at acquisition (18% × 833)	150
	1,418
FV of net assets at acquisition	(833)
Goodwill at acquisition	585

	$000
Goodwill b/fwd	nil
Goodwill acquired (above)	585
Goodwill impairment (bal. fig)	(85)
Goodwill c/fwd	500

chapter

20

Adoption of IFRS

Chapter learning objectives

Upon completion of this chapter you will be able to:

- apply and discuss the accounting implications of the first time adoption of a body of new accounting standards
- evaluate the implications of worldwide convergence with International Financial Reporting Standards
- Discuss the influence of national regulators on International Financial Reporting Standards.

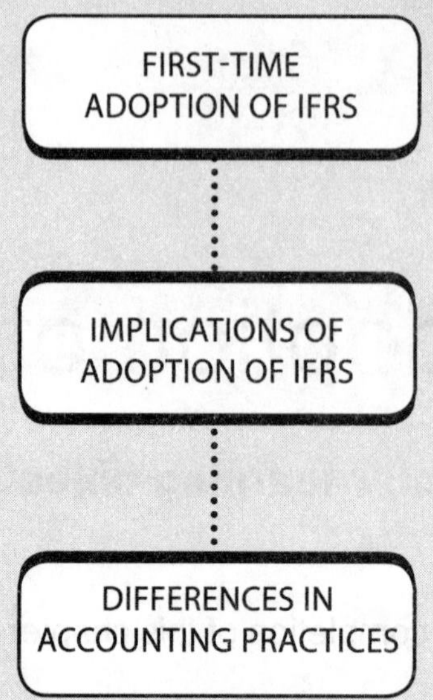

1 IFRS 1: First time adoption of IFRS

Adoption of IFRS

Although not as significant as they once were, differences remain between IFRSs and national standards. Therefore, there is an accounting issue when a company adopts IFRS for the first time.

An entity may adopt IFRS for a number of reasons:

- An entity may be seeking a listing, and listing rules may require the use of IFRS.
- Entities who have no expectation of seeking a listing may choose to adopt IFRS if they perceive that IFRS is more relevant to their situation.
- Unlisted multinational corporate groups may choose to adopt IFRS as the basis for financial reporting throughout the group. This may save time and resources in the preparation of management information throughout the group, and streamline group annual financial reporting requirements.
- Entities may believe that adoption of IFRS could assist in their efforts to raise capital. For example, if potential capital providers are familiar with IFRS, it may ease their evaluation of any capital investment opportunity.
- Entities may believe that they are 'doing the right thing' by adopting IFRS as it is already used by other, usually listed and often larger entities.

IFRS 1 First time adoption of IFRS

IFRS 1 First-time adoption of international financial reporting standards sets out the procedures to follow when an entity adopts IFRS in its published financial statements for the first time.

A **first-time adopter** is an entity that, for the first time, makes an explicit and unreserved statement that its annual financial statements comply with IFRS.

There are five issues that need to be addressed when adopting IFRS:

(1) The date of transition to IFRSs

(2) Which IFRSs should be adopted

(3) How gains or losses arising on adopting IFRS should be accounted for

(4) The explanations and disclosures to be made in the year of transition

(5) What exemptions are available.

Date of transition

The **date of transition** is the beginning of the earliest period for which an entity presents full comparative information under IFRS in its first IFRS financial statements.

- IFRS should be applied from the first day of the first set of financial statements published in compliance with IFRS. This is called the opening IFRS statement of financial position.
- Because IFRS require comparative statements to be published, the opening IFRS statement of financial position for an entity adopting IFRS for the first time in its 31 December 20X8 financial statements and presenting one year of comparative information will be1 January 20X7. This is the transition date – the first day of the comparative period.
- The opening IFRS statement of financial position itself need not be published, but it will provide the opening balances for the comparative period.
- If full comparative financial statements for preceding periods are published, then these too must comply with IFRS.
- If only selected information is disclosed about preceding periods, then these need not comply with IFRS. However, this non-compliance must be disclosed.

Which IFRSs should be adopted?

- The entity should use the same accounting policies for all the periods presented. These policies should be based solely on IFRS in force at the reporting date.
- A major problem for entities preparing for the change-over is that IFRSs themselves keep changing. Therefore an entity may apply an IFRS that is not yet mandatory if that IFRS permits early application.
- IFRS 1 states that the opening IFRS statement of financial position must:
  - recognise all assets and liabilities required by IFRS
  - not recognise assets and liabilities not permitted by IFRS
  - reclassify all assets, liabilities and equity components in accordance with IFRS
  - measure all assets and liabilities in accordance with IFRS.

Reporting gains and losses

Any gains or losses arising on the adoption of IFRS should be recognised directly in retained earnings. In other words, they are not recognised in profit or loss.

Explanations and disclosures

- Entities must explain how the transition to IFRS affects their reported financial performance, financial position and cash flows. Two main disclosures are required:
  - The entity's equity as reported under previous GAAP must be reconciled to the equity reported under IFRS at two dates.
    - The date of transition (the opening reporting date)
    - The last statement of financial position prepared under previous GAAP.
  - The last annual reported under previous GAAP must be reconciled to the same year's total comprehensive income prepared under IFRS.
- Any material differences between the previous GAAP and the IFRS statement of cash flows must also be explained.
- When preparing its first IFRS statements, an entity may identify errors made in previous years. The correction of these errors must be disclosed separately.
- When preparing IFRS statements for the first time, the fair value of property, plant and equipment, intangible assets and investment properties can be used as the 'deemed cost'. If so, the entity must disclose the aggregate of those fair values and the adjustment made to their carrying values under the previous GAAP.

Exemptions

IFRS 1 grants limited exemptions in situations where the cost of compliance would outweigh the benefits to the user. For example:

- Previous business combinations do not have to be restated in accordance with IFRS. In particular, mergers (pooling of interests) do not have to be re-accounted for as acquisitions, previously written off goodwill does not have to be reinstated and the fair values of assets and liabilities may be retained. However, an impairment test for any remaining goodwill must be made in the opening statement of financial position.
- An entity can choose to deem past translation gains and losses on an overseas subsidiary to be nil.
- An entity need not restate the borrowing cost component that was capitalised under previous GAAP at the date of transition to IFRS. However, all borrowing costs from the transition date should be capitalised if the conditions in IAS 23 are met.
- Under IAS 32, the proceeds of convertible debt are split into a liability component and an equity component. If the debt had been repaid by the date of transition, no adjustment is needed to recognise the equity component upon adopting IFRS for the first time.
- If a subsidiary adopts IFRS later than its parent, then the subsidiary may value its assets and liabilities either at its own transition date or its parent's transition date (which would normally be easier).

There are some situations where retrospective application of IFRS is prohibited. In other words, the carrying values of assets and liabilities in the closing statement of financial position under previous GAAP are brought into the opening statement of financial position under IFRS. These include:

- Derecognition of financial assets and liabilities
  - If a first time adopter of IFRS derecognised financial assets or liabilities under previous GAAP, these are not re-recognised under IFRS.
- Hedge accounting
- Estimates
  - An entity's estimates in accordance with IFRSs at the date of transition to IFRSs shall be consistent with estimates made for the same date in accordance with previous GAAP unless there is objective evidence that those estimates were in error.

- Some elements of government grant accounting:
  - If a first-time adopter did not, under its previous GAAP, recognise and measure a government loan at a below-market rate of interest on a basis consistent with IFRS requirements, it shall use its previous GAAP carrying amount of the loan at the date of transition to IFRSs as the carrying amount of the loan in the opening IFRS statement of financial position. An entity shall apply IFRS 9 to the measurement of such loans after the date of transition to IFRSs.

Implications of adopting IFRS

There are a number of considerations to be made when adopting IFRS for the first time. The key factors on converting from local GAAP to IFRS are discussed below.

Initial evaluation

The transition to IFRS requires careful and timely planning. Initially there are a number of questions that must be asked to assess the current position within the entity.

(a) Is there knowledge of IFRS within the entity?

(b) Are there any agreements (such as bank covenants) that are dependent on local GAAP?

(c) Will there be a need to change the information systems?

(d) Which IFRSs will affect the entity?

(e) Is this an opportunity to improve the accounting systems?

Once the initial evaluation of the current position has been made, the entity can determine the nature of any assistance required.

They may need to:

- engage IFRS experts for assistance. Such experts can provide staff training and assistance on the preparation of the opening statement of financial position and first set of accounts. They can inform the entity of the information that will be needed to ensure a smooth transition to IFRS. It is essential that the entity personnel understand the key differences between local GAAP and IFRS and in particular the IFRS that will most affect the entity

- inform key stakeholders of the impact that IFRS could have on reported performance. This includes analysts, bankers, loan creditors and employees. Head office personnel will not be the only staff to require training; managers of subsidiaries will need to know the impact on their finance functions as there will be budgeting and risk management issues
- produce a project plan that incorporates the resource requirements, training needs, management teams and timetable with a timescale that ensures there is enough time to produce the first IFRS financial statements
- investigate the effect of the change on the computer systems. Establish if the current system can easily be changed and, if not, what the alternatives will be. Potentially the IT cost could be significant if changes need to be made.

Other considerations

Aside from the practical aspect of implementing the move to IFRS, there are a number of other factors to consider:

(i) Debt covenants

- The entity will have to consider the impact of the adoption of IFRS on debt covenants and other legal contracts.
- Covenants based on financial position ratios (for example the gearing ratio) and profit or loss measures such as interest cover will probably be affected significantly by the adoption of IFRS.
- Debt covenants may need to be renegotiated and rewritten, as it would not seem to be sensible to retain covenants based on a local GAAP if this is no longer to be used.

(ii) Performance related pay

- There is a potential impact on income of moving to IFRS, which causes a problem in designing an appropriate means of determining executive bonuses, employee performance related pay and long-term incentive plans.
- With the increase in the use of fair values and the potential recycling of gains and losses under IFRS (e.g. IAS 21 The effects of changes in foreign exchange rates), the identification of relevant measures of performance will be quite difficult.
- If there are unrealised profits reported in profit or loss, the entity will not wish to pay bonuses on the basis of profits that may never be realised in cash.

- There may be volatility in the reported figures, which will have little to do with financial performance but could result in major differences in the pay awarded to a director from one year to another.

(iii) Views of financial analysts

- It is important that the entity looks at the way it is to communicate the effects of a move to IFRS with the markets and the analysts.
- The focus of the communication should be to provide assurance about the process and to quantify the changes expected. Unexpected changes in ratios and profits could adversely affect share prices.
- Presentations can be made to interested parties of the potential impact of IFRS. Analysts should have more transparent and comparable data about multinational entities once IFRS has been adopted.
- Consistency over account classifications, formats, disclosures and measurement will assist the analyst's interpretation.
- Analysts will be particularly concerned about earnings volatility that may affect how they discount future profits to arrive at a present fair value for the business.

Test your understanding 1 – Nat

Nat is a company that used to prepare financial statements under local national standards. Their first IFRS financial statements are for the year ended December 20X5 and these will include comparative information for the previous financial year. Its previous GAAP financial statements are for the years ended 31 December 20X3 and 20X4. The directors are unsure about the following issues:

(i) Nat received $5 million in advance orders for a new product on 31 December 20X3. These products were not dispatched until 20X4. In line with its previous GAAP, this $5m was recognised as revenue.

(ii) A restructuring provision of $1 million relating to head office activities was recognised at 31 December 20X3 in accordance with previous GAAP. This does not qualify for recognition as a liability in accordance with IFRS.

(iii) Nat made estimates of accrued expenses and provisions at 31 December 20X3. Some of these estimates turned out to be understated. Nat believes that the estimates were reasonable and in line with the requirements of both its previous GAAP and IFRS.

Required:

In accordance with IFRS 1, how should the above issues be dealt with?

2 Harmonisation

Reasons for differences in accounting practices

The reasons why accounting practices may differ from one country to another include the following:

- **Legal systems**. In some countries, financial statements are prepared according to a strict code imposed by the government. This is often because the accounts are being prepared primarily for tax purposes rather than for investment.
- **Professional traditions**. In contrast to countries where accounting standards are embedded in legislation, other countries have a strong and influential accounting profession and can rely on the profession to draft relevant standards.
- **User groups**. As mentioned above, in some countries the tax authorities are the main users of accounts, and so a standardised, rule-based approach to accounting emerges. Quite often, depreciation rates will be set by law rather than being based upon useful lives. In countries where businesses are generally financed by loans (rather than by equity) then financial statements will focus on a business' ability to service and pay back its debts. In the UK and the US, businesses are generally financed through equity. In these countries, the shareholders share the risks of profits and losses, and so they demand full disclosure of a business' financial affairs.
- **Nationalism**. Individual countries believe that their own standards are the best.
- **Culture**. Differences in culture can lead to differences in the objective and method of accounting.

Culture and local custom

Financial reporting practice may be influenced by cultural factors in a number of ways.

- Some nationalities are naturally conservative and this may affect their attitude to accounting estimates, particularly when it comes to providing for liabilities.
- Religion may affect accounting practices; for example. For example, Islamic law forbids the charging or accepting of interest.

- Different nationalities have different attitudes to risk. For example, in Japan high gearing is usual and is a sign of confidence in an entity.
- Attitudes to disclosure also vary. Some cultures value openness while others have a strong tradition of confidentiality.
- In the UK and the USA, the main objective of management and shareholders is generally to maximise profit in the short term. However, in other countries, investors and management may have different or wider objectives, such as long-term growth, stability, benefiting the community and safeguarding the interests of employees.

Benefits of harmonisation

Benefits of harmonisation

There are a number of reasons why the harmonisation of accounting standards would be beneficial. Businesses operate on a global scale and investors make investment decisions on a worldwide basis. There is thus a need for financial information to be presented on a consistent basis. The advantages are as follows.

(1) **Multi-national entities**

Multi-national entities would benefit from closer harmonisation for the following reasons.

(a) Access to international finance would be easier as financial information is more understandable if it is prepared on a consistent basis.

(b) In a business that operates in several countries, the preparation of financial information would be easier as it would all be prepared on the same basis.

(c) There would be greater efficiency in accounting departments.

(d) Consolidation of financial statements would be easier.

(2) **Investors**

If investors wish to make decisions based on the worldwide availability of investments, then better comparisons between entities are required. Harmonisation assists this process, as financial information would be consistent between different entities from different regions.

(3) **International economic groupings**

International economic groupings, e.g. the EU, could work more effectively if there were international harmonisation of accounting practices. Part of the function of international economic groupings is to make cross-border trade easier. Similar accounting regulations would improve access to capital markets and therefore help this process.

The role of national standard setters

The role of national standard setters

- The harmonisation process has gathered pace in the last few years. From 2005 all European listed entities were required to adopt IFRS in their group financial statements. Many other countries including Australia, Canada and New Zealand decided to follow a similar process. National standard setters are committed to a framework of accounting standards based on IFRS.
- Additionally, the US are committed to harmonise with IFRS and the FASB and the IASB are aiming for convergence over the next few years.

The role of accounting standard setters and the IASB

- In February 2005, the IASB issued a memorandum setting out the responsibilities of the IASB and national standard setters. It is most relevant to those who have adopted or converged with IFRSs'. It deals with the responsibilities of national standard setters to facilitate adoption or convergence with IFRS.
- It includes the responsibilities of the IASB to ensure that it makes information available on a timely basis so that national standard setters can be informed of the IASB's plans. Sufficient time should be allowed in relation to consultative documents so that national standard setters have sufficient time to prepare the information in their own context and to receive comments from their own users.
- The national standard setters should deal with domestic barriers to adopting or converging with IFRS. They should avoid amending an IFRS when adopting it in their own jurisdiction, so that the issue of non-compliance with the IFRS does not arise. They should encourage their own constituents to communicate their technical views to the IASB and they themselves should respond with comments on a timely basis. They should also make known any differences of opinion that they have with a project as early as possible in the process.

Chapter summary

First time adoption of IFRS

- Five points to consider are:
  - the date of transition to IFRS
  - which IFRS should be adopted
  - how gains or losses arising on adopting IFRS should be accounted for
  - the explanations and disclosures to be made in the year of transition
  - what exemptions are available

Implications of adoption of IFRS

- Consider practical implications – training, IT systems, planning project
- Also consider terms in debt covenants, calculation of performance-related pay and anything that is based on the profit figure
- Communicate with analysts on the expected changes to the financial statements

Differences in accounting practices

- There are historical reasons for differences in accounting systems such as legal, professional, culture
- Some accounting differences remain, but the harmonisation process is taking place
  Many countries are adopting IFRS
- The IASB is aiming to converge with the US standard-setter the FASB to harmonise IFRS with US GAAP

Test your understanding answers

Test your understanding 1 – Nat

Nat's first IFRS period is the period ended 31 December 20X5. However, comparative figures prepared under IFRS for year ended 31 December 20X4 must be presented. Nat's date of transition is therefore 1 January 20X4 and an opening IFRS statement of financial position must be produced as at this date.

Some of the accounting policies that Nat uses in its opening IFRS statement of financial position differ from those that it used for the same date using its previous GAAP. The resulting adjustments arise from events and transactions before the date of transition to IFRSs. Therefore, an entity shall recognise those adjustments directly in retained earnings

Transaction (i)

The sale does not meet the criteria for recognition under IAS 18 because the risks and rewards of ownership have not transferred from the seller. In the opening IFRS statement of financial position as at 1 January 20X4, a liability for deferred income should be recognised. The $5 million loss on recognition of this liability will be accounted for in retained earnings.

Transaction (ii)

The provision does not meet the criteria under IAS 37. In the opening IFRS statement of financial position as at 1 January 20X4, the provision should be derecognised. The $1 million gain on derecognition of this provision will be accounted for in retained earnings.

Transaction (iii)

Although some of the accruals and provisions turned out to be underestimates, Nat concluded that its estimates were reasonable and that, therefore, no error had occurred. In accordance with IAS 8, this should be accounted for prospectively. Therefore the additional expense will be recognised in the IFRS profit or loss figures for the year ended 31 December 20X4.

chapter

21

Specialised entities and specialised transactions

Chapter learning objectives

Upon completion of this chapter you will be able to:

- account for transactions and events occurring in not- for-profit and public sector entities
- discuss solutions to the problem of differential financial reporting
- discuss the accounting treatments not allowable under the IFRS for SMEs including the revaluation model for certain assets
- discuss and apply the simplifications introduced by the IFRS for SMEs including accounting for goodwill and intangible assets, financial instruments, defined benefit schemes, exchange differences and associates and joint ventures
- discuss the key differences between the IFRS for SMEs and UK GAAP (P2 UK only)
- identify when an entity may no longer be viewed as a going concern and outline circumstances when a reconstruction may be an alternative to corporate liquidation
- outline the appropriate accounting treatment required relating to reconstructions.

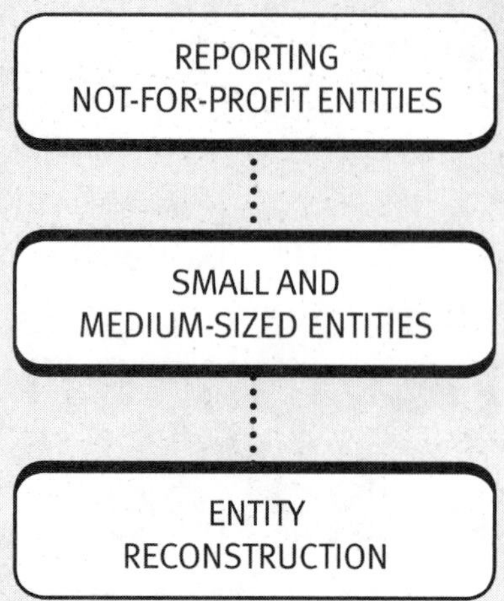

1 Not-for-profit entities

Reporting not-for-profit entities

Definition

A **not-for-profit entity** is one that does not carry on its activities for the purposes of profit or gain to particular persons, including its owners or members; and does not distribute its profits or assets to particular persons, including its owners or members.

The main types of not-for-profit entity are:

- clubs and societies
- charities
- public sector organisations (including central government, local government and National Health Service bodies).

The objectives of a not-for-profit entity

Key points

- The main objective of public sector organisations is to provide services to the general public. Their long-term aim is normally to break even, rather than to generate a surplus.
- Most public sector organisations aim to provide value for money, which is usually analysed into the three Es – economy, efficiency and effectiveness.
- Other not-for-profit entities include charities, clubs and societies whose objective is to carry out the activities for which they were created.

Assessing performance in a not-for-profit entity

- It can be difficult to monitor and evaluate the success of a not-for-profit organisation as the focus is not on a resultant profit as with a traditional business entity.
- The success of the organisation should be measured against the key indicators that reflect the visions and values of the organisation. The strategic plan will identify the goals and the strategies that the organisation needs to adopt to achieve these goals.
- The focus should be the measures of output, outcomes and their impact on what the charity is trying to achieve.

Accounting in a not-for-profit entity

The financial statements of a public sector entity or a charity are set out differently from those of a profit making entity, because their purpose is different. A public sector organisation is not reporting a profit; it is reporting on its income and how it has spent that income in achieving its aims.

The financial statements include a statement of financial position or balance sheet, but the statement of profit or loss and other comprehensive income is usually replaced with a statement of financial activities or an income and expenditure account showing incoming resources and resources expended.

Example of not-for-profit accounts

An example of a statement of financial activities for a charity is shown below.

The Toytown Charity, Statement of Financial Activities for the year ended 31 March 20X7

	$
Incoming resources	
Resources from generated funds	
Grants	10,541,000
Legacies	5,165,232
Donations	1,598,700
Activities for generating funds	
Charity shop sales	10,052,693
Investment income	3,948,511
Total incoming resources	31,306,136

Resources expended	
Cost of generating funds	
Fund raising	(1,129,843)
Publicity	(819,828)
Charity shop operating costs	(6,168,923)
Charitable activities	
Supporting local communities	(18,263,712)
Elderly care at home	(4,389,122)
Pride in Toytown campaign	(462,159)
Total resources expended	(31,233,587)
Net incoming resources for the year	72,549
Funds brought forward at 1 March 20X6	21,102
Funds carried forward at 31 March 20X7	93,651

The statement of financial position or balance sheet of a not-for-profit entity only differs from that of a profit making entity in the reserves section, where there will usually be an analysis of the different types of reserve, as shown below.

Toytown Charity, Balance sheet as at 31 March 20X7

	$
Non-current assets	
Tangible assets	80,500
Investments	12,468
	92,968
Current assets	
Inventory	2,168
Receivables	10,513
Cash	3,958
	16,639
Total assets	109,607
Reserves	
Restricted fund	20,200
Unrestricted funds	73,451
	93,651

Non-current liabilities	
Pension liability	9,705
Current liabilities	
Payables	6,251
Total funds	109,607

The reserves are separated into restricted and unrestricted funds.

- Unrestricted funds are funds available for general purposes.
- Restricted funds are those that have been set aside for a specific purpose or in a situation where an individual has made a donation to the charity for a specific purpose, perhaps to replace some equipment, so these funds must be kept separate.

2 Small and medium sized entities

Definition:

A small or medium entity may be defined or characterised as follows:

- they are usually owner-managed by a relatively small number of individuals such as a family group, rather than having an extensive ownership base
- they are usually smaller entities in financial terms such as revenues generated and assets and liabilities under the control of the entity
- they usually have a relatively small number of employees
- they usually undertake less complex or difficult transactions which are normally the focus of a financial reporting standard.

One of the underlying requirements for financial reporting is that the cost and burden of producing financial reporting information for shareholders and other stakeholders should not outweigh the benefits of making that information available.

IFRS for small and medium-sized entities (IFRS for SME) has been issued for use by entities that have no public accountability. This means that debt or equity instruments are not publicly traded. IFRS for SME reduces the burden of producing information that is not likely to be of interest to the stakeholders of a small or medium company.

The problem of differential reporting

- It can be difficult to define a small or medium entity
- If a company ceases to qualify as a small or medium entity then there will be a cost and time burden in order to comply with full IFRS
- There may be comparability problems if one company applies full IFRS whilst another applies IFRS for SME.

What is the effect of introducing the IFRS for SME?

IFRS for SME will be updated approximately every three years. In contrast, companies that use full IFRS have to incur the time cost of ensuring compliance with regular updates.

Accounting under full IFRS necessitates compliance with approximately 3,000 disclosure points. In contrast, IFRS for SME comprises approximately 300 disclosure points all contained within the one document. This significantly reduces the time spent and costs incurred in producing financial statements.

Key omissions from IFRS for SME

The subject matter of several reporting standards has been omitted from the IFRS for SME as follows:

- Earnings per share (IAS 33)
- Interim reporting (IAS 34)
- Segmental reporting (IFRS 8)
- Assets held for sale (IFRS 5)

Omission of subject matter from IFRS for SME is usually because the cost of preparing and reporting information exceeds the expected benefits which users would expect to derive from that information.

Accounting choices disallowed under IFRS for SME

There are a number of accounting policy choices allowed under full IFRS that are not available to companies that apply IFRS for SME. Under IFRS for SME:

- Goodwill is always recognised as the difference between the cost of the business combination and the fair value of the net assets acquired. In other words, the fair value method for measuring the non-controlling interest is not available.
- Property, plant and equipment and intangible assets must be accounted for at cost less accumulated depreciation and amortisation and impairment. The revaluation model is not permitted.

- After initial recognition, investment property is remeasured to fair value at the year end with gains or losses recorded in profit or loss. The cost model can only be used if fair value cannot be measured reliably or without undue cost or effort.

Key simplifications in IFRS for SME

The subject matter of other reporting standards has been simplified for inclusion within the IFRS for SME. Key simplifications to be aware of are as follows:

- Borrowing costs are always expensed to profit or loss
- Whilst associates and jointly controlled entities can be accounted for under the equity method, they can also be held at cost (if there is no published price quotation) or fair value. Therefore, simpler alternatives to the equity method are available.
- Depreciation and amortisation estimates are not reviewed annually. Changes to these estimates are only required if there is an indication that the pattern of an asset's use has changed.
- Expenditure on research and development is always expensed to profit or loss.
- If an entity is unable to make a reliable estimate of the useful life of an intangible asset, then the useful life is assumed to be ten years.
- Goodwill is amortised over its useful life. If a reliable estimate of the useful life cannot be made, then the useful life is assumed to be ten years.
- On the disposal of an overseas subsidiary, cumulative exchange differences that have been recognised in other comprehensive income are not recycled to profit or loss.
- If an entity is not able, without undue cost or effort, to use the projected unit credit method to measure its obligation and cost under defined benefit plans, the entity is permitted to:
  - ignore estimated future salary increases
  - ignore future service of current employees
  - ignore possible in-service mortality of current employees between the reporting date and the date employees are expected to begin receiving post-employment benefits.
- There are numerous simplifications with regards to financial instruments. These include:
  - Measuring most debt instruments at amortised cost
  - Recognising most investments in shares at fair value with changes in fair value recognised in profit or loss. If fair value cannot be measured reliably then the shares are held at cost less impairment.

Advantages and disadvantages of IFRS for SME

Advantages

- There will be time and cost savings due to simplifications and omissions, particularly with regards to disclosure.
- IFRS for SME is worded in a more accessible way than many standards within full IFRS.
- All standards are located within one document so it is therefore easier and quicker to find the information required.

Disadvantages

- There are issues of comparability when comparing one company that uses full IFRS and another which uses IFRS for SME.
- IFRS for SME is arguably still too complex for many small companies. In particular, the requirements with regards to leases and deferred tax could be simplified.

Technical Article

The P2 Examiner wrote an article discussing the issue of IFRS for SME in the March 2010 Student Accountant magazine. You can access this article from the ACCA website (www.accaglobal.com).

3 UK GAAP

UK GAAP

Old UK GAAP

Since 2005, UK listed groups have been required to prepare their consolidated financial statements in accordance with IFRS.

Most other groups and companies could apply IFRS or UK GAAP. Small companies (defined by Companies Act 2006) could choose to follow the Financial Reporting Standard for Smaller Entities (FRSSE).

New UK GAAP

For periods beginning on or after 1 January 2015, three new Financial Reporting Standards are applicable.

These new standards are FRS 100, 101 and 102.

The accounting standards

FRS 100 does not specify accounting requirements but rather details which particular standards UK companies should apply. The choices detailed are as follows:

- 'Small' companies can still follow the FRSSE.
- It is mandatory for listed groups to prepare their accounts under IFRS.
  - However, the individual financial statements of the companies within the group can be prepared using FRS 101. This is a reduced disclosure framework that will save considerable time for the preparers of the individual financial statements.
- Most other companies can choose to adopt IFRS.
- Companies that do not follow the FRSSE or IFRS must adopt FRS 102.

'Small' Companies

As noted above, companies in the UK which qualify as 'small' can use the FRSSE.

Small companies are private companies that, with some exceptions, comply with two or more of the following criteria:

Turnover	≤ £6.5m
Balance sheet	≤ £3.26m
Employees	≤ 50

These criteria exclude banks, building societies, insurance and financial services companies, regardless of their size.

FRS 102

FRS 102 is a single standard that is organised by topic.

Although FRS 102 is based on IFRS for SME, there are differences. Some of these differences are included in the UK P2 syllabus.

Financial statement presentation

To comply with Companies Act, FRS 102 allows a 'true and fair over-ride'. If compliance with FRS 102 is inconsistent with the requirement to give a true and fair view, the directors must depart from FRS 102 to the extent necessary to give a true and fair view. Particulars of any such departure, the reasons for it and its effect are disclosed.

Statement of cash flows

Under FRS 102, mutual life assurance companies, pension funds and certain investment funds are not required to produce a statement of cash flows. This exemption does not exist under IFRS for SME.

Consolidated and separate financial statements

Under IFRS for SME, a parent need not present consolidated financial statements if the parent is itself a subsidiary, and its ultimate parent (or any intermediate parent) produces consolidated general purpose financial statements that comply with full IFRSs or IFRS for SME.

FRS 102 makes some slight amendments to the above to comply with Companies Act. In particular, consolidated financial statements do not need to be produced if the parent, and group headed by it, qualifies as small. The requirements of Companies Act are dealt with in more detail later in this section.

Investments in associates

FRS 102 explicitly clarifies that an investment in an associate cannot be equity accounted in the individual financial statements of a company that is a parent. Instead, the investment in associate can be held at cost of fair value.

Under FRS 102, the cost of an associate should include transaction costs. These are excluded from the cost of the associate under IFRS for SME.

Investments in joint ventures

FRS 102 explicitly clarifies that an investment in a jointly controlled entity cannot be equity accounted in the individual financial statements of a company that is a parent. Instead, the investment in associate can be held at cost of fair value.

Property, plant and equipment

Under FRS 102, property, plant and equipment can be held under the cost model or the revaluation model. IFRS for SME does not permit the revaluation model.

Intangible assets

Under FRS 102, an intangible asset arising from development activity can be recognised if certain criteria are met. These criteria are broadly the same as under IAS 38. According to IFRS for SME, research and development expenditure is always written off to profit or loss.

Under FRS 102, intangible assets can be held under the cost model or the revaluation model. IFRS for SME does not permit the revaluation model.

Accounting policies

Under FRS 102, the revaluation model is permitted for property, plant and equipment and intangible assets. If an entity switches from the cost model to the revaluation model, this is not adjusted retrospectively. This issue is not relevant under IFRS for SME because the revaluation model is prohibited.

Business combinations and goodwill

Under FRS 102, goodwill is amortised over its estimated useful life. If no reliable estimate of the useful life can be made, then the life must not exceed five years. If the useful life of goodwill cannot be reliably estimated under IFRS for SME, then it must not exceed ten years.

According to FRS 102:

- Negative goodwill (where the fair value of the net assets acquired exceeds the consideration) is recognised on the statement of financial position immediately below goodwill. It should be followed by a subtotal of the net amount of goodwill and the negative goodwill.
- The subsequent treatment of negative goodwill is that any amount up to the fair value of non-monetary assets acquired is recognised in profit or loss in the periods in which the non-monetary assets are recovered. Any amount exceeding the fair value of non-monetary assets acquired must be recognised in profit or loss in the periods expected to be benefited

Under IFRS for SME, negative goodwill is recognised immediately in profit or loss.

Government grants

Under FRS 102, two methods of recognising government grants are allowed:

- The performance model
  - If no conditions are attached to the grant, it is recognised as income immediately.
  - If conditions are attached to the grant, it is only recognised as income when all conditions have been met.

- The accruals model
  - Grants are recognised as income on a systematic basis, either as costs are incurred (revenue grants) or over the asset's useful life (capital grants).

Under IFRS for SME, only the performance model for recognising government grants is allowed.

Borrowing costs

Under FRS 102, an entity may capitalise borrowing costs that are directly attributable to the construction, acquisition or production of a qualifying asset. Under IFRS for SME, all borrowing costs are recognised as an expense in profit or loss.

Impairment of assets

Under FRS 102, an impairment loss recognised against goodwill can be reversed if the reasons for the impairment have ceased to exist. IFRS for SME prohibits the reversal of impairment losses recognised against goodwill.

Employee Benefits

Under FRS 102, the projected unit credit method must be used to estimate the defined benefit obligation.

In contrast, IFRS for SME allows some simplified estimation techniques if an entity is not able, without undue cost or effort, to use the projected unit credit method to measure its obligation and cost under defined benefit plans. Entities are permitted to:

- ignore estimated future salary increases
- ignore future service of current employees
- ignore possible in-service mortality of current employees between the reporting date and the date employees are expected to begin receiving post-employment benefits.

Related parties

FRS 102 permits an additional exemption from the disclosure of related party transactions than IFRS for SME. FRS 102 states that disclosures need not be given of transactions entered into between two or more members of a group, provided that any subsidiary which is a party to the transaction is wholly owned by such a member.

Income tax

The income tax section of FRS 102 differs significantly from IFRS for SME.

- Profit or loss/statement of financial position
  - FRS 102 adopts a profit or loss approach to the recognition of deferred tax. Timing differences are defined as differences between taxable profits and total comprehensive income as stated in the financial statements that arise from the inclusion of income and expenses in tax assessments in periods different from those in which they are recognised in financial statements.
    - FRS 102 makes an exception to this rule. It states that deferred tax should also be recognised based on the differences between the tax value and fair value of assets and liabilities acquired in a business combination.
  - In contrast, IFRS for SME conceptualises deferred tax through the statement of financial position. The standard states that deferred tax should be accounted for based on differences between the amounts recognised for the entity's assets and liabilities in the statement of financial position and the recognition of those assets and liabilities by the tax authorities.
- Permanent differences
  - FRS 102 uses the concept of permanent differences. Permanent differences arise because certain types of income and expenses are non-taxable or disallowable, or because certain tax charges or allowances are greater or smaller than the corresponding income or expense in the financial statements. Deferred tax is not recognised on permanent differences.
  - IFRS for SME does not use the terminology 'permanent difference'. Instead, it says that deferred tax assets and liabilities are recognised for 'temporary differences'.
- Deferred tax assets
  - Under FRS 102, unrelieved tax losses and other deferred tax assets are recognised to the extent that it is probable that they will be recovered against future taxable profits.
  - IFRS for SME requires the use of a 'valuation allowance'. An entity should recognise a valuation allowance against deferred tax assets so that the net carrying amount equals the highest amount that is more likely than not to be recovered based on current or future taxable profit.

Companies Act

The UK syllabus for P2 specifies that candidates must know the basic Companies Act requirements surrounding when single and group entity financial statements are required and when a subsidiary may be excluded from the group financial statements.

Single entity financial statements

A company is exempt from the requirement to prepare individual accounts for a financial year if:

- it is itself a subsidiary undertaking
- it has been dormant throughout the whole of that year, and
- its parent undertaking is established under the law of an EEA State.

Group financial statements

A company subject to the small companies regime **may** prepare group accounts for the year.

If not subject to the small companies regime, a parent company **must** prepare group accounts for the year unless one of the following applies:

- A company is exempt from the requirement to prepare group accounts if it is itself a wholly-owned subsidiary of a parent undertaking.
- A parent company is exempt from the requirement to prepare group accounts if, under section 405 of Companies Act, all of its subsidiary undertakings could be excluded from consolidation.

Exclusion of a subsidiary from consolidation

Where a parent company prepares Companies Act group accounts, all the subsidiary undertakings of the company must be included in the consolidation, subject to the following exceptions:

- A subsidiary undertaking may be excluded from consolidation if its inclusion is not material for the purpose of giving a true and fair view (but two or more undertakings may be excluded only if they are not material taken together).

- A subsidiary undertaking may be excluded from consolidation where:
  - severe long-term restrictions substantially hinder the exercise of the rights of the parent company over the assets or management of that undertaking
  - the information necessary for the preparation of group accounts cannot be obtained without disproportionate expense or undue delay
  - the interest of the parent company is held exclusively with a view to subsequent resale.

UK focus question – Stream

Stream is a medium sized company which has invested in several smaller companies. The draft profit after tax in the consolidated statements for the year ended 31 December 20X1 is $5m. However, advice is required about the following transactions:

(i) A new subsidiary was acquired on 1 January 20X1. Goodwill arising on the acquisition was $1m. The useful life of this goodwill cannot be reliably estimated. No amortisation has yet been charged.

(ii) During 20X1, Stream spent $500,000 on development activities. These activities are still ongoing as at 31 December 20X1. However, the Directors of Stream firmly believe that this development will lead to future economic benefits. Stream has adequate resources to complete the development. The cash spent to date has been recognised as an intangible asset.

(iii) On 1 January 20X1, Stream took out a $10m 6% bank loan to finance the construction of a new head office building. Construction commenced on 1 January 20X1 and was still ongoing at the year end. Interest on the loan for the year has been charged as an expense.

If a choice of accounting treatment exists, the Directors of Stream wish to select the policy that will maximise reported assets.

Required:

Calculate the revised consolidated profit after tax for the year ended 31 December 20X1 assuming that Stream prepares its accounts using:

(a) **IFRS for SME**

(b) **FRS 102**

Solution

	(a) IFRS for SME	(b) FRS 102
	$000	$000
Draft profit	5,000	5,000
Issue (i)	(100)	(200)
Issue (ii)	(500)	–
Issue (iii)	–	600
Revised profit	4,400	5,400

Explanations

(i) Under IFRS for SME, goodwill whose useful life cannot be reliably determined is amortised over a maximum of ten years. Assuming that the maximum useful life is selected, the annual amortisation charge is $100,000 ($1m/10 years).

Under FRS 102, goodwill whose useful life cannot be reliably determined is amortised over a maximum of five years. Assuming that the maximum useful life is selected, the annual amortisation charge is $200,000 ($1m/5 years).

(ii) According to IFRS for SME, expenditure on development activity must be recognised as an expense. Therefore, if accounting under IFRS for SME, the development asset currently recognised must be written off.

Expenditure on development can be capitalised under FRS 102 if relevant criteria are satisfied.

(iii) Borrowing costs must be expensed under IFRS for SME.

According to FRS 102, borrowing costs can be included within the cost of a qualifying asset. Therefore, if Stream accounted under FRS 102, it would be able to reverse out the interest expense of $600,000 ($10m × 6%) and instead recognise it as part of the cost of its property, plant and equipment.

UK focus question – Sofa

Sofa is a company that has a number of investments. Sofa exercises control over some of these investments and significant influence over others.

Required:

Advise the Directors of Sofa as to the key differences between IFRS for SME and FRS 102 that would impact the consolidated financial statements of the Sofa group. Where possible, discuss the potential impact that these differences would have on profit.

Solution

Under IFRS for SME, negative goodwill is recognised immediately in profit or loss. According to FRS 102, negative goodwill is recognised on the statement of financial position as a deduction against goodwill.

- If a company acquires 'negative goodwill', the treatment under IFRS for SME would lead to higher reported profits in the year of acquisition.

Under FRS 102, goodwill is amortised over its estimated useful life. If no reliable estimate of the useful life can be made, then the life must not exceed five years. If the useful life of goodwill cannot be reliably estimated under IFRS for SME, then it must not exceed ten years.

- Assuming that a company cannot reliably estimate the useful life of goodwill and opts for the maximum period available, profits will be lower under FRS 102.
- However, the carrying value of goodwill will be lower under FRS 102, leading to smaller goodwill impairments in the future.

Under FRS 102, an impairment loss recognised against goodwill can be reversed if the reasons for the impairment have ceased to exist. IFRS for SME prohibits the reversal of impairment losses recognised against goodwill.

- Goodwill impairment reversals could lead to higher reported profits under FRS 102 than under IFRS for SME.

Under FRS 102, the cost of an associate should include transaction costs. These are excluded from the cost of the investment under IFRS for SME and are instead written off to profit or loss.

- Under IFRS for SME, profits will be lower in the year when an associate is acquired than under FRS 102.
- The lower carrying value of the associate under IFRS for SME may mean that impairments are less likely in the future.

4 Entity reconstruction schemes

Key reason for an entity reconstruction

Financial difficulties

If an entity is in financial difficulty it may have no recourse but to accept liquidation as the final outcome. However it may be in a position to survive, and indeed flourish, by taking up some future contract or opportunities. The only hindrance to this may be that any future operations may need a prior cash injection. This cash injection cannot be raised because the present structure and status of the entity may not be attractive to current and outside investors.

A typical corporate profile of an entity in this situation could be as follows:

- Accumulated trading losses
- Arrears of unpaid debenture and loan interest
- No payment of equity dividends for several years
- Market value of equity shares below their nominal value
- Lack of investor and market confidence in the entity.

To get a cash injection the entity will need to undergo a reorganisation or reconstruction.

To consider how a reconstruction may help the entity to survive, the rights and interests of the various stakeholders need to be considered.

Entity stakeholders

The capital structure of a corporate entity is designed to protect its principal stakeholders – normally identified as equity holders and providers of finance. Any changes to this structure are therefore restricted by corporate law in most countries to protect these stakeholders. Some of the ways in which this is achieved are explained below.

An entity with accumulated losses is normally prevented from paying equity dividends, usually until the accumulated losses have been recovered by trading profitably, which could take several years, because of corporate law restrictions on distributions to shareholders. This situation will not make the entity an attractive proposition for prospective equity investors.

Non-payment of equity dividends add to the problem for the following reasons:

- Current equity holders will find it difficult to sell their shares for what they may consider to be a satisfactory price; any potential purchase of their shares is likely to be at a low value.
- Potential investors will not be attracted by the poor dividend payment history, and the fact that this situation is unlikely to improve in the foreseeable future.
- If the market price of equity shares is below their nominal value, a new issue of equity shares is unlikely to be successful as potential investors will seek to pay only market value for the shares. Many countries have corporate law which prevent equity capital being issued at less than its nominal value.

In summary, there is likely to be a lack of confidence in the entity to attract new investors, or to encourage existing investors to retain or increase their investment.

Providers of loan finance are primarily concerned with recovery of their capital and interest. The operational performance and profitability is of secondary importance provided that they can recoup their capital and interest. Existing or threatened arrears of debenture or bank interest are a negative factor when trying to raise finance for the following reasons:

- They tie up any future resources for interest and capital payments which could otherwise be used for expansion.
- They tie up any future profits which could be used for distribution in the form of a dividend.
- They make it difficult to obtain new loan finance as past arrears will make any attempt to raise new finance unattractive to the market.
- Existing providers of loan finance may also have the right to enforce recovery of funds from the entity, perhaps by having security (i.e. collateral) for their loans.
- There may be few, if any, assets available within the entity for use as security (i.e. collateral) to support any future raising of finance.

A reconstruction of the entity's capital may help to alleviate these problems and may involve one or more of the following procedures:

- Write off the accumulated losses.
- Write off arrears of repayment of loan finance
- Write down the nominal value of the equity capital.

How is this achieved?

To do this the entity must ask all or some of its existing stakeholders to surrender existing rights and amounts owing in exchange for new rights under a new or reformed entity.

Why would stakeholders be willing to do this?

The main reason is that a reconstruction may result in an outcome preferable to any other alternative as follows:

- Providers of loan finance and other creditors may be left with little or no prospect of repayment.
- Providers of equity finance may be left with little or no prospect of a return (dividends and capital growth) on their investment.
- Corporate liquidation may provide some return to providers of loan finance, but is unlikely to provide any return to equity holders, depending upon the financial position of the entity.

How could this be agreed between the various stakeholders?

It may be helpful to review the situation faced by each group of stakeholders as follows:

Equity shareholders –This is the last group to be allocated funds in a corporate liquidation, and therefore have a high chance of receiving no return at all. It would therefore seem appropriate that they should bear most of the losses from the present situation, in exchange for potential future benefits if the entity is profitable following reconstruction.

Trade creditors and payables may have some prospect of recovery of at least part of the amounts due to them as they rank ahead of equity holders for repayment upon corporate liquidation. Some trade creditors may also protect themselves from the risk of non-recovery by including the right to retain legal title or ownership of goods delivered to customers until they are paid for. In the event of non-recovery of amounts due to them, they will have the right to take repossession of their inventory.

Debenture holders often have a better chance of recovery of capital under liquidation than other stakeholders because such loans are often secured against entity assets. However, even in this situation, the full amount outstanding of such loans may not be recovered. In this case, any amount not recovered from the assets used as security (or collateral) would then normally be regarded as an unsecured creditor in the same way as trade payables.

There may be a situation where there is more than one debenture loan secured against entity assets. in this situation, the respective rights of each debenture holder would need to be examined to determine who would be paid off first in the event of there being insufficient assets to meet the claims of all secured loans. It could be, for example, that secured loans are paid off or settled in the order in which they were created; i.e. the oldest loans would be paid off first from available assets, then more recent loans would be paid off out of any available surplus.

It may therefore be in the best interests of all stakeholders to agree to a scheme of reconstruction. In effect, they give up existing rights and amounts owing (which are unlikely to be recovered) for the opportunity to share in the future profitability which may arise from the extra cash which can be generated as a consequence of their actions. This can only be achieved if all stakeholders are willing to compromise by waiving some or all of their existing rights, and if they can be convinced that there is an improved prospect of future returns as a result of a reconstruction scheme.

In examination questions, be alert to identify any information relating to the order in which liabilities are to be settled or paid off, and what happens to any amounts not paid due to inadequate security or collateral. This information should then be applied to ensure that liabilities are paid off in the correct order, having identified those liabilities secured by assets or collateral.

One additional factor is that there may be **professional fees** incurred as part of any reconstruction scheme. Carefully review the information in the question to determine whether:

- such creditors rank ahead of unsecured creditors for payment
- whether their fees are paid by any particular stakeholder group, depending upon who initiates the reconstruction scheme.

Capital reduction scheme

Using this scheme, an entity may:

- write off unpaid equity capital – this situation may arise, for example, if there are partly-paid shares in issue. The entity is effectively reducing the nominal value of its equity share capital by the amount not yet called up and paid by the equity holders. For example, partly paid equity shares with a nominal value of $1, may be reduced to the amount currently paid up, say, $0.75; in doing so, the equity holders will no longer be required to pay the amount still outstanding.
- write off any equity capital which is lost or not represented by available assets – in this situation, the entity has a deficit on retained earnings due to accumulated losses. This prevents payment of an equity dividend and also depresses the share price. In effect, the entity will write off this deficit against any other available components of equity to clear all or part of the deficit on retained earnings.
- write off any paid up equity capital which is in excess of requirements – in this situation, the entity uses surplus cash to repay its equity holders.

This scheme does not really affect creditors as the equity holders have reduced their capital stake in the entity, either by reducing the nominal value of the shares in issue, or by reducing the total number of shares in issue, or a combination of both.

This scheme is normally regulated by formalised procedures detailed in law, such as the Companies Act 2006 s641 in the United Kingdom, which may differ in other countries. In examination questions, it is unlikely that there will be questions set which require a specific and detailed knowledge of law from any particular jurisdiction. However, it is likely that students will be expected to have an understanding of the principles of when such a scheme may be appropriate and how it may be applied. It is also possible that a question could be set which provided the rules to apply in a given scenario.

Illustration – Struggler

Struggler has the following statement of financial position at 30 June 20X8:

	$000
Assets	500
	500

	$000
Equity and liabilities:	
Issued equity shares ($1 each)	600
Share premium	100
Retained earnings/(deficit)	(300)
Liabilities	100
	500

Struggler has the following problems:

- Accumulated losses which prevent payment of a dividend should the entity become profitable at some future date.
- Issued equity capital of $600,000 which is only backed by assets to the extent of $500,000.
- Difficulty in attracting new sources of equity and loan finance.

Required:

Apply a capital reduction scheme and restate the statement of financial position at 30 June 20X8.

Solution

Using the reduction of capital scheme, the deficit on retained earnings could be cleared by reducing both the share premium and issued equity capital accounts. Any balance on share premium account should be utilised first to minimise the reduction of equity capital as follows:

	$000	$000
Dr Share premium	100	
Dr Equity share capital	200	
Cr Retained earnings		300

The resulting statement of financial position would be:

	$000
Assets	500
	500

Equity and liabilities:	$000
Issued equity shares	400
Share premium	nil
Retained earnings/(deficit)	nil
Liabilities	100
	500

The equity holders have effectively recognised the financial reality of their situation by reducing the nominal value of the issued share capital. If the entity begins to make profits following the reconstruction, there is no longer a deficit on retained earnings to clear before a dividend can be paid. Potential equity and/or loan finance providers may also be encouraged by this situation.

The reduction in equity capital could be reflected by either a reduction in the nominal value per share (from $1 down to approximately (400/600) $0.67, or by converting and reducing shareholdings on a pro-rata basis. For example, if a person previously owned thirty shares with a nominal value of $1 each, following conversion and reduction, they would now own only twenty shares with a nominal value of $1 each. In either situation, the total equity share capital would be $400,000.

5 Reconstruction schemes

Reconstruction schemes extend the principles of the capital reduction schemes by including the various creditors within the scheme. In addition to reducing equity share capital, reconstruction schemes may also include:

- writing off debenture loan interest arrears
- replacement of debenture loans with new loans having different interest and capital repayment terms
- write off amounts owing to unsecured or trade payables.

Equity holders and creditors may be willing to do this if the entity is considered likely to survive and return to profitable trading in the future. They are effectively sacrificing their current legal and commercial rights for future legal and commercial rights which will hopefully bring them better financial returns than under their current position. Such reconstruction schemes may be subject to court or law-based formal approval procedures before they can be implemented.

In practical terms, this can only be achieved if all stakeholders agree to forego some of their current legal and commercial rights. For those in the weakest position, usually the equity holders, they would be expected to sacrifice more than others, such as secured debenture loan providers. Secured debenture loan providers could act in their own interest and enforce possession of the assets provided as security (i.e. collateral), but this would often be to the detriment of other stakeholders and could lead to the liquidation of the entity if it can no longer operate. Consequently, due to their stronger position, secured loan providers will be reluctant to sacrifice as much as the equity holders in any reconstruction scheme.

In the United Kingdom, these schemes are governed by the Companies Act 2006 s895. As with the capital reduction scheme considered earlier, it is unlikely that an examination question will be set which requires a detailed knowledge of specific law from any one jurisdiction. However, questions may be set on the application of the principles, possibly including rules to apply in a given situation.

Illustration 1 – Machin

Consider the statement of financial position of Machin at 30 June 20X9:

	$000
Non-current assets:	
Intangible – brand	50,000
Tangible	220,000
	270,000
Current assets:	
Inventory	20,000
Receivables	30,000
	320,000
Equity and liabilities:	$000
Equity share capital @ $1 shares	100,000
Share premium	75,000
Retained earnings	(100,000)
	75,000
Non-current liabilities: Debenture loan	125,000
Current liabilities:	
Bank overdraft	20,000
Trade payables	100,000
	320,000

The following reconstruction scheme is to be applied:

(1) The equity shares of $1 nominal value currently in issue will be written off and will be replaced on a one-for-one basis by new equity shares with a nominal value of $0.25.

(2) The debenture loan will be replaced by the issue of new equity shares – four new equity shares with a nominal value of $0.25 each for every $1 of debenture loan converted.

(3) Existing equity holders will be offered the opportunity to subscribe for three new equity shares with a nominal value of $0.25 each for every one equity share currently held. The shares are to be issued at nominal value. It is expected that all current equity holders will take up this opportunity.

(4) The share premium account is to be eliminated.

(5) The brand is considered to be impaired and must be written off.

(6) Retained earnings deficit is to be eliminated

Required:

Prepare the statement of financial position of Machin immediately after the scheme has been put into effect. Show any workings required to arrive at the solution.

Solution

Begin by opening a reconstruction account:

All adjustments to the statement of financial position as a result of the reconstruction scheme must be accounted for within this account. Any balance remaining on this account will be used to either write down assets or create a capital reserve.

Reconstruction account

	$000		$000
New equity shares (100,000 × $0.25) (Note 1)	25,000	Equity shares @ $1 (Note 1)	100,000
New equity shares (125,000 × 4 × $0.25) (Note 2)	125,000	Debenture loan (Note 2)	125,000
Brand impaired (Note 5)	50,000	Share premium (Note 4)	75,000
Retained earnings (Note 6)	100,000		
	300,000		300,000

The note references refer to the details of the reconstruction scheme.

The debenture holders may be prepared to sacrifice their rights as a creditor if they believe that Machin will trade profitably following the reconstruction scheme. They will forego the rights of a creditor in exchange for the rights of an equity holder – i.e. future dividends plus growth in the capital value of their equity shares.

The resulting statement of financial position for Machin will be:

	$000
Non-current assets:	
Intangible – brand	nil
Tangible	220,000
Current assets:	
Inventory	20,000
Receivables	30,000
Bank ((20,000) + 75,000) (Note 3)	55,000
	325,000
Share capital (W1)	225,000
Share premium	nil
Retained earnings	nil
	225,000
Non-current liabilities: Debenture loan	nil
Current liabilities:	
Bank overdraft (eliminated by cash receipt from share issue)	nil
Trade payables	100,000
	325,000

(W1) **Confirmation of equity share capital following reorganisation:**

		No
Note 1	Issue of one new equity share for one old equity share	100,000
Note 2	Convert debenture loan into new equity shares: 125,000 x 4	500,000
Note 3	Issue of new equity shares for cash	300,000
		900,000

Share capital is therefore $225,000 (900,000 × $0.25).

e.g

Illustration – Bentham

Bentham has been making losses for several years, principally due to severe competition, which has put downward pressure on revenues whilst costs have increased.

The statement of financial position for Bentham at 30 June 20X1 is as follows:

	$000
Non-current assets	7,200
Current assets	10,550
	17,750
Equity and liabilities	$000
Equity share capital ($1 shares)	20,000
Retained earnings (deficit)	(17,250)
	2,750
Non-current liabilities:	
11% debentures 20X3 (secured)	7,000
8% debentures 20X4 (secured)	5,000
Current liabilities	3,000
	17,750

The entity has changed its marketing strategy and, as a result, it is expected that annual profit before interest and tax will be $3,000,000 for the next five years. Bentham incurs tax at 25% on profit before tax.

The directors are proposing to reconstruct Bentham and have produced the following proposal for discussion:

(1) The existing $1 equity shares are to be cancelled and replaced by equity shares of $0.25.

(2) The 8% debentures are to be replaced by 8,000,000 equity shares of $0.25 each, regarded as fully paid up, plus $3,000,000 6% debentures 20X9.

(3) Existing shareholders will have their $1 equity shares replaced by 11,000,000 $0.25 equity shares, regarded as fully paid up.

(4) The 11% debentures are to be redeemed in exchange for:

- for:$6,000,000 6% debentures 20X9, and
- 4,000,000 equity shares of $0.25, regarded as fully paid up.

In the event of a liquidation, it is estimated that the net realisable value of the assets would be $6,200,000 for the non-current assets and $10,000,000 for the current assets.

Required:

- **Prepare a statement of financial position for Bentham at 1 July 20X1, immediately after the reconstruction scheme has been implemented.**
- **Prepare computations to show the effect of the proposed reconstruction scheme on each of the equity shareholders, 11% debenture holders and 8% debenture holders.**
- **Comment on the potential outcome of the scheme from the perspective of a shareholder who currently owns 10% of the equity share capital on whether to agree to the reconstruction scheme as proposed.**

Solution

Bentham – the revised statement of financial position at 1 July 20X1 following reconstruction would be:

	$000
Non-current assets	7,200
Current assets	10,550
	17,750

	$000
Equity and liabilities:	
Equity share capital (23 million shares × $0.25)(W1)	5,750
Retained earnings	nil
	5,750
Non-current liabilities:	
6% debentures 20X9 (W1)	9,000
Current liabilities	3,000
	17,750

(W1) The reconstruction account would be as follows:

Reconstruction account

	$000		$000
New 6% debentures	6,000	11% Debentures redeemed	7,000
New equity shares: 4m × $0.25	1,000	8% Debenture redeemed	5,000
New equity shares: 11m × $0.25	2,750	Equity cancelled	20,000
New equity shares: 8m × $0.25	2,000		
New 6% debentures	3,000		
Deficit on retained earnings	17,250		
	32,000		32,000

If Bentham was to be put into liquidation, rather than undergo the reconstruction, the following could be the consequence:

	$000
Net realisable value of non-current assets	6,200
Net realisable value of current assets	10,000
	16,200
Repayment of 11% secured debenture loan	(7,000)
Repayment of 8% secured debenture loan	(5,000)
Available for unsecured creditors	4,200
Unsecured creditors	(3,000)
Available for equity holders	1,200

It can be seen that, whilst secured creditors will be paid off, and there should then be sufficient assets available for payment of unsecured creditors, equity shareholders would not fully recover the nominal value of their shareholding. The equity holders would receive only (1,200 / 20,000) $0.06 for each $1 equity share held. Note that this does not include any legal and professional fees that may be payable to implement such a scheme.

If the scheme is implemented, the debenture holders would forego part of their prior claim for repayment in exchange for equity shares. If they are to agree to this, they must be satisfied regarding the reliability of the profit forecast for future trading, so that they can receive future dividends and enjoy capital growth on the value of their shares. Additionally, they will have a significant equity holding of 12 million out of 23 million equity shares. This is just enough to give them a majority of the equity capital; they could then use their voting power to appoint or remove directors as they see appropriate.

If the reconstruction scheme is implemented, the revised capital structure results in significantly more equity shares in issue, with reduced long term liabilities in the form of secured debenture loans. It can be seen that the current debenture loan holders have deferred the repayment date of their loans from 20X3 and 20X4 respectively to 20X9, and accepted a reduced rate of interest on their loans. In addition, they have received some equity shares which will give them the opportunity to share in the future prosperity of Bentham if it becomes profitable following the reconstruction.

From the perspective of someone who holds 10% of the equity before the reconstruction takes place, the following comments can be made:

- The gearing ratio has reduced as follows:

Before:	$000		After:	$000	
Gearing ratio	12,000 / 14,750	= 81.3%		9,000 / 14,750	= 61.0%

The reduction in gearing will be regarded as a decrease in financial risk for the equity holders.

- If the forecast regarding expected profit before interest and tax is reliable, then the following will result:

		$000
Profit before interest and tax		3,000
Less: debenture interest	9,000 × 6%	540
Profit before tax		2,460
Tax (× 25%)		(615)
Profit after tax available to equity holders		1,845

Potentially, there are retained profits available for payment of an equity dividend. Whilst it may not be advisable to distribute all profit after tax in the form of a dividend, it is a positive step to have retained earnings within the entity. Additionally, interest cover of (3,000/540) 5.5 may be regarded as reasonable in the circumstances.

- One further factor is the change in proportionate voting power if the reconstruction scheme is implemented. Previously, someone who owned 10% of the equity share capital would have 10% × 11 million = 1.1 million equity shares in the restructured entity out of 23 million equity shares – i.e. 4.7% of the equity shares. This is a significant dilution of voting power, but it may be a reasonable thing to give up in exchange for the future prospect of the continuation of Bentham, together with the potential receipt of a dividend if the forecast is realistic.

Test your understanding 1 – Wire

Wire has suffered from poor trading conditions over the last three years. Its statement of financial position at 30 June 20X1 is as follows:

	$	$
Non-current assets:		
Land and buildings		193,246
Plant and equipment		60,754
Investment in Cord		27,000
		281,000
Current assets:		
Inventory	120,247	
Receivables	70,692	
		190,939
		471,939
Equity and liabilities:		$
Equity shares ($1)		200,000
Retained earnings (deficit)		(39,821)
		160,179
Non-current liabilities:		
8% debenture 20X4	80,000	
5% debenture 20X5	70,000	
		150,000
Current liabilities:		
Trade payables	112,247	
Interest payable	12,800	
Overdraft	36,713	
		161,760
		471,939

It has been difficult to generate revenues and profits in the current year and inventory levels are very high. Interest has not been paid to the debenture holders for two years. Although the debentures are secured against the land and buildings, the debenture holders have demanded either a scheme of reconstruction or the liquidation of Wire.

During a meeting of directors and representatives of the shareholders and debenture holders, it was decided to implement a scheme of reconstruction.

The following scheme has been agreed in principle:

(1) Each $1 equity share is to be redesignated as an equity share of $0.25.

(2) The existing 5% debenture is to be exchanged for a new issue of $35,000 9.5% loan stock, repayable in 20X9, plus 140,000 equity shares of $0.25 each. In addition, they will subscribe for $9,000 debenture stock, repayable 20X9, at par value. The rate of interest on this new debenture is 9.5%.

(3) The equity shareholders are to accept a reduction in the nominal value of their shares from $1 to $0.25 per share, and subscribe for a new issue on the basis of one-for-one at a price of $0.30 per share.

(4) The 8% debenture holders, who have received no interest for two years, are to receive 20,000 equity shares of $0.25 each in lieu of the interest payable. It is agreed that the value of the interest liability is equivalent to the fair value of the shares to be issued. In addition, they have agreed to defer repayment of their loan until 20X9, subject to an increased rate of interest of 9.5%.

(5) The deficit on retained earnings is to be written off.

(6) The investment in Cord has been subject to much speculation as Cord has just obtained the legal rights to a new production process. As a result, the value of the investment has increased to $60,000. This investment is to be sold as part of the reconstruction scheme.

(7) The bank overdraft is to be repaid.

(8) 10% of the receivables are regarded as non-recoverable and are to be written off.

(9) The remaining assets were independently valued, and should now be recognised at the following amounts:

	$
Land	80,000
Buildings	80,000
Equipment	30,000
Inventory	50,000

If the reconstruction goes ahead, the following is expected to happen:

(1) It is expected that, due to the refinancing, operating profits will be earned at the rate of $50,000 after depreciation, but before interest and tax.

(2) Wire will be subject to tax on its profit before tax at 25%.

Required:

- **Prepare the statement of financial position of Wire immediately after the reconstruction**
- **Advise the equity holders and debenture holders whether or not they should support the reconstruction scheme.**

6 External reconstructions

Such schemes normally involve the assets and liabilities of the current entity being transferred to a new entity on an agreed basis. Typically, this will require information regarding the following:

- details of purchase consideration to acquire the business as a whole, or specified assets and liabilities – this may give rise to goodwill for the purchaser.
- details of what will happen to assets and liabilities currently belonging to the entity which are to be sold, transferred, written off or realised as appropriate – this will lead to a profit or loss on realisation for the vendor.
- how repayment or settlement of capital of the selling entity is to be arranged.

Test your understanding 2 – Smith and Thompson

Smith has agreed to acquire the net assets, excluding the bank balance, and the debenture liability which is to be paid off in cash, of Thompson. The purchase consideration comprises the following:

	$000
50,000 $1 equity shares at a fair value of $1.04	52,000
$30,000 debenture loan issued at par value	30,000
Cash	18,000
	100,000

When determining the consideration to be paid, the directors of Smith valued the land and buildings of Thompson at $40,000, inventory at $15,000 and receivables at carrying value, subject to a 3% write off for bad debts.

After the sale, Thompson is liquidated.

The statement of financial position of Thompson immediately before the acquisition is as follows:

	$
Non-current assets:	
Land and buildings	24,000
Plant and machinery	22,000
	46,000
Current assets:	
Inventory	19,000
Receivables	20,000
Bank	5,000
	90,000

	$
Equity and liabilities:	
Equity shares ($1)	30,000
Share premium	10,000
Retained earnings	16,000
	56,000
Non-current liabilities:	
6% debentures	20,000
Current liabilities:	
Trade payables	14,000
	90,000

Required:

- **Prepare the closing entries for Thompson**
- **Prepare the opening statement of financial position for Smith**

Reconstructions and UK law

Capital reduction scheme

Formalised procedures (s641 Companies Act 2006) are detailed in law if a company wishes to reduce either the number of shares in issue, or the nominal value per share in issue:

- A public company requires a special resolution to be passed by its members which is then supported by the court.
- A private company requires a special resolution to be passed by its members, together with a solvency statement provided by all of the directors. .

Administration

Administration involves the appointment of an insolvency practitioner, known as an administrator, to manage the affairs, business and property of a company. It was first introduced by Schedule 16 IA 1986, but has subsequently been amended by the Enterprise Act 2002. An administration may be used in order to:

- rescue a company in financial difficulty with the aim of allowing it to continue as a going concern, or
- achieve a better result for the creditors than would be likely if the company were to be wound up, or
- realise property to pay one or more secured or preferential creditors.

An administrator can be appointed by any of the following persons:

- the court, in response to a petition by, e.g. a creditor, the directors or the company itself, or
- the holder of a qualifying floating charge over the company's assets, or
- the company or its directors provided that winding up has not already begun.

Liquidation

This is the winding up of a limited company to bring its existence to an end. It may be a:

- **Compulsory liquidation** (s122 Insolvency Act 1986) whereby a petition is presented to the court, and a winding up order is granted. The most frequently used grounds for use of these proceedings is where a judgement debt of £750 or more is unpaid after more than three weeks, or where the court considers that it is 'just and equitable' to wind up the company. A liquidator will be appointed to realise the assets and distribute then in accordance with the respective claims of the various classes of creditor, and also to the members if there is any surplus.
- **Voluntary liquidation**, which identifies that the members have passed a special resolution to wind up the company. This can be done for any reason, but may reflect that the company is expecting to encounter financial difficulties. In principle, a liquidator is appointed who then realises and distributes the assets based upon the respective rights of the different creditors, with the ordinary shareholders taking any surplus thereafter. There are two types of voluntary liquidation:
  - **a members' voluntary liquidation.** In this case, a declaration of solvency must be made by the directors (s89 insolvency Act 1986). A liquidator will then be appointed by the members (s91 Insolvency Act 1986). In principle, as creditors will be paid in full, they have no rights in respect of this process, other than being paid what is due to them.
  - **a creditors' voluntary liquidation**. In this case, the directors are unable to provide a declaration of solvency. A meeting of creditors will follow that of the members. Due to the risk that they will not be paid in full, the creditors' choice of a liquidator prevails over that of the members (s100 Insolvency Act 1986).

7 Chapter summary

Reporting not-for-profit entities

- These entities are in the public sector or are charities
- The objective of these entities is to achieve their aims, not to make a profit
- Guidance is provided in SORP 2005 and the ASB's Statement of Principles for public benefit entities

Small and medium-sized entities

- These entities need exemptions from some of the requirements of IFRSs
- Two possible solutions: exemption or differential reporting

Entity reconstruction

- Going concern issues
- Possible alternative to liquidation
- Accounting treatment

Test your understanding answers

Test your understanding 1 – Wire

Wire – statement of financial position at 30 June 20X1 (after reconstruction)

	$
Non-current assets:	
Land and buildings at valuation	160,000
Equipment	30,000
Financial asset – investment in Cord	nil
	190,000
Current assets:	
Inventory	50,000
Receivables (70,692 × 90%)	63,623
Bank (W2)	92,287
	395,910

Equity and liabilities:	$
Equity shares ($0.25 each) (W3)	140,000
Share premium (W3)	17,800
Retained earnings	nil
Capital reserve (W1)	1,863
	159,663
Non-current liabilities:	
9.5% debentures (W4)	124,000
Current liabilities:	
Trade payables	112,247
	395,910

Wire – workings:

(W1) **Reconstruction account**

	$	$
Carrying values:		
Land and buildings	193,246	
Equipment	60,754	
Investment in Cord	27,000	
Inventory	120,247	
Receivables written off (70,962 × 10%)	7,069	
Deficit on retained earnings written off	39,821	
Revised valuations:		
Land and buildings		160,000
Equipment		30,000
Investment in Cord		60,000
Inventory		50,000
Share capital reduced (200,000 @ $0.75)		150,000
Capital reserve (bal fig)	1,863	
	450,000	450,000

(W2) **Bank account**

		$
Overdraft		(36,713)
New equity share issue	200,000 × $0.30	60,000
New debenture issue	9,000 at par value	9,000
Sale of investment – Cord		60,000
		92,287

(W3) **Shareholdings**

	Equity shares		Share premium
	Number	$	$
Redesignated existing shares ($0.25 each)	200,000	50,000	
New issue ($0.30 each)	200,000	50,000	10,000
Part-exchange of 5% debenture	140,000	35,000	
Debenture interest (12,800 – 5,000)**	20,000	5.000	7,800
	560,000	140,000	17,800

**8% deb interest on $80,000 p.a. for 2 years = $12,800 – $5,000 (20,000 × $0.25) = $7,800 share premium.

(W4) **Debenture loan**

	$
8% debenture 20X4 deferred to 20X9 with 9.5% interest rate	80,000
New 9.5% debentures 20X9 – nominal value	9,000
New 9.5% debentures 20X9 – part conversion of 5% debenture	35,000
	124,000

Advice to equity and debt holders:

Based upon the situation at 30 June 20X1 before the reconstruction scheme was devised, the following can be ascertained:

(1) There are sufficient assets to repay the secured debentures and perhaps most of the arrears of interest.

(2) Unsecured creditors would be unlikely to receive payment in full for amounts owed.

(3) Equity shareholders are unlikely to receive anything upon liquidation.

If a reconstruction scheme is to be agreed between the various parties, those who are in the strongest position (secured creditors) would expect to give up the least. Those in the weakest position (unsecured creditors and equity holders), would be expected to sacrifice more of their current entitlement to have any chance of recovery in the future.

The position of Wire if it was to go into liquidation is as follows:

		$
Land and buildings		160,000
Plant and equipment		30,000
Investment		60,000
Inventory		50,000
Receivables (70,962 × 90%)		63,623
Assets available		363,263
Secured liabilities (80,000 + 70,000)		(150,000)
		213,623
Current liabilities:		
Overdraft	36,713	
Interest	12,800	
Trade payables	112,247	
		(161,760)
Available to equity holders		51,863

The above summary identifies the position of the various stakeholders if there was no reconstruction scheme and Wire was liquidated. The debenture holders would be sure to receive their loan repayment, together with probably all of the arrears of interest, depending upon realised values of the assets and no other significant liabilities being uncovered.

The equity holders would not receive a full return of the nominal value of their capital, receiving only approximately (51,863/200,000) $0.26 per share.

Consequently, if the reconstruction scheme is implemented:

(1) The debenture holders are to be offered an increased rate of interest, but must also accept extension of the lending period to 20X9. It continues to be secured against land and buildings. Their position is relatively strong and safe.

(2) Some of the debenture holders have exchanged some of their legal rights as creditors for rights as equity holders. They must hope that Wire becomes profitable so that they can receive dividends in future years and that the share price increases. In addition, they must hope that, even if Wire gets into financial difficulties at a later date, there are still sufficient assets available to repay them, after the secured creditors have been repaid.

(3) It would appear that Wire will make profit after tax if the reconstruction goes ahead. If the profit forecast is reliable, this will be as follows:

	$
Profit before tax and interest	50,000
Less: debenture interest (9.5% × $124,000)	11,780
Profit before tax	38,220
Tax (× 25%)	(9,555)
Profit available to equity holders	28,665

Earnings per share would therefore be: $28,665/560,000 = 5.1 cents per share (i.e $0.051 per share).

Test your understanding 2 – Smith and Thompson

Closing accounting for Thompson

(W1) **Realisation account**

	$	$
Carrying values:		
Land and buildings	24,000	
Plant and equipment	22,000	
Inventory	19,000	
Receivables	20,000	
Creditors		14,000
Purchase consideration		100,000
Profit on realisation (bal fig) (W3)	29,000	
	114,000	114,000

(W2) **Bank and cash**

	$	$
Balance b/fwd	5,000	
Cash received for sale of business	18,000	
Debenture stock paid off		20,000
Cash to shareholders as part of winding up (W3)		3,000
	23,000	23,000

(W3) **Capital settlement on winding up**

	$	$
Equity shares received at FV	52,000	
Debenture received	30,000	
Cash return to equity holders (W2)	3,000	
Share capital		30,000
Share premium		10,000
Retained earnings		16,000
Profit on realisation (W1)		29,000
	85,000	85,000

(W4) **Receivable Account – Smith**

	$	$
Purchase consideration due		
Equity shares	100,000	
Shares at FV		52,000
Debenture loan		30,000
Cash		18,000
	100,000	100,000

Smith – Statement of Financial Position

Assets	$
Goodwill*	17,600
Land and buildings	40,000
Plant and equipment	22,000
	79,600
Current assets:	
Inventory	15,000
Receivables	19,400
	114,000

Equity and liabilities	$
Equity share capital ($1)**	50,000
Share premium**	2,000
Non-current liabilities: Debenture loan	30,000
Current liabilities:	
Trade payables	14,000
Bank overdraft	18,000
	114,000

Notes:

* Goodwill is the difference between the consideration paid and the net assets acquired:.

	$	$
Consideration		100,000
Land and buildings	40,000	
Plant and equipment	22,000	
Inventory	15,000	
Receivables ($20,000 × 97%)	19,400	
Trade payables	(14,000)	
		(82,400)
Goodwill		17,600

** The fair value of equity shares issued is $52,000 (50,000 × $1.04).

Of this the nominal value will be $50,000 (50,000 × $1) giving rise to a share premium of $2,000 (50,000 × ($1.04 – $1)).

chapter

22

Non-financial reporting

Chapter learning objectives

Upon completion of this chapter you will be able to:

- discuss the increased demand for transparency in corporate reports, and the emergence of non-financial reporting standards
- discuss why entities might include disclosures relating to the environment and society
- appraise the impact of environmental, social and ethical factors on performance measurement
- evaluate current reporting requirements in the areas of environmental and social reporting, including the development of integrated reporting
- discuss the progress towards a framework for integrated reporting.

Non-financial reporting

Non-financial information, in the form of additional information provided alongside the financial information in the annual report, has become more important in recent years.

While financial information remains important, stakeholders are interested in other aspects of an entity's performance. For example:

- how the business is managed
- its future prospects
- the entity's policy on the environment
- its attitude towards social responsibility.

Although these activities do have an impact upon financial position and performance, some users of financial statements may have a particular interest in these activities. For example, potential shareholders may be attracted to invest in a particular entity (or not), based upon their environmental or social policies, in addition to their financial performance. Regulators or consumer pressure groups may also have a particular interest in such policies and disclosures to manage their activities or monitor the effectiveness of their activities.

Additional reports and disclosures go some way towards providing transparency for evaluation of entity financial performance, position and strategy. Transparency fosters confidence in the information which is made available to investors and other stakeholders who may be interested in both financial and non-financial information.

Management Commentary

Purpose of the Management Commentary (MC)

The IFRS Practice Statement (PS) Management Commentary provides a broad, non-binding framework for the presentation of management commentary that relates to financial statements that have been prepared in accordance with International Financial Reporting Standards (IFRSs)

It is a narrative report that provides a context within which to interpret the financial position, financial performance and cash flows of an entity. Management are able to explain its objectives and its strategies for achieving those objectives.

This PS helps management to provide useful commentary to financial statements prepared in accordance with IFRS information. The users are identified as existing and potential members, together with lenders and creditors.

Framework for presentation of management commentary

The purpose of a management commentary is:

- to provide management's view of the entity's performance, position and progress, the reasons for this, and the implications for the future
- to supplement and complement information presented in the financial statements, and
- to explain the main trends and factors that will influence future performance, position and progress.

Consequently, the MC should include information which is forward-looking and adheres to the qualitative characteristics of information as described in the Conceptual Framework for Financial Reporting.

This type of commentary will help users of the financial reports to understand risk exposures and strategies of the entity, relevant non-financial factors and other issues not otherwise included within the financial statements.

Elements of management commentary

Although the particular focus of management commentary will depend on the facts and circumstances of the entity, management commentary should include information that is essential to an understanding of:

- the nature of the business
- management's objectives and its strategies for meeting those objectives
- the entity's most significant resources, risks and relationships
- the results of operations and prospects, and
- the critical performance measures and indicators that management uses to evaluate the entity's performance against stated objectives.

It can be adopted by entities, where applicable, any time from the date of publication in December 2010.

Environmental reporting

Environmental reporting is the disclosure of information in the published annual report or elsewhere, of the effect that the operations of the business have on the natural environment.

Environmental reporting in practice

There are two main vehicles that companies use to publish information about the ways in which they interact with the natural environment:

(a) The published annual report (which includes the financial statements)

(b) A separate environment report (either as a paper document or simply posted on the company website).

The IASB encourages the presentation of environmental reports if management believe that they will assist users in making economic decisions, but they are not mandatory.

IAS 1 points out that any statement or report presented outside financial statements is outside the scope of IFRSs, so there are no mandatory IFRS requirements on separate environmental reports.

The content of environment reports

The content of an environment report may cover the following areas.

(a) **Environmental issues pertinent to the entity and industry**

- The entity's policy towards the environment and any improvements made since first adopting the policy.
- Whether the entity has a formal system for managing environmental risks.
- The identity of the director(s) responsible for environmental issues.
- The entity's perception of the risks to the environment from its operations.
- The extent to which the entity would be capable of responding to a major environmental disaster and an estimate of the full economic consequences of such a future major disaster.
- The effects of, and the entity's response to, any government legislation on environmental matters.
- Details of any significant infringement of environmental legislation or regulations.
- Material environmental legal issues in which the entity is involved.
- Details of any significant initiatives taken, if possible linked to amounts in financial statements.
- Details of key indicators (if any) used by the entity to measure environmental performance. Actual performance should be compared with targets and with performance in prior periods.

(b) **Financial information**

- The entity's accounting policies relating to environmental costs, provisions and contingencies.
- The amount charged to profit or loss during the accounting period in respect of expenditure to prevent or rectify damage to the environment caused by the entity's operations. This could be analysed between expenditure that the entity was legally obliged to incur and other expenditure.
- The amount charged to profit or loss during the accounting period in respect of expenditure to protect employees and society in general from the consequences of damage to the environment caused by the entity's operations. Again, this could be analysed between compulsory and voluntary expenditure.

- Details (including amounts) of any provisions or contingent liabilities relating to environmental matters.
- The amount of environmental expenditure capitalised during the year.
- Details of fines, penalties and compensation paid during the accounting period in respect of non-compliance with environmental regulations.

Accounting treatment of environmental costs

Environmental costs are treated in accordance with the requirements of current accounting standards.

(a) Most expenditure is charged to profit or loss in the period in which it is incurred. Material items may need to be disclosed separately in the notes to the accounts or on the face of the statement of profit or loss and other comprehensive income as required by IAS 1.

(b) Entities may have to undertake fundamental reorganisations or restructuring or to discontinue particular activities in order to protect the environment. If a sale or termination meets the definition of a discontinued operation, its results must be separately disclosed in accordance with the requirements of IFRS 5. Material restructuring costs may need to be separately disclosed on the face of the statement of profit or loss and other comprehensive income.

(c) Fines and penalties for non-compliance with regulations are charged to profit or loss in the period in which they are incurred. This applies even if the activities that resulted in the penalties took place in an earlier accounting period, as they cannot be treated retrospectively as prior period adjustments.

(d) Expenditure on non-current assets is capitalised and depreciated in the usual way as per IAS 16 Property, plant and equipment. Any government grants received for expenditure that protects the environment are treated in accordance with IAS 20 Accounting for government grants and disclosure of government assistance.

(e) Non-current assets (including goodwill) may become impaired as a result of environmental legislation or new regulations. IAS 36 Impairment of assets lists events that could trigger an impairment review, one of which is a significant adverse change in the legal environment in which the business operates.

(f) Research and development expenditure in respect of environmentally friendly products, processes or services is covered by IAS 38 Intangible assets.

(g) The fact that the entity's activities have caused environmental contamination does not in itself give rise to an obligation to rectify the damage. However, even if there is no legal obligation, there may be a constructive obligation. An entity almost certainly has a constructive obligation to rectify environmental damage if it has a policy of acting in an environmentally responsible way and this policy is well publicised. If this obligation will lead to a probably outflow of economic benefits that can be measured reliably, then a provision should be recognised in accordance with IAS 37,

Test your understanding 1 – Two transactions

You are the chief accountant of Redstart and you are currently finalising the financial statements for the year ended 31 December 20X1. Your assistant (who has prepared the draft accounts) is unsure about the treatment of two transactions that have taken place during the year. She has written you a memorandum that explains the key principles of each transaction and also the treatment adopted in the draft accounts.

Transaction one

One of the corporate objectives of the enterprise is to ensure that its activities are conducted in such a way as to minimise any damage to the natural environment. It is committed in principle to spending extra money in pursuit of this objective but has not yet made any firm proposals. The directors believe that this objective will prove very popular with customers and are anxious to emphasise their environmentally friendly policies in the annual report.

Your assistant suggests that a sum should be set aside from profits each year to create a provision in the financial statements against the possible future costs of environmental protection. Accordingly, she has charged profit or loss for the year ended 31 December 20X1 with a sum of $100,000 and proposes to disclose this fact in a note to the accounts.

Transaction two

A new law has recently been enacted that will require Redstart to change one of its production processes in order to reduce the amount of carbon dioxide that is emitted. This will involve purchasing and installing some new plant that is more efficient than the equipment currently in use. To comply with the law, the new plant must be operational by 31 December 20X2. The new plant has not yet been purchased.

In the draft financial statements for the year ended 31 December 20X1, your assistant has recognised a provision for $5 million (the cost of the new plant). This has been disclosed as a separate item in the notes to the statement of profit or loss for the year.

The memorandum from your assistant also expresses concern about the fact that there was no reference to environmental matters anywhere in the published financial statements for the year ended 31 December 20X0. As a result, she believes that the financial statements did not comply with the requirements of International Financial Reporting Standards and therefore must have been wrong.

Required:

Draft a reply to your assistant that:

(a) **reviews the treatment suggested by your assistant and recommends changes where relevant. In each case your reply should refer to relevant International Accounting Standards**

(b) **replies to her suggestion that the financial statements for the year ended 31 December 20X0 were wrong because they made no reference to environmental matters.**

Social reporting

Corporate social reporting is the process of communicating the social and environmental effects of organisations' economic actions to particular interest groups within society and to society at large.

Social responsibility

A business interacts with society in several different ways as follows.

- It employs human resources in the form of management and other employees.
- Its activities affect society as a whole, for example, it may:
  - be the reason for a particular community's existence
  - produce goods that are helpful or harmful to particular members of society
  - damage the environment in ways that harm society as a whole
  - undertake charitable works in the community or promote particular values.

If a business interacts with society in a responsible manner, the needs of other stakeholders should be taken into account and performance may encompass:

- providing fair remuneration and an acceptable working environment

- paying suppliers promptly
- minimising the damage to the environment caused by the entity's activities
- contributing to the community by providing employment or by other means.

Reasons for social reporting

There are a number of reasons why entities publish social reports:

(a) They may have deliberately built their reputation on social responsibility (e.g. Body Shop) in order to attract a particular customer base.

(b) They may perceive themselves as being under particular pressure to prove that their activities do not exploit society as a whole or certain sections of it (e.g. Shell International and large utility companies).

(c) They may be genuinely convinced that it is in their long-term interests to balance the needs of the various stakeholder groups.

(d) They may fear that the government will eventually require them to publish socially oriented information if they do not do so voluntarily.

Test your understanding 2 – Social and environmental

(a) **Explain why companies may wish to make social and environmental disclosures in their annual report. Discuss how this content should be determined.**

(b) Company B owns a chemical plant, producing paint. The plant uses a great deal of energy and releases emissions into the environment. Its by-product is harmful and is treated before being safely disposed of. The company has been fined for damaging the environment following a spillage of the toxic waste product. Due to stricter monitoring routines set up by the company, the fines have reduced and in the current year they have not been in breach of any local environment laws.

The company, is aware that emissions are high and has been steadily reducing them. They purchase electricity from renewable sources and in the current year have employed a temporary consultant to calculate their carbon footprint so they can take steps to reduce it.

Discuss the information that could be included in Company B's environmental report.

Sustainability

Sustainability is the process of conducting business in such a way that it enables an entity to meet its present needs without compromising the ability of future generations to meet their needs.

Introduction

A sustainability report is a report published by a company or organisation about the economic, environmental and social impacts caused by its everyday activities.

More and more business entities are reporting their approach to sustainability in addition to the financial information reported in the annual report. There are increased public expectations for business entities and industries to take responsibility for the impact their activities have on the environment and society.

Reporting sustainability

Reports include highlights of non-financial performance such as environmental, social and economic reports during the accounting period. The report may be included in the annual report or published as a stand alone document, possibly on the entity's website. The increase in popularity of such reports highlights the growing trend that business entities are taking sustainability seriously and are attempting to be open about the impact of their activities.

Framework for sustainability reporting

There is no framework for sustainability reporting within IFRS. This lack of regulation leads to several problems:

(a) Because disclosure is largely voluntary, not all businesses disclose information. Those that do tend to do so either because they are under particular pressure to prove their 'green' credentials (for example, large public utility companies whose operations directly affect the environment) or because they have deliberately built their reputation on environmental friendliness or social responsibility.

(b) The information disclosed may not be complete or reliable. Many businesses see environmental reporting largely as a public relations exercise and therefore only provide information that shows them in a positive light.

(c) The information may not be disclosed consistently from year to year.

(d) Some businesses, particularly small and medium sized entities, may believe that the costs of preparing and circulating additional information outweigh the benefits of doing so.

However, the benefits of sustainability reporting are widely known. In particular, shareholders, banks and the public are more likely to see the rewards of long-term sustainable behaviour rather than short-term profit seeking.

Integrated reporting and the IIRC

What is the IIRC?

The International Integrated Reporting Council (IIRC) was created to respond to the need for a concise, clear, comprehensive and comparable integrated reporting framework.

The IIRC define an integrated report (IR) as 'a concise communication about how an organisation's strategy, governance, performance and prospects, in the context of its external environment, lead to the creation of value in the short, medium and long term.'

The IIRC believe that intergrated reporting will contribute towards a more stable economy and a more sustainable world.

What is the role of the IIRC?

At present a range of standard-setters and regulatory bodies are responsible for individual elements of reporting. No single body has the oversight or authority to bring together these different elements that are essential to the presentation of an integrated picture of an organisation and the impact of environmental and social factors on its performance. In addition, globalisation means that an accounting and reporting framework needs to be developed on an international basis. At present, there is a risk that, as individual regulators respond to the risks faced, multiple standards will emerge.

The role of the IIRC is to:

- raise awareness of this issue and develop a consensus among governments, listing authorities, business, investors, accounting bodies and standard setters for the best way to address it;
- develop an overarching integrated reporting framework setting out the scope of integrated reporting and its key components;
- identify priority areas where additional work is needed and provide a plan for development;
- consider whether standards in this area should be voluntary or mandatory and facilitate collaboration between standard-setters and convergence in the standards needed to underpin integrated reporting; and

- promote the adoption of integrated reporting by relevant regulators and report preparers.

Who are the members?

The IIRC brings together a powerful cross section of representatives from the corporate, accounting, securities, regulatory, and standard-setting sectors. Membership will comprise international representation from the following stakeholder groups: companies, investors, regulators, standard-setters, inter-governmental organisations, non-governmental organisations, the accounting profession, civil society and academia.

Further information on the IIRC can be found at www.integratedreporting.org

The International Intergrated Reporting Framework

The consultation draft of the Integrated Reporting (IR) Framework is an examinable document for P2.

Objective of the Framework

The IR Framework establishes 'guiding principles' and 'content elements' that govern the overall content of an integrated report. This will help organisations to report their value creation in ways that are understandable and useful to the users.

The IR Framework is aimed at the private sector, although could be adapted for use by charities and the public sector.

The key users of an integrated report are deemed to be the providers of financial capital. However, the report will also benefit employees, suppliers, customers, local communities and policy makers.

The Framework is principles based and therefore does not prescribe specific KPIs that must be disclosed. Senior management need to use judgement to identify which issues are material. These decisions should be justified to the users of the report.

Those charged with governance are not required to acknowledge their responsibility for the integrated report. It was felt that such disclosures might increase legal liability in some jurisdictions and therefore deter some companies from applying the IR Framework.

Fundamental concepts in the IR framework

An integrated report concerns how value is created over the short-, medium- and long-term. To this extent, a number of fundamental concepts underpin the IR framework. These are:

- The capitals
- The organisation's business model
- The creation of value over time.

The **capitals** are stocks of value that are inputs to an organisation's business model. The capitals identified by the IR are financial, manufactured, intellectual, human, social and relationship, and natural.

- The capitals will increase, decrease or be transformed through an organisation's business activities.
  - The use of natural resources will decrease natural capital, making a profit will increase financial capital.
  - Employment could increase human capital through training, or reduce human capital through unsafe or exploitative working practices.

Central to integrated reporting is the overall impact that a business has on the full range of capitals through its business model.

The **business model** is a business' chosen system of inputs, business activities, outputs and outcomes that aims to create value over the short, medium and long term.

- An integrated report must identify key **inputs**, such as employees, or natural resources. It is important to explain how secure the availability, quality and affordability of components of natural capital are.
- At the centre of the **business model** is the conversion of inputs into outputs through business activities, such as planning, design, manufacturing and the provision of services.
- An integrated report must identify an organization's key **outputs**, such as products and services. There may be other outputs, such as chemical by-products or waste. These need to be discussed within the business model disclosure if they are deemed to be material.
- **Outcomes** are defined as the consequences (positive and negative) for the capitals as a result of an organisation's business activities and outputs. Outcomes can be internal (such as profits or employee morale) or external (impacts on the local environment).

Value is created over time and for a range of stakeholders. IR is based on the belief that the increasing financial capital (e.g. profit) at the expense of human capital (e.g. staff exploitation) is unlikely to maximize value in the longer term. IR thus helps users to establish whether short-term value creation can be sustained into the medium- and long-term.

The content of an integrated report

An integrated report should include all of the following content elements:

- **Organisational overview and external environment** – 'What does the organisation do and what are the circumstances under which it operates?'
- **Governance** – 'How does the organisation's governance structure support its ability to create value in the short, medium and long term?'
- **Opportunities and risks** – 'What are the specific opportunities and risks that affect the organisation's ability to create value over the short, medium and long term, and how is the organisation dealing with them?'
- **Strategy and resource allocation** – 'Where does the organisation want to go and how does it intend to get there?'
- **Business model** – 'What is the organisation's business model and to what extent is it resilient?'
- **Performance** – 'To what extent has the organisation achieved its strategic objectives and what are its outcomes in terms of effects on the capitals?'
- **Future outlook** – 'What challenges and uncertainties is the organisation likely to encounter in pursuing its strategy, and what are the potential implications for its business model and future performance?'

Including this content will help companies shift the focus of their reporting from historical financial performance to longer-term value creation.

Test your understanding 3 – Integrated reports

AA is a UK-based public limited company that purchases shoes directly from manufacturers and then sells them through its own UK-based shops. AA has been profitable for many years and has continued to expand, financing this through bank loans.

AA's shoes sell particularly well amongst lower income families and AA has therefore specifically targeted this demographic. AA offers a discount of 50% on school shoes if the child is entitled to free school meals. This discount is partly subsidised by a government grant.

AA maximises its profits by buying its inventory from overseas. In the past year there have been several press reports about poor working conditions and pay in factories where AA products are manufactured. AA is conscious that it needs to monitor its supplier's employment conditions more closely.

AA has also been criticised in the press for the quality of its products. Some customers have complained that the shoes are not well-made and that they must be regularly replaced. A major consumer magazine has strongly argued that AA products are a 'false economy' and that customers would save money in the long-term if they bought slightly more expensive but better quality shoes

Staff who work in AA's shops are paid the national minimum wage. Training is minimal and staff turnover is extremely high.

AA does not fully engage with local or national recycling initiatives. The directors of the company believe these initiatives would increase operating costs, thus reducing the affordability of its products for its target demographic.

The success of the AA business model has led to an increased number of competitors. Although these competitors do not yet have the same high street presence as AA, some of them have invested more money into developing online stores. Although AA has a website, its products cannot be purchased online.

Required:

Why would an Integrated Report provide useful information about AA?

1 Chapter summary

Non-financial reporting

Management commentary

- Provides management's view of the entity's performance, the reasons, and the implications.

Environmental reporting

- Details the effect of the business on the environment

Social reporting

- Details the organisation's impact on society

Sustainability reporting

- Details actions and policies towards helping future generations meet their needs.

Integrated reporting

- Communication about how value is created in the short, medium and long term
- Aimed at investors

Test your understanding answers

Test your understanding 1 – Two transactions

MEMORANDUM

To: Assistant Accountant

From: Chief Accountant

Subject: Accounting treatment of two transactions and disclosure of environmental matters in the financial statements

Date: 25 March 20X2

(a) **Accounting treatment of two transactions**

Transaction one

IAS 37 Provisions, Contingent Liabilities and Contingent Assets states that provisions should only be recognised in the financial statements if:

– there is a present obligation as a result of a past event

– it is probable that a transfer of economic benefits will be required to settle the obligation

– a reliable estimate can be made of the amount of the obligation.

In this case, there is no obligation to incur expenditure. There may be a constructive obligation to do so in future, if the board creates a valid expectation that it will protect the environment, but a board decision alone does not create an obligation.

There is also some doubt as to whether the expenditure can be reliably quantified. The sum of $100,000 could be appropriated from retained earnings and transferred to an environmental protection reserve within other components of equity, subject to formal approval by the board. A note to the financial statements should explain the transfer.

Transaction two

Again, IAS 37 states that a provision cannot be recognised if there is no obligation to incur expenditure. At first sight it appears that there is an obligation to purchase the new equipment, because the new law has been enacted. However, the obligation must arise as the result of a past event. At 31 December 20X1, no such event had occurred as the new plant had not yet been purchased and the new law had not yet come into effect. In theory, the company does not have to purchase the new plant. It could completely discontinue the activities that cause pollution or it could continue to operate the old equipment and risk prosecution under the new law. Therefore no provision can be recognised for the cost of new equipment.

It is likely that another effect of the new law is that the company will have to dispose of the old plant before it would normally have expected to do so. IAS 36 Impairment of Assets requires that the old plant must be reviewed for impairment. If its carrying value is greater than its recoverable amount, it must be written down and an impairment loss must be charged against profits. This should be disclosed separately in the notes to the statement of profit or loss and other comprehensive income if it is material.

(b) **Reference to environmental matters in the financial statements**

At present, companies are not obliged to make any reference to environmental matters within their financial statements. Current international financial reporting practice is more designed to meet the needs of investors and potential investors, rather than the general public. Some companies choose to disclose information about the ways in which they attempt to safeguard the environment, something that is often carried out as a public relations exercise. Disclosures are often framed in very general terms and appear outside the financial statements proper. This means that they do not have to be audited.

Several companies publish fairly detailed 'environmental reports'. It could be argued that as Redstart's operations affect the wider community, it has a moral responsibility to disclose details of its activities and its environmental policies. However, at present it is not required to do so by IFRSs.

If a company has, or may have, an obligation to make good any environmental damage that it has caused, it is obliged to disclose information about this commitment in its financial statements (unless the likelihood of this is remote).

If it is probable (more likely than not) that the company will have to incur expenditure to meet its obligation, then it is also required to set up a provision in the financial statements.

In practice, these requirements are unlikely to apply unless a company is actually obliged by law to rectify environmental damage or unless it has made a firm commitment to the public to do so (for example, by promoting itself as an organisation that cares for the environment, as the directors propose that Redstart should do in future).

Test your understanding 2 – Social and environmental

(a) The way in which companies manage their social and environmental responsibilities is a high level strategic issue for management. Companies that actively manage these responsibilities can help create long-term sustainable performance in an increasingly competitive business environment.

Reports that disclose transparent information will benefit organisations and their stakeholders. These stakeholders will have an interest in knowing that the company is attempting to adopt best practice in the area. Institutional investors will see value in the 'responsible ownership' principle adopted by the company.

Although there is no universal 'best practice', there seems to be growing consensus that high performance is linked with high quality practice in such areas as recruitment, organisational culture, training and reduction of environmental risks and impact. Companies that actively reduce environmental risks and promote social disclosures could be considered to be potentially more sustainable, profitable, valuable and competitive. Many companies build their reputation on the basis of social and environmental responsibility and go to substantial lengths to prove that their activities do not exploit their workforce or any other section of society.

Governments are encouraging disclosure by passing legislation, for example in the area of anti-discrimination and by their own example in terms of the depth and breadth of reporting (also by requiring companies who provide services to the government to disclose such information). External awards and endorsements, such as environmental league tables and employer awards, encourage companies to adopt a more strategic approach to these issues. Finally, local cultural and social pressures are causing greater demands for transparency of reporting.

There is no IFRS that determines the content of an environmental and social report. While companies are allowed to include the information they wish to disclose, there is a lack of comparability and the potential that only the positive actions will be shown.

A common framework that provided guidelines on sustainability reporting would be useful for both companies and stakeholders. An important example of this would be the Integrated Reported Framework produced by the International Integrated Reporting Council.

(b) Company B's environmental report should include the following information.

- (i) A statement of the environmental policy covering all aspects of business activity. This can include their aim of using renewable electricity and reducing their carbon footprint – the amount of carbon dioxide released into the environment as a result of their activities.
- (ii) The management systems that reduce and minimise environmental risks.
- (iii) Details of environmental training and expertise.
- (iv) A report on their environmental performance including verified emissions to air/land and water, and how they are seeking to reduce these and other environmental impacts. Operating site reports for local communities for businesses with high environmental impacts. Company B's activities have a significant impact so it is important to show how this is dealt with. The emissions data could be graphed to show it is reducing. If they have the data, they could compare their carbon dioxide emissions or their electricity usage over previous periods. Presenting this information graphically helps stakeholders see how the business is performing in the areas it is targeting.

(v) Details of any environmental offence that resulted in enforcement action, fine, etc. and any serious pollution incident. They can disclose how fines have been reducing and state that there have not been any pollution incidents in the current period.

(vi) A report on historical trends for key indicators and a comparison with the corporate targets.

Test your understanding 3 – Integrated reports

An integrated report might highlight a number of positive issues about AA:

- AA's financial capital has increased as a result of its profitable current business activities.
- Financial capital has increased due to the receipt of government grants and this will help AA to repay its debts in the short and also, potentially, the medium term.
- AA's has a positive impact on social capital by helping low income families to buy essential items of clothing. This is likely to foster brand loyalty from these customers, as well as generating good publicity. This may lead to a further increase in financial capital in the future.

However, it could be argued that the AA business model will not create value in the long-term. An integrated report might refer to the following issues:

- The government grants may not continue indefinitely. This could be due to government budget cuts, increasing competition or, perhaps, as a result of ongoing quality issues with AA products.
- AA does not invest highly in human capital. Unskilled and untrained staff are unlikely to foster brand loyalty and could lead to a loss of custom over time.
- AA uses cheap labour from overseas. Although this is likely to increase financial capital, it may lead to a net decrease in other capitals
  - AA may be criticised for not investing in local communities, or for exploiting overseas workers. By not investing in human capital there may also be a negative impact on social and relationship capital.
  - AA's recognition of the need to increasingly monitor its suppliers indicates that current economic benefits may not be sustainable in the longer-term.

- Purchasing goods from overseas will increase AA's carbon footprint. Moreover, AA does not widely recycle. Its activities thus place an overall drain on natural capital and this may deter some investors and consumers.
- A focus on high street expansion may leave AA vulnerable to online competitors, who will be able to offer the same products more cheaply. AA's lack of investment in staff may compound this because the retail stores are unlikely to offer a greater experience or level of service than can be obtained online. The current business model may therefore not be resilient in the medium or long term.

Summary

AA's business model is currently profitable. Such information could be obtained from the historical financial statements. However, an integrated report that looks at value creation and stability in the medium and longer term may offer a more pessimistic outlook. Banks are more likely to invest in companies who have sustainable business models and therefore integrated reports will help them to make stronger investment decisions. Other investors, such as potential or current shareholders, would also be able to make more informed decisions.

Producing an Integrated report is not mandatory. Businesses which have a detrimental net impact on capitals (particularly non-financial capitals) are unlikely to voluntarily produce an integrated report. In contrast, companies who create value in sustainable ways are more likely to want to disclose this to users. However, if the production of an integrated report was mandatory, then it might motivate a company like AA to shift its focus from increasing short term financial capital to the generation of an array of capitals over the medium and long-term.

chapter

23

Assessing financial performance and position

Chapter learning objectives

Upon completion of this chapter you will be able to:

- develop accounting policies for an entity that meet the entity's reporting requirements
- identify accounting treatments adopted in financial statements and assess their suitability and acceptability
- select and calculate relevant indicators of financial and non-financial performance
- identify and evaluate significant features and issues in financial statements
- highlight inconsistencies in financial information through analysis and application of knowledge
- make inferences from the analysis of information taking into account the limitation of the information, the analytical methods used and the business environment in which the entity operates.

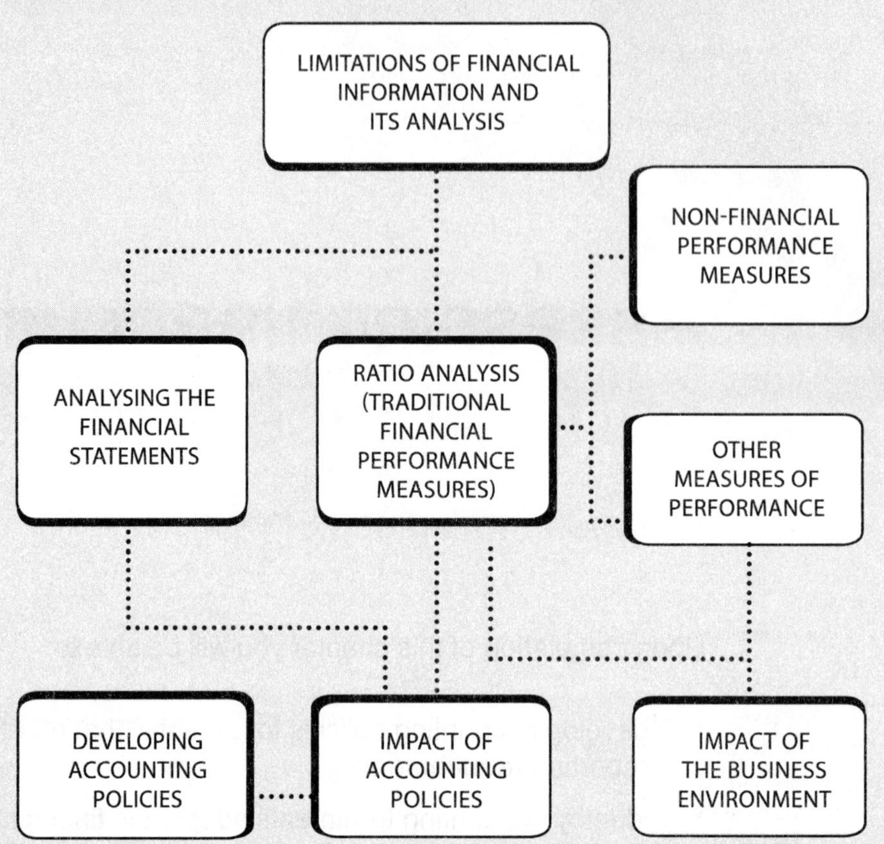

IAS 8

IAS 8 Accounting Policies, Changes in Accounting Estimates and Errors states that where a Standard or Interpretation exists in respect of a transaction, the accounting policy is determined by applying the Standard or Interpretation.

- Where there is no applicable Standard or Interpretation, management must use its judgement to develop and apply an accounting policy.
- The accounting policy selected must result in information that is both relevant to the needs of users and reliable, in that the financial statements:
  - represent faithfully the financial position, financial performance and cash flows of the entity
  - reflects the economic substance of transactions, other events and conditions, and not merely the legal form
  - are neutral, i.e. free from bias
  - are prepared on a prudent basis
  - are complete in all material respects.

IAS 8 provides a 'hierarchy' of sources that the management should use to develop an appropriate accounting policy in the absence of a Standard or Interpretation that specifically applies. These sources should be used in the following order:

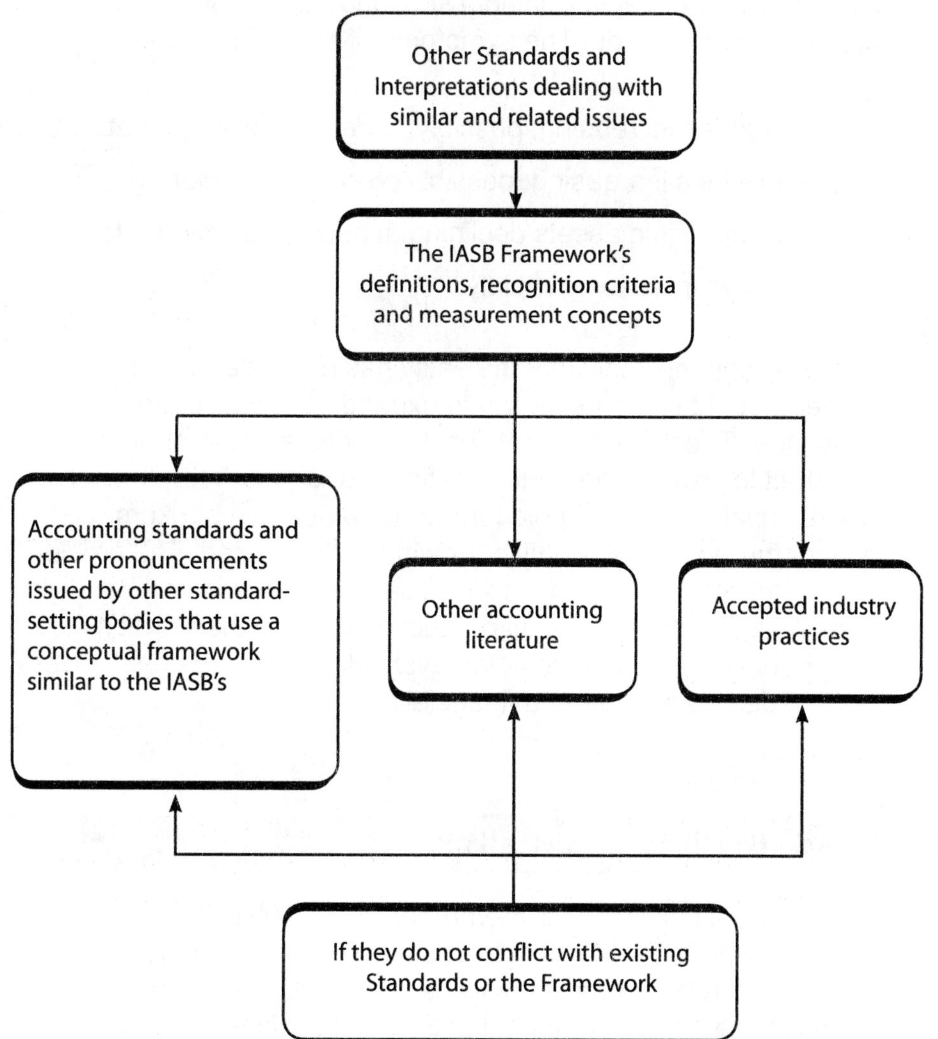

An entity must select and apply accounting policies consistently for similar transactions.

An entity should only change its accounting policies if the change:

- is required by a Standard or Interpretation
- results in reliable and more relevant information.

Overtrading

Overtrading is the term used to describe the situation where an entity expands its sales rapidly without securing additional long-term capital adequate for its needs. The symptoms of overtrading are:

- inventories increasing, possibly more than proportionately to sales
- receivables increasing, possibly more than proportionately to sales
- cash and liquid assets declining at a fairly alarming rate
- payables increasing rapidly.

These symptoms imply that the entity has expanded without giving proper thought to the necessity to expand its capital base. It has consequently continued to rely on its suppliers and probably its bank overdraft to provide the additional finance required. It will reach a stage where suppliers will withhold further deliveries and bankers will refuse to honour further cheques until borrowings are reduced. The problem is that borrowings cannot be reduced until sales revenue is earned, which in turn cannot be achieved until production is completed, which in turn is dependent upon materials being available and wages paid. Overall result – deadlock and rapid financial collapse!

Interpreting financial obligations

As well as calculating and interpreting liquidity ratios, it is important to be aware of other potential obligations that may affect liquidity and cash flow. These may not necessarily be recognised in current liabilities or even included in the statement of financial position at all.

(a) **Earn out arrangements**

Where one company acquires another, part of the consideration may be deferred to a later date because it is dependent (contingent) on the performance of the acquired entity. If this deferred consideration is recognised in the financial statements, the amount is likely to be based on an estimate. Alternatively, the acquirer's management may not have provided for the obligation because they believe that it is unlikely to become payable.

(b) **Redeemable debt**

A company may have raised finance by issuing loan notes that it is committed to redeem or repurchase, possibly at a premium.

(c) **Contingent liabilities**

Contingent liabilities are not recognised in the financial statements but must normally be disclosed in the notes.

(d) **Interpretation**

In all cases such as these, the obligation may involve a material cash outflow in the near future.

Where there are either provisions based on estimates or contingent liabilities, it is possible that the situation may have changed since the reporting date (for example, a contingent liability could have become an actual liability). It is necessary to use whatever information is available (e.g. selected notes to the financial statements, details of events since the publication of the latest financial statements) to determine the likelihood of the cash outflow occurring, its timing and whether the entity is likely to be able to meet the obligation in practice.

Non-financial performance measures

Non-financial performance measures are measures of performance based on non-financial information. They are becoming increasingly important both to management and to shareholders and other interested parties external to an entity.

Ratio analysis and other interpretation techniques based on the financial statements cannot measure all aspects of performance. For example, the effect of a business on the environment cannot be measured using financial criteria, but is increasingly regarded as an important aspect of performance.

- Where an entity presents an Operating and Financial Review or a Management Discussion and Analysis it may include Key Performance Indicators (KPIs) based on non-financial information.
- KPIs may also be included in an environmental or social report. Reports prepared in accordance with the Global Reporting Initiative (GRI) Sustainability Guidelines should contain economic indicators, environmental indicators and social indicators.

- Examples of non-financial performance measures are:
  - trend in market share
  - number of customers at the year end
  - sales per square foot of floor space (for a retailer)
  - percentage of revenue from new products
  - number of new products being developed at the year end
  - number of instances of environmental spillage per year
  - reduction in CO_2 emissions during the year
  - amount of waste (kg) arising from packaging on each $1,000 of products
  - employee turnover
  - training time per employee
  - lost time injury frequency rate (relating to employees).
- Non-financial performance measures are likely to be particularly relevant to 'not for profit' organisations, because these organisations need to measure the effectiveness with which services have been provided. Examples of non-financial performance indicators for public sector bodies could include:
  - pupil-teacher ratios
  - population per police officer
  - serious offences per 1,000 of the population
  - proportion of trains arriving on time
  - number of patients who wait more than one year for treatment.
- Where an entity presents non-financial measures:
  - the definition and calculation method should be explained
  - the purpose of the measure should be explained
  - the source of the data on which the measure is based should be disclosed
  - the measure should be presented and calculated consistently over time (and ideally, there should be comparative figures for the previous year)
  - any changes in the measures or in the way they are calculated should be disclosed and explained.

Illustration – non-financial measures

Verdant is an entity that manufactures hazardous substances. There have been several escapes of toxic gases from its plant over the last few years and the directors are concerned that this will damage the entity's reputation.

The directors decide to publish a key performance indicator to assess the effectiveness of the management of hazardous substances (and to demonstrate that the entity is taking steps to reduce the problem).

The measure is the number of significant incidents during the year. Significant incidents are defined as escapes of gas exceeding 10,000 cubic feet.

The data is taken from all Verdant's manufacturing plants.

In 20X6 there were 15 significant incidents compared with 21 gas escapes in 20X5.

Other measures of performance

In recent years, investment analysts have developed a number of new financial performance measures. These attempt to overcome the limitations of traditional ratios, such as earnings per share and return on capital employed.

- Earnings before interest, tax, depreciation and amortisation (EBITDA) is an approximation to operating cash flow and is therefore believed to be a better point of comparison between entities than earnings per share.
- Free cash flow is calculated as cash revenues less cash expenses, taxes paid, cash needed for working capital and cash required for routine capital expenditure. Analysts attach importance to this measure because cash is essential for an entity's survival and it is also less easy to manipulate than profit.

Shareholder value is created by generating future returns for equity investors that exceed the returns that those investors could expect to earn elsewhere.

- Many entities are adopting the enhancement of shareholder value, rather than the generation of profit, as their primary objective.

- A number of ways to measure shareholder value have been developed. The most important of these is probably Economic Value Added (EVA).
- EVA = adjusted net operating profit after tax – (weighted average cost of capital × adjusted invested capital). It is a variation on return on capital employed that adjusts the numerator and the denominator to remove the effects of accruals accounting and some of the effects of the entity's choice of accounting policies.

Alternative measures of performance

A number of ways of measuring shareholder value have been developed as follows. Measures of shareholder value have a number of common features.

- They focus on cash flow rather than on profit.
- They emphasise the 'whole' business. The idea behind the concept of shareholder value is that there are several 'drivers' within a business that can be managed to create value, e.g. growth in sales, increase in the operating profit margin, reduction in the cash tax rate. These are summarised into a single performance measure.
- They are essentially forward looking. In particular, calculating SVA involves estimating future performance.

(a) **Shareholder value analysis (SVA)**

SVA calculates a value for the entity that is based on projected future cash flows, discounted to their present value at the entity's cost of capital. The market value of debt is deducted from this figure to give shareholder value.

(b) **Market value added (MVA)**

MVA is the additional value that is added to an entity by its management in excess of the actual value of the funds invested by the shareholders.

MVA = Market value of entity – capital employed

The market value of the entity is the market share price multiplied by the number of shares in issue. Performance can be measured by calculating the yearly change in MVA.

(c) **Economic value added (EVA)**

EVA is calculated as follows:

EVA = adjusted net operating profit after tax – (WACC × adjusted invested capital)

EVA was developed as a sophisticated version of return on capital employed and similar methods of measuring the return on an investment. It can be argued that the normal calculation is distorted by the following factors:

- the effect of accruals based bookkeeping, which tends to hide the true 'cash' profitability of a business
- the effect of prudence, which often leads to a conservative bias and affects the relevance of reported figures (although this is less of a problem following the issue of IAS 37 Provisions, contingent liabilities and contingent assets)
- the effect of 'successful efforts accounting' whereby entities write off costs associated with unsuccessful investments. This tends to understate the 'true' capital of a business and subject profit or loss to 'one off' gains and losses.

Therefore adjustments are made to operating profit and asset values. These can include the following:

- removing non-recurring gains and losses such as restructuring costs
- capitalising intangible assets such as research and development expenditure
- adding back 'unnecessary' provisions (such as deferred tax)
- capitalising the net present value of future operating lease payments.

A positive EVA for a single year does not necessarily mean that value has been created and a negative EVA for a single year does not necessarily mean that value has been destroyed. EVA is probably most helpful when it is used to interpret an entity's performance over a period of several years.

Analysing the financial statements

The best way to start to analyse the financial statements is by observation. This can often tell a reader more, more quickly, than calculating ratios (and it does not depend on selecting the correct ratios).

Analysis should take into account:

- the nature of the entity's business
- any particular concerns of the users of the information (for example, a shareholder may suspect that the financial statements have been manipulated)
- any important issues facing the business
- the accounting policies adopted by management (if these are known).

The statement of financial position

The main areas of interest in the statement of financial position are set out below.

Non-current assets	• Significant additions/disposals ? • Evidence of business expanding ? • Any unusual items (e.g. intangibles) ? • Revaluations ? • How are assets valued ? • Depreciation/amortisation/useful lives? • Any associates or joint ventures (equity accounting)?
Current assets/current liabilities	• Significant movements? • In line with revenue and cost of sales? • Any unusual items? • Cash position? • Financial instruments: accounting policy?
Equity	• Share issues in the year? • Reason (e.g. to finance asset purchases/ acquisitions)? • Any significant/unusual movements on reserves? • Increases/decreases in minority interest?

Non-current liabilities	• Increase/decrease in year? • When do loans fall due?

The statement of comprehensive income and statement of changes in equity

The main areas of interest in the statement of comprehensive income and statement of changes in equity are set out below.

Revenue	• Increase/decrease? How significant?
Cost of sales/ Gross profit	• Movement in line with revenue? • Sales growth v profit growth?
Operating expenses/ Operating profit	• In line with revenue (especially selling costs)? • Any unusual items?
Finance costs	• Reasonable given level of loans/overdraft? Movement? Interest cover?
Profit before tax	• Any investment income, interests in associates, joint ventures?
Income tax expense/ Profit for the period	• Effective rate of tax? (This should be reasonably constant from year to year).
Dividends	• Trend, level, cover? A fall is usually a very bad sign.
Other comprehensive income	• revaluations?

Operating expenses may include various items that affect the analysis, for example:

- one-off unusual items
- depreciation and profits or losses on disposal of non-current assets
- research and development expenditure
- advertising expenditure
- staff costs that may have risen in line with inflation (rather than sales)
- pension costs including any surpluses or deficiencies (dealt with according to IAS 19 **Employee benefits**)

- amortisation of intangibles
- impairment losses (including goodwill)
- directors' emoluments (including share-based payment).

Trend analysis

Comparative figures for one or more years provide information about the way in which the performance and financial position of a business has changed over a period. Published accounts give comparative information in two main areas:

- the corresponding amounts for items shown in the statements of financial position, comprehensive income, cash flows and changes in equity and notes. Such amounts are required by IAS 1 **Presentation of financial statements** for virtually all items disclosed in the accounts
- historical summaries of information covering several years.

It may be possible to predict future performance from trend information, particularly if the figures are very stable.

- The extent to which amounts and ratios are stable or volatile can reveal a great deal. Figures that are very volatile, or sudden changes in trends, may indicate that the company will experience problems in the future, even if performance is apparently improving.
- Trend information should be interpreted with caution because it does not take account of the effect of inflation.

Impact of accounting policies and choices

Introduction

Accounting policies can significantly affect the view presented by financial statements, and the ratios computed by reference to them, without affecting a business's core ability to generate profits and cash.

The potential impact of accounting policies is especially important where:

- accounting standards permit a choice (e.g. cost v fair value)
- judgement is needed in making accounting estimates (e.g. inventory valuation, depreciation, doubtful receivables, provisions)
- there is no accounting standard (e.g. some forms of revenue recognition).

Asset valuation

A key area is the measurement of non-current assets. Measuring assets at fair value rather than historic cost has the following effects (assuming fair value is increasing each year):

- earnings reduce (profits decrease due to the additional depreciation)
- return on capital employed reduces (capital employed increases while profits decrease)
- gearing reduces (capital employed /equity increases, while debt remains the same)
- another effect of fair value accounting is that profits and trends in ratios may become more volatile and therefore harder to interpret.

Illustration – impact of accounting policies

Three entities are identical in all respects, except for the way they finance the major productive capacity they need. The following information has been extracted from the financial statements of the three entities for the year ended 30 September 20X4:

	A	B	C
Profit or loss	$000	$000	$000
Revenue	200	200	200
Operating costs	(160)	(190)	(170)
Profit from operations	40	10	30
Statement of financial position			
Share capital	50	50	50
Retained earnings	90	60	50
Revaluation reserve	–	210	–
Capital employed	140	320	100
Operating profit margin	20%	5%	15%
Asset utilisation	1.43	0.63	2
Return on capital employed	28.6%	3.1%	30%

Entity A

A obtained the capacity needed by purchasing a non-current asset costing $200,000 four years ago. The asset is being depreciated on the straight-line basis over 10 years. Therefore, $20,000 of depreciation has been charged to this year's profit and the asset has a carrying value of $120,000 in the statement of financial position.

Entity B

B also purchased a non-current asset four years ago for the same price but revalued it to its fair value of $350,000 at the start of the current year. As a result, a revaluation gain of $210,000 has been recognised within other comprehensive income. With seven years, life remaining, the depreciation charge has been increased to $50,000 per annum.

The revaluation has caused the operating profit margin to fall due to the extra depreciation. Asset utilisation has also fallen due to the revaluation reserve being included in capital employed.

Hence the entity appears to be generating a lower return.

Entity C

C has obtained the capacity needed under an operating lease agreement, paying an annual rental of $30,000, which has been charged to operating expenses.

This causes its operating profit margin to be lower than A's, because the lease payments are higher than A's depreciation charges. However, the asset utilisation is higher than A's since the non-current asset is not recognised in the statement of financial position.

Recognition of assets and liabilities

Another key area is the recognition (or non-recognition) of assets and liabilities. IAS 1, IAS 8 and the IASB's Framework set out the general principle that an entity should report the substance of a transaction rather than its strict legal form.

- There is no accounting standard that specifically deals either with specific types of transaction (e.g. sale and repurchase agreements, debt factoring) or with substance in general.
- It is still possible for a company to account for complex transactions so that significant assets and liabilities are not recognised on in the statement of financial position.

- Non-recognition of assets normally improves ROCE while non-recognition of liabilities normally improves gearing. For example, leasing obligations increase debt and therefore increase gearing.
- Management may seek to keep liabilities off the balance sheet in order to manipulate the gearing ratio.

Illustration: impact of accounting policies

The following ratios have been calculated for Laxton, based on its financial statements for the year ended 31 December 20X4:

Return on capital employed	$45m/$160m	= 28%
Gearing	$80m/$160m	= 50%

During the year, Laxton sold a property with a carrying value of $40 million to a bank for $50 million. Laxton has treated this transaction as a sale, even though it continues to occupy the property and has agreed to repurchase it for $55 million on 31 December 20X9.

The substance of the transaction is that it is not a sale, but a secured loan. The difference between the sale proceeds and the amount at which the property will eventually be repurchased represents interest.

If the agreement is treated correctly, the effect is:

- profit before interest and tax is reduced by $10m (the profit on disposal)
- capital employed increases by $40m (the property continues to be recognised at its carrying value)
- debt increases by $50m (the amount received from the bank).

(Depreciation is ignored).

The ratios now become:

Return on capital employed	$35m/$200m = 17.5%
Gearing	$130m/$200m = 65%

Illustration – choice of accounting treatment

Below are some examples where reporting standards permit a choice of accounting treatment:

Goodwill on acquisition of a subsidiary – IFRS 3 permits goodwill on acquisition to be accounted for using the full goodwill method or the proportionate goodwill method.

Property plant and equipment – IAS 16 permits property, plant and equipment to be measured using the cost model or the valuation model.

Required:

Briefly explain how choices in accounting treatment may affect the financial statements.

Solution

When goodwill has been accounted for using the full goodwill method, there will be recognition of an asset at a greater carrying value in comparison with goodwill calculated on a proportionate basis. This may give rise to possible sources of inconsistency in making comparisons between reported information from two separate groups as follows:

- one group may have prepared financial statements where goodwill for all subsidiaries has been calculated using the full goodwill method; the other may have applied the proportionate goodwill method upon acquisition of subsidiaries
- the carrying value of non-controlling interest in the group financial statements will be affected by the choice of goodwill accounting policy
- any subsequent write-off for impairment of goodwill in the group financial statements is likely to be greater under the full goodwill method.

When property, plant and equipment (or any single class of asset under this heading) is measured by valuation, this will lead to a greater carrying value in comparison with being measured at cost. There will be a consequent impact upon equity on the statement of financial position, which will impact upon net assets and gearing. Profitability will also be affected as any depreciation charge based upon a revalued amount will lead to a greater charge in profit or loss for the year. This will reduce earnings per share.

Intangible assets and intellectual property

A traditional manufacturing business generates profits mainly from the use of property, plant and equipment. Its financial statements can be interpreted fairly easily because there is a clear relationship between the plant and equipment and working capital in the statement of financial position and the statement of profit or loss and other comprehensive income.

Business practice has changed very significantly over the last 20 years. Many businesses now depend on assets such as copyrights, patents, customer databases and the technical or interpersonal skills of their staff.

These assets are not normally recognised in the statement of financial position, and there are important implications for analysis of the financial statements. Key ratios, such as ROCE and gearing may be virtually meaningless. Interpretations of performance have to be based on profit margins and sales growth. It can be much harder to predict future performance because this is more likely to be significantly affected by unpredictable events than in a business such as manufacturing or retailing. For example, in some situations it could be disastrous if several key members of staff left the company.

Creative accounting

Creative accounting is a form of accounting which, while complying with all regulations, nevertheless gives a biased impression (usually favourable) of the company's performance.

Management may have strong incentives to present the financial statements in the best possible light. For example:

- the directors want to sell the company in the near future
- the company is going through a difficult period (e.g. falling profits, lack of shareholder confidence, a possible takeover)
- directors' remuneration is strongly linked to performance (e.g. bonuses if earnings per share exceeds a certain amount or share based payment that depends on the entity's share price)
- the company is in danger of breaching loan covenants (for example, if the current/quick ratio or the gearing ratio falls below or above a certain figure).

There are a number of ways in which creative accounting can take place.

- **Off balance sheet finance**: transactions are deliberately constructed to allow the non-recognition of assets and (particularly) liabilities for loans. Examples include sale and repurchase agreements and the use of special-purpose entities (quasi-subsidiaries). Note that the issue of IFRS 10, IFRS 11 and IFRS 12 dealing with aspects of accounting for investments in other entities could be seen to be an attempt to close apparent loopholes in how investments in other entities are accounted for.
- **Aggressive earnings management**: recognising revenue before it has been earned. Note that there are current developments which consider how revenue recognition for goods and services provided can be more consistently reported, which may have the benefit of reducing the extent of variation or earnings management which may happen in practice.
- **Unusual assets**: an attempt to recognise an asset which, strictly speaking, is not an asset but an expense. Examples include marketing or advertising costs and recruitment costs (particularly where these have been incurred to recruit staff with essential skills or technical knowledge).
- **Unjustified changes to accounting policies or accounting estimates**: for example, extending the useful lives of assets with the object of reducing the depreciation expense and increasing earnings.
- **Profit smoothing:** manipulating the profit figure by setting up assets or liabilities in the statement of financial position and releasing these amounts to profit over time.

Question

Egremont, a mining company, has been fined for environmental pollution of the area in which it operates. The fine has been treated as an intangible asset and is being amortised over 15 years, the estimated remaining useful life of the quarry in which the pollution incident took place. The directors argue that this treatment is logical because operating the quarry brings them economic benefits in the form of revenues.

Required:

Comment on this accounting treatment.

Solution

An intangible asset is a resource controlled by the company as a result of past events and from which future economic benefits are expected to flow (IAS 38 **Intangible assets**).

The directors seem to be trying to argue that the fine is an unavoidable cost of operating the quarry and that economic benefits result from it. But the fine is avoidable and therefore it is an expense and not an asset.

The fine should be recognised in the profit or loss in the current year and possibly disclosed as a material item under IAS 1 **Presentation of financial statements**.

Limitations of financial information and its analysis

Limitations of financial information

During the last few years, users of traditional financial statements have become increasingly aware of their limitations.

- Preparing financial statements involves a substantial degree of classification and aggregation. There is always a risk that essential information will either not be given sufficient prominence or will be lost completely.
- Financial statements focus on the financial effects of transactions and other events and do not focus to any significant extent on their non-financial effects or on non-financial information in general.
- They provide information that is largely historical. They do not reflect future events or transactions, nor do they anticipate the impact of potential changes to an entity. This means that it is not always possible to use them to predict future performance.
- There is often a time interval of several months between the year-end and the publication of the financial statements. Most financial information is out of date by the time it is actually published.

Limitations of financial analysis

Ratio analysis and other types of analysis such as trend analysis are a useful means of identifying significant relationships between different figures, but they have many limitations, including the following.

- Profit and capital employed are arbitrary figures. They depend on the accounting policies adopted by an entity.
- Many businesses produce accounts to a date on which there are relatively low amounts of trading activity. As a result the items on a statement of financial position are not typical of the items throughout the accounting period.
- Ratios based on historical cost accounts do not give a true picture of trends from year to year. An apparent increase in profit may not be a 'true' increase, because of the effects of inflation.
- Comparing the financial statements of similar businesses can be misleading for a number of reasons, including the effect of size differences and of operating in different markets.
- There are particular problems in comparing the financial statements of similar businesses that operate in different countries. There can be significant differences in accounting policies, terminology and presentation.

The type of business

It can often be helpful to consider whether the statement of profit or loss and other comprehensive income and statements of financial position appear as they should for a particular type of business.

For example:

- Manufacturing industries are capital intensive, therefore they have relatively low asset turnover.
- Service industries depend mainly on people rather than capital assets, therefore asset turnover should be relatively high.
- A builder should have high inventories and work in progress, therefore inventory turnover is usually relatively low.
- A supermarket has perishable inventories, therefore inventory turnover should normally be high.

Groups and individual companies

Being part of a group can have quite a significant effect on the financial statements of an individual company. Intra-group transactions often take place on terms that are different (so more favourable to one of the entities, less favourable to the other) than between two independent companies trading at arms' length:

- Profit margins in the seller may be unusually high.
- The rate of Interest payable on intra-group loans may be unusually low.
- A group company may exist (for example) only to supply essential goods or services to another, so that it has a guaranteed market for its output.
- Services (e.g. administration) may be supplied free of charge.

Events in the period

Events taking place during the period

A significant event during the year often distorts the financial statements and accounting ratios for that year, particularly if it takes place near the year-end. This can make it harder for a user to predict future performance.

Illustration – events in the period

An entity increases its long-term borrowings from $40 million to $100 million just before the year end. Operating profit for the year is $25 million, interest for the year is $5 million and profit after tax for the year is $15 million. The average rate of interest on long-term borrowings is 10%.

Interest cover can be calculated as five times. However, the accounts do not include a full year's interest charge on the new borrowings.

Assuming that operating profit, tax charge and total long-term borrowings remain at the same level, interest cover for the next year will fall to approximately 2.5 times (25 ÷ (100 × 10%)) and profit after tax will fall to approximately $10 million (25 – ((100 × 10%) – 5 charged in current year)).

Significant events may include:

- acquisition or disposal of a subsidiary during the year
- management actions (e.g. price discounting to increase market share) or changes in the nature of the business (e.g. diversification or divestment)
- raising finance just before the year end
- significant asset sales or purchases just before the year end.

It can be useful to ask the following questions:

- What effect do these events have on performance (including cash flow) and key ratios for the current year?
- What effect might they be expected to have on performance and key ratios in the next period and in the longer term?
- What is the apparent or possible reason for the event? Has it taken place for a legitimate business reason, or is it a deliberate attempt to improve the appearance of the financial statements in the short term?

Other business factors

These may include the nature of the business, for example, whether it is highly seasonal or vulnerable to changes in fashion or the market. Other factors to consider are the quality of management and the state of the economy and market conditions.

- Better managed businesses are likely to be more profitable and have better working capital management than businesses where management is weak.
- If the market or the economy in general is depressed, this is likely to affect companies adversely and make most or all of their ratios appear worse. The impact may differ between market sectors.

Preparing a report

An exam question may ask for a report.

REPORT

To

- The report should be focused on the reader(s) and their information needs.

From

Date

Subject

Introduction

- **Brief** introductory paragraph setting out the purpose of the report/terms of reference.

Discussion

This should:

- be structured with headings (usually the specific issues highlighted in the scenario)
- refer to calculations (including ratios) in an appendix (unless the question requires otherwise)
- (if required) interpret the information and any performance measures calculated (for example, possible reasons for a feature or a change)
- make connections between different areas, if the question asks for interpretation/analysis
- state what other information might be needed/would be useful (if appropriate or required by the question).

Conclusion

- Summarise findings and make a recommendation (if required).

Illustration –analysis of financial statements

The consolidated financial statements of TW for the year ended 30 April 20X4 are due to be published in June 20X4. The first draft of the 20X4 financial statements has just been prepared. Extracts from these statements are set out below:

Statement of comprehensive income – year ended 30 April:

	20X4 (draft)	20X3 (final)
	$m	$m
Revenue	3,600	3,400
Cost of sales	(2,300)	(2,250)
Gross profit	1,300	1,150
Other operating expenses	(700)	(600)
Profit from operations	600	550
Profit on sale of subsidiaries	350	Nil
Finance cost	(250)	(120)
Profit before tax	700	430
Income tax expense	(200)	(140)
Profit after tax	500	290
Other comprehensive income:		
Item that will not be reclassified to profit or loss in future years:		
Gain on property revaluation	800	–
Total comprehensive income	1,300	290
Profit attributable to:		
Owners of the parent	440	235
Non-controlling interest	60	55
	500	290

Total comprehensive income attributable to		
Owners of the parent	1,200	235
Non-controlling interest	100	55
	1,300	290
Earnings per equity share	176 cents	94 cents

Statement of financial position at 30 April:

	20X4 (draft)		**20X3 (final)**	
	$m	$m	$m	$m
ASSETS				
Non-current assets:				
Property, plant and equipment	2,400		1,350	
Financial assets	180		250	
		2,580		1,600
Current assets:				
Inventories	430		400	
Trade receivables	600		550	
Deferred marketing costs	100		Nil	
Cash and cash equivalents	940		Nil	
		2,070		950
		4,650		2,550
EQUITY AND LIABILITIES				
Equity:				
Equity capital ($1 equity shares)	250		250	
Share premium	150		150	
Revaluation reserve	800		Nil	
Retained earnings	1,050		610	
		2,250		1,010
Non-current liabilities:				
Long-term borrowings	2,000		1,000	
Deferred tax	180		100	
		2,180		1,100

Current liabilities:

Trade payables	220		200	
Short-term borrowings	Nil		240	
		220		440
		4,650		2,550

Notes to the draft financial statements

(i) During the financial year, the group decided to change the nature and focus of its operations. Consequently, on 31 March 20X4, the group disposed of two subsidiaries for total cash proceeds of $1,000 million. In the year to 30 April 20X4, the two subsidiaries that were disposed of contributed $800 million to group revenue, $320 million to group gross profit and $175 million to group profit from operations.

(ii) During the last few months of the year ended 30 April 20X4 the group embarked on an extensive marketing campaign to underpin the new operational focus. Marketing costs are normally charged to cost of sales but, in the draft financial statements, the directors of TW have included them in the statement of financial position on the basis that the new operational focus is likely to generate future economic benefits for the group.

(iii) The revaluation reserve is caused by a group-wide revaluation of property, plant and equipment on 31 March 20X4, immediately after the disposal of the two subsidiaries. Depreciation was charged on the revalued amounts from 1 April 20X4. The average remaining useful lives of the revalued assets at 1 April 20X4 was eight years.

Ms A is a newly-appointed non-executive director of TW. She wishes to seek your advice prior to the board meeting and her request is set out below.

'The papers contain an assertion from the Chief Executive that the financial statements show a very pleasing financial performance and position. The Chief Executive highlights the increase in revenue, profits, earnings per share and cash balances as evidence to support this assertion. I would like you to evaluate this assertion and to highlight any relevant issues.'

Prepare a reply to the question Ms A has raised.

Solution

Financial performance and position of TW

It is true that the draft financial statements show that revenue, profits, earnings per share and cash balances have all increased. However, the notes to the financial statements reveal a number of issues that should be taken into account when interpreting the figures. The potential effect of these issues on the gross profit margin and the operating profit margin are illustrated in the Appendix.

Disposal of subsidiaries

The group has disposed of two subsidiaries during the year, but their results have not been separately presented within the statement of comprehensive income. In fact the two subsidiaries contributed 22% of total revenue (800 as a percentage of 3,600); 25% of total gross profit (320 as a percentage of 1,300); and nearly 30% of total profit from operations (175 as a percentage of 600). In other words, the discontinued operations appear to be more profitable than the rest of the group. This suggests that the group may be less profitable in future years.

Profit before tax has increased by nearly two-thirds in the year, but this includes the exceptional profit on disposal of $350 million. This profit will not recur and without it profit before tax would have fallen, due to the fact that finance costs have doubled as the group has also doubled its long-term borrowings.

The group has experienced a total cash net inflow of $1,180 million (940 + 240) for the year. However, most of this increase results from the sale proceeds of $1,000 million. The group's cash flow position does not appear to be as healthy as the Chairman suggests.

Marketing costs

The treatment of the marketing costs of $100 million is not justified. An asset can only be recognised if it is probable that the group will obtain future economic benefits from the expenditure as a result of past events or transactions and if these benefits can be measured reliably. It is impossible to measure the economic benefits attributable to specific marketing costs (rather than to other factors, such as the reputation built up over many years), so IAS 38 **Intangible assets** prohibits the capitalisation of marketing costs. Profits are overstated by $100 million.

Revaluation

When non-current assets are revalued, the depreciation charge must be calculated on the revalued amount. This means that depreciation charges increase and profits are reduced. Because the revaluation took place on 1 April 20X4, the financial statements show the increase in property, plant and equipment, but only reflect one month's additional depreciation. However, the full depreciation charge will be reflected in the statement of comprehensive income for the year to 30 April 20X5. The effect of this can be estimated from the increase in the revaluation reserve: there will be a reduction in profit of approximately $92 million (800 ÷ 8 × 11/12).

Conclusion

The potential impact of all these issues is significant, particularly in relation to reported profit. On the face of it, the group's results for the current year may be good, but this trend is unlikely to continue into the future. The financial statements should be interpreted with caution.

Appendix

	Gross profit margin	**Operating profit margin**
20X4 as reported	1,300/3,600 =36.1%	600/3,600 =16.7%
20X4 adjusted:		
Removal of discontinued operations	980/2,800 =35%	425/2,80 =15.2%
As above less marketing costs now charged to income	880/2,800 =31.4%	325/2,800 =11.6%
As above less additional depreciation now charged to cost of sales	788/2,800 =28.1%	233/2,800 = 8.3%

Chapter summary

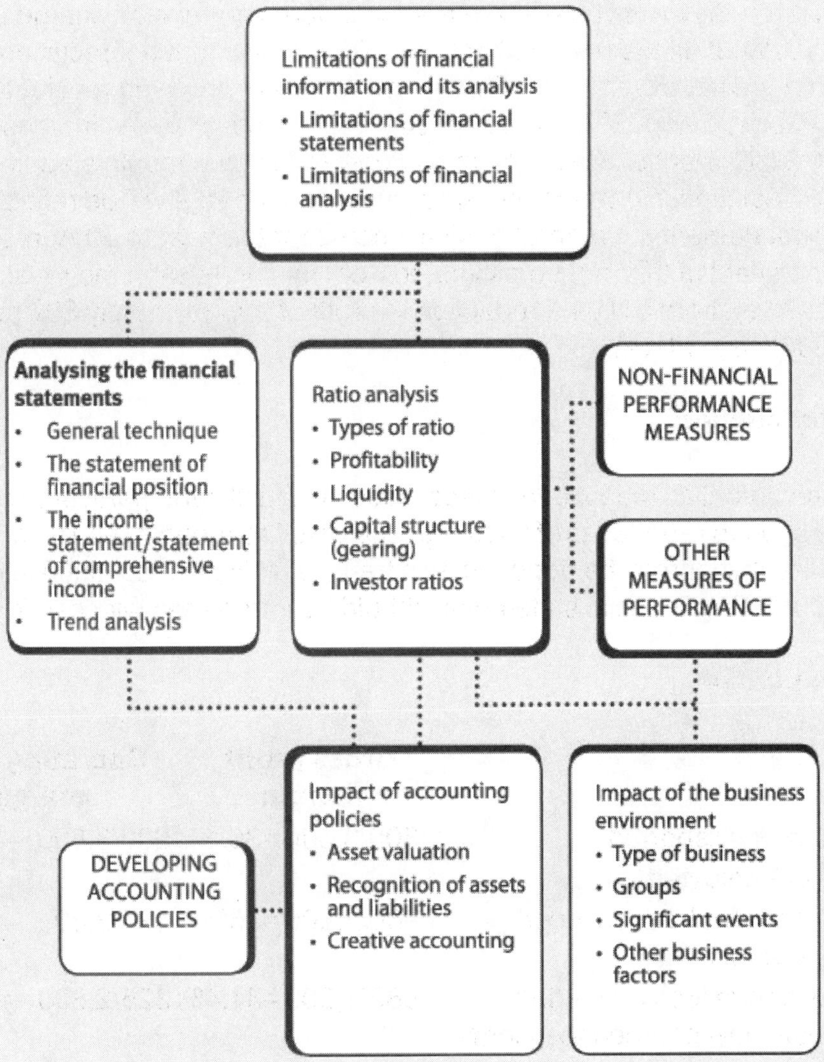

Limitations of financial information and its analysis
- Limitations of financial statements
- Limitations of financial analysis

Analysing the financial statements
- General technique
- The statement of financial position
- The income statement/statement of comprehensive income
- Trend analysis

Ratio analysis
- Types of ratio
- Profitability
- Liquidity
- Capital structure (gearing)
- Investor ratios

NON-FINANCIAL PERFORMANCE MEASURES

OTHER MEASURES OF PERFORMANCE

DEVELOPING ACCOUNTING POLICIES

Impact of accounting policies
- Asset valuation
- Recognition of assets and liabilities
- Creative accounting

Impact of the business environment
- Type of business
- Groups
- Significant events
- Other business factors

chapter

24

Current issues

Chapter learning objectives

Upon completion of this chapter you will be able to:

- discuss current issues in corporate reporting
- identify the issues and deficiencies that have led to a proposed change to an accounting standard
- apply and discuss the implications of a proposed change to an accounting standard on the performance and statement of financial position of an entity

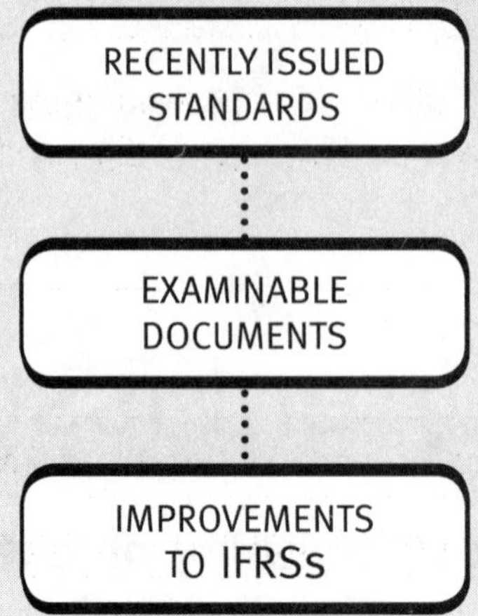

Introduction

The IASB is continually engaged in projects to update and improve existing standards and introduce new ones.

At any time there are a number of discussion papers (DPs) and exposure drafts (EDs) in issue as part of these projects.

In addition, the IFRIC continues to issue interpretations addressing newly identified reporting issues not covered in standards and issues where conflicting interpretations have arisen.

A good source of up to date information is the current projects page of the IASB website at www.iasb.org.

Examinable documents

The following table outlines documents and statements (other than IFRSs/IASs) that are examinable in P2 and indicates where these are covered in this text.

Statement/Document	**Textbook chapter**
The Conceptual Framework for Financial Reporting	1
Practice Statement on Management Commentary	22
Consultation Draft of the International IR Framework	22
ED 2013/3 Financial Instruments: Expected Credit Losses	12
ED 2011/6 Revenue from Contracts with Customers	3
ED 2013/6 Leases	6
Draft IFRS 9: Chapter 6 Hedge Accounting	12
ED 2012/2 Improvements to IFRSs	24
ED 2012/3 Equity Method: Share of Other Net Asset Changes	14
ED 2012/6 Sale of Contribution of Assets between an Investor and its Associate or Joint Venture	14
ED 2012/7 Acquisition of an Interest in a Joint Operation	14
Discussion Paper: A Review of the Conceptual Framework for Financial Reporting	1

Improvements to IFRSs

The IASB has adopted an annual process to deal with non-urgent minor amendments to existing standards. These amendments tend to focus on areas of inconsistency in IFRSs or where clarification of wording is required.

Each year the IASB discusses and decides on proposed improvements to IFRSs as they arise throughout the year. In the third quarter of the year, an omnibus ED of the collected proposals is published for public comment, with a comment period of 90 days. After the IASB has considered the comments received, it aims to issue the amendments in final form in the following second quarter, with an effective date of 1 January of the subsequent year.

Improvements to IFRS

In P2, ED 2012/2 Improvements to IFRSs is an examinable document. It suggests relatively minor technical amendments to four reporting standards as follows:

IFRS	**Subject of amendment**
IFRS 1 First-time Adoption of IFRSs	The IASB will clarify that if a new IFRS is not yet mandatory but permits early application, that IFRS is permitted, but not required, to be applied in the entity's first IFRS financial statements.
IFRS 3 Business Combinations	The IASB will clarify that IFRS 3 is not applicable to the accounting for the formation of a joint arrangement in the financial statements of the joint arrangement itself..
IFRS 13 Fair Value Measurement	IFRS 13 permits an entity to measure the fair value of a group of financial assets and financial liabilities on a net basis if the entity manages that group of financial assets and financial liabilities on the basis of its net exposure to either market risk or credit risk. This is referred to as the portfolio exception. The IASB wishes to clarify that the portfolio exception applies to all contracts within the scope of IAS 39 or IFRS 9 regardless of whether they meet the definitions of financial assets or financial liabilities as defined in IAS 32.
IAS 40 Investment Properties	The IASB plans to amend IAS 40 to state that judgement is required to determine whether the acquisition of investment property is the acquisition of an asset, a group of assets or a business combination in the scope of IFRS 3.

Key issues for regulators

The European Securities and Markets Authority (ESMA) has highlighted areas of focus for European national regulators when they review financial statements. The financial reporting topics ESMA has identified are:

- financial instruments
- impairment of non-financial assets
- defined benefit obligations
- provisions.

Financial instruments

Transparency of information relating to financial instruments is important for users of the financial statements, particularly as a result of the financial crisis. The disclosure requirements of IFRS 7 are therefore a key area for concern. Entities must include relevant quantitative and qualitative disclosures that reflect the nature of their risk exposure.

Impairment of non-financial assets

The current economic environment increases the likelihood that the carrying value of assets will exceed their recoverable amounts. Therefore, users must be provided with sufficient information, in accordance with IAS 36, about impairment reviews conducted during a reporting period.

When calculating value-in-use, ESMA emphasises the need to use realistic assumptions. Disclosures should include entity-specific information related to assumptions used when preparing discounted cashflows (such as growth rates, discount rate and consistency of such rates with past experience) and sensitivity analyses.

Defined benefit obligations

A defined benefit obligation should be discounted using the yield on high-quality corporate bonds. However, if a country does not have a deep market in such bonds then the market yields on government bonds should be used instead. As a result of the economic crisis, some entities will need to change their approach. ESMA emphasises the need for entities to be transparent about the yields used and the reasons for using them.

Provisions

Information about provisions is key because it highlights the risks and uncertainties that an entity is subject to. Yet the information provided is often over-aggregated and overly standardised in nature. ESMA emphasises that, in accordance with IAS 37, entities should disclose descriptions of the nature of the obligations concerned, the expected timing of outflows of economic benefits, uncertainties related to the amount and timing of those outflows as well as major assumptions about future events. This should be done for each class of provision and should reflect the risks specific to the entity.

Existing standards

Although knowledge of developments in the accountancy profession and upcoming standards are a central part of the P2 syllabus, the Examiner has also noted the importance of being able to critique existing accounting standards.

Critiques of existing standards can be found within the relevant chapters in this text. You could also attempt Test Your Understanding 2 ('Applying the Framework') in Chapter 1 of this text as a way of assessing your knowledge of this area.

Chapter summary

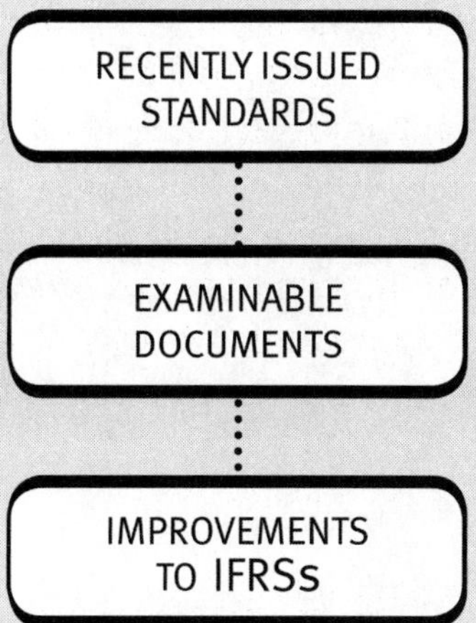

chapter

25

Questions & Answers

Test your understanding 1 – Exotic

The Exotic Group carries on business as a distributor of warehouse equipment and importer of fruit. Exotic is a listed entity and was incorporated over 20 years ago to distribute warehouse equipment. Since then the group has diversified its activities to include the import and distribution of fruit, and it expanded its operations by gaining control of two listed entities, Melon in 20X1 and Kiwi in 20X3, either directly or indirectly.

Accounts for all entities are prepared up to 31 December.

The draft statements of total comprehensive income for Exotic, Melon and Kiwi for the year ended 31 December 20X6 are as follows:

	Exotic	**Melon**	**Kiwi**
	$000	$000	$000
Revenue	45,600	24,700	22,800
Cost of sales	(18,050)	(5,463)	(5,320)
Gross profit	27,550	19,237	17,480
Distribution costs	(3,325)	(2,137)	(1,900)
Administrative expenses	(3,475)	(950)	(1,900)
Profit from operations	20,750	16,150	13,680
Finance costs	(325)	–	–
Profit before tax	20,425	16,150	13,680
Tax	(8,300)	(5,390)	(4,241)
Profit for the period	12,125	10,760	9,439

There were no items of other comprehensive income during the year.

Notes

	Exotic	**Melon**	**Kiwi**
Dividends paid in the year	9,500		
Retained earnings brought forward	20,013	13,315	10,459

The draft statements of financial position as at 31 December 20X6 are as follows:

	Exotic	Melon	Kiwi
	$000	$000	$000
Assets:			
Non-current assets (CV)	35,483	24,273	13,063
Investments:			
Shares in Melon	6,650	–	–
Shares in Kiwi	–	3,800	–
Current assets	1,568	9,025	8,883
Total assets	43,701	37,098	21,946
Equity and liabilities:	$000	$000	$000
Equity shares ($1)	8,000	3,000	2,000
Retained earnings	22,638	24,075	19,898
Total equity	30,638	27,075	21,898
Sundry liabilities	13,063	10,023	48
Total equity and liabilities	43,701	37,098	21,946

The following information is available relating to Exotic, Melon and Kiwi:

(1) On 1 January 20X1 Exotic acquired 2,700,000 $1 equity shares in Melon for $6,650,000 at which date there was a credit balance on the retained earnings of Melon of $1,425,000. No shares have been issued by Melon since Exotic acquired its interest.

(2) On 1 January 20X3 Melon acquired 1,600,000 $1 equity shares in Kiwi for $3,800,000 at which date there was a credit balance on the retained earnings of Kiwi of $950,000. No shares have been issued by Kiwi since Melon acquired its interest.

(3) During 20X6, Kiwi had made inter-company sales to Melon of $480,000 making a profit of 25% on cost and $75,000 of these goods were in inventory at 31 December 20X6.

(4) During 20X6, Melon had made inter-company sales to Exotic of $260,000 making a profit of 33⅓% on cost and $60,000 of these goods were in inventory at 31 December 20X6.

(5) On 1 November 20X6 Exotic sold warehouse equipment to Melon for $240,000 from inventory. Melon has included this equipment in its non-current assets. The equipment had been purchased on credit by Exotic for $200,000 in October 20X6 and this amount is included in its liabilities as at 31 December 20X6.

(6) Melon charges depreciation on its warehouse equipment at 20% on cost. It is company policy to charge a full year's depreciation in the year of acquisition to be included in the cost of sales.

(7) It is group policy to account for non-controlling interest on a proportionate basis. Since acquisition, the goodwill of Melon has been fully written off as a result of an impairment review which took place two years ago. The goodwill of Kiwi has been impaired 60% by 31 December 20X5 and a further 50% of the remaining balance of goodwill was impaired in the year ended 31 December 20X6.

Required:

(a) **Prepare a consolidated statement of comprehensive income for the Exotic Group for the year ended 31 December 20X6 including a reconciliation of retained earnings for the year.**

(12 marks)

(b) **Prepare a consolidated statement of financial position as at that date.**

(13 marks)
(Total: 25 marks)

Test your understanding 2 – Howard

Howard, Sylvia and Sabrina are three entities preparing their financial statements in accordance with International Financial Reporting Standards. Their statements of financial position as at 30 September 20X5 are given below:

Statements of Financial Position	**Howard**	**Sylvia**	**Sabrina**
	$000	$000	$000
Non-current assets:			
Property, plant and equipment	160,000	60,000	64,000
Investments	80,000	–	–
	240,000	60,000	64,000
Current assets	65,000	50,000	36,000
	305,000	110,000	100,000

	$000	$000	$000
Equity capital ($1 shares)	50,000	20,000	15,000
Retained earnings	185,000	43,000	42,000
	235,000	63,000	57,000
Non-current liabilities	25,000	18,000	20,000
Current liabilities	45,000	29,000	23,000
	305,000	110,000	100,000

Note 1 – Investment by Howard in Sylvia

On 1 October 20X3, Howard acquired 70% of the equity share capital of Sylvia for $45 million in cash, when the balance on Sylvia's retained earnings was $28 million. It was determined that at this date, land with carrying value of $40 million had a fair value of $45 million.

On 30 September 20X5, Howard acquired a further 10% of the equity shares of Sylvia paying $10 million in cash.

Note 2 – Investment by Howard in Sabrina

On 1 January 20X2, Howard acquired 60% of the equity shares of Sabrina for $21 million in cash, when the balance on Sabrina's retained earnings was $15 million. It was determined that the book value of Sabrina's net assets on 1 January 20X2 were equal to their fair values.

On 30 September 20X5, Howard disposed of one quarter of its shareholding in Sabrina for $15 million cash. Howard's remaining 45% holding enabled Howard to exercise significant influence over the operating and financial policies of Sabrina. The fair value of the remaining 45% holding was $35 million at 30 September 20X5.

Howard have recorded the proceeds of $15 million by debiting cash and crediting investments, but no other entries have been made.

Note 3 – Intra-group trading

During the year ended 30 September 20X5, Howard sold goods to Sylvia for $8 million.at a gross profit margin of 25%. Half of these goods remain in Sylvia's inventory at the reporting date.

Note 4 – Non-controlling interests and goodwill

Howard's policy is to value the non-controlling interests at acquisition at fair value. The fair value of the non-controlling interest in Sylvia was $17.4 million and the fair value of the non-controlling interest in Sabrina was $13 million at the relevant dates of acquisition. No impairment losses have arisen on goodwill.

Required:

Prepare the consolidated statement of financial position of the Howard group as at 30 September 20X5.

Test your understanding 3 – Hail

On 1 July 20X4, Hail, who has the $ as its functional and presentation currency, acquired eighty per cent of the equity share capital of Snow for cash consideration of $10 million.

Snow is based in a different country to Hail and has the dinar (Dr) as its functional currency. At the date of acquisition, Snow had issued equity capital of Dr5 million and retained earnings of Dr25 million. At that date, the carrying values of the separable net assets of Snow approximated to their fair values. The fair value of the non-controlling interest in Snow on 1 July 20X4 was Dr7.5 million

At the date of reporting date, Hail had retained earnings of $15 million and Snow had retained earnings of Dr43.5 million.

Relevant rates of exchange are as follows: .	Dr to $1
1 July 20X4	4.0
30 June 20X5	5.0
Average for the year	4.5

Required:

Calculate the following amounts that would be included in the Hail group financial statements for the year ended at 30 June 20X5:

(a) **Foreign exchange gain or loss on retranslation of net assets**

(b) **Foreign exchange gain or loss on retranslation of goodwill**

(c) **Non-controlling interest at 30 June 20X5**

(d) **Group retained earnings at 30 June 20X5**

(e) **Group foreign exchange reserve at 30 June 20X5**

(f) **Amount taken to other comprehensive income for the year ended 30 June 20X5**

Test your understanding 4 – Large & Little

Little was incorporated over 20 years ago, operating as an independent entity for 15 years until 1 April 20X0 when it was taken over by Large. Large's directors decided that the local expertise of Little's management should be utilised as far as possible, and since the takeover they have allowed the subsidiary to operate independently, maintaining its existing supplier and customer bases. Large exercises 'arms' length' strategic control, but takes no part in day-to-day operational decisions.

The statements of financial position of Large and Little at 31 March 20X4 are given below. The statement of financial position of Little is prepared in francos (F), its functional currency.

		Large		**Little**
	$000	$000	F000	F000
Non-current assets:				
Property, plant and equipment	63,000		80,000	
Investments	12,000		–	
		75,000		80,000
Current assets:				
Inventories	25,000		30,000	
Trade receivables	20,000		28,000	
Cash	6,000		5,000	
		51,000		63,000
		126,000		143,000

Equity:				
Equity capital (50 cents/1 Franco shares)		30,000		40,000
Revaluation reserve		–		6,000
Retained earnings		35,000		34,000
		65,000		80,000
Non-current liabilities:				
Long-term borrowings	20,000		25,000	
Deferred tax	6,000		10,000	
		26,000		35,000
Current liabilities:				
Trade payables	25,000		20,000	
Tax	7,000		8,000	
Bank overdraft	3,000		–	
		35,000		28,000
		126,000		143,000

Notes to the SFPs

Note 1 – Investment by Large in Little

On 1 April 20X0 Large purchased 36 million shares in Little for 72 million francos. The retained earnings of Little at that date were 26 million francos. It is group accounting policy to account for goodwill on a proportionate basis. Goodwill has been impairment tested annually and, in the year to 31 March 20X4, had reduced in value by ten per cent.

Note 2 – Intra-group trading

Little sells goods to Large, charging a mark-up of one-third on production cost. At 31 March 20X4, Large held $1 million (at cost to Large) of goods purchased from Little in its inventories. The goods were purchased during March 20X4 and were recorded by Large using an exchange rate of $1 = 5 francos. (There were minimal fluctuations between the two currencies during March 20X4). On 29 March 20X4, Large sent Little a cheque for $1 million to clear the intra-group payable. Little received and recorded this cheque on 3 April 20X4.

Note 3 – Accounting policies

The accounting policies of the two entities are the same, except that the directors of Little have decided to adopt a policy of revaluation of property, whereas Large includes all property in its statement of financial position at depreciated historical cost. Until 1 April 20X3, Little operated from rented warehouse premises. On that date, the entity purchased a leasehold building for 25 million francos, taking out a long-term loan to finance the purchase. The building's estimated useful life at 1 April 20X3 was 25 years, with an estimated residual value of nil, and the directors decided to adopt a policy of straight line depreciation. The building was professionally revalued at 30 million francos on 31 March 20X4, and the directors have included the revalued amount in the statement of financial position. No other property was owned by Little during the year.

Note 4 – Exchange rates

Date	**Exchange rate (francos to $1)**
1 April 20X0	6.0
31 March 20X3	5.5
31 March 20X4	5.0
Weighted average for the year to 31 March 20X4	5.2
Weighted average for the dates of acquisition of closing inventory	5.1

Required:

(a) **Explain (with reference to relevant accounting standards to support your argument) how the financial statements (statement of financial position, statement of profit or loss and other comprehensive income) of Little should be translated into dollars for the consolidation of Large and Little.**

(5 marks)

(b) **Prepare the consolidated statement of financial position of the Large group at 31 March 20X4.**

(20 marks)

Note: Ignore any deferred tax implications of the property revaluation and the intra-group trading. and assume that the Large Group uses the proportion of net assets method to value the non-controlling interest.

(Total: 25 marks)

Test your understanding 5 – Arc

Arc owns 100% of the ordinary share capital of Bend and Curve. All ordinary shares of all three entities are listed on a recognised exchange. The group operates in the engineering industry, and are currently struggling to survive in challenging economic conditions. Curve has made losses for the last three years and its liquidity is poor. The view of the directors is that Curve needs some cash investment. The directors have decided to put forward a restructuring plan as at 30 June 20X1. Under this plan:

(1) Bend is to purchase the whole of Arc's investment in Curve. The purchase consideration is to be $105 million payable in cash to Arc and this amount will then be loaned on a long-term unsecured basis to Curve; and

(2) Bend will purchase land and buildings with a carrying amount of $15 million from Curve for a total purchase consideration of $25 million. The land and buildings has a mortgage outstanding on it of $8 million. The total purchase consideration of $25 million comprises both ten million $1 nominal value non-voting shares issued by Bend to Curve and the $4 million mortgage liability which Bend will assume; and

(3) Curve had also entered into a finance lease obligation on 1 July 20X0 for an asset with a useful economic life of six years. The present value of the minimum lease obligation at that date was $3 million, and the implicit rate of interest associated with the lease obligation was 10.2%. The lease required that annual payments in arrears of $700,000 must be made. No entries had been made in respect of the lease in the draft financial statements of Curve; and

(4) A dividend of $25 million will be paid from Bend to Arc to reduce the accumulated reserves of Bend.

The draft statements of financial position of Arc and its subsidiaries at 30 June 20X1 are summarised below:

	Arc	Bend	Curve
	$m	$m	$m
Non-current assets:			
Tangible non-current assets	500	200	55
Cost of investment in Bend	150		
Cost of investment in Curve	95		
Current assets	125	145	25
	870	345	80

Equity and liabilities			
Ordinary share capital	100	100	35
Share premium			8
Retained earnings	720	230	5
	820	330	48
Non-current liabilities:			
Long-term loan	5		12
Current liabilities:			
Trade payables	45	15	20
	870	345	80

As a result of the restructuring, some of Bend's employees will be made redundant. Based upon a detailed plan, the costs of redundancy will be spread over three years with $2.08 million being payable in one year's time, $3.245 million payable in two year's time and $53.375 million in three years' time. The market yield of high quality corporate bonds is 4%. The directors of Arc consider that, based upon quantification of relevant and reliable data at 30 June 20X1, it will incur additional restructuring obligations amounting to $3 million.

Required:

(a) **Prepare the individual entity statements of financial position after the proposed restructuring plan; (13 marks)**

(b) **Discuss the key implications of the proposed plans, in particular whether the financial position of each company has been improved as a result of the reorganisation. (5 marks)**

Professional marks will be awarded in part (b) for clarity and expression of your discussion.

(2 marks)

(Total: 20 marks)

Test your understanding 6 – Kelly

Extracts from the consolidated financial statements of Kelly are given below:

Consolidated statements of financial position as at 31 March

	20X5		**20X4**	
	$000	$000	$000	$000
Non-current assets				
Property, plant and equipment	5,900		4,400	
Goodwill	85		130	
Investment in associate	170		140	
		6,155		4,670
Current assets				
Inventories	1,000		930	
Receivables	1,340		1,140	
Short-term deposits	35		20	
Cash at bank	180		120	
		2,555		2,210
		8,710		6,880
Equity and liabilities				
Equity capital	2,000		1,500	
Share premium	300		–	
Other components of equity	50		–	
Retained earnings	3,400		3,320	
		5,750		4,820
Non-controlling interests		75		175
Total equity		5,825		4,995
Non-current liabilities				
Interest-bearing borrowings	1,400		1,000	
Obligations under finance leases	210		45	
Deferred tax	340		305	
		1,950		1,350

Current liabilities				
Trade payables	885		495	
Interest payable	7		9	
Income tax payable	28		21	
Obligations under finance leases	15		10	
		935		535
		8,710		6,880

Consolidated statement of comprehensive income for the year ended 31 March 20X5

	$000
Revenue	875
Cost of sales	(440)
Gross profit	435
Other operating expenses	(210)
Profit from operations	225
Finance cost	(100)
Gain on sale of subsidiary	30
Share of associate's profit	38
Profit before tax	193
Tax	(48)
Profit for the year	145
Other comprehensive income	
Items that will not be reclassified to profit or loss in subsequent accounting periods	
Gains on land revaluation	50
Total comprehensive income for the year	195
Profit attributable to:	
Equity holders of the parent	120
Non-controlling interests	25
	145

Total comprehensive income attributable to:	
Equity holders of the parent	170
Non-controlling interests	25
	195

Notes:

Dividends

Kelly paid a dividend of $40,000 during the year.

Property, plant and equipment

The following transactions took place during the year:

- Land was revalued upwards by $50,000 on 1st April 20X4.
- During the year, depreciation of $80,000 was charged to profit or loss.
- Additions include $300,000 acquired under finance leases.
- A property was disposed of during the year for $250,000 cash. Its carrying amount was $295,000 at the date of disposal. The loss on disposal has been included within cost of sales.

Gain on sale of subsidiary

On 1 January 20X5, Kelly disposed of a 80% owned subsidiary for $390,000 in cash. The subsidiary had the following net assets at the date of disposal:

	$000
Property, plant and equipment	635
Inventory	20
Receivables	45
Cash	35
Payables	(130)
Income tax	(5)
Interest-bearing borrowings	(200)
	400

This subsidiary had been acquired on 1 January 20X1 for a cash payment of $220,000 when its net assets had a fair value of $225,000 and the non-controlling interest had a fair value of $50,000.

Goodwill

The Kelly Group uses the full goodwill method to calculate goodwill. No impairments have arisen during the year.

Required:

Prepare the consolidated statement of cash flows of the Kelly group for the year ended 31 March 20X5 in the form required by IAS 7 Statement of cash flows.

Test your understanding 7 – Bahzad

Bahzad has singled out the inventory control director for an employee option scheme. He has been offered 3 million options exercisable at 20c, conditional upon him remaining with the company for three years and improving inventory control by the end of that period. The proportion of the options that vest is dependent upon the inventory days on the last day of the three years. The schedule is as follows:

Inventory days	Proportion vesting
5	100%
6	90%
7	70%
8	40%
9	10%

The options also have a vesting criteria related to market value. They only vest if the share price is above 25c on the vesting day, i.e. at the end of the third year.

This is the second of the three years. At the end of year one it was estimated that the inventory days at the end of the third year would be 7. However, during year two inventory control improved and at the end of the year the estimate of inventory days at the end of the third year was 6. The relevant market data is as follows:

Date	Share price	Option price
Grant date	20c	10c
End of Year One	19c	6c
End of Year Two	37c	19c

The option price is the market price of an equivalent marketable option on the relevant date.

Required:

(a) **Show the effect of the scheme on the financial statements of Bahzad for year two of the share option scheme.**

(b) **Explain the significance of any conditions attaching to the share option scheme and how they are dealt with in accounting for such a scheme.**

Test your understanding 8 – Asif

Asif has set up an employee option scheme to motivate its sales team of ten key sales people. Each sales person was offered 1 million options exercisable at 10c, conditional upon the employee remaining with the company during the vesting period of 5 years. The options are then exercisable three weeks after the end of the vesting period.

This is year two of the scheme. At the end of year one, two sales people suggested that they would be leaving the company during the second year. However, although one did leave, the other recommitted to the company and the scheme. The other employees have always been committed to the scheme and stated their intention to stay with the company during the 5 years. Relevant market values are as follows:

Date	Share price	Option price
Grant date	10c	20c
End of Year One	24c	38c
End of Year Two	21c	33c

The option price is the market price of an equivalent marketable option on the relevant date.

Show the effect of the scheme on the financial statements of Asif for Year Two.

Test your understanding 9 – Fourkings

Fourkings is a marketing and public relations entity which provides a 'one-stop-shop' for all aspects of market research and product promotion activities, both domestically and abroad, including hire of staff, venues and marquees, and other associated requirements. In recent years, Fourkings has experienced significant expansion, fuelled mainly by the growth experienced by entities in the financial sector. More recently, the business environment has become more challenging as a result of the global financial crisis and Fourkings has requested advice on a number of financial reporting issues in respect of the financial statements for the year ended 31 October 2010 as follows:

(1) Fourkings requires clients to pay a 15% initial amount at the time of booking an event plus facilities required, with the balance payable by the date of the event. The initial amount is not refundable in the event of the client cancelling at any stage prior to the due date of the event. Currently, the initial amount is taken to revenue immediately upon receipt as Fourkings does not foresee any circumstances when it would need to cancel their service provision.

Required:

Advise Fourkings on the appropriateness of the accounting policy adopted.

(5 marks)

(2) Fourkings purchased a country manor house in extensive grounds to make available to potential clients as an event venue. The property cost $5 million (of which the grounds accounted for $1 million) on 1 November 2006. Both the manor house and the grounds require regular expenditure to keep them in excellent condition to attract clients and bookings. The expenditure has always been expensed but Fourkings now intends to capitalise this expenditure.

The number of bookings for the manor house and grounds for the current year fell in comparison with earlier years. For the year to 31 October 2010, the property was utilised for only 150 days, when the average annual utilisation in earlier years had been 200 days, with the average spend per client day also reduced from previous levels. Fourkings is currently reviewing alternative uses for the house and grounds, including disposal to a property developer who is willing to pay $4.5 million to purchase the manor house and grounds to convert it into a theme park.

Required:

Advise Fourkings on the accounting issues associated with this situation.

(8 marks)

(3) Fourkings spends a considerable amount of time and effort to recruit, train and retain staff. They regard this as a crucial element of their success to date as many competitor companies hire staff on a casual basis and pay minimum wages to keep costs as low as possible. Fourkings is considering capitalisation of recruitment and training costs as it believes that the benefits of staff training are received over several years. It introduced an employee share-option scheme on 1 November 2009 in an effort to retain staff loyalty. A pre-defined group of one hundred employees were selected to join the scheme on the following terms:

(a) Each employee eligible would be granted 500 share options, with a three-year vesting period; the options would become exercisable immediately thereafter.

(b) To be eligible to exercise the options, employees would be required to still be employed by the company at the vesting date. At the date the scheme was established, it was expected that ten employees would leave during the year; however, only five actually left during the year to 31 October 2010.

(c) Fourkings has provided the following information relating to the share option scheme:

Date	Number expected to leave in year	FV of option
1 Nov 2009		$6.00
31 Oct 2010		$7.50
31 Oct 2011	5	(est) $8.25
31 Oct 2012	7	(est) $9.95

Required:

Advise Fourkings on the accounting issues associated with this situation.

(6 marks)

(4) Fourkings has undertaken the organisation of several major product launches during the year. One such event required making payments to an exclusive venue to reserve, pay for the use of facilities and to meet catering and hospitality costs. Fourkings paid a deposit on 31 August 2010 for rental of a villa in the Seychelles on 31 December 2010 amounting to 100,000 Seychelles rupees. The terms of the agreement are that the villa rental can be cancelled at any time up to 31 December 2010 and the deposit returned without penalty. The balance outstanding for the villa rental is due on 1 February 2011 and amounts to 150,000 Seychelles rupees. The table below summarises the rates of exchange during the relevant period:

Date	**Rupees per $**
31 August 2010	1.25
31 October 2010	1.30
31 December 2010	1.20
1 February 2011	1.35

Additionally, Fourkings is considering opening a Euro currency bank account during 2011 to facilitate payments made to third parties within the Euro zone but is unsure about how this should be included within the financial statements for the year ended 31 October 2011.

Required:

Explain the accounting treatment for this situation and calculate the amounts to include in the financial statements for the year ended 31 October 2010 and explain how transactions passing through a Euro currency bank account should be treated in the financial statements for the year ending 31 October 2011.

(6 marks)

(Total: 25 marks)

Test your understanding 10 – Seejoy

Seejoy is a famous football club but has significant cash flow problems. The directors and shareholders wish to take steps to improve the club's financial position. The following proposals had been drafted in an attempt to improve the cash flow of the club. However, the directors need advice upon their implications.

(a) **Sale and leaseback of football stadium (excluding the land element)**

The football stadium is currently accounted for using the cost model in IAS 16 Property, plant, and equipment. The carrying value of the stadium will be $12 million at 31 December 20X6. The stadium will have a remaining life of 20 years at 31 December 20X6, and the club uses straight line depreciation. It is proposed to sell the stadium to a third party institution on 1 January 20X7 and lease it back under a 20-year finance lease. The sale price and fair value is $15 million which is the present value of the minimum lease payments. The agreement transfers the title of the stadium back to the football club at the end of the lease at nil cost. The rental is $1.2 million per annum in advance commencing on 1 January 20X7. The directors do not wish to treat this transaction as the raising of a secured loan. The implicit interest rate on the finance in the lease is 5.6%.

(9 marks)

(b) **Player registrations**

The club capitalises the unconditional amounts (transfer fees) paid to acquire players. The club proposes to amortise the cost of the transfer fees over ten years instead of the current practice that is to amortise the cost over the duration of the player's contract. The club has sold most of its valuable players during the current financial year but still has two valuable players under contract.

Player	Transfer fee capitalised	Amortisation to 31 December 20X6	Contract commenced	Contract expires
	$m	$m		
A. Steel	20	4	1 Jan 20X6	31 Dec 20Y0
R. Aldo	15	10	1 Jan 20X5	31 Dec 20X7

If Seejoy win the national football league, then a further $5 million will be payable to the two players' former clubs. Seejoy are currently performing very poorly in the league.

(5 marks)

(c) **Issue of bond**

The club proposes to issue a 7% bond with a face value of $50 million on 1 January 20X7 at a discount of 5% that will be secured on income from future ticket sales and corporate hospitality receipts, which are approximately $20 million per annum. Under the agreement the club cannot use the first $6 million received from corporate hospitality sales and reserved tickets (season tickets) as this will be used to repay the bond. The money from the bond will be used to pay for ground improvements and to pay the wages of players.

The bond will be repayable, both capital and interest, over 15 years with the first payment of $6 million due on 31 December 20X7. It has an effective interest rate of 7.7%. There will be no active market for the bond and the company does not wish to use valuation models to value the bond.

(6 marks)

(d) **Player trading**

Another proposal is for the club to sell its two valuable players, Aldo and Steel. It is thought that it will receive a total of $16 million for both players. The players are to be offered for sale at the end of the current football season on 1 May 20X7.

(5 marks)

Required:

Discuss how the above proposals would be dealt with in the financial statements of Seejoy for the year-ending 31 December 20X7, setting out their accounting treatment and appropriateness in helping the football club's cash flow problems. (Candidates do not need knowledge of the football finance sector to answer this question.)

(Total: 25 marks)

Test your understanding answers

Test your understanding 1 – Exotic

Key answer tips:

This is not a past exam question, but it is a great question to revise complex groups. If you can work your way through this, then you should be feeling comfortable with this topic and can attempt some of the more difficult questions.

(a) **Consolidated statement of comprehensive income for the year ended 31 December 20X6**

	Exotic	Melon	Kiwi	Adjusts		SOCI
	$000	$000	$000	$000		$000
Revenue	45,600	24,700	22,800	(980)	)	92,120
Cost of sales	(18,050)	(5,463)	(5,320)	740	)	
Cost re equip't sale	200				)	(27,915)
URPS made by M & K (W5)		(15)	(15)		)	
Excess dep'n adj (W6)		8			)	———
Gross profit						64,205
Distribution costs	(3,325)	(2,137)	(1,900)			(7,362)
Administration expenses	(3,475)	(950)	(1,900)			(6,325)
Goodwill impaired (W3)						(259)
						———
Profit from operations						50,259
Finance costs	(325)					(325)
						———
Profit before tax						49,934
Tax	(8,300)	(5,390)	(4,241)			(17,931)
		———	———			———
Profit for the period		10,753	9,424			32,003
		———	———			———
Attributable to:						
Equity holders of the parent (bal fig)						28,289
Non-controlling interests (W8)						3,714
						———
						32,003
						———

There were no items of other comprehensive income during the year.

Reconciliation of retained earnings:

Retained earnings brought forward (W9)	34,115
Profit for the period	28,289
Dividends paid	(9,500)
Retained earnings carried forward	52,904

(b) **Consolidated statement of financial position as at 31 December 20X6**

	$000
Assets:	
Non-current assets (35,483 + 24,273 + 13,063 – 32 (W6))	72,787
Goodwill (W3)	259
Current assets (1,568 + 9,025 + 8,883 – 15(W5) – 15(W5))	19,446
Total assets	92,492
Equity and liabilities:	
$1 equity shares	8,000
Group retained earnings (W7)	52,904
	60,904
Non-controlling interest (W4)	8,454
Total equity	69,358
Sundry liabilities:(13,063 + 10,023 + 48)	23,134
Total equity and liabilities	92,492

Workings

(W1) **Group structure**

2,700 / 3,000 =	90%	Exotic		
	90%		Effective interest of Exotic in Kiwi (90% × 80%) =	72%
		Melon	Effective NCI in Kiwi =	28%
	80%			
1,600 / 2,000 =	80%	Kiwi		

(W2) **Net assets**

	At date of acquisition		**At reporting date**	
	$000	$000	$000	$000
Melon				
Equity capital		3,000		3,000
Retained earnings	1,425		24,075	
Excess depreciation (W6)			8	
Unrealised profit (W5)			(15)	
		1,425		24,068
		4,425		27,068

	At date of acquisition		**At reporting date**	
	$000	$000	$000	$000
Kiwi				
Equity capital		2,000		2,000
Retained earnings	950		19,898	
Unrealised profit (W5)			(15)	
		950		19,883
		2,950		21,883

(W3) **Goodwill**

	In Melon	In Kiwi
	$000	$000
Cost of investment to the group	6,650	
90% × 3,800		3,420
Melon: NCI% of CV of NA at acq'n (10% × 4,425)(W2)	442	
Kiwi: NCI% of CV of NA at acq'n (28% × 2,950)(W2)		826
	7,092	4,246
Fair value of all net assets at acquisition:		
Melon: (W2)	(4,425)	
Kiwi: (W2)		(2,950)
	2,667	1,296
Impairment – in previous years (100%) / 60%	(2,667)	(778)
	-	518
Impairment current year (50% × 518) (I/S)	-	(259)
Statement of financial position	-	259
Charged against retained earnings	2,667	1,037

(W4) **Non-controlling Interest – proportionate basis for both subsidiaries**

Melon

CV of NCI at acquisition (10% × 4,425) (W2)	442.5
Share of post-acq'n retained earnings (10% × (27,068 – 4,425)) (W2)	2264.3
(rounded)	2,707

Kiwi (use effective interest %)

CV of NCI at acquisition (28% × 2,950) (W2)	826
Share of post-acq'n retained earnings (28% × (21,883 – 2,950)) (W2)	5,301
Less: NCI share of cost of investment by Melon in Kiwi (10% × 3,800)	(380)
	8,454

(W5) **Unrealised profit in inventory**

Kiwi – Melon	75,000 × 25 ÷ 125	= 15,000
Melon – Exotic	$\frac{60,000 \times 33.333}{\div 133.333}$	= 15,000

(W6) **Inter-company transfers of non-current assets**

Exotic – Melon	240,000

Therefore Exotic has made an unrealised profit.

Debit group statement of comprehensive income	40,000
Credit group non-current assets	40,000

Total intra-group revenues (480 + 260 + 240) = $980,000

Total intra-group adjustment to cost of sales (480 + 260) = $740,000

Total intra-group addition to NCA re equipt sold by Exotic to Melon = $240,000 when original cost was $200,000.

Depreciation is charged on $240,000 at 20% on cost (i.e. $48,000 each year). This should be charged in the group accounts at 20% on $200,000 (i.e. $40,000).

Therefore $8,000 extra depreciation has been charged each year and must be added back.

Debit depreciation group	8,000
Credit statement of comprehensive income group	8,000
Therefore net impact $40,000 – $8,000 =	32,000
Net non-current assets credit	32,000
Statement of comprehensive income debit	32,000

(W7) **Consolidated retained earnings carried forward**

	$000
All of Exotic	
Per the question	22,638
Unrealised profit re equip't (W6)	(40)
	22,598
Share of Melon	
90% (24,068 – 1,425) (W2)	20,378
Share of Kiwi	
72% (19,883 – 950) (W2)	13,632
Goodwill impairment (2,667 + 1,037) (W3)	(3,704)
	52,904

(W8) **Non-controlling interest in profit**

Melon (10,753 × 10%)	1075
Kiwi's profit (9,424 × 28%)	2,639
	3,714

(W9) **Consolidated retained earnings brought forward**

	$000
All of Exotic	20,013
Share of Melon	
90% (13,315 – 1,425) (W2)	10,701
Share of Kiwi	
72% (10,459 – 950) (W2)	6,846
Goodwill impairment (2,667 + 778) (W3)	(3,445)
	34,115

Test your understanding 2 – Howard

Howard – Consolidated Statement of Financial Position at 30 September 20X5

Assets:	$000
Goodwill (W3)	9,400
Property, plant & equipment ($160,000 + $60,000 + $5,000 (W2))	225,000
Investments ($80,000 + $15,000 (W8) – $45,000 (W3) – $21,000 (W3) – $10,000 (W7))	19,000
Investment in associate (W8)	35,000
Current assets ($65,000 + $50,000 – $1,000 (W6))	114,000
	402,400

Equity and liabilities:	$000
Equity Capital	50,000
Retained earnings (W5)	223,500
Other components of equity (W7)	(2,700)
Non-controlling interest (W4)	14,600
	285,400
Non-current liabilities ($25,000 + $18,000)	43,000
Current liabilities ($45,000 + $29,000)	74,000
	402,400

Workings:

(W1) **Group structure**

Howard

1 Oct X3	70%	1 Jan X2	60%
30 Sept X5	10%	30 Sept X5	(15%)
Rep date	80%	Rep date	45%
	Sylvia	Sabrina	

Note that Howard controls Sylvia from 1 October 20X3. The purchase of additional shares on 30 September 20X5 does not change this situation. An equity transfer is required between the group and NCI to reflect the purchase of additional shares.

Note that Howard controls Sabrina from 1 January 20X2. The sale of shares on 30 September 20X5 results in a loss of control, on which a group gain or loss disposal should be computed and included in the group statement of profit or loss and other comprehensive income. The fair value of the residual holding should be included in the calculation of the group gain or loss on disposal and, as significant influence over Sabrina is retained, is also the deemed 'cost' of the associate.

(W2) **Net assets**

	Sylvia		**Sabrina**	
	Acq'n date	**Rep date**	**Acq'n date**	**Rep date**
	$000	$000	$000	$000
Share capital	20,000	20,000	15,000	15,000
Retained earnings	28,000	43,000	15,000	42,000
FVA – Land (45,000 – 40,000)	5,000	5,000		
	53,000	68,000	30,000	57,000

(W3) **Goodwill – Calculated at the date control is achieved**

	Sylvia	**Sabrina**
	$000	$000
FV of consideration	45,000	21,000
FV of NCI at acquisition	17,400	13,000
	62,400	34,000
Less: FV of net assets at acquisition (W2)	(53,000)	(30,000)
Goodwill	9,400	4,000

(W4) **Non–controlling interest**

	Sylvia	Sabrina
	$000	$000
NCI at acquisition date (W3)	17,400	13,000
NCI share of Sylvia's post-acq'n retained earnings (30% × ($68,000 – $53,000) (W2))	4,500	
NCI share of Sabrina'a post-acq'n retained earnings (40% × ($57,000 – $30,000)(W2))		10,800
NCI before equity transfer	21,900	23,800
Equity transfer due to purchase of additional shares by group (W7)	(7,300)	N/A
NCI at reporting date/disposal date	14,600	23,800

(W5) **Retained earnings**

	$000
Howard	185,000
Provision for unrealised profit (W6)	(1,000)
Howard's share of Sylvia's post-acquisition retained earnings (70% × $15,000 (W2))	10,500
Howard's share of Sabrina's post-acquisition retained earnings (60% × $27,000 (W2))	16,200
Gain on disposal of Sabrina (W8)	12,800
	223,500

(W6) **Provision for unrealised profits**

The profit on the intra-group sale was $2 million ($8m × 25%).

The profit on this sale that remains in inventory at the reporting date is $1 million ($2m × 50%).

The adjusting entry is:

Dr Retained earnings $1m (W5)
Cr Inventory $1m

(W7) **Equity transfer between group and NCI**

	$000
Cash paid by Howard to buy additional shares	10,000
Decrease in NCI (10/30 × $21,900(W4))	7,300
Net decrease in equity of the group	2,700

The adjusting entry is:

Dr NCI (W4) $7,300
Dr Equity $2,700
Cr Investments $10,000 (to reverse the original accounting entry for the receipt of the disposal proceeds)

(W8) **Profit on disposal of Sabrina**

	$000	$000
Proceeds	15,000	
Fair value of residual interest	35,000	
		50,000
Less: interest in Sabrina disposed of:		
Net assets at disposal date (W2)	57,000	
Unimpaired goodwill at disposal date (W3)	4,000	
		(61,000)
Less: NCI at disposal date (W5)		23,800
Profit on disposal (W5)		12,800

After the disposal, Sabrina is accounted for as an associate. Its deemed cost is $35 million (the fair value of the residual interest).

In subsequent periods, the investment in Sabrina will be increased by Howard's share of its profits.

Test your understanding 3 – Hail

(a) Foreign exchange gain or loss on retranslation of net assets:

	Acq'n date Dr000	Rep date Dr000	Rate	Rep date $000
Equity capital	5,000	5,000		
Pre-acquisition earnings	25,000	25,000		
		30,000	4.0	7,500
Post-acquisition earnings (43,500 – 25,000)		18,500	4.5	4,111
FX loss on retranslation of net assets			Bal fig	(1,911)
	30,000	48,500	5.0	9,700

Allocate loss on retranslation as follows:

Group (80% × $1,911) = $1,529 loss

NCI (20% × $1,911) = $382 loss

(b) Foreign exchange gain or loss on retranslation of goodwill

Full goodwill in functional currency of subsidiary	Dr000
Cost to gain control $10m × 4	40,000
FV of NCI at acquisition	7,500
	47,500
FV of net assets at acquisition	(30,000)
Full goodwill at acquisition	17,500

Retranslation of goodwill:	Dr000	Rate	$000
Goodwill at acquisition	17,500	4.0	4,375
Impairment of goodwill in year	(N/A)	4.5	(N/A)
FX loss on retranslation of goodwill		**Bal fig**	**(875)**
	17,500	5.0	3,500

Allocate retranslation loss as follows:

Group (80% × $875) = $700 loss

NCI (20% × $875) = $175 loss

(c) Non-controlling interest at the reporting date:

	Dr000	Rate	$000
NCI at acquisition	7,500	4.0	1,875
NCI % of goodwill impairment in year	(N/A)	4.5	(N/A)
NCI % of profit for the year (20% × Dr18,500) (part (a))	3,700	4.5	822
NCI % of FX retranslation loss on retranslation of net assets (part (a))			(382)
NCI % of FX retranslation loss on goodwill (part (b))			(175)
			2,140

(d) Group retained earnings at the reporting date:

	Dr000	Rate	$000
Hail retained earnings per question			15,000
Group share of goodwill impairment in year	(N/A)	4.5	(N/A)
Group share of profit for the year (80% × Dr18,500) (part (a))	14,800	4.5	3,289
			18,289

(e) Group foreign exchange reserve at the reporting date

	$000
Group share of FX loss on retranslation of net assets (part (a))	(1,529)
Group share of FX loss on retranslation of goodwill (part (b))	(700)
	(2,229)

(f) Amount taken to other comprehensive income for the year

	$000
Total of FX loss on retranslation of net assets (part (a))	(1,911)
Total of FX loss on retranslation of goodwill (part (b))	(875)
	(2,786)

Test your understanding 4 – Large & Little

Group accounting – foreign currency Large and Little

Answer 1

(1) It is clear from the information contained in the question that, on a day-to-day basis, Little operates as a relatively independent entity, with its own supplier and customer bases. Therefore, the cash flows of Little do not have a day-to-day impact on the cash flows of Large. The functional currency of Little is the Franco, rather than the dollar. For consolidation purposes, the financial statements of Little must be translated into a presentation currency: the dollar (the functional currency of Large, in which the consolidated financial statements of Large are presented). In these circumstances, IAS 21 The effects of changes in foreign exchange rates requires that the financial statements be translated using the closing rate (or net investment) method (the presentation currency method). This involves translating the net assets in the statement of financial position at the spot rate of exchange at the reporting date and income and expenses in the statement of profit or loss and other comprehensive income at the rate on the date of the transactions, or as an approximation, a weighted average rate for the year.

Exchange differences on the translation of an overseas subsidiary are reported as other comprehensive income and classified as 'Items which may be reclassified to profit or loss in future periods'.

(b) **Group statement of financial position – Large Group**

Non-current assets:	$000
Goodwill	2,268
Property, plant and equipment ($63,000 + (F80,000 – F6,000)/5)	77,800
Current assets:	
Inventories ($25,000 + F30,000/5 – F1,250/5)	30,750
Trade receivables ($20,000 + F28,000/5 – $1,000)	24,600
Cash ($6,000 + F5,000/5 + $1,000)	8,000
	143,418

Equity and liabilities	$000
Equity share capital	30,000
Retained earnings (W5)	35,926
Group foreign exchange reserve (W7)	2,437
Non-controlling interest (W4)	1,455
	———
Total equity	69,818
Non-current liabilities ($20,000 + (F25,000/5))	25,000
Deferred tax ($6,000 + F10,000/5)	8,000
Current liabilities	
Payables ($25,000 + (F20,000/5))	29,000
Tax ($7,000 + (F8,000/5))	8,600
Overdraft	3,000
	———
	143,418
	———

Workings

(W1) Group structure

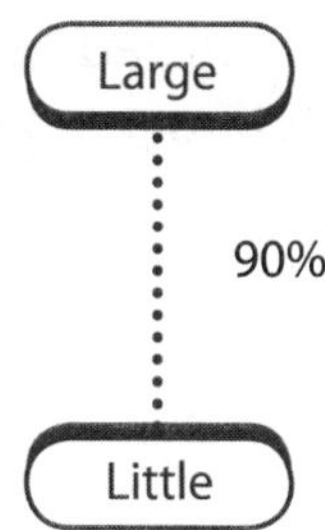

(W2) **Net assets of subsidiary in functional currency**

	Acq'n Date	**Rep date**
	F000	F000
Equity capital	40,000	40,000
Retained earnings	26,000	34,000
Revaluation reserve		6,000
Accounting policy adjustment**		(6,000)
PURP*		(1,250)
	———	———
	66,000	72,750
	———	———

*Calculation of unrealised profit on closing inventory sold by subsidiary:

	%	F000
Cost	100.0	3,750
Profit element	33.3	1,250
Selling price	133.3	5,000

**Accounting policy adjustment:

This arises due to the parent and subsidiary having different accounting policies relating to property. At the reporting date, the property has been owned by the subsidiary, and depreciated, for one year (F25m / 25 year = F1m per annum), giving a carrying value of F24m before the revaluation is accounted for at the reporting date. The revaluation reserve created is therefore (F30m – F24m) F6m. This needs to be removed from both non-current assets and revaluation reserve of the subsidiary.

(W3) **Goodwill**

	F000
Consideration	72,000
NCI at acquisition (10% × 66,000 (W2)	6,600
	78,600
Fair value of net assets at acquisition (W2)	(66,000)
Goodwill at acquisition	12,600
Impairment in year - 10%	(1,200)
Goodwill at reporting date	11,340
Translated at closing rate @ 5 for SOFP	$2,268

Reconciliation of movement in goodwill:

	F000	Rate	$000
Goodwill at acquisition	12,600	6.0	2,100
Impairment	(1,260)	5.2	(242)
Exchange gain		bal. fig	410
Goodwill at reporting date	11,340	5.0	2,268

As goodwill has been calculated on a proportionate basis, all of the impairment is taken to retained earnings in (W5). The whole exchange gain is also attributable to the group and is taken to the foreign exchange reserve (W7).

(W4) **Non-controlling interest**

	F000	Rate	$000
NCI at acquisition (W3)	6,600	6.0	1,100
NCI % of profit for the year (10% × (F72,750 - F66,000)) (W2)	675	5.2	130
NCI % of exchange gain (loss) on retranslation of net assets			225
			1,455

(W5) **Group retained earnings**

	F000	Rate	$000
Large			35,000
Group share of profit for year (90% × (72,750 – 66,000) (W2))	6,075	5.2	1,168
Goodwill impaired in year (W3)	(1,260)	5.2	(242)
			35,926

(W6) **Exchange gain on retranslation of opening net assets and profit**

	F000	Rate	$000
Net assets at acquisition (W2)	66,000	6.0	11,000
Profit for the year	6,750	5.2	1,298
Exchange gain/(loss)		bal fig	2,252
Closing net assets (W2)	72,750		14,550

The exchange gain arising on retranslation of net assets is then allocated between the group and NCI based upon their respective shareholdings as follows:

	$000
Group (90% × 2,252)	2,027
NCI (10% × 2,252)	225

(W7) **Group foreign exchange reserve**

	$000
Arising on retranslation of goodwill (W3)	410
Arising on retranslation of opening net assets and profit (W6)	2,027
	2,437

Test your understanding 5 – Arc

(a) **Arc – restatement**

	Initial	Adjusts	Notes	Final
	$m	$m		$m
Non-current assets:				
Tangible non-current assets	500			500
Cost of investment in Bend	150			150
Cost of investment in Curve	95	(95)	(1)	
Loan to Curve		105	(2)	105
Current assets	125	105	(1)	150
		(105)	(2)	
		25	(3)	
	870	345		905
Equity and liabilities:				
Ordinary share capital	100			100
Retained earnings	720	10	(1)	755
		25	(3)	
	870	35		855
Non-current liabilities:				
Long-term loan	5			5
Current liabilities:				
Trade payables	45			45
	870	35		905

Notes:

(1) Disposal of investment in Curve for $105m, resulting in a profit of $10m.

(2) Long-term loan made to Curve.

(3) Dividend due from Bend.

(a) **Bend restatement**

	Initial $m	Adjusts $m	Notes	Final $m
Non-current assets:				
Tangible non-current assets	200	25	(3)	225
Cost of investment in Curve		105	(1)	105
Current assets	145	(105)	(1)	40
	345	25		370
Equity and liabilities:				
Ordinary share capital	100	10	(3)	110
Share premium		11	(3)	11
Retained earnings	230	(25)	(2)	205
	330	(4)		326
Non-current liabilities:				
Long-term loan		4	(3)	4
Current liabilities:				
Trade payables	15			15
	345	25		370

Notes:

(1) Purchase of investment in Curve for $105m.

(2) Dividend due to Arc.

(3) Purchase of land and buildings from Curve – comprising:

	$m
Non-voting shares of $1 each	10
Share premium (bal fig)	11
Mortgage liability taken over	4
	25

3 – Finance lease obligation as follows:

	Bal b/fwd	Int @ 10.2%	Cash paid	Bal c/fwd
	$000	$000	$000	$000
Y/end 30/06/X1	3,000	306	(700)	2,606
Y/end 30/06/X2	2,606	266	(700)	2,172

Current liability element = $2,606,000 – $2,172,000 = $434,000

(a) Curve – restatement

	Initial	Adjusts	Notes	Final
	$m	$m		$m
Non-current assets:				
Tangible non-current assets	55	(15.0)	(2)	40.0
Finance lease assets		3.0	(3)	2.5
		(0.5)	(3)	
Cost of investment in Bend		21.0		21.0
Current assets	25	105.0	(1)	129.3
		(0.7)	(3)	
	80	112.8		192.8
Equity and liabilities:				
Ordinary share capital	35			35.0
Share premium	8			8.0
Retained earnings	5	10.0	(2)	14.2
		(0.5)	(3)	
		(0.3)	(3)	
	48	9.2		57.2
Non-current liabilities:				
Long-term loan	12	(4.0)		8.0
Loan from Arc		105.0	(1)	105.0
Finance lease obligation		3.0	(3)	2.2
		0.3	(3)	
		(0.7)	(3)	
		(0.4)	(3)	
Current liabilities:				
Finance lease obligation		(0.4)	(3)	0.4
Trade payables	20			20.0
	80	112.8		192.8

Notes:

1 – Loan from Arc of $105m.

2 – Sale of land and buildings to Bend as follows:

	$m
Disposal proceeds (Mort tfr at + shares at FV $21m)	25
CV of land and buildings	15
Profit on disposal	10

(b) The plan has no impact on the group financial statements as all of the internal transactions will be eliminated on consolidation but does affect the individual accounts of the companies. The reconstruction only masks the problem facing Curve. It does not solve or alter the business risk currently being faced by the group.

A further issue is that such a reorganisation may result in further costs and expenses being incurred. Note that any proposed provision for restructuring must meet the requirements of IAS 37 Provisions, Contingent Liabilities and Contingent Assets before it can be included in the financial statements. A constructive obligation will arise if there is a detailed formal plan produced and a valid expectation in those affected that the plan will be carried out. This is normally crystallised at the point when there is communication by the company with those who are expected to be affected by the plan.

The transactions outlined in the plans are essentially under common control and must be viewed in this light. This plan overcomes the short-term cash flow problem of Curve and results in an increase in the accumulated reserves. The plan does show the financial statements of the individual entities in a better light except for the significant increase in long-term loans in Curve's statement of financial position. The profit on the sale of the land from Curve to Bend will be eliminated on consolidation.

In the financial statements of Curve, the investment in Bend should be accounted for under IFRS 9. There is now cash available for Curve and this may make the plan attractive. However, the dividend from Bend to Arc will reduce the accumulated reserves of Bend but if paid in cash will reduce the current assets of Bend to a critical level.

The purchase consideration relating to Curve may be a transaction at an overvalue in order to secure the financial stability of the former entity. A range of values are possible which are current value, carrying amount or possibly at zero value depending on the purpose of the reorganisation. Another question which arises is whether the sale of Curve gives rise to a realised profit. Further, there may be a question as to whether Bend has effectively made a distribution. This may arise where the purchase consideration was well in excess of the fair value of Curve. An alternative to a cash purchase would be a share exchange. In this case, local legislation would need to be reviewed in order to determine the requirements for the setting up of any share premium account.

Test your understanding 6 – Kelly

Consolidated statement of cash flows for the year ended 31 March 20X5

	$000	$000
Cash flows from operating activities		
Profit before tax	193	
Gain on sale of subsidiary	(30)	
Share of associate's profit	(38)	
Finance costs	100	
Depreciation	80	
Loss on disposal of property ($250 – $295)	45	
	–––	
Operating profit before working capital changes	350	
Increase in inventory ($1,000 – $930 + $20))	(90)	
Increase in receivables ($1,340 – $1,140 + $45)	(245)	
Increase in payables ($885 – $495 + $130)	520	
	–––	
Cash generated from operations	535	
Finance costs paid (W2)	(102)	
Tax paid (W3)	(1)	
	–––	

Cash flows from investing activities

Proceeds from sale of property	250	
Purchases of property, plant and equipment (W4)	(2,160)	
Dividends received from associate (W5)	8	
Net proceeds from sale of subsidiary ($390 – $35)	355	
		(1,547)

Cash flows from financing activities

Repayments of finance leases (W6)	(130)	
Cash proceeds from borrowings (W7)	600	
Proceeds from issue of shares ($500 + $300)	800	
Dividends paid to equity shareholders of parent	(40)	
Dividends paid to non-controlling interests (W8)	(40)	
		1,190
Increase in cash and cash equivalents		75
Opening cash and cash equivalents ($120 + $20)		140
Closing cash and cash equivalents ($180 + $35)		215

(W1) **Goodwill**

Goodwill on acquisition of subsidiary disposed of during the year

	$000
Fair value of consideration	220
Fair value of NCI at acquisition	50
	270
Less: Fair value of net assets at acquisition	(225)
Goodwill	45

(W2) **Interest**

	$000
Balance bfd	9
Profit or loss	100
Cash paid (bal. fig)	(102)
Bal cfd	7

(W3) **Tax**

	$000
Balance bfd ($21 + $305)	326
Profit or loss	48
Disposal of subsidiary	(5)
Cash paid (bal. fig)	(1)
Bal cfd ($28 + $340)	368

(W4) **Non-current assets**

	$000
Balance bfd	4,400
Revaluation	50
Finance leases	300
Depreciation	(80)
Disposal of property	(295)
Disposal of subsidiary	(635)
Cash paid (bal. fig)	2,160
Bal cfd	5,900

(W5) **Dividend from associate**

	$000
Balance bfd	140
Share of profit of associate	38
Dividend received (bal. fig)	(8)
Bal cfd	170

(W6) **Repayment of finance leases**

	$000
Balance bfd ($10 + $45)	55
New leases (W4)	300
Lease repayments (bal. fig)	(130)
Bal cfd ($15 + $210)	225

(W7) **Interest bearing borrowings**

	$000
Balance bfd	1,000
Disposal of subsidiary	(200)
Cash received (bal. fig)	600
Bal cfd	1,400

(W8) **Dividend paid to non-controlling interests**

	$000
Balance bfd	175
Share of profits	25
NCI in subsidiary disposed of (W9)	(85)
Dividends paid (bal. fig)	(40)
Bal cfd	75

(W9) **NCI in subsidiary at disposal date**

	$000
FV of NCI at acquisition	50
NCI share of post-acquisition retained earnings (20% × ($400 – $225))	35
	85

Test your understanding 7 – Bahzad

(a) At the end of year two the amount recognised in equity is $180,000 (3m × 10c × 90% × 2/3).

At the end of year one the amount recognised in equity should have been $70,000 (3m × 10c × 70% × 1/3).

Therefore the charge to profit or loss for year two is $110,000 (180,000 – 70,000).

(b) Conditions attaching to a share option scheme may be either service conditions or performance conditions. An example of a **service condition** is that each member of a share option scheme must remain employed by the entity throughout the vesting period. If an individual member of the scheme is no longer employed by the entity at any time prior to the vesting date, they will lose their eligibility to remain as a member of the scheme. Service conditions are regarded as non-market conditions (see below) and are taken into account when estimating the number of options that are likely to vest at the end of the vesting period.

A **performance condition** relates to specified service conditions and/or specified performance targets which should be complied with if a scheme member is to become eligible to exercise their options at some point following the vesting date performance conditions may be either market or non-market conditions.

Market conditions are taken into account when arriving at the fair value of a share option at the grant date. The fair value of an option could be determined by on option pricing model such as Black-Scholes, although other models could be used. This would include, for example, attainment of a minimum share price by the vesting date, or growth in the share price in relation to a specified index. Within this question, one of the conditions of vesting is a 'market condition' (the share price must be above 25c on the vesting day). This should already have been taken into account when the option price was fixed and it does not affect the calculations required to determine amounts included in the financial statements at each reporting date.

Non-market conditions are relevant at each reporting date to estimate the number of options which are likely to vest at the vesting date. Examples of non-market conditions include achievement of a profit or earnings target by the vesting date.

Test your understanding 8 – Asif

The expense is measured using the fair value of the option at the grant date, i.e. 20c.

At the end of year two the amount recognised in equity should be \$720,000 (1m × (10 – 1) × 20c × 2/5).

At the beginning of year two the amount recognised in equity would have been \$320,000 (1m × 8 × 20c × 1/5).

The charge to profit for Year Two is the difference between the two: \$400,000 (720 – 320).

Test your understanding 9 – Fourkings

Revenue recognition
IAS 18 deals with revenue recognition. The principles which underpin the basis on which revenue is recognised are as follows;

- The revenue earned should be capable of reliable measurement
- Economic benefits will probably flow to the provider of services
- The costs incurred can be measured reliably.

If a contract, including the terms of service provision and a price has been agreed, it would appear that the first condition has been met. Similarly, if the contract cannot be cancelled by the client, this would go some way towards regarding the flow of economic benefits to Fourkings as being probable.

Ideally, the deposit should only be released to revenue at the point when the service is provided. However, this principle should be examined more closely, even though Fourkings cannot foresee any circumstances when it may need to cancel attendance or provision for an event, there could be circumstances when it may have no practical alternative. For example, any of the following circumstances could occur which would result in the accounting treatment used by Fourkings being inappropriate:

(a) The venue for an event (whether or not at their own property) could be closed by court or other public order announcement, such as travel and other restrictions imposed during an outbreak of foot and mouth disease. Such an eventuality may be beyond the control of Fourkings.

(b) Illness of Fourkings staff, such as swine fever where staff must stay away from work to prevent the spread of an infection.

(c) The venue could become unavailable due to a freak natural disaster, such as flooding or subsidence due to unusual weather conditions.

In these circumstances, there would be a failure to supply the service or support for an event which would not be the fault of either the client or Fourkings. Consequently, it may be that the deposit should either be returned, or retained pending provision of the service at an alternative date or location. Fourkings may have done little, if anything, to justify recognising the revenue under such circumstances. Where some cost has been incurred, for example ordering catering supplies, it would seem reasonable to recognise some revenue to offset those costs. Reliable measurement of costs would appear to be a straightforward issue. The principal elements of cost will typically include staff hire, ordering of catering supplies and hire of external premises etc should be capable of reliable measurement.

Fourkings should undertake a thorough review of the risk that deposits may need to be refunded or deferred to other dates if the service is not provided when the client is not responsible. It is possible that this could be challenged by an unhappy client and there may need to be a provision recognised in accordance with IAS 37 for refund of deposit.

If revenue was to be recognised only at the point of service provision, it would mean that deposits would be released to revenue only when earned. This may reduce revenue in the first accounting period the practice was applied. It is unlikely to be material or significant enough to require a prior period adjustment, but the change of revenue recognition policy should be disclosed in the financial statements.

Manor house and grounds

One issue to consider is the nature of the expenditure to maintain the manor house and grounds in excellent condition. Any expenditure which is purely repairs and maintenance should be expensed in accordance with the current accounting policy. If there are any elements of improvement, such as expanding the car park, improving access to or from the property, improving drainage etc, it would be reasonable to capitalise these items. In accordance with IAS 16, any capitalised expenditure should be depreciated over their expected useful life to the business.

A further issue is the nature of any cyclical or periodic repairs; IAS 37 prevents building up a reserve in advance of incurring such expenditure or recognition of a provision where no legal or constructive obligation exists. If expenditure is incurred which may help to generate economic benefits over a number of years, it may be possible to capitalise and depreciate this expenditure. One example of this could be periodic replacement of the hobs and ovens in the kitchen, perhaps every ten years.

The fall in business activity and profitability is an indication of possible impairment. Based upon the available information, there could be impairment if the possible sale proceeds (less selling costs) is less than the carrying value. The question identifies initial cost of $5 million and an offer from a potential purchaser amounting to $4.5 million before selling costs. Further information regarding the carrying value of the land and depreciated building would be necessary to make more specific comment on any impairment review. Fourkings should also consider value in use when doing an impairment review. Value in use would comprise the net revenues expected from continued use of the manor house and grounds as currently used. However, it should consider alternative uses (such as opening as a hotel or using the premises as a conference centre); it may also be possible to generate revenue from the sub-letting of part of the property to a third party. Any impairment recognised should be charged in full immediately to profit or loss. If, however, the property had previously been revalued, it would be possible to apply part of the impairment against the revaluation reserve.

If the decision is made to dispose of the property, it may need to be classed as held for sale in accordance with IFRS 5. For this to apply there must be a commitment to sell the property in its current condition at a realistic price. It would also be expected that disposal would be completed within twelve months and that there was little chance of the management reversing the decision to dispose of the property. If the criteria applied, the property would be removed from non-current assets and measured at the lower of carrying value and recoverable amount and presented separately on the statement of financial position.

Staff issues

The capitalisation of recruitment and training costs requires careful consideration. These costs should only be capitalised if there is a reporting standard which requires such treatment, or if it meets the definition of an asset in accordance with the Framework.

Whilst it would be accepted that entities employee staff to help them to generate future economic benefits, the key issue is whether there is a right to receive such benefits and, even if there is, can this be reliably measured for inclusion in the financial statements. Another issue would be that employees may resign after receiving training, and therefore no economic benefits would accrue to Fourkings. Whilst it may be possible to reliably measure both internal and external costs associated with recruitment and training, the problem arises of how benefits are to be identified and quantified. Capitalisation would also require amortisation – over what time period should such costs be amortised?

In conclusion, it would appear inappropriate to capitalise recruitment and training costs; such costs should be expensed as incurred.

The introduction of an employee share option scheme should be accounted for in accordance with IFRS 2. The fair value of the share option at the grant date is used, together with the number of employees who are expected to remain as employees at the vesting date. This information is applied to the number of share options and the costs spread over the three-year vesting period. The accounting treatment creates an equity reserve and also a remuneration expense. For the year ended 31 October 2010 the amounts are as follows:

Year ended 31 October 2010	**SOFP**	**P/L**
	equity reserve	payroll expense
	$000	$000
(100 – 5 – 5 – 7) × 500 × $6.00 × 1/3	83	83

Foreign currency

IAS 21 requires transactions designated in foreign currency are translated using the exchange rate ruling at the date of the transaction. The payment made on 31 August will be translated at the rate 1.25 Seychelles rupees to the $, giving a value of $80,000. As the payment made is a refundable deposit, it will be accounted for as a receivable. The risks and rewards associated with the payment have not yet been transferred as the event could be cancelled at any time up to 31 December 2010 and the deposit refunded in full.

At the reporting date, the receivable of 100,000 Seychelles rupees should be retranslated at the rate ruling at that date – i.e. 1.3 rupees to the $. This will be the best estimate of the dollar value of the receivable as at the year end at an amount of $76,923. The difference in the carrying value of the receivable $3,077 is an exchange loss which is taken to profit or loss.

Whether or not the event is cancelled after the reporting date and prior to the date on which the financial statements are approved by the directors will not be relevant. It would be a non-adjusting event per IAS 10, as would the dollar value of the deposit refunded. If considered to be material, a non-adjusting event could be disclosed by note in the financial statements for the year ended 31 October 2010.

If a euro-denominated bank account was to be opened, any dollar transfers in would be translated at the rate ruling at the date of the transaction. Similarly, any transfers out of the euro bank account into dollars would be translated at the rate ruling at the date of the transaction. At the year-end, the balance on the euro bank account would be translated at the closing rate at that date for inclusion in the financial statements within either current assets or current liabilities as appropriate.

Marking Scheme

(i)	Revenue recognition	5.0
(ii)	Manor house issues	8.0
(iii)	Staff issues	6.0
(iv)	Foreign currency transaction	6.0
		25

Test your understanding 10 – Seejoy

(a) **Sale and leaseback**

A sale and leaseback agreement releases capital for expansion, repayment of outstanding debt or repurchase of share capital. The transaction releases capital tied up in non liquid assets. There are important considerations. The price received for the asset and the related interest rate/rental charge should be at market rates. The interest rate will normally be dependent upon the financial strength of the 'tenant' and the risk/reward ratio which the lessor is prepared to accept. There are two types of sale and leaseback agreements, one utilising a finance lease and the other an operating lease.

The accounting treatment is determined by IAS 17 Leases. The substance of the transaction is essentially one of financing as the title to the stadium is transferred back to the club. Thus a sale is not recognised. The excess of the sale proceeds over the carrying value of the assets is deferred and amortised to profit or loss over the lease term. The leaseback of the stadium is for the remainder of its economic and useful life, and therefore under IAS 17, the lease should be treated as a finance lease. The stadium will remain as a non-current asset and will be depreciated. The finance lease loan will be accounted for under IFRS 9 Financial instruments in terms of the derecognition rules in the standard. The transaction will be recognised by the club as follows in the year to 31 December 20X7:

	Dr $m	Cr $m
Receipt of cash 1 January 20X7		
Cash received	15	
Stadium		12
Deferred income		3
Assets held under finance lease	15	
Finance lease payable		15
Depreciation (15 ÷ 20 years)	0.75	
Assets held under finance lease		0.75

Statement of profit or loss and other comprehensive income:

		$000
Deferred income	($3m/20 yrs)	150
Depreciation		(750)
Finance charge	($15m – $1.2m) × 5.6%	(773)

Statement of financial position:

		$000
Non-current assets - stadium	($15m – $0.75m)	14,250
Non-current liabilities:		
Deferred income	($3m – $0.15m)	2,850
Long-term borrowings	(($15m – ($1.2m × 2) + 0.773)	13,373
Current liabilities - rental payment		1,200

This form of sale and leaseback has several disadvantages. The profit for the period may decrease because of the increase in the finance charge over the deferred income. Similarly the gearing ratio of the club may increase significantly because of the increase in long term borrowings although the short term borrowings may be reduced by the inflow of cash. Unsecured creditors may have less security for their borrowings after the leasing transaction. It may be worth considering a sale and leaseback involving an operating lease as in this case the profit on disposal can be recognised immediately because the sale price is at fair value. The stadium will be deemed to be sold and will be removed from the statement of financial position. Similarly no long-term liability for the loan will be recognised in the statement of financial position, and the sale proceeds could be used to repay any outstanding debt. This form of sale and leaseback would seem to be preferable than the one utilising a finance lease although any increase in the residual value of the stadium would be lost. However the secured loan approach which the directors do not wish to use may better reflect substance over form.

(b) **Player registrations**

The players' transfer fees have been capitalised as intangible assets under IAS 38 Intangible assets because it is probable that expected future benefits will flow to the club as a result of the contract signed by the player and the cost of the asset can be measured reliably, being the transfer fee. The cost model would be used because the revaluation model has to use an active market to determine fair value and this is not possible because of the unique nature of the players. IAS 38 requires intangible assets such as the player contracts to be amortised over their useful life. Intangible assets with indefinite useful lives should not be amortised and should be impairment tested annually. If the player is subsequently 'held for sale' i.e., becomes available for sale to other clubs and satisfies the criteria in IFRS 5 Non-current assets held for sale and discontinued operations, then amortisation ceases.

The amortisation method should reflect the pattern of the future economic benefits. The amortisation of the contracts over ten years does not fit this criterion. IAS 38 recommends an amortisation method that reflects the useful life of the asset and the pattern of economic benefits and, therefore, the proposed method over ten years cannot be used as an accounting policy. The current amortisation level should be maintained and a charge of $9 million ((20 ÷ 5) + (15 ÷ 3)) would be shown in the statement of comprehensive income for the year-ending 31 December 20X7. This proposal in any event would only mask the poor financial state of the club. It is a book entry which may help prevent negative equity but will not give a cash benefit. The fundamental strategy for the club should be to contract players which it can afford and to spend at levels appropriate to its income.

There does not appear to be any probability that the contingent liability will crystallise. Under IAS 37 Provisions, contingent liabilities and contingent assets, a contingency is a possible obligation arising out of past events and whose existence will be confirmed only by the occurrence or non-occurrence of one or more uncertain future events not wholly within the control of the entity. At present the club is performing very poorly in the league and is unlikely to win the national league. Therefore, the contingent liability will not become a present obligation but will still be disclosed in the financial statements for the year-ending 31 December 20X7.

(c) **Issue of bond**

This form of financing a football club's operations is known as securitisation. Often in these cases a special purpose vehicle is set up to administer the income stream or assets involved. In this case, a special purpose vehicle has not been set up. The benefit of securitisation of the future corporate hospitality sales and season ticket receipts is that there will be a capital injection into the club and it is likely that the effective interest rate is lower because of the security provided by the income from the receipts. The main problem with the planned raising of capital is the way in which the money is to be used. The use of the bond for ground improvements can be commended as long term cash should be used for long term investment but using the bond for players' wages will cause liquidity problems for the club.

This type of securitisation is often called a 'future flow' securitisation. There is no existing asset transferred to a special purpose vehicle in this type of transaction. The bond is shown as a long term liability and is accounted for under IAS 39 Financial instruments: recognition and measurement. There are no issues of derecognition of assets as there can be in other securitisation transactions. In some jurisdictions there are legal issues in assigning future receivables as they constitute an unidentifiable debt which does not exist at present and because of this uncertainty often the bond holders will require additional security such as a charge on the football stadium.

The bond will be a financial liability and it will be classified in one of two ways:

- Financial liabilities at fair value through profit or loss include financial liabilities that the entity either has incurred for trading purposes or, where permitted, has designated to the category at inception. Derivative liabilities are always treated as held for trading unless they are designated and effective as hedging instruments. An example of a liability held for trading is an issued debt instrument that the entity intends to repurchase in the near term to make a gain from short-term movements in interest rates. It is unlikely that the bond will be classified in this category.

- The second category is financial liabilities measured at amortised cost. It is the default category for financial liabilities that do not meet the criteria for financial liabilities at fair value through profit or loss. In most entities, most financial liabilities will fall into this category. Examples of financial liabilities that generally would be classified in this category are account payables, issued debt instruments, and deposits from customers. Thus the bond is likely to be classified under this heading. When a financial liability is recognised initially in the statement of financial position, the liability is measured at fair value. Fair value is the amount for which a liability can be settled between knowledgeable, willing parties in an arm's length transaction. Since fair value is a market transaction price, on initial recognition fair value will usually equal the amount of consideration received for the financial liability.

In this case the company does not wish to use valuation models nor is there an active market for the bond and, therefore, amortised cost will be used to measure the bond.

The bond will be shown initially at $50 million × 95%, i.e. $47.5 million as this is the consideration received. Subsequently at 31 December 20X7, the bond will be shown as follows:

	$m
Initial recognition	47.5
Interest at 7.7%	3.7
Cash payment	(6.0)
Amount owing at 31 December 20X7	45.2

(d) **Player trading**

The sale of the players will introduce cash into the club and help liquidity. The contingent liability will be extinguished as the players will no longer play for Seejoy. The club, however, is not performing well at present and the sale of the players will not help their performance. This may result in the reduction of ticket sales and, therefore, cause further liquidity problems. The proceeds from the sale of players may be difficult to estimate at present as the date of sale is significantly into the future. (The players will not constitute held for sale non-current assets under IFRS 5 Non-current assets held for sale and discontinued operations at 31 December 20X6 as the players are not available for immediate sale. As a loss on sale is anticipated on the players, an impairment review should be undertaken at 31 December 20X6.)

If the sale proceeds are $16 million, then a loss on sale will be recorded of $2 million if the players are sold on 1 May 20X7.

	Transfer fee	Amortisation	Carrying amount
	$m	$m	$m
A. Steel	20	4 + 4/12 of 4	14.7
R. Aldo	15	10 + 4/12 of 5	3.3
			18.0
Sale proceeds (estimated)			16.0
Loss			2.0

If the players are not sold by 31 December 20X7, they may constitute non-current assets held for sale, if the conditions of IFRS 5 are met. Immediately before the initial classification of the asset as held for sale, the carrying amount of the asset will be measured in accordance with applicable IFRSs and the non-current assets if deemed to be held for sale will be measured at the lower of carrying amount and fair value less costs to sell. Impairment must be considered both at the time of classification as held for sale and subsequently. Non-current assets that are classified as held for sale are not depreciated. Thus amortisation of the transfer fees will stop if the non-current assets are held for sale. Assets classified as held for sale must be presented separately on the face of the statement of financial position at 31 December 20X7.

Marking Scheme

(i)	Sale and leaseback	9.0
(ii)	Player registrations	5.0
(iii)	Bond	6.0
(iv)	Player trading	5.0
		25

Index

A

ACCA Code of Professional Ethics.....226
Acquisition costs.....384
Acquisition method.....379
Adjusting events.....173
Adoption of IFRS.....691
Agricultural produce.....112
Agriculture (IAS 41).....110
Amortisation.....108
Amortised cost.....290
Assessing financial performance.....685
Asset.....5
Asset ceiling.....243
Associates and joint ventures (IAS 28).....392, 413

B

Biological assets.....110
Borrowing costs (IAS 23).....92
Business combinations and deferred tax.....360
Business model test.....300

C

Capital reduction scheme.....636
Capitalising interest.....92
Cash equivalents.....550, 555
Cash flow characteristics test.....300
Cash flow hedge.....317
Cash flows from financing activities.....551
Cash flows from investing activities.....551
Cash flows from operating activities.....551
Cash generating units.....81
Cash-settled share-based payments.....269
Changes in accounting estimates.....43
Changes in accounting policies.....42
Classification of financial instruments.....287, 289, 302
Classifying a lease.....143
Codes of ethics.....26
Comparability.....4
Complex groups.....431
Compound instruments.....293
Conceptual framework.....2
Confidentiality.....27
Consolidated financial statements (IFRS 10).....374
Consolidated statement of profit or loss.....405
Consolidation.....395
Consolidation of a foreign operation.....522
Constructive obligation.....177
Contingent assets.....180
Contingent consideration.....384
Contingent liabilities.....180
Control.....374
Current cost.....6
Current issues.....715
Current service cost.....232
Curtailments.....232, 233

D

Date of transition.....603
Deferred tax.....347
Defined benefit plans.....229
Defined contribution plans.....229
Depreciation.....74
Derecognition of financial instruments.....303
Derecognition of provisions.....179
Derivatives.....307
Differential financial reporting.....620
Diluted earnings per share.....59
Direct method: cash flows.....552
Disclosure of interests in other entities (IFRS 12).....416
Discontinued operation.....50, 479
Discontinuing hedge accounting.....319
Disposal group.....95
Disposal of a foreign entity.....536
Disposal of a subsidiary.....477
Disposal of non-current assets.....76
Disposal without losing control.....487

E

Earnings per share (IAS 33).....53
Economic value added.....693
Elements.....5
Embedded derivatives.....312
Employee benefits (IAS 19).....227
Environmental provisions.....184
Environmental reporting.....666
Entity reconstruction schemes.....632
Equity.....5
Equity accounting.....393, 536
Equity instrument.....285, 287
Equity-settled share-based payments.....260
Ethical conflicts of interest.....27
Ethics and ethical issues.....25
Events after the reporting period (IAS 10).....172
Exchange differences.....129, 130
Exchange differences on retranslation of foreign subsidiary.....526
Expense.....5

Index

F

Fair value adjustments.....381

Fair value hedge.....315

Fair value hierarchy.....14

Fair value measurement (IFRS 13).....11

Fair value of net assets.....381

Fair value of share options.....260

Fair value option for financial liabilities.....297

Faithful representation.....4

Finance lease.....145, 147

Financial asset.....285, 299

Financial assets at amortised cost.....300

Financial assets at fair value through profit or loss.....300, 301

Financial assets at fair value through other comprehensive income.....301

Financial asset impairment.....305

Financial instruments Disclosures (IFRS 7).....320

Financial instruments (IFRS 9).....286

Financial instruments derecognition.....303

Financial instruments derivatives.....307

Financial liabilities.....285, 287

Financial liabilities at amortised cost.....289

Financial liabilities at fair value through profit or loss.....289

Financing activities: cashflows.....551

First-time adoption (IFRS 1).....601

Foreign currency transactions.....125

Foreign subsidiary.....521

Forward contract.....308

Forward rate agreements.....308

Free cash flow.....691

FRS 100-102.....622

Full goodwill method.....383, 388

Functional currency.....126

Future operating losses.....182

Future repairs to assets.....183

Futures contracts.....309

G

Going concern.....40, 176

Goodwill.....381, 386

Goodwill impairment.....388

Government grants (IAS 20).....89

Grant date.....261

Group accounts – basic groups.....371

Group accounts – change in group.....467, 513

Group accounts – complex groups.....431

Group accounts – foreign currency.....521

Group accounts – statement of cash flows.....549

Group reorganisation.....513

Groups: exclusion of subsidiary.....376

H

Hedge accounting.....313

Hedge effectiveness.....314

Hedged item.....313

Hedging instrument.....314

Held for sale.....95

Historical cost.....6

I

IAS 1 Presentation of financial statements.....34

IAS 2 Inventories.....114

IAS 7 Statement of cash flows.....550

IAS 8 Accounting policies, changes in accounting estimates and errors.....42, 686

IAS 10 Events after the reporting period.....172

IAS 12 Income taxes.....345

IAS 16 Property, plant and equipment.....72

IAS 17 Leases.....141

IAS 18 Revenue.....44

IAS 19 Employee benefits.....227

IAS 20 Accounting for government grants and disclosure of government assistance.....89

IAS 21 The effects of changes in foreign exchange rates.....126, 522

IAS 23 Borrowing costs.....92

IAS 24 Related party disclosures.....213

IAS 27 Separate financial statements.....416

IAS 28 Investments in associates and joint ventures.....392, 413

IAS 32 Financial instruments: presentation.....287

IAS 33 Earnings per share.....53

IAS 34 Interim financial reporting.....62

IAS 36 Impairment of assets.....77

IAS 37 Provisions, contingent liabilities and contingent assets.....177

IAS 38 Intangible assets.....105

IAS 39 Financial instruments: recognition and measurement.....286

IAS 40 Investment property.....100

IAS 41 Agriculture.....110

IFRS 1 First-time adoption of IFRS.....602

IFRS 2 Share based payment.....257

IFRS 3 Business combinations.....379

IFRS 5 Held for sale and discontinued operations.....50, 95, 479, 491

IFRS 7 Financial instruments: disclosures.....320

IFRS 8 Segment reporting.....195

IFRS 9 Financial instruments.....286

IFRS 10 Consolidated financial statements.....374

IFRS 11 Joint arrangements.....411

IFRS 12 Disclosure of interests in other entities.....416

IFRS 13 Fair value measurement.....11

IFRS for SME.....620
Impairment of assets (IAS 36).....77
Impairment of financial assets.....305
Impairment of goodwill.....388
Impairment loss reversals.....86
Impairment test.....77
Income.....5
Income tax (IAS 12).....345
Indirect method: cash flows.....552
Intangible assets (IAS 38).....105
Integrated Reporting.....673
Integrity.....27
Interim reporting (IAS 34).....62
Inventories (IAS 2).....114
Investing activities: cash flows.....551
Investment entities.....377
Investment property (IAS 40).....100
Investment property and deferred tax.....355

J

Joint arrangements (IFRS 11).....411
Joint control.....413
Joint operations.....412
Joint venture.....412

L

Leases (IAS 17).....141
Liability.....5
Long-term employee benefits.....247

M

Management commentary (PS1).....665
Market value added.....692
Materiality.....4
Measurement.....6
Mixed groups.....446

N

Negative goodwill (bargain purchase).....387
Net interest component.....232
Non-adjusting events.....174
Non-controlling interest.....383
Non-current assets.....71
Non-current assets held for sale (IFRS 5).....95
Non-financial reporting.....664
Non-financial performance measures.....689
Not-for-profit entities.....616

O

Objectivity.....27
Offsetting financial assets and financial liabilities.....289
Onerous contracts.....182
Operating lease.....146, 148
Operating segment.....196
Operating activities: cash flows.....551
Option contracts.....309
Other comprehensive income (IAS 1).....35

P

Parent.....374
Past service costs.....232, 233
Performance conditions.....263
Performance reporting.....33
Post-employment benefits.....229
Potential voting rights.....374
Present value.....6
Presentation currency.....127
Presentation of financial statements (IAS 1).....34
Principal or most advantageous market.....12
Prior period errors.....43
Professional behaviour.....27
Professional ethics.....25
Property, plant and equipment (IAS 16).....72
Proportionate goodwill.....383, 390
Professional competence and due care.....26
Provisions (IAS 37).....177
PS1 Management commentary.....665
Purchase consideration.....384
Purchase of additional shares after control acquired.....476

Q

Qualitative characteristics.....3

R

Realisable value.....6
Recognition of elements of financial statements.....5
Reconstruction schemes.....639
Recoverable amount.....78
Related parties (IAS 24).....213
Relevance.....3
Remeasurement component.....233
Reportable segments.....197
Research and development expenditure.....108
Restructuring provisions.....185
Retranslation of monetary items.....130
Revaluation and deferred tax.....354
Revenue recognition (IAS 18).....44
Reverse acquisition.....519

Index

S

Sale and leaseback.....152
Segment reporting (IFRS 8).....195
Separate financial statements (IAS 27).....416
Service cost component.....232
Settlements.....234
Share-based payment (IFRS 2).....257
Share options and deferred tax.....357
Shareholder value.....692
Short-term employee benefits.....245
Significant influence....392
Small- and medium-sized entities.....619
Social reporting.....670
Social responsibility.....670
Specialised entities.....615
Statement of changes in equity.....38
Statement of cash flows (IAS 7).....519
Statement of financial position.....35
Statement of profit or loss and other comprehensive income.....35
Step acquisition.....473
Subsidiary.....374
Subsidiary acquired with view to disposal.....491
Sustainability.....672

T

Tax.....345
Tax base.....348
Temporary difference.....348
Termination benefits.....246
Timeliness.....4
Total comprehensive income.....35
Transactions between equity holders.....476, 487
Trend analysis.....696

U

UK syllabus focus.....622
Understandability.....5
Unremitted earnings and deferred tax.....361
Unused tax losses and deferred tax.....359

V

Value in use.....78
Verifiability.....4
Vertical groups.....432
Vesting conditions.....261, 263
Vesting date.....261
Vesting period.....262